D1445057

Also by RAYMOND BONNER

Weakness and Deceit: U.S. Policy and El Salvador

WALTZING
WITH
A DICTATOR

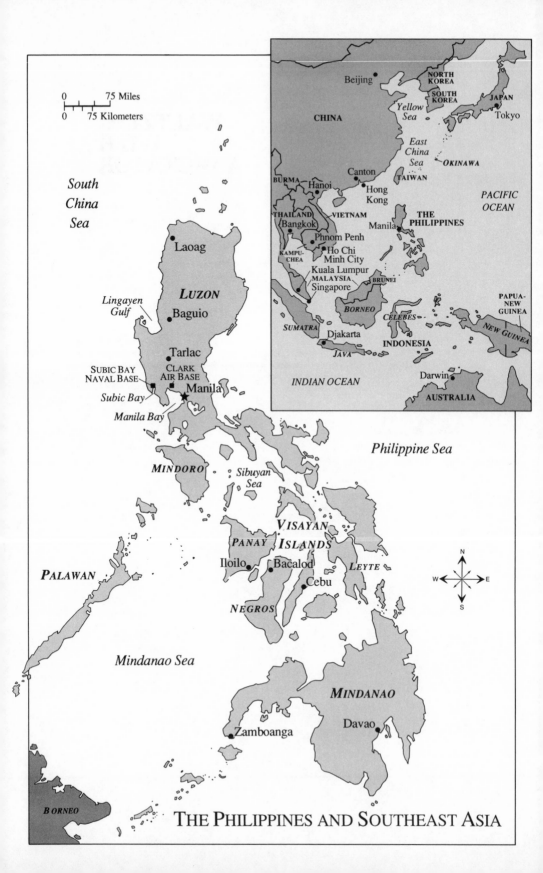

THE PHILIPPINES AND SOUTHEAST ASIA

WALTZING
WITH
A DICTATOR

The Marcoses and
the Making of American Policy

RAYMOND BONNER

M
MACMILLAN
LONDON

First published in the United States of America 1987 by Random House, Inc., New York

First published in the United Kingdom 1987 by
MACMILLAN LONDON LTD
4 Little Essex Street, London WC2R 3LF
and Basingstoke

Associated companies in Auckland, Delhi, Dublin, Gaborone, Hamburg, Harare, Hong Kong,
Johannesburg, Kuala Lumpur, Lagos, Manzini, Melbourne, Mexico City, Nairobi, New York,
Singapore and Tokyo

ISBN 0-333-45764-1

Book design by Andrew Roberts

Printed in the United States of America

8/10 Times Roman (3)
B133   1T   vh

Random House (E. Vanook)   Copyright Raymond Bonner 1987   msp 1/1
13570   1P   4-7-87   Galley 1   REPRO / NEW COPY

FOR JANE

Contents

WALTZING
WITH
A DICTATOR

Prologue

When the CIA officer arrived at the modern, sprawling Forbes Park residence of the American ambassador to the Philippines, he found the occupant, Henry Byroade, relaxing with his evening drink. The diplomat was handed a neatly typed document of about fifteen pages. It was Proclamation 1081, the justifications, skillfully drafted by Ferdinand E. Marcos, for placing his country under martial law. Earlier that evening it had been handed to a Central Intelligence Agency officer by one of the "Rolex 12," as they were to be dubbed, the principal planners of martial law—ten military officers, the minister of defense, and a businessman—to whom Marcos later presented gold Rolex watches in appreciation of their participation.

Talk about the possibility of martial law had been buzzing through Manila for weeks. But it had been little more than that—rumors and concern. Then, on Sunday, September 17, 1972, a Filipino who had been recruited by the agency to provide information earned his keep: He informed the station that martial law would be declared on Tuesday. The next day he called back: Martial law had been postponed until Thursday or Friday. That was the most concrete intelligence the embassy had received—until it was handed Proclamation 1081.

Byroade read the decree slowly. Another ambassador probably would have consulted Washington. Byroade, however, was anything but a typical diplomat. Indeed, he was one of the most extraordinary men in the annals of the soldier-statesman. He had been the youngest general in the history of the American army, promoted by George Marshall in China, where Byroade once went wading with Zhou Enlai. "An authentic Horatio Alger character," *Look* magazine

3

wrote, in a column about "Men Who Fascinate Women," when he was forty-one years old, "Prototype of the grown-up American boy, he could pose for patriotic posters." As a soldier he was at the center of the Berlin blockade crisis; as a diplomat he was involved in the planning of the CIA coup that put the Shah in power in Iran. "The John Wayne of ambassadors" as one aide remembered him, Byroade frequently crashed his career on the shoals of his own fiercely independent streak and his womanizing. But he always managed to recover. The Philippines was his fifth ambassadorial post, Pakistan would be his sixth, a record surpassed by only one other American in the twentieth century; and when Henry Byroade finally retired, the CIA honored him in a private ceremony at the agency's headquarters in Langley, Virginia, a very rare tribute for an ambassador.

Not surprisingly, Byroade didn't ask Washington what he should do about Marcos's proposed action. After reading Proclamation 1081, he called Marcos, asked if he could come over to discuss a matter, without saying what. Marcos, closer to Byroade than he had been or would be to any other American ambassador during his twenty years in power, said of course. Without changing from his sport shirt, Byroade slipped into the back seat of his chauffeured black limousine, with the miniature American flags fluttering on the front fenders, for the twenty- to thirty-minute drive across town to Malacañang, the presidential residence. He did not take the proclamation with him, concerned that his possession of it might reveal to Marcos who among the twelve was his Judas.

Byroade told Marcos that Washington would react strongly if the Philippine president toppled Philippine democracy, especially the Congress. It was the same argument the ambassador had made in earlier discussions with Marcos about martial law, though never very forcefully. Byroade thought he had succeeded in persuading Marcos not to take this drastic action. But he was wrong about Marcos, and he was wrong about the Washington reaction.

After leaving Marcos, Byroade advised Washington of what he had done. The cable was sent not through the regular channels to the State Department but through the CIA transmission facilities, "back channel" to the National Security Council (NSC), headed by

Henry Kissinger.* It was marked Eyes Only. The CIA station sent Langley several of its own messages, one of which contained the text of Proclamation 1081.

In Manila the CIA was prepared for what now seemed to be the inevitable. Worried that when martial law came, there would be a curfew and other restrictions on movement which would make it difficult for the CIA agents to maintain contact with their sources, the station had distributed shortwave radios to some of its most important assets. The assets had code names: Eagle Two; Eagle Three, etc. The station chief was Eagle One.

On Friday, September 22, Eagle Two reached Eagle One. "This is it. All systems are go" was the cryptic message. The CIA knew what it meant. Earlier in the day another of the CIA's Philippine assets had provided the station with a list of the persons Marcos planned to arrest and imprison. At nine o'clock Ferdinand Marcos declared martial law.

The reaction of Washington was mostly silent detachment, except for its emphatic insistence that suggestions the United States had any advance knowledge were "flatly wrong." The United States had not been consulted, the State Department said, and it "was not informed in advance of President Marcos' intention to declare martial law." From Manila it was reported that American embassy officers had "spent the day seeking information about the surprise martial law decree."

At best the denial was a half-truth; the "surprise," feigned. Yet over the years these official statements have held. The standard history of the imposition of martial law maintains that the United States was not involved; it knew nothing. Maybe the United States didn't know the exact hour and minute, but it knew just about everything else.

On September 13 the embassy alerted Washington that Marcos was studying "emergency" measures, "including martial law." That had prompted the State Department to cable back for more details.

---

* The back channel is a means for diplomats in the field to communicate directly with the White House and NSC without the message going through the State Department. As head of Nixon's National Security Council, Kissinger encouraged ambassadors, and other senior officials, to use back channel messages, which are sent via the CIA or National Security Agency (NSA).

And on the nineteenth, three days before martial law was declared, the State Department in a highly classified cable—it was marked Secret with a further restriction that it was to be distributed not through the normal channels but only to the very highest-level officials—asked Byroade for his "evaluation of likelihood that Marcos will impose martial law in near future."

If Washington had wanted to defend democracy in the Philippines, it could have sent a very strong message to Marcos that martial law would not be tolerated, that there would be a cutoff of aid, or some other step taken, if he usurped democracy. No such message was ever sent. And Marcos had reason to be confident that it wouldn't be.

Marcos said afterward that he had "prayed to God for guidance" before making the fateful decision. Contrary to what was officially stated, he had also consulted with Washington, specifically with the president of the United States, Richard M. Nixon. In the days before his proclamation of martial law Marcos spoke with Nixon at least once, telling the American president what he was about to do. He heard no objection.

Democracy mugged, the stage was set for Ferdinand and Imelda Marcos, for their conjugal dictatorship. It was the stage they had calculatingly designed. They were driven by what seemed to be a modern-day third world version of the divine right of kings. He wanted the power to rule, forever and ever. She was obsessed with society and money, with accumulating—possessions and people. They made possible their future by erasing and fictionalizing their pasts. Marcos had beaten a murder charge as a teenager, covered up his father's wartime collaboration, then set about fabricating a legend about himself as a fearless, decorated guerrilla. She squandered a few million dollars to build her "ancestral home," an attempt to buy a heritage of family wealth and prominence when the reality was that her father was the family ne'er-do-well and that as a child she had lived in a garage.

The Marcoses carried on through five American administrations—three Republican and two Democratic. American governments watched as the Marcoses robbed the Philippine people of between $5 and $10 *billion,* larceny and looting that began even before Marcos had declared martial law. Washington looked on as he emasculated the country's democratic institutions: the courts; the schools; the political parties. He corrupted the superb army that had been created by General Douglas MacArthur, sapping it of the ability and morale to fight the Communist-led insurgency. During the Marcos reign and *because* of Marcos, the Philippine Communists grew stronger and stronger; by 1985 they were closing in on taking power. Yet through it all Marcos remained Washington's man in Manila.

After 1972 Ferdinand Marcos was a dictator, in the dictionary definition: He had the authority and control to issue the decrees by which the people were governed without their consent. He was not, however, the classic dictator, less ruthless, probably much smarter and shrewder than most. He was not above bribery and intimidation, employing both whenever they were needed to achieve his goals. But he was a brilliant political tactician, a match for Lyndon Johnson, and, at the beginning of his career, a charismatic speaker, reminiscent of John F. Kennedy. And he was an absolute master of the American political system. He knew more about that system, its intricacies and nuances, and about the men who ran it than they ever did about his country and the man who ran it. He deployed his knowledge, ingenuity, and cunning to extract far more from Uncle Sam than he ever gave. At each turning point, each showdown, whether over Vietnam or human rights, Marcos stood his ground. It was always the powerful United States that blinked.

1 : The Man
and the Woman

From the beginning of his political career Ferdinand Marcos had been frank about his ambitions. "If you are electing me just to get my services as a Congressman for the pittance of seventy-five hundred pesos a year, don't vote for me at all," he shouted at rallies during his first campaign, in 1949, for the seat that his father had held when the archipelago was an American colony. "This is only a first step. Elect me a Congressman now, and I pledge you an Ilocano President in twenty years. . . ."

He was elected, at the age of thirty-two the youngest member of the House of Representatives. And this was one political promise Marcos kept, en route to never suffering an electoral defeat; in his 1959 quest for a Senate seat he won a landslide victory, gathering far more votes than any of the CIA-backed candidates. It took Marcos only sixteen years, not twenty, to deliver on his boast. Not surprisingly. It seemed he was always in a hurry, a bit ahead of everyone else. "Ferdinand Edralin Marcos was in such a hurry to be born that his father, who was only eighteen years old himself, had to act as midwife," according to the authorized Marcos biography. "In fact, young Ferdinand scarcely waited for his parents to graduate from normal school before he put in his appearance, thus bringing to light a secret marriage."

Ferdinand's father, Mariano, became a lawyer and politician; his mother, Josefa, the daughter of well-to-do landowners, was a schoolteacher. Their roots were in Ilocos Norte, the northernmost hardscrabble region of the archipelago, where Ferdinand began life on September 11, 1917. While a strong sense of obligation, along with boundless hospitality, is generally considered common to all Filipinos, inhabitants of the various geographic regions exhibit unique

9

characteristics. In the south are the Muslims, adventuresome and freedom-loving, said to be the best friends and worst enemies one can have. The northern Ilocanos are a hardy, industrious people renowned for their frugality. Above all, the Ilocanos are known as survivors.

Beyond the date of his birth and a few other bare bones details, such as names of his parents and brothers and sisters and the dates of his political victories, to write with confidence about Marcos's early years is made difficult by the extensive misinformation, conflicting "facts," and intentional disinformation. The biographical caution is underscored by an observation of Ferdinand's mother while her son was growing up. He would probably be a novelist, she thought, considering the well-constructed imaginative tales with which he entertained the family. That's a mother's way of saying what it took U.S. diplomats and journalists twenty years to discover: Marcos could tell the most brazen lie with the straightest of faces, then continue telling it until it became accepted as fact.

There is only one full-length account of Marcos's life, *For Every Tear a Victory*, released in 1964 as part of his presidential campaign. Over the years the material in the book became the basis for what journalists wrote and American officials believed. It is styled as a biography, written by Hartzell Spence, who had been an editor of *Yank* during World War II. It is really an autobiography, as told to Spence. The book is without footnotes and contains few internal references; most of the material could have come only from Marcos, embellishing and prevaricating to create himself in his own grandiose image.* Doubts about the reliability of the book begin with the original title, which comes from what Marcos purported to tell his mother when informing her that her husband had been killed by the Japanese during the war. "I promise you, Mother, after this war,

---

* The book was updated and reissued in 1982, this time with an index, but still no footnotes, and a new title, *Marcos of the Philippines*. The references here are from that edition. Several noted journalists, including Colin Campbell, who later covered the Philippines for *The New York Times,* were approached about writing the updated version. Campbell, who was told that Imelda Marcos wanted to present the book to her husband as a birthday present, said that he might be willing to do it for $50,000. The money was no problem, he was told; in addition, he was assured that he would have "lots of fun in Manila," a not very subtle reference to the fact that some journalists who covered the Philippines were regularly provided with lavish gifts as well as women.

for every tear you shed now, a victory." Whether Marcos indeed said that is irrelevant, for his father was killed not by the Japanese but by an anti-Japanese guerrilla unit; Mariano Marcos was a collaborator.

According to the Marcos-Spence account, Marcos was always the first, the youngest, the best in everything. By the age of ten, so their story goes, Marcos had been taught by his grandfather to shoot, ride, and track wild animals in the jungle. During summers in Davao, on the country's southernmost island of Mindanao, where his father had been appointed governor, one of the young boy's duties was to shoot the deer grazing among the cattle, without disturbing the domestic stock. He was trilingual—Ilocano, English, and Spanish—and added a fourth language, Latin, for his school essays, "and, of course," wrote Spence, "read the classics in all four of these tongues."

Even discounting the mythmaking and boasting, Marcos's accomplishments were extraordinary. Even if he wasn't the outstanding athlete of his time, he was certainly a valued member of the university's wrestling, boxing, and swimming teams and captain of the rifle and pistol teams. As president, Marcos, five feet six inches and a wiry 130 pounds, who neither smoked nor drank, was probably one of the most fit and athletic world leaders. Whether or not, while in college, he was the country's best orator, he did use the campus soapbox with success—on the same campus that would breed those students who railed against him a generation later. There is no gainsaying that Marcos was extremely intelligent. While studying for the bar exam, he boasted that he would have the highest scores. He did, the accomplishment all the more remarkable considering that he must surely have been distracted by the arrest and murder charge hanging over him.

On September 20, 1935, a rainy, windy night—"black as sin" was how the prosecutor later described it—someone hidden in a fruit grove fired a bullet into the back of Julio Nalundasan as he stood, some twenty-five feet away, starkly silhouetted in the window, about to rinse his mouth after dinner. Nalundasan had been cut down with a single shot. The murder weapon was a pistol used in competition, with an eight-inch barrel. Ferdinand Marcos, who had celebrated his eighteenth birthday nine days before the murder, was a crack shot on the ROTC pistol and rifle teams.

Marcos had a motive, one that reflected the often violent nature of Philippine politics and the ferocity of family loyalty. Nalundasan had just defeated Ferdinand's father, Mariano, in the first national elections under the archipelago's commonwealth status with the United States. On top of the political humiliation, on the day before the murder, Nalundasan's followers had heaped public ridicule upon Mariano: They placed a coffin labeled "Marcos" in a rumble seat, then drove through the villages, finally arriving at the home of Mariano Marcos. While a band played a mocking dirge, the victors, wiping away false tears, hooted and jeered, "Marcos is dead! Long live Nalundasan."

The wheels of justice ground slowly, and it was not until December 7, 1938, that Marcos was arrested, seized while he was sitting in an evening law class. He was charged with having fired the fatal shot; his father and uncle were charged with conspiracy to commit murder. The case was made for Philippine newspapers, which delighted in sensational stories. Marcos was a student leader, at the top of his class academically, about to be graduated as valedictorian. When the trial began, reporters and photographers scrambled each day with the locals who wanted one of the forty or so spectator seats in the small courtroom. The trial dragged on for nearly two months. Marcos's mother appeared every day, and the fresh law graduate participated in his own defense. "He deeply impressed the court whenever he took an active part in the defense of his own case," the judge wrote in his opinion.

The judge was also impressed by young Marcos's accomplishments and potential, hailing him as "one of the brilliant among our young men. . . . In the opinion of this court, he is a youth with a great future. . . ." But the evidence was overwhelming, and the judge found him guilty of murder, sentencing him to up to seventeen years in prison. (His father and uncle were acquitted.)

Once the verdict had been delivered, Marcos assumed almost complete responsibility for his own defense. His impassioned thirty-minute argument to the trial judge that he be allowed to remain free to prepare his appeal before the Supreme Court brought tears to the eyes of spectators, court employees, and even the judge himself. The daily papers printed it in full. The *Lawyers' Journal* declared that even "shorn of its emotionalism," the plea was "a clear and brilliant piece of legal argumentation." But again Marcos lost.

Marcos became a jailhouse lawyer, though he was allowed to work in a sunny hall rather than spend all his time confined in his windowless cell in the 200-year-old prison in Laoag. Marcos's flair was reflected in his Supreme Court brief. Though impressive in length—830 pages, in three volumes—it was, the court noted in its opinion, "more valuable" for its "literary value" than for the strength and exposition of legal argument. When he appeared before the black-robed justices, Marcos was a vision in white—a white, double-breasted sharkskin suit and white shoes—a sartorial statement of his purity.

Marcos claimed that the trial and appeals had drained the family's resources (this, if true, makes all the more acute questions about the prodigious wealth he subsequently amassed). But he prevailed. The weekly *Philippines Free Press* (which Marcos was to close when he declared martial law) put his photo on the cover—a "public hero."

In reversing the conviction, the Supreme Court cited a number of trial court errors, but it is widely believed that the justices, in order to reach the desired outcome, had stretched to find the narrow technical grounds. What likely swayed the justices were the arguments to his brethren by Justice José P. Laurel that the fledgling democracy needed young people with the intelligence and leadership potential the young Marcos had already displayed, that saddling him with a criminal conviction would do more harm to the country than to the individual. Whatever the reasons, legal or emotional, Marcos was forever grateful to Laurel, who wrote the high court opinion, and his family. During the war Laurel collaborated with the Japanese, and records in U.S. archives suggest that Marcos helped him. When Laurel died, in 1959, Marcos delivered a eulogy, and he later became a trustee of the José P. Laurel Foundation, set up to perpetuate the memory of Laurel "in grateful recognition of his patriotic endeavors. . . ." Later, when Marcos declared martial law, he used his dictatorial powers to destroy many of the country's economically and politically potent families. One of the few families left un-

touched was the Laurels, allowed to keep their extensive landhold-
ings, a bank, and a beach resort. The chief justice's son, Salvador
("Doy") Laurel, was a loyal Marcos political ally until the late 1970s,
and when Laurel did eventually split with Marcos, he was not, as
were so many anti-Marcos politicians, jailed or forced into exile.

In displaying this loyalty to the Laurels, Marcos was exhibiting
utang na loob ("debt of gratitude"), the obligation that one owes
to a friend or person who has helped him. It is a deeply rooted trait,
one that permeates Filipino relationships. The fierce loyalty to family
and to one's region is somewhat comparable to Sicilian loyalty. In
the understanding of Philippine politics, these loyalties cannot be
overemphasized. "Almost invariably," notes the eminent Philippine
historian Teodoro Agoncillo, "the Filipino believes that a candidate
from his province or region, no matter how repugnant, is better
than one who comes from another region." These loyalties explain
in large measure why Marcos would not dismiss General Fabian Ver
as the armed forces chief of staff in spite of U.S. pressure to do so
in the aftermath of the assassination of Benigno ("Ninoy") Aquino
in 1983, a murder in which U.S. officials insisted Ver was involved.
Ver and Marcos had been playmates on the beaches of Sarrat, and
as Marcos acquired more power, so did Ver, rising from the president's chauffeur to chief of palace security to armed forces chief of
staff. Marcos would not turn his back on Ver even though sticking
with his fellow Ilocano cost Marcos critical support in Washington.

The murder rap beaten, Marcos soon found himself at war.
If Marcos, through his biographer, stretched the truth about his
early life, it snapped when he recounted his military years. About
all that can be written with certainty about Marcos's war years is
that he was a guerrilla fighter, he was captured and imprisoned by
the Japanese, and he was decorated. Spence's account of Marcos's
war years begins: "General Douglas MacArthur, pinning on Ferdinand Marcos the Distinguished Service Cross for valor in battle
far beyond the call of duty, commented publicly that without Ferdinand's exploit, Bataan would have fallen three months sooner
than it did."

If Marcos did so perform, it would have been one of the most
significant actions in the defense of Bataan. Yet MacArthur, in his

Reminiscences, doesn't mention any such heroic action by Marcos, nor is it mentioned in the many books about MacArthur, according to John Sharkey, the *Washington Post* reporter who was the first American journalist to challenge Marcos's war medals claims. Moreover, Marcos's name does not appear on official U.S. government lists of Filipinos and Americans who were awarded Distinguished Service Crosses for their bravery at Bataan, one of which was compiled by MacArthur's headquarters in Tokyo after the war's end. Marcos's alleged bravery at Bataan also earned him a recommendation for the U.S. Congressional Medal of Honor, according to Marcos and Spence. But there are no records in the U.S. Army archives of any such recommendation. Marcos also claimed to have won two U.S. Silver Stars.

Altogether Marcos said he received at least thirty awards, medals, and citations (the exact number varies in his accounts, usually between twenty-seven and thirty-three). If he did, not only was he, as claimed, the most decorated Filipino soldier in history, but Audie Murphy, who received twenty-seven awards, becomes a footnote. It all was a monumental fraud, and Marcos was nothing if not daring in perpetuating it. According to the Spence-Marcos account, one day Marcos, who was in Washington lobbying for Philippine veterans' benefits, passed General Omar Bradley. Seeing Marcos's six rows of medals, the four-star general saluted the lieutenant. Marcos carried it off for thirty years.* At the time of Marcos's victory in

---

* Marcos quietly dropped his claim to the Medal of Honor in 1977, after a *New York Times* correspondent, Henry Kamm, had discovered the fraud somewhat serendipitously. Kamm was in the Philippines to write about Southeast Asian refugees (for which he won a Pulitzer Prize). Imelda Marcos had planned a typically ostentatious bash for her husband's sixtieth birthday; Kamm, thinking it would be an entertaining diversion, decided to "crash" the party. With money she had extracted from government contractors and other businessmen, Mrs. Marcos had built a museum dedicated to Marcos's life. While the invited were milling around, Kamm and his companion slipped under the rope and went upstairs, where he found a case displaying Marcos's war medals. When the Philippine president and his wife arrived upstairs, Kamm inquired dryly, "Mr. President, did you get the Congressional Medal of Honor?" Marcos, realizing he had been caught, reacted quickly, summoning an aide standing nearby to remove the Medal of Honor from the case, leaving a conspicuous space. Back downstairs, Imelda Marcos, more concerned about not offending *The New York Times* than about any affront to her husband, treated the uninvited Kamm and his friend as special guests. She insisted that they take seats beside her at the table of honor, then from a buffet groaning with food—Kamm thought it must have been supported by steel girders—she ordered an aide to serve them. "He brought a plate that was filled in direct proportion to the servility that the man serving it thought he owed Imelda," Kamm recalls.

1965, *The New York Times* in its "Man in the News" feature said that he had won twenty-two American and Philippine medals, that he had been "commended by General Douglas MacArthur for his exploits in the defense of Bataan," and that his father had been "bayoneted by the Japanese."

As for some of Marcos's other medals, the ones bestowed upon him by the Philippine government, he did receive them, but the reasons are somewhat suspicious. Five of them were "awarded" in the early 1950s—while Marcos was a leading member of the House Defense Committee. And eighteen years after the war was over, in 1963, Marcos received an astonishing ten medals, nine of them on a single day in December: two Distinguished Conduct Stars; two Distinguished Service Stars; two Gold Cross Medals; three Wounded Personnel Medals. This burst of medal mania might well have been prompted by the Defense Department's desire to earn reciprocal gratitude from Marcos, who was chairman of the Senate Appropriations Committee.

Marcos's medals claims make him the "biggest liar in history," says Romulo Manriquez. Five years after graduating near the top of his class from the Philippine Military Academy, Manriquez joined the American army, in which he reached the rank of lieutenant colonel. He left the Philippines in the mid-1950s, eventually becoming a loan officer with the Veterans Administration in Washington, D.C. Manriquez confirms that Marcos was captured by the Japanese at Bataan in April 1942—Marcos says he was brutally tortured during his imprisonment—but that after Marcos's release a month later "he did nothing—he traded in the black market." From November 1944 until March 1945 Manriquez was Marcos's commanding officer.

Other military commanders agree that Marcos's war record is bogus. "I think a lot of what Manriquez says is true," says Gregory Swick, who was a U.S. Army major in the Philippines during the war. "Marcos never got all the medals he says he got." Swick was honored by Marcos during a celebration commemorating the twenty-fifth anniversary of the fall of Bataan; during the ceremony Swick talked with six or seven officers who had known Marcos well during the war. They described Marcos's claims as "pure BS."

According to Marcos, he had been the commander of Filipino guerrillas who belonged to a unit he claimed to have organized, Ang

Manga (Mga) Maharlika ("The Nobles"). After becoming president, Marcos named a palace auditorium Maharlika Hall, a major north-south road the Maharlika Highway, and even sought to change the country's name from the Philippines to Maharlika. It was appropriate tribute for a guerrilla unit that distinguished itself. The only problem was that the unit was little more than a typewriter organization, a fiction spawned by Marcos's quest for hero status and money. After the war Marcos prepared a twenty-nine-page document containing the purported history of the unit, which he claimed had 8,300 members. If Marcos's claims had been accepted, all the men would have been entitled to back pay and benefits from the United States—at the time of the Japanese occupation of the Philippines MacArthur promised that Filipinos who fought against the Japanese would be compensated after the war—and Marcos, for his "services," would have enriched himself considerably.

The Maharlika unit that existed during the war never consisted of more than 100 or so men, and its military activities were "of very little value," according to American army records. An extensive investigation by the U.S. Army in 1948 concluded that Marcos's claim to have led a unit of this size was not only "fraudulent" but a "malicious criminal act."

Finally, and perhaps even more incredibly, in view of Marcos's attempts to depict himself as a wartime hero, Marcos was arrested during the war by a U.S. Army captain "for illegally collecting money." Normally he would have been held until after liberation, but he was released, for even back then, as an American army officer wrote, Marcos had "enough political prestige to bring pressure to bear where it is needed for his own personal benefit." There is further evidence that Marcos, far from being the leader of a guerrilla unit and deserving of decoration, may have been a collaborator. His father had welcomed the Japanese to Laoag, the capital of Marcos's home province of Ilocos Norte, in 1942 and later became a propagandist for the occupation, a job for which he said he had been recommended by his son, Ferdinand.

When the war ended, Marcos launched his successful political career. It was from his mother that Marcos acquired "a desire to excel so fierce that he cannot abide to be second to anyone in anything," as Spence put it. It was from his father that he learned the "rules" for how to get to the top. To Marcos's father, said to be stern and humorless, the cliché applies: Winning isn't everything; it's the only thing. "The father's emphasis was not sportsmanship— it was on the victory," writes Spence. For his political rallies, Mariano Marcos gathered crowds by arranging boxing matches between the local boys and his two sons, Ferdinand and his younger brother, Pacífico.

"Don't start a fight until you know you can win it," Marcos advised his sons. And the corollary: "Never make an important move until you can choose your own battleground."

These admonitions became the political principles to which Ferdinand Marcos rigidly adhered. For nearly four decades he never lost an election, never suffered a political defeat (until the final ignominious one). But it wasn't just his intelligence, canniness, booming baritone oratory, and phony war record which Marcos parlayed into a stunning political reign. He had another asset: Imelda Romualdez. A "proudly packaged 36-23-35" was how *Time* once described her. Ferdinand Marcos wasn't the first man of power felled by her beauty, nor would he be the last. And she would not stay the submissive, remain-in-the-background politician's wife. It was she, more than he, who put the bite on businessmen for large and regular "donations." In addition to accumulating money, she acquired political power. She was to become governor of Manila, a virtual head of state, and de facto foreign minister, and in the latter capacity she seemed to challenge Henry Kissinger's record for most miles traveled and heads of state met—from Castro to Qaddafi to the leaders of the Soviet Union and six American presidents.

Imelda Marcos's early years are as clouded by her own myth-making as are Marcos's by his. There is, however, a reliable biography about her, *The Untold Story of Imelda Marcos,* written by Carmen Navarro Pedrosa, a journalist. When the manuscript was finished, in 1969, Pedrosa gave it to Imelda Marcos to read. "She moved heaven and earth to keep it from coming out," Pedrosa recalled. Pedrosa withheld publication until after the 1969 campaign; after martial law had been declared, she and her husband were forced into exile. Pedrosa characterizes Imelda Marcos's life as a "Cinderella story."

But as Imelda Marcos would prefer to have her life depicted, she was bred to be, if not a royal queen, certainly a first lady. Her official biography prepared for the 1965 inaugural souvenir program begins: "She considers herself to be of the South, being a Romualdez of Leyte, where her forebears founded the town of Tolosa and established a family that has become one of the mightiest political clans of the country."

The small, idyllic seaport town of Tolosa was founded by the Spanish two decades before the Romualdez family sailed there, leaving behind their life in a dusty suburb of Manila. It is true, however, that after arriving, they did establish a political dynasty. One of her uncles, Norberto, who had been appointed by President William Howard Taft to the prestigious post of fiscal of Leyte, later became a Supreme Court justice, and helped draft the preamble to the Philippine Constitution. Another uncle, Miguel, became mayor of Manila. Imelda Marcos claimed that her father "was such a scholar" that he had a Ph.D. in law with the highest honors and that he had been a dean of the college of law. "He was also an artist, a composer, a painter. He was a Renaissance man." In reality, however, by comparison with his brothers, Vicente Orestes Romualdez, the youngest of the three, was the family ne'er-do-well.

After his first wife died, leaving him with five children, ages seventeen to eight, his mother and brothers began a systematic search for a new wife in the Catholic convents, which, in addition to running orphanages, took in young girls, who in exchange for room and board performed domestic chores. At the Asilo de San Vicente de Paul they looked over five girls, approving two of them as suitable for Vicente Romualdez. The next Sunday the mother superior dispatched the two to Norberto's house, telling them only to wait for a reply to the note in the tightly sealed envelope they carried. But there was only a blank piece of paper inside; what the girls didn't know was that they were being sent for a tryout. The first girl stunned the gathered clan when she said she didn't know how to sing. But the second girl, Remedios Trinidad, daughter of a jewel merchant, enthralled the family, her song communicating the "essence of sadness." She had won the contest, though it would be a year before Vicente Romualdez could convince her to marry him.

Imelda was born on July 2, 1929, the first of Remedios and

19

Vicente's children. It was not a happy household. Quarrels were followed by Remedios's fleeing, followed by Vicente's prevailing upon her to return, followed by more quarrels, separations, and children—six within eight and a half years. When Imelda was eight, her mother died—"of a broken heart," a niece told Carmen Pedrosa. After her husband's inauguration in 1965 Imelda Marcos laid wreaths on the tomb of her father and that of a politically prominent cousin. But she ignored her mother's memory; she wanted everyone, it seemed, to erase it. Though she later spent a few million dollars to build what she claimed was her "ancestral home," squandered more and more millions on edifices to her honor, and erected a gigantic Mount Rushmore–imitation bust of her husband, she did nothing to perpetuate the memory of her mother, who has neither a tomb nor a marker on her grave site.

Imelda Marcos's official biography says that "she spent her childhood in the shadow of Malacañang." It may have been close to the palace, but in fact, while her mother was still alive and the family was living in Manila, Imelda and her five siblings lived in what, in better days, had been maids' quarters, a small, rickety garage with a cement floor a foot from the dirt. After his wife's death Imelda's father took the family back to Leyte, where his position as dean of the law school was ceremonial, not academic, and the courses he taught were insignificant: legal history and legal bibliography. The family lived in a "poor man's quonset hut," which so ashamed Imelda that when the nuns from the Benedictine school she attended came to call, she would not invite them in.

When she was fifteen, "Meldy," whose friends used this childhood nickname even after she had become first lady, wrote on the appropriate spaces in a classmate's autograph book that her motto was "To try to succeed." Her hobbies: "Singing, reading, going to the movies, letter writing." Her favorite actress: Ingrid Bergman. Her favorite dance: rumba. Her favorite subject: "Lovemaking. Ha!" While still in high school, she was crowned the Rose of Tolosa. After graduating with grades a bit above average—about 80 percent—she received a bachelor's degree in education at St. Paul's College. Her extracurricular activities revolved around her singing (friends insisted she perform at their weddings); parties (three successive nights to celebrate her election as student body president); and entertaining politicians who came from Manila.

20

At the age of twenty-three Imelda Romualdez left the provincial backwaters. The woman who fled in 1986 leaving behind department store-size closets of dresses, more than a thousand pairs of shoes, 500 black brassieres, and vats of perfume and who hoarded sacks of pearl rings, diamond earrings, and ruby necklaces worth millions and millions of dollars, arrived in Manila in 1952 with her entire wardrobe in a small suitcase, no jewelry, and five pesos. She moved in with a cousin, Daniel Romualdez, a powerful politician; he was the means by which the young beauty entered the dens of wealth and political power.

Though she was now in Manila permanently, she had been born and reared in the Visayans,* a heritage which is fundamental to understanding the ostentatious, fun-loving, jet-setting life-style of the woman who emerged years later. Among Filipinos, Visayans are noted for their love of music and hedonism. "Give him a jug of 'tuba' (palm wine) and a piece of dried fish and he will sing the wilderness into Paradise," writes historian Agoncillo about Visayans. Upon arriving in Manila, Imelda Romualdez worked, first at the P. E. Domingo music store, singing and playing for potential piano buyers, then as a clerk in the Central Bank. Most of her considerable energy, however, was dedicated to pursuing acclaim—she was named Miss Manila after making a personal, tear-filled appeal to the mayor, who had already declared another young woman the winner—and chasing power.

Among her escorts was a man three years her junior, a dashing, bachelor-about-town, Benigno ("Ninoy") Aquino, who within a few years had become Marcos's most formidable political opponent and forever after a tormentor who would not go away, even after he had been assassinated in 1983. In the early 1950s Aquino would pick up Imelda Romualdez at the music store. The young couple enjoyed days on out-of-the-way beaches and strolls in Luneta Park, sharing sandwiches on the promenade as they watched the fabulous sunsets over Manila Bay. Some of Aquino's friends say that he saw the relationship as a politically expedient one, considering her fam-

---

* Seven large well-populated islands, grouped like a Rorschach blot around the Visayan Sea, make up the Visayan Islands. Including the scattered islets, the Visayans comprise more than half of the archipelago's islands. One of the largest of the Visayan Islands is Leyte, where Imelda Marcos was born and where General MacArthur triumphantly waded ashore, fulfilling his historic promise to return.

ily's political connections. Aquino himself said years later that he had quit dating her because she was too tall. In 1954 Aquino married Corazon ("Cory") Cojuangco, causing Imelda Marcos sometimes to remark to friends that she had been abandoned for an heiress: Cory Aquino could legitimately claim to be from a wealthy family.

Eight months earlier Imelda Romualdez had conquered Marcos, following a chance first encounter and an impetuous courtship. As the story has been told and retold, they met late one evening, when after a hard day on the House floor, Marcos had adjourned to the congressional cafeteria. Imelda, who had come with a friend to fetch her cousin, the speaker of the House, was in a simple dress and slippers, eating watermelon seeds. But Marcos had seen her recently in a much more alluring pose: on the cover of the *Manila Chronicle*'s Sunday magazine, full red lips, arching eyebrows, low-cut dress, looking serious as well, with a pen in hand, writing on notecards. He inveigled an introduction, then proceeded to resolve the one thing that bothered him: He asked her to stand, then stood back to back with her. Satisfied that she was shorter than he—though by only about half an inch—Marcos turned to a congressional colleague and announced, "I'm getting married." How different history might have been had Imelda Romualdez, at five feet six inches unusually tall for a Filipina, been wearing heels that evening or had her hair piled in her customary bun.

Eleven days after that fateful evening, Marcos gave her a ring, encircled with eleven diamonds (eleven, along with seven, would be their lucky number). On May 1, 1954, the thirty-six-year-old Ferdinand Marcos, who already had at least one child out of wedlock, and twenty-four-year-old Imelda Romualdez were joined together. It was a union of love, no doubt, of intelligence and beauty, to be sure, but as important, at least for each of their ambitions, it was a coming together of two of the most powerful political machines in the country. The Marcoses controlled Ilocos Norte; the Romualdezes, Leyte. She bore him three beautiful children, became a dogged and effective campaigner—her appearance and singing alone attracted crowds—and was attentive to the needs of other politicians' wives. She sent them cakes, took them bowling, picked them up to go shopping, bought them gifts. She was everything that an ambitious politician could want.

"She's lost the bloom she had then," an embassy political officer, who knew her in the 1960s, recalled twenty years later. "She was really a beautiful creature. And a very charming personality when she wanted to be. She was quite a delight. . . . She hadn't gotten— as far as I know—this intense interest in being a politician herself that she later seemed to have. She was just, you know, a good wife, supporting her husband, being a charming hostess."

After three terms in the House and one term in the Senate, Marcos, by 1965, was chafing to be president. The incumbent, Diosdado Macapagal, had been saying that he would not run again; then he changed his mind. With that, Marcos switched parties, from the Liberals to the Nationalists. Such a switch was no big thing for Philippine politicians, who viewed politics more as a vehicle for adding to their principals than for advancing principles; they moved back and forth between parties with the frequency and ease of teenagers joining first one side, then the other in a pickup basketball game.

The Nationalist gathering became "a convention based on the highest bidder," as one delegate recalled. And that was Marcos, whose enthusiastic backers "flung 100-peso bills about like confetti." While some of the other candidates were providing sandwiches for the 1,500 or so delegates, Marcos served them chicken dinners— and on their plates were envelopes stuffed with pesos. He wined and entertained them on a barge on Manila Bay, transported them to the Bayside, an expensive nightclub, for even more merrymaking.

And perhaps most important of all, Marcos had total control over the staff of the Manila Hotel, where the convention was held. A few years later, when Imelda Marcos was in Washington, she summoned William Bundy, assistant secretary of state for East Asia, to the Philippine embassy, ostensibly to talk about money for the Philippine government. That subject took only a few minutes. Then the former beauty queen told the very proper patrician (Groton, Yale, Harvard Law) that she had some political advice which he ought to pass on to Vice President Hubert Humphrey, whose political career had begun when she was still a shy schoolgirl. Humphrey was preparing for the 1968 convention in Chicago, and Imelda

Marcos told Bundy, "You've got to control the site; you've got to have your people everywhere. We had the bellhops; we had the waiters; we had the elevator boys; we had the desk clerks; we had everybody talking up Marcos: 'It's going to be Marcos.' " But the most important thing, she stressed, was that "we had all the telephone operators, so the other side never got their calls."

Once he had obtained the party's nomination, Marcos went to work on one of his convention rivals, Fernando Lopez, to be his vice president. Marcos needed Lopez because he had prestige, influence, and money. His father had been a provincial governor at the turn of the century, and Lopez himself had been the country's vice president after independence. Fernando's brother, Eugenio, was the publisher of the family-owned *Manila Chronicle,* one of the two largest dailies. While Imelda Marcos still had only fantasies about a socially active, jet-set life, the Lopez clan was already the first family of extravagant bashes. But Lopez and his family were strongly opposed to his running for the number two spot. "If you want to help your country, either you run as president, or no more politics," Lopez's wife argued. Her husband agreed—until he faced Imelda Marcos. Entering the Lopez suite at the Manila Hotel, she respectfully—and theatrically—dropped to one knee, summoned up a few tears, and pleaded with Lopez. "Imelda was probably the sweetest person you ever met in your life back then," said Lopez's grandson, Robert Puckett, recalling the scene many years later. Lopez accepted.

"I will give you everything you want," Marcos promised voters in numbing day and night rallies when the campaign began. "Except my wife." But she gave everything for his election, with some commentators suggesting she was worth a million votes. Her mere presence drew thousands to rallies. Her tender songs wowed them. Sometimes she and the presidential candidate warbled duets. But she was more than just a pretty face and melodious voice. She was a tireless organizer as well, focusing on women. Philippine women had then, as they do today, more status and opportunities than women in other Asian countries. They also had the right to vote, and a substantial percentage of the eligible ones exercised it. So Imelda Marcos recruited them, the debutantes and the social matrons. They drove cars, answered telephones, catered receptions.

They also wore blue dresses, and thereafter the hangers-on around Mrs. Marcos, the retinue that traveled and shopped with her, in Rome, New York, Teheran, Tokyo, were known as the Blue Ladies.

It was a bitter campaign, a "year-long propaganda orgy," as the American embassy in Manila described it. It had not been a year of debating issues, there being little ideological difference between the two parties. It was, rather, a campaign about personalities, one of the costliest and dirtiest in the country's history. The Liberals charged that Marcos, described at the time by the CIA as a "brilliant lawyer" and a "ruthless politician," had employed slick legal tactics to acquire lands from impoverished peasants, that he had padded his payroll while a senator, that he had issued bad checks in business deals, that he had filed fraudulent war damage claims with the U.S. government (his claims for damage allegedly done to his property during the war were rejected by Washington), that he had taken money from a flamboyant American businessman in exchange for political favors, then made out a false receipt to make it appear he had repaid the money, thus adding the charge of forgery to the Liberals' litany. The Liberal assault on Marcos's character was so excessive that the correspondent for the *Far Eastern Economic Review* suggested, "few are willing to believe anyone can possibly be so bad." Even Imelda Marcos wasn't spared during the campaign. Liberal backers spread stories that they had seen her in the nude in magazines and porn films, though it seemed no one else ever saw them.

Marcos couldn't attack Macapagal's personal integrity, but he could criticize the president—"barely a middleweight in terms of political know-how, administrative ability, and intellectual capacity," the CIA reported—for having failed to do anything about the corruption. The Philippines "suffers from too much politics, too much selfishness and greed, as well as from serious mal-administration and venality on the part of government officials, amounting in some cases to flagrant graft and corruption," said the American ambassador to the Philippines from 1964 to 1967, William McCormick Blair, Jr. A mural in the dining room of the National Press Club in Manila depicted a politician with one hand grabbing a pile of gold coins. By getting a road, school, or other pork-barrel project

25

for his district, a congressman whose salary was only $1,800 a year could up his income, from kickbacks, to $250,000. The easiest and most profitable way to earn a living wasn't by producing sugar, pineapples, or bananas but by smuggling—anything and everything, from American cars and cigarettes to Japanese cameras and Italian shoes. Congressmen ran their own smuggling rings and cut off funds to government agencies when they tried to crack down. Voters expected to be bought—and they were. In one 1965 congressional race the opposing candidates, cousins, each spent nearly $2 million, buying voters meals, paying their medical bills, or simply giving them money, which because of the competition might be as much as $25 per voter, more than most families earned in a month.

On the eve of the 1965 vote the embassy in Manila advised Washington that the presidential race was too close to call. While the incumbent administration normally had the edge in vote fraud potential, the embassy noted, "countermeasures by Marcos forces to checkmate such action may be more effective than those applied previously by opposition candidates."

Marcos buried Macapagal, amassing a plurality of some 650,000 votes out of 8 million cast.

At the time of the election the CIA wrote that the Philippine electorate "craves efficient and honest government." The agency noted that "a generalized condition of discontent and lawlessness" existed in the Philippines, fed by a number of fundamental factors, foremost among them being "widespread rural poverty," and by "deep social and economic cleavage between upper and lower classes," along with "widespread graft, corruption, and favoritism in government and business." Without basic government programs to address these problems, the agency went on, "nationalism and discontent are likely to lend themselves to leftist exploitation. This would present increasing problems to the Philippine government in domestic administration and in the maintenance of a strong pro-US and pro-West position."

It was a trenchant analysis of the fundamental, and deep, problems afflicting Philippine society. And without intending to be, it was prescient. Marcos didn't provide the honest government but rather more graft and corruption than before. The rural poverty became more crushing; the gap between the rich and poor widened.

The conditions were indeed exploited by the left; anti-Americanism grew.

It was all the more painful because the Philippines was the country America had tried to develop in its own democratic image. It was where Americans had first fought a counterinsurgency war in the name of protecting freedom and defeating communism.

2 : Once a Colony, Always a Colony?

America acquired the Philippines (along with Guam, Puerto Rico, and Cuba) as part of the spoils of its war against Spain, a war fought in pursuit of the country's "Manifest Destiny." It was the war precipitated by the sinking of the battleship *Maine* in Havana Harbor. Several weeks later the conflict was carried to the other side of the world. In what might be considered the avenging of the humiliating loss of the *Maine,* Admiral George Dewey sank the Spanish fleet in Manila Harbor, an event remembered not for its being an impressive military feat—the Dewey warships faced a pitiful Spanish flotilla of seven unarmored boats—but for Dewey's memorable cry "You may fire when you are ready, Gridley." Seven months later the Spanish-American War ended with the signing of the Treaty of Paris. The United States gave Spain $20 million. Spain gave the United States the Philippine archipelago, a 1,000-mile elongated S of 7,107 islands, all but 154 smaller than 5 square miles, with the two largest, Luzon in the north and Mindanao in the south, constituting about 65 percent of the country's land area.

Filipinos generally were most appreciative of Dewey and the Americans for having tossed out the Spanish, who had ruled since 1565, forty-four years after Ferdinand Magellan had "discovered" the islands on his voyage to prove the world was round. (Magellan was killed in the Philippines by a local chieftain.) But that didn't mean they were anxious for another colonial master. Under the leadership of Emilio Aguinaldo, they took up against the Americans where they had left off against the Spanish. America's crushing of that independence movement is largely forgotten, mentioned, if at all, as a footnote to the Spanish-American War. Aguinaldo is dismissed in American history as a "rebel"; his guerrilla war, which it most certainly was, as an "insurrection." But in the Philippines Aguinaldo is still honored—the country's Pentagon is named after him—for his role in what Filipinos call the "Philippine-American War." And a war it was. The Philippines lost a staggering 16,000 men in combat (nearly three times the number of Americans who had died fighting for independence), and another 200,000 died from war-related hunger or disease. It was a dirty war, marked by racism and atrocities. The Filipinos were considered "savages, barbarians, a wild and ignorant people." Entire towns were burned to the ground; in one village every male over ten years old was ordered shot.

The war was fought for businessmen who wanted new profits; generals who wanted bases; and other Americans who just wanted to do good—the "white man's burden," as Rudyard Kipling wrote in 1899. President William McKinley called it "benevolent assimilation," a policy designed to "uplift and Christianize" Filipinos. To understand McKinley's messianic ambitions, translate "Christianize" to "Protestantize," for the Filipinos had been hearing about Christ for three centuries, His life and lessons ingrained by Roman Catholic priests and nuns sent out by Spain (who kept Protestant missionaries out of their colonies). What McKinley was really all about was Americanizing the Filipinos.

By 1910 nearly 1,000 teachers, the forerunners of the Peace Corps, had forsaken their relatively comfortable positions in America for the unknown dangers in a steamy tropical land an ocean away. The first group arrived on the USS *Thomas,* and to this day one hears older Filipinos talk warmly about the Thomasites. (Marcos's mother was taught by a Thomasite.) When the Spanish left, barely 5 percent of Filipinos could read and write; before the American teachers had been there long enough to graduate one generation of students, literacy had risen to nearly 50 percent, and it continued climbing, until it is today probably the highest in Southeast Asia. A public education system was established, from elementary schools through the university. Americans inculcated democratic values and were handmaidens to a political consciousness, which in turn gave birth to political parties and spirited elections. The country's Constitution, which had to be approved by President Franklin D. Roosevelt, was a virtual rewrite of the American Constitution. Adopted in 1935, it contained a bill of rights, ensuring freedom of speech, travel, and religion, as well as recognizing the sanctity of private property and the home. Just as in the United States, governing power was shared by three separate and independent branches: legislative; judicial; executive. While the Philippine president was the commander in chief of the Philippine armed forces, he, unlike his counterpart in Washington, had one constitutionally granted extraordinary power: Whenever he deemed it necessary in order to prevent violence, invasion, insurrection, or rebellion or when the public safety required, he could legally "place the Philippines or any part thereof under martial law." It was this provision that Marcos was to invoke in 1972, at a tragic turning point in Philippine history; he noted at the time, and often thereafter with great satisfaction, that as president he was granted that power in a clause of the American-influenced Constitution.

Maybe the U.S. conquest and rule of the islands were imperialistically motivated, but they were defended as "enlightened imperialism" and as "colonialism with a conscience," comparable to British colonial rule and certainly far better than the records of the Spanish and Portuguese. For all that, however, "the American self-image of colonial benevolence is not fully warranted," writes Robert Pringle, a career Foreign Service officer with a doctorate in Southeast Asian history who served in the Philippines in the early 1970s. In a scholarly book Pringle says:

> Myth number one is that we created democracy in the Philippines; that our colonialism was more enlightened than European colonialism, both in its motivations and its consequences. In fact, American rule bolstered a preexisting landed elite, encouraging it to express itself through representative forms. The result was perhaps as "democratic" as Mississippi in 1900.

The "landed elite" extracted tremendous profits from vast agricultural estates, while the mass of the impoverished peasants were kept in their place, which was working in the fields for wages set at barely subsistence levels by the political system which the elite controlled. This feudal system has stalked political stability in the Philippines. In 1952 agrarian unrest underlay the revolution in which the United States intervened. In 1972 Marcos promised that he would use his martial law powers to break up the landed oligarchy. He didn't. And in 1986 old women and teenage girls worked alongside weathered men and small boys, toiling in the merciless sun for a dollar a day, in sugarcane, cotton, and rice fields owned by a few immensely rich and powerful families and American corporations. It was a situation ripe for harvesting by the Communist New People's Army (NPA).

In 1934 the U.S. Congress passed the Philippine Independence Act, which provided for a ten-year commonwealth period prior to complete sovereignty. But before independence came, of course, World War II had to be fought and won. Within hours after the attack on Pearl Harbor, Japanese bombers dropped their loads on Manila. The war saw a new bonding on the American-Philippine relationship, a "special relationship" fashioned from the shared hardships and horrors, victories and defeats, tears and joys. Corregidor; the Bataan death march; General Douglas MacArthur's departing promise—"I shall return"—and his wading ashore at Leyte when he did—they are equally part of American and Philippine culture, history, and lore. Ten months after MacArthur had accepted the Japanese surrender aboard the battleship *Missouri,* the Philippines became an independent country. The July 4 date reflected the seeming oneness of the two countries; in 1962, when independence day was changed to June 12—to commemorate the day Aguinaldo had declared independence from Spain—it reflected a rising nationalism and incipient anti-Americanism.

In the weeks and months preceding independence Filipino and American leaders negotiated the postindependent relationship between the two countries. But it was hardly a negotiation between equals. The Philippines was staggering from war wounds; if it didn't accept what the United States offered, Uncle Sam might just let it collapse and die. The United States received far more than it gave, which was $620 million to rehabilitate the ravaged archipelago. Though it was the first time that the United States had agreed to pay for war-related destruction and while that might seem to be a generous amount, many Filipinos justifiably found it piddling, considering the sacrifices they had endured and the crumbling shell of a nation left after the war. During the Japanese conquest and occupation and the American liberation of the islands, more than a million Filipinos had died. The country was devastated. The infrastructure (bridges, roads, and railroads) had been destroyed; the financial system was virtually nonexistent because the Japanese-issued currency was now worthless; even most of the country's carabao, the beast of burden, had been killed.

Similarly, Filipinos were incensed by the Philippine Trade Act, which was passed by the U.S. Congress in 1946 and set the terms of the economic relationship between the two countries. Though the act brought some definite benefits to Filipinos, its provisions were far more favorable to Americans. The provision that most rankled was the one which gave Americans the same rights as Filipinos to exploit the island's agricultural and mineral resources and to own and operate public utilities. This "parity" clause violated the Philippine Constitution, which mandated that Filipinos must own 60 percent of any business engaged in the development of the country's natural resources. Under pressure from the United States, the Philippine legislature approved a constitutional amendment—after expelling on specious grounds leftist members who opposed it. (In 1954 the Laurel-Langley Act, passed by the American Congress, provided that the most galling of the unequal trade provisions would expire in 1974.)

Along with its economic stake the United States departed the Philippines with its military interests protected. The issue of what to do or not to do with U.S. military installations in the Philippines had been debated in Washington since Dewey had selected Subic Bay as the site for an American naval base. In 1946 General Dwight David Eisenhower recommended that all U.S. Army units be withdrawn from the archipelago. Eisenhower argued that more important than any strategic value of the bases were good relations between the countries, a prescient understanding that the bases would be an obstacle to smooth bilateral relations. In the end an agreement signed by the two countries in 1947 allowed the United States to keep all its bases in the Philippines, from the military cemetery to the Camp John Hay rest and recreation center in the mountain resort town of Baguio, with the most important, Clark Air Base and Subic Bay Naval Base, soon to become among the largest overseas U.S. military installations.

Independence ended the colonial relationship between the two countries, but the United States had no intention of relinquishing control over the islands. The nature of the relationship was very quickly dictated by the fears of communism and the cold war.

It was George Kennan who set the course for American policy toward postindependence Philippines, an interventionist course that displayed little respect for Philippine sovereignty. In the early 1940s Kennan was arguing, often without much success within the government, about the threat of Soviet communism. After postings in Europe, Poland, and the Soviet Union, Kennan, in 1947, was asked by Secretary of State George Marshall to be the first director of the State Department's Policy Planning Staff, which was established to provide for long-range thinking in American foreign policy. It was in that capacity that Kennan, a brilliant man and prolific writer, detailed what American policy should be in the Far East in order to keep the United States safe from the Soviet Union. While his Top Secret memorandum might seem to be a steely analysis of America's interests and a callous prescription for how to pursue them, it is a far more honest description of American policy in the Philippines, and throughout the third world, during the past four decades than all the rhetoric and speeches about helping others, human rights and democracy. Kennan wrote:

> . . . we have about 50% of the world's wealth but only 6.3% of its population. This disparity is particularly great as between ourselves and the peoples of Asia. In this situation, we cannot fail to be the object of envy and resentment. Our real task in the coming period is to devise a pattern of relationships which will permit us to maintain this position of disparity without positive detriment to our national security. To do so, we will have to dispense with all sentimentality and day-dreaming. . . .
> . . . We should dispense with the aspiration to "be liked" or to be regarded as the repository of a high-minded international altruism. We should stop putting ourselves in the position of being our brothers' keeper and refrain from offering moral and ideological advice. We should cease to talk about vague and—for the Far East—unreal objectives such as human rights, the raising of living standards, and democratization. The day is not far off when we are going to have to deal in straight power concepts. The less we are then hampered by idealistic slogans, the better.

Kennan concluded that in the Pacific U.S. policy should concentrate on ensuring that two countries "remain in hands we can control or rely on." The countries were Japan and the Philippines. American policy, Kennan urged, should be shaped to allow for Philippine independence "in all internal affairs but to preserve the archipelago as a bulwark of U.S. security in that area."

That policy was, in effect, put into practice a few years later when the United States waged a secret counterinsurgency war and thoroughly meddled in Philippine domestic politics. What Washington was seeking to crush was a peasant guerrilla army known as the Huks, born of the union of the Communist and Socialist parties in order to deal with legitimate grievances, the Japanese having served as the midwife. The covert war was led by Edward G. Lansdale. Such were Lansdale and his exploits, in the Philippines and later Vietnam, that he was portrayed in not one but two novels, widely read and talked about because they raised troubling questions about what America had in mind for strange lands and cultures in the 1950s. In *The Ugly American,* Lansdale was the model for Colonel Hillandale, the prototype "good American." In Graham Greene's *The Quiet American,* he was Alden Pyle, the young, idealistic American diplomat obsessed with naïve notions of saving Asians from communism. "I never knew a man who had better motives for all the trouble he caused," Greene's foreign correspondent says about Pyle. Three decades later Lansdale, in his seventies, was still influencing American covert activity abroad, brought in by the Reagan administration to advise on how to get rid of the Sandinistas in Nicaragua and consulted about possible solutions in the Philippines as the Communists grew stronger. One young military officer whom Lansdale impressed was Oliver L. North, the marine lieutenant colonel who from his position at the NSC was a major actor in the Iran-contra scandal.

Lansdale's anti-Huk counterinsurgency war, a mix of paramilitary operations, psychological warfare, and old-fashioned electoral politics, was to become the prototype of U.S. anti-Communist counterinsurgency wars elsewhere: Colombia; Venezuela; Vietnam. "The United States' fateful entanglement in Vietnam began in Manila in the early 1950s," writes Joseph Smith, referring to Lansdale's activities in the Philippines, where Smith also served as a CIA operative. After the French defeat at Dien Bien Phu, Lansdale was rushed to Vietnam. Employing the psywar, or "dirty tricks," he had honed in the Philippines, Lansdale counterfeited documents, invoked soothsayers, and beamed broadcasts that "the Virgin Mary is going South"—in order to frighten peasants into fleeing the Communist North, an operation so successful that the United States ignored the provision in the Geneva accords which called for elections to unify North and South Vietnam with the argument that the people of the North had "voted with their feet." Politically Lansdale looked to Ngo Dinh Diem as Vietnam's Ramón Magsaysay, the man Lansdale and the CIA had nurtured and financed into the Philippine presidency.

When a bearded revolutionary began to implant communism in an island much closer to home, Lansdale not surprisingly found himself with a new third world mission. To train anti-Castro guerrilla forces, Lansdale turned to a Philippine colonel, Napoleon Valeriano, who had been his sidekick in the Huk war. (Valeriano had followed Lansdale to Vietnam, taking with him the wife of a wealthy Philippine businessman. The husband responded by putting out a contract on Valeriano, continually forcing him to find employment elsewhere. One of Emma Valeriano's sons by her first marriage many years later married Marcos's youngest daughter.) After the Bay of Pigs debacle Lansdale was put in charge of the supersecret Operation Mongoose. Lansdale's timetable called for the anti-Castro forces to march triumphantly on Havana by October 1962. As in the Philippines and Vietnam, Lansdale invoked the Deity, broadcasting his message surreptitiously. Christ had picked Cuba for His Second Coming, went the Lansdale-inspired Gospel, but He wanted the Cubans to get rid of Castro before He arrived. Christ never arrived, Castro remained, and Lansdale went back to Vietnam, arriving after the fall of Diem, to continue his covert operations. During a meeting sometime later with Diem's successor, Nguyen Cao Ky, whom Lansdale was urging to adopt a constitution, thus putting at least a democratic façade over his rule, Ky remarked: "I'm just thinking of you Americans. You want us to write a constitution and elect someone every four years. Like Marcos, huh?" Then he laughed. Ky proceeded to recall a meeting he had had with Marcos in Baguio. Imelda Marcos, who had been present, had gone on and on about the poor, explaining all that the Marcos government had done for them. Her fingers, Ky noticed, were laden with jewels. "Is that what you want?" Ky asked Lansdale.

The United States and Lansdale had been more successful in the Philippines in the early 1950s. The Philippine Communist party was founded in 1930, with the openly avowed goals of overthrowing the United States colonial government and replacing it with an independent Philippines patterned after the Soviet Union. Three months after the attack on Pearl Harbor, and Manila, the leaders of the Communist and Socialist parties and of the country's numerous peasant organizations established the Hukbo ng Bayan Laban sa Hapon ("Army of Resistance Against Japan"). With ample arms, and even better equipped with their knowledge of the jungles and mountains, the Hukbalahaps, or Huks, fought with honor and critical success during the war. When the war ended, however, the Americans, fearful of the Huks' political goals, ordered them to be disarmed; one Huk unit was seized, thrown in jail, and all of its members were eventually executed, "with the knowledge of the American military police." Several Huk leaders were jailed, the most prominent being Luis Taruc.

But the Huks were far from defeated, and with the Japanese gone they returned to their fight against the feudal land tenure system. It was class warfare, the Marxist indoctrination reinforced by the fact that while the peasants had been fighting and dying for liberation, a substantial portion of the nation's wealthy elite had fled the country, sought refuge in the cities, or in many cases become collaborators. When the fighting ceased, the landowners returned to their villages, demanded back rents from the tenant farmers, and employed military police and their own paramilitary armies to enforce their "rights." As with the revolution in the Philippines in the 1970s—as well as in El Salvador and Nicaragua—the peasants who joined the Huks had little knowledge or understanding of Marxism, Leninism, or socialism. "The rebellion's main impetus was peasant grievances, not Leninist designs," conclude the authors of a book prepared by the Foreign Area Studies Program at American University, under contract with the Department of the Army.

The peasants fought back with the ballot as well as the bullet, and in 1946 several Communists, including Taruc, were elected to

Congress. The Communists and other leftists were promptly thrown out on the ground that they had won by resorting to fraud and violence, a pretext which, if applied across the board, might have reduced the legislative body to fewer than enough members for a good poker game. The real reason for the expulsion: The leftists were opposed to the trade act and the parity amendment, and they had enough votes to block their adoption. The blatant action reinforced the peasants' conviction that their enemies were the landlords and their U.S. backers.

All, or even a substantial portion, of the tactics employed by the United States to defeat the Huks in the early 1950s remain hidden, safely secure in Lansdale's memory and in documents, still classified three decades later. For that reason, what Lansdale himself has chosen to reveal becomes even more chilling. Playing on the Filipino peasant's taboos, fears, and myths, Lansdale concocted his "eye of God" scheme, which he had borrowed from the ancient Egyptian practice of painting watchful eyes on the tombs of pharaohs to scare away would-be plunderers. Lansdale made a sketch of these eyes, and at night members of his team would slip into villages and paint them on a wall facing the house of a suspected Huk. The twentieth-century version of the "eye of God" also involved using light aircraft, which were flown over Huk-occupied areas, with Lansdale's psywar crews broadcasting in the native languages from above the clouds so that the listeners would think they were hearing from one of their gods. The psywar teams also broadcast curses that would descend on any villagers who gave food or support to the Huk combatants, with the result, which Lansdale omits to mention, that some Huk villages were starved into surrender.*

---

* Young CIA recruits in the 1950s would hear about Lansdale's tactics in their course on how to disseminate information, or disinformation, and disguise the source, which was, of course, the United States. Disinformation was categorized—light, medium, and dark gray—according to how well the source was disguised. The best propaganda, the students were taught, was "black propaganda," and Lansdale was its master. Another example of a black propaganda operation, the young men learned, was one devised by E. Howard Hunt, who later acquired unwanted fame with his involvement in the Watergate break-in. When Hunt was with the CIA in Mexico, he, upon learning that a Communist organization was planning a reception for some visiting Soviet dignitaries, had obtained an invitation. He made 3,000 copies, which he passed out. When the "invited" guests arrived, either they couldn't get into the crowded hall, or if they did manage to, they discovered that all the food and drinks had been consumed. They departed with anything but a good feeling about the Communists.

Another psychological operation played upon the people's dread of the *asuang* ("vampire"). Lansdale's psychological warfare teams would move into a village and tell peasants about the presence of an *asuang* among the Huks. After sufficient time for the stories to have been spread among the villagers, the soldiers ambushed a Huk patrol as it moved along the trail in the dark of night. Snatching the last man in the patrol, the soldiers "punctured his neck with two holes, vampire-fashion, held the body up by the heels, drained it of blood, and put the corpse back on the trail." When the Huks found their comrade, they quickly fled the area—and Lansdale's soldiers moved in.

It wasn't only a bloody war in the jungles. The United States also meddled in Philippine politics—heavily. In the late 1950s and through the 1960s American officials, as well as scholars and journalists, were contemptuous of Philippine politics. They spoke, and wrote, derisively and snidely of "democracy—Philippine-style," or "election—Philippine-style." What the cynics overlooked was America's contribution to the political process. The United States hardly bears full responsibility for the aberrant behavior, but it certainly didn't set an enlightened example, starting with the election of Ramón Magsaysay. As always, American intervention was motivated by the best of intentions. Lansdale and the American ambassador at the time, a retired admiral, Raymond A. Spruance, knew that the peasants had legitimate grievances, that reforms were needed if a revolution was to be defeated. Their candidate was Magsaysay.

As minister of defense Magsaysay, prodded by Lansdale, purged the army of its corrupt officers and disciplined soldiers who abused the peasants. Above all, Magsaysay, a burly, powerfully built man, nearly six feet tall, went out into the countryside, among the peasants, listening to their concerns, seeking their views. "Magsaysay's humane approach electrified the populace and one by one, the Huks surrendered to him," writes Philippine historian Teodoro Agoncillo. And every time a Huk surrendered he was photographed handing his gun over to Magsaysay. He became a national hero. He was also a humble man, the son of a farmer and teacher. "Bare feet will always be welcomed in the president's palace," he said after becoming president.

Magsaysay resigned as minister of defense to begin his campaigning; on that same day in 1953, half a world away in Iran, Prime Minister Mohammed Mossadegh was driven from his palace by crowds loyal to the shah Mohammad Reza Pahlavi—part of the CIA's covert intervention in domestic politics there. Magsaysay's opponent was the incumbent president, Elpidio Quirino, whom Lansdale, Spruance, and others disapproved of because they thought he was too corrupt. The CIA ran Magsaysay's campaign as if the agency were the Republican or Democratic National Committee and he were its man for the White House.

Just how extensive the American participation in the Philippine domestic politics was may never be determined. The CIA didn't record what was being done, and the station chief had instructions from his superiors in Washington not to tell the State Department what the agency was doing. Among other things, the CIA drugged President Quirino's drinks before he was to give a speech so that he would appear incoherent.

CIA director Allen Dulles offered Lansdale $5 million for the campaign, but Lansdale said he needed only $1 million, which was delivered to him in cash in a suitcase. The funds from Washington were supplemented by business "donations" from American corporations in the Philippines; Lansdale did the arm-twisting. It must have seemed a bit strange to corporate officers that an American military officer—for that was what Lansdale was to them—was acting as finance chairman in a foreign campaign, or maybe it wasn't, considering America's colonial legacy—but they gave. A "big contributor" was the Coca-Cola franchise in the Philippines, whose director told his board, "Ed made me an Eagle Scout, so I gave money to the Magsaysay campaign."

Several CIA agents worked on Magsaysay's campaign. One was David Sternberg. A paraplegic who once shot an intruder "squarely in the forehead," Sternberg disguised his CIA status by acting as a consultant to the U.S. government and as a correspondent for the *Christian Science Monitor,* in which his articles appeared from 1946 until at least 1972; he also contributed at least one article to *Foreign Affairs.* During and after the campaign Sternberg wrote speeches for Magsaysay. On one occasion when Magsaysay insisted on delivering a speech that had been written by a Filipino, Lansdale reacted in a rage, finally hitting the presidential candidate so hard that he knocked him out.

Another American, a New York lawyer and unsuccessful Republican candidate for Congress, Gabriel Kaplan, was recruited by the agency and sent to Manila with instructions "to help Lansdale elect Magsaysay." Kaplan's cover was the Committee for Free Asia, which later became the Asia Foundation. Working with various community organizations, such as the Chamber of Commerce, Rotary, and veterans' groups, Kaplan, with funds from the agency, set up a nationwide organization called NAMFREL, the National Movement for Free Elections—the same organization that was resuscitated after a decade of martial law and played a critical role in the 1986 election. (Some of the Filipino community leaders who were involved in NAMFREL later moved over to Laos and Vietnam as the nucleus for Operation Brotherhood, a CIA-funded and -controlled "humanitarian" organization, principally assisting, at least at first, the refugees from North Vietnam. "We taught a lot of Filipinos how to tap telephones and bug offices," remarked William Sullivan, who as ambassador had carried out the secret war in Laos in the late sixties.) Throughout the campaign United States officials, including Secretary of State John Foster Dulles and President Eisenhower, brazenly denied there was any American involvement.

The United States had "neither the authority nor justification" for interfering in the election, and Spruance had been "wrong" in doing so, writes Thomas Buell in *The Quiet Warrior: A Biography of Admiral Raymond A. Spruance.* Washington's conduct was "contrary to the lawful relations between two sovereign states," and Spruance "deceived the American people and the world through his false and misleading statements" that America was remaining neutral in the election. It would have been "more fitting," Buell writes, had Spruance "resigned as Ambassador rather than to compromise his integrity. . . ." It might have been more fitting, but it would have been a rare act for the ambassador to have resigned. The Foreign Service has not stressed that ethic, as became even more evident in Vietnam and Cambodia during the 1960s and early 1970s and in Nicaragua in the 1980s. Many Foreign Service officers thought that American conduct in those countries was without authority or justification. But it is considered more appropriate for a

Foreign Service officer to work within the system, dutifully carrying out orders of the president he serves, than it is to resign.

On election day in 1953 the Philippines was swarming with foreign correspondents, their presence "orchestrated" by the CIA, which had encouraged major newspapers and magazines to send their best reporters to cover the elections because, the agency told editors, that's where the action was in Asia. The agency, which had secretly set up the National Press Club in Manila, had also been successful in planting newspaper articles and editorials "echoing" its anti-Huk, pro-Magsaysay themes. Whether at the CIA's urging or on their own initiative, *The New York Times* editorial writers were unrestrained about Magsaysay, a man they saw as being "on our side in the present alignment of the forces of freedom against the minions of enslavement." He was, the paper said, a man "of integrity, imagination, courage and simplicity." *Time* magazine put him on the cover when he was still defense minister, a man of "unchallenged reputation for honesty," who was carrying out the "U.S. experiment in transplanting democracy."

America was transplanting democracy by doing whatever was necessary to put Magsaysay in Malacañang. The agency had even smuggled guns into the Philippines, for use in a coup, if Magsaysay was defeated at the polls. But Magsaysay defeated Quirino, decisively. All the clandestine—and illegal—activities appeared to have been justified—that is, if the ends justify the means. Magsaysay was "America's boy," unabashedly so in foreign affairs, consulting with the Manila CIA station before making any important foreign policy decision; Sternberg continued to write his speeches.

Transplanting democracy meant going after Magsaysay's domestic political opponents, the most effective of whom was Senator Claro M. Recto, as unrelenting in his opposition to American foreign policy in the region as Magsaysay was slavish in following it. Recto, who was proud of his complete collection of *Foreign Affairs,* considered himself not anti-American but pro-Philippine. He criticized the bases agreement on the grounds, correctly, that the U.S. agreements under NATO and with other countries were far more favorable to the host country than was the U.S. arrangement in the Philippines. In Spain the Spanish flag flew over the bases; in the Philippines it was the American flag. When Washington claimed that the United States owned the lands on which the bases were situated, Recto prepared memorandums setting out the Philippine position that the United States had only leasehold rights, an argument eventually accepted by the United States. Recto was the "spearhead and brains of the national reawakening."

The CIA set about to destroy Recto, who had been a principal drafter of the 1935 Constitution. It planted stories that he was a Communist Chinese agent who had been infiltrated into the Philippine Senate. To derail Recto's electoral ambitions, the agency prepared packages of condoms, which it labeled "Courtesy of Claro M. Recto—the People's Friend." The condoms all had pinprick-size holes in them at the most inappropriate place. The agency went further. The CIA station chief, General Ralph B. Lovett, and the American ambassador, Admiral Spruance, discussed assassinating Recto, going so far as to prepare a substance for poisoning him, an assassination plot that has not been publicly discussed before.

Recto wasn't assassinated, the idea abandoned "for pragmatic considerations rather than moral scruples" (and with Lovett later suggesting that the bottle containing the poison was tossed into Manila Bay). He died of natural causes in 1960 at the age of seventy. Magsaysay was killed when his helicopter crashed in March 1957. He was forty-nine years old. Even though the Huks had been defeated and communism was no threat to the Philippines, the United States was still intent on controlling the country.

"Find another Magsaysay," the chief of the agency's Far East division instructed Joe Smith when he headed out to the Philippines. (His cover was as a civilian air force employee.) The first stage focused on the 1959 off-year elections, in which eight of the country's twenty-four senators were to be elected. Because senators did not represent separate provinces but were elected in at-large races, the candidate who received the most votes immediately became a national political leader and a serious presidential contender. Smith worked assiduously to put together a slate, holding endless clandestine meetings with various Philippine politicians who wanted to be on the American-backed slate. One of those involved in the negotiations was Marcos, at the time the Liberal party's forty-two-year-old leader in the House of Representatives. Marcos was "always much cagier" than the other politicians, recalled Smith. He would never commit himself to any of the slates, always seeming to agree to whatever coalition was being proposed.

In the end Smith was able to put together a slate of six. It became known as the Grand Alliance, and the agency gave it $200,000, funneling the money through one of the candidates who didn't raise any suspicions because of his own wealth. It gave $50,000 to Diosdado Macapagal, who became president in 1961. "We were breaking Philippine law against foreign intervention in their elections," Smith acknowledged later. The intervention reflected the same arrogance that marked American involvement in the election of 1986, the belief that it was justified, as Smith put it about the 1959 effort, "in order to change their country for the better." America's Grand Alliance was clobbered, the top vote getter finishing tenth overall, with two of the candidates pulling up the very rear. Marcos, who was not on the Grand Alliance slate, finished at the top, an impressive 300,000 votes ahead of number two.

The agency's failure was reversed two years later, when, according to Smith and other CIA officers, it again backed Macapagal, this time successfully for president. The CIA backing of Macapagal in two key elections would seem to lead to the conclusion that the United States supported him, not Marcos, in 1965. But the United States wasn't particularly fond of Macapagal after his one term. "He was sort of the picture of flightiness," recalled a diplomat who had been senior in Philippine matters at the time. "The man could be talked into anything by the last person who talked to him." Philippine military and intelligence officials who worked closely with the CIA specifically asked the agency not to support Macapagal. These officials wanted the United States to respect Philippine sovereignty by remaining neutral, and there is reason to believe the agency may have done so.

The CIA's Intelligence Memorandum on the Philippine elections, prepared a few weeks before the voting in 1965, noted that both the candidates were "Western oriented and pledged to continue close and equitable relations with the US and the West on matters of mutual interest." While it is possible, of course, that the United States had finally decided to stay out of a Philippine election, in

43

view of this CIA assessment, what seems most likely is that the United States contributed to both camps, as it had in 1959. By doing so, Washington would be in a position to extract the quid pro quo from whoever was elected. At this point in the American-Philippine relationship what the superpower wanted above all from its former colony was some support for the escalating U.S. war in Vietnam from the new Philippine president, Ferdinand E. Marcos.

3: Debut and Conquest

Luneta Park, with its newly planted grass rolling to the waters of Manila Bay, was jammed for the inauguration of the country's sixth postindependence president. Spectators arrived early on December 30, 1965, their umbrellas offering some respite from the blazing sun when the drifting clouds parted and moved on. They were to witness the coming of Camelot to the Philippines. Imelda Marcos seemed equipped, and determined, to be her country's Jackie Kennedy, who had been born in the same month of the same year. The Luneta crowd erupted when the first lady, her rich black hair piled in a bun, stepped out of the limousine. She looked svelte in a simple ecru designer terno, with an unusual paisley design hand embroidered on the short butterfly sleeves and bodice, and a wrap-around, inverted tulip skirt with two overlapping petals. She flashed a V sign and kissed the ring of Rufino Cardinal Santos without kneeling. In tow were the first couple's three children, ten-year-old Marie Imelda ("Imee") and five-year-old Irene outfitted in identical designer dresses, pink velvet ribbons for their hair and sashes; their seven-year-old brother, Ferdinand, Jr. (then and into adulthood called Bong Bong), attired like his father—white barong over striped dark pants, and black shoes—sent the security detail scurrying when he asked for chewing gum. Their father labeled his inaugural message "A Mandate for Greatness," and when the boyish-looking forty-eight-year-old orator boomed it out, American reporters present flashed back to JFK's inaugural a few years earlier.

Listening was Vice President Hubert Humphrey, who worked the crowd as if the Filipinos would be able to vote in his next campaign. The vice president was the highest-ranking American ever to attend the inaugural of a Philippine president. Other coun-

tries didn't consider it such a momentous occasion, Indonesia sending its minister of budget, India the minister of petroleum, and Japan
a *former* prime minister. Humphrey's presence, it seemed, had less
to do with the personage of Ferdinand Marcos than with the war in
Vietnam. On Christmas Day 1965 U.S. President Lyndon B. Johnson had ordered a halt to the bombing of North Vietnam in an
attempt to achieve a negotiated settlement. Then, as part of his
grand peace offensive, LBJ dispatched his most trusted team of
foreign advisers (UN Ambassador Arthur Goldberg; Ambassador
W. Averell Harriman; National Security Adviser McGeorge Bundy)
to world capitals with the mission of gaining support for the U.S.
strategy. Humphrey had the same assignment in Tokyo, Taipei, and
Seoul as well as with the new president in Manila, where Humphrey
also discussed the war with Lansdale, who had come over from
Vietnam for the occasion.

In his inaugural Marcos never used the word *Vietnam,* referring
to the war only very obliquely in a couple of sentences, even though
he had promised the American ambassador that he would use the
occasion to endorse American policy. As the temperature rose to
a tropically muggy eighty-six degrees, Marcos, cool in his barong
tagalog, the sheer shirt worn outside the trouser and without a coat,
delivered an oration that was a paradigm of hypocrisy. The man
who soon had his hand in the public treasury and who within a few
years had handed over practically the entire economy to his cronies
for plunder on this day condemned public officials who "combine
with unscrupulous businessmen to defraud the government and the
public—with absolute impunity." The man whose wife was to push
consumption beyond ostentation was now promising that "Every
form of waste—or conspicuous consumption and extravagance, shall
be condemned as inimical to public welfare." And the man who was
to rape his country's judicial system called "upon all to join hands
with me in maintaining the supremacy of the law." And so it went,
for thirty-one minutes—eleven minutes longer than his prepared
text—without his even glancing at a note. He delivered the inaugural
in a rolling cadence, effective pauses followed by his voice driving
to crescendos. He was interrupted nineteen times by applause, the
loudest when he declared that he had been given "a mandate for
greatness."

"It was a tour de force," Jack Valenti remembered twenty years later. In a memorandum for LBJ written at the time, Valenti, who was the president's special assistant, was unrestrained, heralding Marcos as "one of the most magnetic speakers you have ever heard." The address had "stunned" Valenti, not exactly a neophyte in speechmaking, who described it as "perfectly timed, ingeniously shaped, in a voice that must tritely be compared only to an organ." Moreover, Marcos was "enormously intelligent," he was "tough," and he had "guts," Valenti told his president.

Valenti was one of the first Americans of power and prominence whom the Marcoses captivated. "It's amazing how much time we spent with him prior to his inauguration," Valenti recalled. "We had lunch with him, dinner with him, spent an enormous amount of time with him." On the day before the inauguration Marcos said, "Let's play golf tomorrow."

Valenti was taken aback. "Mr. President, you're being inaugurated tomorrow."

"I know," Marcos replied, "so we'll tee off at six in the morning."

And sure enough, while Filipinos were praying for their new president at inaugural day masses throughout the land, Marcos and Valenti were driving down the manicured fairways of the Wack Wack Golf and Country Club (in a residential district where the streets are named Harvard, Yale, Princeton, Stanford, Berkeley, Northwestern, Duke, Fordham, Notre Dame, Holy Cross, Colgate, and Cornell).*

The Valenti-Marcos friendship flourished. Once or twice a year Valenti returned to the Philippines, always as a special guest of the first family, put up in the lavish guest quarters at Malacañang. On

---

* Marcos was an avid golfer, and LBJ later presented him with a custom-made set of clubs. The American embassy in Manila cabled Washington: "His swing weight is D-zero (i.e., one step lighter than D-one), he prefers quote regular unquote shaft flexibility, and for present has length of 43 inches for woods and 38½ inches for irons." When "playing regularly," the embassy noted, Marcos's handicap was eight, which is quite good. Marcos's handicap was kept that low by caddies, who altered the numbers on his scorecard, and solicitous security men, who, upon arriving at balls before Marcos, nudged them into better lies. What some U.S. diplomats most remembered about a round of golf with Marcos, however, was the scene in the locker room afterward: Marcos's aides would sit the president on a locker room bench, remove his golf spikes, loosen his belt, remove his golfing shorts, slip on a fresh pair of trousers, then tighten his belt.

one occasion, at about three in the morning, Valenti sought to escape a nightclub party in order to get some sleep. Imelda Marcos reluctantly let him go, but only if he would agree to see her later. When Valenti explained that he had a noon flight, she said, OK, they'd meet for breakfast. She continued partying. At 7:00 A.M. she appeared, fresh and sharp, in her palace suite. Doodling on a napkin to illustrate her points, she talked politics. "I thought, my God," Valenti said many years later, vividly remembering the scene, "she could go before a Yale political science class and do very well as a teacher." Valenti remained loyal to the Marcoses even when most of the rest of the world was condemning them. He escorted Imelda Marcos to parties, and in 1985 Valenti said of Ferdinand Marcos, "I think he is one of the great men of Asia."

Valenti taught the Marcoses the importance of having powerful men in the right places. Upon returning from the inauguration, Valenti became, in his own words, "kind of his [Marcos's] man in the White House." At critical moments he interceded for the Marcoses, one of the first and most important times occurring when a state visit for Marcos was at stake. Rare is the world leader who doesn't covet an invitation from the American president. An official welcome in Washington is a seal of approval, redeemable in the guest's home country and around the world. It is in part for that very reason that the invitations are not lightly issued; an administration doesn't want to cheapen their value, reserving and doling out invitations in exchange for something Washington wants from the honored world leader. In addition, of course, state visits are taxing on the bureaucracy, from the Secret Service, which has to provide protection, to the State Department, whose involved officers must devote their attention to caring for the visiting dignitaries. Marcos wanted a state visit for his own domestic image; LBJ wanted it for Vietnam.

Within the Johnson administration there were some serious reservations about inviting Marcos. "Marcos is acting more and more like a Philippine President than the tough and far-sighted New Dealer/pragmatist that he appeared to be," James C. Thomson, Jr., the Asian expert on the National Security Council (NSC), wrote in a Secret memorandum, the subject of which was "A Marcos Visit: The Plot Thickens." Marcos did not want to come to Washington "unless he can return with some highly tangible goodies," Thomson explained, "with his hands very full." That "message," Thomson added, was being carried to the State Department and White House by Benjamin Romualdez, Marcos's brother-in-law. While in town, Romualdez presented, as a gift from Marcos to LBJ, the mounted head of a tamarau, a wild and dangerous version of the domestic water buffalo, which, if Romualdez was to be believed, Marcos had shot on a hunting trip to Mindoro Island. Imelda Marcos's brother Benjamin, fourteen months younger than she, was every bit as avaricious, unscrupulous, and ambitious—but not as smart—as his sister. At twenty-four years old Kokoy, as he was known, had attached himself to Marcos when the then congressman had married his sister. Romualdez became a political huckster. He was the first of the sycophants in the Marcos court, tireless and shameless in promoting the self-interests and images of his brother-in-law and sister. After declaring martial law, Marcos amply rewarded Romualdez, naming him ambassador to Saudi Arabia, where he squandered a few million dollars to build a new residence and embassy befitting an oil sheikh; to China; and later to the United States. Simultaneously with some of these posts he was governor of Leyte, one of the largest and politically most significant Philippine provinces. And of course, in keeping up with the rest of Marcos's family and cronies, Romualdez amassed a prodigious personal fortune, including an estate in Southampton, on Long Island, in New York State, for which he paid, in 1980, well over $1 million.

Romualdez, who had earlier pushed for Humphrey to attend Marcos's inauguration, was now campaigning for the state visit. He was assisted by Jack Valenti, who even though he had left the White House to become president of the Motion Picture Association of America, remained close to Johnson. On Motion Picture Association stationery, Valenti weighed in, recommending that LBJ invite Marcos to visit and to address a joint session of Congress. Valenti was as effusive as always, pitching Marcos as "handsome, a war hero . . . earned the highest grades ever gained by a lawyer . . . is married to the reigning beauty of the Islands." Turning to the State Department's concerns about the costly demands Marcos would make, Valenti responded: "I can dispose of this argument by asking one simple question: What is too high a cost for the presence of 2,500 Philippine fighting men in Viet Nam?"

Getting Philippine boys in Vietnam was part of LBJ's "More

Flags" crusade, designed to assure the American people that the Vietnam War wasn't just an American war. The effort had netted contingents from South Korea, Thailand, Australia, and New Zealand. The Philippines, it would have seemed, should have been eager to enlist. The nation was only 600 miles across the South China Sea from the Indochina peninsula; if the dominoes had started falling, surely they would create a red wave that would engulf the archipelago. Marcos's predecessor, President Macapagal, had offered to send a combat battalion to Vietnam. But in the Philippine Senate the opposition had been led by one Ferdinand Marcos. The Vietnam War wasn't much more popular in the Philippines than it was in the United States, students marching and demonstrating against it, often in front of the American embassy. The Vietnam legislation died. After Marcos had been elected president, the pressure on him became intense. He was visited by Humphrey a second time, then by Harriman, and by Lansdale, who was back in Vietnam and made several pitches, directly and through emissaries. The Johnson administration also agreed to pay the expenses of the Philippine troops in Vietnam, though this was not disclosed publicly.

Eventually Marcos was persuaded. But he didn't do much. South Korea sent 50,000 troops to Vietnam; Thailand, 11,500; and Australia, 7,500. The Philippines, which had three times the population of Australia, sent a 2,000-man engineer battalion. In September 1966 the first contingent of the Philippine Civic Action Group (Philcag), as it was called, boarded two Philippine Navy LSTs, bound for Tay Ninh, South Vietnam. On the same day Marcos departed for Washington. He was in an "excellent mood" and "obviously pleased with the prospects for his visit," the American ambassador, William McCormick Blair, Jr., reported. "I have seldom seen him in a better frame of mind."

But Blair, a lawyer from a wealthy and socially prominent Chicago family who had been active in Democratic politics before President Kennedy had named him ambassador to Denmark, had some reservations. "The combination of a genuine war hero who speaks eloquently and a beautiful, charming, and talented First Lady is almost certain to receive unusual attention of U.S. press and other media," Blair had cabled Washington when the state visit was being considered. "I am concerned that enthusiastic response which I expect President and Mrs. Marcos to evoke from American people may give rise to extravagant expectations of him on our part, and veil profound continuing problems."

The cautionary communiqué was far more prophetic than Blair could ever have imagined. One month after the cable *Life* magazine became one of the first in the media to provide the unusual attention. "Not since the days of Jackie Kennedy in Washington's White House has a First Lady moved into her role with the verve and style of Imelda Marcos," *Life* exclaimed in an August 1966 cover story for its Asia edition. The title of the article told it all: "The Philippines' Fabulous First Lady." Mrs. Marcos, *Life* proclaimed, possessed not only the "grace and attractiveness of Jackie" but the "energy reminiscent of Eleanor Roosevelt." *Parade* magazine followed a few weeks later with a gushing story, complete with the obligatory photo of a smiling, happy family (along with another of Imelda Marcos dancing with South Vietnamese Premier Nguyen Cao Ky). "Besides magnificent honey-colored skin, eyes of fiery topaz and the figure of a beauty queen, she has brains and energy to boot," the article opened. Ferdinand Marcos was on the cover of *Time,* the first Filipino president in two decades to be so honored, heralded for his "dynamic, selfless leadership." The magazine found him to be a "perpetually grinning man who walks with a military spring, drives a golf ball with the tense fury of Ben Hogan, and spends 20 hours a day on the job." He had, according to *Time,* been recommended for the U.S. Congressional Medal of Honor (he hadn't) and had won a "second Silver Star" (also false). And all that press adulation was in the first year of the reign of Ferdinand and Imelda; for twenty years, Imelda Marcos was to be ever attentive to journalists, wining and dining them, presenting them with gifts, massaging their egos.

The state visit, in September 1966, became a prelude to, and preview of, the next twenty years of the U.S.-Marcos relationship, from the charm of Imelda Marcos to the cunning effectiveness of her husband. Everything about the state visit was in keeping with the Texas-size grandeur that marked the Johnson years—including the biggest Washington downpour of the Johnson presidency. Four and a half inches of rain fell during the hours surrounding the landing at Andrews Air Force Base of the U.S. Air Force VC-137 with the Marcos party, which included Imelda Marcos's brother Kokoy Romualdez; then Major Fabian Ver, of the palace security force; a coterie of Blue Ladies; and a handful of American diplomats, who sang with the first lady during the long flight.

In an emotional address to a joint session of Congress Marcos, who had been introduced as a "war hero," displayed the ease with which he cut his convictions to fit his audience. Even though he had refused to send combat troops to Vietnam, he now spoke glowingly about America's involvement there, sounding more militant than Johnson. He proposed that after the United States defeated the Communists in Vietnam, it establish a cordon sanitaire around China. Speaking at the United Nations, he called for a "new Tashkent for Southeast Asia" as the vehicle for ending the war. (In January, with the Soviet Union acting as intermediary, India and Pakistan had ended their war over Kashmir, signing a truce in the central Asian city of Tashkent.) Marcos's bold initiative was reported at the top of the front page of the *Washington Post,* under an eight-column banner headline announcing that Undersecretary of State George Ball was resigning because of his doubts about the escalating Vietnam War.

Marcos might speak boldly, but his actions didn't match. LBJ still wanted more Philippine soldiers in Vietnam, including combat troops. Marcos was reluctant to provide anything more. But he wanted more money, lots more, which Johnson's advisers were reluctant to provide. Marcos, they noted, was seeking the money for "political purposes" and had not proposed "effective means of using the large sums." In addition to two fifty-foot Swiftcraft patrol boats and rifles for a combat battalion that was *not* going to Vietnam, Marcos was seeking equipment for ten engineering battalions; he had already been promised equipment for three. Secretary of Defense Robert McNamara was opposed to the increase. It would be enough, McNamara suggested to Johnson, for Marcos to be told during the state visit that he would receive equipment for two more battalions. Those five battalions, McNamara argued, "should be ample for the very small contribution the Philippines have made in Vietnam." Moreover, the secretary of defense noted, "the 10 battalions are not essential to the military security of the Philippines."

They were, however, essential to Marcos's domestic "political purposes." He used them to build roads, which he pointed to as one of his accomplishments during the next presidential campaign. They were also used to enrich his friends. Marcos awarded one of his cronies, Rodolfo Cuenca, the contract to build a highway outside the mountainous resort town of Baguio. Instead of using his own men and equipment, Cuenca used four of the U.S.-supplied engineer battalions.

In the end Marcos prevailed, hauling away a commitment for ten battalions, plus $45 million in economic assistance; $31 million in settlement of Philippine veterans' claims; and, finally, from the Special Education Fund, $3.5 million, which would be for Imelda Marcos's Cultural Center. Marcos had prevailed in spite of the reservations of just about all of Johnson's advisers because, as was his nature, he had been relentless, dogged, determined—and because Johnson, like his successors, gave in to Marcos, rather than forcefully stand up to him.

In a state visit the diplomats are supposed to take care of all the details in advance, the short meeting between the American president and the foreign head of state being largely ceremonial, for pleasant chatter and pictures. But when Marcos found the State Department resisting his demands, "he insisted on going head to head with the president," recalled William P. Bundy, assistant secretary for East Asia at the time. That didn't please LBJ. "He got mad as hell at me," Bundy remembered, adding, "It was a messy visit, just a messy visit." Johnson never got over his dislike of Marcos, according to Bundy, principally because the Philippine president only modestly supported the Vietnam War while never relenting in his demands for concessions. In December 1967 Johnson and Marcos met in Australia, where they were attending the funeral of Prime Minister Harold Holt, who had drowned while swimming off the southern coast of Victoria. Marcos used the solemn occasion to press LBJ again for more American aid. An angry Johnson told Bundy, "If you ever bring that man near me again, I'll have your head."

The tension of the state visit was hidden behind the glamour and glitter. At the White House dinner the stiff card beside every plate informed the select guests that their crabmeat Chesapeake, roast sirloin, and garden salad would be followed by Trappist cheese. For dessert? Glace Imelda.

The thirty-seven-year-old former beauty queen was at the head table, on her left the president of the United States, on her right the secretary of state, Dean Rusk. Across the table was His Eminence Francis Cardinal Spellman, archbishop of New York, next to whom had been placed Catherine Gerlach Blair, an intelligent, sophisticated lady, often on "best-dressed" lists, and the wife of the American ambassador. (Having to share a table with Mrs. Blair must have rankled Imelda Marcos, for she was loath ever to be in the presence of anyone more beautiful or charming than she, even to the point of staying away from parties, which she so loved. Joseph Smith, the CIA man in the late 1950s, recalled how Senator Marcos, but not his wife, showed up for Smith's going-away party, with everyone laughing and telling Smith that it wasn't that Mrs. Marcos didn't like him, just that the host's wife was prettier.)

When the strolling musicians, nine army violinists and cellists in red jackets, played a Filipino song, "Planting Rice" ("Planting rice is never fun, bent from morning to the set of sun . . ."), Imelda Marcos sang along, joined by a few Americans accustomed to singing with her in the Philippines. In his toast LBJ recounted how Humphrey, Valenti, Rusk, and the others all had returned from trips to the Philippines with glowing reports about the new president. And he said, each agreed, "He sure has a beautiful wife." Her low-cut, pale yellow, butterfly-sleeved gown—one of the forty she had brought for the visit, along with boxes and boxes of jewels—prompted the president to quip, "You must have a pretty good CIA yourselves," explaining that yellow was his favorite color. "It's my favorite color, too," she replied, with political savvy, for, in fact, she was more partial to red (a taste that caused her some consternation years hence when she wore a red dress on a visit to Libya's Muammar al-Qaddafi, whose color is green). After dinner, when the band struck up "Hello, Dolly," LBJ's favorite, he led the Philippine first lady in a dance, gliding across the marble foyer, joined by President Marcos and Lady Bird Johnson. Then, it was on to the East Room for "Moments from Great American Musicals." Imelda Marcos looked "like a bright-eyed teen-ager watching her first show," notes author and journalist Jim Bishop in his book *A Day in the Life of President*

Johnson. Ordinarily the American president and first lady retired about 11:00 P.M., but tonight the singing and dancing were only just beginning at that hour. LBJ, escorting Mrs. Marcos from guest to guest, exclaimed that she was the prettiest woman in attendance. It was 1:08 A.M. when the Johnsons escorted the Marcoses down the steps of the north portico and into their waiting limousine.

The next evening the festivities moved up Connecticut Avenue a couple of miles, to the redbrick Shoreham Hotel, where the Marcoses laid it on as if they were from the wealthiest country in the world: 3,000 Chinese egg rolls, 650 pounds of beef, 800 pounds of shrimp, 150 pounds of caviar, 150 pounds of crabmeat, 75 pounds of mushrooms, and tray after tray of pastries. But again the evening was remembered for Imelda Marcos. Wearing cherry-size drop earrings of yellow pearls, she was accompanied by Peter Duchin's Orchestra as she sang "Because of You" in Tagalog, her starry-eyed gaze fixed on the American president.

"Bravo," cried a radiant LBJ, standing to applaud, as did Washington's society columns. IMELDA STOLE SPOTLIGHT, declared the *Washington Post.* The *Washington Star* thought her worth two stories, with photos. Betty Beale, chronicler of the after-hours doings of Washington's powerful, acclaimed Mrs. Marcos as "talented, beautiful and aristocratic." A longer story appeared that day written by Ymelda Dixon; Imelda Marcos, displaying her mastery of flattery, suggested that she might change the spelling of her name, because " 'I' sounds so egotistical." Dixon gushed, and in print heralded Imelda Marcos as "a blessing not only to her own country, but to the world."

That was Washington, dismissed as a shallow "political town" by "sophisticated" New Yorkers. But Imelda Marcos was prepared to storm the cultural capital as well. This was not her first trip to New York. Her earlier visit, however, had been and would remain secret: She had come for psychiatric treatment. She was diagnosed as a manic-depressive, treated first with heavy tranquilizers and later with lithium. Her spending binges are a classic manifestation of the manic stage, according to doctors.

On her first full day in the big city, in September 1966, Imelda Marcos started off with a fashion show. But the Philippine beauty, stunning in a turquoise and white terno, "ended up being the star attraction herself," reported the *Washington Post* in a short item on the front page of its Sunday paper. "U.S. fashion may never be the same again," the paper declared. That evening, after she had attended a performance of *Man of La Mancha,* New York Mayor John Lindsay, handsome, urbane, and young, gave a dinner for Mrs. Marcos in the Belasco Room at Sardi's, the Times Square hangout where Broadway stars, politicians, and newspapermen (*The New York Times'* presses are on the other side of the walls) went to see and be seen. Angela Lansbury and Johnny Carson provided some impromptu entertainment; then Imelda Marcos sang.

After a few hours' sleep Mrs. Marcos, resplendent in a tight, flowing skirt and a revealing deep V royal blue bodice, alighted from a limousine, then kissed the ring of the round-faced, bespectacled Cardinal Spellman. Following mass at St. Patrick's Cathedral and an appearance on NBC's *Meet the Press,* Marcos spent a sunny Sunday afternoon on the links at the Rockefellers' Tarrytown estate, with Nelson, Laurance, David, and John. Throughout the week it was a litany of celebrities, the powerful and important. New York Governor Nelson Rockefeller called on President Marcos in the presidential suite of the Waldorf Towers; David Rockefeller, president of Chase Manhattan Bank, gave a luncheon in the Marcoses' honor at 1 Chase Manhattan Plaza; Mayor Lindsay hosted a black-tie dinner at the Cloisters; *Reader's Digest* hosted a luncheon for them at the Starlight Roof of the Waldorf-Astoria; five hours later, in the same room, the Marcoses gave a reception for New York editors and publishers; *Newsweek*'s top staff met with them at the presidential suite of the Waldorf Towers; the president of Time, Inc. hosted a black-tie dinner in the Ponti Auditorium of the Time-Life Building at Rockefeller Center. (Within less than one month Marcos was to make his appearance on the cover of *Time.*)

Squeezed in between all that was a quick hop to the Midwest, aboard a U.S. Air Force special flight. After breakfast with Chicago's Mayor Richard Daley, Marcos flew across Lake Michigan to receive an honorary degree. Marcos had been desperately seeking an honorary, but he wanted the prestige of Harvard or Yale. At every opportunity his brother-in-law Kokoy Romualdez pressed State Department officers. "The President is quite a scholar, you know," Romualdez told the embassy's political officer during a lunch at the

Seafront Restaurant in Manila. During a meeting in Washington William Bundy, a Yale alumnus, told Romualdez that despite Washington's "best efforts," an honorary degree at either Yale or Harvard was not possible. It may have been one of the few times that Washington put one over on the Philippine leader, instead of vice versa, for what Marcos and his brother-in-law didn't know was that nothing had been done to obtain either of those prestigious honoraries. In the end Marcos received his honorary from the University of Michigan, a center for Philippine studies.

Ferdinand got what he coveted; so would Imelda. That was to be present at the opening of the Metropolitan Opera House in Lincoln Center. It was an extravaganza-cum-supergala, described by one matron there in a gold lamé evening dress as "quite possibly the greatest social event since the Nativity." Among the 3,800 men in white ties and tailcoats and women in long gowns and sparkling diamonds were "tycoons, aristocrats, nabobs, bankers, moguls, diplomats, potentates, fashion plates, grande dames and other assorted Great Society over-achievers," according to Charlotte Curtis's capture of the evening on the front page of *The New York Times.* Wearing a full-length gown with butterfly sleeves and a diamond and pearl tiara, Imelda R. Marcos appeared in a picture in *The New York Times* the next day. Front page. At the top. In the center. Standing next to the first lady of the United States in an intimate cluster with the Met's general manager, Rudolf Bing, and John D. Rockefeller III, chairman of the board of Lincoln Center. In a full-page photo in the *New York Post,* there was Imelda Marcos amid the likes of Mrs. Henry Ford II; the Cornelius Vanderbilt Whitneys; Ethel, Joan, and Rose Kennedy; Governor and Happy Rockefeller; Senator and Mrs. Jacob Javits; Ambassador and Mrs. Arthur Goldberg; Mrs. Richard Rodgers.

Mrs. Marcos was center stage. But this time it wasn't her charm and beauty that accounted for her presence. When the embassy first suggested that the Marcoses might like to attend an opera at the newly opened opera house, the response (from Kokoy Romualdez) was that the Marcoses "would have no interest in opera unless it were opening performance." Not even *Il Trovatore,* with sets by Cecil Beaton and of almost equal significance to the premiere? No. The premiere or nothing. There was opposition in both the White

House and State Department, but then "Kokoy went to work," recalled Paul Kattenburg, a career diplomat who was handling Philippine matters in Washington at the time. "I don't know how much money they spent, but they must have spent thousands of dollars." It's not clear exactly what Romualdez did; perhaps he simply shelled out a large amount of money for tickets; that is how many people buy their way into a New York event.

After New York it was on to San Francisco, where Imelda Marcos and her Blue Ladies spent several thousand dollars in an after-hours shopping spree at Magnin's, the fashionable Powell Street emporium; and down to Los Angeles, where Ferdinand Marcos golfed with Valenti, Bob Hope, and Lloyd Hand, LBJ's chief of protocol, who had been with Valenti at Marcos's inauguration.

On the way home the Marcoses stopped in Hawaii, where the next Johnson-Marcos pirouette caught some State Department officials napping. "It came out of nowhere," recalled Edna Barr Hubbert. "I bolted off the couch." Hubbert was responsible for the Philippine matters in the State Department's Bureau of Intelligence and Research (INR) at the time, but it was from the evening news that she learned about what was to become the Manila Summit.

With his popularity slipping and the war growing increasingly unpopular, LBJ wanted to do something about the war—and get out of the country so that he would not have to campaign for those Democrats who were facing certain defeat in the looming elections. Johnson's domestic political advisers came up with the idea of the president's going to Manila in LBJ's first trip outside the Western Hemisphere since becoming president. Altogether he would travel 31,500 miles, visiting seven countries in seventeen days. When the idea for a gathering in Manila was presented to Marcos, he "went for it like a hungry trout," as Bundy phrased it.

"It is with great feeling of pride and joy to learn of your forthcoming visit to my country," a Filipino farmer, from Baco, Oriental Mindoro, a province on the impoverished island south of Luzon, wrote the American president. The letter was addressed "c/o U.S. Embassy, Manila."

You will, no doubt, be feted in the grand circles of my leaders as the honor of your person and office befits. They will, no doubt too, impress upon you their much vaunted, grandiose achievements in the interest of my people. . . .

I wish, with all my heart that you would prolong your stay so that you could come to my barrio and see for yourself how the common Filipino lives, for how could we better fight communism except by preventing these people from turning to it? You would see roads being neglected in spite of a budget that is unparalleled in my country's history. You would notice, if you would travel the entire length of my province that broad tracts of land, fertile and waiting, left untilled, because roads are so bad and transportation so costly that it is useless to till the farm anyway. You would find peasants eating rice only once a day or not once at all.

I would advice [sic] you, Mr. President, not to be impressed by my leaders' pronouncements. We never had a leader who had the welfare of the common man at heart except, possibly, the late Ramón Magsaysay. . . .

To the common man, Mr. President, it seems illogical that my President could initiate a Summit Meet [sic], the primary goal of which is to achieve peace in Southeast Asia when we the barrio people of my country are being left harboring within himself [sic] a sense of being uncared for, unnoticed, neglected.

It was signed, "A filipino farmer." It could have been written by a peasant in El Salvador, Brazil, Zaire, India, or Thailand, in 1986, as in 1966. Just as it would effectively be ignored by LBJ, so would the essential message fail to penetrate many American policymakers (and journalists) in the Philippines and in most of the third world. The glitter and modernity of most third world capitals are a façade over the grinding semifeudal poverty that grips most of the country.

The Marcoses were unrestrained in their efforts to present their Philippines as they wanted it to be seen. Potholes were filled, streets cleaned, buildings scrubbed, and whitewashed walls erected so that the visiting dignitaries wouldn't have to look at the slum poverty; other eyesores were camouflaged by coconut fronds. There was even a moral renovation, albeit only slight and temporary: Manila's racketeers and gangsters were rounded up; taxicab drivers and bar girls, asked to observe a moratorium on padding the bills for foreign visitors.

Imelda Marcos led the charge, her visions of status and grandeur, her formidable energy—the "Lyndon Johnson of Asia" as one American described her—propelled by the fresh memories of Texas size and New York style. She was everywhere, all the time, her need for only three or four hours' sleep now serving not just as a luxury to allow more time for partying but an essential. She had the almost inconceivably short time of one month to prepare for the caring of seven heads of states (in addition to Johnson: Chairman Nguyen Van Thieu and Premier Nguyen Cao Ky, of South Vietnam; Thailand's Prime Minister Thanom Kittikachorn; South Korean President Park Chung Hee; Australia's Prime Minister Harold Holt; and New Zealand Prime Minister Keith Holyoake), their wives, aides, hangers-on, plus 1,000 or so reporters. Imelda Marcos succeeded. She scurried about Malacañang, checking the teaspoons and crystal goblets, supervising the six men teetering precariously atop tall ladders and working around the clock. "It will be done tomorrow night, or else," one of the workmen told a Philippine journalist, repeating her orders. She sent her Blue Ladies on lawn patrols: Litter was gathered; weeds were picked; shrubs were trimmed; grass was manicured. She persuaded some fifty wealthy families to "donate" everything from their silver and china to rugs, furniture, and chandeliers, which she relocated in the suites of the Manila Hotel, the stately bayside establishment used by General MacArthur for his headquarters during World War II. She ordered each of her Blue Ladies to learn—fast and completely—about the country and individual for whom she would be hostess. As for Mrs. Johnson, Imelda Marcos's minions set upon her the minute she arrived, to measure her for Filipino fashions, which Mrs. Marcos in the years to come always made sure were on the hotel beds of the wives of visiting VIPs.

While the men deliberated the curse and course of the war—the closing joint communiqué called for the withdrawal of all foreign troops from South Vietnam—Imelda Marcos sparkled. No one could match her for always looking so fresh. Even then, barely ten years after she had arrived in Manila with all her clothes in one suitcase, her possessions were awesome. She had closet after closet of dresses, divided into Western-style ones and butterfly dresses, and, as an aide to Lady Bird Johnson still vividly remembered twenty years later, an "astounding wall of shoes," arranged like a prism, from

shades of blue to violet to red. At each stop during a tour she led
for the wives of the heads of state Mrs. Marcos, who had three of
every outfit, would change from the one with creases and sweat
marks into a fresh one handed to her by a maid.

The grand finale, the culmination of the courting and catering,
was the Barrio Fiesta, a colorful jubilee which Spanish priests had
converted from a pagan festival into a ceremony for the cleansing
of sin. Under Mrs. Marcos it became a Roman orgy. "I have rarely
seen a night to equal it," exclaimed Mrs. Johnson. It was a preview
of the show that was put on for every American dignitary during
the next two decades.

The heads of state arrived at Malacañang in two-wheel carts
draped with bright crepe paper, a grinning LBJ hunched forward
pulling on the pony reins, with Mrs. Johnson on the seat next to
him. On the palace's expansive lawns the acacia trees and banana
palms were illuminated with 7,800 bright paper lanterns of traditional Malay design. The 3,000 guests mingled with the powerful,
entertained by Philippine beauties and strolling guitarists playing
and singing romantic ballads. Malacañang, a stately Spanish colonial
structure, quarters for Spanish and later American governors, was
awash with 400 dozen African daisies "and enough assorted flora
to eclipse Holland in tulip time," as *Life* magazine described the
scene in its eleven-page spread about the summit pageantry. From
the food booths, arranged in groups of seven (one of the Marcoses'
lucky numbers), the guests piled their trays woven out of leaves
with pieces of unhatched duckling parboiled in the egg, stuffed crabs,
rice cakes, and sweet, sticky baby coconuts. As the guests gorged
themselves, beautiful young girls gracefully placed a tiara of tiny
white flowers on the head of each first lady. On the peak of each
modern-day emperor they fixed a crown of flowers (which LBJ acknowledged with a smile at Imelda Marcos, then quietly removed
and laid beside his plate). Filipino dancers entertained with native
dances, and the orchestra dedicated a number to each potentate:
"Waltzing Mathilda" for Australia's Holt; "Arilang" for General
Park of Korea; a Maori farewell song for New Zealand's Holyoake;
and "Deep in the Heart of Texas." Imelda Marcos, of course, sang—
and danced. In the stifling, muggy tropical heat a small boy with a
large fan stayed near Johnson, who in the morning was to slip away

to Vietnam, the first American president since Lincoln to get so close to an actual battlefield. But tonight the lanky American president, wearing a barong and a bright kerchief around his neck to absorb some of the sweat, enjoyed leading the Philippine first lady in a fox-trot.

LBJ was so smitten by Mrs. Marcos that he honored her, in May 1968, at a private White House dinner, the American president making a special trip back from his Texas ranch in order to attend. It was nearly the equal of an affair for a head of state. "Mrs. Marcos would enjoy some star types," noted the suggested guest list, which along with senators and justices included socialites and power brokers. Her brother Kokoy Romualdez and two of her Blue Ladies were also guests. In his toast Johnson heralded Imelda Marcos as the "jewel of the Pacific." While in Washington, she was also honored at a luncheon on Capitol Hill hosted by Senate Majority Leader Mike Mansfield, during which she was photographed shaking hands with Senator Edward Kennedy; up in New York she breakfasted with Terence Archbishop Cooke. During this trip to the United States Imelda Marcos also wanted a visit to Cape Kennedy, for twelve-year-old Bong Bong. Senator Daniel K. Inouye of Hawaii, who over the years was probably closer to the Marcoses than any other member of Congress, urged that the request be granted, for "it could prove to be a 10-strike in relations with the Marcos family and the Filipino people." The State Department thought it would be sufficient, and less expensive, if the youngster visited NASA headquarters in Washington or the Goddard Space Flight Center in nearby Maryland. But Mrs. Marcos didn't want anything second-best for her son. Johnson's national security adviser agreed, adding that "NASA should provide an escort who is both an expert, a good teacher, and a good baby-sitter. Let him go to Cape Kennedy to see the real thing." Young Marcos went to Cape Kennedy. Imelda Marcos would keep coming back to Washington.

4: Chasing Power

The Marcoses' spell over American policy continued to hold, long after their popularity at home had begun to erode. In the streets and at the polls Filipinos registered their disapproval of the Marcos administration. But the Marcoses discovered that they could rely on American leaders to bail them out when it seemed that many Filipinos wanted to throw them out. Ferdinand Marcos turned out to be not that much different from many of the worst of Philippine politicians, using high office to enrich himself, buying and stealing political power. Imelda Marcos raised corruption to a tasteless art form. During the first Christmas in the palace she planned a party for orphans and needy children. She sent letters to and telephoned businessmen, soliciting donations, collecting several hundred thousand dollars. All the checks and cash went not toward the party "but into Imelda's pockets," a presidential aide of the time recalled.

Washington became aware early of the sordid manner of the Marcos rule when Senator Stuart Symington conducted hearings into the conduct of the Vietnam War. But the United States remained silent. It was Mrs. Marcos's task to bring home the influential and mighty; she did so methodically and seriatim.

Richard Nixon was exposed to the Marcos press, as LBJ had been, on what was his first trip outside the United States after becoming president. Nixon's stop in Manila, in July 1969, came during a lightning twelve-day circumnavigation of the globe. The journey had begun with Nixon on the deck of the USS *Hornet*, present for the splashdown and recovery of *Apollo 11;* Nixon welcomed the first man to walk on the moon, Neil Armstrong. Continuing westward, the presidential party stopped at Guam, the tiny island runway for B-52 strikes into Vietnam, and, thought secret at the time, of Cambodia as well. But the process of extricating the

United States from Vietnam had also begun. The term *Vietnamization* was being tossed about, and Nixon had, a month earlier, announced the withdrawal of 25,000 (of about 500,000) American troops in Vietnam. While on Guam, Nixon outlined for reporters the future limits of American military involvement in Asia: In order to avoid another Vietnam, the United States would not dispatch troops to fight in Asia except in the event of a threat from a major power involving nuclear weapons. In other words, the Asian governments would have to fight their own wars against internal enemies. The "Guam doctrine" became, with the help of Nixon's image makers, the "Nixon doctrine."

Arriving in Manila, President and Mrs. Nixon received the Marcos welcome. The Philippine honor guard played "California, Here I Come"; the six-and-a-half-mile route from the airport to the palace was jammed with government employees, students, ROTC students (in civilian clothes) who had been turned out, along with thousands of Filipinos who genuinely wanted to greet the American president. They waved miniature American flags, tossed rose petals at the first ladies, and carried placards: FLY US ALSO TO THE MOON, MR. NIXON and THE MOON BELONGS TO EVERYONE BECAUSE OF PRESIDENT NIXON.

The visit also brought out the protesters. Peasants in straw hats gathered in front of the American embassy, carrying flaming bamboo torches and shouting, "Stay on the moon, leave Asia alone," and "Give Asia back to the Asians." Students carrying placards saying UNCLE DICK, GO AWAY QUICK and AFTER VIETNAM WHAT NIX burned American flags torn from the boulevard welcome arches and effigies of the American president. In the days before Nixon's arrival a Molotov cocktail was thrown at the U.S. Information Service library, blowing up a moon trip exhibit and killing an eighteen-year-old youth who was looking at it; another grenade landed at the gate of the American embassy; and a third shattered windows at the American military headquarters. The demonstrations reflected not only an anti-Vietnam sentiment but, more, a growing nationalism. The protesters were shrill in their rhetoric and occasionally violent in their actions, but they were very few in number. Indeed, if there had been a plebiscite on statehood or some other form of formal affiliation with the United States, it almost certainly would have passed with an overwhelming majority.

The Marcoses understood well the depth of Filipino respect, admiration, and almost reverence toward the United States. And Nixon was their man of the moment to tap it. Though the American president wouldn't be in Manila long enough for the earth to complete one rotation on its axis, it was long enough for the Marcoses to extract what they wanted, and it had more to do with appearances and domestic politics than with substance or foreign affairs.

The Philippine presidential election was just six months away. For Marcos the task was formidable, for no Philippine president since independence had been reelected. Marcos knew that sidling up to the Americans would win him votes. So did everyone else. "The visit itself is a domestic political windfall for Marcos," the embassy reported. "President Nixon's mere presence in Manila will convey to the average voter a US endorsement and protect Marcos from opposition charges that he is not a good friend of the US."

Among Filipinos, personal relationships are of supreme importance. Consequently, Nixon's visit would convey even more, would allow Marcos to reap an even bigger political windfall if it contained a personal element. That could be demonstrated if the Nixons slept in Malacañang. Imelda Marcos went to work.

The Nixons were scheduled to stay in the presidential suite on the twelfth floor of the Intercontinental Hotel. For the very reason that the Marcoses wanted the Nixons at Malacañang, U.S. diplomats did not want them to stay there: to avoid the appearance that the United States was tilting toward Marcos in the upcoming election. This was before Imelda Marcos had squandered several million dollars refurbishing Malacañang; it was long on old-world charm but short on the space and amenities for an American president and his wife. But Mrs. Marcos was determined to make room for the Nixons. The Marcos children were moved into a gymnasium downstairs, and if the palace still had to be altered, it would be—and it was. "It was incredible," remembered a senior U.S. diplomat who was stationed in the Philippines at the time. Imelda Marcos drove workers in around-the-clock shifts, polishing and scrubbing, installing new bathrooms, knocking down walls to enlarge the living quarters.

She had an ally in the effort and in many of her future ventures, an American diplomat by the name of James Rafferty. "Rafferty was as busy as hell during that period," recalled the same official.

One would have to search the crusted crevices of American

diplomatic lore long and hard—and probably without success—to find another diplomat who had a role like Rafferty's, though considerable confusion surrounds the man and his activities in the Philippines. "He was always an enigma to me," said Evelyn Colbert, a senior officer in the State Department's Bureau of Intelligence and Research when Rafferty was in the Philippines. "What was his relationship to the first family? What was he doing? I don't know. He was a mystery man." It was widely believed, by Filipinos and Americans, then and now, that Rafferty worked for the CIA. "He was introduced to everyone as a CIA man," recalled Jovito Salonga, a Philippine senator when he dealt with Rafferty. "I've always assumed the agency sent him, and I'd be surprised if I were wrong," says Lewis Gleeck, Jr., an unwavering right-winger who was U.S. consul general in the Philippines from 1962 to 1969, then remained, in 1986 publishing the *Bulletin of the American Historical Collection.*

According to several CIA agents who were in the Philippines while Rafferty was, Gleeck and the others are wrong. "Most people thought he was CIA," said one CIA man, "which was very convenient for us because it meant all the loonies went to him." Another station chief, however, didn't find it so humorous; so pervasive was the belief among Filipinos that Rafferty was the station chief that the real station chief had to reveal his identity to certain Filipinos so that they would know to deal with him, not Rafferty. For his part, Rafferty won't say for whom he worked and delights in all the confusion. "I used the CIA and FBI as my cover," he says with a laugh.

In the end it's really not so important whether Rafferty worked for the CIA or was in fact a State Department officer (which, it seems, he was). What is significant is what Rafferty was expected to do, and did, and that was to take care of the Marcoses, to be attentive to their wants and whims, to provide them with another channel to the American government. Rafferty and his mission were a manifestation of the special nature of Washington's relationship with the Marcoses at the time and thereafter.

Rafferty remained in Manila from June 1966 until September 1973. That's a seven-year hitch, an almost unprecedented tour, during which he served four ambassadors and three station chiefs. Rafferty was around that long serving so many different bosses because he did his job well, doing what his superiors wanted done but often didn't want to be caught doing themselves. Rafferty became legendary for his work habits—usually from midnight until 6:00 A.M. "He was my after midnight guy-around-town," recalled one ambassador. "He knew what was going on in every bedroom in Manila."

Rafferty, who was only thirty-four years old when he arrived in Manila, was well suited for his duties and relationship to the Philippine first family. He was an affable man who enjoyed intrigue and good times. And he kept his mouth shut. "One of the reasons I had that job [in the Philippines] was that I don't talk," he said over the phone years later. His duties seemed to have no boundaries. He advised Marcos's defense minister that American ships with nuclear weapons were in port, and he hustled out of the country a woman who decided that Marcos's bank account was as ripe for picking as he had been for seducing.

Marcos was a notorious philanderer, but most of his affairs went unnoticed. In Philippine society, with an emphasis on machismo, an affair wasn't just tolerated but was expected, and it often enhanced a man's image. Even Marcos's carrying on with the wife of an American navy lieutenant commander assigned to the embassy was quietly taken care of: The navy man was reassigned. But that was not the case with his dalliance with Dovie Beams, a B-grade Hollywood starlet out of Nashville, who was thirty-eight years old but claimed to be twenty-three. It's not exactly clear what induced her to go to the Philippines. Some Filipinos believed she had been sent by the Mafia as some sort of payoff to Marcos. Imelda Marcos once ranted to the CIA station chief that the CIA had sent Beams in order to blackmail Marcos. Beams said she went there innocently enough, to star in a movie about Marcos's war exploits. She was soon, however, the lead in a real-life pornographic script, with goons and diplomats scampering amid the comic moments. The affair became public when Imelda Marcos called the wife of the editor of the *Philippines Free Press,* Teodoro Locsin, and demanded to know why the magazine had put her husband's mistress on the cover. Mrs. Locsin didn't know what Mrs. Marcos was talking about. Nor did Mr. Locsin. He had no idea who Dovie Beams was. His magazine was a serious one; but he knew that cheesecake sold, and because he was too cheap to pay models, he had sent his photographer one day to shoot some pretty girls who wouldn't want to be paid. Dovie Beams just happened to be one of them.

The Dovie Beams issue of the magazine also provided a few moments of mirth, and some answers, for the usually staid diplomats at Foggy Bottom. The *Philippines Free Press* with Beams on the cover arrived in Washington about the time that the U.S. mission in Hong Kong was sending frantic cables wanting to know who Dovie Beams was and just what the mission was to do with her. Hong Kong had become involved because that was where the U.S. embassy had decided to send her, to protect her from the Marcos goons who were gunning for her. It seems that when Marcos had grown tired of Miss Beams, she said, fine, but how about a separation allowance of a few hundred thousand dollars? Marcos balked, sending death threats instead. Beams ran for help to the American embassy, for one of the missions of every embassy is to protect the lives of American citizens in danger in a foreign country. The diplomats soon discovered that they had not only a seductively attractive woman on their hands but also a cleverly sinister one. Beams wasn't just the kiss-and-tell type. She was of the modern age: kiss and tape. During all those trysts and turns with the Philippine president, some of them in the palace with Imelda Marcos in the next bedroom, Dovie Beams had had going under the bed a tape recorder which even picked up sounds of Marcos singing to her in the shower.

At one point after Marcos had tossed her out of his life, Beams called Ninoy Aquino, asking him to meet her for breakfast at an out-of-the-way restaurant. She wasn't setting out to seduce Marcos's chief rival; she just wanted him to hear the tapes. The X-rated tapes were worth $100,000, or at least that's what Beams claims to have been offered by American diplomats, a bribe she thought was coming from Imelda Marcos. American officials say Beams has reversed things a bit, that she was the one demanding the $100,000. In any event, she held a press conference, at which she played parts of the tapes; soon the coos, groans, and love songs of the Philippine president were wafting over the airwaves. Then she departed the country, led onto the plane by an American diplomat, in full view of photographers. The press coverage angered Rafferty, for he had arranged with Marcos's men for Beams to leave the country without the public involvement of the American embassy.

While Rafferty occasionally got involved in looking after the Philippine president, his principal mission was "holding hands with Imelda," as both a CIA official and a senior Marcos aide phrased it. Whatever Imelda Marcos, her Blue Ladies, or her friends wanted, Rafferty procured, from American visas to all those televisions, stereos, and other goodies available and inexpensive at the PX stores. When William Sullivan arrived in the Philippines as ambassador in 1973, he got rid of Rafferty. "I fired him," Sullivan says. "I don't say that we introduced a puritan tenor, but at least enough of a difference so that it was quite clear there was a change in dealing with the Americans." But a few years later, sent by the Carter administration, Rafferty was back in Manila.

In 1969 Imelda Marcos instructed Rafferty to deliver an ultimatum: Either Nixon stayed at Malacañang or he didn't come to the Philippines. Nixon came, of course, and he stayed at Malacañang, where workers were actually laying tiles in the bathroom as Air Force One touched down. There was little substantive purpose behind the Nixon visit; as the Philippine foreign minister, Carlos P. Romulo, noted in a burst of undiplomatic candor, "We know he is only coming because the *Apollo 11* splashdown was in this area and if he did not come there would be a hue and cry." While the presidents conferred, the indefatigable Imelda Marcos was dragging Pat Nixon on a tour of her projects: a fifteen-minute stop at a children's center at Bago Bantay; on to an orphanage on the South Superhighway; a dash through the sprawling and, at the time, unfinished model of traditional Philippine villages. "At the end of the day Mrs. Nixon was utterly exhausted," recalled an American official who was on the trip. But the sating dinner, Barrio Fiesta, and revelry at Malacañang were still ahead.

The 400 dined on pâté de foie gras, followed by Mindoro turtle soup, lapu-lapu fish, and stuffed pigeon, washed down with red and white wines, champagne for the toasting. As Mrs. Marcos had been honored with a dessert in her name during the White House dinner three years earlier, Mrs. Nixon, wearing a gown provided by Mrs. Marcos, was honored with a mango dessert called Délice Patricia. In his toast President Nixon quipped that if he were in a campaign, he sure wouldn't want Mrs. Marcos to be on the other side. The

Philippine first lady joined in the laughter, the import of the remark perhaps having failed to penetrate. (In a cable a few days before the Nixons were to arrive, the embassy reported, "Despite almost round the clock pressure on palace, Mrs. Marcos has still not reached final decisions on Mrs. Nixon's schedule, which would permit development of detailed itinerary. We have used every available channel to her, but the Philippine First Lady simply will not be moved.") Then came the hours of entertainment, dancing music provided by two bands, the guests refreshing themselves at the well-stocked bars. "Have you ever seen anything like it?" an overwhelmed Nixon aide asked Robert Semple of *The New York Times*. Semple had to admit that he probably hadn't.

All nations at all times spend inordinately on entertaining dignitaries and heads of state. But the Marcoses carried it to excess. The Philippines wasn't just a poor third world country. It was desperately impoverished. Per capita income was less than $250 a year, one of the lowest in the world. More than half the country's children under the age of ten suffered from malnutrition. In a slum district of Manila adjacent to Ermita, where the wealthy had their swimming pools and finely tended gardens, families of eight and more jammed into a warren of squat, dirt-floor shanties. Only one of every ten children was normal; the rest were seriously retarded because of poor diet. This wasn't what the Marcoses wanted Americans, and certainly not American reporters, to see. But on the morning after the Malacañang blowout the press buses, because of the rains, had to take a detour to the airport, passing some of Manila's slums as a result. "I remember being horrified at the poverty in contrast to the lavishness I'd seen the night before," Semple could still recall twenty years later. When Marcos was deposed by the people rising up against him in 1986, Semple thought, "I'd gotten the visual portrait back then of why."

Only two months later Imelda Marcos was feting, charming, and dancing with another American politician, though not as influential at the time as he would be a decade later, when he would return the hospitality. The man was Ronald Reagan. The occasion was the opening of the Cultural Center of the Philippines, an $8.5 million colossus inspired and driven to completion by Mrs. Marcos's obsession with anything and everything grandiose and international.

The edifice was built under the auspices of a cultural commission set up by Marcos; she was chairman and one of the seven trustees was Juan Ponce Enrile, a prominent lawyer who was to accumulate extreme power and concomitant wealth during twenty years of loyal service to Marcos until breaking with the Philippine president at the last moment in 1986. The commission's mandate was to "awaken the consciousness" of the Philippine people in "our cultural heritage" and "to cultivate and enhance . . . appreciation of distinctive Philippine arts."

The country's leading writers, artists, and intellectuals bitterly criticized the Cultural Center, arguing that it was hardly intended for the advancement of Philippine culture, but rather to entice international artists with whom Imelda Marcos wanted to cavort. The critics were right: during the first month alone, there were performances by the London Philharmonic Orchestra, the New York Chamber Soloists, and American pianist Eugene Istomin; the first season added the Grand Classique from France, the Dance Company of India, and the Japanese and Chinese operas.

The center was being built "to enshrine the name Imelda, as 'Imelda the Patroness of the Arts,' " shouted Benigno Aquino in a speech on the Senate floor. And indeed, inside the edifice, prominently displayed, on the second tier above the sweeping lobby, hung (until the February 1986 revolt) a life-size portrait of Imelda Marcos, in a full-length white gown, a sash with a medal over each bare shoulder. The Cultural Center was criticized for being, as Aquino put it, "a monument to the nation's elite bereft of social conscience," built at a time "when the impoverished mass groans in want."

The American government contributed $3.5 million for the center, from a Special Fund for Education, set up in 1963 in settlement of Philippine war damage claims, "for the purpose of furthering educational exchange and other educational programs to the mutual advantage" of the Philippines and the United States. The connection between the Cultural Center and education—at least as envisioned by the 1963 legislation—seems tenuous at best. As for the private funds that were used for the center, *Parade* magazine praised Imelda Marcos for having raised them. "In a nation still battling poverty and corruption," the magazine wrote, she had inspired the wealthy "to dig into their pockets for her causes." They were digging into their pockets, or more appropriately into their corporate treasuries, for $10,000, $15,000, $25,000, but it was anything but voluntary. Developing a technique she later perfected, she would send a letter to company executives, bank presidents, and individuals, informing them of the expected amount of their "donation." Then a messenger would be sent to pick it up—in cash. She also utilized the federal taxing power for all her projects as well as for her personal benefit. One day when the tax commissioner came into the palace with two large suitcases, Jaime Ferrer, an executive assistant to Marcos, asked innocently, "What's that for?"

"For the first lady," the tax collector replied.

"How much?" asked Ferrer, one of the most honest and independent men in Philippine politics.

"Five million" (in pesos—the equivalent at the time of roughly $1,250,000). When the tax commissioner came out, Ferrer noticed that he was perspiring and shaking. Asked what was wrong, the tax man replied, "She's not satisfied."

Before the center could be built, tons of rock and earth had to be hauled to fill in Manila Bay, about a half mile or so on a straight line south from the American embassy. Thought by some Filipinos to resemble the Parthenon, the Cultural Center has dancing fountains, and inside, behind the towering glass doors, hang three gigantic chandeliers. The carpets are the traditional red and gold opera colors. There are six elevators; two escalators. There is seating for 2,598, in contour chairs, upholstered with oxblood cushions. Between the audience and the stage—which Imelda Marcos boasted was as large as that of the Metropolitan Opera in New York—is the full orchestra pit. In the basement, below the level of the bay, is a rehearsal area that is a mock-up of the main stage. Patrons of New York's Lincoln Center or of Washington's Kennedy Center would feel comfortably at home.*

---

* Mrs. Marcos's penchant for spending profusely on projects in her own country which would bear some testimony to herself didn't extend to projects in other countries, or at least not to the Kennedy Center. Some thirty countries—including Thailand, Pakistan, Indonesia, and nearly every other East Asian nation—contributed to the Kennedy Center, but not the Philippines, which might have been expected to, considering the "special relationship." Early on Imelda Marcos had promised to provide Philippine mahogany for the dance floors. But the wood never arrived, and when the dance floors were finished, Mrs. Marcos, expressing disappointment, promised to provide the wood for one of the conference rooms. The cost would have been about $4,500. The promise was never kept.

For the gala opening Imelda Marcos wanted "somebody really high-powered," Ambassador Byroade recalled. He passed on the request to Washington. Working one day at the Western White House in San Clemente, Nixon, after seeking National Security Adviser Kissinger's approval, picked up the phone and called Sacramento. Nixon and the United States would be represented by Governor and Mrs. Reagan, who brought along seventeen-year-old Patti and thirteen-year-old Ronald, Jr., as well as Michael Deaver, one of Reagan's most trusted aides, who later followed him to the White House and to a role in Manila after Aquino was assassinated. It was the fifty-eight-year-old Reagan's first official visit outside the United States except for a brief jaunt to Mexico.

The Reagans stayed with the Marcoses at Malacañang, and there was, of course, dinner and dancing. The select 500 heard Marcos joke that he had stopped watching movies since Reagan had switched from acting to politics. Reagan responded with the expected salute to a head of state, then, raising his champagne glass a third time, proposed a toast "to the wives of all of us," adding, "With special reference to Mrs. Marcos." Then they danced, the handsome former movie star, the ravishing former beauty queen.

While all this public celebrating was going on in Manila, in Washington another face of the Marcos rule was being revealed privately. The forum was the Senate Subcommittee on United States Security Agreements and Commitments Abroad, chaired by Missouri Democrat Stuart Symington. On the last day of September 1969 the subcommittee began holding highly charged hearings about the conduct of the war in Vietnam, specifically the role, usually secret, of other Asian countries in supporting the U.S. war. The first country examined was the Philippines. For four days the committee heard senior U.S. military officers and diplomats describe the rampant crime, official corruption, and virtually wide-open smuggling in the Philippines and how the Marcos administration had done little to combat it.

At the insistence of Nixon and Kissinger the hearings were held behind closed doors, and when they were concluded, the administration fought to keep the testimony from the public. The Pentagon was worried about the discussions regarding the bases and the extent

73

of American military activity in the Philippines, including some highly sensitive, top secret intelligence-gathering activities. The State Department was concerned that the remarks by its diplomats about the Marcos government might rankle the Philippine president. In the end a 1,146-page transcript of the hearings was made public. But it was highly sanitized. It was not just a word here and there or even a few paragraphs; pages, sometimes many successive pages, were expunged. While some of the censored material pertained to military matters, entire chunks related to the manner in which Marcos ruled.

On the matter of smuggling, for example, which Marcos had pledged to combat, the released testimony contained a statement by James Wilson, who had been the deputy chief of mission in Manila since 1966, that the United States had been "encouraged by some improvement which has taken place." But censored out was Wilson's opinion that Marcos "always was a part of that system and is likely to remain so." Much of the testimony by State and Pentagon officials focused on the "atmosphere of general lawlessness" around Clark Air Force Base; members of the old Huk movement, the committee was told, were looting about $1 million a year. The Huks were no longer guided by Communist political ideology but had degenerated into common street gangs, often fighting among themselves, "rather reminiscent of the situation in Cicero, Illinois, at the turn of the century," as Wilson described it. In the police department of Angeles City, the seedy district outside the Clark gates, between 50 and 90 percent of the members were Huk supporters; all the Filipinos working at the Voice of America radio facility had to be cleared for employment by the Huks; the contractors who provided material to or ran concessions on Clark had to pay off the Huks.

In testimony that was censored, Wilson noted that there was a general lack of "political motivation" to deal with the problem, that the Marcos administration had "not put sufficient political, military, social and economic muscle" into wiping out the Huks. It was not surprising. The Huks, the committee was told in testimony that was censored, often operated in collusion with local politicians and police chiefs.

But the focus of the testimony was Vietnam, and members of Congress now learned for the first time that Washington had been

74

secretly paying the Marcos government in exchange for his sending Filipinos to Vietnam. At least $39 million was spent by the United States to equip, train, and pay the Philippines Civic Action Group (Philcag) in Vietnam. That testimony or at least some of it was made public. When it was, Marcos issued an emphatic denial: "The Philippines has received no fee nor payments of any kind in support of Philcag, or its personnel, nor has there been any grant given in consideration of sending the Philcag to Vietnam."

The denial wasn't just perfunctory, an expected lie from a government that had been caught misleading its people. Nor was the lie motivated solely by Marcos's interest in defending the honor of the Philippine nation from the taint of having been an American mercenary. Marcos had some very persuasive personal reasons for the denial: During the preceding four years—that is, throughout Marcos's first term—the U.S. embassy had been delivering quarterly checks, each in the amount of several hundred thousand dollars. All were delivered pursuant to agreement "between officials of the Department of State and President Marcos that the Philippine Government could conceal the receipt of these payments from the Philippine public in its national defense budget," the General Accounting Office determined. (The GAO's report is still classified Secret, only a censored summary having been released in 1970.) Consequently, the GAO, the investigating arm of the Congress, went on to point out that "it is quite conceivable that few officials in the Marcos administration were aware of the cash payments by the United States or of the purpose for which they were actually intended." Nor did Washington know where the money went either, for as the GAO noted, in a portion of the report that is classified: "U.S. officials exercised no control or supervision over the utilization of funds" provided to Marcos for the payment of Philippine soldiers in Vietnam.

U.S. intelligence, military, and diplomatic officials who were in the Philippines at the time have no doubt that many of the millions that the United States sent Marcos for the Philippine task force went into his pockets or, more accurately, into his overseas bank accounts. Some of the American checks were made out to the Philippine minister of defense, then deposited in the Philippines Veterans Bank. After he had declared martial law in 1972, Marcos systematically drained the bank through loans to cronies—frequently never re-paid—for projects in which the Marcoses were often hidden part-ners. Marcos may have siphoned off some of the millions more directly. What the GAO investigators didn't discover—they were "seriously hampered" in their investigation by the State and Defense departments—was that Rafferty sometimes delivered checks directly to Marcos.

Even those portions of the Symington committee hearings and the GAO report which were eventually made public were not re-leased until after the 1969 Philippine election. The State Department argued, with support from Ambassador Henry Byroade, that to release them before that might affect the outcome. Perhaps. But Marcos was prepared to cheat and steal and do whatever else was necessary to win.

"Marcos succeeded himself by backing up trucks to the Central Bank," remarked a CIA officer who had been in the Philippines at the time of the election. He was speaking figuratively; but it was very nearly a literal observation. Two weeks before the election Marcos's campaign manager, Ernesto Maceda, withdrew 100 million pesos (roughly $25 million). Then, with an air force plane and mil-itary security, he hopped around the islands, dispensing peso-filled envelopes: Barrio captains received 2,000 to 3,000 pesos, mayors up to 100,000 pesos, and favored congressional candidates as much as a million pesos. "We were prepared to cheat all the way," Maceda said in an interview many years later. The election cost Marcos a staggering $50 million, which was $16 million more than Nixon had raised for his successful presidential bid the year before. Marcos used some of it to pay for the consulting services of a couple of Washington political pros, Lawrence F. O'Brien, former Demo-cratic national chairman, and Joseph Napolitan, who had master-minded Humphrey's media program during the 1968 campaign.

What votes Marcos couldn't buy, he stole, not very subtly. In one election district in Ilocos Norte, for example, the "official" tally showed Marcos got 5,322 votes; his opponent, the Liberals' Senator Sergio Osmeña, Jr., 3. In a schoolhouse in central Luzon election workers filled out ballots for Marcos's Nationalist party while being watched over by two armed men in civilian clothes, one with an M-16, the other with a .45-caliber pistol. "I have covered several

Asian elections where dirty tactics were used," *Newsweek*'s Everett Martin wrote. "But never have I seen so much personally."

It was all operation overkill, so that Marcos could not merely defeat but humiliate Osmeña, political chieftain in Cebu, the fiefdom inherited from his father, who was the country's president from 1944 to 1946. Marcos swamped the rather lackluster Osmeña by nearly 2 million votes out of 9 million cast.*

When Vice President Spiro T. Agnew showed up in Manila for the inauguration, he was the fourth American president or vice president to bless the Marcoses in four years, more than all his predecessors had achieved in twenty. In its "Man in the News" feature on the occasion of Marcos's reelection, *The New York Times* heralded the Philippine leader as "a debonair, slender but combative man," with "abounding energy," and reported again that he was the "most decorated Filipino soldier in World War II, with 22 medals, including the Distinguished Service Cross of the United States." Similarly, *Time*, after commenting on his "pleasing, youthful good looks," pointed out his war record, crediting him with twenty-seven medals.

Foreigners might be fooled by Marcos, but at home he was beginning to run into trouble; his popularity was eroding, and ultimately, after the usual gambits of money, threats, and violence didn't work, he would be forced to seize power in order to hang on to it.

When the first couple stepped outside after the president had delivered his state of the nation address in January 1970, they were

---

* Did the United States help Marcos in 1969? "I can tell you in all honesty that I came away with the very strong impression that we were helping him get reelected," says Paul Kattenburg, who had been director of Philippine affairs at the State Department and at the time of the 1969 election was teaching at the Foreign Service Institute, where he received the State Department's Meritorious Honor Award. "Now, how we specifically did it, whether we just put money in there, or whether we printed things or helped him stuff the boxes or God knows what, I just don't know. But it seems to me that everyone I spoke with said that this election was just crooked as hell." Other Foreign Service officers involved in Philippine matters at the time agreed that the United States was somehow involved in the election. On the other hand, James Wilson, the deputy chief of mission in Manila at the time of the 1969 election, insists "categorically that we didn't help Marcos." The United States didn't have to provide any assistance to Marcos, say Wilson and others, who also insist there was no U.S. involvement because he was running against a weak opponent and had all the money and resources he needed and could steal.

met by 20,000 jeering students, workers, and peasants. The mob pelted them with a papier-mâché replica of a crocodile, rocks, and bottles. It was a shocking occurrence, the first time since independence that a Filipino leader, let alone the president, had been so disgraced. Then, four days later, the worst peacetime riots in the country's history erupted when demonstrators marched across Mendiola Bridge and tried to storm Malacañang, in front of which the protesters then burned candles near a realistic coffin, mourning the death of democracy. The violence escalated. During a daylong demonstration that began with a march and ended with a mock trial of President and Mrs. Marcos and the United States, a twenty-three-year-old university student was shot in the head. The next day rampaging demonstrators, many with white bandannas around their foreheads, assaulted the American embassy. Shouting, "Down with imperialists," "Yankee, go home!" and "Imperialist pigs!" they ripped the large, circular U.S. seal off the embassy's outer brick wall. Stones and homemade firebombs were hurled at the embassy, shattering glass doors and windows. When the U.S. marine security detachment lobbed tear gas grenades, the mobs retreated to the nearby business district, smashing windows in restaurants and offices, tossing a Molotov cocktail into the Manila Hotel, burning cars, and mauling people on the streets who got in their way.

The turmoil became known as the First Quarter Storm. Twice during it Marcos publicly raised the possibility of martial law, once after a soothsayer had told him he was about to be assassinated. He dropped the idea, in large measure because one of his most trusted military advisers told him the army would not be able to enforce it if the people rose in protest. Marcos blamed the unrest and the riots on the Communists. Indeed, many of the protest leaders were influenced by the thoughts of Marx, Lenin, and Mao, which were being taught at the University of the Philippines, which barricading students had renamed Stalin University. But the students didn't appear to be all that ideologically motivated. During one riot they smashed windows of a restaurant called The Front, which displayed portraits of Marx and Mao, while leaving untouched a nearby restaurant called the American; shouts of "Yankee, go home" were often accompanied by a stage-whispered "And take me with you." In some measure the students were mimicking, somewhat belatedly, their counterparts in France, Japan, and the United States. The vast bulk of the demonstrators knew little of Marx or Mao. What they were protesting, as the State Department noted in a Secret report, "Philippines: The Radical Movements," were the "social inequities," which were, "if not the greatest among the countries of Southeast Asia, certainly the most visible." The protests were also against Marcos as president. As *Time* concluded, "Filipinos are increasingly cynical about Marcos' 2,000,000-vote margin of victory in last November's presidential campaign—a feat that they quite reasonably believe could only have been achieved by widespread vote buying."

Whatever the motivations, the First Quarter Storm dissipated in April, when students left Manila for the provinces and the start of summer vacation. But the democratic opposition to Marcos continued to build and organize; by the time of the 1971 congressional elections the Liberal party was prepared to face Marcos at the polls. The opening salvo in the campaign was a violent one, rocking even a nation which seemed to accept bloodshed and balloting as the coefficients of elections.

Shortly before 9:15 P.M. on August 21, 1971, during a Liberal party rally of more than 10,000 supporters at Plaza Miranda—in the heart of downtown, Manila's Hyde Park—two fragmentation grenades were hurled at the speakers' platform; other explosives were detonated beneath the stage. In the bloody heap of bodies just below the microphones were those of a ten-year-old cigarette vendor and two newspaper photographers. At least six other persons were killed. All of the Liberal party's eight senatorial candidates were among the more than 100 seriously wounded. "I saw my boss tossed in the air by the force of the shrapnel before dropping to the floor," said an aide to Senator Osmeña, the former presidential candidate. Senator Jovito Salonga, the party's leading candidate, had the bones in one ear shattered; deep canyons cut by the shrapnel permanently scarred his forearms. The wife of one senator had both kneecaps smashed.

The *Philippines Free Press,* the least sensationalist of the country's newspapers, called it the "most villainous, outrageous and shameful crime in the annals of local political violence . . . a night of national tragedy and infamy as democracy—Philippine style—bared itself in all its terrifying ugliness."

Marcos, reacting to the incident by immediately suspending the writ of habeas corpus, charged that the Communists were responsible for the bloodshed and repeated his accusations that Aquino was aiding and abetting them with money and weapons. Though Aquino was the Liberal party leader, he escaped the carnage, arriving late because he had been attending a dinner. He also said that he had received an anonymous phone call warning him of the attack and that after the party he was further delayed when he went home to put on his bulletproof vest. Aquino's absence led to suggestions that he, in a desperate effort to eliminate all challengers to his power within the party, had been behind the attack. No one was ever convicted, and in late 1986 it was still being reported that the Plaza Miranda bombing "remained a mystery."

It wasn't a mystery to American intelligence and diplomatic officers who were in the Philippines at the time or who looked into the incident later. They are convinced that the bombing was not the work of the Communists. "Without question" it wasn't, one CIA officer said. The Communists at the time were a fledgling organization with fewer than 100 members, and they were very disorganized. Moreover, their efforts were concentrated in rural areas, building for a peasant revolution along the lines of Mao's in China. They had no urban capability.

Nor was the bombing the work of any of Marcos's opponents. Rather, according to American diplomats and intelligence officers, it was carried out by Marcos loyalists within the military—the grenades were traced to an army arsenal—though they don't know whether or not Marcos himself ordered it.

The attack, instead of hurting the Liberals in the election, may have created sympathy for the party. Of the eight senators elected in the at-large voting, only two were from Marcos's Nationalist party. Six of Marcos's handpicked candidates were defeated. They included Enrile, who finished near the bottom of the pack. The top vote getter was Salonga, who had campaigned in a wheelchair, his wounds from the Plaza Miranda attack heavily bandaged. Salonga even defeated Marcos's party in the president's home district, Ilocos Norte; Imelda Marcos's province, Leyte, also went for the Liberals.

The results of the 1971 elections stunned Marcos. He had known that he couldn't succeed himself; the Constitution limited a president to two terms. But he had thought he could choose his successor. He was considering Enrile, his suave defense minister. Imelda Marcos was also seriously positioning herself to succeed her husband. But it was now painfully apparent that Aquino and the Liberals would defeat Enrile, Mrs. Marcos, or anyone else Marcos and the Nationalists selected. Marcos still believed that he himself could defeat Aquino. There was, however, the constitutional obstacle. Thus, if Marcos were to remain in power democratically, the Constitution would have to be amended or that restriction removed.

For many years Philippine leaders of both political parties had been calling for a constitutional convention. Rightists, leftists, and independent observers felt a need to replace the 1935 Constitution, which had been pressed on the Filipinos by their American colonial masters. Finally, in the summer of 1971, with nationalism on the rise, 320 delegates, who had been chosen by the people in a special election, began debate on a new charter. The Constitutional Convention (dubbed "Con-Con" by Filipinos) provided opportunities for Marcos but also posed some risks. On the plus side for the Philippine president, the delegates could eliminate the restriction on two terms, or they might, as Marcos urged, adopt a parliamentary system, which would allow Marcos to run from his home district, then seek to be named prime minister. On the other hand, the new constitution might keep the two-term restriction and, moreover, add a specific prohibition, which the delegates considered, that would bar Imelda Marcos from succeeding her husband. The dangers were very real. Polls showed that 80 percent of the Filipinos were opposed to a third term for Marcos and to his wife's succeeding him. Marcos had to control the convention, or in the event that he was unable to, he had to prepare the way for discrediting it with the Americans, by arguing that it had been controlled by the Communists. The latter was Imelda Marcos's task.

It is unlikely that any third world leader, and certainly no spouse of a third world leader, ever demanded and received as many audiences with the highest-level officials in Washington as did Imelda Marcos over the years. Her beauty was her calling card, delivered on a platter thick with flattery, a lethal combination in a city where men are easily intoxicated with power and ego. In 1970, after a journey that had begun with a stop in Rome, where she had a private audience with Pope Paul VI, Mrs. Marcos was accorded a thirty-minute session with Nixon and Kissinger in the Oval Office, according to President Nixon's logs, followed by a White House luncheon in her honor. During that visit there had been a minor controversy over her quarters. She wanted to stay in Blair House, the historic building across from the White House (Andrew Johnson lived there for five weeks between his inauguration as vice president and Lincoln's assassination; it was home for President Truman and his family for three years while the White House was being renovated), which was the official residence for visiting heads of state—which Mrs. Marcos was not. "No precedent whatsoever exists for a wife of a Chief of State or Head of Government" to stay at Blair House, Nixon's chief of protocol noted. Eventually, because Blair House was being renovated, Nixon offered her "the hospitality of the Presidential Suite in the Madison Hotel or comparable accommodation in any other hotel of her choice in Washington." She chose the Madison, which she later departed without paying her bill of $1,608.87, much of it for liquor miniatures. The National Security Council and the State Department argued about who would have to pay the bill, neither wanting to since Mrs. Marcos had not been on an official visit. State paid.

State Department officers suffered most from the demands of the unrelenting Philippine first lady; after all, they could ill afford to say no to a woman who had been embraced by presidents. "I can remember Bill Bundy putting his head in his hands when he would hear that Mrs. Marcos was coming to town, and saying, 'Oh, Jesus,' " recalled a State Department officer referring to the head of the East Asian bureau during the Johnson administration. Bundy's successor, Marshall Green, once having met the arriving Mrs. Marcos after midnight at the airport, discovered that it wasn't enough, that she insisted on talking with him further. In spite of the hour and the presence of his wife, who had dutifully accompanied him to the airport, Green acceded, his wife going home alone. Once they entered Imelda Marcos's suite at the Madison Hotel, she "clapped her hands, and all those Filipinos stuffing the room just disappeared," Green recalled. Green, a red-headed, most properly ed-

ucated (prep school, followed by Yale), distinguished career diplomat, found himself alone in the room with the Philippine beauty
queen, and when he took a seat on a small sofa, she crowded down
right next to him, rejecting the nearby couch. As she talked about
the poverty of the Filipino people, tears began to roll through her
mascara. She excused herself, and when she returned, she had changed
from her dress into skintight leotards. The next morning Green
called a colleague who was scheduled to meet Imelda Marcos and
warned him that he might have been a bit too generous with his
promises the previous night, but, Green added, "You will certainly
find it to be an interesting experience."

Another State Department official who was summoned to Mrs.
Marcos's suite was Richard Usher, who had known her when he
was political officer in Manila. He was now the Philippine desk
officer. The Philippine first lady was wearing tight black slacks and
a tight-fitting, low-cut leopard-skin top and, for added effect, spike
heels, which made her taller than Usher, who felt more than a mite
embarrassed in his off-the-rack Sears, Roebuck suit. To compound
his discomfort, when he started to sit in one of the two chairs across
from her, she patted a spot on the love seat next to her. Then, gazing
on him with her heavily made-up big eyes, her voice taking on a
sultry whine, she said, "Dick, you're not taking care of your baby.
The Philippines is your baby, and you're not taking care of your
baby." The flustered Usher didn't know what she was talking about.
So she proceeded to explain how the Communists were controlling
the Constitutional Convention. Thirty minutes later Usher stumbled
out. Over the next two days he began receiving calls from furious
senators. Imelda Marcos, who was savvy to the ways of American
politics, had gone courting in the Senate, and they wanted to know
what the State Department intended to do about the Communists
who were trying to write the new Philippine Constitution.

Imelda Marcos's pilgrimage to Washington in 1971 had been
preceded by a stop in Iran for the gargantuan celebration at Persepolis of the 2,500th anniversary of the Persian Empire. She had
invited Cristina Ford, wife of Henry Ford II, to "share the tent,"
as the embassy reported in a highly classified cable, a reference to
the air-conditioned "tents" erected in the desert for the occasion at
$120,000 apiece. From Persepolis Mrs. Marcos had traveled to Dear-

born, Michigan, where she was the Fords' houseguest. Coming to Washington, she was preceded by Rafferty and her brother Kokoy Romualdez, whose missions were to arrange for her to stay in Blair House and to meet again with President Nixon. The State Department agreed. "It should be born [sic] in mind," the department wrote in a memo to the White House Protocol Office, that "Mrs. Marcos is a political figure of considerable stature in her own right," and there is "the possibility that she might some day herself be a candidate for the Presidency of the Philippines." The Protocol Office blocked her from staying in Blair House. But she did get her meeting with Nixon.

It was a brief meeting, and Imelda Marcos's major theme was that the Communists were going to take over the Philippines through the Constitutional Convention. Nixon wanted an immediate response, and a NSC member was instructed to call the State Department. After some scurrying about, department officers discovered that the Bureau of Intelligence and Research (INR) was preparing a report on the Constitutional Convention. "Oh, crap," the INR officer, Edna Barr Hubbert, thought when told what Imelda Marcos had been saying over at the White House. But Hubbert, who had served in the Philippines in the 1950s, was more diplomatic in her response to the White House aide: "The people who control that convention are spelled M-A-R-C-O-S."

The idea that the Communists controlled the convention didn't even rise to the level of feverish paranoia. The convention was controlled, Hubbert noted, by "vested oligarchial [sic] interests." The vast majority of the delegates were lawyers and businessmen, and conservative ones. That didn't mean they were pro-Marcos; indeed, many thought the power ought to shift to them and their friends. Marcos, however, was "confident of his ability to keep the bulk of" the delegates in line, Hubbert wrote in another Secret INR report, "through the traditional tactics of manipulation, coercion, concession and bribery."

Marcos wasn't alone in his fear of what the constitutional delegates might do if not controlled. The Americans also were. And they resorted to methods just as unsavory and undemocratic as his. What concerned Washington was the desire of many delegates to ban foreign bases (which meant American bases), to declare the

Philippines a neutral country, and to restrict the activities of the large American corporations, which had investments of more than $1 billion in the Philippines. In the Manila coffeehouses and the convention corridors there was talk about the CIA and American businessmen's passing money to the delegates. According to several diplomats who were in the Philippines at the time, the reports and stories were accurate. (If so, the Philippines, of course, wasn't the only country in Asia where at this very time the United States was subverting democracy in the name of democracy. In Vietnam the CIA was bribing members of the National Assembly to ensure the passage of favorable legislation.) But it wasn't only the CIA at work in the Philippines. It was also Ambassador Byroade. In the security of the golf shack on the other side of the sluggish Pasig River from Malacañang, he and Marcos hatched a plot to defeat some of the "anti-Marcos" and "anti-American" provisions being considered by the delegates. The scheme was carried out under such extreme secrecy that not even the CIA station was told about it in advance, and it never learned any more than that Byroade and Marcos had collaborated successfully. Byroade has said that he will take the details of what they did to his grave. It wasn't the only time that Byroade demonstrated his fondness for Marcos; it was, of course, on his watch that Marcos declared martial law, without the American ambassador's expressing any public disapproval.

There may not be another diplomat quite like Henry Alfred Byroade. Little is known about him publicly, astonishingly little, for to insiders his life and career became a legend, a combination, it seemed, of George Patton, Clark Gable, and maybe Paul Bunyan. With legends come myths. For instance, more than one diplomat and CIA official who worked with Byroade attributed his diplomatic successes to his having been, they said, George Marshall's son-in-law. It was said he swam with Mao. Both stories were more than slightly askew. Byroade's first wife was his high school sweetheart; many years later, while ambassador in Afghanistan, he met and carried off the wife of a mid-level embassy officer, a scandal that many thought would end his career. And it was Zhou Enlai, not Mao, who Byroade joined in the water—and it wasn't swimming.

It was during World War II, when the two men were trying to ferry troops and heavy trucks across a rain-swollen river. When Zhou, who had stripped down to his undershorts, reached the middle of the raging waters, Byroade snapped his picture. Years later, when Kissinger was preparing to go to China, Byroade sent him the snapshot, with a note: "I got him down to his shorts. See if you can do better."

There was little in Byroade's humble beginnings to portend his greatness, dashing, and daring. He was born on July 24, 1913, and his home was an Indiana farm, at a crossroad four miles from the nearest town, which had a population of 499. When the Depression closed in, he went to work, driving a school bus. He didn't just drive the bus. He built it. Displaying a mechanical aptitude and interest that were to serve him well during dull moments in his career, he took a Maxwell touring car and a Model T truck, cut them in two, then welded the halves together. With no family money for an education, he applied to West Point, which he entered in 1933 along with about 400 other young men, only 255 of whom hung on until graduation. Byroade, who finished fifty-sixth overall, was in the top ten in mathematics and science. Following his earning an advanced degree in engineering from Cornell University, he was given responsibility for forming an experimental aviation engineers regiment at Langley Field, Virginia. While there, he and three others developed the concept of using rolls of pierced metal for temporary runway strips, which soon were in use around the world and were still used for temporary military runways forty years later. After the attack on Pearl Harbor he was sent to China, volunteering for what became the "Hump" operation.

Thirty years old and already a lieutenant colonel, Byroade was placed in command of logistics and supplies for the eastern half of China, his primary mission being to support General Clare Chennault's Fourteenth Air Force. Utilizing a half million Chinese laborers, Byroade supervised the construction of forty-three bases, which were to accommodate the new B-29 heavy bombers, a "task compared in engineering to building the pyramids in Egypt," the *New York Herald Tribune* declared. In September 1944 Byroade, thirty-one years old, a full colonel, and chief policy coordinator for the China-Burma-India theater of operations, was transferred to the

Pentagon. His boss was General George C. Marshall, who promoted him to brigadier general. At the age of thirty-two, he was the youngest man in the history of the American army to wear one star, "unless," says Byroade, "you consider Custer, and according to my research, he died before his commission arrived." Newspapermen remember the handsome general at a Manchurian banquet, seriously conversing with Chinese elders while discreetly looking over the Chinese beauties in the background.

After the war he worked on German affairs at the Pentagon, which had responsibility for the administration of Germany and Japan. Much to the displeasure of the generals, Byroade argued that the State Department should take over these responsibilities. Eventually the transfer happened, with Byroade also being shifted to the State Department. He was quickly promoted from director of the German-Austrian bureau to assistant secretary of state for Near East, South Asian, and African affairs, which included the Middle East. In an address to the American Council for Judaism, Byroade suggested that a major cause of the Middle East tension was Israel's immigration policy, which, in effect, was that all Jews in the world were welcome there. In view of the country's very small land area, this generated fears among neighboring Arab countries that Israel would pursue an expansionist course. "Surely it is not asking too much to ask Israel to find some way to lay at rest these fears of her neighbors," Byroade told the anti-Zionist audience. The Israeli government lodged an official protest, charging that Byroade's comments imposed "a severe strain on Israeli-American friendship." The chairman of the Jewish Agency for Palestine denounced the speech as "ungracious and harsh advice resulting from dubious political expediency." Letters soon began arriving at the White House about Byroade's "sex life"—sent by Zionists, Byroade was convinced.

Byroade decided that he wanted another assignment, one that would take him away from the Washington bureaucracy and out into the field, where there was more space for a man of his independence. President Eisenhower named him ambassador to Egypt, but Byroade ran into Indiana's Republican Senator William Jenner, a conservative isolationist who wanted to haul Byroade before his committee to answer questions about "who lost China." Unlike other diplomats who would have considered it improper, Byroade lobbied vigorously on behalf of his own nomination, with his friends on the Hill and out in Indiana, seeking the endorsement of the state's newspapers. Finally, Byroade decided he had to confront Jenner. On a bitter cold December 24, as Jenner was preparing to sit down to Christmas Eve dinner, Byroade knocked on the door. Byroade apologized for disturbing the senator, explaining that he had tried to reach him by phone, but it had been constantly busy.

"Well, why did you come to see me?" Jenner growled.

"I didn't want to, Senator. I'm only here because I've been told that I have to," Byroade answered. Then, with equal lack of diplomacy, tried to explain that Jenner really had no right to block the nomination because even though Byroade had been born in Indiana, he hadn't lived there in twenty years.

"You've told me what you've come to tell me; now get the hell out," Jenner sputtered.

As Byroade reached the door, he turned to Jenner. "And Merry Christmas to you, too, you son of a bitch."

Eventually Jenner came around, but Byroade lasted only a year in Cairo. Byroade's problem was his relationship with Gamal Abdel Nasser. It was too cozy for John Foster Dulles and the Israeli lobby. Byroade and Nasser were about the same age, and both were military men. Nasser had a "high regard" for Byroade, whom he found to be "a warm, sympathetic friend who fully lived up to the pro-Arab promise of his earlier speeches." That, of course, angered American Jews, who leaned on Dulles. But Byroade also crossed Dulles, recommending that the United States supply military arms to Nasser in order to keep him from drifting closer to the Communist bloc. Dulles thought that anyone who even considered talking to the USSR was an enemy. Byroade was exiled to South Africa, not a place where much was happening in the mid-1950s, and he passed the time conducting his own big-game safaris.

Byroade was a free spirit and a bit of a rogue; neither is a trait sought by the diplomatic corps. But in the Foreign Service, as in any corporation, whom you know may help overcome what you are. And Byroade knew Dean Rusk from their days in the China theater during World War II. Nevertheless, after Byroade's fling in Afghanistan (where he was sent after South Africa), the State Department must have scoured the atlases before coming up with his next assignment: Burma. Byroade passed the time in that sleepy post rebuilding a 1939 Rolls-Royce Phantom III, which had once served as Churchill's wartime touring car in North Africa. Byroade stripped it down to its bearings, then put it together again. He replaced all the teak on the dashboard, paneled the doors with leopard skins, covered the armrests with lizard skins, and placed python-skin-covered tea trays in the back of the stretch limousine. The car having been built, and there being only so much boredom that any man can endure, Byroade began pestering Rusk for a transfer. He got nowhere, Rusk giving Byroade the impression that the Israeli lobby was still against him. Finally, Byroade, as independent and irreverent as ever, notified State that he was leaving Burma. If that wasn't enough to relay his feelings to the bureaucrats, he added a good measure: He didn't send an embassy cable; rather, he sent his message from the Western Union office in downtown Rangoon.

"Do you still have your moxie?" President Nixon laughingly inquired when he discussed with Byroade his assignment to the Philippines. It was a "rehabilitation" for Byroade, who worked well with Nixon and his national security adviser, Henry Kissinger, agreeing with their aggressive control of foreign policy and obsession with secrecy. When the *Pentagon Papers* began appearing in *The New York Times,* Byroade cabled Washington: "There can be little doubt Marcos . . . will be deeply shocked that a major secret U.S. foreign affairs document has been obtained and is being published by an American newspaper." Byroade was expressing his own reaction, but it wasn't really shock. It was outrage, for he believes that foreign policy cannot be conducted with leaks all the time. His reaction to congressional meddling—at least in Byroade's eyes it was meddling—in foreign affairs was just as strong. When the staff members from the Symington subcommittee, which was looking into the secret activities of Asian countries in support of America in Vietnam, came to the Philippines to investigate, Byroade was so furious that he seriously considered resigning; he fired off a back channel message to Nixon and Kissinger, saying that the congressional investigation "challenges who's running the foreign policy in the United States."

The person supposedly in charge of foreign policy was William Rogers, the secretary of state. Rogers and Byroade didn't get along.

Not only did Byroade go around Rogers, using the back channel to Kissinger,* but he brazenly ignored requests from the secretary of state. After Byroade gave "a hell of a thumping speech" critical of the Symington subcommittee hearings, Rogers asked for a transcript; Byroade said there wasn't one, and that the tape had been destroyed. The friction between the two men was reflected in— maybe it was exacerbated by—their differing attitudes toward Mrs. Marcos. Byroade got along extremely well with her, dancing with her and joining in songs by fires on the beach, World War II ditties sung by American GIs that she had learned as a young girl. The secretary of state didn't care for her. He pointedly refused to call her the first lady or even the president's wife. Instead, he referred to her as "Byroade's girlfriend" or, when he was talking with Byroade, "your girlfriend."

Byroade's only concern as he departed for Manila, he told friends and colleagues, was that his reputation as a womanizer would precede him and that Imelda Marcos would attempt to compromise him. "An attractive rascal," as one journalist remembered him, Byroade, tall (five feet eleven inches), dark, with wavy hair and that correct military bearing, had a reputation, well earned, for pursuing, and being pursued by, beautiful women. Prior to heading off on one diplomatic mission, he and an American president enjoyed a private dinner with a woman both men were dating—and all three were married. In Manila Byroade continued to charm. "Oh, God, he was so handsome," a prominent Filipina journalist said with a slight gasp twenty years later. There was continual gossip about his girlfriends and liaisons. This gave him something in common with Marcos, and the two men frequently laughed about their playboy reputations.

Byroade remained in the Philippines for nearly four years, minus a few months, the longest tenure of any American ambassador since Philippine independence. Marcos had been a democratically elected president when Byroade arrived; on the ambassador's watch Marcos seized power. Byroade has to bear some of the responsibility for allowing that to happen. Though he would like to be remembered as a great soldier-statesman and, for much of what he did, he de-

---

* Byroade insists that he very rarely used the back channel, once when he urged Kissinger to attend Nasser's funeral. Byroade's top aides, however, along with CIA and NSC officers, say that he used the back channel frequently.

serves to be, Henry Byroade had, it seemed, a blind spot when it came to Ferdinand Marcos. Of all the rulers Byroade knew, Marcos was his favorite. Marcos was equally fond of Byroade; he was the only American ambassador regularly invited back to stay in Malacañang when his tour was over. Maybe they were too close, too similar in style and thinking for the ambassador to see the worst in Marcos. Whatever the reasons, Byroade did not act forcefully to deter Marcos from imposing martial law, and once Marcos had acted, he had Byroade's complete support.

5 : Countdown to Martial Law

In the summer of 1972—while the American Democrats were nominating their most liberal candidate in many years and the Republicans were breaking into the Democratic party headquarters, then trying to hush up the break-in—the Philippines was a nation under siege. Not by a foreign power, but from excesses—of man and nature. Torrential rains—68.6 inches in greater Manila in July alone—turned highways into raging rivers and central Luzon into a huge lake, the worst natural disaster in modern Philippine history. Before the rains hit, a boat had been found on an abandoned shoal; the government said it had been loaded with weapons for the Communist New People's Army. And Manila was racked by bombings, every few days, in public and private buildings; the government blamed "subversives." Filipinos could not, of course, control nature, they couldn't explain the boat (those who didn't believe the government), and they were terrified by the bombings, which some thought Marcos might be responsible for in order to create the conditions that would justify some emergency measures. It did seem, at least on the surface, that the Philippines needed some strong governmental action to restore order and discipline. Many American diplomats certainly thought so.

Manila had the air of a modern-day Sodom and Gomorrah: gambling; prostitution; mistresses; pervasive political corruption. But as much as it was Sin City, Manila was Dodge City. The Philippine national homicide rate, which was eight times higher than in the United States, was about 35 per 100,000, compared with a rate of 29 in Thailand and 25 in Colombia, one of the most violent societies in Latin America. For the Filipino man the handgun was "a symbol of male virility and as common an item in the male

92

wardrobe as a tie clasp," an embassy political officer remembered. He carried his firearm in the small of his back, bulging beneath the loose-fitting barong. Car owners packed pistols in their glove compartments. Given that the slightest provocation, real or imagined, was likely to trigger their use, wise—and still alive—was the driver who when involved in an auto accident jumped out of his car, shouting, "It's my fault! It's my fault!" Nightclubs posted notices asking patrons to check their sidearms. Few macho Filipinos did—certainly not those who had a healthy respect for staying alive. And many a man who survived the drinking and shooting didn't live to brag about it. Each morning Roxas Boulevard, wide and majestic along Manila Bay, was littered with automobiles wrapped around the stands of palm trees.

The attitude of the embassy in Manila, and probably many Americans, was summarized by the political officer from 1969 to 1971, Francis T. Underhill. "This place is a hopeless mess," he wrote years later. "Power is so dispersed that nothing can be done. Graft and corruption are rife. The streets are unsafe. The Philippines needs a strong man, a man on horseback to get the country organized and going again. Look at the progress being made by Park in Korea, Suharto in Indonesia, and Lee in Singapore."

Comments like these, which American diplomats made in cocktail party chatter, may have encouraged Marcos to impose martial law, but there is no concrete evidence of more direct or active U.S. involvement in the planning. The United States was, however, very much aware of Marcos's intentions and the details of the countdown and did not take decisive actions to deter him.

The CIA station in Manila had sent its first reports about the possibility of a Marcos takeover back in 1971. Now, in the summer of 1972, it was beginning to analyze more ominous signals. Some of them came from what Imelda Marcos was saying to her Blue Ladies, several of whom talked loosely and caustically among themselves and friends—who, in turn, talked to the CIA. She was saying things like "This country really needs my husband, don't you think? My husband really should stay on. Don't you agree?" Since he couldn't stay on under the Constitution, and the Constitutional Convention was mired in rancorous debate and making very little progress, the only way Marcos could stay in power was by seizing it.

93

The station's belief that Marcos was preparing to do just that was reinforced when he began shuffling military commanders. Officers who believed that the army's duty was to defend democracy, not to subvert it, were transferred out of positions where they had command over troops. As commanders of two military units responsible for the areas in and around Manila, where the repression would have to be swift and total if martial law were to be enforced, Marcos named two loyalists. Soon the three were conferring regularly, and secretly, in Malacañang. The embassy, through the CIA's assets, was aware of the meetings, though it couldn't penetrate them sufficiently to learn the details of what was being discussed. But the embassy and the CIA knew full well that the gatherings could not be explained by any military threat to the Marcos government, which was nonexistent, although an incident in July 1972 generated a lot of talk about the incipient Communist insurgency.

The incident was the discovery of the ninety-one-ton, ninety-foot-long *Karagatan,* found drifting in the azure waters fewer than 100 yards from a white sand beach on the isolated northeast coast of Isabela Province. Local tribespeople—short black men with Afro haircuts, loincloths and bamboo-pierced ears—led government soldiers to a weapons cache which they said had been unloaded from the *Karagatan* for the New People's Army. There were several hundred M-14 rifles, the kind the American army used before it was replaced by the M-16; more than 100,000 rounds of ammunition; and some rocket launchers, copies of a Soviet model.

"Everything about it was as curious as could be," recalled a CIA official who had been in the Philippines at the time. The rifles had strange serial numbers; the ammunition had been produced in 1960, with no record of its whereabouts since; the *Karagatan* was a fishing vessel, but there wasn't any fishing equipment on board. The Philippine Congress investigated, but never resolved the mystery, nor did the CIA, which called in a couple of log experts to read the wood on the rifle stocks in an effort to determine their origin. But they failed, concluding only that the weapons had not been used in combat. The agency eventually decided, according to a Secret report, that it was "likely" that the weapons had been purchased in Hong Kong, from "gun-smuggling circles."

Marcos's critics hollered that the whole thing was a sham, a government setup designed to create the conditions that would justify the imposition of martial law. This time, however, the cynics were wrong, though, like the Plaza Miranda bombing, the mystery surrounding the *Karagatan* has not previously been resolved publicly. According to two leaders of the Communist party, who discussed the incident more than a decade later, the weapons were, in fact, intended for their revolution; they had come not from China but from North Korea. One of the men explained that the gun-smuggling effort had been bungled from the beginning. "We were not prepared for such an operation," he said. Moreover, the whole affair led to some friction within the party, with one local guerrilla commander executed by a firing squad. The death sentence was imposed because the commander, as part of a party power struggle, had spread stories—"intrigues" they called them—that the NPA guerrillas who had been infiltrated into the region to take the weapons from the *Karagatan* were in fact there, he charged, to take power away from the local cell. None of this, however, was known back then, and even if it had been, it would not have justified martial law to deal with the NPA, which simply was not a threat; the bungling of the *Karagatan* operation was indicative of its capabilities.

But the Marcos government said that the Communists were well organized, well armed, and violent. An outbreak of bombings seemed to prove that. In March two men on a motorcycle threw a bomb at the Arca Building, shattering windows on the ground floor; a month later four men in a light blue Impala threw their bomb at the entrance of the Filipinas Orient Airway's office; in May two hand grenades exploded on the porch of the South Vietnamese embassy; in June the target was a branch of the Philippine Trust Company. In July there were three separate incidents, one explosion shattering the glass walls of the Phil-American Life Building, apparently aimed at the Far East Bank and Trust Company and the American Express office, and two weeks later a bomb was found in the Senate's publications office.

In early August, in a meeting with Minister of Defense Enrile and a handful of his most trusted military commanders, Marcos decided to declare martial law sometime within the next two months. Several tentative dates were discussed, all ending with the number seven or divisible by seven. Though the Americans were not aware of this meeting, Marcos was now discussing the possibility of martial law more frequently with Ambassador Byroade, sometimes in the secrecy of the golf shack across the Pasig River from Malacañang.

Byroade agreed with Marcos that some strong measures were needed to deal with the increasing chaos. But he told Marcos that martial law would never be accepted by Washington, that it would generate a maelstrom of protest in Congress. This was Byroade's principal argument; he had made it repeatedly to Marcos. At no time, however, was Byroade forceful. He never said, "Mr. President, if you impose martial law, you will jeopardize economic and military aid," as would have been the policy, and the message, if the Nixon administration had been serious about defending democracy in the Philippines. It was not even "Mr. President, we urge you not to impose martial law." Byroade never expressed more than the "undesirability" of martial law, and even that position was "not stated in so many words," Byroade wrote in a cable that was highly classified—marked "Secret" and further limited in its distribution to only the very highest-level officials in Washington.

Byroade was not acting totally on his own this time; he was implementing the policy, not making it. It had been set by Nixon and Kissinger. In the course of one of Byroade's discussions with Marcos, the Philippine president said that while he understood the ambassador's views, he wanted a more specific reading of the attitude in Washington. Byroade flew home for consultations. In an Oval Office meeting with Nixon and Kissinger, the ambassador outlined the potential negative consequences of martial law, explaining that significant sectors of the Philippine population would probably rebel against it and that they would transfer their anger into anti-Americanism if the United States went along. For the most part Nixon didn't pay much attention to what Byroade was saying. "He seemed bored," recalled a member of the NSC who was present. But an agreement was reached on what the policy should be, and on returning to Manila, Byroade delivered the policy message to Marcos.

The policy was, and Byroade told Marcos, that if martial law were needed to put down the Communist insurgency, then Washington would back the Philippine president. One didn't have to be as savvy as Marcos to see that as an encouraging yellow light, if not a wholly green one. All he had to do was create the conditions, say the right things.

The bombings escalated. On August 15 the Philippine Long Distance Telephone Exchange Office was bombed; seven minutes later the Philippine Sugar Institute was the target. Two days later the Department of Social Welfare was hit, and two days after that a powerful plastic explosive tore a huge hole in a water main in Quezon City. The month staggered to a conclusion: On August 30, at 12:30 A.M., the Phil-Am Life Building was the target again; fifteen minutes later an explosion destroyed an armored car in front of the Philippine Banking Corporation; a few hours later an attaché case containing a twelve-pound bomb was found on the ground floor of the Department of Foreign Affairs Building.

On the evening of September 5 a powerful device exploded inside Joe's Department Store. A woman was killed and forty-one persons were injured. It was one of the only attacks in which people were hurt. The other bombings occurred late at night or early in the morning, when few, if any, people were around, or the explosives were discovered before they were detonated. Two days later a few blocks away, at the foot of the escalator on the ground floor of the Good Earth Emporium, a homemade explosive—a small bar of soap with a timing device, three matchsticks, and a blasting cap—was discovered. On the ninth a nighttime explosion in the Manila City Hall demolished three rooms. On the eleventh, between 12:20 and 12:55 A.M., three power company substations were hit, causing widespread blackouts. The next morning, again shortly after midnight, a bomb destroyed a forty-eight-inch pipe and a twenty-six-inch main of the water and sewage system. Thousands of homes in the southern section of Manila and adjacent suburbs were left without water; again, no one was injured, leading to increasing speculation that Marcos was responsible for the bombings in order to justify emergency measures.

The next day, while emergency crews worked to repair the damage, Senator Aquino dropped his own bombshell on the Senate floor. He exposed a government plan to put Greater Manila, along with parts or all of the adjacent provinces of Rizal and Bulacan, under martial law. The plan had the code name Oplan (Operation Plan) Sagittarius. Always anxious to ingratiate himself with the

Americans, Aquino advised the embassy political officers about Oplan Sagittarius the day before he revealed it to Filipinos. Among those present at the luncheon was the embassy's recently arrived political officer, Frank Maestrone. When Imelda Marcos, who did not take kindly to American officials talking with the "enemy," learned about the lunch, she called Rafferty, demanding to know who was the "Macaroni," a nickname that stuck with Maestrone. After first denying the existence of the plan—Marcos branded it a "typical Aquino concoction"—the government admitted that it existed, but contended that it was merely a contingency plan, prepared in 1966 and periodically updated.

In fact, Marcos was now in the final countdown of his martial law takeover of the country. Aquino's disclosure prompted the martial law planners, the principal one being Defense Minister Enrile, to heighten their security measures. A few days after the Aquino revelations, CIA sources had fully informed the agency. Then Marcos was betrayed when one of his most trusted confidants handed the embassy the smoking gun, a copy of Proclamation 1081, the martial law decree.

On Tuesday there was another bombing, this one of the Quezon City Hall where the Constitutional Convention was in session. Military security around the hall was tight, but somehow the bombers had managed to slip through, planting what military bomb disposal experts said were sticks of dynamite with timing devices. The first bomb exploded in the men's room on the fourteenth floor, causing panic among the spectators packed into the adjacent public gallery, sending delegates diving for cover under their desks. Seconds later another bomb went off, this one in the sixth-floor bathroom, adjacent to a courtroom where nine persons were being tried on charges of subversion. Eleven persons were injured, none seriously.

Marcos, meanwhile, was in direct contact with Nixon. The day after declaring martial law, when one of Marcos's top assistants expressed concern about how the American president might react, Marcos told him not to worry because he had already cleared martial law with Nixon. General Romulo, Marcos's foreign minister at the time, told Raúl Manglapus, a former foreign minister and in 1972 a senator, that the two presidents spoke on or about the eighteenth. Romulo told another friend that Marcos spoke with Nixon twice.

During the first conversation Marcos asked Nixon how he would react if martial law were declared. Nixon replied that he would get back to Marcos, and he did, according to Romulo, four days later, saying that the United States would have no objection. Though Byroade and other high-level American officials who were in the Philippines at the time were not aware of any telephone conversations between Nixon and Marcos prior to martial law, they don't doubt that there probably was direct contact. As a senior CIA official who was in the Philippines when martial law was declared and who knew Marcos very well says, "I just don't see him [Marcos] doing it [declaring martial law] without clearing it with someone up the ladder—and very high up the ladder. . . . He just would not have gone ahead without some assurance that he was not going to get clobbered." And that assurance, this CIA officer says, could have come only from Nixon.

On Friday the twenty-second, Marcos met again with Byroade around noontime. The agenda was the need for martial law. Following the meeting, Byroade returned to the embassy and, gathering up the recent events, observations, conversations, and thoughts, organized them into a three-page cable for Washington. The cable was classified Secret and ExDis, which means that it was not placed in the normal distribution channels. Byroade concluded that "for the time being, possibly for next six weeks or so, likelihood of martial law declaration has now lessened."

At the very moment Byroade was writing, however, martial law was only a few hours away. There are several possible explanations for Marcos's having misled the ambassador. Marcos, as cagey and careful as a guerrilla warrior, knew the value of surprise; he wanted no leaks. And Marcos the deceitful politician also knew the value of "deniability." By not informing the ambassador of the details and even more, by misleading him, Marcos permitted the ambassador and Washington to say, as they did—but only by speaking very narrowly and technically—that martial law was a surprise. The only surprise, if any, was the day and hour of the issuance of the decree.

As Byroade, in his office overlooking Manila Bay, finished the final paragraphs of his cable, on the other side of the city, at Camp Aquinaldo, Defense Minister Enrile was placing a call to Marcos, telling the president that it was time to act: now or never. All the troops were in position, and their commanders were ready. Journalists were asking him about reports that martial law was imminent. It was too risky to wait. Enrile had been the principal martial law architect, and many diplomats and CIA officers who worked closely with Enrile thought that he wanted martial law for his own purposes, that the defense minister believed that after a few years Marcos would turn power over to him. He was wrong.

Within an hour after Enrile spoke with Marcos, a colonel arrived at Enrile's office bearing sealed envelopes. Inside were the presidential orders. After notifying the general staff, Enrile headed home. As the defense secretary's blue Ford with tinted windows, accompanied by a heavily armed security detail, rounded the back of the Wack Wack Golf Course, gunmen opened fire. Bullets riddled the right front and back doors of the Ford and shattered the windshield. Enrile, however, wasn't in the Ford, having decided, miraculously it seemed, to ride in his security car. "God saved him," Enrile's wife, Christina, told an American official at the time. But God had had nothing to do with it. Marcos and Enrile had staged the "ambush," as the final justification for martial law. At 9:00 P.M. the order implementing martial law was signed.*

Marcos's military struck first at the Manila Hilton, room 1701, where Senator Aquino was discussing tariff matters with colleagues from both parties. Earlier in the evening Aquino had received a couple of phone calls warning that he was to be arrested, but he ignored them. Just after midnight there was a gentle knock on the door. It was Colonel Romeo Gatan, a personal friend of Aquino's from the days when Gatan had been the head of the constabulary in Tarlac. Gatan asked his friend to step outside. Just as he had

---

* The long document spelling out the justifications for martial law, Proclamation 1081, was dated September 21, a Thursday, the day before Marcos gave the orders to implement it, giving rise to a long-unsolved puzzle: Had Marcos signed the proclamation on the twenty-first, then waited for an event (which the staged attack on Enrile provided) to implement it? Or had the proclamation been backdated? The answer is the latter. Marcos's signature on the proclamation was witnessed on Saturday morning, the twenty-third, by Roberto Reyes, acting as executive secretary in lieu of Alejandro Melchor, who was in Washington. And the man who was the most intimately involved in the drafting of the martial law papers, Defense Minister Enrile, in an interview many years later, confirmed what had long been suspected: Marcos had backdated the proclamation to the twenty-first because of his superstition about the number seven.

passed up the chance to escape earlier, Aquino now declined to call on his always present well-armed bodyguards to help him resist. Returning to the group, Aquino said, "I'm sorry I can't address the meeting. I'm being arrested."

Aquino's arrest, a few minutes after midnight, preceded all others and came before any of the other military actions. Had Aquino managed to avoid being picked up that evening—either by fleeing or by fighting—Marcos might not have declared martial law at that moment, for as he knew, Aquino was the one person who could rally Filipinos against it.

The Marcos-Aquino duel, fought over three decades, pitted two men marked, it often seemed, more by what they had in common than by their differences. They were dashing men-about-town in their bachelor days; as politicians they were equally charismatic and driven in their quests for power. Both were great prevaricators; U.S. officials who knew both men were divided on which concocted the biggest whoppers. The difference in the two men may lie in Aquino's having been imprisoned for nearly eight years; that may be enough to change any man, and according to those who knew him before and after, it did Aquino.

Unlike Marcos, Benigno Simeon Aquino, Jr., born on November 27, 1932, had an undistinguished scholastic record; "I got bored with class," he said. During his first year in college he regularly cut classes to participate in the presidential campaign and to work as a copyboy at the *Manila Times*. When the Korean War broke out, he volunteered as a correspondent, arriving at the front lines before he was eighteen years old; the grizzled, hard-drinking veterans would toast him as "Aquino, milk boy." He compensated for his youth and lack of experience with seemingly unharnessable energy and an obsession to learn; one of his principal tutors was Marguerite Higgins, the renowned and hard-line anti-Communist correspondent for the *New York Herald Tribune,* whom Aquino had befriended by offering to drive her jeep and who may have tempered some of his liberal political ideas. After eleven months of sloshing through mud and snow and surviving the vicious winter—"I don't brush my teeth anymore because the water is so cold it hurts," he wrote his mother—

relieved by frequent weekend jaunts to Tokyo, Aquino returned home, honored with a military ceremony, the "boy wonder." He pursued his law studies, though his serious "book learning" would not come until his years in prison, when, it is claimed, he voraciously devoured 5,000 books, from the Bible to Dostoevsky and all volumes of the *Encyclopaedia Britannica*. But when he was a restless young man, his principal education came from his travels.

In 1952, with classes in summer recess, he set out on a journalistic sweep of Southeast Asia. In Taiwan he scored an interview with Generalissimo Chiang Kai-shek. "The internal problems of Asia can never be solved until the root causes—the Kremlin and Peiping—are crushed," the general told him. Aquino witnessed firsthand the efforts of European powers to crush uprisings that were nationalistic in origin, communistic in political ideology. In Vietnam he flew to watch the French Foreign Legionnaires raid three small Vietminh-controlled villages, an early battle in what would become one of the greatest counterinsurgency failures. Dropping south, down the spiny peninsula to the British-controlled country of Malay, he accompanied a regiment of specially trained British soldiers on a jungle operation against the liberation-minded guerrillas, most of whom were Chinese and Communists. (The British won that war, still widely considered the "model" for how to conduct a counterinsurgency campaign.) He went to recently independent Burma and Indonesia, which Sukarno had wrested away from the Dutch. It was something of a political passage for the not yet twenty-one-year-old Aquino. He had believed in the domino theory, saying about Vietnam that "should this state fall into the hands of the Communists the Free World might as well write off Southeast Asia as lost!" But the roving three months of seeing, asking, listening, thinking, and writing apparently changed him. He concluded:

> To the Asian, the western argument that "if Communism wins, Asians stand to lose their civil liberties" is meaningless. To the Asian now jailed by the French in the numerous prisons of Vietnam for being "too nationalistic," civil liberties have no meaning. To the Asian jailed on St. John's Island in Singapore for possessing intelligence and nationalistic spirit above the average, civil liberties are likewise meaningless. The Filipino is aware of and has enjoyed America's benevolence; but to the rest of Asia, the American looks

like the Frenchman, the Britisher and the Dutchman. To Asians, these people are the symbols of oppression. And many Asians would prefer Communism to western oppression.

But his political views were anything but fixed, perhaps reflecting his youth or his ambition. As an adviser to President Magsaysay in the early fifties, Aquino prepared position papers that, contrary to what he had written earlier about America in Asia, defended the Formosa Strait resolution and supported the Diem regime in Vietnam. It was also while working for Magsaysay that Aquino participated in the surrender of the Huk leader Luis Taruc, though the exact nature of Aquino's role in that dramatic incident depends on who is telling the story. In Aquino's version, he, after gaining Magsaysay's approval, set out to meet with Taruc, hiking over perilous mountain trails crowded with jungle growth to a clandestine rendezvous. Some months later the redoubtable Taruc surrendered. Aquino claimed credit.

Taruc's version is that he surrendered because he feared that he was about to be liquidated as part of a struggle for control within the Communist party leadership. According to the CIA's man in the war against the Huks, Ed Lansdale, Aquino's role in the matter has been exaggerated: Taruc's surrender had already been arranged, and when Aquino learned about it, he rushed into the hills to grab some glory. Moreover, contrary to a widely held belief, Aquino was not working for the agency, according to Lansdale.

The issue of Aquino's ties to the CIA bobbed around his life, set afloat by Magsaysay's sending Aquino to the United States in 1954. During four months Aquino "observed training methods in American spy schools and did a report on them for Magsaysay," an Aquino biographer, Nick Joaquin, writes. Whether Aquino "observed" or actually participated in the training is unclear, but he later boasted often about his relationship to the agency. In the late seventies Aquino denied that he had ever been under contract to the agency. But he added, he had worked "with the CIA," an assertion he repeated two years later, when he said, "I've worked with your CIA on many operations." He claimed, for example, that in 1958 he had secretly flown to Indonesia as part of the CIA's covert paramilitary operation in support of rebels seeking to overthrow President Sukarno. The operation was aborted by Washington when an American pilot, Allen Lawrence Pope, was shot down and captured after his plane had accidentally bombed a church, killing most of the worshipers. Aquino later complained to friends that the CIA had abandoned him, that he had survived in the jungle for several weeks before managing to escape back to the Philippines. While it is true that the Indonesian operation was run by the CIA out of the Philippines and that Filipinos had been recruited by the agency for the mission, and while Aquino did clandestinely go to Indonesia and could not have done so without CIA knowledge and approval, considering the CIA's complete control over the operation, CIA officials with intimate knowledge of the operation deny that Aquino was working for the agency.

"Absolutely not," says Joseph Smith, when asked if Aquino was working for the agency in Indonesia. Nor adds Smith, whose CIA assignments in the 1950s and 1960s involved him in the Philippines and Indonesia, was Aquino ever on the agency's payroll. Smith's emphatic denial of any direct Aquino-CIA relationship is confirmed by a half dozen CIA officials, including former station chiefs in Manila. They all add, however, that Aquino knew all the station chiefs well and that he frequently provided them with important information. They assumed that Aquino was motivated by the excitement and intrigue offered by working with the CIA and that he wanted to curry favor with the Americans. Moreover, back in those days associating with the American spies had a certain badge of honor, rather than, as later, dishonor. What puzzles, and often amuses, American intelligence officers is the ludicrousness of many of Aquino's statements. Aquino, for example, once boasted about having purchased a plane from one CIA agent although the two men had not yet met at the time of the alleged sale. Even more astonishingly, Aquino often made his CIA claims directly to ranking CIA officials, whom he knew to be CIA and who he must have certainly realized would know that what he was saying was a brazen fabrication.

As with Marcos, Aquino found that love and politics were a comfortable match. When he was one month shy of twenty-two, he married Corazon Cojuangco. They had first met as nine-year-olds, with Cory later recalling that Ninoy "kept bragging that he was a year ahead of me in school; so I didn't even bother to talk to him."

She was a member of one of the country's most socially prominent, aristocratic, and wealthy families: sugar plantations, banks, and other real estate. In later years the clan would split, pitting her and a brother against their cousin Eduardo ("Danding") Cojuangco, who sided with Marcos (he was the only civilian involved in the martial law planning) and became one of the country's two or three most grotesquely wealthy individuals, fleeing his native land with the felled leader in 1986. At the age of thirteen Cory was sent to the United States for schooling, seven years at convent schools, first at the Notre Dame School for girls, then the College of Mount St. Vincent, in Riverdale, New York, where she majored in French and mathematics.

With his marriage to Cory Cojuangco, small (five feet two inches) and quiet, Aquino, short, stocky, and a perpetual talking machine, acquired an 18,000-acre sugar plantation, Hacienda Lusita, which accounted for about 10 percent of the country's sugar production. He often described himself as a "radical rich guy." His approach looked a lot like the New Deal or welfare capitalism. With partial financing from a World Bank loan, he built a $10 million sugar refinery, which was painted yellow, "the influence of the women in our family," he said at the time. (Yellow became Mrs. Aquino's symbol in her presidential campaign in 1986.) Sugar production and profits rose, the latter 160 percent in the decade after he took control, he claimed; but so did the sugar worker's wages—120 percent—and standard of living. Aquino allowed his workers to organize a union, provided them with free medical and dental care, free electricity, water, and housing. "From cradle to grave—that was my concept," he explained.

Aquino's political fiefdom was Tarlac, which had been controlled by his family for generations. "An Aquino in Tarlac is like a Taft in Ohio," he once observed. His grandfather had been a general in the Philippine revolt against first the Spanish, then the Americans; his father had been a senator, speaker of the Assembly and cabinet minister. Voters invested Ninoy Aquino with his political crown when they elected him mayor, at the age of twenty-two the youngest in the archipelago. Matching "firsts" with Marcos, Aquino became the youngest vice-governor in 1957 and the youngest governor, at the age of twenty-eight, two years later. At the age of thirty-two he

105

became the youngest senator in the country. Aquino ran his Tarlac empire from what he called his "economic war room," where sophisticated radio communications gear allowed him to keep in contact with distant village leaders—as well as fueled talk that he was really working for the CIA. He kept in touch with his constituents by flying around the vast province in his own private plane and every forty-five days conducting public opinion surveys, tabulating the results with the help of IBM computers.

That is the benign version of Aquino's early political years—accurate but incomplete. Contrary to Mark Antony's oration at Caesar's funeral, it is the good that men do that lives after them, the evil is often interred with their bones—at least in the case of martyrs, which Aquino became with his assassination in August 1983.

In the tradition of most successful Philippine politicians, Aquino maintained order and control in his kingdom with his own private army, keeping more than 100 of his own guns in his basement. He was often autocratic, ruthless when it was necessary. As governor Aquino once personally arrested a rape suspect, jailed him without any due process, and roughed him up. He captured another rapist, whose victims were usually schoolteachers, going to Manila himself, locating a bar girl, then placing her in a rural school as a seductive, and successful, lure. He personally engaged in shoot-outs with cattle rustlers, and political violence was as endemic in Tarlac as in many other parts of the country. As with Marcos, many Filipinos and Americans are convinced that there is political blood on Aquino's hands, but again as with Marcos, the allegations remain little more than that.

Whatever his methods, Aquino, who could hold forth for hours in political analysis, impressed Americans, even those who didn't share his liberal political views. "He is probably one of the smartest young men I've met in my life," the president of the Rand Corporation said after meeting him in the mid-1960s. That was quite an accolade in view of the conservative orientation of Rand, the first of America's think tanks.

Smart, politically skillful, cunning, well connected, and wealthy—all it took to become president, which many Filipinos hoped, and Marcos feared, Aquino would be. Martial law would save Marcos from having to face him at the polls; to save martial law, Marcos knew that Aquino, and all other democratic opponents, had to be silenced.

With Aquino in jail, Marcos's military units moved swiftly and efficiently throughout the city. By 4:00 A.M. scores of prominent Filipinos had been seized: politicians, journalists, publishers, priests, students, and others who were Marcos's opponents and might be expected to lead the opposition to martial law. Radio and television stations were padlocked; newspaper presses, turned off.

Most of the coming issue of the *Philippines Free Press* had already been printed when the soldiers marched in. There was a story following up on the recent floods, an article illustrated with a caricature of Richard Nixon riding a tiger labeled "Vietnam War," and a two-page spread, with color photos, on "The Art of Aguilar Alcuaz." It was standard fare for the magazine, which had been founded in 1908. But the cover was ominous. There was Ninoy Aquino, with his thick, bushy black hair, tortoiseshell glasses set on his square face. Wearing an ornately embroidered white barong with French cuffs, he stood at a tilted podium, speaking into a silver microphone, emphasizing a point with the index finger of his extended right arm. He was framed in a circle. His upper body was bisected by rifle crosshairs—a most eerie portrait considering Aquino's fate eleven years later. The issue never hit the streets.

Marcos had effectively ensured that there would be no outcry in the Philippines against his seizure of power, but he still had Washington to worry about. Regardless of whatever assurances he might have received from Nixon, Marcos understood the workings of the American political system as well as his own. He knew there were other voices in Washington; Byroade had been telling him there would be a congressional uproar. Moreover, Marcos wasn't a leader who left anything to chance. He wanted to be absolutely certain that no one in Washington spoke out against him. Opposition there, from whatever quarter, might spark demonstrations in Manila, might encourage professional, democratically inclined military officers to oppose him.

Alejandro ("Alex") Melchor, Marcos's executive secretary with cabinet rank, was given the task of making sure everybody in Washington was on board with Marcos. Often referred to as the "Little President," Melchor was to Marcos what H. R. Haldeman was to Nixon, what James Baker and later Donald Regan were to be to Ronald Reagan. Though he was stripped of his official duties in 1975, after he had angered Mrs. Marcos with a plan to purge the government of corrupt officials, Melchor remained close to the president. And he was always so close to the vortex of American power that it was sometimes difficult to know whom Melcor served. When a new U.S. ambassador arrived in Manila, Melchor was often the first to host a dinner for him. Reports he prepared for the president—he had served Macapagal before joining Marcos—were often read by the U.S. embassy before they were sent over to Malacañang. Melchor's standing with Americans was rooted in the connections his father had made when he worked in Washington for the Philippine government. After graduating from a D.C. high school, Melchor had attended the Naval Academy. All those years in the United States had made him so American that a standard joke among Philippine political pundits was that Melchor could easily be elected president—except he couldn't speak Tagalog. But he could speak to Washington power. Indeed, it is unlikely that any Filipino leader, including the Marcoses, had as much cachet and respect in Washington as did Melchor. During the final forty-eight hours of the Marcoses' reign, in February 1986, Melchor was actually in the secure situation room at the White House, advising on how to deal with the crisis.

Melchor's first call when he arrived in Washington, less than twenty-four hours after martial law had been declared, was to John Holdridge, on the National Security Council. During lunch at the Hay-Adams Hotel, Melchor assured Holdridge that American business interests would not be negatively affected by martial law, the same assurance he made in a later meeting with the director of the Agency for International Development (who wanted his picture taken with Melchor). After lunch Melchor went over to the Pentagon, where he met with the chairman of the Joint Chiefs of Staff, Admiral Thomas Moorer, who needed no assurances; he was positively enthusiastic about the implementation of martial law. "That's the best thing" for the Philippines, the admiral told aides. After listening to

Melchor, Robert McNamara, director of the World Bank, promised to double World Bank loans if indeed Marcos was going to use his powers to carry out the country's development. World Bank loans quadrupled; about all that ultimately developed were the bank accounts of the president and his friends. During six days Melchor touched all the power bases except one. He didn't even bother going over to the State Department, for he knew well that foreign policy was being set not by the professionals at Foggy Bottom but by Kissinger and Nixon. Melchor went to the Hill, meeting with Hawaii Senator Inouye, Marcos's loyal friend; Senator Mansfield, the Senate majority leader; and William Fulbright, chairman of the Foreign Relations Committee.

The reaction was universal: There was no opposition to what Marcos had done. No one was even concerned enough to ask how long martial law would be in effect. The only probing question was whether martial law would affect American business interests. Only at the *Washington Post,* where he met with reporters and editorial writers, did Melchor encounter some flak. The testy session ended when Melchor said, "Gentlemen, the final judge of whether martial law is good for the Philippines is not going to be the *Washington Post,* but the Filipino people." Then he turned and walked out.

The press in general treated Marcos's seizure of power most benignly, if not outright effusively. "I tend to think Marcos is sincere" in his desire to use his martial law powers for the benefit of Filipinos, "although his actions are hardly without self-interest," *Newsweek*'s Tony Clifton concluded. The *Washington Star,* which was influential in shaping the attitudes of Washington policymakers, discarded nearly all caution, save for a single sentence: "Marcos' critics say he is a ruthless, ambitious dictator who is ending 39 years of American-style democracy solely to perpetuate his personal power." The correspondent, Richard Critchfield, clearly didn't agree, praising Marcos as an "impressive, highly intellectual social theoretician . . . a devout Roman Catholic and his country's most decorated hero in World War II." Adding to the kindly aura enveloping Marcos, Critchfield noted that during his interview with the Philippine president, in early December, "the sound of carols floated in from a grand salon next door, where his wife Imelda was then decorating a Christmas tree." He went on: "Interviewing some national leaders

is like expecting to meet the Wizard of Oz and finding it's only Frank
Morgan. Marcos was the reverse. At first he seemed tough, commanding, the rather two-dimensional figure one sees on Manila's
front pages and television screen. Then, gradually one saw the man:
pale, worn, visibly overworked, highly intelligent, quoting Gunnar
Myrdal and unfamiliar Japanese economists, capable of charm and
disarming friendliness, almost professorial." The article concluded:
"Here is a man who is obviously carrying out a complex plan of
action he has thought about for years and with his responsibility to
the Philippine nation and history clearly in mind."

A few weeks later *The New York Times* added its endorsement.
In its "Man in the News" feature, the paper declared that "to friends
and critics" Marcos "has become the symbol and the person of
strength in a nation of uncertainty. . . . He hardly looks the role of
the tough dictator. His private manner is quiet, gentle, almost self-
effacing." Then followed a recital, for the third time in seven years
in a "Man in the News" item, of all the acclamations: "excellent
student," "brilliant trial lawyer," "an outstanding guerrilla fighter"
who was wounded five times, survived the Bataan Death March and
was "the nation's most decorated soldier." Not surprisingly, the
CIA man in Manila, David Sternberg, posing as a journalist, gave
the readers of the *Christian Science Monitor* a full dose of super-
latives about martial law, without a splash of negatives.

In Congress the maelstrom of protest Byroade had expected did
not develop; there was barely a breeze. Indeed, there was bipartisan
support for Marcos's actions. Marcos wanted Senator Mansfield to
come to the Philippines to look at the situation, an idea endorsed
by Byroade, who had long been friendly with the Senate majority
leader. Mansfield's schedule didn't permit him to get away, but he
sent the secretary of the Senate, Frank Valeo, in December. Valeo's
report was effusive. "The Philippine Republic has rarely been more
serene," he wrote. Manila, "rich with the characteristic human bus-
tle of Asian cities," was "in the midst of an enthusiastic cleanup-
beautification campaign, one of a number of civic projects to which
Mrs. Marcos is lending her talents and energy at the present time."
Perhaps more important to law- and order-minded Americans, Valeo concluded that "a violent opposition has been silenced and a
measure of order and discipline has been introduced into Philippine

affairs." Valeo had accepted, as did the key policymakers, that the opposition to Marcos was violent, when in fact the overwhelming majority of opposition to Marcos was nonviolent and democratic.

The official reaction of the White House and the State Department to Marcos's declaration of martial law was complete silence. Not even in private conversations with Marcos and other Filipino leaders did U.S. officials register any concern. By contrast, when martial law was declared in Korea three weeks later, the secretary of state and the deputy undersecretary of state for political affairs expressed misgivings, albeit muted, to the Korean ambassador in Washington, and the State Department said that the United States "quite obviously" was "not associated with it," implying that Washington saw no need for it. Though that rebuke was, at most, extremely mild—it came from the State Department's press officer, not from a senior official—it was more than was said about the Philippines. The only thing the department's spokesman would say about what had happened in the Philippines was that the United States had not been consulted or informed in advance, a reaction which even in the most charitable light can be characterized as dissembling.

To all other questions about the passing of democracy the United States had "No comment."

6: American
Acquiescence

It is one thing to question why the United States ever accepts a dictator as a partner. But the inquiry becomes particularly acute, returning like Job's plea, in the case of the Philippines. This was, after all, the "showcase of democracy" in Asia, the country where the United States had inculcated the democratic values and traditions, the country where, in the name of preserving democracy and defeating communism, Washington, the CIA, and Ed Lansdale had fought the counterinsurgency war against the Huks. Now Washington watched as democracy was defeated.

Marcos said the Communists were again threatening the Philippines, that he needed martial law to defeat them. He knew this cry would appeal to Washington, even though it had little, if any, foundation in reality. But if Marcos trumped up the threat of communism to justify his actions, and he did, American officials exaggerated the breakdown of law and order in Philippine society and distorted Filipino reaction to martial law as rationalizations for their support of Marcos's seizure of power. Not everyone in Washington, however, bought the Marcos takeover. A few in the State Department saw it for what it was: a grab for power, pure and simple. They provided trenchant analyses and prophetic warnings. But they were ignored, an echo of Vietnam and, before that, of China.

The ultimate responsibility for allowing Marcos to become a dictator rests not with Byroade and the embassy, not with American businessmen in the Philippines, not with the U.S. generals and admirals (though the reaction of all was from tacit approval to enthusiastic endorsement) but with the men who were dominating the U.S. foreign policy at the time, Richard Nixon and Henry Kissinger.

Neither man had any particular interest in the Philippines, and each was intensely preoccupied the week that Marcos acted.

For Kissinger, the Philippines was a "backwater," says William Sullivan, his ambassador in the Philippines from 1973 to 1977. In his two-volume, 2,700-page memoirs, Kissinger makes not a single reference to the Philippines. His concerns were with the world's big powers, which consumed him more than ever in 1972. In February he had opened the way for Nixon's historic visit to China; two months later Kissinger went to Moscow to prepare for Nixon's summit meeting with Leonid Brezhnev. And in 1972 Vietnam continued to plague U.S. foreign policy and domestic politics. While, on the one hand, the administration was trying to wind down the U.S. involvement, Nixon was expanding the war, on the other hand. In response to a North Vietnamese attack across the demilitarized zone, he had ordered the mining of Haiphong Harbor and an intensification of the bombings of the North. The administration didn't want another foreign policy crisis, certainly not in the Philippines, not in the country where U.S. bases were being used for the conduct of the war. It was easier to go along with Marcos than to confront him. This was especially so in September 1972, when Kissinger was deep into his secret negotiations to end the war.

For more than three years Kissinger had been shuttling to and from Paris for secret meetings with North Vietnam's Le Duc Tho; in August and September 1972 the pace of the talks quickened, in part because of Kissinger's desire to reach an agreement before the November presidential elections, which pitted Nixon against the antiwar candidate, George McGovern. On September 15, one week before Marcos declared martial law, in another of their secret meetings Kissinger and Le Duc Tho each made several significant concessions; on the twenty-third, the day after martial law was declared, Kissinger sent a message to Saigon, seeking the support of the South Vietnamese government for the deal. Three days later, while Marcos's executive assistant, Alejandro Melchor, was still in Washington, hustling endorsements for martial law, and Marcos's military men in Manila were throwing more people in jail, Kissinger was back in Paris, for more private meetings with Le Duc Tho. Vietnam might still be a quagmire; the Philippines was a placid lake where U.S. policy sailed smoothly.

Kissinger didn't convene any interagency meeting to discuss how the U.S. should react to Marcos's declaration of martial law. He didn't consult the State Department. By mid-1972 Secretary of State William Rogers "had thrown in the towel," Seymour Hersh notes in his book about Kissinger, "intent primarily on keeping the truth of his eclipse from the public." Kissinger simply informed State that the United States would go along with what Marcos had done. "It was a fait accompli," recalled Marshall Green, then assistant secretary for East Asian and Pacific affairs, who was out of favor with Kissinger because of his opposition to the policy in Vietnam. Though Green, a distinguished professional diplomat once described by *The New York Times* as the State Department's "leading expert on everything pertaining to Asia," thought that martial law was warranted in order to deal with the disorder and chaos in the Philippines, he also thought that Washington ought to have demanded some assurances from Marcos that it would be only temporary, perhaps six months or one year. No such assurances were sought.*

As for Richard Nixon, not only was the war in Vietnam plaguing him, but there was also the matter of the break-in at the Watergate office of the Democratic party in June 1972. For the first weeks afterward Nixon had been successful in containing the investigations by Congress, the Justice Department, the FBI. But Watergate wouldn't go away, and by September it was beginning to unravel. One week before martial law was declared, on September 15, a federal grand jury in Washington indicted seven men in connection with the Watergate break-in. That afternoon, Nixon, his chief of staff, H. R. Haldeman, and White House counsel John Dean III met in the Oval

---

* One is left to speculate what might have happened if the United States had done something other than roll over when martial law was declared. While it might or might not have deterred Marcos from his course, many Filipinos, as well as American officials, believe that a voice of concern from Washington would have encouraged expressions of opposition in Manila. Such a suggestion is not paternalistic or arrogant; it is a recognition of the high regard most Filipinos had for America. But even if a U.S. protest might not have had any immediate impact, "if we had come down harder at the beginning," a senior CIA officer who spent many years on Philippine affairs suggested in 1985, a decade later "we wouldn't have been faced with 'Down with the U.S.-Marcos dictatorship.' " Moreover, he added, "We may have been able to have speeded up the restoration of democracy."

Office, with the president expressing his most concern to date about the spreading Watergate affair. Five days later two principal members of Nixon's reelection committee, including his former secretary of commerce, Maurice Stans, were added as defendants in the Democrats' civil suit. The next day, September 21, the day before martial law was declared, the Nixon people made the first of what would eventually amount to $230,000 in "hush money" payoffs to the conspirators.

Even if Nixon and Kissinger had been paying attention to the Philippines, even if they had not been preoccupied, it is unlikely that Washington would have reacted any differently to martial law. While these two men were in control of American foreign policy, America's support for dictators increased, concomitantly with a diminution of concern about democracy. During the first Nixon-Kissinger term, in addition to the Philippines, other dominoes fell—not to the totalitarian Communist left but to the authoritarian military right. In Cambodia in 1970 General Lon Nol ousted the mercurial Prince Norodom Sihanouk, who had been an irritant to Washington because of his reluctance to allow his country to be used as part of the war in Vietnam. While the United States may not have been responsible for this coup, intelligence agents had approached Lon Nol a year earlier, and once he was in place, "we were ready, as usual, to go along with right-wing generals like Lon Nol and his miserable and corrupt brother Colonel Lon Nol," notes Robert Shaplen, the veteran Asian reporter for the *New Yorker*. A year later, in November 1971, in Thailand generals abolished the Constitution, dissolved the Parliament, disbanded the cabinet, and declared martial law. The new military rulers promised not to interfere with the five large U.S. air bases in Thailand, from which B-52 bombers lumbered with the loads dropped on the Ho Chi Minh Trail; in Washington there was no expression of concern about the blow to Thailand's incipient, and struggling, democracy. In South Korea Park Chung Hee, bolstered perhaps by the Nixon administration's endorsement of martial law in the Philippines, put his country under martial law less than one month later. (Pointing to Washington's not having protested against martial law in the Philippines, Korea's opposition leader Kim Dae Jung said, "I expected that this unfortunate thing would happen in my country too.") On

115

the other side of the world, six months before Marcos seized power, the military in El Salvador stole an election from José Napoleón Duarte; the pleas of Duarte's Christian Democrats were answered with silence in Washington. (Ten years later, after the country had been plunged into a brutal civil war, Duarte was Washington's savior.) And farther south in the hemisphere, in Chile, Nixon and Kissinger were engaged in a number of nefarious covert plots, eventually successful, to topple the government of President Salvador Allende Gossens. Allende had been democratically elected, but Nixon and Kissinger wanted him out. He was a Marxist. (Fourteen years later the dictator who replaced him, General Augusto Pinochet Ugarte, was still in power.)

Marcos knew how to gain Washington's backing: Raise the fear of communism. In the very first paragraph of Proclamation 1081, in the first *"Whereas"* clause, Marcos declared that "lawless elements" and "ruthless groups of men" were "waging an armed insurrection and rebellion against the Government of the Republic of the Philippines in order to forcibly seize political and state power in this country, overthrow the duly constituted government, and supplant our existing political, social, economic and legal order with an entirely new one whose form of government, whose system of laws, whose conceptions of God and religion, whose notion of individual rights and common relations, and its political, social, economic, legal and moral precepts are based on Marxist-Leninist-Maoist teachings and beliefs." Then he went on, for a total of twenty-two *"Whereas"* clauses, eighteen of them devoted to marshaling evidence against the Communist-led insurgency. He made reference to the *Karagatan* landing and went through a recitation of the bombings, in order to paint the Communists as a serious threat.

Marcos, of course, wasn't the first ruler (nor would he be the last) to justify his antidemocratic actions by deploying the Communist threat. It is a standard tactic, even when the threat is not real—maybe more so when it is not. "Any idea or activity based on social justice, whether it comes from political, social, or religious sectors, is immediately branded as Communist," an El Salvadoran political leader, José Morales Ehrlich, told a U.S. congressional committee in 1977, when his country had been under the rigid control of U.S.-backed military dictatorships for nearly half a century.

He explained: "With this position of staunch anticommunism and antisubversion, the government is able to justify violations of human rights, even the right of life and liberty of persons who merely disagree with the government, or who seek a more just society, or who work to insure free elections and a democratic process." The tactic worked in gaining Washington support and, in fact, was tacitly encouraged by Washington, because as an American ambassador in Latin America observed in the late 1970s, "We in the United States have made such a big thing about communism. . . ."

Waving the Red flag has convinced Democratic and Republican administrations to surrender to dictators. In 1954 the Eisenhower administration covertly toppled the Guatemalan government of the democratically elected Jacobo Arbenz Guzmán, after he had brought Communists into his cabinet and announced a land reform program that American businesses in the country found positively communistic. In Iran fears of communism led to the CIA coup against Mossadegh in 1953, followed by more than two decades of bipartisan support for the shah because he was a good anti-Communist. In the name of fighting communism the Kennedy administration launched, and the Johnson administration expanded, the war in Vietnam, rallying behind corrupt dictators, who came seriatim after Diem. And no Washington administration until Ronald Reagan's has been more stridently anti-Communist than that of Richard M. Nixon, the man who rode the waves of the cold war fears from California to the White House.

"Communism" is the buzzword, ending the debate and foreclosing any probe into whether or not there really is a threat. A discussion and inquiry, even a superficial one, in 1972 would have revealed that Marcos had created a "Red Peril" that didn't exist. The Huk insurgency had long ago been defeated; the Communist New People's Army (NPA) was an uncertain and wobbling infant.

The NPA was created during a secret gathering that had begun on the day after Christmas 1968, the seventy-fifth anniversary of the birth of Mao Zedong. A small cadre of university student leaders and young professionals convened the Congress of Reestablishment, and before dispersing two weeks later, they had "reestablished" Philippine communism and created the New People's Army as its military force. The old Philippine Communist party (known by its

Tagalog initials as the PKP) and the Huks had been pro-Soviet. The new Communist Party of the Philippines (CPP) and the NPA looked to China as the revolutionary model. Mao was celebrated as the "acme of Marxism and Leninism in the present era," and Mao's eight principles of guerrilla war were to guide the NPA.

The revolutionary movement had trouble gaining adherents. By the summer of 1972 it "was far from reaching the strength of 35,000 it deemed necessary to accomplish its revolutionary goals," the State Department's Bureau of Intelligence and Research (INR) noted in a Secret research study. "Its military operations were at a low level and confined to remote areas, while it concentrated on recruitment and organization-building." Marcos, as part of his justification for martial law, came up with all kinds of exaggerated numbers for the Communist strength. There were at least 8,000 NPA guerrillas, he claimed, supported by 10,000 active cadres and maybe 100,000 sympathizers. The numbers were hyperbole, and Washington knew it. INR, in another Secret report, put the number of military and support cadres at "less than 9,000." Even that number was inflated because when the report was completed, in December 1973, the deputy chief of mission in the Philippines at the time martial law was declared was back in Washington and working at the bureau; an even lower number would have reflected on the absurdity of Marcos's claims and, by extension, on how unjustified the embassy had been in supporting Marcos. According to the Rand Corporation, in a report for the U.S. Army at the time of martial law, there were some 1,000 NPA guerrillas and maybe another 5,000 to 6,000 part-time militia. And they could not be described as "well armed"; many of their weapons were old-fashioned, more likely to misfire than to fire. The NPA in its own history, prepared years later, wrote that at the time of martial law it had only 350 men with first-line rifles. Whatever the numbers, the NPA "was a joke," said a U.S. intelligence official who was involved in Philippine matters in the fall of 1972.

In the only sections of his martial law proclamation that he didn't dedicate to the alarm of the Red tide inundating the Philippines, Marcos addressed the "equally serious disorder in Mindanao and Sulu resulting from the unsettled conflict between certain elements of the Christian and Muslim population." The "conflict" he referred to had been "unsettled" since the days of Spanish rule, when the Muslims in Mindanao began fighting against subjugation by the Christians in Manila. When Spain turned over the archipelago to the United States, the Muslims argued (and still do) that it was illegal to have included Sulu, the droplet of islands trailing from Mindanao which had been wrested from the sultan in 1876, when the Spanish had dispatched 9,000 troops and eleven gunboats, along with twenty-one other ships, to subdue a rebellion in Jolo. Not until the American commonwealth period were Christian Filipinos allowed to settle in the Muslim ancestral lands. Encouraged by the president's cry to go south, they began arriving in droves, in search of land, timber, and the rich mineral deposits. Peter Kann, a reporter for the *Wall Street Journal,* depicted the conflict as it looked in the early 1970s: "The situation bears some striking similarities to the winning of the American West. The Christian settlers can be seen as Nebraska homesteaders; the mineral and timber magnates as the U.S. railroad barons; and the Muslims, sad as it may be, as the Indians."

The war had another complexion, assumed when university students and young intellectuals in Mindanao, like their counterparts in Manila, became active and militant. In 1970, at Mindanao State University in Marawi City, the Moro National Liberation Front (MNLF) was formed, dedicated to promoting the culture of the now minority Muslim population and demanding independence. Support and sympathy came from Libya and other Middle East countries, with weapons often transshipped through Sabah, the vast territory on the northeast corner of Borneo, which the Philippines claimed in a dispute with Malaysia.

By 1972 the MNLF guerrillas were tougher, better organized, and better armed than the NPA units, able to inflict serious casualties on the Philippine military. Though they presented a serious military problem, it was an isolated one. Moreover, the Muslims, who made up only about 5 percent of the country's population, were no serious threat to the government in a country that was at least 85 percent Catholic.

The American diplomats in Manila, including Byroade, knew that the Marcos government was not facing a military threat—not from the Communists or the Muslims. Nevertheless, most of them not only accepted but positively endorsed martial law. Their justifications have become part of conventional history. The first is that U.S. support for martial law was the right policy because the Filipinos welcomed martial law. The corollary is that martial law was needed because the fabric of Philippine society was being shredded by excesses: too much politics, too much crime, too much corruption, and too little restraint and responsibility. Though there is some truth in both these propositions, like most catechism, they rest more on faith, reinforced by repetition over the years, than on reality.

Filipinos did seem to heave a collective sigh of relief when Marcos declared martial law, understandably perhaps, given their society's state of disrepair. Marcos promised a "New Society." He pledged to disarm the private armies; curb the violence; execute drug dealers; eliminate corruption; break up the economic oligarchies (5 percent of the population controlled 95 percent of the country's wealth, said the conservative Rand Corporation); collect taxes (it was, of course, the 5 percent who weren't paying); and give land to the landless peasants who were starving. The "New Society" Marcos had in mind, it would turn out, was even more corrupt and had a greater concentration of wealth than the "old" society, but for that fleeting moment in 1972 it looked as if he just might be serious about reform.

After declaring martial law, he began immediately to disarm the private armies—at least most of them—and required citizens to surrender their handguns and rifles. The wealthy buried their caches by their swimming pools; government agents with metal detectors dug them up. Within a month the government had collected—by voluntary surrender or confiscation—enough weapons to supply a small army, including rows of American M-16s, Soviet AK-47s, Israeli Uzi submachine guns, an antiaircraft gun, and even a couple of armored cars mounted with machine guns. By Christmas nearly 600,000 firearms had been seized, according to the government. (There was one negative effect to this gun collection campaign, and that was among the Muslims, who considered the right to bear arms divinely ordained and who rather than surrender them joined the insurgency.) The crime rate plummeted; murders in Manila dropped

90 percent in the first weeks. For the first time in years a man felt safe going out without his gun.

Parents who were paying college tuition were pleased with martial law; now their kids would have to spend their time in the classroom reading books, not in the streets burning flags and throwing rocks. Wives were grateful to Marcos for doing what they couldn't: keeping their husbands home at night. With the creativity of a benign Dante, Marcos had come up with an ingenious scheme. A curfew went into effect at midnight, and anyone caught on the streets after that was picked up. While suspicious-looking students would be hauled off for a roughing up followed by detention for several weeks or months, otherwise law-abiding men were treated civilly and released the next morning—but not until ten o'clock. Thus, a man who wasn't home by midnight didn't get home at all and was also late for work the next morning. He faced both an angry boss and wife.

The business community rejoiced. A report prepared for the president a few weeks earlier noted that the fear and violence engulfing society were destroying the economy; the growth in the gross national product would be only 3 percent, less than half what had been projected. After a few days of cautious trading following the declaration of martial law, the stock market snapped out of a two-year slump, heading toward a prolonged recovery. Even church leaders, those who in a few years were to lead the opposition to martial law, were largely silent in September 1972, except for a few statements mildly criticizing the arrests and other violations of human rights. The bishops were quite pleased when Marcos banned blue movies and shuttered the casinos.

Though the reaction of the Philippine populace in general, or at least many segments of it, may have been positive, the response was not necessarily as it has been portrayed to justify Washington's endorsement of martial law. What Americans have cited as Filipino support for martial law may have been only resigned acquiescence, the acceptance of something which the populace was largely powerless to change. The futility of challenging martial law was reflected in a report by the embassy after a meeting with Aquino. A week before martial law was declared, Aquino told some U.S. embassy officers that if Marcos imposed martial law, he would support the

121

president. But, as the embassy commented, Aquino "would have little choice" other than to go along with martial law "since he would be one of President's prime targets were he to oppose Marcos actively." Of course, that is precisely what happened: Anyone who was thought to oppose martial law or Marcos was jailed. Senator Mansfield's man, Frank Valeo, wrote that "a violent opposition has been silenced." In fact, it wasn't just the violent opposition. It was all opposition that was silenced. Some 30,000 people were arrested in the hours, days, and weeks following September 22; very few were Communists advocating the violent overthrow of the government. The overwhelming majority of those in prison were Filipinos who expressed their opposition to Marcos in democratic ways. To have protested martial law would have been to meet the same fate. In addition, Marcos had closed off what was probably the most effective means of dissent by shutting down the country's newspapers along with the radio and television stations.

Regardless of the level of support for martial law by the people, should the United States remain silent in the face of an assault on democracy just because the citizens of the country might acquiesce to it? The answer would be yes if the U.S. adhered to a policy of noninterference in another country's domestic affairs. But it does not. Surely, if a left-wing government had usurped democracy, the United States would protest, regardless of the enthusiasm of the people for the new form of government (as, for example, in Nicaragua under the Sandinistas).

Contrary to all the righteous statements about the United States' simply fitting its policy to the apparent desires of the Filipinos, American support for martial law, in fact, had far less to do with what the Filipinos wanted than with what Americans thought they needed, and that was discipline. Americans demand law and order, at home and abroad. They also expect the people of other countries to govern themselves as Americans do; when they don't measure up, the reaction is to assume that they are not capable of the responsibility that a democracy requires and therefore not worthy of the freedom that it allows. In one of the few articles by an American journalist that was critical of martial law, the *Wall Street Journal*'s Peter Kann, writing in *Foreign Affairs,* observed: "There is something both cynical and presumptuous about Americans, or other

Westerners, writing off the Asian continent—and more particularly the Philippines—as somehow unsuited to democracy." That is precisely what many American leaders, and journalists, thought. The Philippines just wasn't ready for democracy.

In exercising their democratic freedoms before martial law was declared, Filipinos seemed to have grafted on the admonition of Thomas Paine that "moderation in principle is always a vice." Excess was the principle of Philippine democracy. Philippine democracy was the child who hears his parent say a dirty word, then runs around repeating it. Maybe the Philippine "showcase of democracy" was badly cracked. But democracy was functioning: Filipinos could vent their frustrations, anger, and disapproval in regular elections, even if it meant only that the corrupt group of politicians they threw out was replaced by another corrupt group.

Probably no segment of Philippine society was more excessive, more irresponsible than the press. To describe it as licentious would not be unfair; it gave yellow journalism a good name. When, for example, Mrs. Marcos had a miscarriage, it was reported in some detail on the front page; American diplomats read the papers each morning not for news but to find out who among them was the subject of the most recent malicious gossip. ("I have a lot of sympathy for the crackdown on the press," said a diplomat who had been in Manila when martial law was declared, a sympathy that revealed what the press was like as well as the condescending attitude toward Philippine democracy.) The price for press recklessness was one of the most prolific (fifteen newspapers, seven TV stations, and twelve radio stations), diverse, and certainly the freest press in Asia, if not in all the third world. Was the price too high?

Just as democracy in the Philippines was not so enfeebled and corroded that it had to be discarded, so was the decay in Philippine society not so deep as to warrant martial law to rout it out. "Our analysis suggests that the crime problem has been overstated as a general nationwide crisis," the Rand Corporation concluded in 1971 after lengthy research for the U.S. government. Crime was not greatly feared by most Filipinos in general and even less so by those living outside Manila, the researchers found. That it was a greater problem in Manila was "symptomatic of the social disorganization attending urban growth."* In other words, it was no worse in Manila than in other large Asian cities. Moreover, was it necessary to impose martial law throughout the country to deal with the lawlessness, which was concentrated in Manila? Further, was it even necessary to resort to martial law in Manila? Why not only a suspension of the writ of habeas corpus? Even that might not have been needed. What was needed was a rigorous enforcement of the laws by the government. As Kissinger's East Asian and Pacific Interdepartmental Group concluded in an exhaustive and highly classified study begun in early 1972 and completed one month before martial law was imposed, the "law and order problem" in the Philippines was "essentially a police matter."

Thus, if Marcos had wanted to restore law and order, he could have. He had enough control over the armed forces and constabulary to ensure their support of his martial law takeover; he certainly had enough authority to order them to enforce the country's criminal laws, to arrest violators, to confiscate illegal weapons. As for the private armies, those, too, could have been disarmed and dismantled without martial law. It wouldn't even have required the use of the regular Philippine Army to have defeated them. The Philippine Constabulary (PC), the country's national police force, could have done it. The private armies weren't coordinated, and they fought each other, not the government. It would have taken "one [PC] company, one morning for each private army—surprise them all," says General Rafael Ileto, one of the most distinguished and respected men in the history of the Philippine military, and who in November 1986 became President Corazon Aquino's defense minister. A West Point graduate, Ileto knew something about defeating enemies, foreign and domestic. During World War II he fought the Japanese as an officer in the U.S. Army; after the war he organized and commanded the Philippine Rangers, tough, disciplined, highly motivated soldiers who were instrumental in defeating the Huks. He then went to Laos and Vietnam, where he worked closely with

---

* The Rand researchers observed that one of the reasons for the growth of Manila, with the attendant increase in crime, was the economic policies adopted in the 1950s designed to encourage the development of import substitution industries, policies advanced by the United States. These industries were located in and around Manila, where they had a large pool of labor and access to the government. "Thus, although direct links between law enforcement policy and crime are undetectable, there may be important and unsuspected links between economic policy and violence."

the American military men who were just beginning their counter-insurgency war. Returned to the Philippines, he served as the director of the National Intelligence Coordinating Agency, which was patterned after the CIA. In 1965 Marcos gave him his first star, promoting him over senior colonels, and assigned him to be the PC zone commander for the country's nineteen northern provinces, where most of the private armies marauded. "If Marcos had given the orders, the PC could have picked up all the firearms from all the private armies," Ileto says.

Marcos, of course, never gave the orders, in part because many of the private armies belonged to politicians loyal to him. Moreover, Marcos didn't want tranquillity; disorder and chaos served his ultimate end of staying in power. Marcos knew that the Philippine people would tolerate the destruction of their liberties only if the conditions demanded strongman rule. What the lawless elements in Philippine society wouldn't do on their own to create those conditions, Marcos would do himself.

"It was created by Marcos," an American intelligence official who was in the Philippines at the time said about the atmosphere of violence that brought on martial law. While many of the demonstrations were organized by young Communist agitators, and others by priests and university students protesting the poverty and economic inequities, not all of them were. Marcos, according to Philippine and American intelligence officials, also organized demonstrations, including many of those in front of the U.S. embassy. Marcos supplied the banners and paid the marchers to carry them. During one of the Marcos-organized rallies the seal with the eagle was ripped from the American embassy. It was more than just noisy and sometimes violent demonstrations. "At the final point," Ileto says, "they were not just aiding and abetting the violence; they were actually committing it. They were doing it to create the situation to demand more stringent measures."

It was government-sponsored terrorism. All those bombings in the weeks before martial law—of the department stores, private companies, government buildings, waterworks—weren't part of the Communists' plan to take over the country. They were the work of the Marcos government, part of the plan to justify seizing control of the nation.

Specifically, according to Philippine and American military and

125

intelligence officers, the bombings were the work of the "Monkees." The name of the popular American rock group had been applied to the armed gangs that had first surfaced in 1969 in central Luzon, where they carried out assassinations and other paramilitary operations.* Philippine officials vehemently denied that the Monkees had any official connections. In reality, however, they were the forerunners of what became known as the death squads in El Salvador a decade later. They were in the service of local landlords and politicians, but they were very much part of the government. The Monkees were the most trusted of the constabulary soldiers, recruited with promises of cars, motorcycles, televisions, and extra pay for their "extracurricular" activities. Their mission was to "execute or liquidate certain persons whom the military establishment wants to be executed or liquidated for various reasons," a member of the Monkees, José Fronda Santos, Jr., explained. Santos, who had been a military intelligence officer in Tarlac Province from 1969 to 1972 (and again from 1973 to 1983), said, in a sworn affidavit, that he was paid by "private corporations controlled by persons connected with President Ferdinand Marcos." During the 1969 presidential campaign "a plan was devised by the military to terrorize the people of Tarlac Province in order to convince them to vote for President Marcos." The plan, Santos said, was "directed by" Eduardo Cojuangco, one of the wealthiest landowners in Tarlac.

In late 1970 or early 1971 the Monkees began operating in and around Manila, and in the months prior to martial law, they carried out the bombings. (Some American intelligence officials are also convinced that the Monkees were responsible for the Plaza Miranda bombing). The bombing targets were carefully selected, as was the time of the attacks, so as to minimize injury while heightening the sense of anarchy that would justify a martial law clampdown. The Monkees operated in Manila under the direction and control of two of Marcos's most trusted constabulary commanders. And Marcos's defense minister, Juan Ponce Enrile, "knew about every

---

* The Monkees' targets were frequently the lawless Huk units, which became known as the Beatles. The shoot-outs between the two groups became so much a part of the landscape that "When children engage in their war games, one side inevitably calls itself the Monkees and the other the Beatles," writes Eduardo Lachica in HUK: Philippine Agrarian Society in Revolt.

goddamn one of those bombings," says an intelligence officer. So did the CIA in Manila, though not in advance.

To posit fifteen years later that in 1972 the United States should have recognized the declaration of martial law for what it was—a grab for personal power and riches—is not Monday-morning quarterbacking. There was ample evidence *then* to justify serious suspicions about Marcos. The embassy knew that Marcos had the power to curb the violence, that he was, in fact, contributing to it. Documents about Marcos's phony war claims, some of them not even classified, were in the American files. "There exists no authority by which an award of the Medal of Honor to President Marcos may be considered," a military aide to LBJ wrote in a letter to a Filipino, in response to an inquiry in 1966. "We all assumed that this [his war record] was just terribly, terribly fraudulent. But nobody much cared," recalled an intelligence officer. And though it would be several years before the full extent of corruption was publicly known, American officials were fully cognizant by 1972 that Marcos was plundering the national treasury. It was documented that the $39 million the United States had given to him for the Philippine troops in Vietnam had "disappeared." It was well known that Imelda Marcos had her hand in every corporate suite, demanding that she be given a 10 percent interest in all businesses. And each year for her birthday she collected "donations" of about $500,000 from businessmen, usually Chinese, with the commissioner of customs as the bagman. If someone didn't give, he would find that his visa, which he had for many years, was suddenly invalid. A psychological profile on Marcos prepared by the CIA in 1969 concluded that Marcos had already stolen several hundred million dollars. And there were big flashing neon signposts all over the place to show that Marcos was headed in the direction of holding power at whatever cost. It wasn't just the bombings. He had purchased his reelection in 1969 with expenditures staggering even by Philippine standards. When the Constitutional Convention began considering provisions that might restrict his powers or that could expand them, Marcos resorted to "bribery and intimidation," as the State Department noted, to control the convention.

And what about the arrests at the time of martial law? If the justification for martial law was to defeat the Communists or even to restore order and discipline, why was it necessary to imprison priests, publishers, politicians, reporters? These people weren't Communists, nor were they in any remote way responsible for the lawlessness. They were, however, anti-Marcos—not all of them altruistically so, many because they had their own designs on wealth and political power. The senators who were detained, in addition to Aquino, were Ramón Mitra and José Diokno. Mitra, a lawyer in his mid-forties, had served for two years with the Philippine mission to the United Nations, resigning from the Foreign Service for a political career. Mitra was released after a few months, but Diokno, fifty years old, was held for two years. A brilliant lawyer, he had served in the early 1960s as the secretary of justice and had been elected to the Senate as a member of Marcos's Nationalist party, splitting with Marcos after the Plaza Miranda attack, which Diokno publicly blamed on the military. In general, U.S. officials in Manila had more disdain for Diokno than they did for Aquino. The former was a stronger nationalist, advocating restrictions on American businesses and calling for the removal of the American bases. No one, however, questioned his independence and integrity; on his office wall hung a picture of him and J. Edgar Hoover, which the FBI director had warmly inscribed. In 1974, Paul Kattenburg, the retired career diplomat who had distinguished himself often, described Diokno as "mature, prudent, cautious and wise." Yet the United States did not protest Diokno's arrest. Nor was there any effort to secure the release of Mitra (who in 1986 became a member of Mrs. Aquino's cabinet), Aquino, or the other political prisoners. The fears and reservations that the embassy officers should have harbored about Marcos, they had instead for his opponents. This may also explain, in part, why the American embassy tacitly embraced martial law: Most officers believed that Marcos was best for American interests, certainly better than Aquino.

The embassy's post-martial law attitude came under some sharp criticism in Washington, from the State Department's Bureau of Intelligence and Research (INR). Sometimes referred to as State's central intelligence agency, the bureau's task, as its name suggests, is to gather intelligence and conduct research, analyze it, then distribute the result to the relevant bureaus within the department. INR has no official policy-making functions, its job being to provide information and analysis to those who do make policy.

"The embassy has adopted the view," INR concluded, "that martial law, or some such drastic step, was needed to arrest the Philippine slide toward chaos; that martial law was a necessary and appropriate response to this situation; that Marcos is sincere in his intention to implement genuine reforms." It was INR's view, on the other hand, "that martial law was not necessary to deal with the country's problems, which have in fact been considerably aggravated by Marcos' corrupt political style; that based on his record of ruthless self-aggrandizement he cannot necessarily be counted on to implement significant reforms."

This INR analysis was one of a series that the bureau produced in the weeks and months following martial law. Most of them contradict what American officials were saying publicly, and in many cases even privately, about Marcos and martial law. All the INR reports were highly classified, usually Secret, with a further restriction on their distribution. And many were toned down from the drafts, because of bureaucratic pressures not to be too harsh on colleagues. But separately, and even more so when read together, the INR reports are an indictment of the U.S. policy of endorsing martial law, more pointed and disturbing because they were prepared by the professionals within the State Department, not by outside politicians.

One month after the Philippine president had declared martial law, INR, in a very short memorandum of "Talking Points" prepared for the secretary of state, wrote: "By one means or another, Marcos clearly intends to control Philippine politics for many more years." There were "basic reasons for skepticism about his [Marcos's] commitment to reform," INR noted. "He has previously (in the 1969 election) raised the banner of reform, then let it fall when his political goals were achieved." As for his law and order crackdown, the bureau observed: "There is as yet no sign that the decrees against private armies and possession of weapons will apply to the 3,000 ex-convicts reported to be in the pay of Marcos."

The analysis, penetrating and prescient on all counts (Marcos never did implement significant reforms and the private armies loyal to him were left untouched), was prepared by Edwin L. Barber III. "Young and liberal," as a colleague remembered him, Barber had embarked on a Foreign Service career in 1961, upon graduation from Amherst, and during his first years it seemed that most of his time was spent packing and unpacking boxes. After a year in Penang, he was assigned to Singapore for one year. He was next sent to Izmir, Turkey, lasting there for only fourteen months. Then General Lansdale, who was conducting his counterinsurgency war in Vietnam, summoned an officer from Indonesia. The State Department, casting about for a replacement in Jakarta, decided on Barber; he spoke Bahasa Indonesia, and since he was a bachelor, it wasn't so inconvenient for him to move again. After three years in Jakarta Barber went to the University of Michigan, for a master's degree in Southeast Asian studies, then moved into INR, where his mentor was Edna Barr Hubbert, who had prepared the reports detailing how Marcos was subverting the Constitutional Convention.

Deciding that he wanted a more stable life, Barber left the State Department in 1973, a loss to the Foreign Service, though probably the best for him, for it seems unlikely that his career would have prospered. The diplomatic corps generally has not been a particularly warm home for those who express views that don't fit the prevailing policy, as John Paton Davies, Jr., and John Stewart Service discovered in China in the 1940s; Paul Kattenburg, in Vietnam in the mid-1960s; and Robert White, in Central America in the 1980s, to list only some of the most notable, though by no means the only ones who have paid with their careers for expressing dissenting views.

In preparing his reports and observations about Marcos and martial law, Barber had the support and encouragement of his boss at INR, Morton Abramowitz, a candid sort whose own career later ran afoul of the Pentagon and right-wingers but who survived, and in 1985, as the director of INR, played a critical role in contributing to a policy that led to the return of democracy to the Philippines. Back in 1972, he and Barber were ignored.

Within five weeks after martial law had been declared, Barber, in an intelligence note entitled "The Philippines Tries One-Man

Democracy," delivered a devastating critique. "Marcos' security measures so far appear aimed more at his own political opponents than at communists, and his 'reforms' have been little more than conventional bids for popular support which could have been initiated without martial law." Addressing specifically the sweeping land reform program Marcos had announced, Barber noted that it could have been implemented without martial law. The announced program provided that some 700,000 peasants would be allowed to buy their land by making annual payments, for fifteen years, of an amount equal to a year's rent, which was a whopping 25 percent of a farmer's harvest income. "Not much of a bargain for the tenant," Barber observed flatly. As for the 4,800 government employees whom Marcos claimed to have fired as part of his pledge to eliminate corruption in government, Barber noted that "most of them are small fry." And in what may have been the most incisive observation, Barber wrote that Marcos's "tirades against wealth and privilege ring hollow, since he himself has amassed one of the largest personal fortunes in the Philippines during his tenure in office." As for the possibility of real change under Marcos, it was not likely, Barber realized, for Marcos had "his own great stake in the present order, and the deeply-ingrained national habits of graft, nepotism, and violence, *which he himself shares and has exploited*" (author's italics).

Barber concluded: "What he [Marcos] is clearly doing is erecting a one-man constitutional regime which permits him to stay in office indefinitely, with almost unlimited powers, under a veneer of parliamentary democracy." This was a reference to the plan Marcos had announced of submitting to a plebiscite a new constitution, one that would, among other things, replace the Philippine presidential system with a parliamentary one. When Kissinger asked during a meeting of his senior advisers why it was that Marcos wanted to adopt a parliamentary system, an aide suggested that "it would have been too naked a maneuver for him [Marcos] to amend the constitution simply to allow him another term." The aide added, however, "Marcos will still have to 'buy' his legislature."

After nearly a full year of martial law, after there had been a sufficient period to determine where Marcos was headed, INR weighed in again: "We believe that Marcos is a supremely skilled, opportunistic political operator with a strong determination to retain control in his own hands; that as a result, nothing he says is to be taken at face value, that his protestations of abiding friendship for the United States are often just political expediency, and that our policies with respect to him should be subjected to the most cold-eyed and skeptical review on a continuing basis." The embassy in Manila, on the other hand, "has appeared to assume automatically that martial law was in our best interests." The bureau was commenting only about the embassy, but the observation applied throughout Washington. Just about everyone, it seemed, except INR, thought Marcos represented America's best interests. He did not, though it would take fourteen years before Washington would realize it. While a dictator like Marcos might serve short-term U.S. interests, he will more often than not be antithetical to America's long-term interests, as Marcos was to demonstrate: After a decade of his strongman rule, the Communists *had* become a threat to the Philippines, the economy had been destroyed, and the army had been corrupted and demoralized.

There are a number of explanations why INR's observations, dire but accurate, were ignored. In part, it was because the bureau had no champion within the foreign policy-making bureaucracy of the Nixon administration. Secretary of State Rogers didn't fight for much. And of course, the Philippine president and his wife had worked hard courting Americans of influence—senators, ambassadors, Presidents, journalists. Now it paid off. On the surface, who could think ill of a beautiful woman who had danced with LBJ and had been brought into private White House meetings with Nixon and Kissinger? But the reasons behind Washington's willingness to overlook the evils of the Marcoses go deeper than the personalities of the individuals involved, American or Philippine.

"Democracy is not the most important issue for U.S. foreign policy," explained a Foreign Service officer who had been in the Philippines when martial law was imposed and was being asked many years later (he was still in the Foreign Service) why the United States had not objected. "The most important thing is the U.S. national interest, our security interest, our economic interest. If the two coincide, fine. If every world leader were a Madison or a Jefferson, it would be great. But they aren't."

No official would ever make that statement, at least not publicly, for fear of being excoriated by editorial writers and hauled before a congressional committee to explain. But it was about as succinct an explanation for U.S. policy as one can imagine, and it wasn't a new concept. It was precisely what George Kennan had expressed in 1948 when he said the United States had to abandon its "unreal objectives such as human rights, the raising of living standards and democratization." America had to pursue America's interests. In 1957 Secretary of State John Foster Dulles told a congressional subcommittee that the purpose of the State Department was to look after U.S. interests, and he didn't much care whether or not that made friends.

Marcos was certainly no Madison or Jefferson; he was in the mold of a Somoza, a shah, a Park Chung Hee, a Diem. And like those strongmen, he would protect U.S. interests, at least in the short term. In foreign policy Marcos had become "America's boy" more than any Philippine president with the exception of Magsaysay. Even if Marcos hadn't done as much as LBJ wanted, he had sent troops to Vietnam. He allowed nuclear-powered warships to dock at Subic and planes with nuclear weapons to land at Clark—without telling the Philippine people. In 1971, according to a Top Secret National Security Council document, the "Authorized Ceiling on Nuclear Weapon Deployments" in the Philippines was 201, including 115 tactical bombs aboard navy ships. Two years later the authorized number of nuclear weapons at Clark and Subic was up to 260. In addition, Marcos allowed the United States to build and operate a sophisticated and very secret (it has never been discussed publicly) electronic spy station, located on the plantation of an American corporation, on one of the country's southern islands. Within hours after declaring martial law, Marcos sent a military aide to the U.S. embassy with the message that he would not use his martial law powers to interfere with the bases. The messenger was bringing coals to Newcastle: No one in the embassy harbored the slightest doubt about Marcos's loyalty to the U.S.A.

Nor did Marcos pose any threat to U.S. business interests. On the contrary, he would enhance them. Some 800 American companies were operating in the Philippines; their investments were in the range of $1 to $2 billion. The largest 200 corporations in the Philippines were at least 40 percent U.S.-owned. The Fortune 500 were well represented: Weyerhaeuser and Georgia Pacific; Colgate-Palmolive, General Foods, Pillsbury, and Del Monte; Exxon, Caltex, and Mobil Oil; Ford, General Motors, and Chrysler; IBM and Honolulu Iron Works. But recent Philippine Supreme Court decisions were causing American businessmen a great deal of anxiety. The high court justices, reflecting the growing sentiment for greater independence from the United States, ruled that U.S. citizens and corporations could not own agricultural lands, a decision that would affect all properties acquired since 1946 and was a serious blow to the American companies and individuals harvesting fat profits from sugar, bananas, pineapples. The court also restricted the right of foreigners to manufacture raw materials, including oil. And the jurists declared that when Laurel-Langley, the 1954 trade and economic agreement between the countries, expired in 1974, foreigners would not be allowed to hold management positions or serve on boards of directors; current law allowed 40 percent of these positions to be held by foreigners.

Marcos promised to annul the court rulings. It was one of the few martial law promises he kept. He went even further for the benefit of American business. The Philippine Congress had rejected a Marcos-sponsored bill that would have provided lucrative incentives to American and other foreign oil companies that wanted to drill for oil. Ten days after declaring martial law, Marcos, by decree, gave the foreign oil companies what they wanted. In another gesture to business Marcos eliminated the taxes on capital gains and on stock transfers.

Businessmen are generally bullish on dictators. Strongmen keep workers from organizing and striking, dictate free trade zones and tax benefits, decree wages for farm laborers that are barely subsistence. But businessmen usually are careful not to display their enthusiasm for the strongman, fearful that it may not reflect well on their corporate image. In the Philippines the enthusiasm could not be restrained. Five days after martial law was imposed, the American business community applauded, sending Marcos its heartiest congratulations: "The American Chamber of Commerce wishes you every success in your endeavors to restore peace and order, business confidence, economic growth and the well being of the Filipino people and nation. We assure you of our confidence and cooperation in achieving these objectives. We are communicating these feelings to our associates and affiliates in the United States."

The confidence was well placed. After declaring martial law, Marcos pushed ahead with his desire for a new Constitution. The economic provisions of the proposed charter "would substantially ease the nationalistic restrictions that have threatened American investment in the Philippines," it was noted with approval during a meeting of Kissinger's Senior Review Group. Reversing the recent Supreme Court decisions, the new Constitution would protect the rights of Americans to own property, allow foreigners to be represented on the governing bodies of corporations, and permit up to 40 percent foreign ownership of companies engaged in the exploitation of Philippine natural resources.

Marcos wanted the new Constitution as a democratic façade on his dictatorship. He was to call his rule "constitutional authoritarianism." What he had to do in order to gain adoption of the new Constitution contradicts the image that was propounded by American officials at the time, and has survived in history: that Filipinos were delighted with Marcos.

The Constitutional Convention, which had been unable to agree on a new charter after more than a year of often contentious debate, quickly reached agreement after Marcos declared martial law. This was not surprising. The most effective and outspoken of Marcos's opponents were in military stockades; Marcos had bought most of the delegates; no one who wanted a political future was about to vote against the dictator; and finally—a clever Marcos twist—only those members of the Constitutional Convention who approved the Constitution would be permitted to be members in the next Congress (which was to begin sitting only when Marcos chose). The new Constitution that the delegates suddenly found to their liking replaced the presidential system with a parliamentary one, which, of course, meant that Marcos could become prime minister. And he retained the power to rule the Philippines for as long as he wanted, for a key provision provided that he alone had the authority to decide when the first parliamentary elections would be held.

Marcos, so desirous of not appearing to be a dictator, agreed to submit the proposed Constitution to a popular referendum. If his one-man rule were as welcome as he and U.S. diplomats claimed, that should not have been a problem. In December he suspended some of the martial law restrictions in order to allow a fuller discussion of the new charter. But no opposition arguments were ever permitted in the newspapers or on radio or television. Nevertheless, so lacking was any mandate for Marcos that he could not survive even a limited debate. He quickly reimposed all martial law restrictions on assembly, speech, and debate in order to silence his opposition. He also postponed the date for the plebiscite until he had everything ready. He organized "Citizens' Assemblies," which were made up of everyone fifteen years and older in villages, towns, and cities throughout the archipelago. Altogether there were some 36,000 Citizens' Assemblies, and for six days in January 1973 they were convened to register their views. The people didn't cast secret ballots. They raised their hands in response to questions put to them by mayors and district captains, who owed their positions to Marcos. While soldiers mingled, the hands were "counted," the results forwarded to Malacañang. The questions and the "official" results: Do you approve of the Citizens' Assembly as the base of popular government? (Yes: 15,290,639; No: 462,852.) Do you approve of the new Constitution? (Yes: 14,976,561; No: 743,869.) Do you want a plebiscite to be called to ratify the new Constitution? (No: 14,298,840; Yes: 1,322,434.) Do you want to hold elections in November 1973 as provided for in the 1935 Constitution? (No: 14,431,057; Yes: 1,206,721.) Do you want martial law to continue? (Yes: 15,224,518; No: 843,051.)

Again, it was INR that trenchantly cut through it all. "President Marcos has dropped the trappings of constitutionality which had hindered his regime," the analysis began. "It seems almost inevitable that he [Marcos] will have to devote an increasing proportion of his time and energy to putting down opponents." Then the bureau sounded the most disconcerting note, and, in retrospect, the most clarion. "The present outlook is that the longer he remains in power, the more likely it is that Philippine politics will be characterized by a climate of polarization and disarray which will not be conducive to American interests and stability of base agreements." Rather than heed that warning, the Nixon administration (and all those that followed) ensured its realization.

INR concluded: "Only the US can provide the financial aid and appearance of political backing he badly needs." Washington was to provide both.

7: Embracing the Conjugal Dictators

The official United States policy toward the Philippine dictatorship was finalized two months after Marcos's Soviet-style victory and Richard Nixon's landslide reelection. The new policy was contained in National Security Decision Memorandum 209, which Henry Kissinger, as the national security adviser, signed on March 27, 1973. NSDM 209 was the conclusion of a review of U.S. policy toward the Philippines that had begun in June 1972, the type of review that was periodic and generic within the foreign policy bureaucracy, but in the case of the Philippines it was necessitated, in part, by the changing situation in Vietnam. The departments of State, Defense, Treasury, Commerce, and Agriculture and the CIA contributed their views to the policy-making process, and representatives from these agencies, who were members of Kissinger's Senior Review Group (SRG), met on at least one occasion, November 30, 1972, two months after Marcos had declared martial law, to thrash out their views. The one-page NSDM 209, classified Secret, provided:

> The United States Government will continue to deal with the Marcos Administration as the effective Government of the Philippines. Assuming that the Marcos Administration will continue to be the effective Government and given the U.S. interests in improved long-term stability in the Philippines, the U.S. Government will continue security and economic assistance to the Philippines on the basis of continued cooperation from the Marcos Administration in our pursuit of fundamental U.S. interests in the Philippines and of implementation by the Marcos Administration of measures aimed at long-term stability for the Philippines.

There it was. Marcos might be a dictator, but he was Washington's man in Manila. And that was to remain the policy under four

138

American presidents and for fourteen years. It might be modified slightly in its implementation during the Carter years—martial law would be a bit more benign—but there was no fundamental change in the U.S. support for Marcos until 1986, and then it was Marcos himself, not Washington, who unleashed the forces that led to his downfall.

There were two faces of the policy. On the one hand, Washington embraced the Marcoses; at the same time it displayed a callous disregard, at times almost a contempt, it seemed, for those who wanted democracy in the Philippines. With the democratic opposition silenced, Imelda Marcos found it easier to carry on in her ostentatious way. She was preparing to become the successor to her husband, she was virtual head of state, and she was responsible for demonstrating to Filipinos and the world that Washington loved the Marcoses.

Her first-post-martial law appearance on the world stage was at Nixon's inaugural in 1973, even though she had to invite herself. Within the administration there was a general opposition to her coming. But the opposition wasn't rooted in any distaste for the Philippine first lady or her husband's dictatorship. Rather, it was a matter of long-established policy, one so clear that it required only fourteen lines of a cable to state it. All U.S. diplomatic and consular posts were advised that on the basis of historical practice, established "because of the essentially American character of the occasion," and in view of the limited space, foreign heads of state and other dignitaries who wished to attend the inauguration of Richard Nixon "should be discouraged." This policy was proclaimed to Imelda Marcos when she began clamoring for an invitation to Nixon's swearing in. She was also told that President Nixon, because of his tight schedule, would, regrettably, not have time for a visit with her. She wasn't daunted. "No one tells her what she's going to do," said an intelligence official who knew her well.

When she didn't think Jim Rafferty and her brother, Kokoy Romualdez, who as usual were pressing her cause, were pushing hard enough, she took up the charge. "My ear was being bent daily by her," recalled the Philippine desk officer, who took Imelda's calls from Manila. "It was enough to keep a desk officer in a tense frame of mind." There were cables back and forth between Washington and Manila, all classified Secret/ExDis, the tight security for a mere social matter being explained by a diplomat involved: "Here we had a pushy wife of a chief of state. We didn't want that leaked to the press."

Once again Imelda Marcos had her way. "She came, and she expected to be treated in regal style, as if she were a guest of the government, even though she had invited herself," said an NSC officer who had to contend with her. She brought an entourage of twenty-four, including her daughters, her brother Kokoy, and the wife of the commissioner of immigration, who had become one of her most effective "fund-raisers," using his power to grant and re-voke visas as leverage for extorting thousands of dollars from busi-nessmen, especially Chinese.

Reporters were told that Mrs. Marcos "had come to the United States on a private visit to go to Walter Reed hospital for treatment." The press accepted that, and it was partially true; she was to be treated for injuries inflicted in Manila a month earlier, when a man in a dark suit had drawn a foot-long dagger and slashed at her right arm. The assailant was shot on the spot. Nixon had called Mrs. Marcos with his personal sympathy and had dispatched to Manila a hand surgery specialist from Stanford University, Dr. Robert A. Chase, who was also the hand doctor for Van Cliburn.

The Marcos-Nixon friendship relationship had been solidified during Nixon's visit in 1969, when he had been lavishly feted. The Marcoses liked Richard Nixon, with Imelda Marcos becoming one of the first international figures to call on him at San Clemente after he had resigned. In Nixon's 1972 campaign the Marcoses contributed generously. During one of the Watergate-related trials federal in-vestigators discovered a $30,000 cash contribution which had not been reported by Nixon's campaign committee, as the law required. The donor, the investigators were told, had been a former Philippine ambassador to the United States, Ernesto Lagdameo.

But he wasn't really the donor; he was just the front man. He had been acting for the Marcoses. Nixon campaign officials later said that they returned the money to Lagdameo once they realized that it was illegal for a foreigner to contribute to an American campaign.

That was not, however, the only illegal contribution from the Marcoses to the Nixon campaign.

140

Two individuals, a palace insider and a personal friend of the Marcoses, told U.S. officials that the Philippine first couple gave President Nixon $250,000 for his 1972 campaign. The officials not only believed the sources, who had provided reliable information on other occasions, but thought the Marcoses had contributed "at least" $250,000 and probably considerably more.* Their suspicions were correct. According to Rafael Salas, the man who was Marcos's executive secretary from 1966 to 1969 and who was personally close to the Philippine first couple, the Marcoses contributed more than $1 million to Nixon's 1972 reelection effort. "Only Mr. and Mrs. Marcos know the exact amount," Salas said. Salas, who was executive director of the United Nations Fund for Population Activities from 1969 to 1987, added that the Marcoses had also contributed approximately $1 million to Nixon in 1968.

For the 1973 inaugural festivities Mrs. Marcos had two seats on the platform for the swearing-in ceremony, along with two boxes for the inaugural ball and one box for the symphonic concert at Kennedy Center. Limousines hauled her and her court between galas. But Imelda Marcos didn't think she was treated properly, and she complained to the director of Philippine affairs, Richard Usher. During the swearing-in ceremony "she felt she hadn't really been seated as would have been appropriate for a First Lady from a friendly country," Usher wrote in a Secret memorandum following his meeting with Mrs. Marcos. He added that "her feelings had also been hurt by what she regarded as the somewhat less than visiting First Lady treatment with respect to the concert and the ball. She then went on at some length about the honors which had been accorded her on the occasion of her visit to Moscow last year."

Mrs. Marcos's inaugural arrangements, including the limousines, had been made by John Sharon, a Washington lawyer long active in Democratic politics, as an aide to Adlai Stevenson and later as

---

* The information about the Marcos contributions to Nixon was considered so sensitive that it arrived at Langley not even in the most highly classified of cables; rather, it was hand-delivered in a sealed letter. The agency did not pursue the matter further. It's not in the agency's charter to investigate possible wrongdoing by the American president, and any agent who thought he ought to would be fired for having "no goddamn judgment," said one senior CIA officer, who laughed when asked why the agency had let the matter drop. "Like a goddamn hot potato," he added.

141

foreign affairs adviser to Kennedy. Mr. and Mrs. Sharon also sent out engraved invitations for a formal dinner in honor of Mrs. Marcos. But Imelda Marcos, miffed by her treatment, didn't appear; she went to the bash thrown by Henry and Cristina Ford, and later in the evening, on the arm of Jack Valenti, showed up at one of the Democrats' counterinaugural parties. (Sharon, who had played a role in Dr. Chase's visit to Manila to treat Mrs. Marcos and who was to assist Imee Marcos when she applied to his alma mater, Princeton,* expected to be reimbursed—not for the dinner but for the cost of the tickets to the inaugural events as well as for some legal work his firm did for Mrs. Marcos. He submitted bills amounting to about $30,000. Imelda Marcos never paid.)

She scurried around Washington to see and be seen, to charm and lobby: tea with Mrs. Spiro Agnew; cocktails with Senator Charles Percy; a meeting with Senator Mansfield, the photograph of them in the *Washington Post* showing the bandages on the fingers of her right hand, her arm in a gold necklace sling (long after the wounds had healed and she was using her arm and hand without any difficulty in private, in public she continued to wear the sling); dinner with Van Cliburn, who was beginning to become a regular member of her social set.

The press reported that Mrs. Marcos didn't see Nixon personally, but she did. The NSC had argued that if she went back without seeing the president, "there'd be hell to pay," explained an NSC official. Nixon had been in Florida when Mrs. Marcos arrived, but "as soon as he had returned to Washington he expressed the desire to see" her.

The Nixon administration wasn't that solicitous about those who were opposed to Marcos. On the contrary, the administration helped Marcos against his foes. One who felt the ironic sting of democracy

---

* Imee, who had attended a Catholic high school in Monterey, California, enrolled at Princeton in 1973, generating a minor controversy about the presence of gun-toting security guards on campus. Though her record was satisfactory, she was never graduated, and her father thought she got mixed up in drugs. He pulled an American diplomat aside once after an early-morning swim and confided, "I'm not sure this Princeton is good for her." Imelda Marcos didn't care for Princeton either, claiming that Imee was "surrounded by 'faggots' there." While at Princeton, Imee lived on a 13.5-acre estate, purchased by a company registered in the British Virgin Islands, which had not listed officers or owners but which was, in fact, owned by the Marcoses.

being employed on behalf of a dictator was Raul Manglapus, a short, compact man whose pro-Americanism could not be questioned. After escaping from a Japanese prison camp, he joined a guerrilla unit attached to the U.S. Eleventh Airborne Division. Eventually as a journalist he reported from MacArthur's headquarters and covered the surrender of the Japanese aboard the USS *Missouri*. After the war he earned a law degree and entered government service, first as President Magsaysay's undersecretary of foreign affairs. Turning to electoral politics, in 1961 he was elected to the Senate, thanks in part to money and backing from the CIA; in the late fifties and early sixties Manglapus was one of the principal recipients of the CIA station's beneficence. Often referred to as the Adlai Stevenson of Philippine politics, Manglapus in 1968 founded the Christian Social Movement. He fortuitously escaped arrest when martial law was declared, having left the previous day for a speaking engagement in San Francisco. His wife and daughter eventually escaped in a boat. In the United States Manglapus founded the Movement for a Free Philippines and soon seemed to be anywhere and everywhere he could gather an audience, churning out newspaper op-ed pieces along with scholarly articles for *Foreign Affairs* and the *Harvard International Review*. He became a regular witness at congressional hearings.

Soon after taking up exile in the United States, Manglapus, who was as proud of his musical talents as his politics, had applied for and received a $12,000 fellowship from the Ford Foundation to study at Cornell University, which has one of the country's finest Southeast Asian studies programs. Imelda Marcos tried to have the fellowship yanked, appealing to her friend Cristina Ford. The foundation's board of directors refused to be cowed.

The United States government didn't acquit itself so honorably when Manglapus was nominated, in 1974, for a fellowship at the Woodrow Wilson International Center for Scholars, the prestigious research center in Washington, D.C. The center, founded in 1968, held as one of its objectives the pursuit of "intellect and moral purpose." It receives congressional funding, and Congress and the executive branch are represented on the board, the latter in 1974 by Kissinger, by that time the secretary of state, and Caspar W. Weinberger, then secretary of health, education, and welfare. When

Manglapus's nomination came before the fellowship committee, the State Department set out to block it, quietly, of course, in order to "minimize ruffled feathers, surprises, and publicity." The department's justification was that it would be "inappropriate" for the U.S. government "to appear to be subsidizing a person who was actively engaged in activities directed against a government with which the U.S. Government enjoys friendly relations." That it might have been more inappropriate for the United States to back Marcos, the dictator who was stifling rigorous academic debate, was apparently lost on the State Department, and the Wilson directors, who acceded. *

In Manila Marcos's political opponents suffered in jail. While few, if any, of the imprisonments could be justified on the basis of national security, the incarceration of three men underscores what the Bureau of Intelligence and Research concluded but what the Nixon administration refused to acknowledge: Martial law had one and only one purpose, and that was to render unto Marcos and his wife all the power and the wealth of the Philippines.

Two of the prisoners were Eugenio ("Geny") Lopez, Jr., and Sergio Osmeña III, arrested ten weeks after martial law had been imposed. They were imprisoned in connection with what Marcos claimed was a plot to assassinate him, a plot led by Osmeña's father, the man Marcos had defeated in 1969. While the elder Osmeña had hired some American drifters and they did engage in some nefarious activities and may even have entertained some fantasies about getting rid of Marcos, it was a caper more befitting a comic opera than a plot to take over the country; and American officials who were aware of what was going on laughed at it all.

The true motivations behind the arrests, and more broadly behind martial law, become apparent upon an examination of Lopez's background and family. The Lopez clan had everything: wealth;

* The State Department is still covering up its role in this shameful incident twelve years later. Pursuant to the author's FOIA request for documents pertaining to the matter, the department located four documents. Only one was released in full, two were heavily censored, and one was withheld in its entirety. It is difficult to imagine what national security is being protected by the withholding of this information, though it is not at all difficult to understand that it might be more than just embarrassing for the government to reveal the petty-mindedness that underlay its support for a dictator.

144

political power; social eminence. In short, the Lopezes were oligarchs, their enterprises worth some $400 million, and a good case could be made for breaking up, and redistributing, their empire. Before martial law the Lopez family "wielded more real power than any Filipino President ever had," Joseph Lelyveld noted in an article in *The New York Times* which provided the personal and societal ethos as well as the facts about the Marcos-Lopez feud. Geny's uncle Fernando was Marcos's vice president in 1965 (Imelda Marcos had tearfully pleaded with Fernando to accept the number two spot) and in 1969, and the family had poured several million dollars into the campaigns. His father, Eugenio, Sr., was one of the wealthiest men in the Philippines, and as Lelyveld noted, he "was never shy about displaying his wealth," celebrating his golden wedding anniversary with champagne bubbling from an ornamental fountain. Everything the Lopezes had Imelda Marcos coveted. When she had wanted to shop after hours in San Francisco at Magnin's, she appealed to Geny's sister Presy, who in turn went to her father, who knew the Magnin family. When Imelda Marcos prepared to go to the United States for Eisenhower's funeral, she again turned to Presy Lopez, with a plaintive request to borrow some of her dear friend's black outfits. Presy Lopez sent over five black suits and a black Spanish leather full-length coat. Mrs. Marcos never returned them.

With martial law it was time to crush the Lopez clan. The first casualty was the *Manila Chronicle,* shut down along with the country's other newspapers. Since Marcos wouldn't let their paper be printed, the Lopezes leased the *Chronicle* presses to a new paper, the *Times Journal,* which had started after martial law. The owner of that paper was Imelda Marcos's brother Kokoy Romualdez. Six months later the Lopez family lost its broadcasting network (twenty-one radio and television stations, with about two-thirds of the national audience), the facilities being simply transferred to Roberto S. Benedicto, who had been Marcos's classmate and fraternity brother during law school; Defense Minister Juan Ponce Enrile "legalized" the takeover with an order executed after the fact. But the real gem in the Lopez collection was Meralco, a holding company that included the Manila Electric Company, the country's largest public utility, plus oil pipelines, a refinery, a construction company, and the nation's second largest bank.

According to Marcos, Eugenio Lopez, Sr., voluntarily signed

over Meralco in order "to democratize wealth and property for the greater good of our people." Marcos also said that Meralco had been transferred to a nonprofit foundation that would eventually be owned by the consumers. "There has been no evidence that Mr. Marcos, his family or friends profited directly from the takeover," Joseph Lelyveld reported, reflecting what was known at the time. In fact, however, the Marcoses and their friends did profit directly, according to U.S. diplomats and intelligence officials. Imelda Marcos "took a big bite of it," said one senior CIA officer, and Cojuangco got most of the rest. And of course, the transfer hadn't been "voluntary." Marcos's takeover tactics had been two-pronged, one financial, the other personal.

First, after declaring martial law, Marcos ordered an arbitrary, across-the-board 25 percent cut in electric rates, a move that was popular with consumers but that was designed to give Lopez incentive to sell. Two months after Geny Lopez had been arrested, the pressure was applied more directly, by Kokoy Romualdez, who conducted the "negotiations" with the senior Lopez. Romualdez led the elder Lopez to believe that if he signed over the assets, his son would be released. (The Marcoses denied there had been any pressure of this nature, but American officials familiar with the transaction are convinced that Kokoy had indeed suggested this quid pro quo.) Lopez, dying of cancer and wanting to see his son, agreed. But Geny Lopez was not released and was still in prison when his father died in a San Francisco hospital. Shortly before his funeral mass a squad of heavily armed men entered the large church in Quezon City. Near the front they placed a high-backed ornate chair, something like those found in the lobbies of Art Deco theaters. Moments later came a large entourage, accompanying a woman in black. Imelda Marcos deposited herself on the throne. American diplomats present were aghast—disgusted would be the more appropriate description of their reaction—that she would show up for the funeral of a man whose property she and her husband had confiscated and whose son they were still holding in jail.

The most prominent political prisoner, of course, was Ninoy Aquino, held for long stretches in solitary confinement. During the first six months of his imprisonment Aquino lost so much weight that he could remove his trousers without unbuttoning them; his companion in politics, and now in jail, José Diokno, had to hold his pants up to keep them from falling down. Washington refused to intercede on Aquino's behalf (and certainly not on Diokno's, who was released after two years), in spite of campaigns by eminent Americans, one a private citizen, the other a former State Department officer.

Aquino was as energetic and determined in prison as he had been free, reading prolifically and writing as he had once talked—seemingly nonstop. After one of his writings had been smuggled out of prison and surfaced in a Bangkok newspaper, he was transferred to a special prison north of Manila. During his ninth month of detention he wrote the following to a political colleague who was a deeply religious man: "I have just finished my night prayers. Yes, believe it or not, I have been averaging 1,200 'Hail Maries' [sic] a day. . . . I want to tell you all about my conversion and my resolve to join you in spreading the good news if and when I regain my freedom. God has been so kind to give me the power to convince and persuade, which have greatly helped in my political career. Now I want to use the same gifts to spread His Word. I am sure this will please my mother no end."

Aquino went on to describe the conditions under which he and Diokno were being held. The windows in their cells had been boarded up with plywood, except for a six-inch gap, the only source of ventilation. A neon light burned day and night. The door had no knobs. The room was completely bare except for a steel bed without a mattress. On arriving, they had been stripped naked, wedding rings, watches, shoes, clothes, everything taken away. The two men were forbidden to talk to each other, so to ensure that each was alive, they sang songs in Tagalog. Aquino continued his letter:

> . . . I expected to be "liquidated" at any moment. I suspected our guards were the dreaded "Monkeys" who were licensed to kill.
> . . . I was haunted by the thought of my family. . . . At this point of my desperation and desolation, I questioned the justice of God. I remembered your famous words: Hindi natutulog and Diyos [God never sleeps] . . . but I felt, at that moment, He was having a very sound siesta, and I was afraid that when He finally woke up I would have gone!
>
> Then, it was as if I heard a voice saying: Why do you cry? I have given you consolation, honour and glory which have been

denied to millions of your countrymen. I made you the youngest war correspondent, presidential assistant, mayor, vice-governor, governor and senator of the Republic, and I recall you never thanked me for all these gifts. I have given you a full life, a great wife and beautiful, lovable children. Now that I visit you in your slight desolation, you cry and whimper like a spoiled brat!

With this realisation, I went down on my knees and begged His forgiveness. I know I was merely undergoing a test, maybe in preparation for another mission. . . .

Aquino closed:

In the loneliness of my solitary confinement in Laur, in the depths of my solitude and desolation, during those long hours of meditation, I found my inner peace. He stood me face-to-face with myself and forced me to look at my emptiness and nothingness, and then helped me discover Him, who has never really left my side; but because pride shielded my eyes and the lust for earthly and temporal power, honour and joys drugged my mind, I failed to notice him.

So long, dear friend, I am sure we will meet again—if not here, in that kingdom where love is eternal.

A few months later Robert Trent Jones, Jr., son of the renowned golf course architect, began his campaign to free Aquino. Jones had met Aquino in the mid-sixties, when he was constructing a golf course on the family estate, and he remained a loyal friend, providing critical assistance to Corazon Aquino in her 1986 campaign against Marcos. In 1974 Jones used his connections in Washington on behalf of the imprisoned Aquino, writing to the deputy director of Nixon's Cost of Living Council, James W. McLane, who had been at Yale with Jones. McLane forwarded Jones's letter to Winston Lord at the State Department, with the opening "You may remember Bob Jones from the Class of 1961 at Yale—captain of the golf team." McLane characterized Jones as "a humanist as well as basically conservative in his views, being in the golf course design and development business." Lord had considerable clout within the State Department because of his relationship to Kissinger, for whom Lord had worked at the NSC. Lord had supported the secret bombing and invasion of Cambodia, which had begun in 1969, after others on Kissinger's NSC staff dissented, and he had been one of five individuals who accompanied Kissinger on his historic, and secret, trip to China. When Kissinger officially took over the State Department, becoming secretary in the fall of 1973, he appointed Lord director of the Policy Planning Staff. A few years later Lord left the Foreign Service to become the head of the elite, establishment Council on Foreign Relations; in 1985 he was appointed ambassador to China by Reagan.

After obtaining "a fresh status report on the Aquino case" from the embassy in Manila (now under the direction of Ambassador William Sullivan), Lord informed McLane of the charges against Aquino: illegal possession of firearms, including machine guns, high-powered rifles, and hand grenades; conspiracy to kill a local official in 1957 in his home province of Tarlac; four counts of subversion; providing weapons and other supplies to the NPA; giving shelter and medical assistance to ten NPA guerrillas; donating 15,000 pesos to the NPA in April 1969 to organize demonstrations; and, finally, providing the NPA with funds to rent a car in a December 1970 raid on the armory at the Philippine Military Academy. Lord added that the conditions of Aquino's detention "appear to be reasonably humane, and although he is kept in solitary confinement, he is allowed regular family visits twice a week." Thus, Lord concluded, "We have therefore felt that the interest of the United States would best be served if we did not attempt to comment on or characterize internal developments in the Philippines."

However "humane" it was to hold a political leader in solitary confinement in a windowless cell, almost as disturbing was the willingness of the embassy and State Department to accept Marcos's charges, which were blatantly trumped up. If Marcos had jailed everyone who had illegal weapons, he would had to have built new prisons. If Aquino had committed crimes in 1957 and 1969 and 1970, why was he just now being charged? At that, why had the charges not been filed until August 23, 1973—a full eleven months after Aquino's arrest? (They probably wouldn't have been filed at all had it not been for growing international pressure, led by Amnesty International, to release Aquino.)

But though Lord's letter and conclusions were appalling, they were consistent with the administration's policy of blessing Marcos, of remaining silent as he committed his crimes against democracy. In his letter back to Jones, McLane noted that "the State Department wants the matter to be left to the judicial processes of the Philippine Government." That was the equivalent of leaving the matter of a Soviet dissident in the hands of that country's "judicial" system. There was nothing "judicial" about the Philippine process. It was a Marcos process. Using his martial law powers, he had seized control of the judiciary. Military courts had jurisdiction over most criminal cases, and the civilian judges were kept in line because Marcos had demanded they submit their resignations, which he could pull out when a judge's ruling displeased him.

A year or so later it was Paul Kattenburg's time to try. Kattenburg, the aggressive, outspoken Foreign Service officer who had raised objections to America's involvement in Vietnam in 1963, long before anyone else, was a career diplomat and Southeast Asia hand. He had worked on Asian affairs for the Office of Strategic Services during World War II. Then, after earning a master's in government from George Washington University and a Ph.D. in international relations from Yale, he had joined the Foreign Service, beginning as a research specialist on Indonesia in 1950. That was followed by special assignments in Saigon in 1952 and 1955, and he had been the second secretary in the embassy in Manila from 1957 to 1959, when he had met, and been highly impressed by Aquino, then the young, enthusiastic governor of Tarlac. Fluent in four languages, Kattenburg was derailed after his opposition to the Vietnam War (which he loyally kept within the councils of government, rather than go public). He was shipped off to Guyana (where he was appalled by the CIA's intervention in that country's election in 1968*), receiving the department's Superior Honor Award for his work there; three years later he received the Meritorious Honor Award for his performance as a teacher of young Foreign Service officers at the Foreign Service Institute. In 1972 he retired, at the age of fifty,

---

* Though the agency's covert efforts in the early 1960s to bring down Guyana's socialist President Cheddi Jagan has been written about, U.S. involvement in the subsequent election has remained secret. In the 1968 election the CIA actively assisted Forbes Burnham, with many of its efforts channeled through the Eagleton Institute for Research at Rutgers University. In addition to providing Burnham with money, the agency engineered an amendment to the Guyanese Constitution that permitted Guyanese citizens residing outside the country to vote. On election day some 16,000 votes for Burnham were "manufactured" in New York City. Then the United States watched as Burnham turned out to have been a closet leftist and moved his country closer to the Soviet Union.

Philippines

FREE PRESS

65 ctvs.

SEPT . 30, 1972

SEN. BENIGNO S. AQUINO

TARGET?

Benigno S. ("Ninoy") Aquino on the cover of the *Philippines Free Press* magazine, September 30, 1972. The issue never hit the streets, Marcos having declared martial law and shut down the presses. Aquino was assassinated eleven years later.

ABOVE: Imelda and Ferdinand Marcos on the campaign trail, 1965. *Time Magazine*
BELOW: President Nixon and Mrs. Marcos at Malacañang, July 1969.

LEFT: Governor Ronald Reagan dancing with Imelda Marcos during festivities marking the opening of Mrs. Marcos's multimillion-dollar Cultural Center in September 1969. BELOW: U.S. Secretary of State Henry Kissinger dances with Imelda Marcos aboard the Philippine presidential yacht on a return trip from Corregidor Island, December 7, 1975. *AP/Wide World*

ABOVE: Vice President Mondale and President Marcos toast each other at a state banquet at Malacañang on May 3, 1978. *UPI/Bettmann*
BELOW: Imelda Marcos with Vice President Mondale and assistant secretary of state Richard Holbrooke in the Roosevelt Room of the White House, July 1978. *AP/Wide World*

LEFT: Patricia Derian, assistant
secretary of state for
human rights during the Carter
administration. *AP/Wide World*
BELOW: Secretary of State
George Shultz greeting
Imelda Marcos as Ambassador
Michael Armacost shakes hands
with President Marcos,
June 1983. *AP/Wide World*

ABOVE: Vice President George Bush and Imelda Marcos attending the inauguration
of President Marcos, July 1981.
BELOW: The Marcoses with U.S. Defense Secretary Caspar Weinberger. At far right, Juan Ponce Enrile
Philippine defense minister, during the Marcoses' official visit to Washington, September 1982.

BOVE: From right to left, Imelda Marcos, Ferdinand E., Jr. ("Bong Bong"), Irene Marcos,
resident and Mrs. Reagan, and President Marcos at a state dinner in Washington in September, 1982.
ELOW: A critical Sunday-afternoon White House meeting forty-eight hours before Marcos left
e country. Special U.S. envoy Philip Habib, gesturing with his hands, briefs President Reagan,
nd from left, Secretary of State Shultz; William Casey, director of the Central Intelligence Agency;
)onald Regan, White House chief of staff. From left, with their backs to the camera, are Defense
ecretary Caspar Weinberger and Vice President Bush. Along the far wall from left are under-secretary
rmacost and assistant secretary Paul Wolfowitz. Others are unidentified. *Terry Arthur/The White House*

RIGHT: Presidential candidate Corazon Aquino during an interview with *The New York Times* at her home in Manila, December 1985. The interview generated considerable alarm within the Reagan administration, motivating her American friends to rally to her campaign. *Susan Meiselas/Magnum*
BELOW: A small portion of the wardrobe Imelda Marcos left behind in Malacañang. *Susan Meiselas/Magnum*

another career cut short by too much independence. He was the director of the Institute of International Studies at the University of South Carolina when he tried to help Aquino.

Kattenburg was ready to do anything to secure Aquino's release, even trying to enlist Muhammad Ali, who was scheduled to fight Joe Frazier in Manila. Not knowing how to contact Ali, Kattenburg, who was at his summer vacation home in Rapid River, Michigan, typed a letter to Howard Cosell, the noted ABC sports announcer. "I wish you would ask Mr. Mohammed [*sic*] Ali, whose ability and intelligence I sincerely respect, how he finds himself able to accept defending his title in Manila," Kattenburg began. Turning to the Muslim problem in the southern Philippines, Kattenburg continued: "Does he not realize that the Philippine Government under President Marcos is daily killing dozens of Southern Philippine Muslims in a cruel war of repression . . . ? That Marcos, his wife and Army are responsible for the murder and misery of Muslim men, women through napalm bombs, village terrorization and prisoner torture in Jolo, Sulu Archipelago . . . ?" If Ali insisted on going ahead with the fight, he should do so, Kattenburg urged, only if Marcos would agree to the unconditional release of Aquino, who "espouses the cause of Muslim rights and freedoms in the Southern Philippines. If he is freed, perhaps Muslims will live."

Ali went ahead with the fight, in October 1975, a characteristically Marcos extravaganza, with tickets selling for up to $300 each (more than the average per capita annual income) and a cost to the Philippine government of $4 million. "Flamboyant events," Marcos assured *Sports Illustrated* in his classic doublespeak, "have their place in the scheme of things in our development plans." They also had a place in his program to legitimize his dictatorial rule. The event would bring publicity, Marcos noted, "but it is not just the common crowd-getting type of publicity. It is the word of truth about the Philippines. . . . Martial law here was proclaimed at the insistence of the people. I sought their advice." Ali, an overweight 229 pounds, defeated Frazier after fourteen rounds. For his beating, Frazier took away $2 million; Ali, who praised Marcos as a "decent and simple man . . . the right man for his country . . . [d]edicated and humble . . . a peaceful and loving man," departed $4.5 million richer. Aquino remained in jail.

Through a more official channel Kattenburg contacted a friend who was the special assistant in the Bureau of East Asian and Pacific Affairs. Kattenburg wrote: "It is about time we did something to spring Aquino; and I hope you agree. I swear, I'm personally going to set out to blast any further U.S. aid to Phils [sic] if we don't at last act in this matter! The point is, we should be able to demonstrate—at least privately—that we've taken some action; and put the monkey on Marcos' back if he still refuses to release him."

Kattenburg also wrote to Philip Habib, the assistant secretary of state for East Asia. Kattenburg, who was in touch with Robert Jones, informed Habib that Mrs. Aquino had indicated that her husband, who had now been in jail nearly three years, was willing to make a commitment in writing through an intermediary that he would accept exile. (He had been insisting that he would not accept exile, for that would be tantamount to an admission of guilt.) Kattenburg suggested that the embassy in Manila, specifically Frazier Meade, the embassy's political officer, who was respected by Filipino opposition leaders, contact Mrs. Aquino. With Aquino's statement in hand, Kattenburg said he would pursue the matter "with the Australians in Canberra," where Australian National University had said repeatedly that Aquino could have a position.

Kattenburg closed with a notation: "It would seem obvious to me that if nothing is done this time, Philippine aid will suffer grievously in the Congress." Kattenburg had too much faith—in Congress and in his own institution. Philippine aid didn't suffer; it increased. And Habib, after communicating with Ambassador Sullivan, concluded, "I do not believe that now is the time to involve ourselves as intermediaries in this case." He explained that "Bill [Sullivan] is confident that Aquino has the means for direct access to Marcos at all times and does not need the services of an intermediary." Stripped of the diplomatic jargon, what that meant was the United States didn't want to irritate Marcos; let Aquino stay in jail.

That Sullivan didn't want to take up Kattenburg's proposal reflected the ambassador's style and his politics. Sullivan was an aggressive, take-charge type; the assignment he most liked was Laos (from 1965 to 1969), where he conducted the CIA's war, acting more as a field general than as a diplomat, picking targets and giving orders for bombing attacks on the Ho Chi Minh Trail. Sullivan didn't like anyone's interfering in his running of the embassy. All Sullivan needed, said an aide later, was "himself, a secretary, and a bank newsletter to report on the economy." And Sullivan, like most high-level American officials, wasn't enamored of Aquino. Robert Jones recalls that one time when he was in Manila on matters unrelated to Aquino, Sullivan learned that he was in the country and asked to see him. Sullivan couldn't understand why Jones was trying to help Aquino, who, Sullivan insisted, had Communist connections with the Huks and probably was guilty of some of the things he had been charged with. (Even if he was, that hardly justified solitary confinement and the kangaroo court proceedings in Marcos's military tribunals.*)

While not working to secure Aquino's release, American officials continued publicly to embrace Marcos, Gerald Ford becoming the third American president to lend the support of the office to the Philippine leader. Ford, of course, had become president in August 1974 after Nixon had been forced to resign, departing the White House grounds in a helicopter (as Marcos was forced to leave Malacañang twelve years later). Mrs. Marcos "deplores what happened to Nixon," Ambassador Sullivan reported, adding that "in general," she was "turned off on the American press." Though Nixon was gone, American policy toward the Marcos dictatorship remained the same, as was expected since Henry Kissinger stayed on under Ford as the secretary of state.†

President Ford visited the Philippines during his ten-day 7,000-mile journey in December 1975. The trip, which took Ford to China and Indonesia before the Philippines, was designed to reassure Asian allies in the aftermath of America's withdrawal from Vietnam, which had been completed eight months earlier with the ignominious lift-off of the helicopters from the roof of the American embassy in Saigon. Ford didn't intend his stop in the Philippines to be an endorsement of martial law, but that was how Marcos intended to

---

* Sullivan doesn't recall the specifics of the Jones-Kattenburg efforts and insists that he had a deal with Marcos to let Aquino go to Harvard but that "Marcos reneged."

† During a major address to Congress in April 1975 Ford failed to mention the Philippines as he listed America's friends in the Pacific. Some observers thought it was a conscious omission meant to be a message of disapproval to Marcos. According to Sullivan, however, the omission was simply an oversight, not intentional. Sullivan relayed that message to Marcos.

portray it. Fully aware of Marcos's desire to wrap himself in the American flag, the embassy's deputy chief of mission, Lee Stull, had been opposed to Ford's coming. But Stull was overruled, in part because Sullivan, like most ambassadors, welcomed a presidential visit. Though such visits require an extraordinary amount of extra work for the ambassador and his staff, they also bring attention, and an ambassador or aide who performs well can be that much more confident of future presidential appointments.

Precisely as expected, Marcos used the visit to advance his hold on power. A columnist for the *Times Journal,* owned by Kokoy Romualdez, observed that the visit by Ford was "confirmation of the truth that the U.S. has never questioned the legitimacy of the martial law regime." And Ambassador Sullivan in a Confidential assessment on the conclusion of the visit recorded that from Marcos's standpoint "President Ford's visit was a success as soon as it was announced. The President's inclusion of Manila in his itinerary provided Marcos with opportunity to personally identify himself with U.S. President, who is a formidable symbol for most Filipinos. Visit of first western head of state since martial law also gives New Society stamp of tacit approval which Marcos professes not to need but obviously craves."

Driven by that craving, the Marcoses "pulled out all stops," preparing a welcome for Ford that, as impossible as it might seem, surpassed Mrs. Marcos's previous prodigious efforts. The embassy said it was "unprecedented." Imelda Marcos forcibly moved squatters, and on arrival day the seven-mile route from the airport to Malacañang was lined with at least 1 million Filipinos, cheering, waving flags, and tossing flower petals at the motorcade. Some 10,000 Filipinos, attired in native costumes, from loincloths to butterfly dresses, performed in the streets—elaborate dances, banging on steel drums, blowing on flutes. It was all "elaborately stage managed" and "carefully contrived," with most of the participants "obliged to be present," the embassy reported. As the motorcade moved slowly through the gathering dusk and sporadic drizzle, two trucks mounted with huge floodlights directed their beams on the two presidents, who stood through the sunroof to wave at the crowd.

The Marcoses didn't ignore the power of the press to endorse their martial law rule either. Each of the 150 reporters accompanying

Ford was handed a two-foot-high stack of books, papers, and other materials justifying martial law and extolling the "New Society." Moreover, as *The New York Times* reporter James M. Naughton noted in his dispatch, "In what seemed an excess of customary Filipino hospitality in a nation with an average annual income of $330, each of the reporters and 50 White House aides was presented with an embroidered 'barong tagalog' dress shirt, $30 worth of cigars in a mahogany humidor box, stationery and matchbooks embossed in gold leaf, a necklace, and an assortment of soft drinks accompanied by a pint of Philippine rum." He then noted that at the lavish palace dinner the guests were served quail eggs, meatball soup, fish, heart of lettuce salad, prime beef steak, fruits, chocolates, red wine, white wine, and champagne.

Not surprisingly the Marcoses directed some of their overweening attention on Kissinger, the real power in the making of American foreign policy. They treated him "very lavishly," recalled one diplomat. Imelda Marcos's task in winning Kissinger was more difficult than she had realized. During the welcoming ceremony at the airport first Marcos made a gracious speech, followed by a gracious "It's nice to be here" from Ford. That was supposed to be it. Then Mrs. Marcos grabbed the microphone and began to talk, at which point Kissinger turned to an aide and in his deep voice, loud enough to be overheard by those close by, said, "I cannot stand this woman." But that was before the partying and the cruise aboard the Marcoses' presidential yacht, *Ang Pangulo,* a 2,200-ton, five-decker floating palace, with a helicopter landing pad and sixteen VIP cabins lined in beige Leatherette. Alongside it the American presidential yacht *Sequoia* would look like a dinghy. Imelda Marcos hauled the secretary of state aside for a private lunch to apply her personalized charm. For two hours the two were locked in conversation in one of the yacht's staterooms, discussing only the two of them know what. At the end of the outing, when everyone was disembarking from the yacht, Kissinger said to Ambassador Sullivan, very seriously, "Bill, she's such a charming woman. Why can't you get along with her?" Sullivan and a Kissinger aide were stunned, having heard Kissinger complaining about the woman just the day before.

Kissinger's conversion was another exhibit in the catalog of Mrs. Marcos's efficacy, his remark a reflection of Sullivan's disapproval of her ways. Though American policy didn't change under the Ford administration, the relationship of the American ambassador to Mrs. Marcos changed dramatically when Sullivan replaced Byroade. Sullivan pointedly refused to refer to her as the "first lady," even in public speeches and toasts saying, "the president and Mrs. Marcos"; in private addressing her as "Meldy."

While Sullivan demeaned her at every opportunity, after the implementation of martial law, Imelda Marcos became much more than just a first lady. On June 7, 1975, in his own tiny scrawl, Marcos wrote out Presidential Decree Number 731. "By virtue of the powers vested in me . . . , I, Ferdinand E. Marcos, hereby decree" that "in the event of my death or permanent incapacity," a commission shall exercise power. And the chairman of the commission, he also decreed, shall be "Mrs. Imelda R. Marcos." She never was to exercise those powers—nor was the "will" ever made public—but Marcos, again by decree, created Metro Manila, which merged the commercial capital of the country, Manila, with the official capital, Quezon City. Then, in November 1975, Marcos named his wife the governor of Metro Manila, replacing the mayor who had been elected in 1971, giving her control over 1,675 square miles, some 6 million people, thousands of jobs, and hundreds of millions of dollars.

Internationally Imelda Marcos seemed to be chasing Henry Kissinger in a contest over who could log the most diplomatic miles, consort with the most heads of state. "Mrs. Marcos may be ready for the world, but is the world ready for Mrs. Marcos?" Sullivan commented to Washington on the eve of her spring 1975 junket. During 1975 alone she scampered from the jungles of Papua, New Guinea, to the heights of the Himalayas, the latter for the coronation of the king of Nepal, another one of those overindulgent affairs where she was accompanied by an entourage of sixty, including Cristina Ford. Mrs. Marcos's travels weren't circumscribed by geography or political ideology. The Arab Middle East or Catholic Latin America; democrats, dictators, or monarchs; right-wingers or leftists—all were one and the same to her. She met with Anwar el-Sadat in Egypt, skipped over to Algeria for a session with Colonel Houari Boumediène, who had seized power in a coup the year Marcos had first been elected president. When King Faisal was assassinated by his nephew, Imelda Marcos rushed to Saudi Arabia, becoming the first woman ever to be officially received in that conservative nation. In the Western Hemisphere she went to La Paz, walking down the brick streets of the 12,000-foot-high capital with an oxygen mask and looking a mite cold in her butterfly dress, to embrace Bolivia's right-wing dictator, General Hugo Banzer. And she called on Latin America's reigning left-wing dictator, Fidel Castro, invading the island with the Philippine dance troupe and a planeload of sycophants. She returned home with stories about all the wonderful things Castro was doing for the poor and claimed that he had begged her to remain and help him.

Imelda Marcos's most remembered trip, and diplomatically her most impressive one, at least on the surface, was to the People's Republic of China in September 1974. It was the era of Ping-Pong diplomacy, with the Philippines and China exchanging trade delegations and basketball teams, just as the United States and China were doing. To demonstrate its independence, the Philippines was anxious to establish diplomatic relations with China before the United States did. Mrs. Marcos was sent to pave the way. China was equally covetous of official recognition from its neighbor in Asia. The Chinese, always grateful and hospitable to foreigners, grabbed Imelda Marcos's massive ego, which it fed and massaged until it was an ideological Red. She was received by the aging Zhou Enlai as if she were a head of state, attended to by Mao's wife, Chiang Ching, as if she were a soul sister.

Zhou, who was ailing, hadn't been seen in public for nearly two months and had recently declined to see a U.S. congressional delegation headed by Senator Fulbright. But on Mrs. Marcos's first full day in his country, Zhou, in a gray tunic and looking a bit more gray-haired than when last seen, got out of his bed to greet Mrs. Marcos at the hospital door, then escorted her down a long corridor to a reception room for an hourlong conversation. With Mao's wife as her escort, Imelda Marcos traipsed to the usual sites, from the Great Wall to the fifteenth-century Ming tombs. She also saw a revolutionary ballet, revolutionary opera, and revolutionary factories. "I am quite impressed," she remarked at the time. Imelda Marcos, who only three months earlier had been received by India's Indira Gandhi, went to China expecting Chiang Ching to be a "radical ideologue" but found her "soft-spoken, very feminine" as well as "open-minded." Chiang, the official host for many important foreign visitors, was dazzled by Mrs. Marcos, entertaining in her "royal proletarian style." So impressed was the Chinese leader that she took the Philippine first lady to a commune on the outskirts of Tianjin, usually barred to foreigners. It was Chiang's model commune, "a tiny utopia of proletarian culture." Thousands of children and workers had been turned out to cheer the Philippine first lady when she arrived in Tianjin, and at the commune the two women sat at a long table in a dirt courtyard, Imelda Marcos in a black suede coat over a print dress, a scarf flowing from her neck; Chiang Ching in a rough-cut man's sport coat, a Mao cap, and heavy-rimmed glasses: the consummate capitalist; the revolutionary Communist. Each was impressed, if not awed, by the other. After Mrs. Marcos had returned to Manila, Chiang continued the courting, with gifts arriving every few days, usually "delectable foodstuffs," the American embassy in Manila reported. (The Imelda Marcos–Chiang Ching relationship "fascinates me," Sullivan cabled, asking for "comments, speculations, and pontification" on what it might mean.)

At Peking University the talk among students was that Chinese leaders were appalled by Mrs. Marcos's extravagance and displays of wealth. Perhaps they were, but it didn't show. For days the *People's Daily* and the *Red Flag* (the official paper of the People's Liberation Army) prominently played the visit on their front pages, with large photographs and banner headlines. Imelda Marcos was taken to Yanan, the shrine of Chinese communism, where for thirteen years Mao had lived in the caves and where the Long March had ended. When she, wearing fashionable sunglasses, spotted a toothless, weathered old man who was a veteran of the march, she embraced him, a gesture which some thought led to an unexpected invitation to meet with the eighty-two-year-old Mao himself. On the substantive agenda, Imelda Marcos signed a long-term contract to buy crude oil from the Chinese, an accomplishment of which she boasted, because it would reduce Philippine dependence on Middle East countries. But the oil she bought was of such horribly inferior quality that it clogged the Philippine refineries.

Like a wide-eyed college student of the 1960s, Imelda Marcos thought she had seen the future, and it was Mao's China; she ignored, or was unaware of, the Cultural Revolution that was devastating the country. She was still bubbling with revolutionary rhetoric when she returned to the Philippines. "She is inclined not only to give Chinese much greater credit than they are due for resolution of all the problems she has tackled in the Philippines (family planning, nutrition, etc.), but she is increasingly critical of the Western system of things, particularly as currently being manifested in the U.S.," Sullivan advised Washington in November 1974. Sullivan sought to snap her out of it. The confrontation, perhaps the most publicly brutal between the two, occurred during the celebration of the thirtieth anniversary of MacArthur's wading ashore at Leyte. She had squandered several million dollars to build what she claimed was her ancestral home on some beachfront property. She even had the wood specially treated so that it would look old. But it was more than just a home; it was a sprawling 1,500-acre resort: two Olympic-size swimming pools; three heliports; an eighteen-hole golf course; an auditorium; guest cabanas of bamboo and coconut wood set among the palm trees; a catacomb-chapel built into the side of a hill; and its own water and power system. This "ancestral" estate was so new that the grass had to be sprayed with green paint for the celebration.

While the bacchanalia was proceeding, Imelda Marcos invited the American ambassador and his wife, along with a priest who was Mrs. Marcos's confessor, for a private lunch. The first lady launched into a discussion about China, offering to be the bridge between the two superpowers. It was a role she was particularly suited to play, she explained to Sullivan, because after Mao died, Zhou Enlai would be pushed aside, and Madame Chiang, with whom she got on so well, would be the new ruler. Against his better diplomatic judgment ("I guess the devil made me do an unchivalrous thing," he said years later), Sullivan told her she didn't know what she was talking about, that Chiang Ching was a "left-leaning deviant," who would be "wiped out" in the purge that would follow Mao's death. Imelda Marcos's chin began trembling; then she burst into tears and fled the table. She had been stung, interpreting Sullivan's remarks, she told friends later, as indicative of what the U.S. attitude would be toward her if she succeeded her husband. After Mao died and his wife was put on trial along with the Gang of Four, Imelda Marcos explained that Madame Chiang's fatal mistake had been in not acting decisively upon her husband's death to take over power. Those who heard her say this assumed she was making it clear that she would not make the same mistake when Marcos died.

Noting that most of Mrs. Marcos's travels had been in the developing world and that she had visited so many Communist countries, the CIA concluded: "Her enthusiasm for third world and communist causes can be explained by the fact that the relationships are new and she does not have to share the spotlight." The agency added that "her foreign policy initiatives are short on substance." Any reported results from the trips, such as obtaining oil supplies from the Middle East or commitments that the Arab countries would not support the Muslim struggle in Mindanao, "were usually negotiated in advance by the responsible government agencies, leaving the publicity for her."

Her travels were also marked, U.S. officials thought, by her desire both to antagonize and to obtain more from the United States, including favorable personal treatment. She apparently believed, or at least Americans who knew her concluded, that if she cozied up to America's enemies, the United States would respond by offering more to bring her back into its camp. Whatever the reason, in addition to Mao and Castro, Imelda Marcos went in pursuit of Libya's Colonel Qaddafi, a leader who impressed her because of what she said was his "incorruptibility." Sullivan cabled Washington: "It remains to be seen whether Mrs. Marcos will be able to work her wiles on the ascetic Libyan colonel, not to mention the MNLF [Moro National Liberation Front] leadership, but she will certainly give it the college try."

Substantively, Imelda Marcos's Libya trip was designed to enlist Qaddafi's aid in negotiating an end to the Muslim rebellion in the Philippines, and what became known as the Tripoli Agreement was signed; but peace never came, and Qaddafi continued shipping arms to the MNLF. Nevertheless, the U.S. embassy in Tripoli concluded that her visit "can only be described as a diplomatic success. In fact it made diplomatic history. For the first time in the memory of local diplomats ladies were invited to the 'State' dinner for Mrs. Marcos. Moreover Mrs. Qadhafi (number 2 of 3) emerged from almost total obscurity to host a dinner (in a tent in her backyard) for Mrs. Marcos and the wives of Tripoli diplomats."

Qaddafi was so smitten by her that he took her to his tent in the desert to meet his father, a rare honor for a woman. The colonel was also reported to have suggested that she remain in his country to study the Koran. "You are a good woman, why don't you become Muslim?" he remarked. He offered to be her tutor. Imelda Marcos, who videotaped the affair, as she did almost every meeting, offered to teach him to dance. When she returned to Manila, she was filled with wild stories. Among friends she ridiculed Qaddafi for being a homosexual. She also said with a laugh that Qaddafi was easy to deal with. She said, "All you have to do is rub his leg." Sullivan, not about to pass up another chance to toss a barb at Mrs. Marcos, commented in a cable to Washington that she "may be entering phase of fascination with Islam similar to period of entrancement with things Red Chinese. . . . If so we may yet see artificial sand dunes in back of the Cultural Center in Manila Bay."

When Imelda Marcos wasn't traveling, she was enriching herself. "What is the biggest industry in the Philippines?" began a joke heard frequently after the implementation of martial law. "Mining" was the answer. "That's mine, that's mine, that's mine. . . ." It was a reference to how Mrs. Marcos acquired her wealth. It was as simple as it was brazen: She just went to businessmen and demanded an equity interest in their companies. Before martial law it had been 10 percent; quickly it became 25 percent. The corporate executives would appeal to Marcos; he would shrug: nothing he could do about his wife, or nothing he wanted to do. Those who didn't comply found themselves hounded by the tax collector or the justice department or this inspector or that one.

Cosmopolitan magazine, in December 1975, acclaimed Imelda Marcos as one of the ten richest women in the world, her photograph appearing in the gallery between Queen Elizabeth of England and Dina Merrill, along with Christina Onassis Andreadis, Barbara Hutton, and Queen Juliana of the Netherlands, among others. The magazine even suggested she might be "the richest woman in the world, *bar none*." Impressive, if not unprecedented, progress for a woman who had no inherited wealth, whose husband had seen his family's wealth depleted in his defense against a murder charge and whose salary as the country's president for the past ten years had been less than $5,000 a year. The CIA in Manila, in 1976, conducted a little informal study. The station determined that Imelda Marcos's portfolio consisted of three to four dozen companies, including several banks. Her net worth was at least $150 million.

In the CIA files at Langley was a Top Secret analysis. Essentially a profile of Imelda Marcos, it was a summary of what she had become in the ten years since her husband had first been elected president. It reveals what U.S. officials knew about her and raises questions about why they continued to court and allow themselves to be charmed by her.

In a section headed "The Steel Butterfly," the CIA analyst, herself a woman, begins:

> Mrs. Marcos is ambitious and ruthless. Born a poor cousin of landed aristocracy, she has a thirst for wealth, power and public acclaim, and her boundless ego makes her easy prey for flatterers. Although she has little formal education, she is cunning.
>
> Her political organization is largely made up of media people and businessmen, plus a scattering of politicians and a few military men. Most are sycophants seeking protection.
>
> Her political advancement has been handled largely by her brother, Benjamin Romualdez, absentee governor of Leyte Province, home of Imelda's family.

The "Marcos marriage," the analyst concluded, was "essentially a business and political partnership." He was head of government; she was head of state. It was a conjugal dictatorship.

It had been founded during the Nixon watch, tolerated during Ford's. While neither administration may have openly condoned what was going on in the Philippines, neither expressed any alarm about it. At no time, not publicly or privately, was it ever suggested to Marcos that he ought to lift martial law and restore democracy. But with the American presidential election of 1976, it seemed that the policy of tolerance for Marcos, indeed for all dictators, had ended.

8: Human Rights: Conflict at Foggy Bottom

The United States was tacking on a new course in the conduct of its relations with the world when James Earl Carter became the country's thirty-ninth president. Human rights would be, as he expressed it, the "soul of our foreign policy." A commitment to human rights fitted the moral character of the new president, an Annapolis graduate and a deeply religious man from Plains, Georgia. But this new emphasis was also a reflection of the times, and they were changing. In the aftermath of Vietnam; the power and abuses of power by Nixon and Kissinger; the secret and illegal bombing and invasion of Cambodia; the clandestine overthrow of the Chilean government; each revelation about nefarious CIA activities, including plots to assassinate world leaders, there was a sense that there had to be another way for the democratic superpower to behave.

Congress led the way, often pulling and pushing a reluctant White House and State Department. During the cold war the deliberative body had generally deferred to presidents' foreign policy ventures, with only occasional individual voices of dissent, for example, when Truman dispatched American boys to Korea and when Eisenhower sent the marines wading ashore in Lebanon. The Gulf of Tonkin Resolution, LBJ's blank check to commit the United States militarily in Vietnam, was approved by all but 2 of the more than 500 members in the Senate and House. But the 1970s brought an activist Congress into the making of U.S. foreign policy.

It was a passionate desire to avoid "another Vietnam" that propelled Congress, in 1973, to enact the War Powers Resolution, which

163

circumscribed the president's power to send American troops into combat without congressional approval. Nixon vetoed the legislation, but so strong was the sentiment in Congress that it was able to override the president. Congress was intent, however, on doing more than keeping American boys out of some foreign wars; it also wanted to inject some morality into America's relations with foreign countries, to put some distance between the United States and repressive regimes. During the last months of 1973 Congressman Donald Fraser, a liberal Democrat from Minneapolis, held fifteen hearings pertaining to human rights and foreign policy. In December Congress enacted legislation which provided that it was the "sense of Congress" that the president "should" deny military assistance to any country that imprisoned people for political reasons. As a "sense of Congress," it was not a stricture, not a flat prohibition; the Nixon administration, with Kissinger as secretary of state, ignored it.

Then came the congressional class of 1974, elected three months after Nixon's resignation; the members were young, liberal, and activist. Fraser accelerated the pace and number of human rights hearings, aided now by a neighbor from Iowa, Thomas Harkin, elected at the age of thirty-four. A former navy pilot in Vietnam, Harkin had become prominent as a congressional aide when he had discovered South Vietnam's infamous "tiger cages," the tiny boxes where prisoners were held. President Ford vetoed some of their efforts, and Kissinger's State Department continued to ignore those that were enacted. Congress pushed on.

By the time the Carter administration arrived in Washington, Congress had created the position of coordinator for human rights and humanitarian affairs within the State Department and required the department to issue a report each year on the human rights practices in countries that received aid from the United States (it was later changed to include all countries on the ground that it was unfair to criticize countries America dealt with while remaining silent about others, such as the Soviet Union). But the most pointed laws were those that pertained to the handing out of military and economic assistance. Two laws prohibited U.S. dollars from going to any country "which engages in a consistent pattern of gross violations of internationally recognized human rights, including torture or cruel, inhuman, or degrading treatment or punishment, prolonged detention without charges, or other flagrant denial of the right to life, liberty, and the security of person." (There are exceptions, in emergency situations for military aid and for economic aid if the latter will directly benefit the needy people in the recipient country.)

The human rights policy was besieged from the right and the left. Conservatives attacked it as being a crusade for ideological liberals and shouted that it was applied only to right-wing regimes. Liberals tended to cloak the human rights issue in moral cloth, and too many human rights advocates displayed self-righteous arrogance. Conservatives failed to see, and liberals too rarely argued, that the human rights policy was anchored not only in morality but in realpolitik. America's interests, economic, military, and political, lie in stability. Violent revolutions come about when the avenues of democratic evolution have been closed. The revolutions are usually directed against repressive regimes that the United States has been backing, driving the militants to look for, and find, support from America's enemies. Thus, when those violent revolutions are successful, as in Cuba, Vietnam, Iran, Nicaragua, the new governments are frequently, and understandably, hostile to the United States, a simultaneous expression of the anger toward the United States for having bolstered the dictators and of the debt owed to those countries, such as the Soviet Union and Cuba, which helped throw them out.

Carter's human rights policy, at least as enunciated at the outset, certainly suggested that the U.S. was no longer going to be quite so cozy with dictators. "Because we are free, we can never be indifferent to the fate of freedom elsewhere," Carter said in his inaugural address. Adopting the positive approach, he added: "Our moral sense dictates a clear-cut preference for those societies who share with us an abiding respect for individual human rights." Marcos's "New Society" did not seem to be one of those. "Of America's allies, none is violating human rights more egregiously than the Government of President Ferdinand E. Marcos," Bernard Gwertzman of *The New York Times* wrote in early 1978.

The first independent look at what had happened to the "showcase of democracy" was delivered in September 1976 by Amnesty

International (AI), which was to receive the Nobel Peace Prize a few months later. Amnesty's report focused on the treatment of political prisoners, of which there were still at least 6,000 in the Philippines four years after martial law had been declared. "Torture was widespread," Amnesty concluded. Electric shock was routinely applied to prisoners' breasts or genitals. One common torture was to force a prisoner to lie with his feet on one bed, his head on another, arms held tight by the side; whenever his body fell or sagged, he was beaten and kicked. It was called the San Juanico Bridge torture, named for the bridge connecting Imelda Marcos's home province of Leyte with Samar, which residents said had been given by the president to his wife for a birthday present. Jean Cacayorin-Tayag, mother of a three-year-old boy, was blindfolded and gagged during interrogation, forced to strip, kicked from behind, beaten with a belt, slapped, and required to squat for hours. Mrs. Cacayorin-Tayag was made to go without sleep for eight days and nights, forced to stand for hours at a time in front of a full-blast air conditioner. The soldiers fondled her, then threatened to ruin her moral reputation by spreading gossip about her having an affair. Her husband was separately interrogated; on the first day for five hours he was tied to a chair and beaten with fists, karate chops, and kicks, then struck in the stomach with a rifle butt. His assailants were a lieutenant, a sergeant, a lawyer, and a police chief. He was removed to a safe house, where the tortures continued for three weeks. He was beaten so severely on the soles of his feet that long afterward he still could not walk. His lips were burned with a cigarette; his mustache, with a cigarette lighter. José Lacaba, thirty years old, who had been a reporter with the *Philippines Free Press,* was subjected to the San Juanico Bridge torture and later was taken to a hospital, where he was injected with "truth serum." He was held incommunicado for two months, as was another journalist, Bonaficio Ilagan, twenty-four years old. Both were arrested because they were publishing an underground newspaper that opposed martial law. A lieutenant stood Ilagan against a wall, then used him for a punching bag. A sergeant forced him to squat and when he collapsed, kicked him in the sensitive parts of his body before passing him to another sergeant for more of the same abuse.

Amnesty's report brought the predictable protests from the Philippine government, which charged that the Amnesty investigators had only talked to "Communists" and Communist "sympathizers." But however gruesome it might be, the report was solid, and the United States knew it was.* Asked by Washington to examine Amnesty's report allegation by allegation, the embassy responded that it was "both essentially balanced and accurate." Indeed, the embassy, noting that the AI team had been limited to Luzon, added that if it had traveled farther, "we suspect their report might have been more critical, since reports of torture, maltreatment, etc., become more common the farther one gets from Manila." The embassy didn't think, however, that "torture and maltreatment" were "explicit government policy at the political level." Rather, the embassy suggested it was merely a case of officers' leaving detainees to the "not so tender mercies of lower-ranking military, many of whom had to drink to be able to inflict the torture."

Amnesty's report included a number of recommendations, which, if implemented, would restore at least a modicum of decency, humanity, and justice in the treatment of prisoners. Several months later, after analyzing each recommendation, the embassy reported that "in sum" the Marcos government had "not repeat not made any major effort to implement" them. As for the recommendation that soldiers involved in torture be punished, the embassy said, "Frankly, we would be surprised if any serious disciplinary action were taken . . ." Turning to Amnesty's recommendation that the right of habeas corpus be restored, the embassy found it "understandable" that Marcos would not comply with this recommendation "since compliance goes against entire martial law system."

Those embassy conclusions should have had a great impact on the Carter administration and the policymakers at State, for implicit within them was the essence of Marcos's rule. He had imposed martial law solely for the purpose of advancing his personal wealth and power. That was precisely what State's Bureau of Intelligence and Research had said when martial law was declared. Just as that

---

* The leader of the Amnesty team was Thomas Jones, a lawyer in his late thirties, described in a State Department cable sent over Kissinger's name as "very mature and balanced." Jones had worked for Covington and Burling, one of the largest law firms in Washington, D.C.; that fact was noted by the department in its cable as a kind of seal of approval that Jones could not be considered reckless or a radical.

reality had been ignored then by the Nixon administration, so would it now be by the Carter administration. In fact, it was even more indefensible to ignore the reality now. Should one accept, for the sake of argument, that Washington had been justified in supporting martial law when it was imposed on the grounds that some strong measures were necessary to deal with the violence, that a new social order was needed, and that Marcos could be trusted and deserved a chance, it was apparent by the time that the Carter administration arrived that none of these premises was valid. The State Department was aware of what Marcos was about. In a Confidential "Briefing Paper," written in November 1975 for President Ford prior to his trip to the Philippines, the department noted, "Martial law was seen as a temporary phenomenon, and the public in general supported Marcos' efforts to restore order, clean house in the government administration and get the economy rolling. It has become increasingly clear, however, that Marcos has no immediate plans for ending martial law or restoring democracy and individual freedoms." The Ford administration had done nothing to press for a restoration of democracy, but certainly, it was thought, the Carter administration would.

On the contrary, Carter's policy "in fact sanctioned Philippine authoritarianism." That was the conclusion of a career Foreign Service officer who served in the Philippines, Robert Pringle. During the Carter years martial law was a bit more benign perhaps: Many political prisoners were released; there was a diminution of the torture. These were important improvements, but they were cosmetic more than fundamental. The core of Marcos's power was not touched. The Carter policy did not persuade Marcos "to liberalize the political system to the point where opposition groups could compete for political power in free elections," the Congressional Research Service concluded. When Carter left Washington after four years, Marcos was still ensconced in Manila, far wealthier than four years earlier, with just as much power, maybe more—and with no thought of turning it over to anyone.

That the Carter administration was reluctant to lean heavily on Marcos, to put the distance between Washington and his regime that even the conservative Reagan administration did a few years later reflects a number of the elements that go into the making of foreign policy: immutable principles; the cautious nature of diplomats; ambitious individuals; domestic politics. Through all these elements runs an ever-present axiom of American foreign policy: Democratic administrations, especially liberal ones, are reluctant to push right-wing dictators. They will not "because of this overweening fear of being accused of being soft on communism," explains Leslie H. Gelb, who has studied and observed foreign policy on the inside and out (in the Defense and State departments; as director of the project that produced the *Pentagon Papers;* as a correspondent for *The New York Times*). JFK launched the Bay of Pigs invasion, in part, to prove that he could be tough on communism; a few years later LBJ sent the marines into the Dominican Republic to keep it from becoming "a second Cuba." Many Democrats in the 1980s voted for aid to contras trying to overthrow the Marxist-oriented Nicaraguan government lest they be charged with being soft on communism.

This fear of being labeled "soft on communism" is rooted in the 1930s, when liberals embraced communism, which meant the Soviet Union, which meant Stalin. Democrats are still atoning. Then came Mao's defeat of Chiang Kai-shek. Since that happened during the Truman watch, the Democrats naturally were to blame. The "Who lost China?" debate began. It wasn't really a question or a debate. It was an indictment—and a conviction. Democrats cowered. McCarthyism seared itself into the American foreign policy psyche, the scars remaining long after those he had destroyed were gone. The "who lost" debates march on, almost inexorably, it seems (and still without any examination of the underlying assumption about what is America's to "lose"). Who lost Vietnam? Who lost Iran? Who lost Nicaragua? To avoid having to answer the shrill charges, in its final days the Carter administration resumed military aid to El Salvador (it had been suspended on human rights grounds) and dispatched military advisers, in quaking fear that the leftist guerrillas who had launched what they boasted was their "final offensive" might just be successful.

After Marcos had been toppled in February 1986, Carter's assistant secretary of state for East Asia, Richard Holbrooke, said, "Thank goodness it happened on a Republican watch. . . . If a Democrat had tried to do this, it would have split the country."

It might not have split the country, but it would certainly have brought blasts from the conservatives. And the Carter administration, from the outset, was engaged in enough initiatives that brought out the wrath of the right. In Asia it sought to advance what Nixon had begun in China and discussed, at least for a couple of years, bringing American troops home from Korea. Carter successfully pursued an arms control agreement with the Soviets and turned over the Panama Canal to Panama, a recognition of the country's sovereignty. In another positive step in the third world, the administration backed the effort which led to majority black rule in what became Zimbabwe. He didn't need to sharpen another sword and hand it to the conservatives.

But all the fears and all the principles are inert matter until propelled by individuals. That may be a truism, but the role of the individual in the making of foreign policy is far greater than is generally perceived. The impact of an Acheson, a Kennan, a Dulles, a Kissinger may be well known, or become so later. But at lower levels and without the public acclaim, or criticism, men (and, in rare cases, women; the Foreign Service until the Carter years effectively had a WOMEN NEED NOT APPLY sign) leave their tattoo on a policy, a country, and a people.

As it turned out, the making and implementation of Philippine policy during the Carter administration were marked by tension and conflict within the foreign policy establishment, with the embassy in Manila discovering that Washington didn't want as active a human rights policy as the rhetoric suggested. Small steps for human rights never became big strides. Heated debates over how much aid the Philippines ought to receive from the United States were resolved in favor of more, not less, a clear signal to Marcos that he wouldn't be required to mend his ways.

The principal verbal pugilists were Richard Holbrooke and Patricia Derian. He was assistant secretary of state for East Asian and Pacific affairs. She was assistant secretary of state for human rights and humanitarian affairs. It was a clash of the policies and personalities of two aggressive, strong-willed, tenacious fighters. Neither would, or could, admit that there was any conceivable way other

170

than his or her own. Neither, on looking back, could see any mistakes in his or her policy for the Philippines, and only a few minor ones anywhere else in the world that had come within his or her policy-making orbit. Had they been on the same side, their formidable energies and abilities combined might have been enough to move countries. Instead, they carried on a guerrilla war against each other from the Foggy Bottom trenches, each with help from the fourth estate. He, an easterner, had received all the proper training, knew the rules, had courted the members of the club, and had been admitted. She, a southerner, was a street fighter, an outsider, who seemed to take more delight in tweaking the establishment than in entering it. He won.

"I made Philippine policy," says Richard Charles Albert Holbrooke. It is a boast, but it is not an exaggeration. Secretary of State Cyrus Vance was more interested in U.S.-Soviet relations; National Security Adviser Zbigniew Brzezinski concentrated on China. The Philippines, for each, was a sideshow. In his memoirs Vance mentions the Philippines only in connection with Cambodia; in his, Brzezinski makes only two passing references to the archipelago, once noting that a presidential review memorandum (the mechanism for triggering a review leading to the adoption of a position or policy) had been ordered on the bases negotiations. Carter's White House memoirs likewise have but one mention of the Philippines, again in connection with U.S.-China relations.

It wasn't necessary for Vance, Brzezinski, or the president to focus on the Philippines because it wasn't a crisis spot. Marcos was firmly in control and seen to be protecting American security and financial interests. In foreign policy the application of the "if-it-ain't-broke-don't-fix-it" principle is: If something isn't a crisis, it will be largely ignored, and certainly no dramatic initiatives will be tried. Indeed, so smoothly did everything seem to be going out there during the Carter years that with the exception of a meeting to discuss the bases there was never a need to convene an interagency or NSC meeting to develop a policy. It all was left to Holbrooke, not just the Philippines but most of Southeast Asia, with the exception of China, where Brzezinski didn't want anyone interfering. Holbrooke came into power in the wake of America's final withdrawal from Vietnam, when the nation was reexamining its commitments in the Pacific. Like Kissinger, Holbrooke wanted the United States to remain a power in Asia, and he established the broad outlines of what is still U.S. policy in the Pacific. In the Philippines Holbrooke joined Lansdale and Byroade in the exclusive club of individuals who had a singular impact on the policy and the country.

"I'm proud of it," Holbrooke says about his Philippine policy. "My reputation will stand or fall on it." Holbrooke desperately wants his reputation to stand, solidly enough to support his longing to be secretary of state someday. Ask a Foreign Service officer about Dick Holbrooke, and invariably the response will include the advice Holbrooke sought from his career counselor soon after arriving at the State Department. In the telling and retelling, the story has acquired different details. One account is that he asked how to become an ambassador or assistant secretary before he was thirty-five years old; the other is that he asked how to become secretary of state. Whichever question Holbrooke asked, the career counselor's response to the impetuous young man was a facetious "Leave the department." Holbrooke doesn't recall having sought that advice, but he doesn't deny that he might have. He left the department twice, returning the first time as an assistant secretary, at the age of thirty-five the youngest assistant secretary in at least forty years. After Carter was defeated, Holbrooke, who says that the secretary of state "shouldn't be a career officer," left the State Department to become a Wall Street investment banker. But he continued to stay active in foreign policy; at a critical moment in late 1985 he returned to the Philippines, meeting with Marcos and his rival, Corazon Aquino, whom he cautioned about running for president.

Becoming secretary of state is a real possibility for Holbrooke in a Democratic administration. Whether he reaches it may depend on how successful his numerous enemies are in pulling the brass ring away. Few question Holbrooke's intellectual prowess: "very smart, . . . very able, very articulate," says a former colleague. "Dick can talk on any side of every issue." But many are troubled by his manner of dealing with people, much too abrasive; and his ambition, too bold even by Washington standards. "He's infinitely ambitious, infinitely egotistical," says the same retired career Foreign Service officer.

While Holbrooke's ambition is obvious, his political orientation

172

is not. He was against the Vietnam War, and after it was over, he worked hard to establish diplomatic relations with Vietnam. He was also a staunch advocate of expanding relations with China, and his contributions to that success during the Carter administration were greater than Brzezinski has been willing to share. Holbrooke considers himself a liberal. "I'm not ashamed to say I'm a liberal," he said in 1986, a time when conservatism was the prevailing gale and when many liberals, as he noted, tried to avoid being labeled as such, preferring "to call themselves pragmatists and progressives." But it's not clear that the label "liberal" fits (a reflection, perhaps, of the danger inherent in any label). After he had left the government, Holbrooke was on a panel at the Johns Hopkins School for Advanced International Studies on the subject of arms control; he agreed on almost every point with Paul Nitze, Reagan's first arms negotiator. Holbrooke also supported the Reagan administration's Central American policies: military aid to El Salvador; arming, training, and equipping the contras in Washington's war to overthrow the Nicaraguan government.

Whatever his politics, a revealing insight into Holbrooke, particularly how he perceived his role in shaping the world, is found in a short essay he wrote for *Harper's*. When he first arrived in Washington, "straight from college," he wrote, he read an article in *Life* written by Theodore H. White about the men in the Kennedy administration. That article "made a great impression on me," Holbrooke remembered. "It described a new group of men . . . who were coming to Washington to determine the destiny of the nation and the world. They were called 'action-intellectuals,' for they possessed a rare combination of intelligence and flair for decisive action. They were, in other words, very very smart."

David Halberstam was to call them "the best and the brightest."* "They were our role models," Holbrooke recalled in 1986. "But when I finally met these guys, I realized, yes, they were bright, but

---

* Though Holbrooke isn't mentioned in Halberstam's book, his copy is inscribed: "For Dick Holbrooke, who taught me everything that I know about Viet Nam, and bears responsibility (or irresponsibility) for the mistakes contained herein. With special affection, David Halberstam." Many have long suspected that Holbrooke was a principal source for Halberstam, and Holbrooke himself, in an interview in 1986, said that he had provided Halberstam with a number of anecdotes that appear in the book.

they were very flawed." (It was how many of his colleagues described him.)

Holbrooke's diplomatic career was born out of a marriage of fortuitousness and failure. His father, a doctor, had moved the family from Manhattan to Scarsdale, the affluent suburb on the commuter line north of New York City, when Dick, born on April 24, 1941, was nine years old. One of the family's neighbors was Dean Rusk, and in high school Rusk's son and Holbrooke were classmates, "very good friends, best friends," says Holbrooke. When Dean Rusk gave a talk at Scarsdale High, it was Holbrooke's introduction to the Foreign Service. But his real interest was journalism. Rusk's son was the editor of the high school newspaper; Dick was the sports editor. At Brown University Holbrooke became the editor of the *Brown Daily.* In May 1960 he sent himself to France to cover the scheduled summit between Eisenhower and Khrushchev. "It was kind of an audacious act" for the Brown paper to cover it, he says. The summit collapsed (in the aftermath of the U-2 spy plane incident), but while in Paris, Holbrooke approached the Paris bureau chief for *The New York Times,* Clifton Daniel. "I presented myself, full of boldness. Here I am." Holbrooke was hired, for $10 a day. After graduating from Brown, Holbrooke applied for a job as a reporter with *The Times*—"Journalism was my only love," he says— but he was turned down. So he took the Foreign Service exam, "in large part because Dean Rusk was someone I admired immensely."

When Holbrooke joined the department, Dean Rusk was secretary of state. Over an end-of-the-day scotch in his seventh-floor office Rusk asked William Sullivan, a career diplomat on the rise and also a Brown graduate, to look after the new Foreign Service officer. Sullivan recommended that the the young man go to Vietnam, where careers were to be made. Holbrooke began as an economic development officer in Ba Xuyen Province, where the eager new diplomat encountered Lansdale and Colonel Valeriano, Lansdale's sidekick since the Huk wars, along with others who had transported anticommunism from the Philippines to Vietnam. Within a year Holbrooke had moved up, as a staff aide first to General Maxwell Taylor, then to Ambassador Henry Cabot Lodge.

While in Vietnam, Holbrooke met many of the young Foreign Service officers who were to be intertwined with his career in the years ahead: Peter Tarnoff, who became Vance's executive assistant; Anthony Lake, Vance's director of policy planning; and John Negroponte (Holbrooke's roommate in Saigon), whom Holbrooke brought on as his chief deputy. Holbrooke displayed the aggressive can-do spirit that was the mark of so many of the U.S. Foreign Service officers in Indochina. "He was so confident, so self-assured," recalled a CIA officer. "He acted as though he had been an ambassador all his life."

After three years in Vietnam Holbrooke was back in Washington, first at the White House, working for Robert Komer, who was conducting what was called the "other war," an assignment that Holbrooke would like to forget about. That "other war" was also called just as euphemistically the "pacification" program; it was the one that provided for the forced resettlement of the Vietnamese peasants into "strategic hamlets," while their villages were bulldozed by American soldiers and the surrounding areas were sprayed with herbicides in order to make sure no one could go home again.

Holbrooke's career received a major thrust in 1968, when he was brought on by Averell Harriman as a member of the U.S. delegation to the Paris peace talks. Harriman liked to travel with a small staff, most of whom were young, and to become a Harriman protégé was to have a guaranteed future. Harriman's deputy to the talks was Cyrus Vance. The talks failed, and when Nixon and Kissinger took over foreign policy, Holbrooke, along with a number of young liberals who had been opposed to the Vietnam War, went off to academia, Holbrooke to the Woodrow Wilson School of Public and International Affairs at Princeton. When that year was up, it was still the time for someone with Holbrooke's views to be far from Washington, the farther the better. A liberal filled with a desire "to see the world," he became director of the Peace Corps office in Morocco. He returned to Washington in 1972, having been recruited to be managing editor of a new magazine, *Foreign Policy*, which was to become, thanks in large part to Holbrooke's talent and energy, the forum for Democratic views about the conduct of foreign policy, an alternative to the more conservative *Foreign Affairs*.

At the age of thirty-three Holbrooke was acclaimed by *Time* in its issue on "Leadership in America." He was in the select galaxy of 200 persons under the age of forty-five who *Time* saw as the leaders of the future, Holbrooke's bio-sketch sandwiched between James F. Hoge, Jr., the thirty-eight-year-old editor of the *Chicago Sun-Times,* and thirty-three-year-old Congresswoman Elizabeth Holtzman, who as a freshman legislator had brought suit to halt the bombing of Cambodia and who from her seat on the House Judiciary Committee was a leader in the effort to impeach Nixon.

Holbrooke's way back into the government side of foreign policy began when he signed on early with a man from Georgia few Americans had ever heard of. Holbrooke and Carter both were members of the Trilateral Commission, an elitist nongovernmental foreign affairs organization founded in 1973 by David Rockefeller, chairman of the Chase Manhattan Bank, and Zbigniew Brzezinski. They selected the members, with Carter probably the most obscure of the politicians allowed in, and Holbrooke, at thirty-two, one of the youngest. Holbrooke, who had wanted to work in a presidential campaign but had sat out 1972 because he considered McGovern too liberal, was invited to a small Georgetown dinner party to meet Jimmy Carter. Holbrooke became one of the Democratic candidate's principal foreign policy advisers. With Carter's victory, Holbrooke coveted the post of national security adviser, and he was on a short list; but there was never serious doubt that the position belonged to Brzezinski. Vance asked Holbrooke to be his executive assistant; Holbrooke declined, preferring to have more operational responsibility. What he most desired was the position as undersecretary for political affairs, the number three job in the department. But Philip Habib, who had known Vance for years and was "Mr. Foreign Service," had a lock on that. Since there were no other positions on the seventh floor, Holbrooke asked to be head of one of the geographic bureaus, particularly East Asia and the Pacific, which was the post his mentor Dean Rusk had once held. It was now Holbrooke's.

Holbrooke's appointment was not enthusiastically received by some of the older, more traditional diplomats at Foggy Bottom. They thought he was too young as well as too aggressive and a bit too mercurial, traits a diplomat shouldn't have. Their concerns became resentments after Holbrooke had taken over, especially since he tended to ignore seniority and age and advanced the younger officers on the basis of merit, as he saw it. An impressive number

on one occasion, however, when he failed to appear for a House subcommittee hearing. He sent his senior deputy, Michael Armacost, with a message that Assistant Secretary Holbrooke deeply regretted he was unable to attend but he was preparing to leave the next day on a trip to Singapore. Holbrooke's nonappearance would probably have passed without comment had it not been for his highly visible social life.

The morning after the hearing Holbrooke's picture was on the front page of the style section of the *Washington Post*. In black tie, holding a drink in his right hand, Holbrooke, strapping and curly-haired, was caught by the photographer engaging in banter with George Stevens, Jr., and Jean Firstenberg, the outgoing and incoming directors, respectively, of the American Film Institute. Cicely Tyson was there, as were Elizabeth Taylor, Jack Valenti, and other notable politicians and celebrities. "Welcome to my house," Holbrooke, ever gregarious, had said in greeting the guests, who drank and chatted in the State Department's Benjamin Franklin Room overlooking the Potomac. That "welcome" was turned on Holbrooke by the chairman of the House subcommittee on Asia, Lester Wolff. After seeing the photograph and article, Wolff wrote a "Dear Dick" letter, partly in jest and partly out of pique: "Earlier in the day you would have been welcome at our House, the House of Representatives."

That was a tweak, embarrassing but not damaging (and not public). But Holbrooke's principal protagonist, Patt Derian, was intent on inflicting mortal wounds, if not on the man, then certainly on his policies. When it was all over, when Carter had been defeated by Reagan, Derian, leaning back in her chair with feet on the desk near a can of Coke, found some consolation. "At least Dick Holbrooke won't be around anymore," she remarked to aides.

Though on her official documents New York City is listed as her place of birth, Patricia Murphy was there "by accident" on August 12, 1929. Her father had taken his wife to the big city, as he frequently did, for a weekend of theater. Patt (a grandfather gave her the double *t*'s in her nickname; an architect, he decided that a single *t* left the name unbalanced) was a southern belle, reared

179

around Danville, Virginia, her father a Washington lobbyist for Anaconda Wire and Cable. While at nursing school at the University of Virginia, she married a medical student, Paul S. Derian. After graduation, they had planned to live in Paris. Instead, they ended up in Mississippi, a place, she notes wryly, she had previously avoided by breaking off one of her many college engagements. It was 1959, the civil rights movement was breaking out, and Derian joined in.

Her involvement began simply enough, out of a gesture on behalf of her cook, who had been snared by appliance dealers and loan sharks in a classic scheme. The woman had purchased some appliances on the installment plan, starting with a refrigerator. When she later bought a washing machine, only $5 remained to be paid on the refrigerator, but the fine print of the installment contract, which had been sold to a finance company, provided that the refrigerator was collateral for the washing machine. When the woman's husband abandoned her, she was no longer able to make the payments. In the middle of the night the sheriff's posse came and took everything. Derian knew nothing about law, but she thought this was wrong. She made some phone calls, and eventually the merchants backed off, returning the appliances. The cook told her friends, and they began coming to the Derian household for advice and assistance.

Derian's experiences and lessons broadened, as did her involvement in the civil rights movement. When James Meredith sought to enter "Ole Miss," she organized a group to push for integration. Mississippians for Public Education, its members grandly called themselves. There were only about twenty-five women in the group— "white ladies in gloves and stockings," she says with slight self-mockery. Derian progressed from issues to candidates. In 1964 she gathered signatures to put LBJ's name on the Mississippi ballot and four years later organized the biracial Loyalist Mississippi Democratic party, which successfully challenged the all-white Mississippi delegation for seating at the riot-strewn 1968 Democratic Convention in Chicago. She toiled for McGovern in 1972, and in 1975, "greatly impressed with his kind of straight-arrow manner," she joined the Carter team. During the campaign her responsibility was, as she says, "liberals, intellectuals, and attitudes."

After Carter's victory Derian, tall and bearing a slight resemblance to the actress Lily Tomlin, was first offered the position of chief of protocol, which she rejected with the quip "I can't tap-dance." Regardless of her ballroom skills, it's hard to imagine Derian in that post. She treated dictators and strongmen, even if they were heads of state, with all the respect she would have shown a redneck southern sheriff. If the tale about Holbrooke's seeking advice on how to get ahead quickly is the one Foreign Service officers most delight in telling about him, the story they call up when asked about Derian is her trip to East Asia to examine the human rights situation. After forty-five minutes of conversation with the Singaporean foreign minister, Derian, feeling that she was not getting straight answers, gathered her papers, picked up her purse, and walked out, leaving the foreign minister and officials from the American embassy aghast. Her meeting with the Singaporean prime minister, Lee Kuan Yew, who had ruled the former British colony since 1959, went only slightly better. For nearly an hour they talked past each other, Derian suffering additionally because she was without a cigarette in the presence of the abstemious Lee, who neither smokes nor drinks. Finally, Derian *had* to have a cigarette; the session was moved upstairs to a larger room with a window, where she sat blowing smoke into the monsoon rains, while Lee listened at some distance.

Derian became the head of the Human Rights Bureau at the suggestion of Richard Moose, who had left the Foreign Service in the late 1960s to work on Senator Fulbright's Foreign Relations Committee, principally in opposition to the Indochina policies. Moose, who had coauthored a committee report shortly after Marcos's martial law takeover, was now on Carter's foreign policy transition team. (Vance selected Moose as his assistant secretary for Africa, and the Human Rights Bureau found him to be the most supportive assistant secretary.) On the patronage ledger, Derian had a number of important political pluses. She was a woman (Carter and Vance were committed to advancing women and minorities in the Foreign Service, long dominated by white males); she was from the South; and she had the endorsement of Hodding Carter, Jr., who was no relation to the president but who had worked in the campaign and was about to become the State Department spokesman—and who, in December 1978, became Patt Derian's husband, her previous marriage having ended in 1976, after twenty-four years.

There was little opposition to Derian's appointment from the career professionals in the State Department. The general feeling in the Foreign Service establishment was that human rights wasn't a very important position. Under Kissinger it had been a sleepy post, and the head of the bureau was a "coordinator," not an assistant secretary. So let a woman have it. Certainly a woman couldn't do much, the chauvinistic establishment thought. Above all, not this woman, for she had never held a paying job before and was a complete novice in foreign policy. In other words, Derian would be a nice—and quiet—token of Carter's commitment, but little more. How wrong they were.

First of all, Congress, in 1977, upgraded the status of the human rights office, giving the director assistant secretary rank, and the Human Rights Bureau was suddenly on the seventh floor, the same floor as the secretary of state and one floor above the regional bureaus. Then, much to the shock of the male diplomats, Derian wasn't a submissive female. She was tough and combative. While she irritated many, at home and abroad, and her style may have interfered with her effectiveness with foreign leaders, she may have been just what was needed in the Human Rights Bureau. "She took an institution that was lethargic and stagnant, and she moved it," says a career Foreign Service officer who worked for her. Whatever her shortcomings in style, and whatever criticisms from the left and right are heaped upon her, Derian's impact was as great as Holbrooke's.

The Reagan administration was to deemphasize, and in many cases to debase, human rights as a plank in U.S. foreign policy, but it couldn't ignore the issue. The Carter administration may have failed to live up to its human rights rhetoric; but it placed human rights firmly in the foreign policy firmament, and Derian deserves much of the credit. While others in the administration backed off from a strong human rights policy, under attack from conservatives, including conservative Democrats, Derian remained unwaveringly committed. It wasn't just her energy and doggedness that made her effective. "She was so goddamn quick," says Mark Schneider, her principal deputy for two years. "She would have made one hell of a litigator . . . one dynamite attorney before a jury. She is really top-notch in terms of presenting a case."

Derian took the same withering approach to the bureaucracy,

182

which often united to defend against her charges, as she did with dictators. She once drafted a cable to the American ambassador in Argentina which sent shudders through Vance's office when it was intercepted. The Argentine government at the time was engaged in what has become known as the "dirty war," a bland euphemism for the kidnapping, torture, and killing of thousands of Argentines, mostly students, by the military dictatorship in its campaign against leftist urban guerrillas. In her cable Derian described Argentina as a "country held in the thrall of a repressive government whose labor leaders are imprisoned and harassed, whose journalists practice their profession in fear of their lives, whose mothers must demonstrate to find out what the government has done with their children, whose prisoners are tortured and killed." Derian turned on the embassy reporting from Buenos Aires. "Your messages suggest that despite all this we should abandon our human rights policy in order to push our trade figures even higher and ensure that visiting U.S. brass get a warmer welcome from the junta." She concluded, in a tone sarcastic and demanding, "We look forward to cables outlining the embassy's human rights goals and suggestions for implementing them." Derian classified the cable ExDis, which meant that it was not to be widely distributed within the department, thus limiting the number of diplomats who would be aware of her stinging rebuke.

Someone, however, leaked the cable—not to the press but to Vance's office. When Peter Tarnoff, Vance's executive assistant, saw it, he sent a crisp memo to Derian, classifying it Eyes Only, which meant it was not to be shown to anyone. He began by chastising her for requesting a response from the embassy in Buenos Aires without having cleared her request through the Bureau of Inter-American Affairs on the sixth floor. That was a bureaucratic sin. Secondly, he noted that even though the cable had an ExDis classification, it would "eventually" become public, as it probably would have. Derian's staff was very good at using the press. "I would rather not see this exchange in the press," Tarnoff wrote. The cable was never sent to Buenos Aires; the exchange never made the press.

Carter himself had presided over the swearing in of Derian, a message to the bureaucracy, even more than to the world's dictators, that this woman and her mission had his personal endorsement.

She didn't stand a chance. She was a woman in a male establishment. She was aggressive and sometimes strident, though no more so than Holbrooke. While Foreign Service officers allowed that diplomatic blemish on him, they were not about to forgive it in a woman. But the heaviest burden Derian carried in the foreign policy wars was her portfolio—human rights.

Contrary to the convictions of many conservatives, the Foreign Service is not dominated by liberals. Quite the opposite. Most Foreign Service officers are rather conservative, with the center about as far left as they stray politically. Given a choice between the status quo and change, they'll opt for the past almost instinctively. It is not, however, so much politics that explains the general opposition to a strong human rights component of foreign policy. The resistance is, rather, embedded in the nature of diplomacy as the practitioners view it. As one Foreign Service officer expressed the attitude of diplomats, "They don't like to make waves, they don't like surprises, and above all, they abhor confrontation." Ambassadors view human rights issues much as they do problems about narcotics. No diplomat looks forward to informing a head of state that his minister of defense, chief of staff of the army, or whoever is placing electric shocks on women's breasts or smuggling cocaine.

Few diplomats bought into Carter's human rights policy. Some, such as Byroade, resigned. Others were hostile to the bureau. Most simply ignored it or implemented the human rights policy only to the extent they were forced to by Derian and her aides. It wasn't only arch conservatives who resisted. Even someone like Marshall Green, as decent a Foreign Service officer as the system ever produced and a self-styled liberal, wasn't comfortable with the Derian approach. It was too much "a crusade," he thought. He argued "for more modesty, mutuality and multilateralism in the conduct of our diplomacy."

For Green, as for all diplomats, the most cherished objective is smooth bilateral relations. And that is what underlies nearly all foreign policy decisions: good relations between the United States and the host country. There are, of course, twists and turns in the policy and nuances to fit each country. But the fundamental policy is always anchored to the rock of smooth relations.

The corollary of this drive for good relations is "clientism," the tendency of a diplomat to perceive the host country as his or her client. The diplomat becomes an advocate, pushing for military or economic assistance or overlooking the country's human rights abuses. One of the more blatant and appalling examples of clientism, as well as a reflection of the institutional opposition to Carter's human rights policy, occurred in Argentina, where the ambassador defended the country and a Foreign Service officer who had been sent out by Derian to monitor human rights was thwarted. The junior diplomat was a big, friendly Texan, F. Allen ("Tex") Harris. When he arrived in Buenos Aires, Harris reached out to the mothers and families of the "disappeared" and the victims of torture. Many a person lived because of Harris, who became a virtual Argentine national hero. It was "amazing," said Jacobo Timmerman, the Argentine editor whose kidnapping and torture became an international cause célèbre. Remembering back to Harris's presence in Argentina, Timmerman said, "This is the first time that the United States is not accused of being the main support of the military dictatorship. It is the first time that the United States is identified with the hopes we had."

Harris's humanity wasn't appreciated by the American ambassador, Raul Castro, who suppressed reports Harris wanted to send to Derian's staff about the human rights atrocities. Harris resorted to the Dissent channel, a process created by the department to allow for, if not to encourage, subordinates at least to state views which might not fit the prevailing thinking. Harris's efforts and activities resulted in his superiors placing negative personnel reports in his file. (In 1984 the American Foreign Service Association, an independent organization, presented Harris with the William R. Rivkin Award, in recognition of his "extraordinary contributions to the practice of diplomacy exemplifying intellectual courage and a zeal for creative accomplishment.")

But clientism and the aversion to a strong human rights policy are not ideological. Each year the department, as required by Congress, submits a thick report on human rights practices in countries around the world. In preparing the report, the Human Rights Bureau begins with submissions from the embassies and from the country desks in the department. Then begin the negotiations, which during the Derian reign frequently became shouting matches be-

185

tween her aides and the desk officers involved. When the report on East Germany came into the bureau, Stephen Cohen, a deputy secretary, was stunned. The report, as remembered and paraphrased by Cohen, began; "The GDR [German Democratic Republic] is committed to improving the economic well-being of its people. During World War II, its economy was devastated. After WW II, it made efforts to improve the economic well-being, but it was hampered by so many people leaving the country. In an effort to correct this, they erected the Berlin Wall."

It was, in short, an apology for the East German regime, a justification for the building of the Berlin Wall. Cohen, a certified liberal (he had been an antiwar activist in the 1960s and had worked in Eugene McCarthy's 1968 presidential campaign), called the desk officer who had prepared the East German report. "Forget what HA [Humanitarian Affairs] wants," Cohen said. "When Congress reads this, you'll be out on the street."

Derian has been criticized not only by conservatives but also by moderates who think that she had a hypocritical, dual standard. Says Holbrooke: "She singled out only the regimes to the right and wasn't evenhanded." In fact, however, Derian was seemingly single-minded in criticizing all governments that violated human rights, whether they were on the left or right. When, for example, the issue of which group was to represent Kampuchea in the UN came up, she argued passionately against the United States siding with a coalition that included the brutal Pol Pot. She was overruled by Holbrooke and Vance, who, even though they abhorred Pol Pot, had to consider more than just human rights, but also the broader geopolitical issues: Pol Pot was supported by China, while the other claimant for the seat, the Vietnamese-backed government of Heng Samrin, was allied with the Soviet Union. (Holbrooke says that voting for Pol Pot was the "single most difficult thing" he ever had to do. "It ran counter to my private views. But as a public official, I had to swallow hard.") Derian also fought with Holbrooke and the East Asian Bureau over the report on China: She wanted to be more critical of the human rights abuses; he wanted to tone it down because the Carter administration was seeking to expand on Nixon's China initiative by establishing diplomatic relations.

It wasn't only in Asia. Derian advocated a more critical and

186

more public posture on violations of the Helsinki accords by the Soviet Union and other Eastern European countries. She wanted to list specifically the human rights violations—such as torture and psychological deprivations—as well as to name the victims. And though she agreed that there should be no linkage between arms control and human rights, she did seek to link human rights to economic and trade issues—for example, that trade might be suspended with Romania or Czechoslovakia if there weren't improvements in human rights. She ran into fierce opposition from the European Bureau and the various country desks, which were supported by the higher-ups at State and in the Carter White House, the policymakers who didn't want human rights questions to interfere with their desires for détente with the Soviet Union.

These skirmishes are a reflection of what happened to Carter's human rights policy: It was derailed, and quickly. The administration had come in with a strong commitment to human rights, and nearly all of the president's political appointees at State were on board. But when the conservatives, from columnists to Democrats, began their attacks, yelling that injecting human rights into foreign policy was naïve and idealistic, that what the United States had to be most concerned about was realpolitik and the country's security, there was widespread defection from the policy, by almost everyone except Derian. She fought with just about every bureau and desk, but she and her aides remember the disagreements with Holbrooke as the most bitter and most frequent. There was little to portend the Derian-Holbrooke face-off. During the campaign Holbrooke had injected human rights themes into candidate Carter's speeches. But when the attacks on the policy started, Holbrooke retreated farther and more quickly than others.

Holbrooke and Derian even fought about personnel. To concentrate on Asia, Derian wanted to assign John Salzberg, who had worked for Congressman Donald Fraser on the human rights hearings and legislation; he and Fraser had met with Aquino in prison in 1973, the first American officials to visit him.

Holbrooke was enraged when he learned of Derian's plans for Salzberg. Their paths had crossed in South Korea, in early 1977, on one of Holbrooke's first trips abroad as assistant secretary. Salzberg, a soft-spoken Quaker, was there as a staff member of a congressional delegation and wanted to meet with a group of Koreans who had recently signed a declaration calling for the lifting of martial law. The American ambassador, Richard Sneider, one of those diplomats who didn't care for Carter's human rights policy, tried to block the meeting. Salzberg, who says, "I take human rights rather passionately," eventually met with the dissidents, the meeting arranged through a Methodist missionary. Holbrooke did not approve of Salzberg's having done what the embassy did not want. "He really chewed me out," says Salzberg. "He said that my behavior had been unacceptable, inappropriate, disrespectful." That wasn't the only incident on the Korea trip that caused Holbrooke to resent Salzberg. During his press conference in Korea Holbrooke neglected to say anything about human rights in a country under one-man rule and with several hundred political prisoners. That "lapse" generated a letter from Representative Fraser to Vance critical of Holbrooke. Two years later Derian hired Salzberg. Holbrooke had not forgotten.

Salzberg quickly realized that the officers in the East Asia section wouldn't talk to him. One day he learned why. "John, this is nothing personal," the Indonesian desk officer told him, "but we have instructions not to talk to you." The instructions had come from Holbrooke. No one on the staff was to talk with Salzberg, not even to return his phone calls. Then, while Derian was on vacation in Maine, Holbrooke took up the issue with Warren Christopher, Vance's principal deputy, and Vance himself. The result: Salzberg was transferred to the African section of the Human Rights Bureau, another victory for Holbrooke, a loss for the human rights effort in Asia.

Holbrooke maintains that he was as committed to human rights as Derian was, that the difference between them was that she was myopically fixed on human rights as the only plank in American foreign policy while he had to be concerned about America's security and economic interests along with human rights. "I had a very complex tightrope to walk," Holbrooke says, "between the human rights people and the Pentagon." Derian and her staff are convinced that he fell off, into the laps of the generals, and the list of human rights accomplishments in the Philippines is short.

While saying that "overall" the Carter human rights record was "impressive," the Center for International Policy, a liberal Washington-based research organization, concluded that "in Asia, especially Korea and the Philippines, Carter's policies and actions were only cosmetically better than those of his predecessors Richard Nixon and Gerald Ford." The center's conclusions reflect the extent to which Holbrooke retreated from Carter's human rights policy, more than other assistant secretaries, and his effectiveness in implementing the policy he wanted.

Though he was locked in constant battle with Derian, Holbrooke did not express public opposition to the principles of Carter's human rights policy, and even in private he was guarded. Not until after he left the administration did he lash out. Appearing before a congressional committee in 1982, Holbrooke charged that the human rights advocates within the administration had been guilty of "preachy moralism" and "excesses." They were, he said, "ideologues of the left." Lumping them with "isolationists of the far right," he accused them all of sharing a "common arrogance" in the belief that the United States "has the right, perhaps even the obligation, to attempt to restructure the world." Within the Carter bureaucracy, he continued, there had been those who sought to use the human rights policy as "American pressure to change governments." He was careful not to mention Derian by name, but there was no doubt that she was the object of his barbs. He also didn't explain what was wrong with trying to change a government, such as the Argentine junta, Marcos, or South Korea's Park, and though he condemned trying to restructure the world, he was supporting Reagan's contra war to change the Sandinista government in Nicaragua. Holbrooke also informed the committee that he didn't think much of the human rights report which Congress requires the State Department to submit each year. The reports, he said, were "morally arrogant" and "politically undesirable."

Some of his friends and former colleagues thought that in expressing these rather harsh views, Holbrooke was striving to keep in step with the conservative swing in American politics in 1982. Derian and her associates were convinced, however, that this had always been how Holbrooke felt about human rights, that while serving Carter, he had kept them private. His strident views in 1982 may have reflected a little of both.

Whatever the explanation, the differences between Holbrooke

and Derian were profound, and it was in the Philippines that the feud between them was most visibly played out. While he labeled her an "ideologue of the far left" and thought she did damage to U.S.-Philippine relations, she considered him "a supplicant for Marcos." As far as she was concerned, Holbrooke had been bewitched by the Marcoses from the very beginning.

Holbrooke was exposed to the manner in which the Marcoses, particularly Mrs. Marcos, snared and seduced American policy-makers on his first trip abroad as assistant secretary, the same one during which he had encountered Salzberg and failed to comment on the human rights abuses in South Korea. From Korea, Holbrooke flew to Manila, where he was met at the airport by the first lady's brother Kokoy Romualdez—"unexpectedly," the embassy reported. No one should have been surprised. Romualdez would surely be on hand to begin massaging this powerful new person from Washington who could affect the Marcoses' future. The Filipino told Holbrooke that he really ought to spend "informal" time with Marcos, just relaxing, getting to know him. While Holbrooke was touring the American military installations at Subic and Clark, for the briefings about the importance of the bases to American security, a message came from Marcos that Holbrooke should scrap his schedule for the next day (it was already set) and pass a night and day aboard the presidential yacht. Ambassador Sullivan was also invited, but he "begged off"; he had had enough of the Marcoses and knew what these outings were all about. It was a twenty-four-hour revelry of waterskiing, dancing, singing. "A lot of frivolity," Holbrooke recalled. The ever-attentive and effective Imelda Marcos had learned that it would soon be Holbrooke's thirty-sixth birthday; she threw a surprise party for him.

What he discussed during his meetings with the Philippine president, his wife, and other top Philippine government officials was classified Secret when it was reported back to Washington. And though some parts of the reporting cable have been released, the bulk was still being withheld more than a decade later. According to Holbrooke—and the released portions of the cable support him—he used the visit to raise human rights issues, including once during a private meeting with Marcos aboard the yacht. In particular, Holbrooke urged Marcos to release Aquino, Osmeña, and Lopez, who had now been in jail for nearly five years. More generally, Holbrooke sought to explain President Carter's human rights policy. He noted that the new administration had not singled out any Asian country for human rights criticism, but he added pointedly that Carter's "willingness to remain reticent is limited" and that at some point he "would have to speak out."

Carter never did speak out against the Marcos government, but for the first few months of his administration there was some activity by the American embassy in Manila which offered hope to the victims of repression.

The first visible suggestion that the human rights rhetoric had some weight came in May 1977 and involved a prisoner named Trinidad Herrera, a wiry thirty-five-year-old political organizer in one of Manila's largest slums, on the edge of the industrial port north of downtown Manila. She had been picked up and jailed but had not been charged. Charles Salmon, a mid-level embassy political officer, was heading off for a weekend of scuba diving and snorkeling off Mindoro when he was alerted by a Philippine priest about Mrs. Herrera's plight. After informing Washington, Salmon went to the beach. Upon returning on Monday, he found instructions from Washington to follow up; he and another embassy officer proceeded to the military camp at Bicutan Rehabilitation Center where Mrs. Herrera was being held. They found her in a state of near shock. She claimed that at one point, after being stripped naked, she was forced to wind an electrode wire around her nipple. A few days after Salmon's visit she was released.

The embassy's intervention in the Herrera case became a symbol. It was cited at the time, and long after, in press stories and in studies of Carter's policies as evidence that the administration had vigorously pursued its human rights goals in the Philippines. In human rights work, symbols are important, and this direct action in behalf of a Philippine political prisoner was dramatic, probably without precedent and certainly something that would not have happened during the Ford and Nixon administrations. Nevertheless, too much has been made of the Herrera case as representative of Carter's human rights policy in the Philippines. Hers was a special

191

situation, which even the Foreign Service officers involved acknowledge. Her activities on behalf of the poor had made her well known in the Philippines and the United States. On a visit to Manila Congressman Fraser had met with her. When word of her detention reached Washington, his office began making inquiries to the State Department. Thus, her release was as much an example of the benefit of knowing people in high places as it was a manifestation of a vigorous human rights policy. The Carter administration did not follow up with efforts to secure the release of the several thousand political prisoners being detained and in many cases tortured in Marcos's jails (except for overtures for the release of Aquino, Lopez, and Osmeña, who had become international symbols of Marcos's dictatorship).

It wasn't the fault of the embassy in Manila that more wasn't done. Indeed, the embassy had other ideas for advancing Carter's human rights policy. But it quickly discovered that Washington's enthusiasm for human rights was not even lukewarm. It was icy, and Lee T. Stull, the man in charge of the embassy between the departure of Ambassador Sullivan in April 1977 (he went to Iran) and the arrival of David Newsom in November, collided with Holbrooke.

Stull, who had spent eleven months as a POW after being shot down during the invasion of Normandy in World War II, had joined the Foreign Service in 1949, after graduating with honors from Princeton University's Woodrow Wilson School of Public and International Affairs. He was filled with idealistic visions. "I wanted to be a diplomat. If you will, I wanted to be a peacemaker," he says. There is a long, reflective pause. "That's a very dangerous aspiration." His career was marked by clashes with men of more power. In 1968 he opposed the resumption of military aid to Pakistan, which was preparing for war against India; a favorable performance report was removed from his personnel file, replaced by a negative one. But that was mild compared to what happened after he had come out early and strongly against the Nixon/Kissinger tilt toward Pakistan in 1971. For that bit of independence and dissent, Stull was placed on Nixon's "enemies list," the only person on that list who had a diplomatic address: New Delhi, where he was political counselor.

Stull's appointment as acting ambassador in the Philippines came by virtue of Imelda Marcos's power and petulance and the Carter administration's refusal to stand up to her. Ambassador Sullivan was to have been replaced with Arthur Hummel, who had been Ford's assistant secretary for East Asia. But Mrs. Marcos wanted someone with more élan and social cachet than Hummel, a career diplomat born and reared in China by American parents. She wanted Lloyd Hand, who had been LBJ's protocol officer and whom she had met at the Manila Summit in 1966. Of course, she couldn't state those reasons directly, so Marcos's foreign minister, Carlos Romulo, made some specious objections to something that Hummel had said about the bases and the mutual defense treaty between the United States and the Philippines.

The young Carter administration was taken aback by the Philippine resistance to Hummel. It is highly unusual for any country to refuse to accept another country's diplomat; it is almost unheard of when the two countries are friends and allies. It wasn't that other countries didn't sometimes try to influence U.S. ambassadorial appointments. Colombia, for instance, also resisted Carter's choice for ambassador but eventually backed down when the president held firm.* There wasn't any merit to the Philippine opposition to Hummel, an Asian specialist who later became Reagan's ambassador to China, but the Carter administration capitulated to the Marcoses. Holbrooke also benefited in the internal bureaucratic wars. Hummel had been the choice of Philip Habib, who was at once Holbrooke's mentor and rival. With Hummel out, Holbrooke could name his own man, someone who would owe him loyalty. While all this was going on in Washington, Stull, who was the deputy chief of mission, became the chargé d'affaires for about six months.

Stull took what Carter said about human rights seriously. "It's not a moral issue," says Stull. "I didn't figure I was earning points with St. Peter because I had done good things in the Philippines.

---

* Carter's choice was José Cabranes. He was rejected by the Colombians because of some bad experiences with a previous ambassador who had been sent because of his Hispanic background. This time the Colombians wanted a professional diplomat. After the administration held firm and Colombia backed down, Cabranes decided he didn't want the post. Carter eventually named him a federal judge in Connecticut; Diego Asencio was sent to Bogotá, where he was seized when guerrillas in jogging gear took over the embassy there.

. . . I wasn't paid to moralize. As a diplomat I am there as a communicator. A policy emphasis had been asserted by my authorities. . . ." But he also believed in the policy. As he saw it, the United States should compete with the Soviet Union by playing to America's strengths—freedom and democracy. If that sounds a bit naïve to the practitioners of realpolitik, there is also a practical component of the human rights policy. As Stull explains, "We can deal more comfortably, more confidently with governments rooted in consensus than with governments that have built into their structure a significant portion of dissent."

Stull seized a tense moment and a dance to broach the sensitive human rights issue with Mrs. Marcos. During a private party someone at the table began to harangue Stull about American policy in the Philippines. He was saved from having to respond when the band struck up a song. "Shall we dance?" Stull asked, turning to Mrs. Marcos. While the lanky diplomat and the first lady twirled on the floor, he whispered into her ear that there were a number of serious matters he would like to discuss with her but that he didn't feel comfortable doing so with so many people around. We should have lunch, Mrs. Marcos suggested. "Your place or mine?" Stull said jokingly. Stull informed Washington about his conversations with Mrs. Marcos in a cable which diplomats long after remembered with amusement for Stull's reference to his having "danced with a lady last night." Then, a few days later, it was lunch at Stull's residence with Mrs. Stull present. Stull presented Mrs. Marcos with a one-page memorandum of itemized suggestions of what the Philippine government could do to enhance its image with the new administration and the U.S. Congress. He was making similar suggestions in meetings with Marcos. He also delivered numerous speeches in public forums about human rights.

Stull also directly confronted Marcos on the issue of human rights. In what Stull described as "not an easy meeting" during which Marcos displayed "considerable agitation beneath the controlled exterior," Stull told Marcos that the police unit in Manila was "permeated from the top down by personnel, attitudes and practices that condone, support and protect the regular use of torture to extract information from prisoners." When charges of torture were filed by victims, it was "customary" that investigations were thwarted, as in the cases, Stull bluntly told the president, of "one lieutenant 'hot iron' specialist . . . and one notorious major. . . ."

These human rights activities by Stull were "on his own initiative" and had been pursued by him in his "characteristically energetic fashion," an evaluation in his personnel file reads. Because of Stull's "skill as a negotiator and persuader," the evaluation says, there had been some improvements in the human rights situation in the Philippines during his tenure as chargé.

Stull's experience rebuts the standard diplomatic opposition to an aggressive human rights policy, which is the fear that it will lead to tensions between the criticized government and Washington. In spite of all that Stull did, energetically and aggressively, U.S.-Philippine relations, which had been "correct but not overly cordial" during Sullivan's tenure, improved under Stull. Marcos even began calling him by his first name, uncharacteristic behavior by the Philippine president, and, upon Stull's departure, warmly invited him to return.

With all that, it might have been thought that Stull would receive one of the department's awards. Instead, he was left out in the cold and eventually took early retirement. It is customary for a returning deputy chief of mission, especially one who has also served for a period as ambassador, to be debriefed upon leaving his post. When Stull returned to Washington at the end of his tour in Manila, Holbrooke did not ask to see him. Moreover, the efficiency report which is supposed to be placed in the personnel file was not completed about his performance as chargé. Above all, he was not given a significant new assignment.

What caused his problems is not clear. Stull thinks it was in part because of his clashes with Holbrooke. Holbrooke wanted to rein in Stull's activist approach, and Stull objected when Holbrooke tried to send out James Rafferty, whom Sullivan had dismissed a couple of years previously, as part of a moral renovation of the embassy. Holbrooke insists that he did not block any new assignment for Stull. The reasons for Stull's failure to receive a promotion may be found in the personnel evaluation (which was completed in lieu of the efficiency report). "In his vigorous administration of the mission, Stull exerted more policy initiative than is customary in a Chargé d'Affaires," the evaluation states. "In fact, some of the senior officers in the Department felt that in some cases he had acted with a little too much zeal." Aggressiveness is not a trait generally rewarded in the diplomatic corps, and when there is at the top someone as strong as Holbrooke, who wants to set the course, neither is policy initiative.

By June 1977, only two months after Holbrooke's visit, "Washington was exhibiting nervousness about even the phased and deliberate human rights approach being pursued by the Embassy," Stull wrote later. After Stull had informed Washington about his human rights discussion with Marcos and asked for guidance, Holbrooke responded, in a highly classified cable (presumably to prevent a leak), that "the intensity of our dialogue with Marcos on human rights is all that the traffic will bear at present time." As a result, according to Stull, within six months after Carter had been sworn in, Marcos was "reasonably confident of deflecting the American human rights thrust with little more than the cosmetic changes of which he was a master."

As was the case in its dealings with so many other countries, the Carter administration was backing off from its strong human rights policy. It was sending mixed signals, speaking eloquently about human rights but not acting to implement the words. At the Notre Dame University commencement in May 1977 Carter "reaffirmed America's commitment to human rights as a fundamental tenet of our foreign policy." Yet in the same month his administration supported $88 million in World Bank loans to the Philippines without a peep about human rights. It was one particular World Bank loan to the Philippines which revealed the split between the rhetoric and reality of the human rights policy, as well as the differences between Stull and Holbrooke.

The State Department, over Derian's objections, had decided to vote in favor of the loan—$15 million for rural development—but at the same time it wanted to let Marcos know that it intended to take human rights matters into account when voting on these loans, thereby implying that in the future the vote might be no. Stull, who was enthusiastic about this approach, was instructed to deliver that message. When the loan first came up for consideration during bank deliberations, a vote was postponed because the representative from Canada wanted to register a protest about the torture of Mrs. Herrera. Meanwhile, in meetings with the Philippine finance minister and other top officials, Stull was delivering the message that if the human rights situation didn't improve in the Philippines, the Carter administration might vote against loans. According to the plan, the U.S. representative to the World Bank was to make the same statement when the $15 million loan was voted on. "Wow!" says Stull. "It would really carry a message." But when the vote came, in May, the United States voted yes, and the representative was silent.

Stull fired off a cable to Washington. "Much Ado in Manila; Zilch in Washington" was the subject. "The Department's total failure to follow through" with a statement about human rights and bank loans, Stull wrote, "has left us in limbo dangling a dud with credibility damaged, and far from the intended signal conveyed." He concluded his brief message: "Human rights in the Philippines is too important an issue for this kind of mismanagement."

It was blunt, all too blunt for Holbrooke. It was one thing for Sullivan to send graphic cables. Holbrooke didn't much care for Sullivan, but Sullivan had too many of his own power bases within the department for Holbrooke to exercise any control over him. Holbrooke was not, however, about to have another outspoken man in Manila. "He really rapped my knuckles," Stull recalled.

Some weeks after Holbrooke's knuckle rapping, Stull received a cable from Washington. Headed "Apologies on the Zilch," it was an apology—but not for the administration's having failed to speak about human rights during the meeting on the loan, only for the department's not having informed the embassy in advance that it was going to remain silent. At that it wasn't from Holbrooke's office but from Derian's. "Please continue efforts to keep us in line," it concluded.

In Washington a committee at the State Department struggled to keep the department's actions in line with the expressed human rights policy and to ensure compliance with the myriad and somewhat complex provisions of the human rights laws, most of which had only recently been enacted. In addition to the prohibitions on bilateral aid from the United States to a country that was violating human rights, Congress, in 1977, mandated that the U.S. representative at the nonprofit multilateral development banks must vote against loans to any country that was a gross violator of human rights unless the assistance would be used to provide for "basic human needs" of the people of that country.*

The committee's formal name was the Interagency Group on Human Rights and Foreign Assistance; it became known as the Christopher committee, named for the chairman Warren Christopher, whom Vance had brought into the department as his chief deputy. Christopher was a lawyer, low-key and self-effacing, who moved back and forth between public service and corporate law with a prominent Los Angeles firm. During the Johnson administration he had been deputy attorney general. Under Carter he was to become the principal negotiator in the Iranian hostage crisis, a role for which he was particularly well suited, not only because of his skills as a mediator but because he believed in being neither seen nor heard. He declined so much as to whisper about anything internal, let alone reveal any secrets. Even though Derian and the Human Rights Bureau lost frequently in the Christopher committee, she and her deputies retained their respect for him. Patiently and incisively probing, Christopher presided over the committee.

It met, at his call, in the seventh-floor conference room. Representatives from the State Department's geographic bureaus, the Joint Chiefs of Staff, the National Security Council, the Export-Import Bank, and the Treasury, Agriculture, Commerce, and Labor departments gathered, on an irregular basis, to thrash about in search of a policy that would be in line with the president's statements about human rights and the congressional laws on the subject. The issue would be framed in a neutral presentation by Lake's Policy Planning Staff. Then the geographic bureau would present its case in support of the loan or aid package, or whatever it was that was being considered, followed by the Human Rights Bureau's arguments in opposition. Then came the debate and shouting. Was the

---

* These development banks, often referred to collectively as the international financial institutions, are the International Bank for Reconstruction and Development (better known as the World Bank); International Development Association; Inter-American Development Bank; African Development Fund; and Asian Development Bank (headquartered on Roxas Boulevard, just south of the American embassy, in Manila).

country a "gross violator of human rights"? Was it engaged in a
"consistent pattern" of human rights violations? Or was the torture
the aberrations of a few sadistic soldiers? Was the loan for "basic
human needs" (a BHN loan, as it was called in abbreviation-prone
Washington), in which case it would be approved regardless of the
country's human rights record? If military aid was involved, one
question was if it was going to be used for abetting the repression,
as, say, pistols might, or if it was for national defense, such as
F-14 jets.

Holbrooke found the Christopher meetings "some of the most
ugly, contentious meetings I ever attended." His reaction may be
attributable to his having lost one encounter with Christopher over
aid to Marcos. Holbrooke argued that the Marcos government was
not a gross violator of human rights. Christopher disagreed. It was
a moment that the Human Rights Bureau cherished. It was also the
last meeting Holbrooke attended, after that sending aides. There is
some question about just how important the meetings were; some
within the department saw the principal purpose of the Christopher
committee to give Derian a forum and at the same time to control
her.

In spite of Marcos's human rights record and the opposition of
Derian and the Human Rights Bureau, the Philippines fared quite
well before the Christopher committee. For the period between May
1977 and September 1980 the Carter administration voted on sixty-
one multilateral development bank loans. The United States never
voted no. It abstained on only eleven loans, which amounted to a
total of $267.6 million. The administration approved fifty, which
added up to $1.9 billion. Military aid also continued to flow, largely
unimpeded, in spite of objections by the Human Rights Bureau,
which seemed intent on shutting off the flow totally but which usually
lost to the other bureaus that wanted to send everything.

A typical debate, and resolution, involved the Philippine request
for submachine-gun pistols, small arms manufacturing equipment,
three sixty-five-foot patrol boats (worth $35.4 million), and fifty-one
armed infantry fighting vehicles ($15.9 million). The Human Rights
Bureau was opposed across the board. But Holbrooke's East Asian
Bureau, along with Policy Planning and the Politico-Military Bureau, favored all the items. Christopher denied the pistols and the

arms manufacturing equipment but approved the patrol boat and light tanks (and even the decision on the first two items was later reversed because of fear that it would jeopardize the bases negotiations). The decision had the ironic, if not perverse, effect of giving to Marcos the big items while denying him the little ones. It was also a reflection of the burden placed on the human rights staff: Rather than those who favored military aid having to justify the need, opponents had to show that the aid was going to be used to advance repression.

The debate about how to implement the human rights policy was misdirected, focusing on minutiae rather than broader concepts. A dictator is not going to end his repressive practices just because he has been denied a loan or an AID project, a few pistols or bullets, or even planes or tanks. The denial of those things might result in some cosmetic changes, the punishment of a token soldier for torturing someone or the release of some political prisoners. But even if it does, this form of diplomatic bribery—the "carrots," as they are often called—encourages the smart dictator to go out and seize more people, then release them in exchange for more aid. While there are justifiable reasons for denying aid on human rights grounds— it probably keeps people alive—something more fundamental has to occur if the objective is to bring about lasting, structural changes in a repressive government. "It's not the materials; it's the political symbols," says Mark Schneider, who worked on human rights and foreign policy issues as a Senate aide before becoming Derian's deputy. "And if you can't make them clear and convincing, then you lose." A dictator has to be convinced that the entire political relationship between his country and the United States is at stake; that if the repression doesn't stop, that if he doesn't open up his country to democracy, he is jeopardizing not just a few more trinkets but his country's good relations with Washington. That's something nearly every dictator needs and desperately pursues. Marcos never believed that his standing in Washington was in peril—with good reason.

Maybe the Marcoses were not treated and received by the Carter administration as they would have liked, but they were accorded more respect and audiences than as corrupt dictators they deserved from an administration with a strong human rights platform. Imelda Marcos was in the White House on five or six occasions for meetings with Vice President Walter Mondale, meetings about which Derian was not consulted or even advised.* She was always pushing for more meetings, but "I had other duties as Vice President," says Mondale, who remembered little about what was discussed except that Mrs. Marcos always seemed to be rambling on about the Communists and how her husband was the only man who could prevent them from taking over the country. Imelda Marcos also managed a meeting with Carter on at least one occasion, possibly two.

Their first meeting was in October 1977 in New York. She had come as the representative of the Philippine government to address the opening of the UN General Assembly, an honor usually reserved for the venerable Carlos Romulo, a cofounder of the United Nations in 1945 and Marcos's foreign minister. Romulo was "downgraded this year in favor of Mrs. Marcos," the U.S. embassy reported. Mrs. Marcos came to New York not only to speak but also to spend. On one day alone, October 13, she parted with $384,000, including a platinum bracelet with rubies for $50,000; a diamond bracelet for $50,000; a pin set with diamonds for $58,000. On the previous day her private secretary in New York, Vilma Bautista, had laid out $18,500 for a gold pendant with diamonds and emeralds; $12,900 for gold ear clips with diamonds and emeralds; $9,450 for a gold ring, with diamonds and emeralds; and $4,800 for a gold and diamond necklace. Two weeks later, on November 2, Mrs. Marcos spent $450,000 for a gold necklace and bracelet with emeralds, rubies, and diamonds; $300,000 for a gold ring with emeralds and diamonds; and another $300,000 for a gold pendant with diamonds, rubies, and thirty-nine emeralds: more than $1 million in one day. It was close to the same amount she and her husband had six days earlier donated to Tufts University in Boston. The $1.5 million was to endow a professional chair in East Asian and Pacific studies at the Fletcher School of Law and Diplomacy. Sinners and gangsters try to buy their way into heaven with large donations to churches. Dictators try to purchase respectability. Tufts presented Mrs. Marcos, on October 27, with a certificate for her "deep humane concern."†

---

* When I asked Derian about the meetings with Mondale during an interview in the summer of 1986, she said, "I never heard about them. Not till this moment."

† When students and professors learned of the gift and award, which had been kept secret, they protested; eventually the university rejected the Marcos funds, but it did hold several conferences and seminars with money from the Marcoses.

Mrs. Marcos's meeting with President Carter was an event which, much to the relief of the administration, the American press failed to cover. The Marcos-controlled Philippine press did, however, for it was a major coup for the Marcos regime—America's moralist, principled president meeting with Mrs. Marcos. They had expected that of Nixon, but not of Carter, not on the basis of all that he had said about human rights. President Marcos had raised the possibility of the meeting with Holbrooke when the latter was in Manila. The assistant secretary notified Washington in a highly classified cable— Secret and not for distribution except to Vance and Brzezinski. The tight security had nothing to do with the contents but everything to do with the administration's desire to keep the press and the public from knowing that Carter would be meeting with Mrs. Marcos. The restriction on distribution also meant that Derian would not know about the proposed visit. Holbrooke urged that Carter meet with her, noting in his cable that "her power and authority are unquestionable." Vance and Brzezinski agreed to the meeting. Derian, who, as the date grew closer, learned of the meeting, opposed it, without success, of course, and the bureau was not even allowed to submit "talking points" (short, snappy memos enumerating the issues that should be discussed). But human rights were not the principal matter on the agenda. Imelda Marcos was granted the meeting in large measure because she brought with her a letter from her husband about the American bases in the Philippines.

9 : The Bases

America's military bases overseas have frequently been the lodestone for the nation's foreign policy, bending it on a course away from democracy. When the right-wing colonels seized democracy from its cradle in Greece in 1967, most European democracies distanced themselves, but not the Johnson administration, which recognized the junta, negotiating with it for the home porting of the American navy's Sixth Fleet. Francisco Franco ruled Spain for three decades with Washington's blessing in exchange for air and naval bases. And in the Philippines the bases had always exerted a heavy pull on the American policy. But during the Carter administration those bases became the tail wagging the policy dog.

There seemed to be little in the bilateral relationship that wasn't tied to the bases, specifically to a renegotiation of the agreement signed in 1947 which set the terms for the existence of the American bases on Philippine territory. Holbrooke's drive and talents were propelled toward that end. He pushed for a renewal of the negotiations which had stalled under Ford and Kissinger; then he shuttled to and from Manila when they bogged down, always remaining attentive to Congress so that when an agreement was reached, the funding body wouldn't buck. A forceful policy calling for a return to democracy was sacrificed to a successful renegotiation; human rights criticisms were muted lest they anger Marcos into a hard-line position on the bases. Multinational development bank loans were approved and military equipment was dispatched because of the bases. "We wanted those bases, and if Marcos knew how much we wanted those bases, he might have gotten more out of us," Holbrooke says. As it was, Marcos got a great deal; the first year alone of the new bases agreement saw a 300 percent increase in military and security assistance. And Marcos gave up virtually nothing, certainly nothing that went to the basis of his power.

As General Eisenhower had foreseen three decades earlier, the American bases in the Philippines became sand in the oil of smooth U.S.-Philippine relations. Their sheer size alone were gaping reminders of the American colonial era, a suggestion that Uncle Sam hadn't really ever left or that if he had, he had placed boulders on the dirt path to independence and sovereignty. Clark Air Base, home to the Thirteenth Air Force, is, in area, the fourth-largest U.S. Air Force base on foreign soil.* With a two-mile-long runway, a parking area large enough for 200 aircraft, Clark can accommodate any aircraft in the air force fleet and has been the home for two F-4 tactical fighter squadrons. A forty-three-mile pipeline runs across Luzon, connecting Clark with the naval supply depot at Subic, which has the capacity to store 110 million gallons of petroleum and lubricants. Subic comprises eighteen square miles (golf course and riding stables included), plus forty square miles of a naturally protected deep harbor. With three wharves and three floating dry docks, Subic has been home port for the U.S. Seventh Fleet, with its full panoply of aircraft carriers, destroyers, submarines, and guided missile cruisers.

Olongapo and Angeles City, the towns that sprang up outside the gates of Subic and Clark respectively, were, and are, seedy districts of honky-tonk bars, strip joints, and massage parlors, maybe no more offensive than other port districts, but that's hardly any consolation to Filipinos. In 1966 Olongapo was a sleepy waterfront town of 40,000; a decade later, as a result of the military buildup begun during the Vietnam War, it was up to 200,000. The town had no industrial base. The biggest employers, after the U.S. military, were the bars, across the fetid canal from the entrance to the base, stocked with teenage prostitutes ("hospitality girls," the euphemism). During briefings for congressional delegations in the 1970s

---

* It is usually said and written that Clark is the largest overseas American air base. In fact, however, the largest is Sonderstrom (462,284 acres), in Greenland, followed by Thule (338,884 acres), also in Greenland. Prior to 1979 the area of Clark that belonged to the United States was 131,000 acres; by virtue of the 1979 agreement about 90 percent of the land reverted to Philippine control, leaving 9,082 acres for the United States. Howard Air Base in Panama is 14,078 acres.

military officers, while ticking off the impressive numbers about the sizes of the ships, the depth of the water, the number of gallons of paint on the hulls, would add, just as seriously, how a sailor could, for $15 or $20 at the most, buy dinner and a girl. It was a sordid two-way street between American servicemen and Filipinos. Periodic assaults on Filipinos by the servicemen reinforced the sense that Americans still considered Filipinos their "little brown brothers." A marine sentry who shot a Filipino boy on a bicycle claimed he thought it was a wild boar. Few American servicemen were ever punished because under the terms of the agreement signed in 1947, the United States retained jurisdiction over virtually all criminal matters, whether committed on the base or by its servicemen off base.

Provision by provision, the U.S.-Philippine bases agreement of 1947 was a contract of adhesion, the terms imposed by a big power on a weak one, unfair even in the abstract, more offensive when compared to America's arrangements with other countries. In Spain, the country to which the Philippines understandably felt the most kinship, the bases were considered Spanish territory that was used by Americans. Spanish sovereignty was acknowledged by the flying of the Spanish flag and by the fact that Spanish military officers were the base commanders. It was the opposite in the Philippines: American flag; American commanders. In the 1950s Senator Recto, the man the CIA wanted to assassinate, had been a lone voice of criticism about the unequal nature of the agreement in the Philippines. By the 1970s the merit of the objections was sinking in, taken up not just by the Communists and strident nationalists but by a broader sweep of leaders, men and women with unassailable democratic credentials: former President Macapagal, university presidents, nuns, and businessmen. To them the bases were an affront to Philippine sovereignty, independence, and national development.

Marcos had been posturing about the bases since assuming office, his oratorical flourishes aimed at two audiences, one domestic, the other Asian. He wanted to assuage his nationalist critics at home. And he was making a bid for himself and his nation to become recognized and respected as leaders in the third world. The price of acceptance as a third world leader was less dependence on the United States and greater neutrality, in rhetoric, if not in reality.

205

The Bangkok Declaration, which gave birth, in 1967, to the Association of Southeast Asian Nations (ASEAN),* provided that foreign bases in all the countries "are only temporary." Imelda Marcos was also, the CIA reported, "behind some of the more strident anti-U.S. rhetoric about the bases," reflecting her "fascinations with the third world," which had developed during her globe-trotting.

In spite of the rhetoric, what Marcos really wanted was what he always wanted: money. Or, as it was put in a Secret/Sensitive National Security memorandum in 1976, he wanted "some form of compensation for use of the bases, such as rent or a guaranteed level of military assistance."

But the Pentagon doesn't pay "rent," not in the Philippines or elsewhere. It's not because the generals are being frugal, protecting the Treasury against raids by foreign rulers. Rather, the American position has always been that its foreign bases, in the Philippines, Greece, Spain, Turkey, Germany, Britain, virtually everywhere, are for the mutual benefit, the mutual defense of the host country and the United States. "We do not pay rent to any of our defense treaty allies, and to do so would seem out of keeping with the spirit of an alliance," Kissinger explained in a Secret briefing paper for President Ford. U.S. military assistance, Washington stresses, is not a quid pro quo for the bases but the aid that the United States would provide to a friendly government for its needs even if there weren't any bases.

But it is financial semantics to say that the United States doesn't pay rent in the Philippines. It might be called military assistance or security assistance or economic aid. In reality, it's rent. "I am sure they recognize, and we do, that military assistance is in return for our bases over there," the assistant secretary of defense for military assistance and sales, Lieutenant General Robert H. Warren, told the Senate Subcommittee on U.S. Security Agreements and Commitments Abroad in a closed-door session in 1969. He added, with a candor that the secrecy of the proceedings allowed, "And, as a practical matter, I think it is really in the form of rent."

That the bases are for the mutual defense of the Philippines and

---

* The original nations were the Philippines, Thailand, Malaysia, Indonesia, and Singapore, with tiny Brunei joining after acquiring independence in 1984.

the United States is another myth. Not since the end of World War II has there been any external threat to the Philippines that justifies the need for either Clark or Subic. In the late sixties China was seen as the "principal threat" to the Philippines, according to the assessment of the Mutual Defense Board, which had been set up in 1958 to coordinate the military activities of the United States and the Philippines. But even that threat was considered "very small, very small," the commander of all American forces in the Pacific (CINCPAC), Rear Admiral Draper L. Kauffman, testified in 1969. Under probing by Senator Stuart Symington, Kauffman acknowledged that indeed, China presented no threat at the moment, only that it might sometime in the future. But the future saw Imelda Marcos being feted in China, followed in 1975 by the two countries' establishing diplomatic relations, which, of course, the United States was also on the verge of doing. China was no longer an enemy; it was nearly everyone's friend. As for the Soviet Union, no one has seriously suggested that it presented any threat to the Philippines. If anything, Philippine-Soviet relations were better than Philippine-American relations, or at least that's how Mrs. Marcos felt. A frequent visitor to Russia, she once complained to Mondale, as she did to American diplomats and her friends, that she received a warmer reception in Moscow than in Washington. Marcos wasn't worried about the Chinese or the Russians. He believed that "the major threat to his security will be from internal subversion," the CIA noted in 1975. He was right. And though the threat was growing, *because* of Marcos, it was still not serious. Moreover, there was nothing in the bases agreement about allowing for the use of the bases against internal enemies, nor did the mutual defense agreement obligate the United States to defend the Philippine government against its own people, though the United States was in the 1970s, as it had been in earlier years, conducting clandestine anti-insurgency operations from the bases.

The reality is that the bases aren't for the Philippines. They are American bases. Their function is to advance American interests. They serve the same interests as the bases in Hawaii and Alaska, in Alabama and Wyoming. And they have always been American bases, for covert operations and overt wars. In the 1950s the U-2 spy plane flew some of its missions out of the Philippines. The CIA carried out operations against China from Subic during the mid-1950s. The CIA's clandestine support for the right-wing generals in Indonesia in 1958 was staged from Clark. At least since the early 1960s nuclear-powered ships have called at Subic, and planes with nuclear weapons have landed at Clark.

While the issue of removing the bases was never considered, for several years a number of technical panels, of American and Philippine representatives (lawyers, diplomats, politicians, and soldiers), did examine and in some cases modify various provisions of the complex 1947 agreement. The negotiations proceeded by fits and starts, often influenced by events in the United States. In the summer of 1974, when the Watergate investigations into Nixon and his activities were intensifying, Marcos saw no reason to negotiate with the Nixon administration if it wasn't going to survive.

Within a year helicopters were evacuating Americans from the roofs of embassies, first in Phnom Penh and quickly thereafter in Saigon, leaving behind the residue of America's long war, a new Southeast Asian political order, and questions about America's future in that part of the globe. Marcos, like other Asian leaders, was shaken by the American defeat, but in it he found opportunities.

The United States had no intention of turning away from the Pacific. It was a power there and would remain so. That message was first delivered in unequivocal military language. When the Cambodian government seized a U.S. merchant ship, the *Mayaguez,* in May 1975, President Ford reacted (some would say overreacted) by ordering U.S. Air Force jets to strafe Cambodian naval vessels and by sending in the marines on a rescue mission.* Six months later, during his visit to the region, Ford delivered the message that America would remain an Asian power. In Manila he and Marcos issued a joint communiqué calling for a reopening of the base negotiations.

---

* The air raids were launched from American bases in Thailand, and in reaction the Thai government accelerated its ouster of the American military. By the end of 1976 all American troops were out of Thailand and the vast network of American air bases built up during the Vietnam War had been closed. In the subsequent decade without the American military presence the country has not toppled to communism.

Though the issues negotiated were considerable in number—twenty-five substantive ones—most of them pertained to insignificant, arcane provisions of the agreement, such as if it should be authentic in both English and Tagalog. All that Marcos really wanted was "some cosmetic changes," Ford's national security adviser, Brent Scowcroft, was advised in a Secret/Sensitive memorandum, so that he could "counter third world criticism that they [Filipinos] do not have control of the bases on their sovereign territory." Thus, the key issues were a Philippine flag over the bases, a Philippine officer in command of the bases, and responsibility for external security in the hands of Filipino soldiers. Since these were the same rights possessed by other countries that were landlords for American bases, the negotiations should have been swiftly concluded. They weren't. Not even the redoubtable William Sullivan, who assumed much of the negotiations himself, with regular back channel communications to Kissinger, was able to break the jam.

Finally, Kissinger, who had received the Nobel Peace Prize for his part in the negotiations that had finally ended the Vietnam War, got involved. But the negotiations were still at an impasse when Jimmy Carter defeated Ford in November 1976. Even though he was now a lame duck, Kissinger continued to negotiate. To some of the professionals at State and Defense it seemed inappropriate that an outgoing Republican administration would make agreements—and obligations amounting to hundreds of millions of dollars—which would bind the incoming Democratic one. At least, it was thought by many, Kissinger should have consulted with the new administration. He didn't. During a meeting in Mexico in late November for the inauguration of President José López Portillo, Kissinger offered Philippine Foreign Minister Romulo, with whom he had been negotiating, a compensation package of $1 billion in exchange for the use of the bases for the next five years. The offer jolted nearly everyone. Kissinger had pulled his offer "out of the blue," says Sullivan, ambassador at the time. In keeping with his usually secretive, independent manner, Kissinger hadn't even bothered to inform, much less consult with, the officials at the Defense Department or in the embassy who were carrying on the negotiations. The embassy learned about the offer only because the National Security Agency, which listens in on phone conversations around the world, had intercepted Romulo's message to Marcos about the Kissinger offer.*

Marcos rejected the offer, though exactly why has never been clear. The reason stated publicly at the time, which has since become the conventional history, was that he thought $1 billion was not enough, that he wanted at least $1 billion in military aid plus more in economic aid. But U.S. officials concluded that something deeper and more profound than dollars explained Marcos's rejection. Marcos understood the American political system as well as, if not better than, any third world leader ever has. In this case he knew that the incoming administration and especially the Congress might not feel bound by an agreement reached by the outgoing administration. So why should he sign it? When the deal finally signed with the Carter administration provided for $500 million in security assistance, it appeared that Marcos had made a blundering miscalculation, and the Carter administration boasted that it had better served American interests and taxpayers than Kissinger had. But military officers and diplomats who were involved in the negotiations during both administrations say that the two agreements were essentially the same. Kissinger's $1 billion figure, hastily thrown together for dramatic impact and without great analysis, included every single dollar of every one of the myriad U.S. aid programs in the Philippines, from the Peace Corps and Food for Peace to bullets and jets, and encompassed projects already funded and in the pipeline as well as future ones. The Carter deal was only for military aid and security assistance, excluding all the economic programs, and only included what was to come in the years ahead. In sum, as a Defense Department official who worked on the negotiations during both administrations says, "There was a lot of phoniness in Henry's deal; a lot of phoniness in Carter's deal. Essentially the two deals are the same."

In all the attention focused on the Philippine bases, the issue that requires the most rigorous debate has generally been ignored.

---

* It wasn't the only occasion on which American officials learned about Kissinger's activities from American spies. During the Vietnam peace negotiations the embassy in Saigon learned about an offer Kissinger had made to Le Duc Tho after a Vietnamese informant within the North Vietnamese government had reported to his CIA handler.

Does the United States need the bases? Can they be moved without jeopardizing American security? These would seem to be the most fundamental questions, to be answered before we become bogged down in how much the United States should pay for them. Given their commitment to expanding American military influence, conservatives tend not to ask these questions. And liberals have simply accepted the premise that the bases must remain, that they are strategically vital. Somehow the sense that there have always been American bases in the Philippines translates into an unthinking assumption that there always should be. "Just as there will always be a General Motors, so will there always be a Clark," an air force officer once said. Thus, liberals and conservatives have sought to fashion a Philippine policy around that given. This is so even though the arguments for moving the bases have been advanced not only by Philippine nationalists, anti-imperialist leftists, and American isolationists but as well by eminent and respected American public officials, civilian and military.

"Immediate, complete, resolute and wordless withdrawal." These words were written in 1977 by George Kennan, the man who had coldly dispensed with any "sentimentality" and "daydreaming" when declaring, in 1948, that the United States must maintain control in the Philippines in order to contain Soviet expansion. When Kissinger's billion-dollar offer was still afloat, Kennan proposed that the United States should bluntly tell Marcos what to do with his demands for a tribute, pack up the footlockers, hoist the anchors, fire up the engines, sail and fly to a new home. "I can see no reason at all to pay any tribute of this nature, whether it is a billion dollars or any other sum; nor can I see any reason why the bases should not be removed at once." The exclamation point was provided by the force of the man, the declarative simplicity of the sentence.

Kennan reasoned that in view of America's "naval and military interests in the region" there no longer appeared to be a "serious need" for the bases. It would therefore be "highly unsound, politically and psychologically, to get into the habit of paying this sort of financial price (which would surely rise with the years) for the privilege of retaining them." He was prescient in his parenthetical note. During the next round of negotiations, with the Reagan administration, Marcos upped the ante a few hundred million a year more,

211

and this time he prevailed without even a struggle. Turning to more philosophical, less strategic thoughts, Kennan commented: "The position of retaining on the territory of a small state military facilities which the government of that smaller state does not want there, and paying huge annual bribes as a form of hush money to keep the leaders of that state quiet and to cause them to accommodate themselves reluctantly, and for the moment, to this practice, is not a position in which the United States should ever choose to appear." Kennan's conclusions, succinctly stated in his book *The Cloud of Danger: Current Realities of American Foreign Policy,* were ignored.

If a person of Kennan's stature couldn't affect policy, it's no surprise that diplomats without his public acclaim couldn't. One who tried was Francis T. Underhill, the political counselor in Manila from 1968 to 1971. During his thirty-one-year Foreign Service career, which began after he had earned a master's from the Fletcher School of Law and Diplomacy and served as a navy lieutenant in the Pacific, Underhill had earned the respect of his peers as a "heavy thinker," and they were in awe of his mastery of cable writing. Byroade, the man who was an ambassador to six countries, considered Underhill the best political counselor who ever worked for him. Underhill knew and understood Southeast Asia, the countries, the people, the cultures. He served in Djakarta; as the officer in charge of Indonesia-Pacific island affairs in Washington; in Kuala Lumpur; back in Washington as the director of the Office of Southwest Pacific Affairs; then as the Indonesian country director. After Manila he was promoted to the number two post in Seoul, and in 1974 he was named ambassador to Malaysia.

"The necessity of maintaining the bases should not be considered as obvious and self-manifest" was how Underhill began a lengthy cable about the bases. "Those that support a base agreement should be required to state and defend their case, as of course should those who question the need for this kind of presence." Underhill was of the latter opinion, and he set out his case, carefully addressing the arguments usually advanced for maintaining the bases. He dispensed with the argument that the bases were needed if the United States intended to project its military power in the region by noting that the nations of Southeast Asia were "not threatened by conventional attack, but by internal subversion and insurgency." And "our ex-

212

perience" in Vietnam, he added cryptically, "has shown the severe limitations of our capacity to intervene successfully in such conflicts. . . ."*

But beyond all the strategic and geopolitical arguments, there was something else troubling about the bases. Underhill trenchantly summarized it in a long paragraph:

Our relations with the Philippines can never be normal while our bases remain. For the Filipinos they [the bases] create contradictions and strains which twist and warp every aspect of their attitudes toward us. On the one hand the bases symbolize the "special relationship" with us. . . . On the other hand the bases are also regarded as an affront to Philippine national pride, and a symbol of imperfect independence and continuing dependency. The Filipinos have long since persuaded themselves that the bases serve only U.S. interests and that their generous acceptance of a serious abridgment of their sovereignty has been inadequately recognized and shabbily rewarded. In the third world circles they yearn to join, the Filipinos are condemned and ostracized because of the bases, and the solatium they now seek they see as modest compensation for the obloquy they suffer on our account. Manuel Quezon [president from 1935 TO 1944] once said, "Better a country ruled like hell by Filipinos than one ruled like heaven by Americans." While Clark and Angeles, Subic and Olongapo are the Jekyll-Hyde sides of the same coin, for the Filipino they put the heaven and hell in stark, immediate, confidence-destroying contrast. The base relationship also helps to perpetuate in the Philippines a neurotic, manipulative, psychically crippling form of dependency. As a consequence it is a country that is difficult to take seriously. We acknowledge Philippine independence, but we still think of bases extraterritorially. Messages still move in our communications channels addressed to "Clark Field, P.I.," the P.I. standing for Philippine Islands, a geographic name as obsolete as "Batavia, Netherlands East Indies." . . .

Underhill had offered his views in response to a request from Mondale and Holbrooke during a meeting in January 1977 in Tokyo. It was Underhill's feeling that he had been asked to meet the new vice president because he was being considered for a high-level post.

---

* Underhill believed strongly that there should be a "scrutiny of the arguments pro and con by the Congress, the press, and the public." For that reason he included nothing in his cable "that cannot be in the public domain." Yet, in response to an FOIA request for the cable from this author, the State Department excised two paragraphs out of nineteen.

But when Underhill's views on the bases arrived in Washington, Holbrooke dismissed them as "stupid," "nutty." And Underhill's service as an ambassador to Malaysia was not followed by another ambassadorial post. Many of his colleagues are convinced that Underhill's views about the bases were the cause. Underhill isn't so certain, but the existence of that perception underscores the extent to which there is a belief within the Foreign Service that one pays a high price for nonconformity, for expressing views out of sync with those at the top.

Few diplomats have been willing to express other than the conventional view about the bases, which is that the United States has to remain on them. This is not surprising considering the strength and direction of the prevailing gales and the Pentagon's virtual veto power over ambassadorial assignments to the Philippines. It takes someone with the convictions of an Underhill or the iconoclasm of a Paul Kattenburg, the Foreign Service officer who was one of the first to see the folly in Vietnam, to express dissenting views. Kattenburg has advocated that the United States "withdraw from and permanently close the bases at Clark and Subic."

The military and geopolitical strategists, of course, have their arguments for maintaining the bases. The admirals present maps showing the sea-lanes and the Indian Ocean theater, slide shows of the big ships being serviced at Subic, and charts with the number of "sailing days" to various points of potential conflict (the Indian Ocean, the Middle East) from Subic, compared with, say, Singapore or the western coast of Australia, which are other possible locations for the American fleet. The generals note how many air miles closer to Korea and Japan the Philippines is, compared with Guam, where Clark might be relocated.

The soldiers' arguments cannot be dismissed lightly. Neither are they to be accepted on the strength of the impressive ribbons, medals, and stars trimming the uniforms of the men or of the aura surrounding their presentations, which are kept purposely complex with dizzying numbers and claims of secrecy, the message being that these are matters best left to the professional fighters. Moreover, there have been some discordant notes sounded, the loudest by a retired Navy admiral, Eugene R. La Rocque. According to him, the U.S. military bases in the Philippines "do not contribute significantly to either offensive or defensive actions by the U.S. in the

214

Western Pacific." La Rocque has been to the Pentagon and the military what Ralph Nader has been to corporations and consumer issues: a constantly questioning voice, irritating to the establishment, toppling shibboleths. Other military men agree with La Rocque, though few speak out.

The most exhaustive public examination of the bases issue by a military officer is a Ph.D. thesis by an air force officer, William E. Berry, Jr. A major when he did his doctoral work and later promoted to lieutenant colonel, Berry looks at the history of the bases and details the negotiations between 1976 and 1979. What is most striking about his thesis is what he doesn't write. Nowhere in the 528 pages is there an argument, strong or weak, that the bases must be maintained in the Philippines. And in congressional testimony in 1983, Berry, then an associate professor at the Air Force Academy, said, "The proper course for the United States to pursue is to seek alternative basing arrangements. . . ."

The proponents of keeping the bases in the Philippines also turn altruistic to support their position. The Chinese are said to want the bases to remain as a check on the Soviets, especially since they took over Cam Ranh Bay after the American retreat. The Soviets, on the other hand, want the bases to stay as a check on Chinese aggressions. Even if we accept the sincerity of these arguments, basing U.S. policy on what the two Communist powers want "seems a dubious rationale," as Underhill noted. It also posits an intriguing and somewhat alarming scenario: On whose side is the United States going to deploy the bases in the event of a war between the two great Communist powers? More realistically and insidiously, the Chinese and Russians may have reasons for wanting the American bases to remain in the Philippines which have nothing to doing with their fear of each other. Indeed, quite paradoxically, they may want the bases to remain because of their ideological war with the United States. The bases, the Communists argue to the third world, are manifestations of America's colonialist and imperialistic behavior. As Underhill put it, displaying a critical knowledge of Marxist-Leninist theory, the Chinese and Russians believe that "the bases will intensify the contradictions in U.S.-Philippines post-colonial relations, strengthen class struggle, and hasten the day of a revolutionary move toward socialism."

It's not just the Communists. All those friendly nations want

215

the U.S. presence as well: the Japanese; the Koreans; all the ASEAN countries. Everybody loves the U.S. military presence in the region—as long it is in the Philippines. That's the rub, at least to many Filipinos. None of these other countries, they note, as did Underhill, has been clamoring for the bases to be located on its soil, infringing on its sovereignty.

One country that would seem to be an appropriate location for the bases is Indonesia. It is far larger than the Philippines, has vastly more natural resources, including oil, and, strategically, commands the straits into both the South Pacific and Indian oceans. But since the country's independence from the Dutch in 1949, the Indonesian leaders have been far too independent even to entertain the thought of American bases on their soil, notwithstanding the fact that Indonesia was receiving almost as much security assistance from the United States in the 1970s as was the Philippines, another matter which understandably irritated Filipinos. There are other potential locations, in countries that have been more favorably disposed than Indonesia to the United States. The Pentagon has been particularly covetous of Cockburn Sound, near the western Australian city of Perth, for some of the functions performed at Subic. Singapore, 1,300 miles closer to the Indian Ocean than the Philippines and adjacent to the Strait of Malacca, is another alternative for some of the Subic ships and repair facilities.

While it would probably not be possible to find any other single port as ideal as Subic (thus necessitating relocating ships and functions to more than one location), moving Clark is a far easier matter. The case for closing Clark is also a stronger one. A congressional study completed early in the Carter administration concluded that Clark wasn't needed "unless the United States intends to maintain a capability to mount and support major military operations on the Southeast Asian mainland." The United States certainly wasn't about to do that, it seemed. That's what Nixon had declared at Guam, and Carter was even more intent on reducing U.S. military influence in Asia. Ambassador Sullivan and his successor, David Newsom, thought Clark could be relocated, expressing their views in highly classified cables and private talks. There wasn't anything daring or heretical about their positions. Highly classified Pentagon reports showed that the air force was prepared to move Clark—if it was ordered to by the president.

Though the Pentagon might acknowledge that it *could* move the bases, that wasn't the same as saying it *wanted* to do so. It would prefer the status quo, adopting change only if forced to. Thus, when, in 1985, the Joint Chiefs of Staff began looking very seriously at the Perth-Fremantle area in Australia, it was precipitated by a fear that the Communists might gain control of the Philippines. As long as Marcos was in control, no serious thought would be given to relocating. Just as businessmen are bullish on dictators, so are generals, in spite of the obvious paradox that the bases are intended to defend democracy.

A dictator is easier to deal with than a rambunctious democracy. "Agreements are much easier to strike when you have an authoritative figure in power such as President Marcos," said a State Department officer who was involved in the negotiations from 1975 to 1977. In the Philippines U.S. nuclear ships called and planes with their tactical nuclear weapons landed. Marcos was the only one who had to be informed. His approval could be purchased. If Filipinos tried to disagree, he could toss them in jail. It wasn't that easy in a democratic country, where the antinuclear movement could express itself, as the United States was to discover in New Zealand in 1985. Similarly, the U.S. military could conduct "training" exercises in the Philippines that might not be acceptable in democratic countries. Jets thunder low over Philippine villages during Cope Thunder exercises, providing realistic combat experience. Clark's Crow Valley, larger than the District of Columbia, is used for aerial bombing and gunnery practice. The Zambales Amphibious Training Area and the Tabones Training Complex at Subic provide sailors and marines "invaluable training," Colonel Berry observed, "for amphibious landings and air-to-surface bombing and ship-to-shore gunnery practice."

The folks around Perth, Australia, might not look kindly on the bombing of their land, might vote out of office the politicians who allowed the American gunnery practice, might organize protest marches and demonstrations. All these democratic exercises were circumscribed by Marcos. The restrictions applied to American military activities by Japan underscore the value, to the United States, of the Philippine bases. The United States is permitted to launch combat missions from bases in Japan only in support of Japan or South Korea. There are "essentially no restrictions by the Philippines on what we may use the bases for," a Defense Department official explained during a closed-door session.

Putting aside the political climate in the Philippines, and stripping away all the military jargon about sailing days and sea-lanes, one reaches the bottom line for keeping the bases. It is also the financial bottom line. Read the speeches, the documents, and the congressional hearings, and what emerges most starkly is how much it would cost to move the bases. It would be a lot. In 1977 the figure was $2 billion; by 1986 it was up to $8 billion. The numbers may be exaggerated to discourage Congress from talking seriously about moving the bases, but whatever the exact number, there is no doubt that it is best for the bases to remain in the Philippines. Best, that is, for the U.S. taxpayer. Filipinos, however, might not agree, or at least they might say, "Share some of those savings with us."

More than just the cost of constructing new facilities is involved. The United States has had a very good deal in the Philippines in regard to cheap labor. In the mid-seventies Filipinos repairing the ships at Subic were earning 45 to 70 cents an hour. A one-year repair bill for the navy at Subic in 1974 which came to $32 million would have cost about $220 million in the States. The cost of repair work at Subic was only $21.50 per worker per twelve-hour shift in 1977; it was $88 at Yokosuka, Japan, another potential location for some of the Seventh Fleet; a staggering $142 at Guam. While labor costs were increasing during the seventies by 400 percent in Yokosuka, the increase at Subic was 65 percent. Little wonder the United States didn't want to move. And it's understandable that Filipinos began to listen when the Marxist-trained university students talked to them about exploitation.

The Carter administration did not have to choose between keeping the bases and pushing Marcos to abandon his dictatorship and return democracy to the Philippines. The administration could have had both: bases and human rights. The current bases agreement didn't expire until 1991. If Marcos wanted a new agreement, let him, not the United States, pay for it. The bases could have been used as a bargaining tactic for Aquino's release; for the release of all political prisoners; for an end to torture; for the lifting of press censorship; for honest elections; for an end to martial law—in general, for a return to democracy.

In the discussions about the bases in Washington, in the questions during congressional testimony, the focus was always on how important the bases were to the United States, as they definitely are. The State Department's Bureau of Politico-Military Affairs, under the direction of Leslie Gelb, did a study in 1977 about the bases. The conclusions were that the bases couldn't be relocated without serious cost, that a relocation would affect our strategic capabilities, and that there would be a particularly severe problem about where to locate the nuclear weapons stored at Clark and Subic. (The study rankled the generals at the Pentagon. They weren't upset with the study's conclusions. It was a matter of bureaucratic turf: They objected to a non-Asian bureau's involving itself in an Asian issue, the same objection that the Asia hands at the NSC and within the State Department raised. But it was the Pentagon that was the most incensed because it was its physical as well as intellectual turf that had, in its views, been violated.) The bureau also said that Marcos very much wanted the bases and was not about to evict the United States. It is this latter conclusion that was overlooked by the Carter administration.

The pressures on Marcos to allow the bases to remain were far greater than the noise for their removal. However vociferous and credible, those Filipinos who wanted the bases closed were a minority. Some 43,000 Filipinos earned their living on the bases. Tens of thousands more indirectly benefited. The bases contributed more than $200 million annually to the economy. For all these reasons, and many of his own—he was thoroughly pro-American and the bases gave him money and leverage—Marcos wanted the bases as badly as did Washington. He wasn't about to evict the United States.

No one in the embassy who knew Marcos, who knew the Philippines, who was involved in the negotiations thought Marcos would. Not Lee Stull ("Marcos was not about to kill the golden bases"); not Robert Wenzel (the embassy's senior political officer); not Michael Connors (who worked for Wenzel, with principal responsibility for the negotiations, and who earned such respect from the military that he was assigned to the U.S. Pacific command in Honolulu after Manila); not Ambassadors Sullivan, Newsom, and Murphy. Not Philippine scholars at American universities. Not journalists who covered the Philippines. In a lengthy analysis of the bases negotiations, in May 1977, Harvey Stockwin of the *Far Eastern Economic Review* concluded that the nationalistic arguments against the bases would be used by Marcos "for improved US guarantees rather than withdrawal." He added, in what was probably the most penetrating observation, "Even if withdrawal arguments are advanced, they would face the same obstacle in the Philippines as they would in the US. The defense establishments in both countries would be most concerned if they were faced with a civilian predilection for the speedy abandonment of Clark and Subic."

There were external pressures on Marcos as well, from neighboring countries. High-level Japanese officials delivered frequent, direct, and persuasive messages that Marcos allow the U.S. bases to remain. And while Washington officials recognized the pressures from China, Indonesia, and the other ASEAN countries on the United States to retain the bases, they conveniently failed to see the other edge of the sword: the cutting influence of these countries on Marcos.

In addition to geopolitical military considerations, Marcos also saw the bases as his trump card against an aggressive human rights policy. "He was correct," says Robert Pringle, the Foreign Service officer who wrote about the Philippines and Indonesia after service in those countries. Once again Marcos was the shrewder and much tougher negotiator, the better poker player. He had a couple of aces; Washington, a full house. If the Carter administration had been serious about its human rights agenda in the Philippines, it could have played its cards accordingly. But the Pentagon didn't want any connection between human rights and the bases negotiations, and if the generals and admirals had to, they'd just wait out Derian. The military was actually willing to wait, satisfied with the current agreement. The principal push for concluding an agreement quickly was from the State Department, which wanted to remove an irritant in the relationship. Washington folded.

Though Ford had started the negotiations, it was Marcos who had suspended them. So there was no obligation on Carter to start them up again. However, it was Holbrooke, not Marcos, as has been claimed, who asked to reconvene the negotiations, raising the issue during his visit to the Philippines in April 1977. Having reopened the negotiations, Holbrooke then gave the Pentagon much more direct responsibility for them than it had had under Kissinger and Ford. "He was absolutely a genius" in doing this, says Robert Oakley, a career diplomat who worked for Holbrooke. "Our military didn't think State was selling them out."

Holbrooke badly wanted, and was to obtain, what had eluded Kissinger. When David Newsom was sent out to Manila as ambassador, his principal assignment was to conclude a bases agreement. That was Richard Murphy's mission as well when he replaced Newsom. Holbrooke's man on the Philippine desk, John Monjo, was on the phone to the embassy in Manila almost daily, extraordinary contact for any embassy at any time except during a crisis. Monjo was calling not about human rights but about the bases negotiations. Though his persistent calls began to grate on the embassy officers, they were even more irritated when Holbrooke revived James Rafferty. Given his close relations with the Marcoses, Rafferty perhaps could pave the way to an agreement. Holbrooke wanted to assign Rafferty permanently to the embassy in Manila, as a special assistant to the ambassador, the same position he had held from 1966 until Ambassador Sullivan sent him packing in 1973. No one in the Manila embassy particularly wanted Rafferty to return, so Holbrooke resorted to special missions for him. Rafferty's presence undercut the embassy's general credibility with Philippine officials, who saw in Rafferty a message that he, not the embassy officers, was the one to deal with. And the embassy officers interpreted Rafferty's missions, as well as the frequent visits by other Holbrooke aides, as indications that Holbrooke didn't particularly trust the embassy.

But Holbrooke wasn't running a popularity contest. He was conducting American policy in the Pacific as he thought it should be conducted. Crossing him was potentially perilous, as Salzberg and Stull had discovered. Another Foreign Service officer who paid with his career for failing to satisfy Holbrooke was Robert Wenzel. A twenty-year diplomatic veteran with service in Vietnam (including Hanoi) from 1954 to 1956 and again from 1970 to 1973, Wenzel was the political counselor (generally considered the number three position in an embassy) in Manila when Holbrooke arrived on the scene. "I fired him," says Holbrooke. Precisely what it was about Wenzel that Holbrooke found objectionable is not clear. Holbrooke remembers only that "he wasn't up to the demands of the job. I put very high standards on it. . . ." It is true that Holbrooke did promote some very bright and capable officers. But his assessment of Wenzel is not supported by Wenzel's career or by Ambassador Sullivan, on whose staff Wenzel served in Washington and Manila. Wenzel, says Sullivan, was "sound analytically . . . [and] his reporting was excellent"; overall he was a "first-class officer." Stephen Cohen, who while working for Derian made two trips to the Philippines, says, "I learned more about the Philippines from Wenzel than from anyone else."

Wenzel was never told by Holbrooke why the assistant secretary went after him, but he thinks it may have been because of his contacts with the political opposition to Marcos, which it was his job as political counselor to maintain. The Marcoses, of course, didn't like the embassy's talking with anyone in the opposition, and Washington didn't want to rankle Marcos lest he become more intransigent on the bases. Wenzel's fall from Holbrooke's grace may have been more directly related to the bases. Wenzel had early delegated much of the political section's responsibility for the bases negotiations to one of his deputies, Michael Connors. At one of the first briefings for Holbrooke in Manila, Wenzel did not appear, continuing to allow Connors to lead. Connors was the expert, having worked in the Defense Department before being assigned to Manila. There he devoted two years to the negotiations during the Ford administration and was consumed by them for two more years in Manila. Holbrooke expressed displeasure to his aides and embassy staff that Wenzel was not more directly involved in the negotiations. Holbrooke's conclusion that Wenzel wasn't interested was a "snap judgment" says a Foreign Service officer who heard Holbrooke's complaints; so was the decision to dismiss Wenzel, many officers who worked for Holbrooke believed.

In February 1986, when Marcos was on the ropes and within days of being ousted, Holbrooke told a congressional committee, "I believe that negotiating the base agreement was in the interest of the human rights policy as well as our strategic interests." But that was not what Holbrooke had said in 1979. In a congressional hearing one month after the bases agreement had been signed, Congressman Clarence Long, a Maryland Democrat who for years was the feisty chairman of the House subcommittee that was supposed to control foreign aid spending, asked Holbrooke if "we could not have gotten some better terms" in the negotiations. "And one of those terms," Long suggested, "might have been to make sure or put some pressure on Marcos to get a more democratic government, a government that was less vulnerable to criticism, and a government which does a better job of trying to improve the well-being of the Philippine people." Holbrooke responded: "Insofar as your second question about linking human rights on the bases is concerned, it is our strong view that you cannot use your leverage two ways at once. And we had to choose between using our bilateral relationship for human rights objectives and using it first for putting our military facilities on a stable basis."

Holbrooke's answer to Long is the accurate history.* The bases had been placed above human rights.

Far more insidious than that the Carter administration failed to use the bases to advance human rights was that Marcos used the bases to perpetuate his dictatorship. The "preoccupation of Washington" with the bases made it "difficult to maximize human rights initiatives," writes Stull. Or as non-Foreign Service analyst Larry Niksch, the Southeast Asian specialist with the Congressional Research Service, put it, the bases were a "disincentive to a stronger U.S. effort to promote human rights."

---

* During that same congressional appearance in 1986 Holbrooke claimed that Osmeña and Lopez, the two young men who had been jailed in connection with that bizarre plot to do in Marcos, had been "released from jail during President Carter's administration, under heavy pressure from the Carter administration." Whether or not the pressure had been "heavy" is debatable. But it is stretching the facts to say that Osmeña and Lopez were "released." They escaped, in a harrowing episode that was fit for Steve McQueen. The escape was masterminded by Steve Psinakis, a full-bearded, Greek-born, naturalized American who was married to Lopez's sister, Presy, the woman who had once been close to Imelda Marcos. The plot involved a twin-engine, six-seater Cessna 320, a swarthy Los Angeles pilot who had flown for Israel during the Six-Day War, a glamorous blonde, the clever switching of passports at the airport, and much more. Everything but a "release."

10 : Visitors to Manila

It wasn't always easy for Ferdinand Marcos to get what he wanted from the United States or for Richard Holbrooke to conduct American policy in the Philippines as he wanted to. Each had to contend with Patt Derian, a bur under both men's saddles. But when Derian irritated Marcos and thereby upset the Washington-Manila relationship, Holbrooke recruited Vice President Mondale, and together they rode in to heal the wounds.

Derian's encounter with Marcos came during her first swing through the Orient, which also included Singapore, Indonesia, and Thailand; she was to have visited South Korea, but the stop was canceled at the last minute, much to the relief of the ambassador, who didn't want her to come. Prior to Derian's departure, her senior deputy, Mark Schneider, sat down at his typewriter. It was December 31, 1977, the end of the Human Rights Bureau's first aggressive year, a year of fighting and losing, not so much with foreign dictators as with American diplomats and bureaucrats. Schneider was accustomed to liberal causes and losing battles. After serving in the Peace Corps in El Salvador in the late 1960s, he had worked for seven years as an aide to Senator Edward Kennedy, fighting for legislation that would link U.S. assistance to a country's human rights performance. Now he had just finished reading the briefing papers prepared by the State Department desks for each country Derian was about to visit, a routine procedure for all high-level officials before their visits to foreign countries. Once again the Foreign Service officers were glossing over human rights abuses, trying to present their countries in the most favorable light. Turning to his typewriter, Schneider banged away at the keys, "using the machine to rid myself of today's feelings of anger at the inclination of some to downplay

224

the corrupt, venal and repressive nature of the Marcos and Park governments."

Schneider had some advice for Derian: "Be inscrutable. Talk about the weather, the flowers, the color of the water; but do not embarrass your hosts by raising nasty subjects directly." Then, he added, sarcasm punctuating his anger, "Actually, that is not what they [the authors of the briefing papers] are saying. They want you to raise human rights but to do it through encouragement of such recent actions as prisoner releases and statements not to torture 'no more.' But do not criticize them for having held people for their political beliefs or for having permitted torture to go on up to the time of the new order." He closed his informal note with a friendly and cheery "Have a good trip, enjoy the mysteries of the orient, and beware of base treaties, buddhas and over-cooked rice. See you next year."

Reading his outrage in cold print caused Schneider to caution Derian to "tear this up after you read it." She didn't, ripping into the region's rulers instead. Before taking on the Asian strongmen seriatim, Derian warmed up on American diplomats, at a chiefs of mission meeting in Hong Kong. "It was a very bitter session," recalled Holbrooke, who chaired the gathering of America's ambassadors or their principal deputies in the region. It was a revealing and, to Holbrooke, astonishing reflection of "the gap between what she wanted to do in the region and what the ambassadors wanted." She wanted to push human rights; they wanted smooth bilateral relations. "To her credit she stood up to these men for three straight hours," says Holbrooke. "It was gutsy." And for Derian, not pleasant. At one point the venerable Mike Mansfield, Montana's former senator and at the time ambassador to Japan, interrupted the talk about human rights and policy to reminisce about Derian's grandfather, who had lived in Montana. In his deliberate manner of speaking, Mansfield talked for several minutes, recalling the man's courage and principles. "And I'm proud to know his granddaughter," Mansfield concluded, to silence. "I'm usually pretty tough," Derian says, recalling the incident. "But I really appreciated this emergency rescue."

From Hong Kong Derian made the short flight to Manila and four days of tense, acerbic confrontations relieved by a few comic moments. Derian's meeting with Marcos horrified Ambassador Newsom. She didn't exhibit the respectful demeanor that he expected from American diplomats with heads of state even if they were dictators. Indeed, in Newsom's thirty years in the Foreign Service—he had been ambassador to Libya and Indonesia—he had never witnessed such a heated exchange between an American official and a head of state. Derian told the Philippine president that Washington had ways of expressing its disappointment with human rights abuses by voting against loans from the international development banks. That was too much for Marcos. He was a man who normally exhibited remarkable self-control. Now he became visibly angry, replying with considerable heat that he had never submitted to dollar diplomacy before, and he wasn't about to start.

Having shaken the steely, inscrutable Marcos, she went for the suave defense minister, Juan Ponce Enrile. Like many military men around the world who have been trained in American military schools, Enrile and his staff had a public relations show all prepared for Derian, with slides, charts, pointers, and officers in crisp uniforms to deliver the performance. She interrupted when she saw all the props. What about all those people in jail who hadn't had any charges filed against them? How about the reports of torture? He'd be happy to answer her questions, Enrile said respectfully, but wouldn't she like to watch the program first? No. Derian wasn't interested in the public relations blitz. She wanted answers. She got lies. Military officers who engaged in torture were punished, Enrile insisted. As for press censorship, he explained that the papers had been closed because they were being used by the "subversives" in their propaganda campaign to overthrow the government; moreover, today's Philippine newspapers, Enrile said, were exercising press freedom with responsibility. Derian tried to explain about democracy in America. Enrile dismissed it as not suitable for the Philippines.

In spite of the multiple collisions, the Marcoses hosted a luncheon for Derian, a testament perhaps to their diplomatic civility and graciousness. Or maybe there was a more pragmatic explanation: The Marcoses thought the discomfort of eating with her was preferable to the congressional reaction if they snubbed her. Whatever, they gathered in the high-ceilinged room in Malacañang, around a banquet table so long that binoculars should have been passed out to guests at each end, and megaphones to those on the sides. Derian thus carried on an essentially private conversation with Marcos, who was sitting next to her. She tried appealing to the man's sense of history, suggesting that it was not too late if he wanted to be remembered as a great leader rather than "a dirty little footnote." All he had to do was restore democracy.

In the middle of the luncheon Imelda Marcos entered, late as usual. As the tall, massive wooden doors opened and she swept in, a dutiful silence fell over the guests. Taking her seat next to Newsom, Mrs. Marcos chatted with the ambassador, then in a burst of enthusiasm launched into an endorsement of a wonderful new medicine. It was made from natural Philippine substances and kept hair from turning white or restored white hair to its natural color overnight, she said. She wanted Derian to have the pills as a gift. She couldn't hand them across to Derian; the table was too wide. So the pills started on a journey around the table, passed from guest to guest, while Marcos and Derian continued their weighty discussion about human rights. Finally the pills reached Derian, at which point Marcos exclaimed that he had been taking them for years. Derian put on her eyeglasses and read the label: "Made in New Jersey."

The embassy also hosted a party for Derian. Regardless of how much the diplomats bristled at her style and policy, she *was* an assistant secretary. It was an evening affair at the ambassador's residence. She wore a strapless gown, and late in the night, the moon full overhead, the CIA station chief, Herbert Natzke, approached. If she wanted to visit Aquino in jail, they had to go now. She sensed he expected her to say no. She said yes, emphatically. She would be the highest-level American to meet with him during the now five-plus years he had been held. Not even an ambassador or a deputy ambassador had called on Aquino. Holbrooke says he and Derian had discussed the meeting, and he had enthusiastically endorsed it. Derian insists she never even broached the matter with Holbrooke, that she neither needed nor wanted his involvement. But the meeting had been arranged, and now Derian borrowed a wrap from Mrs. Newsom, a shawl that had been made by the wives of some political prisoners in Algeria.

On the way to the prison Natzke railed against Aquino to Derian and her aide. Aquino was unworthy of any special attention from the United States, he said, certainly not from anyone who professed to care about human rights; Aquino was nothing but a rich playboy, an adventurer, a seamy character. It was a recitation of what Derian had read in a CIA profile about Aquino. She, too, had some reservations about Aquino. He was no saint, she knew. But the man she met that night in an open room in an army barracks had changed, she was convinced. For ninety minutes they talked—no, he talked, she listened, about his life and imprisonment. "Some other person had emerged," she thought. "And who emerged was a democrat, a small *d* democrat, with an honest-to-God full understanding of the history of the idea of democracy, of the necessity of it, the mechanism, the games of it. It was simply a breathtaking exposition. . . . We came away with the sense that we had met somebody of monumental stature. Intellectually and in terms of democracy. Like Churchill. A giant." Newsom, upon listening to Derian speak so glowingly about Aquino, thought he had put on a performance for her in the same manner, and with the same success, as the Marcoses did for other Americans.

Derian's visit to the Philippines became the talk of Manila. The comments about Derian were most unflattering, and even some of the opposition leaders who, though pleased that a high-level American had finally shown some interest in democracy, were a bit put off by her style. Imelda Marcos, avoiding the substance of Derian's visit, prattled on about Derian's skin and how old she looked, the CIA reported to Washington, its cables passed around by chortling Foreign Service officers who didn't much care for either woman. But it was the crusty Carlos Romulo, Marcos's foreign minister, who came up with the epithet that put Derian where the Marcos crowd, and even some moderate Filipinos, thought she belonged. The seventy-nine-year-old Romulo had been offended by Derian, hadn't liked what she had to say about human rights or the manner in which she had said it. "She was a schoolgirl," he said. When their thirty-minute tête-à-tête ended and Romulo was asked by reporters what he thought of her, he said she reminded him of the durian. There was great laughter. Patt Derian became Patt Durian. The durian is a southeastern Asian tree fruit that is edible—if one can get past the foul odor.

When Romulo visited Washington a few months later, he boycotted a meeting of Asian allies because Derian was scheduled to
make a brief appearance. That was the peg for another attack on
Derian by Rowland Evans, Jr., and Robert Novak, the conservative
columnists who waged a four-year war against Derian and her human
rights policy. They particularly took her to task for her criticisms of
the Argentine junta, which they staunchly defended.* This time
Evans and Novak wrote: " 'She was rude to President Marcos,' one
ranking diplomat told us." The "ranking diplomat" was Holbrooke,
or so Derian was told by an ally in the department who said he had
overheard Holbrooke talking with Evans on the telephone. Derian
stormed into Holbrooke's office. "He got wildly excited and furious," Derian says, "waving his arms and yelling. . . . But he wasn't
able to deny it." Holbrooke acknowledges having had a close working relationship with Evans, but he doesn't recall the encounter with
Derian or if he gave Evans the quote.

That particular Derian-Holbrooke encounter was but a minor
skirmish. The real slugfest, which ended with a punch which put
her human rights policy for the Philippines down if not out, came
a few weeks after Derian returned from Manila. At issue was a
proposed trip there by Vice President Mondale. Derian was against
it, her opposition more passionate because she had tremendous
respect and admiration for Mondale. She considered him a decent,
principled liberal; many years earlier she had hosted a dinner for
him in Mississippi. She didn't want him used by Marcos. She didn't
want any American vice president to embrace a dictator. All dictators skillfully manipulated those visits, turning them into endorsements of their rule. Marcos was the master at doing that.

Holbrooke was equally insistent that Mondale go to Manila. He
wanted to "repair the damage" he thought Derian had done, "to
assure Marcos that she'd be reined in," explained a State Department officer. Holbrooke also wanted a bases agreement, which he

---

* Referring to congressional testimony in which Derian had accused the Argentine
government of widespread killing, torture, and kidnappings, Evans and Novak described it
as "undiplomatic ravages . . . language seldom used by one friendly power to another." They
reported that "horrified officials" in State's Latin American bureau had attempted to delete
her testimony from the transcript that was made public. Moreover, the columnists ridiculed
reports by Derian's bureau that the Argentine junta had "executed 3,000 persons" and that
another 5,000 were missing. The numbers were indeed wrong; they were understated.

229

still didn't have. Coinciding with the third anniversary of the fall of Saigon, the trip would also send a message that the United States was still an Asian power, that the Carter administration wasn't abandoning that part of the world. Until now Carter had been focusing on the Middle East, relations with the Soviet Union, and handing control of the Panama Canal to Panama. Mondale, with Holbrooke at his side, was to stop in New Zealand, Australia, Thailand, and Indonesia. How could he go to all those countries and bypass the Philippines? "I don't know what good not going would have done," Mondale said, looking back years later.

What it might have done was send a message that the Carter administration didn't approve of Marcos's corrupt, undemocratic ways. By Mondale's going, the opposite message was conveyed. There was a personal, as opposed to political, message in the Mondale visit as well: Richard Holbrooke could deliver. Vice presidents visit few countries; even secretaries of state don't make it to that many. An assistant secretary who can deliver someone high-level, the higher the better, gains status, prestige, and influence—with the leader of the foreign country as well as within the bureaucracy in Washington.

No one except Derian and the Human Rights Bureau was opposed to the Mondale visit. Not Brzezinski or his deputy and close Mondale aide David Aaron at the NSC; not Vance or Christopher at the top of State. Against that lineup, Derian didn't stand a chance. And Holbrooke didn't give her one. "He sideswiped us," says Schneider. Holbrooke was exceptionally skillful and effective in working the bureaucracy, especially this bureaucracy because he was on good terms with all the key players. Holbrooke had them all on board for the Mondale visit before Derian could even register her views. When she discovered what had happened, she exploded, demanding a meeting with the vice president. Derian thought if she could talk to Mondale, he would understand, that once he had a view of Marcos other than the one Holbrooke was providing, he would never agree to the trip.

Holbrooke wasn't about to allow Derian to talk with the vice president on a matter pertaining to his part of the world without his being present. When the elevator opened in the State Department basement, Derian, on her way to the White House, found Holbrooke standing by her limousine, "furious," according to Derian. Their rising voices echoed in the basement. Derian got into the car; Holbrooke followed. "We rode over to the White House with him screaming at me the whole way," Derian says, recalling the incident eight years later. They found Mondale leaning back in his chair, in his shirtsleeves, smoking his big cigar (as he did regularly, though he did not allow himself to be photographed with one). Derian tried to present her case; she was repeatedly interrupted by Mondale and Holbrooke. Mondale argued that the United States couldn't interfere in the internal politics of another country, that promoting human rights was a great idea, but it had to be subordinated to national security; that you had to be polite, you couldn't just slam American ideas down the throats of other cultures; that it wasn't like the civil rights movement in the South, well-meaning Americans couldn't just go to another part of the world and work their will. "He gave me a lecture on human rights—at the most elementary level," she says. It was the same lecture she heard from conservatives and Foreign Service officers.

"It was as unpleasant and disappointing a meeting as I ever had with a U.S. government official," Derian said years later with what would seem to be a bit of hyperbole. But she was emphatic. "I came away with no respect at all for Mondale. I was just disgusted."*

Some of Derian's aides realized later that the approach to Mondale could have been handled better. Instead of confronting the vice president and putting him on the defensive, Derian and the bureau should have said in effect, "look, the issue of your going has been decided; now let's talk about what you do." Above all, Derian should have stressed that the decision had been made without any input from the Human Rights Bureau. "How can we avoid that happening in the future?"

Holbrooke was acutely aware of the potential positives and the lurking negatives in the Mondale visit; he knew it could be used to advance democracy or could be viewed as bolstering dictatorship. The risks were magnified because the vice president would be arriving in Manila one month after an election for a Philippine national

---

* Mondale doesn't recall the meeting, but he says that Derian "was wrong" in her opposition to his going.

assembly. It was the first election since Marcos had taken over in 1972, other than the five plebiscites on martial law, in each of which he had received 90 percent "approval." Holbrooke wanted this election to be honest, and he expected some progress on other human rights issues. He sent strongly worded instructions to the embassy in Manila.

"We are counting upon you to convince Marcos that U.S.-Philippine relations are at a turning point," Holbrooke bluntly informed Ambassador Newsom in a Secret cable. Marcos should be made to understand, Holbrooke continued, that if there were "real progress in human rights," it could "lead to a reduction in criticism from Congress and the press and to a long-term improvement in our relations." It was particularly important that Marcos "move in a clear, credible way on elections and martial law" if Congress was to be persuaded not to cut military aid and to come up with a compensation package for the bases. Holbrooke added that it was imperative for Newsom to "impress upon Marcos the necessity of convincing outside observers, including USG [U.S. government] and Congress that elections will be a truly free one in which Philippine voters are given genuine choice."

Holbrooke had some specifics on what Marcos should do. Newsom was instructed to try to "persuade Marcos" to "permit temporary release of Aquino and other non-radical detainees who wish to campaign." As for martial law, Holbrooke, of course, wanted that lifted. But while it would be nice if Marcos did so before the election, Holbrooke advised Newsom that he should not press so hard for a lifting of martial law "as to upset the chances of its being done at the time of the vice-president's visit."

The cable provides a succinct and unique insight into the Carter administration's policy in the Philippines. It reveals that Holbrooke, in his suggestions about postponing the lifting of martial law, was willing to put partisan politics above foreign policy and humanitarian concerns. But more important, it penetrates the rhetorical fog that obscured the administration's foreign policy and allows some glimpses into its application of that policy. Rather than use the levers the State Department and White House controlled, such as canceling the Mondale visit or voting against multilateral development bank loans, Holbrooke and the administration were trying to move Marcos by invoking Congress and public opinion. And though Holbrooke and the administration did, and continued to, claim publicly that they pushed relentlessly and forcefully for Aquino's release, in fact, they weren't pushing Marcos that hard. Holbrooke, in his cable, didn't suggest that Aquino be permanently released, as he should have, considering the trumped-up nature of the charges, but only that he be temporarily released so that he could campaign.

The cable becomes most telling about the Carter administration and Holbrooke, however, when it is examined in light of what happened. Martial law wasn't lifted; Aquino wasn't released to campaign; the elections were fraudulent. Holbrooke and Washington capitulated; the administration's support for Marcos continued unabated.

The legislative elections tested the Carter administration's commitment to democracy in the Philippines. At stake were 165 seats in what was to be the Interim Batasang Pambansa, as the legislature was called. Marcos would appoint another 35 members from his cabinet and organizations representing various sectors of society. In reality, however, nothing was at stake, at least not for Marcos. Under the Constitution and rules, which he had written, regardless of the outcome of the voting he would remain president; he would have absolute veto power over any and all actions by the assembly; and he could dissolve it at any moment, for any reason—or without reason.

To the Filipinos a little democracy was better than none at all, and they loved to play politics. If this were the only game in town, they'd play. Even Aquino, now under a death sentence imposed by a military court, campaigned from his jail cell. He was the leader of the Lakas 'ng Bayan, Tagalog for "People's Power." Laban, as it was known by its acronym, was the same party that eight years later his widow led to triumph over Marcos. Aquino was a candidate for one of the twenty-one Metro Manila seats in the Assembly. His seven-year-old daughter, Kris, appeared at the rallies. "Please vote for my father," was the gist of her plea, "so that he can come home." By her seventieth appearance she was able to recite the names of the other twenty Laban candidates without the benefit of notes.

Imelda Marcos was also a candidate in Metro Manila, as leader of the Kilusan Bagong Lipunan (KBL), or New Society Movement.

She campaigned tirelessly, appearing at rally after rally, most of them in the slums, from early morning, during the punishing noonday heat, late into the night. She sang. She cooed: If the people didn't vote for her, "I won't love you." She cautioned: The ladies' auxiliary brigade would be watching at the polls, "and they will know who does not vote for KBL." She told jokes: A recent fire, which had destroyed twenty square blocks in the waterfront district, left 21,000 people homeless—and without toilet paper. She suggested they had found a use for the Laban campaign leaflets.

The crude joke was a fitting description of the whole election. It was a burlesque, a virtuoso performance conducted and directed by Marcos, for the benefit of world opinion and particularly Carter's human rights policy. If the U.S. president wanted him to hold an election, if that would satisfy the American Congress and keep the aid flowing, fine, Marcos would allow an election. He had never been as extreme in his use of brutality and repression as most dictators. As long as the power was his and his alone, as long as he and his wife didn't have to answer for their pilfering of the country's treasury, he'd have this contest. He'd even let Aquino play—if that's what Washington wanted. But the Marcoses wouldn't lose; they wouldn't let Aquino win.

The elections had been fraudulent ab initio. The embassy knew it, and the embassy reported it. Six weeks before the voting, which was to be on April 7, Lee Stull, the deputy chief of mission who was always trying to advance democracy and human rights, sent Washington a cable about the election. It was a remarkably candid assessment, stripped of the diplomatic caution and the clientism that generally varnish the sordid reality about a friendly government. Stull's opening: "The results of the forthcoming legislative elections are virtually certain. Oppositionists will likely win but a few seats, and President Marcos will be assured of an overwhelming majority in the new Interim Parliament."

Stull wasn't basing his conclusion on any political prognostication skills, nor was he being cynical. He was just stating the reality. He explained: "It is not particularly meaningful, in the context of martial law, to dwell on 'fairness' of the campaign and the elections. While the polling itself could be reasonably valid, this has limited significance when viewed in the unbalanced political setting." And that was just his summary. The details followed: How Marcos would allow a few opposition candidates to win, for appearances' sake; how his "political lieutenants" had encouraged the formation of "pseudo-opposition groups" in the provinces "to spar with KBL."

Marcos also gathered all the powers of the government available to him, and he used them, "with a lack of even elemental subtlety," Stull wrote. The Philippine president used the "carrot," as the embassy described his promises to raise the pay of teachers and other civil servants, and the "stick," which was "thinly veiled threats to government employees to vote KBL, or else. . . ." Those uses of incumbency weren't new to Philippine elections, or even unique to them, but in the context of martial law they took on "a larger and more insidious dimension," with retribution more certain and swift, the embassy noted.

So great was the antipathy toward Marcos, however, that he would have to cheat even more massively to arrange the outcome he desired. The embassy knew that as well, and reported it. This was a particularly good embassy staff, maybe an exceptional one. It reported the situation as it was, not as it thought Washington wanted to hear it, so unlike what was to come in the last two years of the Carter administration and what was even more pronounced during the first Reagan term. Three weeks before the election Theresa Tull, the U.S. consul in Cebu, reported being told by one of Imelda Marcos's confidants that "Marcos will permit approximately 10 percent of the 165 elected IBP seats to be won by non-KBL candidates." It would be "in the counting and not in the casting of votes that the election will be decided," Tull was told.

But it was about Manila, where Aquino was leading the opposition, that the Marcoses were the most concerned. Three days before the voting the embassy had reached an astonishing conclusion. "We believe that in an honest vote, Laban would win a substantial number, perhaps a majority of the Metro [Manila] seats." It was even "quite likely" the embassy reported, that some of the Laban candidates, of whom Aquino was the most popular, might, if the election were honest, "come in ahead of Imelda."

That Aquino and his Laban party could do so well was a piercing manifestation of the dissatisfaction with Marcos and his martial law rule. Laban's success was even more remarkable considering Mar-

235

cos's control of everything from the pay raises for teachers to the media, with Aquino allowed only one television and one newspaper interview.

But there was no way Aquino was going to be permitted to finish ahead of Imelda Marcos. Her ego wouldn't permit that. (When a magazine supplement to a Philippine newspaper conducted a poll of college students asking who their heroes were, she finished sixth, behind Aquino and José María Sison, the imprisoned chairman of the Philippine Communist party. Not mollified by the fact that Jesus Christ had finished ninth, she ordered the magazine destroyed.) Moreover, she was the standard-bearer for Marcos's New Society. If she didn't win and win big, it would cast doubts on Marcos's rule. On the eve of the voting the embassy reported, "Marcos will likely resort to major fraud and manipulation to assure KBL sweep in Metro Manila." He did. Aquino finished twenty-second. Imelda Marcos was first, even ahead of Carlos Romulo, who had been leading until the Marcoses counted the ballots as they wanted to. It was a KBL sweep.

The fraud the embassy had feared had come to pass. There were "flying voters"—200,000, the embassy reported—brought in from the Marcoses' provinces to vote in Manila. They, and others, were paid between 100 and 200 pesos (roughly $15 to $30; or the equivalent of a month's wages for many) to vote for the KBL. Marcos and his party also "printed and marked one million fake ballots for use in the process as necessary to assure an overwhelming KBL victory," the embassy said. Voters who arrived at the polls within minutes after they opened found the boxes already stuffed. Teachers recruited by the federal elections commission to supervise the polls were paid 200 pesos ($30)—"under the table," the embassy reported—to ensure a favorable count for the KBL. A group of parents, angry that their children's teachers had been used in what they described as the "dirtiest election in our whole lifetime," sent an open letter to school officials. "We had been quite proud of the fact that most of us studied in, or graduated from, the nation's public schools. But today, we feel we have no right to be proud. Instead, we bow our heads in shame. . . . Our children should have reason to greet [their teachers]: 'Good morning, teacher,' instead of 'Good morning, cheater.' "

When all that failed to produce the outcome Marcos desired, he ordered it. In Cebu all thirteen Assembly seats were won by the opposition party, its victory "undeniably," Tull reported, "an anti-Marcos, anti-martial law protest." But after some negotiations it was decided that the tally would show that nine opposition and four KBL candidates had won. Then Marcos stepped in, ordering that the opposition candidates be declared the winners. He hadn't been overcome by a stroke of democracy. It was much more pragmatic. He wanted the elections to have some semblance of credibility, and the nine KBL candidates Marcos knocked out had been building a political base that was independent of the Marcoses'.

It took Filipinos only two days to react to the cruel hoax Marcos had played. He had dangled democracy in front of them, then snatched it away. They took to the streets to protest, the second time in a week. On the night before the voting Manila residents had carried out what they called a noise barrage. At precisely 9:00 P.M. church bells began pealing, while drivers laid on their car horns, housewives banged on kitchen pots, and tens of thousands of Filipinos—even the call girls—clogged the streets in a shrieking, cacophonic, defiant protest against Marcos and martial law. Then had come the voting. Now, on Sunday, April 9, two days after the voting, there was another protest. Under the fierce tropical sun several hundred people gathered at St. Theresa College for a peaceful march to a mass at the Manila Cathedral. Mostly students and workers, they were led by priests carrying a coffin—the death of democracy. A year earlier a Pakistani election marred by widespread fraud was followed by street demonstrations, which led to a coup against Prime Minister Zulfikar Ali Bhutto, who was arrested and sentenced to death. Marcos was taking no chances that the demonstrations in Manila would get out of hand as they had in Karachi, Lahore, and Islamabad.

Government troops broke up the march, arresting 600 Laban followers, including former Senator Lorenzo Tañada, a Harvard-educated lawyer who had prosecuted collaborators during World War II. As the seventy-nine-year-old Laban campaign manager was loaded into a police van, he raised a clenched fist and shouted, "Laban" (which means "fight"); the young marchers returned the salute. Herded off to jail in buses that had been commandeered by the police, the demonstrators sang a haunting Philippine protest song from the days when the archipelago had been under first Spanish, then American rule: "The Philippines, my beloved country, you are like a bird. You want to fly away, but you are imprisoned in a cage. My country is imprisoned." Within a few days all but eight were released, though they were formally charged by a military tribunal with illegal assembly, sedition, and inciting to sedition. One of those arrested and charged was a Jesuit priest, and the day after the demonstration the Jesuit seminary, the Loyola House of Studies, was raided by government agents in civilian clothes. They hauled away two young seminary students and took them to a military base. One, a seventeen-year-old, died, from brutal beatings and torture, the Jesuits said. His intestines had been ripped out. "Acute pancreatitis," said the government.

The *Washington Post*'s political cartoonist Herblock seemed to capture it all best: the election; the fraud; the reaction. An incensed Marcos, fists clenched, watches a police van speed away, prisoners peering through the slats. He snaps to the general standing next to him, "Ingrates! You let them vote and the next thing, they want their ballots counted." There was another message in the Herblock cartoon, one which pertained not to the Philippines but to Washington. Herblock didn't have access to the classified cables. He had been reading the newspapers, his own and *The New York Times*. They had been reporting the fraud, not with as much detail as, and to the extent that, the embassy did in its secret cables, but enough so that anyone who cared to would have realized that the elections stank. Indeed, Malacañang became so furious with the *Post*'s Jay Mathews and *The Times'* Fox Butterfield that the two were called in for a lecture by the government's information czar; a "Malacañang insider" complained loudly to American diplomats, especially about Butterfield and Michael T. Malloy, of the *Wall Street Journal*, whose stories the insider told the embassy's press officer were full of "outrageous lies."

On the other hand, a palace insider told the embassy that the *Time* and *Newsweek* stories about the election had been "quite good." *Time* managed to believe that the election was "A Real Contest." The *Time* account did not even mention that the election

238

had been carried out under martial law conditions, with all the restrictions on liberties which that wrought. Marcos himself was so delighted with *Newsweek*'s coverage that a week after the election he invited the magazine's Barry Came for a game of pelota and an "exclusive" interview; Came wrote about Marcos's "trim figure" and "cheerful" nature and dismissed the Filipinos and their desire for democracy: "Most Filipinos seemed unconcerned with the idea of election fraud," he wrote.

Marcos's conviction that Butterfield and Mathews were "unfair" in their reporting was unfounded. Both *The New York Times* and the *Washington Post* treated the campaign seriously, covered Imelda Marcos's campaigning, and gave Marcos space in their papers when, typically, he went on the offensive, accusing the opposition of fraud, to avoid being put on the defensive about his fraud. Even more out of touch with reality was Marcos's fear that the reports would make any difference. They didn't. In one story Mathews suggested that the fraud charges "could hurt" U.S. congressional approval of a "lucrative new bases treaty." Two days later, in a front-page story about the arrests of the opposition leaders during the April 9 protest, Mathews concluded: "A return to the pattern of harsh repression and underground rebellion of the early days of martial law could severely jeopardize Marcos' chances of winning U.S. approval for a new and more lucrative military bases agreement." Any reasonable reporter who had heard all the Carter administration's proclamations about human rights and had read the congressional laws would have reached the same conclusions. Mathews was wrong, of course. The fraud and the return to repression didn't jeopardize the bases agreement or any of the other aid.

At the polls and in the streets Filipinos had registered their disapproval of Marcos. But the Carter administration wouldn't. Eight years later, in 1986, when the Reagan administration pulled the plug on Marcos, Holbrooke and others in the Carter administration defended their not having done so with the argument that they had not had the opportunities, that the conditions had not been the same. In fact, the elections of 1978 were an opportune moment for Carter. Those elections or, more precisely the strength of Aquino and Laban, the noise barrage, and the post-voting protest revealed, as the embassy reported, the "serious cracks" in Marcos's New Society.

It was an opening for the administration. It wasn't necessary, nor would it have been justified, for the United States to have engaged in a covert operation to topple Marcos. That was for the Filipinos. All the Carter administration had to do was cut aid or otherwise strongly express its disapproval.

During a meeting with Mondale Father James Reuter, an American Jesuit who had been in the Philippines for four decades and was highly respected by American officials, was asked how long Marcos would remain in power if the United States cut off aid. "I said about two days," Reuter recalled. It was a reflection of the depth of respect in the Philippines for the United States; the protesters were a small minority. Reuter's statement was, of course, not literal. Maybe it would have taken two years, or four. Maybe it wouldn't have happened at all, but at least the Carter administration would have backed democracy instead of a dictator. It wasn't even necessary to cut off aid. All the administration had to do was put some distance between itself and Marcos, to speak out for democracy. It had an opportunity to do so, but let it pass. George McT. Kahin, acclaimed professor of Southeast Asian and international studies at Cornell University, who had observed the April elections in the Philippines, told a congressional committee that in his three decades of studying elections in Southeast Asia he had encountered few "that were so blatantly rigged."

The Carter administration could have loudly and unequivocally denounced the election as fraudulent. Instead, it viewed the election as "a step toward eventual restoration of representative government." But Carter did more than just fail to condemn. The administration tacitly endorsed the fraudulent elections, patched up the cracks. In the first two months after the election, the Christopher committee, at the urging of Holbrooke and the East Asian Bureau and over the objections of Derian and the Human Rights Bureau, approved three separate aid packages for the Philippines, including $17 million worth of bullets, fifty-one armored vehicles, and patrol boats.

If the Carter administration had wanted to send a message about democracy, it would have been so simple yet so potent not to have sent Mondale. Canceling the Mondale visit would have demoralized Marcos. Instead, Mondale went ahead, bolstering Marcos, demoralizing his opposition.

Mondale didn't intend that result, nor did Holbrooke. Both men came away from Manila convinced, and have so remained, that the vice president's visit had advanced America's security interests and human rights. While there can be little disagreement that Mondale advanced U.S. security interests—or at least advanced the bases negotiations—there is considerable question about what the visit accomplished in the human rights arena. The American vice president did raise the issue of human rights in his meeting with Marcos. "It was a lively discussion," Marcos said. The discussion also made it clear that human rights was of concern not just to Derian and the bureaucracy but to the highest levels of the administration, a message which neither the Ford nor the Nixon administration had sent (nor would Reagan). But beyond that the Mondale visit appears to have had little, if any, impact. Aquino was imprisoned for two more years, and martial law was not lifted while Carter was president.

Mondale's was an impossible mission, almost by definition. It was like trying to waltz without embracing. No matter what he said about human rights, his mere presence in the country, in the company of the Marcoses, was a louder message of approval. The Marcoses were brilliant at disseminating that message. A photo of Mondale's nineteen-year-old son Theodore was on the front page of one of the Marcos-controlled newspapers, his dirt bike off the ground as he flew over the tracks at Fort Bonifacio with the son of Defense Minister Enrile, the man who had been an architect of martial law, who held the keys to the prisons where men and women were tortured. Joan Mondale was exploited, too, hauled on the usual tour by Imelda Marcos, her photograph on the front page another day. And of course, the Marcoses wined and dined the Mondales. Vice President Mondale did offend Mrs. Marcos, though not with any political intention. She became perturbed because during the prolonged Malacañang extravaganza David Aaron, the number two man on the National Security Council, excused himself from the head table, returned moments later, and whispered in the vice president's ear. Then the two conversed in hushed tones. This happened several times. Finally, Imelda Marcos remarked to Mondale that she would appreciate it if he would pay more attention to the show. "I'm happy to be your guest, Mrs. Marcos," Mondale replied graciously, but with slight irritation, "but I'm still vice president of the United States." Aaron's calls had been from the U.S. commanders in Hawaii about the bases negotiations, which Mondale was discussing with Marcos. During the course of the evening's gala, when the lights were dim, someone whispered to Elizabeth ("Bess") Abell, formerly Lady Bird Johnson's social secretary, who had done some of the advance work on this trip for Mrs. Mondale. "Mrs. Marcos wants you to have this," the person said, handing Abell a tiny box. Opening it later, Abell found a ring with a large pearl set in diamonds. At the airport Mrs. Abell politely, but forcefully, handed the ring to Mrs. Marcos, who tried to resist, saying, "Oh, it's nothing. Keep it. Nobody will ever know."

While in Manila, Mondale signed four aid agreements totaling some $41 million, the signing ceremony shown on Marcos-controlled television and reported on the front pages of the government-controlled newspapers. It was a ringing endorsement of the Marcos government, sounded even louder because the agreement was signed so publicly in Manila, instead of quietly in Washington. In furtherance of the Carter administration's effort to appease and appeal to Marcos, Mondale took careful measures to avoid offending him. In spite of all the talk by Holbrooke and others about how much they were doing for Aquino, Mondale declined to meet with him after Marcos had passed the word that such a meeting would be "absolutely unacceptable."

The U.S. vice president did meet with other opposition leaders, as well as with the archbishop of Manila, Jaime Cardinal Sin, meetings which Mondale and Holbrooke, as well as American reporters, considered highly significant. But all the meetings were as secret as possible, with photographers not permitted, to keep from offending Marcos. At that they, even the meeting with Sin, were not the bold gestures or strong statements for democracy which they were portrayed to be. Sin, as he said himself, was a "critical collaborator" with Marcos and martial law; in the American embassy the feeling was that he was more of a collaborator than he was critical. As the *Far Eastern Economic Review* noted in an article at the time of the Mondale visit, "With rare exceptions, Sin has pretty much toed the line of the regime."*

---

* *The New York Times* reporter described Sin as "sharply critical" of the Marcos regime. *The Times* reporter, Terence Smith, regularly covered the White House, not the Philippines; this probably explains his mischaracterization of Sin.

While struggling not to upset Marcos, the U.S. officials displayed what most charitably can be described as insensitivity and arrogance in meeting with the opposition political leaders.* The meeting was scheduled for Mondale's suite in the Philippine Plaza Hotel. The hotel was owned by Imelda Marcos, though her ownership was hidden. It was one of fourteen first-class hotels rushed to completion in 1976 so that Manila and the Marcoses could be hosts for the annual meeting of the World Bank and International Monetary Fund. Most of these hotels were owned by Marcos's cronies, and they were financed with government loans and government guarantees to banks. At least $75 million for the Philippine Plaza came from the Government Services Insurance System, which handled government employee pensions. All the hotels were appropriate to Hong Kong, London, or New York but were an ostentatious waste in the Philippines. Altogether the government spent at least $500 million on the hotels, compared with $13.3 million in the same year for public housing, desperately needed in a country where the per capita income was less than $400 a year and where at least half the population lived in hovels. Within months the hotels were largely vacant, the owners couldn't pay on their loans, and Marcos, with a stroke of his dictatorial pen, rescheduled the loans, to avoid government foreclosure.

Located behind her Cultural Center, Imelda Marcos's Philippine Plaza, with its balconies looking over Manila Bay, was the largest (730 rooms) of the crony hotels, and the most expensive. Because of kickbacks and windfall profits from the rushed construction, the cost per room was at least $100,000, making it at the time the most expensive hotel ever built anywhere in the world. The lobby is massive; an escalator descends to a pond stocked with fish; outside, rocks have been fashioned into falls to carry water into the pool, which has a floating bar in the center.

The opposition political leaders, offended by being asked to

---

* *The New York Times* reported that Mondale's agreement to meet with the opposition was a "compromise" between canceling the trip, which is what Derian and her bureau wanted, and going ahead with it, which is what Holbrooke wanted. Derian rejects that, insisting that she remained firmly against the trip. "Damage limiting" is how she describes her pressure on Mondale to, at a minimum, meet with the opposition if he felt he had to go ahead with the trip.

enter Imelda Marcos's posh hotel, wanted a change of venue. They suggested the historic Manila Hotel. Even though it was owned by the government, which had lavished $40 million on its refurbishing, it harbored memories of MacArthur and the better days of U.S.-Philippine relations. But the Mondale people wouldn't budge. As a result, Jovito Salonga, the former senator who had nearly been killed at the Plaza Miranda bombing and was one of the most principled of the opposition leaders, respected even by those American diplomats who didn't care much for Aquino, refused to meet with Mondale. Salonga was also incensed because after the meeting with the other opposition leaders Mondale refused to issue a statement. "There was nothing to be ashamed of," says Salonga.

The opposition leaders who did meet with Mondale were also bitter, though not immediately. "He sure tricked me," says Diosdado Macapagal, the former president. "He misled us because he made us believe he was here in order to help the opposition in promoting democracy. But it turned out that he came here to assure President Marcos of the support of the Carter administration. The visit was a signal that Carter was going to continue the policy of the Nixon and Ford administrations." The Carter administration, Macapagal argues, "did nothing to alleviate the subjection of the Filipinos to the rule of martial law."

Father Reuter, the American-born Jesuit, was also disappointed. The Americans had sought a meeting with him, but the priest was requested by the Mondale people not to pass through the hotel lobby but to enter the back way, in order to minimize the chances of antagonizing Marcos. Reuter's request to Mondale was a simple one: "Don't help this guy anymore. Don't give him any more military aid because he's only using it to kill Filipinos." After the meeting Reuter thought "maybe something would happen. But it didn't." Reuter was disappointed with the Carter administration in general. "The hopes went up," he said, explaining the reaction after Carter's victory. "There was a change of tone, but no action." Around the world, within a year and a half after Carter had come into office, church and political leaders in countries ruled by dictators were registering similar disappointment. In May 1978 the archbishop of San Salvador, Oscar Arnulfo Romero, who two years later paid with his life for his outspoken criticism of the government's repression, said, "I feel greatly disappointed because we had hoped the U.S. policy on human rights would be more sincere."

The Philippine opposition was so angered by the Mondale visit that most of its members stopped talking with the U.S. embassy. When UN Ambassador Andrew Young came to Manila a year later, the embassy found it difficult to find any opposition leaders willing to meet with him (and the visit was just as devastating to the democratic opposition as Mondale's had been, with Young so effusive in his praise of the Marcoses that Holbrooke's office was stunned). Contacts with any opposition to an existing government are always sensitive because the nature of diplomatic relations is government to government. Usually a second- or third-level embassy officer in the political section is assigned to maintain a liaison with opposition leaders. The job isn't difficult in a democratic country, where the opposition is an accepted part of the system, but conversely, it is more difficult in a dictatorship where the opposition is not tolerated. Still, those opposition contacts are critical, not because of any abstract moral principle but because of a very pragmatic one: The opposition may someday become the government. Indeed, two of the opposition leaders arrested after the April 9 protest march in Manila (and who were still being detained when Mondale arrived, further underscoring the inappropriateness of his visits) were Aquilino Pimentel and Joker Arroyo, who eight years later became high-level members of Corazon Aquino's cabinet.

After the Mondale visit the embassy reduced its efforts to reach out to the opposition. There was a definite "squeamishness" in Washington about the embassy's contacts with the opposition, Robert Wenzel, the political counselor who ran afoul of Holbrooke, and others in the embassy felt. Overall, after the Mondale visit, "the Administration's human rights diplomacy was less active," two scholars on the Philippines, Larry Niksch and Marjorie Niehaus, concluded in an analysis for the Congressional Research Service. "There were fewer public statements," they explained, and "fewer direct initiatives above the ambassadorial level."

Three years later Vice President George Bush was to travel to Manila and praise Marcos's "adherence to democratic principles and to the democratic processes." He was heckled and jeered by American editorial writers, the words hung on him, tightened around his

245

neck the harder he ran. But Mondale's visit, it may be argued, was maybe even a stronger endorsement of the Marcos dictatorship than Bush's Orwellan toast. Bush, after all, was the member of a conservative administration which made no effort to disguise its sympathy for and admiration of strong, conservative, anti-Communist, pro-American dictators. Mondale, on the other hand, was a liberal in an administration that professed a commitment to human rights. Whatever Mondale might have said about human rights, and notwithstanding his perfunctory meetings with the opposition, his visit was seen by Marcos and Filipinos as an endorsement of the regime. The *Bulletin Today,* a paper owned by a former Marcos military adviser, summed it up when it declared that Mondale's visit "proved that the irritants in the relationship of the two countries are minor in relation to the overall picture." The editorial concluded: "His visit affirmed the warmth of the relationship."

With Mondale's visit the Carter human rights policy was fully exposed for what it was: much ado about little. Holbrooke had said during the administration's first month in office that U.S. military and economic assistance to the Philippines would not be cut because of Marcos's human rights abuses. One year later the administration reiterated that there would be no cuts in military aid; the State Department's report at the time accused the Marcos government of torture, electric shock, long isolations, beatings, and the "severe curtailment of human rights of individual citizens." Moreover, this announcement of "aid-as-usual" came three weeks after the Derian visit, so whatever message she had delivered about human rights, Marcos could now ignore. Forget the words; look at the deeds. Then came the fraudulent elections, followed by Mondale's visit, at a time when *The New York Times* reported that none of America's allies was violating human rights "more egregiously than the Government of President Ferdinand E. Marcos." What was left? Why should Marcos believe that he had to do anything toward improving human rights, toward restoring democracy? Marcos had taken on Carter's human rights policy and rendered it impotent. In what has to be regarded as a silent taunt, after the election and before Mondale's visit, Marcos charged Trinidad Herrera, the slum organizer whose release from prison in early 1977 was heralded as a demonstration of Carter's commitment to human rights, with "subversion."

Yet for all that had been done for Marcos, for Mondale's having extended the cloak of respectability, for the continuing aid and the efforts not to offend Marcos, the administration still did not have what it desperately coveted: a bases agreement. Mondale and Marcos had issued a statement pertaining to the bases, one which recognized Philippine sovereignty and at the same time provided for unhampered U.S. access. But there was still no final agreement. Then along came Imelda Marcos, on a visit to the United States, imperiously demanding to be received, supremely confident of her ability to charm, and venting her pique when she failed to be treated in a manner which did not accord with her exalted sense of self-importance.

Mrs. Marcos had been chafing at home for what for her was an inordinately long hiatus, at least six months. In July she set off again, first stop Moscow, her third visit to the Soviet Union; she viewed each of them as means to deliver affronts to the United States. Lest the message be lost, this year she met with Prime Minister Aleksei Kosygin on July 4. The picture of them together, framed in silver, was prominently displayed years later in her music room in Malacañang. At the cosmonaut community and training center twenty-five miles from Moscow, she laid flowers at the base of the huge memorial statute honoring Yuri Gagarin, the first person in space. For her birthday, on July 2, she handed out "Happy Birthday" T-shirts. During the dinner in her honor, she toasted the Soviet Union for demonstrating "the noble dimensions of the maximum wholeness which man can achieve," for bringing "fullness to the lives of man."

After nine days of spartan communism, Mrs. Marcos was ready for some unbridled capitalism. On her first full day in New York City, it was antiques, $193,320 worth, including a $12,000 Ming-period side table; a pair of Georgian mahogany Gainsborough armchairs ($24,000); a Sheraton double-side writing desk ($6,240); a George II wood side table with marble top ($11,600). The purchaser was listed as the Philippine consulate on Fifth Avenue. That meant that Philippine government money had been spent and that the purchases were exempt from New York sales tax. But all the antiques were for Imelda Marcos. A week later it was time for some personal shopping, Mrs. Marcos storming through Manhattan's elegant jewelry stores. In a one-day spree: $2,181,000. A platinum and emerald bracelet with diamonds from Bulgari alone cost $1,150,000. She also paid $330,000 for a necklace with a ruby, emeralds, and diamonds; $300,000 for a ring with heart-shaped emeralds; $78,000 for eighteen-carat gold ear clips with diamonds; $300,000 for a pendant with canary diamonds, rubies, and emeralds on a gold chain.

After sating herself in New York, Imelda Marcos, with her thirty-six person entourage dutifully in step, dropped down to Washington for a bit of democracy; she was to learn that it couldn't always be purchased. The lesson was delivered somewhat abrasively by a group of congressmen, in a manner to which she was not accustomed. Why she had sought the meeting with the members of Congress who had signed a letter protesting the fraud in the recent Philippine elections was understandable. She had been charming political potentates for years. She had bestowed gifts on them, danced with them, sung with them, Democrats and Republicans. Surely she could handle a few lowly congressmen. Her advisers tried to dissuade her. Berkley Bedell, a mild-mannered Democrat from Iowa who had initiated the letter expressing concern about the electoral fraud, also had reservations, fearing what his colleagues would do to this imperious woman. Imelda Marcos was undeterred.

She had made an error in judgment. These were mostly liberals, men and one woman, who cared about human rights, who weren't about to be satisfied with her sweet verbal wanderings about love, truth, justice, beauty, holes in the skies, through which beams directed power on to the Philippines. For this audience she summoned a few tears when she talked about World War II. It didn't work. Father Robert Drinan, a Jesuit from Massachusetts, who was forced to give up his seat a few years later under an edict from Pope John Paul II that priests and politics don't mix, asked about persecution of the church. Yvonne Burke, a black congresswoman from a Los Angeles district of Filipino voters, wanted to know about Trinidad Herrera. Imelda Marcos said Mrs. Herrera was a Communist. That led to questions by Fortney ("Pete") Stark, from the San Francisco Bay Area, about whether it was illegal to be a Communist in the Philippines, whether the penalty was death, imprisonment, or expulsion, a fitting line of inquiry considering that Mrs. Marcos had just come from praising the Soviet Union. She avoided a direct answer, saying, "We believe in free enterprise and we don't intend to have a Communist ideology." Stark, who had been a wealthy banker, and John F. Seiberling, from Akron, Ohio, and heir to a tire and rubber fortune, asked Mrs. Marcos about her wealth and spending. She told them about her nutrition programs, then joked that if she had as much money as everyone said, perhaps she should help New York City (which was in the midst of its fiscal crisis). Leo Ryan, whose South San Francisco district included a sizable Philippine population (as well as a number of young people who had headed off to Jonestown, Guyana, where Ryan was killed), asked her about the reports of the electoral fraud.* She insisted the elections had been "clean." It took Tom Harkin, the resident human rights liberal, to put the punctuation point on the session. "Mrs. Marcos, this reminds me of a meeting I had in the Presidential Palace in Saigon in 1970. . . ." The Vietnamese president "went on and on about how we had to stay in Vietnam—how we had to support the regime because of the Communist threat—and that the Communists were exported by the Chinese and if we didn't stop the Chinese there, the Chinese would take over in Vietnam, the Chinese would be in Japan, the Chinese would be in the Philippines, and on and on and on. The next thing we know, they'd be in Los Angeles."

"Barbarians," Mrs. Marcos said after the session. She compared it to the Spanish Inquisition. She told the Philippine embassy staff in Washington, "I have been to Peking. I have been to Moscow. I have been to Libya. Nobody ever treated me so rudely."

The next day, still smarting, she went to the White House. She had been seeking an audience with Carter, though she hadn't made an official request for fear that it would be rejected. As expected, Derian and the Human Rights Bureau were opposed to any meeting between Carter and Imelda Marcos, not even a short one, a "drop-in," as it is called, when the president sticks his head in, usually while the American first lady is entertaining over tea. Holbrooke's

---

* Ryan was killed in 1978 when he went to investigate the People's Temple; his murder was followed by the bloody suicide-massacre.

249

bureau wanted a meeting, and the Philippine desk officer, John Monjo, became "exasperated" with Derian and her staff for their intransigence. In the end Mrs. Marcos met with Mondale, Newsom (back in Washington as the number three man in the State Department), and Holbrooke. The president stopped by for a perfunctory hello. The meeting didn't mean much to any of the high-level Americans, but it meant a great deal to Imelda Marcos. There on the front page of the *Bulletin Today* was the Philippine first lady chatting with the vice president of the United States, Holbrooke listening intently from across the heavy table in the Roosevelt Room. Holbrooke's scrapbook photo shows them all "sharing a laugh." The photos and stories in the Manila papers were yet another message to Filipinos that even the human rights-oriented Carter administration courted Marcos. And as if Washington had not done enough for Marcos, while in the capital, Imelda Marcos signed an $88 million loan agreement with the World Bank.

Then she headed home, and when she arrived, the woman who had been roughed up by the congressional liberals and had not received the audience from Carter that she thought she deserved unleashed her fury. The next day Marcos announced that he was suspending negotiations on the bases. Then came a succession of stories in the government-controlled newspapers that were critical of the bases. There were anti-bases rallies and protests by a government-sponsored youth organization, Kabataang Barangay. During one rally an attractive twenty-two-year-old woman, neatly dressed, with her dark shoulder-length hair in a flip, led the chanting of "Yankee, go home." "Step up the drumbeat," she shouted. And who was the leader? Imee Marcos. She wasn't rebelling against her parents; she was assisting them, principally her mother, in rebelling against the United States.

It wasn't a serious rebellion, not one of politics but of personal pique. A month later, in September 1978, Marcos, anxious for an agreement, resumed negotiations. Senator Inouye went to Manila to tell his friend that he would be wise to accept what the administration was offering because Congress wasn't likely to cough up any more money. But Marcos wanted a bit more, perhaps, some of the American negotiators thought, only to demonstrate that he could score last. Washington was offering a military aid package that amounted to $450 million for five years. Marcos wanted $500 million.

Up at Ilocos Norte for the Christmas holidays, Marcos made his pitch to Ambassador Murphy, who had succeeded Newsom and wasn't about to go on any year-end vacation, or let Marcos enjoy one, until there was a bases agreement. Murphy called Holbrooke, who called Vance, who called Carter. Add $50 million, and we've got a deal, the secretary of state told the president. OK, said Carter. Then the message went down the line in reverse—Vance to Holbrooke to Murphy to Marcos.

The Philippine opposition was furious when the agreement was announced. On Christmas Day 1978 forty-two of them signed and sent a letter of protest, outlining their reasons for opposing the continuation of the bases on Philippine soil. They condemned "the Marcos martial law regime for bartering the survival, the development and the welfare of the Filipino people for compensation which will help perpetuate it in power without the free consent of our people." The signers weren't Communists. They were prominent, respected Filipino leaders. Among them were seven ex-senators, including José Diokno, who had been jailed for two years after martial law; Jovito Salonga, the man badly injured at the Plaza Miranda bombing; Ramón Mitra, also jailed at the time of martial law, who in 1986 joined Mrs. Aquino's cabinet; Ninoy Aquino, still in jail; and Lorenzo Tañada, the feisty seventy-nine-year-old who had been arrested during the demonstrations after the fraudulent election in April 1978. It was also signed by former President Macapagal; the former president of the University of the Philippines, Salvador López; four Catholic sisters and two bishops. At a time when outspoken criticism of Marcos could mean jail, the letter was an act of conscience and courage.

More remarkable than the criticisms of Marcos, and what should have been more troubling to Carter, was the condemnation of his administration: "We denounce the Carter administration for advocating respect for human rights while at the same time generously subsidizing a dictator and imposing the continued presence of its bases upon a people shackled by martial law, thereby denying them the most basic of all human rights, namely, their right to survival." It was the first time a group this diverse had joined on any issue. The price of U.S. support for the Marcos dictatorship was beginning to emerge, only barely, but it was beginning.

In Washington, however, December 1978 was a time for rejoicing for Holbrooke and his staff. "We were euphoric," Holbrooke recalled. "We'd had a hell of a December." The bases negotiations were completed, and something else Holbrooke cared about, and had played a role in achieving, had come to fruition: Carter announced on December 16 that U.S.-China relations would be normalized. The next day the administration revealed that China's vice-premier Deng Xiaoping would make an official visit to the United States, becoming the highest Chinese leader to visit in more than three decades.

But Southeast Asia was in turmoil, the countries being rearranged on the geopolitical checkerboard. In November Vietnam and the Soviet Union had signed a treaty of friendship and cooperation, which obligated the superpower to come to Vietnam's defense if the latter was attacked. A few weeks later Vietnam was the aggressor, invading Kampuchea, capturing Phnom Penh on January 7, 1979, leading to the ouster of the genocidal dictator Pol Pot. Six weeks later the Chinese invaded Vietnam.

Yet with all the activity in Southeast Asia it was events in another part of the world that burst the Carter administration's euphoria and appeared to raise the most disturbing questions about U.S. policy in the Philippines.

11 : Marcos
Grows Stronger

The year 1979 was not a good one for dictators or for the Carter administration. It became an embattled and eventually a defeated administration in the aftermath of the fall of Mohammad Reza Pahlavi. The shah of Iran was chased out of his country in January 1979, replaced by the ayatollah Ruhollah Khomeini, beginning one of the most traumatic periods for American foreign policymakers. Six months later the Sandinistas marched into Managua, sending Anastasio Somoza Debayle on a hasty flight, first to Miami, then to Paraguay, the culmination of a prolonged guerrilla war against the Somoza family.* Only three months after the Sandinista triumph, in neighboring El Salvador a coup by moderate military officers marked the beginning of the end of nearly half a century of repressive military rule in that tiny country. Eleven days later, on October 26, on the other side of the world, South Korea's General Park Chung Hee, who had ruled his country for sixteen years, was assassinated by the chief of the Korean CIA.

Was Marcos next? It seemed the obvious question, more so when one looked at the parallels between the shah, Somoza, and Marcos. During their reigns the three had amassed prodigious personal fortunes while their country's poor were strangled by poverty. Many of the American diplomats and Filipinos who knew Imelda Marcos well thought that her sojourn to Persepolis for the blowout there in 1971 was the turning point for her, that after it she matched, if not outdid, the shah in excessive ostentation. Like Marcos, the shah and Somoza held elections, but they were fraudulent, façades for one-man rule, designed to please and appease Washington. Admin-

---

* Somoza was assassinated in Paraguay on September 17, 1980.

istrations, Democrat and Republican, regularly genuflected before the pro-American, anti-Communist dictators. The Somoza family dynasty reached back to 1932, when the United States handpicked a Somoza to head the country's army, which had been created by the United States. The shah had been placed in power by the CIA in 1953. Nixon had Somoza to the White House for dinner; Carter and his wife spent New Year's Eve in 1977 with the shah. The American president toasted Iran as "an island of stability" and waxed enthusiastic about the shah's rule.

When it finally penetrated that neither the shah nor Somoza served America's best interests (much less his own nation's), Washington withdrew support. Imelda Marcos's reaction to the Shah's ouster was that her nemesis, William Sullivan, who was now ambassador in Iran, had succeeded in doing there what he had tried but failed to do in the Philippines. But in both Iran and Nicaragua the United States had waited too long before moving away from the dictator; as a consequence, it was unable to influence the events that came after their falls. Khomeini's rabid revolutionaries seized the American embassy and hostages, and along with them the American psyche. The Sandinista takeover was far less radical, the anti-Americanism confined principally to rhetoric, but within the Carter administration there was considerable dissatisfaction with the outcome in Nicaragua. David Aaron, Carter's number two man on the National Security Council and a close adviser to Mondale during the 1984 campaign, told friends after Carter had been defeated by Reagan that there were only two things he blamed Jimmy Carter for: Ronald Reagan and the Sandinistas. It was said with wry cynicism, but Aaron, along with Brzezinski and Holbrooke, was not pleased with the Sandinistas and became a supporter of Reagan's contra war to overthrow their government.

Yet in spite of the ominous similarities between the Philippines under Marcos, Somoza's Nicaragua, and the shah's Iran and the potential for similarly disastrous outcomes—at least from the perspective of the Carter administration—there was no reexamination of America's Philippine policy in 1979. Long-range thinking and planning are not prevalent among diplomats, their absence as glaring a weakness of American foreign policy as of American business.

At the conservative Rand Corporation Guy Pauker, a Southeast

Asian expert who had been studying and writing about that part of the world for the benefit of the U.S. government for a couple of decades, wrote a memorandum after the fall of the shah suggesting a look at the potential instability and succession problems in three Asian governments: South Korea, Indonesia, and the Philippines. Washington wasn't interested. It explained to Rand that U.S. relations with each of the three countries were solid, that there was no need for concern. After Park had been assassinated in October 1979, someone in Washington lamented that Pauker had not been commissioned to do the study, and in 1981, as Marcos's rule began to look more tenuous, Pauker was finally asked to look at the what-happens-next question.

The analogies between the shah and Marcos consumed outsiders, but not the policymakers. "The Philippines: The Next Iran?" became a stock title for articles by journalists and scholars. Holbrooke, however, did not convene any high-level or interagency meetings to probe for lessons. "After the shah falls, you don't have a meeting on the Philippines," he says. "You have a meeting on Iran, which you should have had earlier." All the concern about the Philippines' becoming another Nicaragua or another Iran, he says, was "journalistic talk. You, of course, make the analogy, but it doesn't affect anything. It's just background noise."

In a narrow sense there were significant differences between the Philippines and Iran. The former is a Catholic country; in Iran fundamentalist Islam added the fever and fervor to the revolution. The Philippines also has a democratic tradition, and there exists a deep reservoir of goodwill toward the United States, both of which augur against an outbreak of violent anti-Americanism. In a broader sense, however, there were disturbing parallels, and these were what the policymakers should have seen. In the Philippines—as in Iran, as in Nicaragua—the United States was backing a corrupt dictator who was looting his people, was growing increasingly isolated from them, and had lost their support.

But far from leading to a policy that put some distance between Washington and Marcos, the overthrow of the shah and Somoza saw a strengthening of the Philippine dictator's position vis-à-vis the Carter administration. If that outcome seems to be an irony, and a tragic one, it was also inevitable. The Iranian hostage crisis so weakened the Carter administration that it had little influence over world events. At home the administration was under siege from conservatives for having "lost" Iran and Nicaragua. It was not an environment for Carter to take on another right-wing dictator. Consequently, there were even fewer talks with Marcos about human rights than before. Marcos was welcomed in Honolulu by Holbrooke in the Philippine leader's first trip to America since 1966, and there were discussions about inviting him to Washington for a state visit. When some members of Congress who were worried about another Iran sought to withhold a little of the money that the United States was giving Marcos, the Carter administration resisted with stunning determination. As the administration watched, the Marcoses plundered.

The State Department once described the Somoza family dynasty as a "kleptocracy." A new word will have to be found to depict the Marcoses. Somoza's personal wealth was put at $500 million. The Marcoses make him look like a piker. The depth of the Marcoses' greed wouldn't begin to register fully with the public until 1985, but the corrupt accumulation had begun far earlier and was known to the Carter administration. By 1979 Ferdinand Marcos, who had no inherited wealth and whose annual salary for the past fifteen years had been less than $6,000, and his wife were almost certainly the wealthiest couple in Asia and quite possibly in the entire world, with the exception of an oil sheik or two.

How much wealth had the Marcoses accumulated through corruption? "Enough to break the strongest computer in the house," just trying to calculate it, CIA station chief Herbert Natzke said in 1979. A billion dollars? he was asked. "At least that," he answered flatly.* The Marcoses flaunted it on the occasion of their twenty-fifth wedding anniversary. For the silver celebration, a planeload of royalty was flown in from Europe. Cardinal Sin, the "critical collaborator," officiated as the Philippine first couple renewed their vows, Imelda Marcos, her head bowed reverentially beneath a white

---

* Natzke left the agency to go to work for a Philippine banker closely allied with Imelda Marcos. Many of Natzke's colleagues and superiors were chagrined.

veil, fondling a rosary two feet long, each bead a diamond. It was probably worth at least $1 million. Music was provided by the Manila Symphony; there was dancing until dawn. None of this opulence was shown on TV or even reported by the Marcos-controlled press, not to the millions of Filipinos who were lucky to be earning $500 a year.

Marcos was a brilliant man, Natzke once observed, but he had two flaws: "He can't avoid stealing everything in sight, and he can't control his wife." Marcos made no effort to control his wife. On the contrary, he gave her more authority to abuse. By 1979 she was "functioning increasingly as the head of Government," noted the Defense Intelligence Agency in a highly classified analysis from Manila (classified Secret and not to be shared with *any* foreign governments). Three years after naming her governor of Metro Manila, Marcos, in 1978, created something called the Ministry of Human Settlements; she was named minister. She talked about the development of the "whole" man, who was "at the center of all things." She explained her theory of man and development to everyone, from journalists to cabinet ministers to visiting dignitaries, doodling on a napkin or drawing on a blackboard. She'd draw a triangle to represent the people. Then she'd draw a square—the means or tools—followed by a circle—the whole man. All these together equaled the heart, which she would draw. One of her projects had the acronym BLISS. There were agencies, and subagencies: the National Electrification Commission; National Food Authority; National Housing Corporation: National Home Mortgage Corporation; National Pollution Control Commission; Rural Waterworks Development Corporation. She was chairwoman or director of all of them—and through them passed hundreds of millions of American aid dollars. She came up with cute little sayings. "I am S and S," she would say, "their slave and star," by way of explaining her relationship to her country's poor. She devised a program for the country's prisoners: She gave each a pet rabbit or plant to keep in his or her cell, to teach the prisoners love and caring. Other projects were simple but effective. She outfitted 10,000 poor Filipinos, men and women, in yellow T-shirts, with red letters—"Metro-Manila Aide"—paid each less than $2 a day, and had them sweep the streets.

Mrs. Marcos spent and built—the more, the larger, the better.

She built a hospital. It wasn't just any hospital; it was a heart hospital. She didn't name it the Manila Heart Hospital or even the Heart Hospital of the Philippines. It was the Philippine Heart Center *for Asia*. It was ultramodern, cost at least $50 million, and had only 100 beds, in suites. Meanwhile, at least three out of every five Filipino children suffered from malnutrition. Proportionately there were fewer doctors in the Philippines than in North or South Korea (the doctor to population ratio 1:3,000 in the Philippines; 1:1,000 in North Korea; 1:2,000, South Korea).

The Philippine first lady moved about sprawling Manila in a black Cadillac with the license plate IM777, a light in the back not for reading but to shine on her face. For longer trips into the countryside she had a custom-built bus, used most frequently for taking important people, U.S. officials and reporters, on tours of her pet projects. Between stops they would be entertained with music and video tapes of her in action, from holding Mao's hand to smiling with Qaddafi.

She hardly had time to govern, spending so much time outside the country. After her husband had nationalized Philippine Airlines (the owner made the mistake of submitting a bill for expenses Imelda Marcos had incurred), PAL became a virtual private commuter line for her and her entourage of Blue Ladies and sycophants, often numbering more than 100. When she grew impatient, she ordered pilots to violate airport regulations in order to land or take off, drawing fines, which the Philippine government paid. Sometimes, after ferrying Imelda Marcos and her retinue to their destination, say, Honolulu, the planes would fly back to Manila empty to continue their commercial runs, then return to wherever she had gone to pick her up. On other occasions PAL's paying passengers were simply forced to wait, as they did when Mrs. Marcos once decided to take a side trip from Rome to Copenhagen; for two days PAL passengers were stranded in Rome until the plane returned and continued to Manila. When she traveled to the United States, officials were kept busy arranging for special landing rights and parking privileges for the jet and Secret Service protection for her, even though she was not a head of state and therefore not automatically entitled to it. Imelda Marcos was always treated with special care.

New York was her favorite city, the place where she could spend the most. In September 1976 the Marcoses purchased a condominium in the Olympic Towers on Fifth Avenue; five months later they bought the three adjoining apartments, altogether paying some $4 million. But when in New York, Imelda Marcos usually stayed at the Waldorf-Astoria on Park Avenue, where her vast suite was always so filled with flowers that American diplomats she summoned there for meetings thought they were entering a funeral parlor. When she arrived in New York, one of her first calls was often to Harry Winston, the Fifth Avenue jeweler. A man would quickly come over, lugging two suitcases, with two bodyguards. Mrs. Marcos would spill out the contents onto her bed and fondle and kiss each of the necklaces, earrings, brooches, rings of diamonds, pearls, rubies, sapphires. And then she would be out to spend more. The money came from the New York branch of the Philippine National Bank, brought to her hotel room in suitcases, sometimes as much as $250,000 at a time; between 1973 and 1986 some $30 million was taken out of the bank in cash and hand delivered to Imelda Marcos.

The Marcoses took care of family and friends as well, divvying up the economy, from coconuts to casinos, and giving a piece to this relative, that friend. It would be dubbed "crony capitalism." Rarely, if ever, in history have so few stolen so much from so many.

Imelda Marcos's youngest sister and her husband owned 60 percent of Manila's Century Park Sheraton, a plush five-star hotel: a one-acre lobby; an indoor waterfall; a lagoon in which a harpist performed on an island. It was financed by the government's Development Bank of the Philippines. They also owned a block-square shopping mall, built on city property which had been cleared of squatters by the Marcos government supposedly to prepare the land for a zoo. One of Imelda Marcos's younger brothers, Alfredo Romualdez, operated the jai alai fronton, having been given the franchise in 1975, when Marcos took it away from the former owners. The government agency responsible for supervising the jai alai play and gambling was chaired by an Imelda Marcos appointee. In 1977 the jai alai company took in about $57 million; $28.5 million was paid to gamblers, and $13 million to the government, leaving $15.5 million to be split up according to the Marcos family's wishes.

Additional gambling revenues came in from the floating casinos. Marcos had closed the casinos when he declared martial law—part of his drive for a "New Society"—but in late 1975 a 5,000-ton vessel, subsequently dubbed the "Philippine tourist," was purchased in Oslo, Norway, for $4 million. It had 68 gaming tables (roulette, blackjack, and baccarat) and 110 slot machines. Later a 10,000-ton vessel with 80 gaming tables and 150 slot machines was purchased. On January 1, 1977, Marcos by decree created the Philippine Amusement and Gaming Corporation (Pagcor). It was exempt from taxes; its employees were not protected by civil service or wage and labor regulations, and they were prohibited from striking. When the floating casinos opened, Imelda Marcos came up with a clever phrase: "We will legalize virtue, we will not legalize vice." It was legalized theft for the Marcoses. In 1977 the Manila casinos generated about $165 million in income; $82 million was paid back to customers in winnings; $16 million to the government for public works projects. That left $67 million for the owners and operators of the casinos—the first lady's brother Alfredo and Roberto Benedicto, who had been Marcos's classmate and fraternity brother during law school in the 1930s and had remained a very close friend.

Benedicto, described by the embassy as "one of the most notorious of the presidential cronies," also owned the largest television and radio network in the Philippines—the one Marcos had expropriated from the López family. But that wasn't enough. Marcos, using his martial law powers, nationalized the sugar industry, creating two government agencies, one to regulate the sugar production, the other to control the marketing and sale of all the country's sugar at home and abroad. Benedicto was named the head of both. The sugar operations were financed by the government-owned Philippine National Bank, which was headed for a while by Benedicto, who was also ambassador to Japan. Later, in 1978, Marcos decreed that a commercial bank, Republic Planters, was to be the lending facility for sugar growers. The bank's chairman? Benedicto.

During the first year of the government sugar monopoly, 1973, growers were paid thirteen cents a pound for their sugar, which the government then resold on the international market for forty cents a pound; the profits that should have been going to private growers went, instead, to the government, so that there was more for Marcos, Benedicto, and others to siphon off. Expecting world prices to go even higher, Marcos and Benedicto did what all good monopolists do: They hoarded. Philippine sugar piled up in warehouses, school gymnasiums, swimming pools, tennis courts, and even churches around the country. But they had gambled wrong: Instead of rising further, the world price of sugar plummeted (as corn sweeteners began to replace sugar and as sugarless soft drinks caught on). The losses were staggering, in the hundreds of millions of dollars. Those were, of course, government losses, which meant losses to the people of the Philippines. Neither Marcos nor Benedicto suffered. Indeed, in 1976 Benedicto purchased not one but two houses in Beverly Hills and with money from a Swiss bank account opened a bank in Los Angeles, the California-Overseas Bank, into which, during the next few years—when sugar losses were mounting—he channeled more than $30 million.

Another who made it rich in sugar was Antonio O. Floirendo. Until Marcos became a dictator, Floirendo had been a struggling Ford dealer in the southern city of Davao, his franchise worth about as much perhaps as one in Billings, Montana, in 1940. He worked for Marcos in his 1965 and 1969 campaigns, and Imelda Marcos reciprocated by arranging for Floirendo to receive the lease on 17,000 acres of public land where the Davao penal colony was located—which he converted into one of the largest banana plantations in the world. The convicts were an always available supply of cheap labor, even cheaper than the dollar or two a day other Philippine farm workers received. Branching out from bananas to sugar, Floirendo brokered a deal, in 1976, for the SuCrest Corporation, a New York-based refinery, to buy the glut of Philippine sugar. Floirendo's commission was nearly $1.2 million. It was a sweet deal—for SuCrest. The sugar-purchase contract provided that SuCrest could take out all expenses and a fixed profit *before* remitting anything to the Philippine government, which was *not* guaranteed any profit. A year later SuCrest sold the lucrative contract, as well as its refineries in Chicago, New York, and Boston to Floirendo, who was, not surprisingly, acting as a front for, and in partnership with, Marcos.

Benedicto and Floirendo, who was a regular in Imelda Marcos's flying retinue, had their counterparts in the coconut industry, principally Eduardo Cojuangco, who had been the only civilian involved in the martial law takeover. Cojuangco was godfather to Marcos's son and had named his eldest son Marcos. He was also Corazon

Aquino's cousin, and some of his initial post martial law acquisitions were grabbed from the Aquinos as part of Marcos's destruction of his rival. The Aquino family had been forced to sell its holding company when its bus company ran into serious financial difficulties—in large measure because the Marcos government would not approve a fare increase in 1973 in spite of the spiraling cost of oil and fuel. Shortly after declaring martial law, Marcos also set new capitalization requirements for banks, the effect of which was that the First United Bank, owned by the Aquino clan, had to be sold.

The Marcos government refused to approve the sale to four prospective buyers; then Mrs. Marcos's brother Kokoy Romualdez suggested selling the bank to Cojuangco. Marcos, of course, approved, with the purchase financed in part by loans from the government-owned Philippine National Bank. The new bank was appropriately named the United Coconut Planters Bank since the money came from coconut planters, part of another Marcos defalcation. Using his decree powers, Marcos, in 1973, imposed a levy on the country's coconut planters. The idea for the levy and bank had come from Defense Minister Enrile, who was named the bank's chairman; he was also the chairman of the Philippine National Bank. Enrile insisted at the time that he owned only a few shares of the UCPB, just enough to gain a seat on the board of directors; in fact, he held a large chunk. He hid his involvement by placing the shares in the name of a corporation, which he and his wife secretly controlled. Cojuangco was president of the UCPB.

Over the years the coconut planters, through the government-imposed levies, paid more than $1 billion into the bank. Where it went, nobody knows—nobody, that is, except Marcos, Cojuangco, and Enrile. But there can be little doubt that it went into their ostentatious life-styles. Cojuangco, one of the richest men in the Philippines, owned most of Palawan, the elongated island that stretches southwesterly from below Manila, and a $20 million stud ranch in Australia. Enrile, who had been in government service since 1965, had by 1979 already purchased two condominiums in a luxurious building on Broadway in San Francisco, one of the most expensive hills in the City by the Bay. Enrile's wife, Christina, was the registered owner, and in 1982, when the Enriles purchased a $1.9 million apartment one block away, the other two apartments were transferred to a corporation called Renatsac, which was the backward spelling of Christina Enrile's maiden name. But coconut wasn't the only source of Enrile's extracurricular wealth. He also acquired a near monopoly of the country's logging and timber industry, one of the most lucrative after coconut and sugar, using his military muscle to force competitors out of business or to sell their operations to him.

How was it, Roy Rowan of *Fortune* magazine asked Imelda Marcos in 1979, that all these relatives and friends had managed to become so wealthy? "Sometimes you have smart relatives who can make it," she began simply and with conviction. "My dear," she added, "there are always people who are just a little faster, more brilliant, and more aggressive."* Her answer gave rise to the title of a study clandestinely published by a group of Philippine businessmen and professionals about the extent of crony capitalism: "Some Are Smarter Than Others."

The reality, of course, was that financial success during the Marcos reign bore as meager a relationship to intelligence or ability as Marcos's elections did to democracy. Many of those in the gallery of the Philippine nouveau riche, especially those hung there by Imelda Marcos, weren't entrepreneurs; they were money leeches.

It wasn't just money that drove Marcos to monopolize the economy for himself and his friends. In fact, for him, money was almost secondary. He wanted power. In explaining the coconut and sugar monopolies, the embassy noted that he was motivated "first" by the "intense drive to power that placed Marcos in the Presidency in the first place and which has kept him there." With control, the embassy added, he had acquired "additional political and financial leverage to remain in power." Marcos utilized his "feudal type" economic

---

* Back in the United States, writing his article for *Fortune,* Rowan received a phone call from Manila. It was Mrs. Marcos, who always thought she could influence anyone, especially a journalist, with a few soft words. It was nearly midnight for Rowan, but she talked on and on. Finally, to get her off the line, Rowan reminded her that he had been in Manila for her twenty-fifth wedding anniversary, which he had covered for *Life* magazine, and that he really should go to bed because the next day was his twenty-seventh wedding anniversary. The next morning a truck with a floral spray arrived at Rowan's Greenwich, Connecticut, home; it had come from Manhattan, not a local florist. There were so many flowers that they smothered a large table. "It looked like we'd won the Preakness," Rowan recalled.

system to reward, and ensure, loyalty from military officers as well as businessmen.

A case study of how the Marcos system functioned, the extent to which corruption didn't just permeate his regime but was both the oil which kept it running and the glue which held it together, and of how Washington aided and abetted the fraud and waste is provided by the details of a nuclear power plant project built in the Philippines by Westinghouse.

It was not surprising that Marcos decided, in 1973, that his country ought to have a nuclear power plant. Nuclear energy was considered the future for the modern world. The Philippines had to have it, to accord with the grandiose image Marcos had of himself and his nation. It was highly questionable, however, whether nuclear energy was wise or needed in the Philippines, questions raised not just by Luddites and antinuclear activists but also by those who thought about the welfare of the majority of the Philippine people.

Even on the basis of the most optimistic and exaggerated projections, only 15 percent of the population on the island of Luzon would receive their power from the nuclear plant Marcos proposed to build on the edge of the South China Sea in the province of Bataan. Three-quarters of the Philippine population lived in rural areas. They walked to wells for water or lugged it from polluted streams and rivers, where caribao sloshed, children frolicked, and women washed clothes. Only about one in ten rural shacks had any electricity, at most a bare light bulb. The Philippines was the poorest of the world's nations embarking on the nuclear path. In East Asia, only Japan, Taiwan, and South Korea were building or planning to build nuclear plants, and those countries were far more advanced economically and technologically than the Philippines.

There were also grave safety issues about the Philippines plant. The plant is located less than 100 miles from five volcanoes, four of which U.S. scientific officials consider active, and near three geologic faults. Six miles from the site is Subic Naval Base, with all its American military hardware, including nuclear weapons. A similar site would never have been approved in the United States.

From the beginning Washington was an enthusiastic backer of the project. The stack of cables to and from the embassy in Manila and Washington is nearly six inches thick. Not just the State Department was involved. This was the largest and most expensive construction project in Philippine history. The Philippine government couldn't begin to finance it from its own treasury, so it turned to the Export-Import Bank in Washington for assistance. While the bank, whose main purpose is to assist American companies doing business abroad by providing loans and guarantees, was considering the application, the projected cost of the plant escalated by 400 percent, to $1.2 billion. At that price it had serious repercussions for the Philippine economy, amounting to almost one-fifth of the country's foreign debt. It was also the most expensive nuclear plant project in the world, more than triple the cost of a similar size plant built by Westinghouse and financed by the Ex-Im Bank in Pusan, South Korea.

In spite of all this, the Ex-Im Bank, in 1975, agreed to provide $277 million in direct loans and $367 million in loan guarantees. Even more would come later, but it was already the largest loan package the Ex-Im Bank had approved anywhere in the world. The bank's chairman was William J. Casey, later CIA director under Reagan and until the bitter end one of Marcos's staunchest defenders. Casey approved the financing after meeting with Marcos in Malacañang and after conferring with Westinghouse officials in Washington.

The losers were the Philippine people—the poor, on whose behalf the billion dollars could have been better spent, as well as the middle class and the wealthy, who would have to shoulder this economically backbreaking colossus (and at the end of 1986 it was still not operating). The winners were Westinghouse, Marcos, and a man named Herminio Disini.

General Electric had appeared to have won the contract, with a bid of $700 million for two reactors, when Westinghouse, in desperate competition with its archrival, enlisted the services of Disini. In the land of fast riches, he was the king of speed. In 1970, after working for a decade as an accountant, Disini, at the age of thirty-four, started his own business—a tobacco filter company which he ran from a one-room rented office. His only employees were a secretary and the secretary's younger brother, who ran errands. Disini later hired the son of a high-level official in the Bureau of Internal Revenue to sell filters, the message to cigarette makers clearly being that if they wanted to avoid audits, they should buy from Disini.

Within a few years after this humble beginning, Disini, who regularly golfed with Marcos and whose wife was Imelda Marcos's cousin and had been governess for the Marcos children, was presiding over his Herdis Group, Inc., an agglomeration of more than some fifty companies—petrochemicals, airline charters, oil exploration, textile manufacturing, insurance—worth at least a billion dollars. It had been assembled with the help of millions of dollars in loans and loan guarantees from the government-owned Philippine National Bank, one for $25 million in order to buy the Caterpillar tractor franchise. Disini was granted the exclusive rights to log 500,000 acres of pine forest in Marcos's home region, which was twice the legal limit for a private concession and which the president granted after he had prohibited the previous holder from cutting the timber for environmental reasons. Disini's biggest break came in 1975, when Marcos levied a 100 percent duty on acetate tow, the raw material used to make filters. The tax put Disini's competitors out of business; he survived because a provision of Marcos's decree exempted Disini's company from paying any more than a 10 percent tax.

Shortly after retaining Disini, Westinghouse submitted a $500 million bid for two nuclear power plants. It was devoid of any details about cost or even specifications. By contrast, GE had invited Philippine officials to visit its nuclear plant in California, had conducted seminars on nuclear power in Manila, and had submitted four thick volumes on costs and specifications. Nevertheless, during a cabinet meeting Marcos announced that the contract would go to Westinghouse. He cut short all objections, refusing to allow any discussion. GE wasn't the only big loser. Also left out of the profits was Amex Bank Ltd., a London-based subsidiary of American Express. Amex was the leader of a syndicate of banks that was to lend $256.6 million to the Philippines for the nuclear project. Marcos yanked Amex and selected a consortium led by a subsidiary of New York's Citibank—after Disini had intervened on behalf of Citibank, which earned $2.5 million on the deal.

After it had locked in the contract, Westinghouse set about submitting a serious proposal. When it came in, it was for $1.2 billion for *one* reactor, or 400 percent higher than its original bid.* Little did Marcos care. He was guaranteed his take, which altogether would amount to nearly $80 million. Westinghouse didn't hand the money directly to Marcos. It paid Disini, through a maze of channels, cutouts, and stratagems. Disini owned a construction company, which he had purchased with a government-backed loan and which had been awarded, without bids, a cost plus fixed fee contract for all civil construction at the nuclear power plant site. The price of the equipment for the project "was inflated, as a way to cover the cost of the fees to Disini," a lawyer who worked on the project explained to Fox Butterfield of *The New York Times*. Westinghouse set up a subsidiary in Switzerland, which funneled the money into Disini's European bank accounts. The Swiss subsidiary, after entering into the deal with the Philippine government, assigned the contract to the Westinghouse International Projects Company, which had been established solely to handle the Philippine project. Westinghouse International, in turn, entered into a subcontract with the Westinghouse Electric Corporation, the parent company in Pittsburgh. Westinghouse officials repeatedly denied any wrongdoing in connection with the project.

In 1985 the *San Jose Mercury News* published a series of articles about crony capitalism in the Philippines, focusing on the real estate that the Marcoses and their friends—Benedicto, Floirendo, Enrile, Cojuangco, et al.—had purchased in California and New York. The series generated public outcry and congressional investigations, and the three reporters who conducted the investigation later received a Pulitzer Prize for their work. But it wasn't the first time that Marcos's corrupt system had been exposed. Articles had begun appearing in the mid-seventies in the *Los Angeles Times* (a front-page story about Imelda Marcos's hotels) and the *Wall Street Journal* (Disini and the Westinghouse deal) and regularly in the *Far Eastern Economic Review*. A free-lance writer, Brennon Jones, wrote about corruption in the sugar industry for the *Nation*,

---

* By 1986 the inoperative reactor had already cost the Philippines $2.1 billion. Interest costs alone were $210 million a year, nearly 10 percent of the total Philippine foreign debt.

the facts of which were repeated in many major journalistic articles several years later, when it became fashionable to criticize Marcos. In the *Washington Post* Jay Mathews and Bernard Wideman (the *Far Eastern Economic Review* correspondent whom the U.S. embassy considered one of the most knowledgeable reporters in the Philippines in the 1970s) wrote a front-page story about Marcos's nationalization of PAL, another about the Marcos family and gambling, and a longer piece about crony capitalism in general. Fox Butterfield of *The New York Times* wrote a series of articles in January 1978—about how Marcos, Cojuangco, and Enrile had taken over much of the Aquino empire; the Disini-Westinghouse deal; and how the National Grain Agency, which, like the sugar and coconut industries, had been monopolized by Marcos, had made at least $100 million in three years by keeping the price of wheat artificially high and misusing cheap credits from the U.S. Department of Agriculture. They were long articles, and all appeared on the front page. But they fell flat. Mondale went ahead with his visit to Manila four months later. Congress didn't undertake any investigations and, what's more, continued to pour hundreds of millions of U.S. dollars into the Marcoses' Philippines. There wasn't an outpouring of editorial rage.

Even for all that reporters revealed in 1978, there was more—and it was known to U.S. officials in positions to do something about it. CIA and embassy officers in Manila were, for example, well aware of the Westinghouse-Disini-Marcos connection by late 1978, if not much earlier; they thought the amount that Westinghouse had paid Disini was between $25 and $40 million, and they knew Disini was fronting for Marcos. After the accident at the Three-Mile Island nuclear plant in Harrisburg, Pennsylvania, in March 1979, Marcos suspended work on the Philippine project; Westinghouse began to complain. Ambassador Richard Murphy thought it a bit unseemly for Westinghouse to complain about anything, given its own conduct. Yet no action was taken by the Carter administration publicly or even privately. On the contrary, the administration continued to push the project. Washington advised Manila in October 1979, when the Nuclear Regulatory Commission was considering Westinghouse's license application, that the "executive branch had done its part by submitting favorable recommendation to NRC."

Similarly, the Carter administration protected Marcos in another payoff case, this one involving the purchase of the Philippine Long Distance Telephone Company. The General Telephone and Electronics Corporation owned 28 percent of the Philippine company, which GTE decided to sell in 1966 when it was beginning to appear that the rights of American companies to own Filipino utilities might be terminated. GTE located a group of purchasers, but during the negotiations the company suddenly decided to sell to another group, one of whose members was Ramón Cojuangco. Ten years later, in early 1977, the American Securities and Exchange Commission (SEC) charged that "officials at the highest level" of the Philippine government had intervened to force the sale to the Cojuangco group. Not only did GTE sell to the handpicked group, but it also made payments to it of at least $4.5 million, the money funneled through secret "commissions," credits, and uncollected loans. And who were the "officials at the highest levels" that the SEC would not publicly identify? One of them was Marcos. He had acquired shares, which were worth $15 million at the time he fled in 1986.*

It wasn't only that Marcos, his spouse, and their friends were acquiring such fabulous wealth that made the American policy so tragic. More painful was that it was done on the backs of the poor, grinding the overwhelming majority of Filipinos deeper into misery, malnutrition, and poverty—and turning them into willing recruits for the Communist New People's Army. "I never could get away from the disparity between wealth and poverty in the Philippines," says David Newsom, the ambassador for a brief period under Carter, who had seen crushing poverty during postings in Karachi, Baghdad, Africa, and Indonesia. "There was something about the conspicuous consumption, exemplified by Imelda, which ran counter to what we should stand for in the Philippines."

Perhaps the best picture of the Philippines was captured in this sentence, written in December 1977: "Almost eight decades after Admiral Dewey steamed into Manila Bay, a visitor to many rural

---

* American companies, such as Westinghouse and GTE, weren't the only ones making secret payments to Marcos. Indeed, according to Philippine businessmen and government officials, Japanese companies were considerably more willing to engage in this type of activity. Among the Japanese companies that made payments to Marcos: Kawatetsu Bussan Co., Ltd. ($311,874.08); Sumitomo Corporation ($212,708.75); and Kanematsu-Gosho Ltd. ($404,747).

areas of the Philippines today would see conditions similar to those first seen by Americans in the last century—a farmer in the field with his water buffalo; women washing clothes in the stream; homes without electricity, water, or toilets; malnutrition, especially among infants and children; no paved roads at all; no irrigation; no doctors or dentists."

This description of Philippine backwardness and poverty is the very first sentence in a report by the Agency for International Development (AID), the agency responsible for America's economic assistance program. No doubt it was intended as a justification for more millions in economic assistance. But it raised questions, unintentionally, about the effectiveness of Washington's aid programs. The amount of economic assistance the United States had sent to the Philippines from 1953 (in other words, *after* the World War II reconstruction period) through 1977 was slightly more than $1 billion; add another half billion for military assistance; then there was the indirect U.S. assistance in the form of loans and loan guarantees from the World Bank, Asian Development Bank, Ex-Im Bank, and International Monetary Fund. What the United States had helped perpetuate was a two-class system. The very wealthy, along with a small middle class, lived in Manila, a crowded, noisy metropolis with posh residential areas, a high-rise business district astride divided boulevards, mass transit, and shopping centers. The rest of the country—the rural poor—lived as they had for centuries.

If far too little of that American aid seemed to be trickling down during the 1950s and 1960s, the class system was exacerbated by Marcos after martial law. Marcos had promised a "New Society," a cornerstone of which was land redistribution. "If land reform fails, there is no New Society," he declared a few weeks after imposing martial law. It failed because Marcos never had any intention of implementing it. The original program gave a tenant farmer the right to buy a plot from the landowner whose property exceeded seven hectares (approximately seventeen acres). (Again, cutoff size was selected for no other reason than that seven was Marcos's lucky number.) It wasn't a very radical program. It didn't apply to the two-thirds of the country's agricultural lands—those that were planted with commercial crops, such as sugar, coconuts, and pineapples. But even the minimal plan was not implemented. By 1979 only 1,500 tenants, or about 0.5 percent of the entitled total, had received titles to 0.3 percent of the land reform area.

Marcos had promised a redistribution of wealth. On that he delivered—but he redistributed the wealth from the poor to the rich. Overall, by the mid-1970s seven out of every ten Filipinos were worse off economically as the result of martial law. Real wages for factory workers fell by about 30 percent in the first years of martial law, while consumer prices nearly tripled. The gap between the rich and the poor, already the most skewed in Asia when Marcos took over, worsened under his stewardship. Two out of every three Filipinos were living—"barely surviving" would be more accurate—below the poverty line, a substantially greater percentage of persons shoved into that squalor than when Marcos had become president.

Philippine soil is rich, there is plenty of rain and sunshine, and the people are hardworking. Yet, under martial law, while the palace royalty and their guests stuffed themselves on caviar, the Filipino people had become the poorest fed in all Asia. The per capita calorie intake was less in 1976 than it had been in 1960. This in spite of the United States' having provided the Philippines with more than $300 million under the Food for Peace program since 1960. In the 1950s Filipinos had probably been the best fed in Asia; now the people in India, Indonesia, and perhaps even Bangladesh were eating better than they. Malnutrition ravaged areas of the country outside Manila. A staggering 40 percent of all the nation's deaths were caused by malnutrition. The infant mortality rate was nearly twice as high in the Philippines as in South Korea. Nearly 20 percent of all the country's deaths were children aged one to four years, a figure nine times that of China and sixteen times that of Japan. Part of the reason for the malnutrition, according to a confidential World Bank study in 1979, was that "one-third to one-half of the population is too poor to purchase and consume enough food."

Negros, the country's fourth-largest island, was a political, social, and economic laboratory, about to explode. "Sugarlandia" it was called. Sugar was king, the fields flowing to the edge of mountains. Ownership of the sugar lands was in the hands of less than 2 percent of the island's 1.9 million people; 98 percent were virtual serfs. In late 1974 Joseph Lelyveld of *The New York Times* visited Negros. It was the year of booming world prices for sugar. A planter

271

with 125 acres, a relatively modest holding, earned a net profit of between $25,000 and $40,000, while a 2,500-acre estate could generate a profit of $750,000. A family of six or seven barefoot children next to their mothers and fathers, who planted and then later cut the cane under a blistering sun, were lucky if they earned $225 a year. Six years later a *Wall Street Journal* reporter, Barry Kramer, wrote from Negros. The past years had been ones of depressed sugar prices; nevertheless, the sugar barons, Kramer noted, lived in a "world of giant estates, fine antiques, luxury foreign cars (Mercedes-Benz is a favorite), and country clubs with immaculate golf greens." The workers continued to suffer, maybe more than before. The legal minimum wage was $1.36 a *day,* barely enough to buy a meal of rice and salt, with perhaps a bite of dried fish. But even that was too much of a burden for the sugar owners. Most workers received 81 cents a day. A man consumed all of his day's wage to buy five pounds of rice (compared with twenty pounds a few years earlier), and there were only about 180 workdays in the year.

Behind the cold numbers was the numbing reality. "The young patients seem to have been transplanted from the famines in Bangladesh and the sub-Sahara earlier in the decade," *Time* magazine's Ross H. Munro wrote in September 1979, after visiting the malnutrition ward in Bacolod, the provincial capital of Negros. "Big eyes staring from skeletal heads, matchstick limbs, bloated bellies." The children Munro saw were the fortunate ones; they were receiving treatment. Around Negros the ugly, horrifying look of starvation was on the faces of tiny children crowded into shacks in the dirt. On Negros malnutrition was epidemic, "one of the worst [instances of malnutrition] in the world," Theresa Tull, the American consul in Cebu, said in 1979. At least three out of every four Negrito children suffered from second- or third-degree malnutrition.

Bangladesh and Africa brought cries of compassion. But about its former colony Washington seemed uninterested.

POWDER KEG OF THE PACIFIC was the headline of *Time*'s September 1979 story. Those were the same words used at the time by the CIA station chief in Manila to describe the situation in the Philippines. In spite of it, the Carter administration did not alter its course. Not all the corruption, political and economic; not the repression of human rights; not the oppression of the human spirit and dignity; not the conspicuous consumption amid the dehumanizing poverty—nothing precipitated a change of policy.

There were, however, some State Department officials who saw the need for a shift in Washington's relations with Marcos. They weren't heeded. One was Robert Wenzel, the quiet political officer in the Manila embassy whom Holbrooke sought to have removed from his post. While the policy of Holbrooke and the State Department was based on the belief that Marcos could be moved to reform, "I'm persuaded he's not going to change," Wenzel told Stephen Cohen, Derian's deputy, in the summer of 1979. Or as John Maisto, one of Wenzel's deputies in the political section, who within in a few years played a key role in affecting the policy, said at the time, "The longer people stay in this post, the more cynical they become in terms of believing Marcos."

Maisto and Wenzel thought the United States ought to begin distancing itself from Marcos, looking toward the day when he would be gone. "We should develop our relationship with the opposition, be more open and forthcoming," Wenzel said then. He added: "We need to find ways to step up the dialogue on human rights a few notches. We have to ask, 'Mr. Marcos, when are you going to step down or give someone a fair chance to compete?' We should consider going public a little bit more than we have." Marcos was never asked. The policy was quiet diplomacy.

In the State Department the principal advocate of a policy of putting greater distance between Washington and Marcos (the policy the Reagan administration ultimately adopted) was Stephen Cohen. Having been active in the antiwar protests first at Amherst, then at Yale Law School, Cohen delights in recounting how it was that he came to work for the government. When Carter and the Democrats won, Cohen was teaching tax law at the University of Wisconsin, but his real interest was foreign policy, particularly arms control. "I admired Paul Warnke," he says about Carter's first arms control negotiator. "But I didn't know Paul Warnke from a hole in the ground." A friend recommended to Cohen that he call Leslie Gelb, who had been named by Cyrus Vance as director of the Bureau of Politico-Military Affairs. But Cohen didn't know Gelb either, so he called journalist Seymour Hersh, who arranged for a meeting. Hersh had worked with Cohen on Eugene McCarthy's 1968 presidential campaign and as a reporter had become a nemesis to every administration. "I got my job in the State Department through Seymour Hersh," Cohen recalled, laughing at the irony.

After two years in Policy Planning, Cohen transferred to Derian's Human Rights Bureau as a deputy assistant secretary. Cohen, wiry and balding with a heavy black beard, was as organized and incisive in his thinking as he was disheveled in appearance; Derian repeatedly suggested that it wasn't appropriate for a senior State Department officer to keep a pile of dirty clothes in his office. But he won the respect of the professionals, including many who detested Derian's principal deputy, Mark Schneider. When Schneider would go to a country for an inspection visit, a Pentagon official would advise the military attachés not to cooperate. But he so trusted Cohen that he provided him with classified information and urged other military officers to cooperate to the fullest.

In June 1979 Cohen traveled to the Philippines. It was not the usual quick-fix forty-eight- or seventy-two-hour trip. Cohen, who had read extensively on the country before going, spent two weeks in the archipelago, a long period for a working visit. And he didn't spend all his time in Manila, with the good restaurants and starched hotel room sheets. He traveled widely: Cebu, Naga, and Legaspi (where poverty was acute); Davao (where the NPA was growing rapidly); and Zamboanga (center of the Muslim rebellion). Cohen met and talked with Philippine priests and American Peace Corps workers (the corps directors, a man-and-wife team, were "very impressed" by Marcos, thought that he really cared about the Philippine people and rural development, and wished that Carter would say some of the same things in his speeches that Marcos did); members of the Philippine Supreme Court and the officers from the American embassy; high-level Philippine government officials and businessmen.

When he returned to Washington, Cohen set about putting his findings and conclusions on paper. In the end it became a letter, thirty pages long, to Ambassador Murphy, Newsom's successor. Among other thoughts, comments, and observations, Cohen, reflecting the views of Wenzel, Maisto, Tull, and others in the embassy, recommended that Washington start preparing for the post-Marcos era. Marcos was sixty-two years old and ailing; he might rule for another fifteen years, Cohen acknowledged. But he didn't think so. That's not what he had heard from the embassy officers. "The odds are that one way or another—due to popular rebellion, natural causes, or something we can't foresee—he won't be here in ten years. And I believe the odds are significant that he will be out in five." Consequently, Cohen wrote, "I think we need very carefully and deliberately to begin to distance ourself from Marcos." How well Cohen had listened, learned, and understood in July 1979; the "popular rebellion" came within ten years, as he had predicted.

The East Asian Bureau's response to Cohen's exegesis came from Robert Oakley, one of Holbrooke's principal deputies. "The breadth and depth of your inquiries during a short visit are genuinely impressive," Oakley wrote. But that didn't mean there was going to be any shift in Washington's approach. As for a policy of "distancing" (Oakley thought it might better be called "balancing"), Oakley said that would be up to Ambassador Murphy. If there were to be a distancing policy, it would have to be directed by Holbrooke's bureau. And that wasn't what Holbrooke wanted. Murphy wasn't about to distance himself or his embassy or any part of the U.S. government from Marcos. Those weren't his instructions. Indeed, his instructions were to the contrary.

Murphy was a surprise and an unusual choice to be ambassador to the Philippines. He was a Middle East scholar and expert; he spoke Arabic, had served in Beirut, Jidda, and Amman. He had not had a single posting in any part of Asia, let alone the Philippines or even Southeast Asia. After the Philippines he returned to the Middle East, as ambassador to Saudi Arabia, his departure from Manila coming as abruptly as had his arrival, when Secretary of State Alexander Haig angrily fired the American ambassador in Saudi Arabia and Murphy replaced him.

Murphy himself didn't think his assignment to the Philippines was particularly wise, believing that it was generally not sound foreign policy to send as an ambassador a person without any experience in an area or country. The posting had come about because Newsom had been summoned by Vance (after only five months in Manila) to become the number three man in the department after

Philip Habib had suffered a heart attack. To replace Newsom, Vance and Holbrooke exhausted a long list. Holbrooke's first choice was Morton Abramowitz, a career officer who at the time was detached to the Defense Department, where he had been deeply involved in the bases negotiations. Although Abramowitz was exceptionally able, Vance was reluctant to send him to the Philippines for his first ambassadorial assignment. Instead, Vance sent him to Thailand, which was considered a less significant post but which became active and important when the Vietnamese boat people and refugees from Pol Pot's Cambodia began streaming into the country. Holbrooke had a couple of other candidates, but they weren't available. Vance had his own list, but Holbrooke vetoed each person on it. One diplomat who should have been an obvious choice was Frank Underhill. He had been political officer in Manila prior to martial law, was then promoted to number two man in Seoul, followed by four years as ambassador in Malaysia. But Underhill wasn't on anyone's short list. It requires more than qualifications to become an ambassador, especially to a class one post, which the Philippines is. It is critical to have an advocate within the department, a "rabbi," and Underhill lacked one. Moreover, he had fallen from grace with Holbrooke and the Defense Department because of his cable expressing nonconformist views about the bases.

Finally, after many desperate weeks, Oakley told Holbrooke, "I have just the man for you": Richard Murphy. Holbrooke remembered Murphy favorably because when Holbrooke was Peace Corps director in Morocco in the early 1970s, Murphy, then ambassador to Mauritania, had visited him, the only ambassador to call. That was a definite plus in Holbrooke's ledger, and he was relieved that someone had been found. Murphy was incredulous. "Are you sure you have the right Murphy?" he asked when Oakley reached him in Syria, where he was ambassador.

Holbrooke gave Murphy, who arrived in Manila in the summer of 1978, two principal missions. The first was to secure a bases agreement, and Murphy did that. The second was to improve relations with the Marcoses, which had begun to sour under Sullivan and had curdled with Derian's visit; Murphy was to repair the damage. Since the Marcoses were a team, the assistant secretary told Ambassador Murphy and his wife that he expected them to work as a team, especially on Imelda Marcos. They carried out their instructions well. Once during a dinner party a CIA officer began talking about Imelda Marcos and her prodigal ways. Mrs. Murphy quickly came to Mrs. Marcos's defense—to the surprise of the CIA man, who diplomatically fell silent.

Murphy's reports from Manila painted a picture of the Marcos regime that wasn't justified by the reality. He told Washington that land reform was progressing when in fact, it was an abysmal failure. He wrote that the gap between the rich and poor was narrowing; the CIA station chief at the time said, "The gap between the rich and the poor is greater than ever before." Murphy's tendency to see the glass half full while his staff was seeing it half empty, as one aide put it, was a reflection of his mission. Marcos was Washington's man in Manila. It wasn't for the ambassador to send back bleak reports about Marcos and his rule. Murphy's successor, Michael Armacost, was to be severely criticized and ridiculed for being close to the Marcoses. Murphy was just as friendly, just as close. "I thought he was an agent of Marcos," José Concepción, a prominent businessman, remarked to Stephen Cohen about a year after Murphy had arrived. Concepción recalled how during a meeting with about a dozen businessmen Murphy kept asking, "Isn't martial law good for business? Doesn't it produce stability?"

The answers Philippine businessmen had long been giving were yes. Now, however, they were beginning to question the pact they had made with Marcos, an informal one, the effect of which was that in exchange for Marcos's maintaining peace and order, the businessmen would surrender their constitutional rights. They discovered that they had also lost their economic rights to Imelda Marcos and the cronies. But though many Philippine businessmen were growing increasingly restive with martial law, American businessmen were still very bullish on Marcos. At one of the regular monthly meetings of the American Chamber of Commerce in the Philippines, in late 1977, chairman William Dunning, head of Caltex Petroleum in the Philippines, explained to an American embassy officer how the businessmen were working with Imelda Marcos to help the Marcos government improve its image abroad. The board members stressed that they eschewed politics and human rights. They acknowledged that they were being criticized in the United

States for "being in the pocket" of the Philippine government, but they said they acted that way voluntarily because of the benefits arising to business from the effects of martial law. The Philippines, they thought, had a better investment climate than Indonesia, Malaysia, and Thailand. By "better investment climate" they meant, of course, lower wages for workers, restrictions on strikes, and generous tax breaks.

Marcos was "very sensitive to the needs and position of the foreign investor," George F. Suter, Jr., president of Pfizer, Inc., the multinational drug company, and president of the American Chamber of Commerce in Manila in 1979, told *Business Week*. The embassy described Suter as "a known apologist for the martial law regime." What particularly pleased the businessmen was the cost of labor. The minimum daily wage for factory workers, including cost-of-living allowances, was about $3 a day. That wasn't enough to put rice on the table—a struggling family of six would spend about $4 a day for food, excluding rice—or to keep children in shoes and in school. But Marcos had seen to it that Philippine labor was, by the end of the 1970s, among the cheapest in the world. His minister of finance boasted that the "effective cost of labor" in the Philippines (fringe benefits plus actual wage) was 47 cents an hour, compared with 85 cents in Taiwan and 95 cents in Singapore.

With business happy and the bases secure, there was no pressure on the Carter administration to adopt a policy of moving away from Marcos. Besides, neither Murphy nor Holbrooke considered Marcos all that evil; Holbrooke described him as a "soft dictator."

By the standards of Idi Amin or Pol Pot, Muammar al-Qaddafi, or even the military junta in El Salvador at the time, the Marcos regime wasn't particularly bloody. But surely those shouldn't have been the standards for measuring human rights performances anywhere, certainly not in the Philippines, the country where America had instilled democratic values. Marcos might not be a Pol Pot, but he was a dictator, willing to resort to ruthless tactics to remain in power. "The Philippines has one of the worst human rights records in the so-called free world" was how ABC correspondent John Martin began a one-hour documentary, *The Politics of Torture,* which aired in December 1978. It was the "story of murder, torture, and repression" in three countries that were America's allies: Augusto Pinochet's Chile, the shah's Iran, and Marcos's Philippines. Another ABC correspondent, William Sherman, posing as a priest, had smuggled cameras and a tape recorder into a Manila prison. He interviewed twenty-five-year-old José Duran, who had been picked up two weeks earlier. Duran explained how he had been subjected to electric shocks for three to four hours. Julius Giron, twenty-six years old, had been stripped naked; then "electric wires were attached to my index finger and to my genitals, and for several times, at different intervals, the electrodes went through my body." A thirty-nine-year-old journalist jailed for more than a year said, "They poured cold water over my body, and then they attached the electrodes on my right finger and then the other on my penis. They applied lighted cigarettes on my toenails and my breasts . . . burned my genitals." And a couple told of being picked up for illegal political activities less than twenty-four hours after Vice President Mondale had departed. The husband had been subjected to electric shock for almost an hour, resulting in second-degree burns on his fingers. His wife, who was two months pregnant, was stripped naked, then made to squat for long hours. "They put the electric wire on my thumbs. Afterwards they wanted to transfer it to my breasts and vagina."

Rather than express concern about torture and violence by the Philippine government, the State Department attacked the press. "As perhaps might have been expected, a 12-minute segment did not accurately portray the full magnitude of the Philippine scene," the department advised the embassy in Manila two days after the show had aired. "Nevertheless, we might have hoped for a more professional, less obviously biased presentation." If anything, a segment longer than twelve minutes could only have been worse. But the department assured the embassy that there was no need to become too concerned; the show had "attracted little attention," being "far overshadowed by events" in other parts of the world, particularly Iran, "giving the Philippines a day off from media interest." When the Philippine government launched official protests about the program, it was an opportunity for the Carter administration to suggest that perhaps the government might want to consider no longer applying electric shocks. Instead, the State Department recommended to Ambassador Murphy that he suggest to the Philippine government officials that they "may wish to consider asking American Broadcasting Company for opportunity to present its side of story." Murphy made the recommendation.

The human rights situation worsened in subsequent years, after the impact of the Derian visit had worn off, after the effective message of the Mondale visit had sunk in, after the bases agreement had been signed, after, in sum, it had become clear that there wasn't much but talk, and less and less of that, in Carter's human rights policy. "Political human rights conditions in the Philippines have on balance deteriorated in the past year," James Morrell of the Center for International Policy told a congressional committee investigating the status of human rights in non-Communist Asia in 1980. Holbrooke disagreed, telling the same committee three weeks later, "I do not see a significant deterioration in the area of human rights." Holbrooke, the East Asian Bureau, and the State Department generally might dismiss Morrell as just another of those "liberals" who were always tilting at dictators. But there were some Republicans who agreed with Morrell. After a trip to the Philippines, Representative James M. Jeffords, a Vermont Republican, reported, during the same hearings attended by Holbrooke, that the "unanimous consensus" of the Philippine groups and individuals he had met with was that "the overall situation in the Philippines, and not just the human rights situation, has deteriorated in the past year, and in essence, things are getting worse, not better." Among the Filipinos sharing that view were many conservatives. On the eve of the seventh anniversary of martial law, Cardinal Sin, who, contrary to how he was portrayed in the American press, was, as the *Far Eastern Economic Review* noted, "conservative" and was seeing and being seen with the Marcoses, said about martial law in general, "It is becoming worse every day, the abuses, the killings." The church leader added, in an interview at his residence with Henry Kamm of *The New York Times,* "We expected that if the human rights plan of Mr. Carter was to have any authentic meaning at all, it should have been attempted here to rescue Philippine democracy."

Within the administration Derian and her human rights voice had been reduced from a lion's roar to a puppy's whimper. It wasn't that she was shouting any less; it was just that no one seemed to be paying much attention to anything other than the hostages in Iran and, after December 1979, the Soviet invasion of Afghanistan. Those two events alone reduced the Carter administration's effectiveness in the world; at home they moved the president to use tougher language, to adopt the more traditional anti-Soviet cold war posture. There was little room anymore for human rights. Derian lost more and more fights.

Not all members of Congress were in accord with Holbrooke's policy in the Philippines. A few thought it might be time for the United States to use some of its economic muscle on Marcos, in an effort to move him toward democracy. They didn't get very far, defeated by an administration determined to back him.

The leader of the congressional effort was a somewhat unlikely congressman, Tony P. Hall, unlikely because he was from Dayton, Ohio, an industrial district with no significant Filipino population. Moreover, he was a freshman, and though he was a Democrat and had served in the Peace Corps in Thailand from 1964 to 1966, he did not arrive with a reputation as a liberal human rights activist. Hall, whose father had once been mayor of Dayton and who had worked as a real estate broker while a member of the Ohio legislature, was approached on the Philippine issue by priests as well as some anti-Marcos Filipinos who had been forced into exile. Carter's human rights policy had given birth to a cottage industry in human rights monitoring and lobbying. A legacy of the policy may be this collective institution; long after Carter was gone, the human rights organizations stayed on to fight. Many of them, with their modest offices near the capital, were staffed by dedicated Americans lobbying on behalf of human rights in El Salvador, Chile, South Africa. By contrast, the anti-Marcos, human-rights-in-the-Philippines advocates tended to be Filipinos, perhaps because they spoke English and were familiar with the U.S. legislative process, and it was relatively easy for them to enter the country. At their request Hall, who was a member of the Subcommittee on Asian and Pacific Affairs, introduced legislation in 1979 to cut $7.9 million from the $95.7 million in military assistance that the Carter administration was requesting for the Philippines. The administration lobbied hard to defeat Hall's cut. Secretary of State Vance, Secretary of Defense

Harold Brown, Holbrooke, and even Carter himself wrote letters and made phone calls. They were successful.

Hall tried again the next year "to send a signal" to Marcos. Out of the $100 million in military aid, Hall proposed to cut a mere $5 million. And it wasn't really a cut. It was just a suspension of that amount until Marcos took some positive steps toward restoring democracy. With Holbrooke in the lead, the administration intensified its lobbying. Hall was "flabbergasted at the opposition" and a bit bemused that as a freshman congressman he would draw such attention, especially for such a relatively small amount of money. Murphy was brought back from Manila to lobby Congress. Hall found him "very arrogant" but "less harsh and strident than Holbrooke." Holbrooke invited Hall to the State Department for breakfast. "It was the worst breakfast I've ever had with any top State Department official—*any* official," Hall says. "He got red and mad." It wasn't the demeanor Hall expected from a diplomat.

Holbrooke's general argument, which is commonly made by Foreign Service officers, was that foreign policy should be left to the professionals, not to congressmen, who have to concentrate on getting reelected. Holbrooke also argued that he and others in the State Department were talking to Marcos about human rights. Above all, Holbrooke raised the subject of the bases agreement. As part of the agreement Carter had sent Marcos a letter pledging his administration's "best effort" to obtain from the Congress $500 million in overall military assistance for the next five years. The "best effort" clause had been proposed during the negotiations by Holbrooke to counter Marcos's demands for rent and a definite financial commitment. The Pentagon wouldn't go along with rent out of principle, and as Holbrooke knew, Congress wasn't about to commit itself to any long-term agreement. Consequently, the administration could promise only that it would use its "best effort" to obtain the $500 million from Congress. In his discussions with Holbrooke Hall argued that the agreement did not require that $100 million be appropriated every year, that it would be within the agreement to send $95 million this year, then $105 million next year—after Marcos had stopped the torture, or lifted press censorship, or something.

Regardless of how lawyers might decide what the best effort clause meant, it was specious to argue that the clause required the administration to pull out its heaviest hitters, as it did, and give them weighted bats. Wasn't it enough that the administration had *requested* the full amount? Or that Assistant Secretary Holbrooke had lobbied? More important, if the administration had wanted to send a serious message to Marcos about human rights, it would have welcomed the cut, then gone to Marcos and in effect said, as Holbrooke had earlier, "Look, Mr. President, this is the way Congress feels about human rights; unless you do something, there's not much we can do."

Not surprisingly, Imelda Marcos played her part, asking for and being granted a meeting with the Ohio congressman. She arrived at his office with an entourage of thirty, including bodyguards and cameramen who filmed the session, as they did at nearly all her activities. For half an hour she talked almost nonstop, as was her tactic. "She's smarter than you are," Hall explained later. "She purposely leaves no time for questions." As she rambled on, about how there were no human rights abuses in her country, about how much the people loved her husband, about the Communists who were trying to take over the country, Hall was transfixed—by her red fingernails. "Out to here," he remembered, holding his right hand several inches from the fingertips of his left. "She's one tough lady," Hall thought at the time. But he wasn't charmed by her any more than he had been bullied by Holbrooke.

The Carter administration had more success in the Senate when the $5 million cut was debated there. Representative Stephen Solarz, a Democrat from Brooklyn, New York, presented the case for the cut to the Senate-House conference committee. A colleague read a list of the church organizations that endorsed Hall's bill: the United Church of Christ, the Lutheran Council of the U.S.A., the United Presbyterians, the Mennonites, the Church of the Brethren, American Baptists, Maryknoll Fathers and Brothers, National Council of Churches, Friends Committee, and the Episcopal Church.

The conferees were overwhelmed. Holbrooke sent a representative. The Pentagon sent a general. The secretary of state and secretary of defense each sent a letter, arguing in identical language that the cut would "erode American credibility." Murphy sent a confidential cable from Manila, saying much the same: that the issue was "a measure of America's reliability as an ally." Philippine of-

283

ficials, he added, "tend to see the issue as a matter of principle." The arguments about "credibility" and "reliability" were warped. It *was* a matter of principle, but the credibility the Congress, as well as the administration, should have been trying to protect was America's as a nation that supports democracy. Murphy also claimed that "a cut could affect . . . the maintenance and unhampered use of our military facilities." That argument bordered on the ludicrous. Was Marcos really going to toss the Americans out for a mere $5 million? His wife could spend that in a few days. (While the administration was trying to save Marcos money, Imelda Marcos in two days in New York, in April 1979, had spent $280,000 for a necklace set with emeralds and diamonds; $18,500 for a yellow gold evening bag with one round cut diamond; $8,975.20 for twenty-karat gold ear clips with twenty-four baguette diamonds; $8,438.10 for eighteen-karat gold ear clips with fifty-two tapered baguette diamonds; and $12,056.50 for twenty-karat gold ear clips with diamonds.)

During the conference committee session the opposition to Hall's proposed cut was led by Senator John Glenn. (When the former astronaut launched his presidential bid in 1984, he sought the backing of his fellow Ohioan Hall, who reminded the senator that he had not supported him on the Philippine issue.) Glenn argued that the United States needed to continue supporting Marcos, reading approvingly from a *Wall Street Journal* editorial. However "authoritarian" and "riddled with corruption" the Marcos regime might be, the *Wall Street Journal* and now Glenn argued, "we have seen nothing to suggest that an opposition regime would be a better one." It was the classic argument for supporting dictators, fundamental to the Carter administration's policy as it would be to Reagan's that there were no competent democrats to replace Marcos. But it was an argument that ignored reality and reflected contempt. It was true that the democratic leadership had been weakened by Marcos; nevertheless, there were any number of qualified men and women to lead the Philippines. They might not have seemed so to American officials, but that was a reflection of American arrogance: it is difficult for Americans to accept that they don't always know what is best for the rest of the world.

The administration and Congress thought Marcos was best for the Philippines, and the spigot to the Philippines was opened wide.

In addition to the $100 million in military assistance, which was called for in the bases agreement, there was more in economic assistance—$72 million in 1979; $83 million in 1980—and yet more from the multinational development banks. In 1980 there was only one abstention, on a $4.5 million industrial gas project loan, while loans totaling at least $721 million were approved. One of them, for $25 million from the Asian Development Bank, was approved even though the State Department had been advised that the recipient, a private investment house called the Philippines Investment Systems Organization (PISO), was a conduit for funds to the Marcos family and its cronies.

The Marcoses had plenty of money, if not enough to sate Imelda Marcos's cravings. In 1977 they purchased a house on Makiki Heights Drive in Honolulu, for $717,000; two years later they bought the house and lot next door. They also had two houses in Cherry Hill, New Jersey, purchased in 1978 and 1979, for use by their son and their daughter Imee. And in June 1980 they were principals in a partnership, which included several doctors connected with Imelda Marcos's heart hospital, that purchased the Webster Hotel in San Francisco for $5.3 million. The Marcoses didn't need more money. What they wanted was that stamp of approval, more personal blessings by American leaders, like those Mondale had bestowed. Marcos wanted to be invited for another state visit. Holbrooke thought he should be and was lobbying for it within the administration. Marcos had to settle for less, but only slightly less.

In 1980 Marcos was invited to the United States, his first visit since 1966, though of course, his wife had been coming two and three times a year. The opportunity was provided by the American Newspaper Publishers Association (ANPA), which invited Marcos to address its annual meeting.* The gathering, in April 1980, was in Honolulu (where Floirendo, the banana and sugar crony, had purchased a $1 million mansion on Makiki Heights Drive in March).

---

* It's difficult to fathom why an organization dedicated to a free press would invite a dictator whose government censored and controlled the press; had deported the bureau chief for the Associated Press, Arnold Zeitlin; had charged Bernard Wideman, of the *Far Eastern Economic Review* and *Washington Post,* with being an undesirable alien for writing "scurrilous libel against personalities," among the personalities being the Marcoses, Defense Minister Enrile, and sugar baron Benedicto; and tortured Philippine journalists.

It was a public relations triumph for Marcos. As the embassy observed, Marcos would "use his visit to mute foreign critics and, through wide media coverage at home, bolster domestic support." Indeed, the government-controlled and crony-owned newspapers wrote long stories about the invitation and convention. The implication was clear: If such an organization honored Marcos, then he certainly wasn't an evil dictator. As the articles noted, Jimmy Carter had been the keynote speaker the previous year, and in earlier years speakers had included Vice President Nelson Rockefeller and Henry Kissinger. To wrap Marcos further in cloaks of credibility and respectability, his press prominently pointed out that newspaper publishers who were members included Arthur Ochs Sulzberger of *The New York Times,* Katharine Graham of the *Washington Post,* and Warren Phillips of Dow Jones & Company, which publishes the *Wall Street Journal.* Moreover, "Mrs. Graham, publisher of the *Washington Post,* which broke the Watergate story, is treasurer of the Association," and "she has been nominated for the ANPA presidency," one story noted.

Since Marcos was coming to the United States, both Ambassador Murphy and Assistant Secretary Holbrooke thought he should be received at the highest possible level, preferably by President Carter. "You know how sentimental Marcos is about the U.S.," Murphy cabled Holbrooke, with the recommendation that if Carter were "unavailable" to meet with Marcos, then Brzezinski should. "I suspect their chemistry might be particularly good," Murphy wrote. Holbrooke was at work in Washington. "Ideally, I would propose that Marcos be invited to Washington to meet with the President, yourself and other key members of the Administration," Holbrooke wrote in a memorandum to the secretary of state. In making his argument, he added, "One final point worth mentioning is that Jeff Carter [President Carter's son] has been in Manila . . . and was warmly treated by the Marcoses."

Vance vetoed the idea of Marcos's coming to Washington, and of himself, or his chief deputy, Warren Christopher, or Brzezinski going to Honolulu, Holbrooke's other suggestions. Vance gave approval to Holbrooke and Newsom, the number three in the department, welcoming Marcos in Hawaii. That had been Holbrooke's last choice, and he told Vance that he considered it "inadequate."

Holbrooke persisted. Eventually, he says, "we concocted this idea of Rusk going out there to represent the president."

And so Holbrooke and Dean Rusk, as Carter's personal representative, embraced Marcos on behalf of the American government. There was still more for Marcos. Holbrooke drafted a very warm letter from Jimmy Carter to the Philippine president. Carter apologized for not being able "to greet you in person. I am pleased, however, that my good friend Dean Rusk has agreed to receive you on my behalf." After thanking Marcos for his support of the U.S. position on the summer Olympic Games in Moscow, which the administration boycotted because of the Soviet invasion of Afghanistan, Carter concluded that "in these times of challenge nations and peoples are being called upon to stand up for their values and their interests." There was nothing about the values of democracy that Marcos was suppressing. Rather, Carter wrote, "We are proud that our time-tested friendship with the Philippines has once again shown its enduring value to both our nations." He ended: "Finally, I want you to know how much my son Jeff and his wife enjoyed their recent visit to the Philippines and the gracious hospitality extended to them by you and Mrs. Marcos."

The same letter could have been sent by Nixon or Reagan, and, indeed, the Carter administration's human rights policy in the Philippines was much the same as Reagan's would be. It was "quiet diplomacy," as Holbrooke's senior deputy, Michael Armacost, who later was Reagan's ambassador to Manila, told Congress in February 1980. It was the same around the world. But in the Philippines even Ambassador Murphy thought it was quieter than in most places. It was so quiet that Marcos didn't hear it. Either that or Holbrooke and the Carter administration had been ineffectual in implementing their policies.

After three years, after a bases agreement which gave the Philippines $100 million a year in military aid, after voting in the multinational development banks for loans to the Marcos government, after visits by Mondale, Holbrooke, and Rusk, and after a personal letter from Carter, after everything, the administration had little to boast about, least of all the matters of human rights and democracy. Even applying its own criteria, as set out by Holbrooke prior to Mondale's visit, the administration had failed. Martial law was still in place. There had not been a free and honest election. There was no free press. Aquino was still in jail.

Finally, in May 1980, Aquino was freed. Then and thereafter Carter administration officials trumpeted the release as demonstrable proof of the effectiveness of the human rights policy. Aquino himself said often after his release that he owed his life and his freedom to Carter and the human rights policy. "Nixon and Ford never talked about human rights," Aquino said to one interviewer. "When Carter came onto the scene and spoke about human rights it gave us new hope. . . . It was the best thing that ever happened to the Third World."

Aquino's release was certainly the most visible manifestation of the Carter administration's human rights policy in the Philippines. But however tempting it might be to allow the tributes and positive memories to constitute history, factors other than Carter's human rights policy were decisive in the release. Even Ambassador Murphy said at the time, and to his colleagues in the department later, that these other factors, more than pressure from Washington, had influenced Marcos to free Aquino.

The principal factor was the fear of death. It was stalking two of the most powerful and cunning men in Philippine history. Specifically it was the fear of Aquino's death. He had been struck by chest pains one day while doing push-ups. Doctors diagnosed him as needing a heart bypass. Marcos didn't want Aquino to die on his watch, in his prison. It was Imelda Marcos who brought Aquino the message that Marcos would release him to go to the United States for a heart operation. Then, for two hours in her heart hospital, where he had been taken for examination after the chest pains, two of the most garrulous figures in the Philippines—Imelda Marcos and Ninoy Aquino—carried on. At the end he even gave her his gold necklace with a crucifix, which he had worn for the past seven years in prison. She hung it on the wrist of the statue of the Santo Niño, which rested in a niche in Malacañang, on display for all to see.

In their first discussion about Aquino, on the presidential yacht back in April 1977, Marcos had expressed concern to Holbrooke that if he released Aquino to live in the United States, the Carter administration would lionize him. "What do you mean, 'lionize'?" Holbrooke asked. Marcos responded that there would be press conferences, that Carter would personally receive Aquino, that he would be invited to address Congress. Holbrooke assured him to the extent that he could, telling Marcos: "The press does not pay attention for too long to that kind of thing; it's a quick story, and it's over, except in the very small groups that pay close attention." He added: "If you will let him out of jail, I can assure you we would not make a big deal of him at the White House or the State Department."

Even with those concessions, it was three years before Marcos released Aquino; this suggests that it was Aquino's health and Marcos's acutely tuned sense of what could trigger a Filipino uprising against him, not the Carter human rights policy, that were the principal motivations for setting Aquino free. Still, Holbrooke kept his promise. Aquino was not received by Carter or afforded any official reception. Once again, when provided an opportunity to make a statement about its preference for democracy over dictatorship, the Carter administration chose silence. Holbrooke and his staff did, however, regularly talk with Aquino, who after heart surgery was at Harvard on a fellowship. But in the final days of the Carter administration, when the crunch came, the State Department capitulated—to Marcos, to the Reagan administration, and to its own bureaucratic penchant for avoiding controversy.

At issue was Aquino's invitation to speak at the State Department's Open Forum, in December 1980. The invitation set off a final round of testy volleys between Derian and Holbrooke, who was supported by Anthony Lake in Policy Planning. The Open Forum had been established in 1967 during the Vietnam War, when dissenting views about the U.S. involvement there were being stifled within the Foreign Service. The forum was designed to serve "as an in-house means for encouraging creativity, openness, and the free expression of views in the foreign policy process." It sought "to conduct a vigorous and intellectually honest examination of the full range of foreign policy issues confronting the United States." In view of these principles, it was understandable that Aquino should be invited to speak on "The Developing Crises in the Philippines." It was to be off the record, attendance limited to State Department employees. It was certainly a timely topic, and considering all the credit that the Carter administration had, and has since, gathered unto itself for Aquino's release, what was not understandable was the opposition to his appearance.

When Holbrooke learned of the invitation, he called Aquino at

Harvard, urging him either to decline the invitation or to restrict the size of the audience to which he would speak. The sides became so entrenched that it was sent to the secretary's office for resolution. The chairman of the Open Forum, George S. Dragnich, argued, "Both Mr. Lake and Mr. Holbrooke evidently believe that the regional bureaus should be able to censor the Open Forum's speakers program when foreign nationals are involved." Such interference, he went on in his memo to the secretary, "fundamentally undermines the Forum's unique policy of openness which has been so carefully built up over the past thirteen years." Derian's memo was less circumspect and diplomatic, but characteristically caustic, directing the harshest language at Holbrooke's phone call to Aquino. Such a phone call, she said, can have a "chilling effect on an alien." She added: "This is not a police state. And no one in the Department should operate in any way as though it were."

Derian and the Open Forum lost. Though Aquino was invited, the audience was limited to no more than fifty people whose IDs were checked at the door.

While Lake agreed that the bureaus, in this case East Asia, should not "be in a position to 'censor' the Open Forum," he also believed that the forum should not be able to decide for itself "that it can invite *foreign* speakers in ways which could embarrass the Department or complicate our foreign relations." Lake, who had defended the Open Forum on numerous occasions, thought there had to be a distinction between foreign and domestic speakers and that to invite Aquino, an outspoken Marcos opponent, to speak at the State Department would have been "interpreted abroad as a calculated political signal" against Marcos. Therefore, Lake, in one memorandum, suggested that Aquino's talk not be public. Holbrooke, concerned that his position on the Open Forum issue not be misinterpreted as "my being an adversary of Aquino," says that he was motivated by a desire to protect his aides, principally John Negroponte, who would have to work for the incoming Reagan administration. He was also worried that "some conservative columnist—Evans and Novak—would write it up as a gratuitous slap" at the Marcoses.

Holbrooke was friendly to the Marcoses until the end—that is, until the end of the Carter administration and his role in making foreign policy. During the final days of 1980, after Carter had been defeated and only a few weeks before Reagan was sworn in, the assistant secretary traveled to Manila for one final bash. He flew with the Marcoses up to Ilocos Norte, the president's hometown, where Marcos had built his own golf course, a museum to himself (in which Holbrooke's photo hung), and an airport. Holbrooke went with Imelda Marcos in her elaborate touring bus with the large windows. "We start barreling down these little back roads in northern Luzon, Frank Sinatra singing 'Have Yourself a Merry Little Christmas,' hundred-degree heat, and chickens and pigs racing out of the way, and she waving to the adoring people. We're looking at this bizarre sight. Imelda really thinks the people love her." For New Year's Eve everyone traveled back to Manila and the blowout at Malacañang. Holbrooke, Ambassador Murphy, and others from the embassy staff attended, along with diplomats from other countries. The music was loud; the dancing, wild. People were throwing money at each other. There was a raffle, the goods obtained by Imelda Marcos through "requests." Holbrooke was honored by being asked to draw the first number; the Russian ambassador the second. At four in the morning, Mrs. Marcos assembled the revelers for prayer at a sixteenth-century Spanish altar which she had expropriated from a church. Then they sat down to watch a forty-five minute videotape of a dinner she had hosted for Richard Nixon in New York a few weeks earlier.

"So that's life in Imelda's fast lane," comments Holbrooke.

The Carter administration had been in that lane for four years, but it had not caused the Marcoses to slow down. The human rights policy had been a yellow light at most. The administration's intentions had been the right ones: to express a preference for governments that didn't oppress their people. The will to implement the principled commitments was lacking. It wasn't that the administration was under any great delusions about the Marcoses. "We knew his was a repressive government. We knew it was corrupt," says Mondale, who once remarked to an aide that Mrs. Marcos had the "smell of corruption."

Nevertheless, U.S. officials continued to see and be seen with the Philippine dictator. The Carter administration's attitude toward the Marcoses was an extension of what has become the nature of U.S. relations with dictators. It was expressed bluntly by President Franklin D. Roosevelt in 1939. In response to reservations by the State Department to a state visit by Nicaragua's Anastasio Somoza García, FDR said, "He may be a son of a bitch. But at least he's our son of a bitch."

How was Marcos to be persuaded to reform? Quiet diplomacy was the Carter administration's answer. Quiet diplomacy, when applied, is the diplomatic equivalent of Christian redemption, based on the belief in the goodness of humankind; American officials believe that dictators can be persuaded to become democrats. Or "quiet diplomacy," as the Reagan administration was to demonstrate, is an excuse for not doing anything, for not criticizing pro-American dictators.

12 : A New Day for Dictators

Ronald Reagan's defeat of Jimmy Carter was the occasion for another raucous all-night party at Malacañang, a celebration in which the past was exorcised and the future drunkenly toasted. Not that the Carter administration had done much, if any, damage to the Marcos empire. Derian and the others had been flies at the Marcos picnic, pestering but harmless. Now, however, even they were gone. The Marcoses had a true friend when Ronald Reagan arrived in Washington. He and his wife, Nancy, had known the Marcoses since they had been feted in Manila for the opening of the Cultural Center in 1969. Ronald and Nancy Reagan liked Ferdinand and Imelda Marcos, and for Ronald Reagan, personalities were as important as policies, maybe more so. But the policies of the Reagan administration favored the Marcoses as well.

The intellectual high priest of the new administration's foreign policy was Jeane J. Kirkpatrick, a hard-line anti-Communist born in Oklahoma in 1926. She was a registered Democrat in 1981 but had lost faith in that party years earlier when many Democratic leaders questioned American intervention in Vietnam. When McGovern became the party's nominee in 1972, Kirkpatrick became a central figure in the neoconservative movement. After years of toiling in the relative obscurity of academia, churning out articles and books which few people read, Kirkpatrick, a professor at Georgetown, wrote an article entitled "Dictatorships and Double Standards," which discussed the difference between "authoritarian" and "totalitarian" regimes. It was a distinction familiar to political scientists, but when Kirkpatrick's article appeared in 1979 in *Commentary,* the neoconservative magazine, Reagan's foreign policy adviser, Richard V. Allen, showed it to the candidate, who was impressed. With Reagan's victory, Kirkpatrick secured a job as ambassador to the United Nations, with cabinet rank. And with the coming into fashion of conservatism and neoconservatism, Kirkpatrick acquired a special cachet; she appeared so often on ABC's *Nightline* that some viewers began to think she was a consultant. (She wasn't.)

In Kirkpatrick's dichotomy, authoritarian regimes—her examples are the shah's Iran and Somoza's Nicaragua—deserve U.S. support because they are pro-American and eventually can be democratized. Totalitarian regimes, on the other hand—Castro's Cuba and the Sandinistas' Nicaragua in her view—will never yield to democracy and are generally anti-American. She blasted Carter's foreign policy with its emphasis on human rights. The consequences for the United States had been disastrous, she argued, leading to the overthrow of Somoza and the shah.

In practice, the Kirkpatrick doctrine, as it came to be known, meant that the Reagan administration would wage wars against leftist governments (Angola and Nicaragua principally) while embracing right-wing regimes (the list, very long, ranged from South Korea to South Africa and included most of the governments of South America at the time). When Senator Howard Metzenbaum, an Ohio Democrat, challenged Mrs. Kirkpatrick on the ground that the policy of making "deals with the juntas and dictators and fascists throughout the world in the last 30 years" hadn't been successful, she countered: "Now, if you want to say that other power—the Soviets—can deal with dictatorships, and suffer no loss of prestige or stature, but that if we deal with dictators or autocrats, we lose our moral credentials, then I would simply say, that's mistaken."

It seemed perversely paradoxical that this harsh critic of communism would adopt the Soviet Union as a standard by which to judge American foreign policy. And though it is quite possible to maintain moral credentials while one deals with dictators, she seemed to have lost them when she put her policy into practice. In pursuit of her foreign policy, she appeared to borrow a view of extremism from the conservative leader of the 1960s, Barry Goldwater. ("Extremism in the defense of liberty is no vice," he told the Republican party delegates in accepting the convention's nomination as the 1964 presidential candidate.)

When four American churchwomen were raped and murdered by government soldiers in El Salvador in December 1980, Kirkpatrick exonerated the conservative military-civilian junta ruling the country. "The answer is unequivocal," she said: The government was not responsible. Most American diplomats who were in El Salvador at the time were convinced that senior officers ordered the killing, and a special commission appointed by Reagan concluded that there had been a cover-up by government officials. Kirkpatrick, however, chose to malign the victims, three nuns and a Catholic lay worker. "The nuns were not just nuns," Kirkpatrick declared. "The nuns were also political activists," working, she insisted, on behalf of the Marxist-led revolution. As chilling and lacking in compassion as was that remark (it was also factually wrong—unless providing food, medicine, and religious instruction to impoverished peasants transforms a nun into a revolutionary political partisan), it was matched in cruelty and insensitivity by Reagan's secretary of state, General Alexander M. Haig, Jr. He suggested that the women might have been killed because "the vehicle that the nuns were riding in may have tried to run a roadblock or may have accidentally been perceived to have been doing so, and there may have been an exchange of gunfire."

However incredible these statements may seem, they were consistent with Kirkpatrick's and Haig's views of how the United States ought to go about conducting its foreign policy. It was an administration in which ideology more than realpolitik concerns about national interest guided foreign policy, to a far greater degree than in any previous administration. It was an administration which, as historian Arthur Schlesinger, Jr., observed, "systematically scorned the United Nations, defied the World Court, overrode the interests of allies, dismissed negotiations with adversaries." Above all, it was, as the Kirkpatrick and Haig remarks reflected, an administration which was intent on conducting foreign policy without the interference of any idealistic notions about human rights. The Carter administration's emphasis on human rights "must be abandoned," President-elect Reagan was advised by one of his transition teams. It was. The new administration was also intent on loudly displaying its friendship for those regimes that had been the subject of some criticism by the Carter administration, regardless of how mild the criticism and how corrupt, venal, and dictatorial the regime.

Unlike the often wishy-washy Carter administration, the Reagan administration resolutely practiced what it preached. Reagan hadn't slept in the White House a fortnight when South Korea's dictator, Chun Doo Hwan, was honored with a state visit. Further to appease Chun, a general who had come to power after Park had been assassinated, the State Department held up the release of its annual human rights report, which had been prepared by the outgoing Derian, because it was critical of Korea.

A scant six weeks later it was Argentina's President-designate, General Roberto Eduardo Viola, who was blessed by Mr. Reagan. This visit was a vindication for Kirkpatrick and American conservatives, such as columnists Evans and Novak, who had unmercifully hammered away at Patt Derian for her criticisms of the Argentine military junta. Reagan had also harshly condemned Derian for her views about Argentina. Back when he was a syndicated columnist— between the end of his California governorship and his run for the presidency—Reagan derided, in a column about Argentina, Derian and the human rights activists in the Carter administration as "born-again McGovernites" who were "infesting various foreign policy-making levels." Columnist Reagan defended the Argentine military junta. President Reagan wooed the Argentine generals.

Viola's welcome at the White House was followed by a succession of high-ranking U.S. military officers making highly visible visits to Buenos Aires. And whereas Derian had provided comfort to the victims of the military atrocities, Kirkpatrick, when she went to Argentina, embraced the military dictatorship, refusing even to meet with representatives of human rights organizations. Kirkpatrick adopted the same dichotomous approach in Chile, which was under the boot of "authoritarian" dictator General Pinochet; by 1986 even the Reagan administration realized he wasn't about to provide any transition to democracy unless he was shoved. Kirkpatrick, whose academic concentration had been Latin America, sided with Argentina in its war with Britain over the Falkland Islands (a position that made her a minority in the Reagan administration). After that war was over, and the Argentine military had been humiliated, democracy returned to the country.* Viola and his colleagues, those men Kirkpatrick, Reagan, and other conservatives had resolutely defended, were placed on trial—for murder, torture, kidnapping, and other atrocities. It was an almost unprecedented spectacle in Latin America, as well as in most of the developing world, where it is more customary for defeated generals to go off into luxurious exile than it is for them to be put in the dock. Viola and four other officers were convicted, in 1984, of having directed the terrorist campaign in which at least 9,000 people were killed; Viola, who three years earlier had been a guest of the White House, was sentenced to seventeen years in prison.

When Reagan wasn't dining with dictators, his administration was opening the vaults of the American Treasury and the multinational development banks for them. One month after Reagan's inauguration his administration lifted the ban on exports to Chile. A month after that the president asked Congress to lift the ban on military aid to Argentina (as it obligingly did). On the other side of the world, Pakistan, ruled by Mohammad Zia ul-Haq, who had seized power in a military coup, later ordering the execution of the man he had deposed, Zulfikar Ali Bhutto, was a major beneficiary of Reagan's largess. "Pakistan's biggest success of 1981 was the attainment of an objective that had looked highly elusive during the preceding years," was how the *Far Eastern Economic Review* began its year-end summary. The *Review* explained that "to the annoyance of all of its neighbours except China," Pakistan had managed to secure from the Reagan administration "a reaffirmation of a special relationship" as well as "an economic-cum-military support pack-

---

* After the fall of the junta, and after she had left office (in part because she lost out in her battle to become Reagan's national security adviser), Kirkpatrick, in her syndicated column, sought to credit the Reagan administration for Argentina's return to democracy. It was an attempt to rewrite history, and a shameless one at that. It was the defeat of the generals she had backed that had brought down the military government. And if anyone in Washington deserved credit for the triumph of democracy in Argentina, it was Patt Derian, as President Raúl Alfonsín seemed to recognize, for it was Derian and her principal deputy, Mark Schneider, not Jeane Kirkpatrick, whom he invited to his inauguration. The official Reagan administration representative was Vice President Bush, who was roundly booed by the crowd, as was the representative from General Pinochet's dictatorship in neighboring Chile. When President Carter later visited Argentina, as a private citizen, he was given an extraordinarily warm and enthusiastic welcome. The Argentines knew which administration deserved credit for promoting democracy in their country.

age." The Carter administration, backing off from its human rights policy in Pakistan as elsewhere, had offered Pakistan $400 million for two years. Reagan raised it to $3.2 *billion* for five years. More important, the new administration agreed to provide more sophisticated weapons, including F-16 combat jets.

As for the multinational development banks, Reagan's foreign policy advisers recommended that "foreign policy objectives and the U.S. role in the multinational banks" be regarded "not [as] an economic matter but [as] a political problem that must be seen in political terms." The administration had a "hit list" of countries that were to be denied loans. At the top were Nicaragua, Cuba, Vietnam, Grenada (before the Reagan administration invaded). On the other hand, the administration used its clout to ensure loans to such countries as South Africa and El Salvador. Voting in favor of a $1.1 billion International Monetary Fund loan to South Africa, which was opposed by most other countries because of the apartheid policies, the administration argued that it was improper to consider political factors when voting on loans, that only economic conditions should be taken into account. Yet it repeatedly blocked loans to Nicaragua, even simple ones for fisheries and rural roads, loans which other bank member nations found to be fully warranted if need and the other economic criteria were applied; with Nicaragua, as with South Africa, ideology guided the Reagan administration.

The early 1980s were euphoric times for America's dictators around the world. And few, if any, found the ambience of Reagan's Washington more favorable than the Marcoses. The Carter-Marcos relationship had been an uncomfortable affair, hidden, at least partially, by the blanket of the human rights policy. With Reagan the affair was legitimized. It became a marriage, a happy, joyous one. The Kirkpatrick doctrine was "music to Marcos's ears," said a senior diplomat who had been in Manila in 1981. To the bitter end Kirkpatrick stuck with Marcos; in the final months before his fall she blamed the press and liberals for his problems.

The other side of this closer relationship with the Marcoses was a moving away from Aquino, which he quickly discovered. When he called John Holdridge, who had succeeded Holbrooke, the new assistant secretary for East Asia was always on the other line, in a meeting, or otherwise occupied. And Holdridge never returned the calls, though sometimes one of his deputies might several days later. It wasn't that Holdridge had anything against Aquino. He was just carrying out policy. Holbrooke and the Carter administration had agreed not to lionize Aquino; the Reagan administration ostracized him. It was a policy of distancing from the opposition, not from Marcos. Aquino wasn't the only opposition leader who found himself on the outside when the Reagan administration came in. During the Carter administration Guillermo Manuel Ungo, a democrat who in the early 1970s had been José Napoleón Duarte's running mate but who had later split with him, becoming the most prominent leader of the democratic opposition in El Salvador, had frequent contacts with American officials, as they searched for a peaceful solution to the war in El Salvador. "I was in touch with every ambassador in Central America," Ungo said about the Carter years. After Reagan's inauguration he said, "I saw no one, not even the ones I had met with before."

The message that this new administration would be the Marcoses' friend in Washington was delivered early and personally by Reagan himself, who met Mrs. Marcos in December 1980. It was an extraordinary meeting, not in substance but in the fact that it took place at all. The session was arranged through the efforts of Admiral Thomas Moorer, who, as chairman of the Joint Chiefs of Staff in 1972, had so enthusiastically embraced martial law and was now, after his retirement, acting as a military adviser to the president-elect. When Reagan checked into New York's Waldorf-Astoria, he called Mrs. Marcos and offered to go up to her suite. He was on the thirty-fifth floor in the Tower, she, on the thirty-seventh, in a much larger suite of seven or eight rooms, probably costing between $2,000 and $3,000 a day. She was advised that it would be more fitting for her to go to Reagan's, and she did. Reagan imposed only one condition on the meeting: that there be no publicity. After all, he met with only one other foreign leader prior to his inauguration, and that was Helmut Schmidt, the West German chancellor. Reagan's meeting with Schmidt lasted only fifteen minutes; he passed an hour with Mrs. Marcos. As usual, she did most of the talking while he listened politely. He did tell her that the United States intended to treat the Philippines as "a major ally." There were no substantive discussions. Reagan's aim was to reestablish personal relations between two old friends. The conversation left the Marcoses "almost euphoric."

Even for Imelda Marcos, December 1980 was a remarkable month. Back home in Manila, her husband was receiving the singer Pat Boone and his wife; the Olympic swimmer Mark Spitz and his bride. Before Mrs. Marcos met with Reagan, she had been received by Vice President-elect Bush. And upon her initiative she had been invited to a Sunday lunch at the home of Senator Charles Percy, chairman of the Senate Foreign Relations Committee; she arrived shortly after 1:00 and left at 4:50 P.M. A few days after her private session with the president-elect, she threw a party in honor of former President Richard Nixon. It was the customary lavish Imelda Marcos affair, attended mostly by bankers and oil company executives. At the head table was Nixon, seated between Mrs. Marcos and the widow of General Douglas MacArthur. Imelda Marcos had a videotape made of the evening's activities, the one she showed her New Year's Eve guests a few weeks later; the prize moment came when Nixon, in black tie, toasted her as the "Angel from Asia" who had come to him when he was down-and-out, a reference to her having visited him in San Clemente shortly after he had been forced to resign as president of the United States.

After all those heady meetings Mrs. Marcos rushed home, to be present for the countdown to the eventual lifting of martial law. The ending of martial law was vintage Marcos, from the hype preceding it to the calculating and clandestine maneuvers that rendered it largely meaningless. For several weeks the controlled press ran carefully orchestrated statements, speeches, and stories in which Marcos hinted, and occasionally declared outright, that he was going to lift martial law without ever saying exactly when. He was building the suspense and interest in order to ensure maximum world coverage; like so much of what Marcos did, ending martial law was designed principally to benefit his international image, rather than the Filipino people. By mid-January correspondents for *The New York Times, Time,* the *Los Angeles Times,* ABC, and CBS all were "converging on Manila to cover the Marcos announcement," the U.S. embassy reported.

Marcos officially lifted martial law on January 17, the specific date chosen, his aides told the embassy, because seven was his lucky number and because it was the anniversary of the passage of the 1973 Constitution. With his astute sense of timing it was also three days before Reagan was inaugurated* and one month before Pope John Paul II was to arrive in the Philippines. The embassy reported that most observers, including embassy personnel, thought Reagan's inauguration and the pope's visit were the two factors that contributed the most to Marcos's acting when he did, and it was the pope, not the president, who had been the more influential. "Focus of world attention would be on 'The Martial Law Philippines' if martial law were still in place [at the time of the pope's visit]," the embassy noted. "Literally thousands of foreign news people would be on hand to report it."

"Marcos has lifted everything else around here, so why not lift martial law?" a Filipino politician remarked to Keyes Beech of the *Los Angeles Times*. Cynicism aside, Marcos relinquished virtually nothing when he lifted martial law. He maintained all the control he needed—over the economy, the press, the military, the police, the political system. The U.S. embassy realized that. After eight years of martial law the powers Marcos needed "have been adequately institutionalized in one fashion or another—economic, military, police, media and, of course, political control," the embassy's deputy chief of mission, James Rosenthal, accurately observed. "Marcos is tired of the 'martial law' label, and wants to rid himself of it—but not to the extent of giving up essential powers." To protect all those powers he had given himself during the preceding eight years, Marcos, a few months before lifting martial law, had enacted legislation which allowed him to retain his martial law powers even after he had lifted the decree. "With this legislation," the embassy had reported, "Marcos can have the best of both worlds—he rids himself of the onus of martial law while retaining the broad powers he now holds."

Marcos's powers were broader than anyone even knew. There

---

* According to Imelda Marcos, during her meeting with Reagan at the Waldorf the American president-elect urged her to tell her husband not to lift martial law. She made the claim in subsequent conversations with Aquino and Steve Psinakis, an anti-Marcos activist in San Francisco. Once again, it was Imelda Marcos saying whatever served her interests. American and Philippine officials privy to the Reagan-Mrs. Marcos meeting say that Reagan never made any such request. "Preposterous!" says a State Department officer.

were at least 1,000 *published* decrees restricting the economic and political activities of all Filipinos. In addition, on the eve of lifting martial law, Marcos had secretly signed a considerable number of others. Many of them were in the financial sphere, continuing Marcos's gifts to businesses, such as a thirty-four-page decree that lowered corporate taxes and abolished the income tax on offshore banks. Another prohibited the courts from issuing any orders that would block any government official, or person acting under the government's permission (i.e., a crony), from carrying out a government-sponsored project. That decree was motivated by a lawsuit filed by eighty-four farmers who complained that their land was being taken by the local governor, a Marcos loyalist. Among the more alarming decrees, which few Filipinos ever knew about, was one that provided for the death penalty for anyone who published "sustained propaganda assaults" against the government.

The broadest power Marcos continued to hold after martial law was Amendment Six to the 1973 Constitution; it had been "approved" in one of Marcos's plebiscites. The amendment was, in effect, the institutionalization of one-man rule. It provided that whenever "in the judgment of the President" (i.e., Marcos) there existed a "grave emergency or a threat or imminence thereof," or whenever the Assembly "fails or is unable to act adequately on any matter for any reason that in his judgment requires immediate action," the president may "issue the necessary decrees, orders or letters of instruction, which shall form part of the law of the land." What president or prime minister wouldn't like to have that power when faced with an intransigent legislature controlled by the opposition. As long as that amendment remained in effect, as it did for as long as Marcos was in Malacañang, there could be "no return to normalcy or democratic government in the Philippines," the Geneva-based International Commission of Jurists noted in 1984.

With Amendment Six and all the other decrees in effect, along with those he enacted later, including one giving him the authority to detain indefinitely anyone charged with "subversion" (a power which he allowed Enrile and military commanders to exercise), Marcos was as much a dictator in 1981 as he had been for the previous eight years. He had only put a different face on his rule, demonstrating once again that he was shrewder, more adaptable than other dictators the world has known. He had placed a rose on top of a dung heap, but it was still a dung heap. He would succeed in convincing the Reagan administration to ignore the smell, but he wouldn't succeed with Pope John Paul II, who arrived on February 17 for what became an exhausting six days in the most Roman Catholic of Asian nations.

The Polish-born pope wasted no opportunity to deliver some messages to Marcos, beginning with the opening ceremony. With Marcos seated in his thronelike gilt chair and his wife nearby in hers, the pope, speaking in firm and clear English, declared pointedly, "Even in exceptional situations that may at times arise, one can never justify any violation of the fundamental dignity of the human person or of the basic rights that safeguard this dignity." It was a human rights homily in Malacañang. In the audience were cabinet members, judges, dignitaries, and political associates—all handpicked by the Marcoses. On orders from Mrs. Marcos, all the women were wearing white butterfly-sleeve dresses, the men (including foreign correspondents) white barongs—made from material she had provided. On each dress and shirt was pinned a bronze medal which Marcos had had struck bearing the profiles of him and the pope. During the ceremonies the Marcoses' twenty-one-year-old daughter Irene, accompanied by a choir in the balcony, sang a song her mother composed.

The Marcos government, Imelda Marcos boasted, spent $1.2 million on the pope's visit, even building a "popemobile." The reception at Malacañang repeated the excesses of the Manila Summit fifteen years earlier. On the spacious lawns orchestras played among the trees hung with gaily colored ornaments and lights. Henry Kamm of *The New York Times* described the scene inside: "Outstanding even in the opulent decor of noble woods, rich cloth and lustrous crystal was a table the length of a long hall heaped to its full extent with carefully piled fruit, largely imported, resembling a 17th-century Flemish still life that had proliferated out of the painter's control." The reception, church officials told Kamm, "fulfilled their worst fears that in a country of great poverty the Pope would be surrounded by official luxury."

What grated on Philippine church officials even more was Mrs. Marcos's conduct. Everywhere that the pope went during his hectic six days—in one day he delivered homilies on four separate islands—she was sure to follow, dragging her entourage of forty, including a number of European celebrities and Cristina Ford. Actually Imelda Marcos would arrive at each stop before the pope did, speaking a few words to the waiting throngs. "Public reaction to this was unfavorable," the embassy reported. In Davao, the large southern port city in Mindanao, even as the pope was giving his homily to the Muslims, the four jets that carried Imelda Marcos and her courtiers roared away, drowning out the pope, who had been restricted to the airport for security reasons, so that she could be in Bacolod before he arrived. The day's itinerary also included Cebu, the most fervently religious city in the Philippines, the birthplace of Christianity in the Far East, dating from Magellan's arrival in 1521. In Cebu the pope sounded his conservative themes against divorce and abortion, and to priests and nuns he repeated his admonition not to mix in politics, a pointed reflection that the church along with the nation was becoming increasingly polarized by Marcos's rule, with a few priests having already signed up with the New People's Army and many religious leaders openly sympathetic.

But the pope, who was as opposed to materialism as he was to Marxism, had no comfort for the Marcoses or the nation's wealthy. He delivered his strongest statement on economic injustice in Bacolod, the largest city on the island of Negros. Nowhere in the Philippines, perhaps, were the gap and the conflict between the rich and poor so stark. Peasants toiling in the merciless sun earned less than $2 a day; in recent months at least nine Catholic lay workers who assisted a sugar workers' organization had been executed. His face sunburned from a day under the scorching tropical sun, the pope, who had at times donned a farmer's conical straw hat, urged a crowd of 250,000 peasants to organize. "Injustice reigns," he told the peasants, "when within the same society some groups hold most of the wealth and powers while large strata of the population cannot decently provide for the livelihood of their families even though they spend long hours of backbreaking labor in factories or in the fields." To the peasants who were landless, hung by a feudal system on the mercy of the landed, the pope intoned, "Human dignity must be promoted by the land. . . . Because the land is a gift of God, it is not admissible to use this gift in such a manner that the benefits it produces serve only a limited number of people, while the others—the vast majority—are excluded from the benefits which the land yields."

The pope was describing the reality of the Philippines, not the make-believe of Marcos or the Philippines that American officials saw because they spent most of their time in Manila. These were the conditions that the New People's Army exploited to gain adherents. But Marcos and Washington did not seem to hear the Holy Father, or if they did, they ignored him. Nothing had been done to pressure Marcos to dismantle the feudal system, to set a humane minimum wage, to address the injustices that the pope condemned.

As always, Marcos tried to paper his one-man rule with a democratic façade. In 1981 he conducted elections. When the Sandinistas held an election in 1984, the Reagan administration blasted it as a Soviet-style sham election. It was a paradigm of democracy by contrast with the Philippine voting. Marcos's first step was a plebiscite on an array of complex provisions. Foremost was a constitutional amendment providing for a return to the presidential system of the 1935 Constitution. It would replace the parliamentary-style system Marcos had instituted with a constitutional amendment in 1973. It would be the ninth revision of the Constitution since martial law. Moreover, the new amendment created an even stronger presidential system than the 1935 Constitution. It provided for a six-year presidential term, with the right of unlimited succession, and gave the president the power to name his successor as well as to dissolve the legislature. There was no vice president, in order not to create a competitor for Marcos, and the minimum age for the president was fifty; this eliminated Aquino, who would be a few months shy of his fiftieth birthday at the time of the first election under the new Constitution.

The constitutional plebiscite was on April 7, Marcos's lucky number, though of course, he needed no luck since he controlled all the media and mechanisms for fraud. The only question was how many yes votes would be cast. In some areas Marcos's new Constitution was approved by 99 percent of the voters; overall, by about 80 percent. Marcos was now prepared to run for president. The opposition, knowing the outcome and so severely decimated during eight years of martial law, didn't even bother to participate in the June 1981 charade. Marcos won, of course, with about 86 percent of the vote. Marcos could teach the Communists a thing or two about elections.

From Washington all the notes were joyous. Between the sham plebiscite in April and the sham presidential election in June, the U.S. House of Representatives passed a resolution commending Marcos for lifting martial law. The resolution had been introduced by Stephen Solarz, the liberal Democrat from Brooklyn who was a critic of the Reagan administration's policy in El Salvador and who had recently taken over the chairmanship of the House Subcommittee on Asian and Pacific Affairs, his platform for becoming one of Marcos's fiercest congressional critics. It had the warm endorsements of such previous Marcos critics as Congressman Jeffords from Vermont, one of the few Republicans who had voted in favor of Congressman Hall's proposed $5 million cut a year earlier, and Berkley Bedell, the Iowa Democrat who was an effective champion of human rights. The reasons that Congress, and especially liberals, commended Marcos are complex and varied. In part, it was that the Democrats in Congress were fighting the Reagan administration so hard to restrict military aid to El Salvador, where the paramilitary death squads were engaged in wanton murder, that they didn't want another fight. Also, many members of Congress believed that Marcos really would reform. Others voted for the resolution because they thought there was no alternative than to hope that Marcos would allow democracy. Whatever the reasons, Marcos once again manipulated the action to his advantage, as the members of Congress should have foreseen.

When the resolution passed, the major Philippine newspapers carried it on their front pages. The Philippine News Agency correspondent in Washington wrote: "The House action in effect repudiated charges . . . that the lifting of martial law was a mere paper lifting," and "approval of the resolution represents a recognition on the part of the House, which used to be critical of the Philippines, of the political developments in the Philippines since the President lifted martial law." The Philippine press ignored another provision in the resolution, one that called for "further progress toward the restoration of democracy." So did the Reagan administration.

Reagan sent a personal note to Marcos after his "election" victory. "Please accept my warmest congratulations on your reelection," the U.S. president wrote. "The American people join Nancy and me in extending to you and your fellow citizens all best wishes . . ." Reagan dispatched Vice President Bush as his personal representative at the inauguration. Other countries didn't think quite so highly of Marcos's sham. Japan thought the occasion worth no more than its foreign minister; Australia, the speaker of the upper house of Parliament; Malaysia, its minister of trade and transport. Also present were the president of Gabon; the secretary of the Presidential Council of Hungary; the vice-chairman of the Romanian Council of State.

The American vice president was accompanied by his wife, Barbara. "Mrs. Bush is 5'8" and wears dress size 16," the State Department cabled Manila in response to a request from Imelda Marcos, who wanted to have dresses ready for Mrs. Bush, who had the good sense and independence to ask to play tennis with Mrs. Murphy, the wife of the American ambassador, at the Manila Polo Club rather than go on one of Mrs. Marcos's numbing tours. The remainder of the American delegation was a fitting reflection of Mrs. Marcos, her pursuits and her relationship to Washington. Included were the venerable Republican lady Ambassador Clare Boothe Luce, who in years earlier had championed the interests of that other Asian couple of remarkable wealth and corruption, the Generalissimo and Madame Chiang Kai-shek; the pianist Van Cliburn, who had become a regular recipient of Imelda Marcos's bounty; Cliburn's mother; the actor Efrem Zimbalist, Jr.

The Bush visit is best remembered for the exuberance of the vice president's toast. His tall, athletic body draped in a barong, garlands around his neck reaching almost to his knees, Bush lifted his wineglass: "We love your adherence to democratic principle and to the democratic processes."

"A real clanger" *The New York Times* labeled the toast in an editorial, "even by the Reagan Administration's solicitous standards to allied dictators." Bush and his aides subsequently offered a number of excuses in an effort to make the American vice president not look like quite such a fool. It was said that his remark had been taken out of context, that Bush was speaking of all ASEAN nations, not just the Philippines. But the explanation compounds rather than mitigates: Of the five ASEAN nations, only Thailand and Malaysia could be considered democracies, and the *Far Eastern Economic Review* described them as "semi-democracies." Indonesia had been run by General Suharto since 1966, and Singapore by Lee Kuan Yew since 1959. The other excuse was that Bush was tired after the long flight and little sleep, on top of which had come the tropical heat and the traditional Marcos hospitality. All these had simply caused him a momentary loss of his senses. Whatever that might say about his qualifications to serve as vice president, let alone president, the argument that Bush was simply overcome collapses under the weight of subsequent statements. When he arrived in Hawaii and incredulous reporters asked the vice president about his toast, he did not retract it or even attempt to modify or qualify it. On the contrary, he reinforced it. "I'll repeat it and stand by it," he said. Of course, he would; he was reflecting the policy.

Those who have mocked Bush for his toast have engaged in a variation of shoot the messenger when they should have been examining the message. Indeed, just one month earlier Secretary of State Haig had been in the Philippines for a meeting of ASEAN and ANZUS (Australia, New Zealand, and the United States). He, too, had toasted Marcos's electoral victory. Moreover, though it was barely noticed at the time of Bush's toast, and rarely has been pointed out since (perhaps because it was easier to tar Bush with the statement than to stick anything negative on Reagan, the Teflon president), when asked about Bush's statement, White House spokesman Larry Speakes said, "I'm sure the president was aware of the statement both before it was made and after it was made, and I'm sure he concurs with it."

Although the tribute to democracy was the gaffe repeated around the world, it wasn't the only howler Bush made during the toast. "I couldn't help but notice as I went to my bedroom last night," Bush continued, turning folksy and personal, "the medals that were modestly displayed—but displayed nevertheless—in a corner of the room and I saw the Silver Star, Distinguished Service Cross, the Purple Heart, and many, many others—President Marcos's service to freedom and to our country." However "modestly" displayed they might have been in a guest bedroom, they were medals Marcos had never won. This remark of Bush's went unreported presumably because the press, as well as U.S. officials, still accepted Marcos's tales of heroism.

All the gushing adoration from the vice president of the United States was no match for what Marcos rendered unto himself. The inaugural festivities were held in Luneta Park, beginning at 6:50 A.M. to avoid the heat and afternoon rains. They were televised live, and the U.S. embassy recommended that members of the Bush delegation who weren't required to attend would probably enjoy the show more from their rooms in the Manila Hotel, where they could watch it on television or catch glimpses if their rooms were facing the park. After the national anthem, the ecumenical convocation, the oath taking, and the inaugural address, a 1,000-voice male chorus boomed out the "Hallelujah Chorus" from Handel's *Messiah*. "And he shall reign forever and ever." Some of the American diplomats were stunned. Nothing they knew or had heard about the Marcoses had prepared them for something quite so brazen. But Marcos did, indeed, see himself as a secular messiah, and he had intentions to rule forever and ever.

While Marcos would go on ruling forever and ever, so would Imelda Marcos go on spending, traveling, partying. A month after the inauguration Mrs. Marcos, through her private secretary in New York, Vilma Bautista, went on a binge. On August 25 she laid out $1.1 million for a heart-shaped necklace with pearls and matching earrings; $130,000 for a necklace and matching earrings with rubies and diamonds; $255,000 for a necklace of Egyptian coral and onyx. Two days later it was antiques: $610,640 altogether. Among the purchases were a rare mahogany China cabinet for which she paid $100,000; a pair of eighteenth-century carved and gilt wood Georgian armchairs, for $41,600; an eighteenth-century red lacquer grandfather clock, for $12,000; an eighteenth-century English cut glass six-light chandelier, for $33,600.

Three weeks later she discovered a less taxing way to consume conspicuously. Rather than look at individual items, she purchased an entire estate, for $5.95 million. It had belonged to Fan Fox Samuels, a New York philanthropist, and included rare books, paintings by the masters, stately furniture, everything. Some of the pieces went to Lindenmere, a vast multimillion-dollar estate on Long Island, which Imelda Marcos purchased in February 1981 (one month after Reagan's inauguration), though her ownership was hidden, the registered owners being first Luna 7 Development Corporation and later Ancor Holdings N.V., an Antilles corporation, both of which she controlled. She frequently summoned the chef and kitchen staff from the Philippine embassy in Washington to cook for her guests at Lindenmere, who often included actor George Hamilton and his mother. Many of the other pieces from the Samuels estate were placed in a New York City town house on East Sixty-sixth Street. The legal title to the town house was in the name of the Philippine government—which meant that effectively it was Imelda Marcos's.

On a stately, formal block between Fifth Avenue and Madison, the town house was her gallery, showplace, discotheque, where she could entertain the rich and famous—along with the pseudorich and not-so-famous. Elegance and kitsch were joined. In the wood-floored, expansive rooms, delicate, tasteful paintings by Van Gogh and Picasso hung near massive, oversize romanticized portraits of Imelda, of Ferdinand, of the entire family (the daughters in white sitting at the feet of their parents: the royal family), and of Ronald and Nancy Reagan. They were garish photographs which had been blown up, then painted over with oils. They were worth no more than $1,000 or $2,000, but Mrs. Marcos paid $100,000 for each. There was a music room, a replica of the one she maintained in Malacañang, with two Steinway grand pianos and a 1763 Baker Harris harpsichord; the library had walls of original editions (most from the Samuels estate)—Balzac and Dickens and a 1662 volume of the royal arms of Louis XIV. The house consisted of six stories altogether, with an elevator and a kitchen on every floor. Even though she never slept there, preferring the Waldorf, she maintained a bedroom on the third floor. Adjacent was a bathroom with a Jacuzzi and a sink for the hairdresser to rinse Mrs. Marcos's hair. Her bed had a scalloped canopy. Pillows strewn around the town house had tacky sayings in needlepoint: "Nouveau Rich Is Better Than No Riche at All"; "I love champagne, caviar and cash"; "Good girls go to Heaven. Bad girls go everywhere." There was a hothouse—with plastic plants.

A staff of eight servants lived in the town house with little to do except be on call for the first lady's summons. They were quartered in the musty basement. A seamstress whose job it was to keep the curtains in repair slept and worked in a room in the subbasement

310

without windows or any ventilation. It was so tiny that her cot was wedged under some shelves, the plumbing and gas pipes only a few feet above her head. On the top floor of the house was a discotheque full of mirrors. Here, with the strobe lights flashing and the music pulsating from a sound system as elaborate and expensive as anything in a fashionable New York City club, Imelda Marcos's friends carried on the fast life.

Life continued to be a party for Mrs. Marcos, at the taxpayer's expense. She could buy everything and influence many leading American politicians, but had trouble with her daughter Imee. High-spirited and independent, Imee chose a low-handicap golfer and professional basketball coach, Tomás ("Tommy") Manotoc to be her husband. Mrs. Marcos found him beneath the Marcos station, believing that her daughter ought to marry Prince Charles. Imee and Manotoc were secretly married in a ten-minute $20 ceremony in Arlington, Virginia, on December 4, 1981. They returned to the Philippines, and Manotoc disappeared. He was last seen on the evening of December 29, 1981, driving away in his white car after dining with his wife at Las Conchas restaurant in Makati, the modern, fashionable district of Manila. Manotoc's parents accused the Marcoses. Imelda Marcos accused everybody: the anti-Marcos opposition in the United States; the Manotoc family; the Communists. The U.S. embassy and the State Department covered the real-life soap opera in cables. The first from Manila, "Who Kidnapped Tommy Manotoc?," concluded that it was doubtful that it was "dissidents." A month later the State Department alerted the embassy: "We have heard reports here that 'the Australians' (presumably the Australian embassy in Manila) have what they deem more definitive information on the case."

Whatever the fate of her missing son-in-law, Imelda Marcos didn't grieve, continuing to receive and entertain, from scientists to celebrities. Members of the august National Academy of Sciences arrived in the Philippines shortly after the new year to study simple energy conversion—how rural families could use less wood, thus saving the country's forests, by, for instance, using a hibachi. During their first encounter with Mrs. Marcos, in her music room at Malacañang, the head of the delegation spoke for about ten minutes. Then Imelda Marcos interrupted him and carried on for nearly two hours, talking about love, truth, justice, beauty. They were spared more of the babble when she abruptly departed for another appointment, but she insisted they return the next day for lunch. The next morning the scientists trooped off to the countryside, and when they returned, they were sweaty and dusty. Some thought they could go to the palace as they were after washing up; after all, it was to be a working lunch. When they arrived, Malacañang looked like Versailles under Louis XIV. The palace swirled with beautiful people; the tables were ablaze with candles. There were eight strolling musicians. After the lunch came the floor show, with shapely models, native dances, folk songs, and, of course, Imelda Marcos warbling love songs. Then she summoned the scientists upstairs. One of the scientists tried to explain the energy project to her. She interrupted him and talked nonstop from 5:00 to 8:00 P.M. She told them about her project of giving each prisoner a rabbit, dog, or plant, and then she drew a circle on the blackboard, representing the universe. She made a hole in the circle and drew some lines. She explained that this represented where cosmic forces entered the Philippines. "And my scientists tell me that these forces are so powerful that we can use them to protect you our American friends against Soviet missiles." The bewildered scientists left; the party downstairs continued.

When the scientists departed, Tommy Manotoc was still missing. A few days later he miraculously reappeared. The government said that Philippine soldiers had fought their way into a hideout in the Sierra Madre, about sixty miles east of Manila, and "rescued" him. Few believed it. With Manotoc safe—he eventually became a part of the family, sharing in the ill-gotten wealth—the embassy dropped any formal pursuit of the issue, but embassy officers assumed that Imelda Marcos and her brother Kokoy Romualdez had been the masterminds. "It's just an example of totalitarian power being used to solve a domestic dispute," says an embassy officer. "He's lucky he didn't get killed."

13 : The Best
of Times . . .

In September 1982, sixteen years almost to the day after the Marcoses had arrived in Washington as guests of LBJ, they were once again triumphantly welcomed. For all that the Marcoses had been able to buy and steal, for all the hundreds of millions of dollars in aid they had extracted from the U.S. Congress, for all undeserved respect shown them by American officials, a state visit, that highest of all homages that an American president can bestow on a third world dictator, had eluded them through three administrations. They had come close before. Ford had promised to invite Marcos if he (Ford) were reelected. During Carter's last year Holbrooke had lobbied on Marcos's behalf, and if Carter had been reelected, Marcos might have been received. Within six months after Reagan was elected, the Marcoses were informed that an invitation to come to Washington would be forthcoming.

The coveted trip did not inhibit Imelda Marcos from venturing off, in the summer of 1982, to visit what Reagan called the "evil empire." Once again, to sharpen the jab at the United States, she began her pilgrimage in Moscow on July 4. In the USSR she spent two hours with Foreign Minister Andrei Gromyko, in addition to meetings with other members of the Politburo, signing trade, scientific, and cultural agreements. Marcos sent about half his cabinet with her "because of the great value he placed on Philippine-Soviet friendship," she explained to the Soviet leaders. While she was in Moscow, the Marcos government concluded an agreement whereby the Soviets agreed to finance and construct a $1 million cement plant. Up to fifty Russians would be in the Philippines to work on the project. "Technicians" they were called; most likely many of them were KGB agents.

This was Mrs. Marcos's fourth trip to the Soviet Union in the past few years. Nevertheless, she was warmly received by the conservative Reagan administration when she flew directly to Washington after Moscow. Bush saw her again, on very short notice. She spent more than an hour with CIA Director William Casey, that hard-line anti-Communist who was conducting the war against Nicaragua. (While her mother was meeting with her new friends in Washington, Imee Manotoc, in New York, spent $79,000 for a brooch of rubies, diamonds, and emeralds and $22,000 for a necklace with gold, diamond, and ruby beads.)

Back in Manila, Imelda Marcos told Ambassador Armacost, who had replaced Murphy, how much she appreciated the access she now had in Washington, how much more pleasant it was to go there now than it had been during the Carter years. She was "in a buoyant mood," Armacost noted, "highly pleased with the results of her latest diplomatic gambits." The ambassador added that Mrs. Marcos and her husband were becoming "increasingly preoccupied with the upcoming state visit."

Indeed, the Marcoses were very worried. They were concerned about demonstrations and rallies by the various anti-Marcos organizations in the United States, which were growing in numbers and activities the longer Marcos remained in power and the more Filipinos fled into exile. They were worried about how they would be treated by the press. Marcos was also worried about increasing opposition to his rule and reaction to the visit at home. The visit would again put the media spotlight on the Philippines, and it would be an ideal moment for anti-Marcos demonstrations. To preempt them, Marcos ordered raids on union offices; more than 40 people were arrested, including a seventy-nine-year-old union leader. That sweep, in August, was followed by a draconian crackdown in Manila. A force of 1,000 "secret marshals" in plain clothes killed 45 persons in just eight days. Marcos said they were "subversives" as well as hard-core criminals. Then he gave an order to kill only when absolutely necessary.

Adding to his anxiety about the visit, on the eve of his arrival in Washington, Amnesty International released a report, its first major one about the Philippines since 1976, entitled *Human Rights Violations in the Philippines: An Account of Torture, "Disappear-*

ances," *Extrajudicial Executions and Illegal Detention.* Most of the abuses had occurred *since* the lifting of martial law. The first account of torture in the report was based on the affidavit of a woman who told how after stripping her husband, "the soldiers squeezed his testicles with pliers. They poured vinegar with pepper on his eyes. They poured gasoline on his feet and burned them. . . . They forced him to drink two liters of water through his nose. . . . In addition, they gave him electric shock." After being released to visit his child, he was killed during an early-morning raid.

Marcos need not have worried. Nearly everywhere he went while in the United States, he was accorded all the respect, wrapped in the pomp and circumstance, of an honorable world leader. If he was corrupt and ruled by fraud, force, and fear, no one seemed overly concerned. After Washington, he went to New York, where he addressed the elite Council on Foreign Relations. He flew to Mobile, Alabama, where the United States Sports Academy gave him a Distinguished Service Award and an honorary doctorate in sports science. On the way home he spoke in San Francisco, where he was welcomed by Mayor Dianne Feinstein, who muted some of the criticisms of her receiving Marcos by handing him a copy of the Amnesty report. In Los Angeles Democratic Mayor Tom Bradley honored Marcos and his wife with a key to the city.

Marcos's greatest fears were about how he would be treated by the American press. Only reluctantly did he finally agree to meet with journalists, addressing the National Press Club, appearing on NBC's *Meet the Press* and ABC's *Nightline.* Interviewers asked Marcos about the Amnesty report, but he deflected the questions. At first he claimed that Amnesty investigators had never even been in the Philippines. It wasn't true; they had been there for seventeen days. When that lie was exposed, Marcos claimed that Amnesty had been in the Philippines clandestinely. That also wasn't true, but it's difficult for the press to stay ahead of a consummate liar, which Marcos was. Marcos buoyantly told aides and American officials afterward that he was delighted with how he had been treated by American reporters. (Though Marcos was confident of his own ability to handle American reporters, he was equally aware of his wife's tendency to ramble and make inane statements; thus, he emphatically told her that she could not appear on two of the network's morning news programs, forcing her to cancel commitments she had given.)

To ensure such a smooth and favorable visit, the Marcoses had gone to extraordinary lengths, even by their own standards of excess. Three months before the visit, Kokoy Romualdez was named ambassador to the United States, his sole task being to prepare for the "second coming" of the Marcoses. He was assisted by four others with ambassadorial rank. Public relations executives from Manila's leading corporations and advertising agencies were pressed into service for the affair and sent off to Washington to cultivate reporters. The Philippine embassy prepared more than 300 "press kits," which contained five books (those purportedly written by Marcos, along with the Spence "biography") and a pile of press releases, all packaged in Philippine-made attaché cases. There were numerous luncheons for journalists, including a very exclusive one for the dozen or so recipients of the prestigious Nieman Fellowships at Harvard.

Sometimes Romualdez and his loyal aides reached too far and got caught. The Philippine embassy issued a statement that Mrs. Marcos was to receive an honorary degree from the University of Pennsylvania. An "outrage," said the university, which emphatically asserted in a public statement that it was not planning to honor Imelda Marcos "in any way, shape or form," adding that it "deeply resented" being ensnared "in the machinations of the Marcos regime's propaganda machine."

But usually what the Marcoses wanted, they received—or more accurately, they bought. Altogether at least $5 million, maybe $20 million, was spent by the Marcoses on the state visit. ("Whatever the trip costs," a U.S. diplomat in Manila told William Branigin of the *Washington Post* on the eve of Marcos's departure, "they'll get it back in compensation for the bases.") In the weeks before the Marcoses' arrival, there had been picnics for Filipino-Americans in five American cities, including Alexandria, Virginia, and San Francisco, costing an estimated $410,000. A restaurant was purchased in the fashionable Georgetown district of Washington, D.C., for $270,000. On chic, high-rent M Street, it was called the Manila in Georgetown, and its true ownership was murky, purposefully so. The application for a liquor license was filed by a company called Philtrade, Inc., which, according to the same record, was owned by

316

Food Terminal Inc., a Philippine corporation. No Marcos name was on any document. But Food Terminal was a government corporation headed by Mrs. Marcos. (In 1984 the restaurant was "sold"—"given away" would be more accurate—to the son of a former Marcos press spokesman for $50,000, or one-fifth what had been paid two years earlier.)

Romualdez had worked tirelessly and successfully. On the way from Andrews Air Force Base, Imelda Marcos, looking out the window of the helicopter as it was about to land on the grounds of the Washington Monument, was relieved. "I see Kokoy has done his homework well," she said to her State Department escort. Instead of the protesters she had feared, nearly 1,000 Filipinos were on hand, turned out by Romualdez and his team. They had been bused in from as far away as Norfolk, Virginia, lured with promises of free food, free lodging, and entertainment (provided by dancers brought in from the Philippines). They were supplied with miniature flags and T-shirts reading "I am a Filipino." It was "one of the most carefully orchestrated events of its kind Washington has seen," noted *New York Times* reporter Lynn Rosellini; it "easily could have been scripted by Cecil B. De Mille."

The show was as much, if not more, for the folks back home as it was for Americans, to convince the Filipinos how loved their leaders were in Washington. The Filipinos who were part of the staged welcome on the mall carried banners, in Tagalog and other dialects, proclaiming, "Long live Marcos and Reagan," and "You are the idol of the Filipinos." All of it was broadcast live by satellite back to the Philippines. The Reagan administration, more attuned than any to the ways of show business and television, cooperated. The White House welcoming ceremony, including the twenty-one-gun salute, the bewigged, slow-marching Old Guard Fife and Drum Corps playing "Yankee Doodle," and Nancy Reagan kissing Imelda Marcos on the cheek, began at 10:00 A.M. Washington time, which was 10:00 P.M. in Manila, the heart of prime time there.

Marcos's entourage was staggering: more than half the cabinet, scores of deputies and senior aides, altogether several *hundred* sycophants and hangers-on who filled two 747s, with Marcos in one, his wife in the other, in the event of a crash. Among them were Defense Minister Enrile and sugar baron Benedicto. It was probably the largest contingent ever to come on a state visit; in contrast, when Singapore's Lee Kwan Yew had visited a few months earlier, he had been accompanied by a staff of eight and without any fuss or fanfare conducted business with all the top officials, including Weinberger, Shultz, and Reagan. The Marcoses hosted a reception that was one of the largest ever by any foreign government in Washington, let alone the government of an impoverished third world country. It was held at the Corcoran Art Gallery, only a few blocks from the White House, and more than 2,000 of Washington's elite were invited to pay respects to the first lady of extravaganza. Among those who appeared were Republican Senators John Warner of Virginia and S. I. ("Sam") Hayakawa of California, along with Secretary of State Shultz, Attorney General William French Smith, and Jack Valenti. There was a groaning buffet and entertainment by folk dancers flown over from the Philippines. When without ever explaining what had delayed him, Marcos arrived after the party had begun, his wife grabbed a microphone and sang "Feelings."

And there was, of course, the White House dinner. Imelda Marcos kissed both the Reagans on each cheek when she arrived. It was a dinner under the stars in the Rose Garden, Japanese lanterns swaying in the trees. Though a White House dinner is customary for a state visit, this one was different. Ordinarily a few celebrities are invited, to add some variety and levity to the crowd heavy with senators, Supreme Court justices, and fat cat political donors. But for the Marcoses the guests had been selected from a list provided by Kokoy Romualdez, which meant by Imelda Marcos. Society types, the people who were talked about more in the gossip columns than they were quoted in the *Congressional Record,* predominated, people whose "allegiances" were "largely to Imelda Marcos and Nancy Reagan," reported the *Washington Post* style section, which regularly monitors these affairs. The only former American ambassador to the Philippines invited, the only one for whom the Marcoses retained any affection, was Henry Byroade, the man who had presided over the beginning of martial law and who frequently saw Imelda Marcos on her trips to Washington, talking with her in her hotel room until early-morning hours. The man whom she had wanted to be ambassador in 1977, Lloyd Hand, was there. John Swearingen, chairman of Standard Oil, came, as did Hong Kong shipping mag-

318

nate Y. K. Pao, who flew in specially for the event. There was the artist Andy Warhol; the countess Luis de Romanones of Madrid; Dallas Cowboys quarterback Roger Staubach; Van Cliburn; the actress Arlene Dahl and her escort, Marc Rosen, vice-president of Elizabeth Arden; and Oscar de la Renta, the fashion designer-cum-entertainer, socialite, and swinger. Surprisingly Robert Trent Jones, Jr., the golf course architect, was also there; he had been one of those fighting for Aquino's release from prison (and three and a half years after the state dinner he was to take an active part in Corazon Aquino's campaign).

If the parties were for Imelda, there were some special moments for Ferdinand to cherish as well. It must have been particularly gratifying for the Philippine leader when Secretary of Defense Caspar Weinberger presented him with a plaque on which were mounted replicas of the Distinguished Service Cross, Silver Star, and Purple Heart, all awards Marcos claimed to have received from the U.S. government. Weinberger praised Marcos, the man whose U.S. military records showed he had probably been a collaborator and who had been arrested during the war, as "a compatriot in arms of American fighting forces." Marcos's fraud and hoax of forty years were still holding—not just holding, but perpetuated by the U.S. secretary of defense, the man who ruled over the very agency of the U.S. government that housed the documents that, if anyone had bothered to look at them, would have exposed the fraud. By now, in fact, there were more than just classified and buried government documents that raised questions about what Marcos had done during the war.

The week before Marcos arrived in Washington, his war medals claims had been exposed as fraudulent by the *Philippine News,* the largest Filipino-American newspaper, published in San Francisco. The fraud was reported by Bonafacio H. Gillego, who had the credentials to be taken seriously. A retired Philippine army officer, he had worked in the 1960s with Operation Brotherhood, the CIA's operation, in Laos and Vietnam; he was an elected delegate to the Constitutional Convention at the time martial law was declared and later had been forced into exile because of his opposition to Marcos. Gillego's article was well researched and included a statement by Colonel Romulo Manriquez, Marcos's commanding officer for a period during World War II. "I consider Marcos to be the greatest impostor that World War II has ever produced," Manriquez said. An army captain, Vicente L. Rivera, who had been Marcos's adjutant, corroborated for the *News* what Manriquez said.

It wasn't only Reagan administration officials who ignored Gillego's story; so did the press. Gillego had approached the *Washington Post* with his information before it appeared in the *News*. He had walked in off the street and asked to talk with someone. As it happened, John Sharkey, an assistant foreign editor, was free and saw him. Sharkey began working on the story, and in September, a few days prior to Marcos's arrival in Washington, Gillego, with Manriquez and Rivera along, again went to the *Post* for a meeting with editors. The next day Marcos went to the newspaper for lunch. He was asked about the Gillego-Manriquez-Rivera allegations. Marcos laughingly deflected them. "If you want those medals back, you can have them." Then he turned serious, launching into stories about his exploits as a guerrilla fighter. The *Post* accepted Marcos's word, a reflection of the deference that the press generally accords public officials, domestic and foreign. (Sharkey continued to work on the story, eventually confirming all that Gillego had written, in addition to uncovering more about the hoax, but it would be another year before the story appeared.)

The moment at the *Post* might have been embarrassing for Marcos, but, he was to tell friends and U.S. diplomats upon his return to Manila, the state visit had "greatly exceeded" his expectations. Above all, he had not been prepared for the warmth extended by the Reagans. In welcoming the Philippine president, Reagan heralded Marcos for having "personally fought so valiantly" during World War II. "Liberty, democracy, justice, equality," declared the president of the United States, were the values for which Marcos, like the United States, had struggled. "Yours, Mr. President," Reagan said to the Philippine strongman, "is a respected voice for reason and moderation." There was more. Reagan praised Marcos's "dedication to improving the standard of living of your people" and "continuing interest in better nutrition." That was a cruel burlesque, for the Philippines under Marcos was a country where children were starving and dying from malnutrition. According to a World Bank

320

report, the number of urban poor had increased from 24 percent in 1975 to 40 percent in 1980; typically they lived in hovels along fetid canals where women washed clothes and children bathed. When Marcos, during his speeches in Washington, had made the same claims about the well-being of Filipinos, Cardinal Sin had been prompted to write in response, "I should not believe that there is malnutrition in the Philippines even if, in the centers run by the Archdiocese of Manila, children are daily being snatched from the jaws of death because of slow starvation."

Prior to Marcos's private chat with Reagan, the Marcoses met with Secretary of State Shultz. Most of their concerns were trivial. Imelda Marcos demanded to know, "Who's this Sheenboom? Who's Sheenboom?" A puzzled secretary of state, who had no idea what she was talking about, finally turned to Marcos and said in effect, "Mr. President, is it my understanding that you've traveled halfway around the world and are about to see the president of the United States to complain about someone named Sheenboom?" That silenced Marcos, but Shultz, still mystified, later asked Ambassador Armacost, who had been present during the meeting, who this "Sheenboom" was. Armacost explained that it was Gilbert Sheinbaum, the political counselor in Cebu; the Marcoses were upset because a twenty-one-page report he had written had been leaked to the press. Sent just one month before the state visit, Sheinbaum's report painted a considerably bleaker picture of the Philippines than either the Marcoses or the Reagan administration wanted to admit. "Whatever is bad may only get worse," Sheinbaum wrote. He mentioned one city where the mayor was allowing gambling to "flourish openly" and the Philippine Constabulary is "benefitting financially." In another province the governor complained about the "crime and corruption conducted by" the military. Sheinbaum also reported about how Marcos cronies Benedicto and Cuenca had purchased huge properties at forced sales. The Marcoses' fears were again unnecessary, however. When the *Washington Post* wrote an article based on the memo—it was about the only newspaper to do so, the press, like the administration, still largely ignoring the growing Philippine crisis—the State Department didn't react by condemning the corruption in the Philippines. Instead, the department complained about the leak. "This has got to stop. This is ridiculous," a State

Department official told the *Washington Post.* "This is a serious breach of security."

The Reagan administration foreign policy, which was based on the Kirkpatrick doctrine, can perhaps best be understood by comparing the approaches to the Philippines and to Nicaragua. During the very month that Marcos was being feted, honored, and heralded in Washington, a new CIA station chief arrived in Honduras to conduct the war to overthrow the Sandinista government in neighboring Nicaragua. The Reagan administration recruited, trained, equipped, and paid contras, then provided them with a manual on how and whom to assassinate; clandestinely and illegally mined Nicaraguan harbors; and when Congress curtailed funding, the administration sold arms to Iran and diverted proceeds to the contras. The administration launched a war against the Sandinistas because theirs was a leftist government which, in its UN votes and rhetoric, tended to align with the Soviet Union and against the United States. The Marcos government, on the other hand, was viewed as a rightist regime which was pro-American, notwithstanding Imelda Marcos's trips to the Soviet Union. That was the dichotomy expressed in its simplest terms, which was how the Reagan administration tended to see it. There was no room in the Kirkpatrick doctrine or the ideology of the Reagan administration for a revolutionary Nicaragua that might be leftist and maybe even Marxist but would not allow Soviet military bases or for a Marcos who might say all the right things but whose rule was contrary to America's best interests.

In order to implement a policy of fighting the Sandinistas and embracing Marcos, the Reagan administration had to adopt an inconsistent approach to human rights. Abuses in the Philippines were quietly overlooked while those in Nicaragua were loudly criticized. When the Sandinistas censored the newspaper *La Prensa,* the denunciations were heard around the world, from moderates and liberals as well as conservatives. But in December 1982, just a few months after Marcos's state visit, soldiers raided and closed the offices of *We Forum,* a small Philippine newspaper that was one of the few voices of opposition to Marcos. The publisher-editor was seized, along with nine other reporters and columnists. They were charged with subversion, with publishing "derogatory and libelous articles to undermine the people's confidence." What had the newspaper published? Gillego's articles about Marcos's war medals fraud. While those articles had triggered the closing, the embassy noted, "It is also likely that the crackdown is meant as a forceful reminder that the Marcos administration intends to enforce limits on both press freedom and opposition political activity." The closing of *We Forum* brought no ringing criticism from the Reagan administration, which had just heralded Marcos for his commitment to "liberty" and "democracy."

There was also a church-state battle in the Philippines and Nicaragua. In Nicaragua it was a complex struggle having as much to do with power as with theology: Was it going to be a hierarchical church or a "people's" church? In the Philippines the bishops' council was overwhelmingly conservative; that meant that most of the country's 100-plus bishops were pro-Marcos or stayed out of politics, as the pope admonished them to do. Among the priests and nuns, again most were apolitical, but a substantial number appeared to side with the revolutionary forces by virtue of their working with the poor. Those religious who did side with the poor often found that they had sinned against Marcos; the power of the state, or of the Marcos cronies, was brought down upon them.

During the nine months preceding Marcos's state visit, thirty priests were arrested in the Philippines; many were held incommunicado for long periods before being released and charged, if at all, with "subversion." Two priests, Niall O'Brien of Ireland and Brian Gore, an Australian, who worked in Negros with the poorest of the poor in the midst of the wealthiest of the wealthy, were placed on trial on trumped-up charges of murder. An American Maryknoll missionary, Father Ralph Kroes, was expelled in August 1981 (one month after Bush had praised Marcos for his democracy). The government charged Kroes, who had served in the Philippines for twelve years, with subversion. The real reason he was thrown out of the Philippines is found deep within a twenty-one-page Confidential report from the embassy. Father Kroes had run afoul of an army colonel who was commander of the Philippine Constabulary in Davao del Norte, criticizing him for allowing military abuses to continue. The colonel enlisted the aid of Antonio Floirendo, the banana crony and a "friend of the First Lady," the U.S. embassy noted. Floirendo "arranged for Kroes' expulsion."*

The fate of church lay workers was more severe. In Negros, on the day after Easter, two lay workers in the Christian base communities, which the Catholic Church encouraged in areas without priests, were dragged from their homes by uniformed men. One of the men had played the part of Jesus in the Easter pageant. Their bodies were found five weeks later, hands tied behind their backs with dried banana stalks. They had been strangled. In an adjacent sugarcane field were the bodies of seven men, also church lay workers. Four had their mouths stuffed with rags; three had crushed skulls; some had been buried alive.

President Reagan never professed that human rights were the soul of his administration's foreign policy, as Carter had about his. But the Reagan administration did feel strongly about conservative economic principles. It worshipped the free-market economy, an inviolable conservative tenet. Applying that yardstick, not human rights, the administration should have treated Marcos like a pariah— or as a Communist. The Reagan administration railed against the Sandinistas for seeking to establish a Marxist economy. In fact, however, even though they did confiscate land and companies (most of which had belonged to Somoza or his friends) and set up state farms and industries, government control of the Nicaraguan economy was probably less than half. Marcos made the Sandinistas look like ideological, true-believing, unbridled Adam Smith capitalists.

"Creeping State Capitalism" the American embassy in Manila labeled a 1983 report. It was thirty-six pages solely about the extensive involvement of the government in the Philippine economy— and that didn't include the crony capitalism. During martial law Marcos had issued 688 presidential decrees and 283 letters of in-

---

* Floirendo's role in the expulsion of Kroes was reported by Sheinbaum in the cable that was leaked to the press (though the Kroes matter was not reported). When the Sheinbaum report was released to this author pursuant to an FOIA request, two long paragraphs containing the Kroes matter were deleted, as were other portions of the cable, the State Department still apparently protecting Mrs. Marcos, Floirendo, or both.

struction, which injected the government into the economy in one form or another. There was not only a National Steel Corporation but also a National Stud Farm (which had "sprung from obscure origins," the embassy noted). The government owned outright or controlled more than 300 companies, engaging in everything from coal mining to the making of polyester to the production of mosquito coils. Many had been privately owned until taken over by the government. By 1983 the government had control of between 75 and 80 percent of all the country's financial assets. In addition to the Philippine National Bank, the Development Bank of the Philippines, the National Development Corporation, and the Veterans Bank (which were, in effect, government agencies), the government owned or controlled eight of the country's twenty-eight private commercial banks. Among them were the Filipinas Bank, whose vice-chairman was Ricardo Silverio—"erstwhile 'Crony' " was how the embassy labeled him—the Republic Planters Bank, whose chairman was Roberto Benedicto, who was also the chairman of the government sugar institute; and the United Coconut Planters Bank, Juan Ponce Enrile its chairman while he served as minister of defense.

Many of these 300 companies and the banks, along with most of the five-star hotels that had been built with government funds in 1976, had been taken over by the government because they were failing, and the owners were, of course, Marcos's friends. It was welfare capitalism.

When the Construction and Development Corporation of the Philippines (CDCP), owned by Marcos's golf buddy Rodolfo Cuenca, who had built highways with the engineering equipment provided back in 1966 for the Philippine troops going to Vietnam, was on the verge of bankruptcy, Marcos issued a letter of instruction. Government banks, whose loans or loan guarantees to Cuenca amounted to more than $1 billion, had to convert their loans to equity. This bailed out Cuenca. The government got CDCP's liabilities: an estimated $700 million, which Paul Gigot of the *Wall Street Journal* calculated was to the Philippine budget the equivalent of what $100 *billion* was to the U.S. budget.

Another of the rescued cronies was Herminio Disini, the man who had built some cigarette filters into a multibillion-dollar conglomerate. His vast empire crumbled when a man named Dewey

Dee fled the Philippines, leaving behind some $80 million in unpaid debts, many to Disini's companies. Government banks, whose own exposure to Disini was about $400 million, provided the bailout loans. Altogether the government had dumped an estimated $1 billion into its corporate bailout program by 1983.

Rather than express repugnance, the Reagan administration embraced Marcos and aided and abetted the corruption. The Ex-Im Bank came up with another $204.5 million for Westinghouse's nuclear power plant project, no longer a white elephant, now a gold one, projected to cost $1.89 billion. Ex-Im's action, taken at the time of Marcos's state visit, prompted a thank-you note from Secretary of State Shultz. "This timely action contributed to the success of the Marcos State Visit and helped to further cement our bilateral relations with the Philippines." It also helped sink the Philippine economy into greater debt—American banks and taxpayers were eventually called upon to bail it out—as well as further to enrich Marcos, who received $1,136,590.88 in payments from Westinghouse in 1981, according to his records.

Marcos was not just corrupt; he was anticapitalist, antifree market. He had created more government monopolies than the most dedicated of socialists. There was even a monopoly over the import of peroxide (by Letter of Instruction No. 1255, granted to Peroxide Philippines). The really big ones were, of course, sugar and coconut. Marcos nationalized the sugar industry completely, from milling to marketing. Only one other man and country had as much control of their sugar industry: Castro and Cuba. Philippine sugar planters lost money; just as the textbooks said, monopolies were costly. Because of the monopoly control, producers had to sell to the government at the prices it set instead of being able to secure the best price they could in the free market; Philippine sugar growers by 1983 had lost more than half a billion dollars.

When it came to coconuts, the president and his pals weren't content to drain only Filipino producers who, as with sugar growers, had been forced to sell to the state at prices below what the coconuts could fetch on the open market. No, the monopolists also wanted to squeeze Americans. Control of the coconut industry was in the hands of Defense Minister Enrile and Eduardo Cojuangco, the two men who had been principals in implementing martial law and remained close to Marcos. Their monopolistic scam involved the United Coconut Planters Bank and the United Coconut Oil Mills (UNICOM), which Marcos had created by decree in 1977. Enrile was the chairman of the bank and UNICOM; Cojuangco was president of both. The bank's funds came from levies on coconut producers. With these funds, Enrile and Cojuangco began buying up Philippine millers. As the U.S. embassy reported, within the industry there were stories that Enrile "pulled no punches when he was talking to the owners of the small Filipino-owned mills—it was sell or else!" On one occasion, the embassy reported, Enrile "met with the six producers of domestically-consumed coconut oil and asked them to name a price for their mills. They declined." A few weeks later Marcos issued a decree that only mills owned by the bank would be entitled to a government subsidy; without the subsidy no mill could survive.

Having cornered the domestic market, Enrile and Cojuangco began looking to the United States. UNICOM set up a marketing operation in Los Angeles. That became a veritable slush fund for Cojuangco and other high-living bank executives. Each time a bank director came to the United States, he would draw out cash "advances" of $10,000. "Cojuangco, on the other hand, whenever he needed funds would simply get his girl Friday . . . to draw out money," on one occasion $100,000, according to the general manager of UNICOM operations in Los Angeles, Rafael Fernando. The money went for wild, extravagant living, so outlandish that a bank director remarked that if the coconut farmers in the Philippines ever found out how their money was being spent, they'd line up the bank officers in Luneta Park and have them shot. It was a life-style that many of the nouveau riche executives didn't know how to handle. When they arrived at the Hyatt Regency Hotel on Union Square in San Francisco late one evening, a bank vice-president discovered that his room was not a suite but a single. He began berating the desk clerk, as if the employee had any influence. His voice rising, he vowed to buy the hotel, demanding to speak with "Mr. Hyatt." Wherever the bank executives traveled in the United States, it was in limousines, $250 a day each. In Minneapolis, where UNICOM was negotiating for the purchase of Cargill's Philippine operations, the hotel staff looked in wonderment at all the limos; only when

Vice President Mondale was in town had they seen so many, they exclaimed. UNICOM also purchased a Learjet for $2.3 million, the funds coming from the UCPB but the expenditure recorded on the books as a coconut oil purchase. To secure bank loans, false bills of lading and accounts receivable were prepared.

Borrowing from the methods of the oil-producing nations, which had joined together to keep oil prices high through the OPEC cartel, Enrile and Cojuangco decided to form a group they called CO-COPEC. It would corner the coconut oil market and keep prices high, a relatively simple task because the Philippines produced 70 percent of the world supply of coconut oil and 95 percent of American imports. Coconut oil is a major ingredient in everything from soaps to baby foods and can be used as a substitute for petroleum in industrial chemicals. UNICOM began hoarding and storing in late 1979, waiting for the price to rise. That's price-fixing, illegal under American antitrust laws.*

UNICOM could do as it wished in the Philippines, where Marcos was the law. But in the United States the Justice Department began an investigation during the last year of the Carter administration. A federal grand jury was convened. Rafael Fernando, the manager of the UNICOM's Los Angeles operations, agreed to cooperate; documents were subpoenaed. Marcos reacted by issuing a presidential decree which made it a crime for any Filipino to testify before an American grand jury; in addition, the decree made it a crime to provide any subpoenaed documents. The decree defined documents in precisely the same language as the Justice Department subpoena. The Justice Department lawyers felt they still had enough evidence to file a criminal case against three American-based companies established by UNICOM.

---

* The scheme backfired, just as had Marcos's attempt to hoard sugar, because prices for coconut oil instead of rising to 42 cents a pound, the price at which COCOPEC intended to sell, fell to about 23 cents a pound. The declining prices were caused in part by the grain embargo on the USSR imposed by the Carter administration in response to the Soviet invasion of Afghanistan. One result was that the market was glutted with soybeans, which can be converted to soybean oil, a substitute for coconut oil in some products. Total UNICOM losses were some $15 million, which because of the relationship between UCPB and UNICOM were passed on to Philippine coconut planters. The fact that a scheme fails does not itself protect the perpetrators from prosecution under the U.S. antitrust laws, which do not make an exception for failure.

All this had transpired prior to Reagan's election, and in late January 1981 the grand jury in Los Angeles had heard all the evidence and was waiting for a recommendation from the Justice Department, which had no doubt that it could secure a criminal indictment. If the Reagan administration wanted to send a message about free-market capitalism, this was an opportunity. The administration balked, just as the Carter administration had so many times on human rights.

Cojuangco had been furious with the American investigation, constantly complaining to embassy officers. In February 1981 Philippine government officials were encouraged by the Reagan administration to present their case in Washington, not in court but at the State Department. The Philippine delegation met with State officials at least three times in six days. During one meeting the deputy assistant secretary of state for East Asia, John Negroponte, later Reagan's ambassador to Honduras, where he supervised the contra war, "assured [the Filipinos] that we understood their concerns clearly," as the department advised the embassy. Negroponte also told the Philippine delegation to present its case at the Justice Department. It did. The criminal case was dropped. Nothing untoward, no pressure from the State Department or White House, a Justice Department lawyer said publicly at the time. He said the case was treated no differently from any other; sometimes it's preferable to file a civil case instead of a criminal one. "That's ridiculous for him to say," says Shelley Taylor Convissar, an attorney who worked on the case for the Justice Department. "It was a total political move." In lieu of criminal fines and possible imprisonment, the defendant companies signed a civil consent decree, admitting no wrong but agreeing not to do it again.

The State Department was pleased and relieved. In a classified message to the embassy in Manila it said, "Dept considers Justice's action to be unusually forthcoming and responsive to GOP [Government of Philippine] concerns in light of the fact that price fixing is normally prosecuted as a crime." The outcome, the department added, was attributable in "large degree" to the manner in which it, along with the Philippine delegation, had presented the concerns to the Justice Department. Reagan's State Department had made a choice: Marcos and monopoly rather than competition and the free market.

They were the very best of times for the Marcoses, those first years of the Reagan administration. For diplomats, there was almost a weekly bash at Malacañang, with hard-rock disco and women passed around like peanuts at a cocktail party; making sure there was an available supply was one of General Ver's assignments. The Great Gatsby would have been jealous. Imelda Marcos had dedicated enormous amounts of her formidable, if not frightening, energy to seducing American foreign policy—everyone from journalists to wives of visiting American officials received her gifts and blandishments—but rarely, if ever, it seemed, had she been more successful. The man in charge of the American mission in Manila during those intoxicating days was Michael Armacost.

Armacost protected the Marcoses, taking measures to ensure that they wouldn't be offended or embarrassed. Like the Marcoses, he was upset by the Sheinbaum cable, not by its contents but because it was not classified Secret (only Confidential); the classification almost assured that it would be leaked, as it was. The American ambassador was similarly nervous about a study that the Rand Corporation was doing about the issue of succession in the Philippines, looking at the question of what happens after Marcos, the very question that U.S. officials should have been probing but weren't. That was the study which Guy Pauker had suggested back in 1979 but which had died for lack of interest. When John Holdridge became assistant secretary for East Asia, replacing Richard Holbrooke, he asked Pauker to proceed. Armacost was gravely concerned that Marcos would learn about the study; he worried that Marcos might conclude that the United States was looking for a successor. Thus, Armacost severely restricted distribution of the Rand report: Rather than 100 or so copies, only about two dozen were distributed; the Philippine desk officer didn't receive one, nor did one-star generals at the Pentagon. Had it been more widely distributed, perhaps the United States would have been better prepared to deal with a post-Marcos Philippines when it became a reality, as well as with the growing threat of the New People's Army, which Pauker also addressed.

Hardly a day passed that Michael Armacost wasn't seen with Imelda Marcos. They danced together in Malacañang; at Leyte they sang World War II GI ditties. He once held her parasol for her. That seemed to be the metaphor for it all. He was dubbed "Armaclose," and "Ourmarcos."

All that was to change dramatically and, for Armacost, painfully. When the pervasiveness of the Marcoses' corruption—social, political and economic—finally sank in, he became an enemy, one they couldn't afford to have. In early 1984 Armacost returned from Manila to Washington, becoming the number three man in the State Department; with his influence and credibility he became a point man, leading Secretary Shultz and the department to a policy that contributed to the downfall of the Marcos empire.

Michael Hayden Armacost. At a going-away party for one of the members of his staff at the Manila embassy, an aide, emboldened by alcohol, said to his ambassador, "Why is it, sir, that everything you do you do so fucking well?" It had always been that way. If it seemed that he was a modern Renaissance man now, he had been an all-American boy in high school and college—in the era of all-American boys. Scholar, athlete, accomplished pianist. "Ace in Everything," the *Minneapolis Star* heralded him in 1958, looking back on his career at Carleton College. "Whatever Mike does, he does well." He had led the baseball team in extra-base hits, missed an occasional practice to rack up points for the track team, golfed in the seventies, was a topflight swimmer. But what he did best was play basketball, so well in high school that he had been offered an athletic scholarship from UCLA, which was only a few years away from becoming one of the greatest college basketball dynasties. Armacost stood six feet three inches—tall in the days when the pro game was dominated by six-foot-ten-inch George Mikan of the Minneapolis Lakers.

Young Armacost wanted to attend UCLA, but his father, a conservative man, had some reservations. He was the president of the University of Redlands, a Baptist college in Southern California, where Mike grew up, and how would it look, how would he be able to recruit students, if his own son attended a state school? Handed a list of small, private schools, Mike selected the one that had won its last fifty-five home basketball games; it happened to be Carleton College, in Northfield, Minnesota. On the flat plains south of Min-

331

neapolis, Northfield was still rural in the 1950s. Among the maples, elms, and Victorian houses, Carleton shares the town with St. Olaf's College, giving the small town a heavy academic quotient.

Armacost, class president, began to play the piano in his senior year. Friends wondered why; then they discovered the girl he was dating was a musician. She was also queen of the annual Winter Carnival; he was king; later they married. Armacost excelled in the classroom, as he did in all other endeavors, athletic and social. He was Phi Beta Kappa and a Rhodes finalist, failing to obtain that coveted scholarship, a faculty adviser recalled, because he had been "too humble," hadn't projected himself enough. He "settled" for a Fulbright, spending the year in Bonn, West Germany, followed by a year as a Woodrow Wilson Fellow at Columbia University.

With a Ph.D. in international relations from Columbia, Armacost was apparently headed to professorial life, but in 1968, when he took a sabbatical, from Pomona College, in Claremont, California, he never returned. After his sabbatical year at the International Christian University in Tokyo, he was selected as one of eighteen White House Fellows, a program designed to expose outstanding young men and women from academia, business, and the military to the workings of the highest levels of the executive branch of the government. Armacost's assignment was the Policy Planning Staff of the State Department. His rise was steady, expectedly for the "ace." He touched all the power bases: senior staff member for East Asia on the National Security Council; over to the Pentagon as a deputy assistant secretary; in 1980, back to State as deputy assistant secretary for East Asia. Then it was on to Manila, in 1982, the year he was one of five men selected to the NCAA's annual Silver Anniversary All-American team, awarded for outstanding performance in both intercollegiate athletics and subsequent career.

Manila was Armacost's first ambassadorial assignment. Maybe that was why he was such easy prey, innocent of the blandishments laid on American diplomats in any country, applied so thickly by Imelda Marcos. Perhaps his life had been too sheltered—too much time in small towns, in academia, in the government bureaucracy. Or maybe he was too much a Christian to believe that anyone could be so base. In college he had written an article, "Christianity and the 'Beat' Generation," and in 1982 he wrote that he remained a

332

"reasonably active member of several churches—Methodist until I left Claremont; Episcopalian since." On the other hand, he was too smart not to have seen the corruption—economic, political, and social—that infested and infected the Marcoses' rule. To the extent that he overlooked the destruction that the Marcoses were wreaking, that he tended to accentuate the positive and dismiss, if not ignore, the negatives, it may be a reflection less on Armacost as an individual than it is on the Foreign Service.

The Foreign Service doesn't reward officers who point out that the emperor has no clothes. Ambassadors and their staffs aren't supposed to be naysayers, especially not about a leader who is an American ally. That was the lesson out of China in the 1940s, when diplomats, John Paton Davies and John Stewart Service being the most notable, reported that Chiang Kai-shek was corrupt and brutal, that sticking with him was not in long-run American interests. They were victims of the "who lost China?" crusade, their careers destroyed in the McCarthy era purges.

Just when it had been thought that maybe those ugly ghosts had been exorcised, that an ideological purge wouldn't again sweep through the State Department, along came the Reagan administration. It drew up a "hit list," some sixty ambassadors who were to be removed because they were considered too "liberal." At the top was Robert White, a man who didn't abide dictators and was outspoken about his feelings, offending Paraguay's Alfredo Stroessner and Chile's Augusto Pinochet Ugarte. But it was White's work as ambassador in El Salvador, speaking out against the government atrocities, supporting land reform, that had most riled the Reagan conservatives. His unceremonial ouster from the Foreign Service brought him a note from retired Senator J. William Fulbright, who had left his mark on American foreign policy as chairman of the Senate Foreign Relations Committee during the 1960s and 1970s. "Like Service, Davies . . . and others in China, your wise counsel has been rejected by the government, and the people of our country will pay the price for the folly of their government." Also on the list was Lawrence Pezzulo, a twenty-five-year careerist who as ambassador to Nicaragua had moved the United States away from Somoza and who sought to establish smooth working relations with the Sandinistas.

Liberals were banished; conservatives, promoted. James Cheek, who deserved the highest commendations for having held the Sal-vadoran situation together during the tumultuous first months of 1980, was exiled to Nepal. On the other hand, the conservative John Negroponte, who had been Holbrooke's deputy in the East Asia Bureau, was made ambassador to Honduras, where he enthusias-tically supervised the first stages of the "secret" contra war against the Sandinistas. Another top Holbrooke deputy, Kenneth Bleakley, whose primary responsibility had been the Philippines, which meant implementing a policy that was essentially the same as the Reagan policy, was rewarded with assignment as the number two in the Salvadoran embassy, where he fervently defended the military against reports that it was responsible for brutal atrocities.

The ideological winds ravaged not just Latin America. In South Korea the right-wing target was William Gleysteen, an exceptionally capable career diplomat whom Carter had appointed ambassador in 1978. He was suspected by the right because as deputy assistant secretary (working for Holbrooke) he had been associated with the discussion of a possible Korean troop withdrawal and with the rec-ognition of China. Gleysteen was called back to Washington and found himself "walking the halls," as Foreign Service officers refer to someone who does not receive another assignment; he eventually left the service. He was replaced in Korea by Richard L. ("Dixie") Walker, whose principal qualification was that he spoke Korean. A right-wing academic, Walker became an apologist for the Korean dictatorship while shunning contacts with the democratic opposition.

Fanning the ideological flames, in the process burning many an officer and scarring the Foreign Service, was Senator Jesse Helms, the archconservative Republican from North Carolina. Helms em-braced Roberto d'Aubuisson, the Salvadoran leader tied to the death squads and the assassination of the country's archbishop, Oscar Arnulfo Romero; heralded the racist South African leaders; and stuck with Chile's General Pinochet, even after the Reagan admin-istration was searching for some distance between Washington and the Chilean strongman. If it seemed that Jesse Helms never met a right-wing dictator he didn't like, it also seemed that there were very few Foreign Service officers he did. Helms not only had extrem-ist views but had the power to advance them. He was a senior member of the Senate Foreign Relations Committee, which has to pass on all ambassador and assistant secretary appointments. Helms blocked or delayed the appointments of a substantial number of men, all unquestionably qualified, many even certified conservatives, but lacking in the ideological purity he demanded.

One target in the conservative sights was Morton Abramowitz, and the damage done directly affected U.S. policy in the Philippines. In 1981 Abramowitz was once again being considered for the Philippine post, as he had been by the Carter administration. When he had lost that early time (Vance didn't think he had enough experience), he went to Thailand, where he earned the department's Distinguished Service Award for his humanitarian handling of the Cambodian refugee crises and in 1981 the President's Award for Distinguished Federal Service. Now the generals at the Pentagon and the right wing went to work on Abramowitz. Abramowitz had been assigned to the Pentagon during the early Carter years when the Korean troop withdrawal was under discussion, and since he was there, he favored it—or so "reasoned" the conservatives against Abramowitz. The very conservative General Richard G. Stilwell, once the commander of troops in Korea and now deputy undersecretary of defense for policy under Reagan, spread the story that Abramowitz had favored the troop withdrawal. In fact, Abramowitz had opposed the troop withdrawal, but as a Foreign Service officer his job was to carry out the policy of the president (or resign).

More troubling than the distortion of Abramowitz's position, however, are the implications of the military's having a de facto veto power over a diplomatic assignment. It often does, at least in the Philippines and other countries where there is a significant U.S. military presence. So Armacost, who had been asked by President Reagan to go to Indonesia, was sent to the Philippines. Abramowitz was slated for Indonesia; the right wing in a dirty campaign defeated that appointment as well.* Though by the ideological rigidity of some in and around the Reagan administration, Abramowitz was

---

* An ideological, scurrilous campaign to block Abramowitz from going to Indonesia was conducted by Undersecretary of Defense Stilwell; the former CIA station chief in Bangkok, Daniel Arnold, who had left the agency to work on Bush's 1980 campaign; and Kent B. Crane, another right-winger, who it was widely believed worked for the CIA under State Department cover and had once been a national security adviser to Spiro Agnew. Crane, who soon was using his access to the Pentagon and the Reagan White House on behalf of the notorious Marcos henchman General Ver and Marcos's son-in-law Gregory Araneta, wanted

not a true believer, neither was he a bleeding-heart liberal. When he was at the Defense Department, he supported resumption of aid to the military junta in Argentina, over the objections of Patt Derian and the Human Rights Bureau. After losing the Philippines and Indonesia posts, Abramowitz was named the director of the Bureau of Intelligence and Research, where he had been in 1972 when Marcos declared martial law; Abramowitz's section, alone among the entire Washington policy-making corps, had recognized it as nothing but a power grab by Marcos.

Had Abramowitz been sent to Manila as ambassador in 1981, the situation might not have deteriorated to the extent that it did. He is "an unusual diplomat," William Shawcross notes in *The Quality of Mercy,* his book about the world's response to the Pol Pot-directed genocide in Kampuchea. A man who "spurns elegant diplomatic dress and formal diplomatic manners," Abramowitz, Shawcross writes, "is remarkably candid, he has extraordinary energy, is perpetually restless and rarely suffers foolishness, inefficiency or contrariness gladly." It's almost inconceivable that Abramowitz, undiplomatically blunt, would have suffered Imelda Marcos's charm and Ferdinand Marcos's lies.

While Abramowitz almost certainly would not have been as cozy with the Marcoses as Armacost, the ridicule and criticisms that have been heaped on Armacost are not justified, or so many of his aides insist. His was an unusually loyal staff. They found their ambassador intelligent and easy to work for, the breadth of his knowledge matched by his even temper. They may be correct that the criticisms of Armacost as a toady to Marcos are unfair. Armacost was close to the Marcoses because that's what his assignment required. That's what the Kirkpatrick doctrine was all about: The United States was

---

the Indonesian post. A "Point Paper on Morton Abramowitz" surfaced while Abramowitz was being considered for Indonesia. It accused him of having been the "architect for U.S. troop withdrawal from Korea" and charged that his political philosophy was "akin to McGovern, Muskie and Mondale." Abramowitz's wife, Sheppie, was dragged into the fight, condemned for having "worked on the staff of Muskie, McGovern and Carter." The memorandum was as vile as it was erroneous: Abramowitz hadn't favored the Korean troop withdrawal; Sheppie Abramowitz had worked only for Muskie, for about a year. The memorandum was anonymous, stamped "Confidential" to give it authenticity, provided to the Indonesian government, and leaked to columnist Jack Anderson. The campaign against Abramowitz was successful. The Indonesian government rejected him, without giving any reasons.

supposed to be friendly to rulers who were friendly to the United States. For Kirkpatrick it was a matter of policy to befriend Marcos. For Reagan it was a matter of personality. "We knew who Ronald Reagan was. We knew he liked Marcos," says a senior embassy officer during the Armacost years as ambassador. It wasn't necessary, therefore, for Washington to send specific instructions to the embassy, telling the ambassador and his staff to be nice to the Marcoses. Ronald Reagan didn't want to hear that his friend Ferdinand Marcos, because of his dictatorial rule, was the Communists' most effective recruiter. He didn't want to know that Marcos and his friends were looting the economy. Nancy Reagan didn't want to learn that her friend Imelda Marcos was an avaricious thief. Armacost performed his mission well, just as he did everything.

On the substantive side there was one and only one issue, just as there had been during the Carter administration: a bases agreement. The 1979 bases agreement provided for renewal every five years. The Reagan administration didn't want to go through another prolonged renegotiation, so, therefore, it took great pains not to irritate Marcos. The Reagan renegotiation was successful, beyond imagination. The negotiations were smooth, harmonious—and over within six weeks. The administration, so committed to reducing federal spending, gave Marcos a $900 million five-year package— nearly double the Carter package. During the negotiations there had been only one hitch. When it appeared to the Philippine negotiators that all that remained was for the document to be signed, their American counterparts said there was one other paragraph which needed to be added. It wasn't anything of substance, but the Filipinos were uneasy, as the Americans knew they would be. The agreement that had been reached had seven paragraphs, Marcos's lucky number. To add an eighth paragraph would have irritated Marcos. After a couple of days the Filipinos realized the Americans' joke. Everyone laughed. The agreement was signed.

A few weeks later Secretary of State Shultz arrived in Manila, and the Reagan administration's love affair with the Marcoses was once again on display for the Filipino people. The American secretary of state was photographed kissing Imelda Marcos on the lips. At the lavish Malacañang luncheon Shultz, an economist and businessman, toasted the "courageous moves" Marcos had made on the economy. "We're bound to see a very healthy Philippine economy." All that Marcos had done was devalue the peso. Whether or not that was courageous, he had done nothing about the anticapitalist monopolies. And the economy was seriously, almost terminally ill, thanks to Marcos's economic malpractice.

During the luncheon Imelda Marcos produced her usual three-hour-long Las Vegas-style show, with skimpily clad dancers among the entertainment. "I might say it's the first time I've ever seen a fashion show," Shultz said lightly in his toast. "I hope it isn't the last," he added, to laughter. He was being diplomatic. He privately told aides later that he had been offended by the garish performance. He was also offended by the manner in which Marcos treated him during their closed-door meeting. Marcos was at his desk elevated on a platform, so that Shultz had to look up to him—and the Philippine president could look down on the American secretary of state. Those were costly miscalculations by the Marcoses, although they would never know that. Shultz was a staunch conservative, completely loyal to Reagan, but he was also a simple, plain man, not given to social flamboyance. The Marcoses had violated his democratic sensibilities.

Shultz expressed his resentments only very privately, but they lingered, making it easier for Abramowitz, an enlightened Armacost, and others in State to convince the secretary that Marcos had to go. But that was nearly three years in the future. For now, in June 1983, as all the memorandums and cables prepared at the time of Shultz's trip declared, U.S.-Philippine relations were "excellent."

"Giddy" might more appropriately describe the state of the relationship. At the end of working hours one day in June, after the bases agreement had been signed, after Shultz had departed, Armacost and his staff gathered on the glassed-in porch off the ambassador's office, with the romantic and tranquilizing views across Manila Bay to the blazing sunsets. They sipped their drinks, puffed on cigars, leaned back with their feet on the coffee table. One diplomat remembered the feeling: "Well, shit, I wonder what we're going to be doing in the fall." Nothing, it seemed, could go wrong.

14 : ... and the Worst

The euphoria on which U.S.-Philippine relations were floating collapsed on August 21, 1983, splattered on the tarmac of the Manila International Airport where the body of Benigno Aquino, Jr., lay, a single shot in the back of his head.

The assassination of Aquino "beyond a doubt was the most momentous event in the Philippines since the end of the war," writes Robert Shaplen of the *New Yorker,* who has been covering the Philippines for nearly four decades. It mobilized Filipinos, hundreds of thousands taking to the streets to mourn his death and simultaneously to protest Marcos's rule, the depth of the opposition to Marcos a surprise to American policymakers. The assassination woke up the U.S. Congress, precipitating hearings, principally conducted by Stephen Solarz, chairman of the House subcommittee on Asia, who happened to have left Manila the day before Aquino was killed.

For all that, however, the assassination of Benigno Aquino did not immediately change the policy or change the mind of the American president or any of his top advisers about Ferdinand and Imelda Marcos. It may be that on the tarmac the seeds for a change in U.S. policy toward the Marcos government had been sown, but for at least another year the policy was one of faith in Marcos.

Aquino had been contemplating and calculating his return home for some time. He still very much wanted to be president of his country. And he still believed that Marcos could be persuaded to provide for a democratic transition. It wasn't so much that Aquino was naïve, though there may have been some ingenuousness in his perspective. It was more that he saw Marcos as a product of the Philippine political and social system and not that different from other Filipino politicians. It was the same system that had produced Aquino, who in many ways was like Marcos. There was tolerance for corruption and strongman rule, but there were limits. Aquino also knew that though violence had been almost endemic to Philippine politics, it was only the lower-level officials who were killed: not a Marcos; not an Aquino.

In the summer of 1983 Aquino began to receive information from his contacts in Manila that convinced him the time to return had arrived. What he was hearing was that Marcos was very sick. In early August Aquino read a short item in *The New York Times* that Marcos was going into a "three-week seclusion" to write two books. Aquino correctly translated the announcement to read that Marcos was going into the hospital for treatment. Aquino and many others believed that Marcos might die. If he did, Aquino wanted to be there, prepared to emerge from the chaos as the country's next leader, to challenge Imelda Marcos and Enrile.

What Aquino didn't know was that Marcos was about to undergo his first kidney operation. The operation, which took place on August 7 (again, his lucky number), was kept secret from Filipinos and Americans. Marcos suffered from lupus erythematosus, a chronic disorder of the immune system. Somewhat similar to arthritis, it causes joint pain and swelling but is most commonly characterized by a red rash on the face resembling wolf bites. It was long thought to be a rare and fatal disease; but by 1980 it was more common in the United States than muscular dystrophy or leukemia, and it could be treated with drugs, prolonging the patient's life for ten to thirty years. Lupus frequently attacks the kidneys, and did with Marcos.

Marcos kept the fact of his disease from American knowledge for a long time. When he made his state visit to Washington in 1982, among all the baggage was a kidney dialysis machine, though American officials were not aware of it. The CIA in Manila kept hearing that American doctors were treating Marcos; but the spies couldn't penetrate Malacañang to learn who they were, and without knowing that, they didn't know what Marcos was suffering from. Finally, a CIA officer succeeded in locating the immigration official at the airport who stamped the passports of two American doctors each time they arrived. With enough money, the agency persuaded the immigration officer to divulge that the doctors were from New York and their names.

Marcos denied that he had ever had a kidney operation. He

later told an American confidant that his Japanese doctors convinced him, in August 1983, that a transplant wasn't necessary; they had prescribed drugs which alleviated the condition, Marcos claimed. After Marcos fled, Filipinos discovered five kidney dialysis machines, emergency oxygen equipment, and a hospital bed in the palace.

Aquino knew that he was risking his life by returning. He had been warned several times. Imelda Marcos herself had been quite explicit. During a three-and-a-half-hour meeting in New York with Aquino in May 1983 (it said a great deal about the personal nature of Philippine politics and society, as well as about Aquino and Mrs. Marcos, that the two continued to have contact), she told him of specific assassination plots, supposedly by Communists, and added that some of Marcos's allies simply couldn't be controlled. She named those who might try to kill him. She urged Aquino to remain in the United States, offering him whatever financial assistance he wanted in order to go into business. He was intent on returning.

In the days before his return Aquino talked openly about the possibility of becoming a martyr, whether because he was an obsessive talker and that was the obvious topic or because it relieved the tension. "You have to be very ready with your hand camera," he told a Japanese television crew that would accompany him, "because this action can happen very fast. In a matter of three, four minutes, it could be all over and I may not be able to talk to you again." There were other journalists on the flight—Aquino thought their presence might offer some protection—including Sandra Burton of *Time,* Max Vanzi of UPI, and Jim Laurie of ABC. Also on board China Airlines Flight 811 with Aquino was Ken Kashiwahara, an ABC reporter whose wife was Aquino's sister. Lupita Kashiwahara, an energetic and acclaimed movie producer and television reporter in the days before martial law, had preceded her brother to Manila, to do some of the advance work, turning out the crowds for her brother's return after three years in exile.

Just before the plane began its descent, Aquino rose from his seat across the aisle from his brother-in-law and went to the bathroom. Under his cream-colored safari suit with the patch bearing his initials, BSA, he slipped on a bulletproof vest. "If they hit me in the head, I'm a goner," he had remarked earlier.

341

There was heavy military security at the airport when Aquino arrived, and a squad of uniformed Philippine soldiers escorted Aquino off the plane. As they neared the bottom of the metal steps, a single bullet penetrated Aquino's skull from behind the left ear, exiting through his chin. There was a fusillade of bullets, and a few feet from Aquino fell the bullet-riddled body of a man later identified as Rolando Galman. The government said Galman had been the assassin, that he was a subversive, with connections to the NPA and the Communist party.

The Filipinos' response to the brutal killing was immediate, overwhelming, and prolonged. "All day long and well into the sultry night, the lines have glided past the open coffin in the ample foyer of the house on Times Street," Clyde Haberman, of *The New York Times,* wrote from Manila about the scene at Aquino's house in the suburb of Quezon City, where the martyr's body lay in state. It was estimated that 100,000 people paid their respects within the first few days, filing by the coffin at the rate of one person every two seconds, twenty-four hours a day. The wealthy arrived in chauffeured cars; the poor, on the gawdy jeepneys, the fare six cents. On the day the body was taken from the house to a nearby Catholic church, hundreds of thousands of Filipinos formed a procession behind the hearse. They filled the width of streets, stretched out for miles under the scorching sun, the temperature pushing 100 degrees. It was a mix of religion and politics. "Blowin' in the Wind," the universal protest song of the sixties, mixed with the Philippine national anthem; white-frocked priests, using a loudspeaker on a pickup truck, chanted "Hail Marys." The outpouring of sympathy and solidarity was repeated a few days later, after a funeral mass celebrated by Cardinal Sin at Santo Domingo Church. The crowds lining the route from the church to the cemetery matched or surpassed, in number, those that had turned out for the pope's visit in 1981 and for the funeral of the country's most popular president, Ramón Magsaysay, in 1957. The procession extended for more than a mile. As the coffin passed by, people on balconies of tall buildings tossed the shredded pieces of phone book yellow pages. Yellow streamers were all along the route. A severe thunderstorm drenched marchers and onlookers (lightning killed one person and injured several in Rizal Park), but it didn't much dampen spirits. Filipinos were not just showing respect for Aquino; they were expressing their contempt for Marcos.

The American embassy and officials in Washington were stunned by the public demonstrations. They had not realized the depth of the opposition to Marcos. It was a repeat of what had happened in Iran, where the United States had had no appreciation of the strength of the opposition to the shah and therefore failed to develop a policy that fitted reality. The cost of being so close to the dictator—American officials knew Marcos well, as their counterparts had known the shah—while keeping their distance from opposition leaders, a distance maintained because the Marcoses were offended when American diplomats were seen with the opposition, was that embassy staff and intelligence officers had lost contact with the people of the country they were supposed to know.

There was another surprise reaction to the assassination. This one was from Washington. It was in the swiftness and tone of the official response. Aquino's murder, the State Department said, was "a cowardly and despicable act which the U.S. condemns in the strongest possible terms." Having said that, the department put some pressure on the Marcos government. "The U.S. Government trusts that the Government of the Philippines will swiftly and vigorously track down the perpetrators of this political assassination and bring them to justice and punish them to the fullest extent of the law." And lest there be any doubt of the department's feelings, the statement concluded, "We extend our condolences to Senator Aquino's wife and children in Massachusetts and to his family, friends and supporters in the Philippines." That was far more support than the Reagan administration had ever extended to Aquino, his family, and his supporters during his life.

The person responsible for that strong, if not extraordinary, statement, though it wasn't known publicly, was John F. Maisto, a career Foreign Service officer. From Aquino's death until Marcos was forced to flee two and a half years later, a period during which U.S. policy shifted, Maisto was pervasive and persuasive. He was rarely, if ever, heard or read about by the American public; a few journalists discovered him, and his knowledge, and while they found he could be relied upon not to lie to them, they also discovered he was very discreet, treating as confidential and secret that which was classified as such. Maisto didn't set the policy. He was "just" a lower-level bureaucrat, head of the Philippine desk. From that position he steadily provided the information and analysis that allowed those above him to reach the same conclusions he had; maybe it directed them to those conclusions. And at critical moments he quietly rescued the Reagan administration from the disastrous consequences of its own statements and actions. "For such a relatively low-level guy, he had a disproportionate influence on the policy," says Stanley Roth, staff director of the House Foreign Affairs Subcommittee on Asian and Pacific Affairs.

Of medium height, stocky, and with a slightly graying mustache on his round face, Maisto lacked the pin-striped background of many of his colleagues. Born in 1938 and reared in Braddock, Pennsylvania, the son of a blue-collar worker who rose from shipping clerk to a foreman for American Shipping and Cable, he didn't prepare in the Ivy League. For one year he attended the small, liberal arts, Presbyterian-affiliated Waynesburg College; bitten by "wanderlust," he transferred to the Foreign Service school at Georgetown. There he met, and eventually married, a Filipina, the daughter of a wealthy Negros sugar family. That gave Maisto a special love for the archipelago. He acquired something else as well over the years, something that was unique: experience in the Philippines, the experience that had historically been lacking among officers assigned to Philippine affairs. ("The Philippines seems to be one country in Asia where the U.S. Foreign Service never considered it necessary to have 'old hands,' 'language officers,' or other varieties of specialists," noted Donald R. Toussaint, number two in the Manila embassy under Murphy.) Maisto knew the premartial law Philippines, having vacationed there for extended periods with his wife. And he had served there after postings in Bolivia, Argentina, and Costa Rica. In 1978 he was assigned to the Philippines, where he remained for four years. When he returned to Washington, the department had the good sense to assign him to the Philippine desk, and by the time the crisis was in its most critical stages, Maisto outranked everyone in his knowledge of the country.

When news of Aquino's death reached Washington, Maisto didn't wait for instructions. He immediately called Aquino's widow, Corazon, in Boston, and expressed condolences; then he called leaders of the anti-Marcos opposition in the United States. And he called the American embassy in Manila to discuss the situation. A cautious desk officer would have waited for some input from the embassy, for a message with the ambassador's views of events. Maisto didn't wait for Armacost. Within four hours after the killing, which occurred at 1:30 A.M. Washington time, Maisto had prepared State's response. Then he swiftly massaged it through the bureaucracy (in time to get it approved for a journalist at *Time* who was waiting to get it in the magazine before its deadline).

Besides Maisto's effort, Washington issued other statements—self-serving ones. *The New York Times* reported on the front page that the Reagan administration was "prepared to dissociate itself" from Marcos if any of his top associates were found responsible for Aquino's murder. Bernard Gwertzman of *The Times* wrote: "The Administration is prepared to take whatever steps are needed to demonstrate its outrage if the Marcos Government is found responsible for the killing, a senior State Department official said." The statement was designed to appease public and congressional critics of the Reagan administration's policy of being cozy with Marcos. But the administration didn't demonstrate its outrage, even when it knew that the Marcos government was responsible. It was an empty threat, designed for domestic consumption.

Marcos responded to the intense pressure at home and abroad and ordered an investigation. The first commission he appointed was so blatantly in his pocket that its members resigned within a few weeks after being named. The second Marcos-appointed commission was chaired by Corazon J. Agrava. "As a group, its members are not at the top rung of their professions," the embassy commented about the Agrava commission, though they were "solid and independent citizens." Everyone expected a whitewash, but the evidence was so overwhelming that only a rinse was possible. The commission, which resoundingly rejected the government's contention that Aquino had been murdered by Galman (that means he, too, was a victim of the plot against Aquino), found sufficient evidence for twenty-five military men and one civilian to be placed on trial, including Marcos's closest confidant and the armed forces chief of staff, General Fabian C. Ver. All were acquitted, not surprisingly, since Marcos controlled the process. One of the judges later told a senior

Philippine diplomat that Marcos secretly paid him "enough so that [he] could live well."

Who killed Benigno S. Aquino, Jr.? Who exactly pulled the trigger is not as important as who plotted the assassination. It is unlikely, if not absolutely certain, that the principals will ever be tried—for the same reason that Marcos could never have allowed a full and impartial investigation: The highest-level officials in the Marcos government were involved. A wide range of U.S. officials, men and women at the State Department, at the CIA, at the Pentagon, are convinced of that.

The Marcos government first tried to intercept Aquino's plane and divert it to a local air base, where presumably Aquino could have been eliminated out of the public eye. Two Philippine Air Force F-5 fighter jets were sent on the mission, and Filipino airmen monitored the scrambling and searched for the China Airlines jet from radar consoles and scopes on the ground at two bases. American airmen at these bases, which are used jointly by the two countries, found the Filipino activity highly unusual but were not informed about what was happening; some were told bluntly that it was none of their business. (Six U.S. Air Force personnel later prepared sworn affidavits about what they had observed; these were rejected by the trial court as "irrelevant and immaterial.") The mission was unsuccessful because the China Airlines plane was never located.*

Quite obviously an operation of that magnitude was not possible without the knowledge of the most senior generals, all of whom had been appointed by and were loyal to Marcos. Nor could the murders on the ground at Manila International Airport have occurred without the extensive involvement of higher-ups. The airport was swarming with soldiers and security people. A special military unit went on the plane and escorted Aquino off.

---

* Phil Bronstein of the *San Francisco Examiner* broke the story about the scrambling of the jets to intercept Aquino's plane in July 1985. The State Department said that it was unaware of anything involving the scrambling or the use of the radar systems at the bases on the day Aquino was murdered. Few other papers followed up on the story until September, when the State Department released the affidavits of the six air force personnel.

But culpability doesn't stop at the barracks; it reaches into Malacañang. "I don't think there's a person in the embassy who doesn't think Ver was deeply involved," says an officer who was in the embassy at the time of the Aquino murder and for three years after. Ambassador Armacost concluded that Ver "was in it up to his armpits." An intelligence officer says, "There is no question in my mind, no question" that Ver was involved. This official was told by one of his Filipino sources that he, the Filipino, had been present in a meeting with Ver when the assassination of Aquino was discussed. It's a near certainty that Ver, who was chief of staff of the armed forces, knew about and gave the approval for the air force effort to intercept Aquino's plane. A minority view on Ver's involvement is sounded by another intelligence officer, who was not posted in the Philippines at the time of the assassination but who still had close contacts in the government. He says that Ver was not directly involved in the actual plotting but that he learned of the plot and did nothing to stop it.

If Ver was involved, it's hard to imagine that Marcos was not also. "He wouldn't have acted without checking with God," says an American intelligence official who knew both men well, "and Marcos was his God." Another CIA officer in the Philippines described the Ver-Marcos relationship this way: "The last person Marcos spoke with before he went to bed at night was Ver—and he was the first person Marcos said good morning to." Ver was totally and completely loyal to Marcos. So loyal, went the standard joke, that if the president told him to jump out the window, Ver would reply, "Yes, sir. What floor?" Once asked about this, Ver answered, "Yes, that's true."

As young boys the two had played together on the beaches of Sarrat. When Marcos was elected to Congress, he chose Ver, then a captain in the constabulary, to be his bodyguard and chauffeur. After martial law was declared, Ver, who had received a degree in police administration from the University of Louisville and had taken training courses with police departments in Honolulu and Los Angeles, was placed in charge of palace security. In 1981, a four-star general, Ver became chief of staff of the armed forces as well as head of the National Intelligence and Security Administration (a combination of the FBI and CIA). As expected, Ver had been financially rewarded as well. Seventeen days before Aquino was killed, Ver, whose salary in the military never exceeded $5,000 a year, purchased, through a chain of offshore and Hong Kong corporations, a hotel in Los Angeles for $5 million. In January 1982 a woman named Edna Guiyab Camcam purchased a waterfront house in an exclusive private community on Long Island for $495,000. Among other things, the woman was Ver's "long-time mistress," according to a State Department officer. Two months after Aquino was assassinated, Mrs. Camcam purchased three condominiums on New York's fashionable East Side, two at 80 Park Avenue, another on East Ninetieth Street.

Was Ver acting under direct orders from Marcos? Or was the general carrying out what he thought his commander in chief wanted? Was Marcos Henry II wanting to be rid of "this turbulent priest," with Aquino his St. Thomas à Becket? There is evidence, which Ver would have been aware of, that Marcos wanted Aquino killed. In all that has been written about the Aquino assassination, one secret has remained. In July, after Aquino had made several statements in the United States that he would return soon, Marcos asked some of his most trusted research assistants to compile what they could about political assassinations. He was most interested in knowing more about the killing of Archbishop Romero, the Salvadoran prelate who was an outspoken critic of human rights abuses and was assassinated with a single shot while saying mass in March 1980.

In addition, and also not publicly discussed, U.S. intelligence officials discovered that Marcos had sent agents to the United States "to shadow Aquino." One man with that mission was Colonel Rolando Abadilla, who had a notorious reputation as a torturer. In July 1983 Abadilla,* described by a U.S. diplomat as "a high-ranking hit man," was in the United States, ostensibly to watch his son participate in a soapbox derby. Some U.S. officials believe that he had instructions to assassinate Aquino if the opportunity arose.

Abadilla's mission and other evidence lead one diplomat, who was in a senior position in the embassy at the time of the assassination, to conclude, "It was Marcos. He wanted to get rid of him

---

* In January 1987, Colonel Abadilla was involved in the coup attempt against President Corazon Aquino's government.

[Aquino]. In effect, there was a standing order to shoot on sight. The order had gone out to take care of Aquino. It wasn't an order to kill at the airport." The operative words may well be the last three. Marcos wanted Aquino killed. But he didn't give the order to do so *at the airport.*

Marcos, of course, has always denied any involvement, and some American officials believe that the president himself wasn't directly a participant. They point out that he was too ill, that he was barely functioning on August 21, still recovering from his kidney transplant only two weeks earlier. But on August 18, three days before the assassination, Marcos met with Ambassador Armacost and Congressman Solarz, who knew nothing about the transplant. Solarz thought Marcos "looked awful." His eyes were teary; his face was puffy. He was obviously in pain. But both Armacost and Solarz thought Marcos's mind was as sharp and lucid as ever.

It has also been argued, in Marcos's defense, that he was too shrewd, too calculating, that while he might not hesitate to kill, he certainly would not have been so dumb as to have executed Aquino in broad daylight, with the press everywhere. Seeming to support the theory that Marcos did not order the killing at the airport is an incident that is said to have occurred at Malacañang when Imelda Marcos walked in on her husband after the news of Aquino's murder had reached him. Marcos reacted furiously, throwing something that struck his wife high on the cheek, just below the eye, raising a bruise. She went into a rage, the account goes, throwing and breaking hundreds of thousands of dollars' worth of antiques. She also remained out of sight for several days. Was Marcos angry that Aquino had been killed? Or was he reacting so furiously because the job had been botched?

While American diplomats and intelligence officers are uncertain, and disagree among themselves, about the nature of Marcos's involvement, most believe that the cumulative weight of the circumstantial evidence points to Imelda Marcos and her brother Kokoy Romualdez as principals in the conspiracy. (Kokoy was in Leyte on the day of the killing, all too conveniently, American diplomats say.) The two were motivated, some American officials concluded, by their belief that Marcos was dying and by Mrs. Marcos's desire to run the country if he did.

They knew that Aquino, and Aquino alone, had the popular support to succeed Marcos. Aquino had to be eliminated. Lending weight to the evidence against her was the involvement of General Luther Custodio. The Agrava commission described his role in the assassination as "indubitable." The head of AVESCOM, which had responsibility for airport security on the day of the killing, Custodio "presided over the whole clockwork-like proceeding" on August 21, the Agrava commission found. An American intelligence official said about Custodio and Imelda Marcos: "She owned him lock, stock and barrel."

Regardless of whether or not Marcos gave the order to kill Aquino, at the airport or before, regardless even of what Imelda Marcos and her gang may have done, what's more critical from the perspective of understanding U.S. policy and the workings of the Reagan administration is what the United States knew, when it knew it, and how it reacted to the Aquino assassination.

What the United States knew is that the Marcos government was involved in the killing of Aquino. And it knew this "immediately," says an intelligence officer. On the day after the murder, Marcos called Armacost and asked him to come to the palace. Armacost, in the midst of a working luncheon, asked if it couldn't wait. Marcos said no, so they talked by telephone. Marcos proceeded to spell out his government's theory on the murder: It had been the work of a lone gunman, he was involved with the Communists, and so on. It was a rambling discourse, lasting forty-five minutes. Armacost had initially been inclined to believe that the assassination had been the work of the Communists. He thought they would have the most to gain from the assassination (not that the Communists wanted to be rid of Aquino but that the ensuing turmoil would benefit them), and he didn't think Marcos would be so dumb. But after his conversation with Marcos, Armacost began to have serious misgivings. Marcos's explanation had been *too* detailed; it was obvious that he was protesting too loudly. Armacost cabled Washington with the substance of what Marcos had said. Then the ambassador added his conclusion: The whole thing "sounds mighty fishy."

350

Yet Armacost was uneasy with the strong statement Maisto had drafted, and the embassy adopted the Marcos line that the assassination was the work of the radical left, the Communists. "Our analysis here is that Marcos would have absolutely zero incentive to have this happen," *Newsweek* reported being told by a "well-placed U.S. source" in Manila. (That's journalese for someone high up in the embassy, possibly the ambassador or someone in the CIA.) During a press briefing an embassy officer, responding to reporters who were expressing skepticism about the government's version of the assassination, insisted that only the Communists would benefit from the assassination, the implication being that they were responsible. Another embassy officer who heard his colleague's remarks was appalled, but he said nothing.

It was still the U.S. policy to defend and protect Marcos. That was clear when Reagan announced on the day after the murder that he would go ahead with his planned trip to the Philippines. Much of the advance work had been taken care of by Michael Deaver, who had been working for Reagan since his days as governor of California and who had accompanied the Reagans to the Philippines for the opening of Imelda Marcos's Cultural Center in 1969. There wasn't much, if any, substance to Reagan's proposed trip to the Philippines. It was only for thirty-six hours. "It was all pictures, pictures, pictures," as one embassy official put it, like many of his colleagues frustrated and disgusted with Deaver and his demands. Reagan, as Deaver planned it, would be photographed at familiar World War II sites: Corregidor, Bataan, Leyte, the American cemetery.

Six weeks after the assassination Reagan canceled the visit. But the decision was not made on the basis of foreign policy considerations or because the Reagan administration had adopted a new policy toward Marcos. Indeed, Secretary of State Shultz wanted Reagan to proceed with the trip, as did the NSC and Defense Department. From outside the administration, Henry Kissinger advocated that the president go ahead with the visit. It was Reagan's *domestic* political counselors who called off the trip. The White House had been monitoring the American reaction to the Aquino assassination. In one memorandum for the White House it was reported that of sixteen recent newspaper editorials, fourteen expressed opposition to the trip, while only two favored it. Those two were the conservative *Washington Times* and the *San Diego Union.*

Contrary to the way it was widely reported and interpreted, the cancellation was not an expression of Reagan's disapproval of Marcos. Reagan went to some lengths to make sure Marcos would not be offended. First, the president canceled his entire itinerary, which included Indonesia and Thailand. If Reagan and the administration had wanted to send a message that the United States felt strongly about the Aquino assassination, the president would have gone ahead with his visits to the other countries. Then Reagan handwrote a letter to Marcos, which Deaver personally delivered (slipping in and out of the country without the knowledge of anyone at the embassy except for the ambassador and his top deputy). "Dear Ferdinand and Imelda," Reagan wrote, "I've always had confidence in your ability to handle things." He closed with the assurance that "Our friendship for you remains as warm and firm as does our feeling for the people of the Philippines."

The administration's unwavering support for Marcos was underscored a few days after Reagan had canceled his visit, when Vice President Bush, on October 6, said that the United States could "not cut away from a person who, imperfect though he may be on human rights, has worked with us." Bush, in an interview with the board of directors of AP Broadcasters, Inc., added, "The United States does not want to have another Khomeini." Besides, Bush didn't think Marcos was responsible for Aquino's assassination. "Marcos may be a lot of things," Bush said, "but I don't think he's a dumb guy."

Marcos had lost nothing with the White House, but he was beginning to lose his hold on the American embassy in Manila. Michael Armacost had been burned. The ambassador paid a condolence call on Aquino's widow, Cory. "I was deeply impressed with the power and dignity of Mrs. Aquino," Armacost quietly recalled several years later. Amid all the turmoil she seemed almost serene. The ambassador also called on Aquino's mother. By that time Imelda Marcos was livid, according to reports coming back to the embassy. Armacost went to the funeral mass, a courageous decision, his aides thought, in view of Washington's still-favorable attitude toward the Marcoses. Moreover, the Philippine foreign minister's office had called all the embassies in Manila to say that it would be considered an affront to the Marcos government if their countries sent representatives to the mass. Armacost sat prominently in the front row.

On the evening of the funeral Imelda Marcos threw a bash at Malacañang. It was in honor of Senator Mark Hatfield, the Oregon Republican who was visiting the Philippines. She invited Armacost. "I can't believe it," he said to an aide as they stood on the embassy roof watching the funeral procession move along Roxas Boulevard. The ambassador's response was measured. He simply could not understand how any person could be so cold as to have a party on that night. He was equally incredulous that she thought he would attend. He did not, though he did send the embassy political officer, Scott Hallford, who was not at all comfortable with the assignment. Senator Hatfield attended, then returned to Washington with a report for President Reagan that "fortified" the president's belief in Marcos's ability to govern the Philippines. Throughout the evening Imelda Marcos took guests to the niche in Malacañang where the statue of the Santo Niño rested. There she showed them Aquino's rosary, the one he had presented to her when he had been released from prison; it hung from the statue's wrist. A few days later, when Armacost was in the palace, she took him to the statue. "Santo Niño, Santo Niño," she addressed the statue. "I said to take care of him, but not in this way." Then she laughed; in a macabre way, the ambassador thought.

Though the shift in Armacost's attitude toward the Marcoses was significant, it emerged gradually and cautiously, in keeping with the nature of diplomats and with a policy in Washington that was still very much pro-Marcos. It was not until November 17, 1983, three months after the assassination, that Armacost made any mention of it publicly. In an address to the Makati Rotary Club, the ambassador recognized Aquino for his having articulated beliefs "in a free press, in free elections, in due process of law." Those were probably the kindest remarks any high-level American official had ever expressed publicly about Aquino, and they were doubly cutting since as everyone in Armacost's audience knew, there was no free press, no free elections, no due process in Marcos's Philippines.

After Aquino's assassination American diplomats in the embassy began to reach out to the political opposition, contacts that had been neglected for much too long. Armacost himself began to meet more frequently with Cardinal Sin. Prior to the assassination Armacost's relations with Sin had been quite formal. The few meetings the American ambassador had with the archbishop had been arranged by one of Armacost's aides. Now the ambassador would call the cardinal for a meeting, and he would go to the cardinal's residence.

Armacost had come a long way. Aides and friends talked about his "conversion." Armacost himself says, with obvious pain long afterward, "It was traumatic." To him the assassination was "an illustration of a government out of control." It was not just that the government believed it could get away with the "most brazen activity." What compounded Armacost's reaction was that the whole operation had been so crudely executed, a reflection that "they didn't even care about the consequences."

Eight months after the assassination Armacost returned to Washington. Imelda Marcos, furious that he was no longer her lapdog, boasted at the time and long after that she had been responsible for his transfer. Many journalists wrote that he had been recalled because he had lost his effectiveness, that he had alienated himself and the U.S. embassy from the opposition prior to Aquino's assassination, and now he was offending the Marcoses. While the premises are certainly accurate, the conclusion may not follow. Shultz brought Armacost back to Washington as the undersecretary for political affairs, replacing Lawrence Eagleburger, who was retiring. It was the number three job in the department and generally considered the highest position in the department for a career Foreign Service officer.

Armacost was in a position to begin shifting the policy away from Marcos and toward democracy, but it was not sudden or easy.

15 : In Search of a Policy

As traumatic as the Aquino assassination was for Michael Armacost, as great as its impact was in the Philippines, it did not, contrary to the conventional wisdom, precipitate a fundamental change in the Reagan administration's pro-Marcos stance. Ideology was to guide the policy for at least another year. And when the shift in policy began, when Washington began to try to move Marcos toward reforms of the country's institutions, it was not because the administration had adopted a foreign policy doctrine that emphasized human rights and democracy. Rather, the impetus was the reality that Ferdinand E. Marcos was no longer serving America's best interests. "The question is not whether he's corrupt or not," says a senior State Department official who was involved in making the policy during both the Carter and Reagan administrations. "The question is whether he had political control of the country. They [the Reagan administration] didn't ease him out because he was corrupt. They eased him out because he lost control of the country."

For more than a decade and through four administrations (Nixon, Ford, Carter, and Reagan), Marcos had enjoyed Washington's succor and countenance because he had a tight grip on the archipelago, a hold that sustained America's economic and military interests. Then Marcos began to slip. And it wasn't just that he was losing control to possible chaos, to an unknown future. That would have been troubling enough. It was far more ominous. Marcos was losing the country to the Communists.

That potential catastrophe began to register in Washington when a Secret cable arrived from the embassy in Manila in June 1984. The subject was "Communist Movements in the Philippines: Background, Present Status, and Outlook." It was seventy-six pages long,

355

a virtual treatise on the Communist party of the Philippines, its roots and its rise. The study was undertaken, and the cable written, by James Nach, a member of the embassy's political section.

A graduate of St. John's College in Annapolis, Maryland (the school that emphasizes reading the "great books" and the broadest possible liberal arts education), Nach knew something about Communist insurgencies. One of his first Foreign Service postings, after he had earned a master's degree in international relations from Columbia, had been in Vietnam, from 1970 to 1974. His first exposure to the insurgency in the Philippines had come when he visited the country as the Philippine desk officer in Washington, working for Holbrooke. Holbrooke encouraged aides to get out of Washington, to travel as widely as possible. And when Nach went to the Philippines, he ventured out of Manila. He went to Mindanao, where the insurgency was strongest. There he met a landowner who told how the New People's Army had taken over his property, how they were uniformed and organized. It was evidence to Nach that this was no longer a ragtag group.

When Nach arrived in the Philippines for full-time duty in August 1982, he found that there wasn't much concern in the embassy about the NPA. The general sense was that the Communist activities were isolated. It was argued that the Filipino people would never accept communism, not in this Catholic country. It wasn't that there had been an active conspiracy within the embassy to suppress reports about the insurgency. It was more that Ambassador Armacost and his staff had been too busy being nice to the Marcoses, working toward a smooth bases negotiation, preparing for the state visit.

For Nach, studying the insurgency became an avocation; he devoted nights and weekends to understanding it and drafting his report. He concluded: "There is little optimism that the Marcos Government is capable of turning the situation around. Without new directions from the top, the prospects are for continued deterioration with the eventual outcome—ultimate defeat and a communist takeover of the Philippines—a very possible scenario."

When the cable arrived in Washington, some people in the State Department thought Nach was being a bit of an alarmist. They noted that his wife was Vietnamese, and they believed that Nach still seemed embittered by the Communist takeover in Vietnam. But regardless of those reservations, they were pleased with the cable. At least it began to get some high-level attention focused on the Philippines.

Official Washington really woke up to what Marcos had wrought in the Philippines when Admiral William J. Crowe weighed in. He was commander in chief of all U.S. forces in the Pacific and on track to become the chairman of the Joint Chiefs of Staff. A few months after Nach's cable Crowe was in the Philippines. He talked with all the same people Nach had, plus his own military contacts. The admiral reached the same conclusion the diplomat had: The NPA was a serious threat. Then Crowe flashed another distress signal: The Philippine military was corrupt and demoralized, incapable of fighting a counterinsurgency war. It was the apocalypse now.

The Philippines was beginning to look more and more like Central America. Substitute Marcos for Nicaragua's Somoza; the NPA for the FSLN (Sandinista National Liberation Front) or the FMLN (Farabundo Martí National Liberation Front) in El Salvador. Like the Salvadoran Army, and Somoza's before that, the Philippine Army was a disgrace, officers getting rich and sloppy, while young troops, poorly trained, equipped and motivated, were fighting and dying. The assassination of Aquino seemed a replay of the murder of Pedro Joaquín Chamorro, publisher of *La Prensa,* killed by Somoza's guardsmen in 1978. Chamorro's murder had accelerated the polarization of the country, as Aquino's was rendering the Philippines. The Philippine church was splitting, with Cardinal Sin trying to hold it together; younger priests and nuns were siding with the revolution in disquieting numbers. Liberation theology was sweeping the Philippines as it was Latin America. A committed middle-aged woman wrote a friend about the activities of the Christian base communities and priests in Mindanao: "What they're trying to do next is to give people a powerful weapon in the Gospel of Liberation, the same kind of dynamite that created Sandinista Nicaragua and upset the Conservatives in the Vatican no end. What I got very infatuated with is that this Gospel does not stop at love and peace and beautiful worship but goes inexorably on to community organizing along very clear Marxist lines of analysis." The writer was like so many of the Philippine middle class, who, fed up with Marcos, were beginning to express sympathy for the NPA. "Sometimes for us moderates, we say, 'What is the viable alternative?' " explained a fifty-five-year-old woman, a lay worker in the Catholic Church. "I mean, I don't go for their [NPA's] ideology. But what is our alternative? Who else is organized?"

When the Reagan administration needed a justification for sending military aid and advisers to El Salvador in 1981, it screamed that the insurgency there was a "textbook case of indirect armed aggression by Communist powers through Cuba." But the administration, however willing it was to distort and dissemble to make a foreign policy fit into its existing ideological baggage, couldn't resort to that rhetoric in the Philippines. It wasn't because Cuba was too far away. It was because the Philippine turmoil was a textbook case of a homegrown indigenous revolution. The leaders, in their thirties, were from middle- and upper-middle-class backgrounds. They had studied Marx and Lenin and were devotees of Mao; some of the leaders had secretly been in China in 1967 and 1968. They also borrowed from the Vietnamese insurgency, the Sandinista triumph in Nicaragua, and the mistakes of the Salvadoran guerrillas. This was to be a long, peasant-based war, like those waged by Mao and the Vietnamese. There were to be coalitions with non-Communist sectors, as the Sandinistas had done. And there was to be no premature "final offensive," which the Salvadoran guerrillas had launched in January 1981 only to discover that they had not politically prepared the populace to rise up with them.

Though the Philippine revolutionaries might borrow from anyone and everyone, it was a Filipino revolution. Nach realized that. "Despite the CPP's [Communist Party of the Philippines] 'Maoist' antecedents, the party has no known current ties with China or any other foreign communist state," he wrote. Though China had in the early days provided some minimal support, it had dried up after China and the Philippines had established diplomatic relations in 1975. And of course, the Soviets weren't welcome, the CPP having split from the pro-Moscow Communist party, which gave birth to it and the NPA. "Improper links with the Soviets cannot be demonstrated," Nach wrote. As a result, the NPA was forced to rely on "ambushes, raids, and the black market" for its rifles and bullets; it had "no steady and reliable source" from any outside powers, Nach reported.

If outsiders weren't to blame, who was? The answer was simple. Ferdinand E. Marcos.

In 1972, when he declared martial law, the number of well-armed NPA fighters was somewhere between 350 (the NPA's figure) and 1,030 (the government's number). By 1984 the Philippine government was acknowledging, at least privately, that there were at least 8,000 well-armed guerrillas. This figure was probably on the low side (to have admitted there were more would have reflected poorly on the martial law years), with the NPA putting its armed strength at 12,000 and U.S. officials using numbers of 15,000 to 20,000 (probably an exaggeration to gain congressional support for increasing military aid to the Philippines). More disturbing than the number of men (and women) in arms was the number of NPA supporters, from a few thousand in 1972 to at least 100,000, if not half a million, after a decade of martial law.

Whatever the exact figures, the Communist insurgency had grown, and alarmingly so. By 1984 it was the only government in many parts of the country. There was no official government. "The Filipino people expect the government to provide schools, roads, and personal security. Marcos has failed miserably on all three counts," the American ambassador Stephen Bosworth, who had replaced Armacost, said in 1984. The NPA built schools, helped peasant farmers, dispensed justice. A Secret study by the State Department's Bureau of Intelligence and Research in 1980 noted that in many areas of the Philippines "justice cannot be obtained from" the military. "The NPA, in contrast, usually honors its promises to provide for the poor, who have little influence with" the military.

Everything Marcos touched, including the military, was tarnished. "Corruption permeates the Armed Forces of the Philippines," reported the same INR study. While there had always been some corruption, "the current state of affairs in the military is regarded even by many Filipinos as without precedent." Army officers demanded positions on boards of directors or as "advisers" to companies doing business with the government, "threatening to exclude the firm from government contracts if their demands are not met."

It was a fully politicized army. One week after he had declared martial law, Marcos raised the salaries of officers by 150 percent.

Promotions were based not on ability or merit but on loyalty to Marcos. By 1984 more than half the Philippine generals were past retirement age but were kept on by Marcos in exchange for their personal fealty. (By contrast, in neighboring Thailand, which was struggling with democracy, there was only one general kept on active duty past retirement.) Marcos increased the size of the Philippine military 400 percent, from 50,000 in 1972 to more than 150,000 regulars and an additional 90,000 reservists by 1984. The military budget went from $82 million in 1972 to $1 billion in 1980; the percentage of the GNP that went to the military more than doubled during the decade after martial law. The army wasn't needed to defend against foreign enemies but against domestic ones. But it couldn't fight. It was an army that was proficient at brutally repressing civilians, but in spite of its staggering increase in size, it was mauled by the NPA and MNLF. "The preoccupation with personal gain also lessens military efficiency, distracts officers from normal military tasks, contributes to breakdown in discipline, and diverts resources needed for legitimate military functions," the State Department noted.

In spite of it all—the corruption that was destroying the economy, the repression that was contributing to the strength of the Communists, the evisceration of the army's ability to fight—and even the knowledge that Marcos was the cause of the destruction, one year after Aquino's assassination Reagan administration policy was still to stick with Marcos.

How President Reagan perceived the problem in the Philippines became clear in the second debate of the 1984 presidential race between him and former Vice President Walter Mondale. A question was framed in terms of the shah and Somoza. Since Reagan had criticized Carter's handling of those situations, what did he propose to do about Pinochet and Marcos? "What should you do and what can you do to prevent the Philippines from becoming another Nicaragua?" asked Morton Kondracke of the *New Republic*.

Reagan responded: "I know there are things there in the Philippines that do not look good to us from the standpoint right now of democratic rights, but what is the alternative?" The conservative president supplied his own answer: "It is a large Communist movement."*

The statement reflected the president's simplified view of the world. It was good guys and bad guys. Us and the Communists. In fact, there was a bit of truth buried in what he had said, albeit certainly not one he had intended to reflect. There weren't as many potential democratic leaders as there could have and would have been if Marcos had not crippled democracy. That was another price of the policy of backing Marcos for so many years. Most of the leaders of the democratic opposition were old, their first political battles having been fought twenty and thirty years earlier. Martial law isn't an environment for nurturing a generation of political leaders. Better for a young man or woman to pursue a career in law, business, sports—anything but politics. There are no opportunities in a dictatorship. Nevertheless, there were some men and women in the Philippines who were dedicated, competent, and democratic. Reagan and his administration may not have considered them qualified to run the Philippines, just as the Carter administration had not been impressed with the Philippine opposition leaders. That reflects the arrogance and ignorance—these traits are bipartisan—which lead so many officials in Washington to believe that they know who is fit to govern another country.

Reagan had dismissed out of hand the democratic Filipino opposition leaders who were searching for a non-Communist alter-

---

* For Mondale, it was an opportunity to drive home the corrupt, repressive nature of the Marcos government, how cozy the Reagan administration had been with it, and how the Reagan administration's policies had contributed to the large Communist movement. Mondale responded that he had raised human rights concerns when he went to the Philippines, that he had called for Aquino's release and that the Carter administration had also secured a new bases agreement. It was a rather lame answer, as Mondale himself acknowledged years later. He had intended to answer more forcefully and did not even realize at the time or long thereafter exactly what he had said. When I asked him about the debate and his answer during an interview for this book, in June 1986, he began by explaining how during the debate he had referred to Bush's ridiculous toast praising democracy. I was surprised because I did not recall that, and I respectfully suggested that I didn't think he had and that I didn't think his response had been very critical of Reagan's policy. He disagreed, and I began to have doubts. Fortunately a call came into his office, and while Mondale talked on the phone, I pulled out *The New York Times'* text of the debate, which I had brought with me. I read his answer again. When he was off the phone, I showed it to him. He read it, then said, "It did not come off as strong as I would have liked, as I wanted."

native to Marcos. It was a blow to the professionals in the State Department like Maisto and others who were trying to fashion policy that looked beyond Marcos and who knew that not all the opposition to Marcos was Communist. The embassy in Manila knew that Reagan's statement would incense the democratic opposition in the Philippines, as it did. At the staff meeting the morning after the debate, Allan Croghan, the press officer, suggested going to Washington for a "clarification"—that is, for a statement which would undo the damage done by Reagan's comment.

Forget it, the deputy chief of mission said. Not only was he himself quite conservative, but there was never going to be a clarification of something said during a presidential campaign. Remember the Ford-Carter debate in 1976, when Ford had declared that "there is no Soviet domination of Eastern Europe," then gone on specifically to mention Poland, Romania, and Yugoslavia as countries that were *not* under Soviet domination. It was a colossal blunder, one that haunted Ford for the remainder of the campaign. His advisers had scrambled to blunt the damage, but there had been no official statement from the State Department.

In the aftermath of Reagan's blunder John Maisto drafted a clarification, then ushered it through the State Department hierarchy. "I don't think that the President was narrowing the situation that far," a State Department spokesman said the morning after the debate. "I think there is certainly recognition on everybody's part that there are other forces working for democratic change in the Philippines." It was a victory for the State Department, and there would be other times that Maisto and his colleagues would have to steer the president and the White House gently away from their ideologically set course of staying with Marcos.

By November 1984 the State Department had formulated a new policy, detailed in a National Security Study Directive (NSSD), which had been drafted by Maisto. In January Reagan signed it, with only a few minor changes. This new National Security Decision Directive (which it became after it had the president's signature) was the first official high-level articulation of American policy in the Philippines in twelve years, since just after martial law had been imposed. It was the ultimate paradox, perhaps the most subtle indictment of American policy: The Communists were forcing Washington to push for change in the Philippines, democratic change.

The new policy was not, however, anti-Marcos. "The U.S. does not want to remove Marcos from power or destabilize" his government, the NSSD said. Moreover, while Marcos was seen as "part of the problem, he is also necessarily part of the solution." In other words, the Reagan administration retained its faith in Marcos. All it wanted was for Marcos to "set the stage for peaceful and eventual transition to a successor government whenever that takes place." It all could be on his terms and his timetable. He could select someone from his party, Enrile, his loyal minister of defense, for example. About the only persons excluded, not in writing, but in the minds of many State Department officers, were Imelda Marcos, Eduardo Cojuangco, and Fabian Ver, because of their suspected involvement in the Aquino assassination and other nefarious activities.

At the core of the new policy was reform: economic; political; military. The United States wanted Marcos to end crony capitalism, to disband the monopolies. Political reform meant opening up the system—free press, honest elections. The military had to be purged of its corrupt officers, replaced with men who could fight and defeat the Communists. Above all, Washington began leaning hard on Marcos not to reinstate General Ver as the armed forces chief of staff. Following the Agrava commission findings of Ver's complicity in the Aquino assassination, Marcos had removed Ver; but he had always said it was only temporary, that he would be reinstated, and Marcos had refused to name a permanent replacement, appointing General Ramos only acting chief of staff.

The Reagan administration acted swiftly to implement its new policy, but events were to show it never acted decisively. The president's signature was barely dry on the NSDD when U.S. officials began to descend on Manila, bearing a very different message from what Marcos had heard before from the administration. In January 1985 alone, it was Paul Wolfowitz, assistant secretary of state for East Asia; Richard Childress, the Asian expert on the National Security Council; and Richard Armitage, assistant secretary of defense for international security affairs. It's unlikely that Marcos had been set upon by so many high-level officials from Washington in such a short time since the Manila Summit twenty years earlier. Their message was the same: Reform.

363

Then, in early February, Ambassador Bosworth was called back to Washington for consultations. When an ambassador's presence is needed in Washington, it generally indicates a hitch in the relationship, one that can't be handled with telephone conversations and cables. Bosworth's schedule in Washington was extraordinarily full, the number of meetings and the persons with whom he met reflecting the growing concern within the State Department about the situation in the Philippines. On just one day he had breakfast with Don Oberdorfer of the *Washington Post,* immediately followed by a thirty-minute meeting with columnist Joseph Kraft, then a lunch at the White House, which is far from normal for an ambassador; the guest list added to the significance: National Security Adviser Robert McFarlane; CIA Director Casey; Chairman of the Joint Chiefs of Staff General John Vessey, Jr.; Undersecretary Armacost; Assistant Secretary Wolfowitz. Lunch finished, Bosworth rushed to Capitol Hill for individual thirty-minute meetings with four members of the House Foreign Affairs Committee, including Stephen Solarz, chairman of the Asian subcommittee.

The department desperately wanted to keep Congress from carping at the policy, so Bosworth's next day was consumed by meetings with senators, seven altogether, an exceptional number, and all the sessions were individual. On the Democratic side, he talked with Paul Simon, a newly elected liberal from Illinois, and Christopher Dodd, a frequent critic of the Reagan administration foreign policy; the principal Republicans were Richard Lugar, chairman of the Senate Foreign Relations Committee, and Frank Murkowski, chairman of the East Asian subcommittee. Attentive to the press, and the harm or help it could be, the department arranged for Bosworth to meet with Robert Manning of the *Far Eastern Economic Review* and lunch with Stephen Rosenfeld, editorial writer and columnist at the *Washington Post.*

But Bosworth's most important meeting was also his shortest—with President Reagan. When an ambassador comes to Washington, he doesn't always meet with the secretary of state; perhaps he meets only with the head of his regional bureau. Only when the matter is very serious does a returning ambassador see the president. To make sure Marcos didn't miss the message, photographers were invited into the White House to capture Reagan conferring with Bosworth.

Back in Manila, Marcos asked Bosworth if it was usual for an ambassador to meet with the president. Bosworth knew how much anxiety lay behind Marcos's question. "No," he said flatly. No explanation followed. Let Marcos believe he was losing support in Washington.

The U.S. policy was now oriented toward putting some pressure on the Marcoses and moving Washington just a little further away from them. Stephen W. Bosworth was the right man at the right time in the right place. For all the wisdom and deliberation behind the decision to send him to Manila, chance had played its role, from Bosworth's joining the Foreign Service to his still being around when he was needed. The son of a Michigan schoolteacher, Bosworth had attended Dartmouth on a General Motors scholarship. Though he majored in international relations, he chose it primarily because it was the least restrictive of majors, offering the widest range of courses. Upon graduation he had wanted to go to law school—to put off making a decision about what he was going to do with his life—but couldn't afford to, so he took the Foreign Service exam. By 1984 he was ready to retire, not because of his age—he was only forty-five—but because he had already been an ambassador (Tunisia), the principal deputy in the Latin American bureau, and the chairman of the secretary's Policy Planning Council. There didn't seem to be any challenges left; besides, he was recently divorced and about to remarry and felt he needed to earn more money. He was exploring several opportunities, including an executive position with an international energy agency in Paris, when Shultz approached him about the Philippines. "After some brief thought, I decided I'd kick myself if I didn't accept," Bosworth says. He thought it would be the most challenging assignment of his career. He could not have known how prescient he was.

Bosworth arrived in Manila skeptical about the Marcoses. It wasn't that he was intent on ousting the Philippine president. Rather, he had to be convinced that the man was best for the Philippines and for the United States. He never was convinced. Bosworth didn't succumb to Imelda Marcos's fawning lures, as had so many diplomats for two decades. Maybe it was because he didn't fit into the social circle. He wasn't dashing or flamboyant; his thinning white hair seemed to magnify his age but reinforced his somewhat laconic demeanor. "He doesn't sing, and he doesn't dance much—that's a severe handicap at Malacañang," said a Bosworth aide, explaining why the ambassador never became part of the Marcos clique. The image of Bosworth that lingers with aides is from a ceremony at Leyte commemorating MacArthur's return. Bosworth was at the head table, along with the Japanese ambassador. At one point Mrs. Marcos passed the microphone to Bosworth, expecting him to sing. With a polite, forced smile he turned away. She persisted; he kept resisting. Finally, she nuzzled closer, sticking the microphone in his face. "One hears a few groaning noises that are a bit like music— as Bosworth turns redder and redder," remembered an embassy officer.

Directly proportional to how much Bosworth was disliked in Malacañang were the trust and respect he earned from the opposition and Cardinal Sin, far greater than had any of his predecessors. Bosworth met regularly with Sin, who warmed to him. The cardinal had addressed Armacost as "Ambassador" or "Michael" but never as "Mike." With Bosworth, it was "Steve." But though they certainly liked him, many Filipinos were puzzled by Bosworth, finding him inscrutable. Jaime Ongpin, the businessman who was a leader of the anti-Marcos opposition and was highly regarded by the Americans, invited Bosworth for a weekend at his beach home. For two days the men talked about the political crisis. At the end of the weekend Ongpin realized that in spite of all that Bosworth had said, he had learned almost nothing about the ambassador or his policies. Bosworth was a diplomat's diplomat: cautious; careful; always keeping his options open, protecting his flanks.

Bosworth was to be reproached by American conservatives who thought he had led the charge against Marcos. But he was no liberal. A few years earlier, when he was a deputy assistant secretary in the Latin American bureau, Bosworth had defended the military government in Guatemala, testifying before Congress that the human rights situation there was improving. In fact, it was a time when the Guatemalan Army was carrying out wholesale massacres of Indians the government accused of supporting the revolution in that country. Bosworth's testimony distorted the reality, but it supported the Reagan administration's policy, which was more support for the military government in Guatemala. Secretary of State Shultz knew Bosworth could be trusted to implement the policy in the Philippines.

The administration's reform policy wouldn't work, however. It couldn't work. It was like asking Samson to cut his own hair. The economic system, the political control, the military corruption were the very pillars that sustained Marcos. Weaken them, and he'd fall. But in Washington the top policymakers believed in the reform policy. They believed it as their predecessors a generation earlier had believed that Diem would reform, that he would do what Americans told him to do. They believed it because they had to. Besides, to admit that Marcos was what he was—corrupt, intent on keeping power, incapable of reform—was to admit that for more than a decade the policy had been wrong.

Moreover, the reform policy wouldn't succeed because the Reagan administration lacked the will to implement it. Criticism of Marcos would be tempered by unwarranted praise. The reform policy became irrelevant, lost any legitimacy, because Marcos knew he would continue to receive aid, much as in El Salvador the Reagan administration made speeches about human rights, then adulterated their impact by continuing aid unabated.

After their separate trips to the Philippines in January, Paul Wolfowitz and Richard Armitage, in congressional appearances, were explicit about the need for economic, political, and military reforms. "The Philippines cannot afford a business as usual approach to the insurgency or the urgent need to deal with its root problems," Wolfowitz told the House subcommittee on Asia, with Armitage seated next to him. In a speech to the National Defense University in Honolulu, Wolfowitz declared that "military abuse against civilians" was "one of the most commonly-cited factors in explaining the alarming growth of the communist insurgency throughout the islands."

These were strong statements, at least relatively. They were moderate when compared with the damage that Marcos was inflicting on the country. But they were the first time American officials had expressed even that much criticism of Marcos publicly. Wolfowitz put the administration's position on the need for reforms in a guest editorial in the *Wall Street Journal*. Even Reagan himself was enlisted in the effort to get a message to Marcos. Persuaded by his foreign policy advisers, principally Shultz (who was listening to Armacost, Wolfowitz, Abramowitz, and Maisto), the president used an interview with *The New York Times* in February to draw back from his remark made during the presidential campaign debate four months earlier that the only alternative to Marcos was the Communists. "We realize there is an opposition party that is also pledged to democracy," Reagan said.

The United States also encouraged a group of Philippine military officers who formed, in March 1985, what they called the Reform the Armed Forces Now Movement, known by the catchy acronym RAM and as We Belong. The nucleus was the graduates from the 1970 and 1971 classes at the Philippine Military Academy. American officials, in Manila and Washington, insisted that the movement was legitimate and important, in spite of widespread cynicism about the possibility of reform within the Marcos military. RAM leaders were brought to the United States to meet with members of Congress and other opinion makers, as proof of the possibility of reform in the Philippines. RAM was also secretly funded by Washington, the money channeled through other Philippine organizations. RAM was the hope for Washington (and ultimately it played a role in toppling Marcos, though having tasted power, the officers weren't so willing to return to the barracks).

For all that the administration seemed to be doing to pressure Marcos, it pulled its punches, didn't press its advantage. The moderately negative comments about the Marcos government were repeatedly balanced, and usually overbalanced, with positive ones. Thus, Wolfowitz told Congress that there had been "important progress toward the revitalization of political institutions," and that there was "broad press freedom." The former was a reference to the legislative elections which had been held in May 1984. While the opposition did better than expected, thanks in part to the vigorous surveillance of a citizens' organization, known by the acronym NAMFREL, Marcos had still resorted to excessive fraud and manipulation. More important, whatever the 1984 election demonstrated, it was not that Marcos was moving toward a democratic transition of power, as 1986 was to make clear. The reality, which

Wolfowitz and others refused to acknowledge, was that the political institutions had only the life that Marcos allowed them. It was the same with the press.

After Aquino's assassination there were more opposition newspapers, but it was hardly "broad press freedom." There was probably no more press freedom in Marcos's Philippines than there was in the Sandinistas' Nicaragua, which the administration condemned as a totalitarian, Marxist-Leninist, Communist regime. During 1984 eight Philippine journalists were killed in the Philippines; six more were murdered in the first half of 1985. "Broad" press freedom? Marcos, his friends, and his family controlled all the country's television stations (daughter Imee ran three), all but a very small fraction of the radio stations, and, by circulation, 80 percent of the newspapers. For nearly two years, Marcos kept equipment the Catholic Church had received to operate a television station sitting on the docks, and he wouldn't issue a broadcast license.

In general, the human rights abuses were escalating; the more control Marcos seemed to be losing, the more repressive he had to become to hold on. Torture and "salvagings" (as Filipinos called summary executions, in which a victim was often found, with hands tied behind the back, a bullet in the head, dumped on the street) were on the increase. Three weeks before Christmas 1984 eight masked men armed with automatic rifles seized a group gathered in front of a church in Agdao, a Davao slum, which had been the site of numerous antigovernment demonstrations (and which the residents had named Nicaragdao). The soldiers separated the group into men and women and forced all to lie facedown in the dirt. The soldiers opened fire, killing four, ages fourteen to twenty-one; the others were wounded. On December 10, 1984, Elegio Ponteras, a twenty-eight-year-old farmer and father of five from Zamboango del Sur, on the western finger of Mindanao, was dragged from his house by a group of soldiers from an airborne unit and the civil defense force. A civilian with them, wearing a red bandanna and a machete at his side, said that Ponteras was a member of the NPA. After searching his house and finding no weapons, the soldiers looted the premises of "our chickens, money, and clothing," Mr. Ponteras stated. He was taken to a military base, tied to a post, then beaten with rifle butts until he was unconscious. Soldiers slashed the bottom

369

of his feet and his leg above the knee, he said, pulling up his green work trousers to show the scars. With a bayonet, "they cut my hair and shirt into pieces," which they forced him to eat until he vomited.

In Catbalogan, in western Samar, Corita Siervo's husband was arrested by soldiers from the Fifteenth Infantry Battalion a few days after he had participated in an anti-Marcos demonstration. He was taken to a police station in another town. When Mrs. Siervo arrived, she saw her husband, his hands tied behind his back, being beaten with rifle butts. When the soldiers discovered her presence, they shoved her to the ground; then the twenty-six-year-old woman, pregnant with her third child, was taken to an elementary school and raped. The next day she learned that her husband and his brother, who had been seized at the same demonstration, had been killed.

Marcos and Defense Minister Enrile were forever promising to conduct investigations into the tortures and killings, but the investigators were military officers, and the result generally was a "cover-up," ruefully noted a Philippine Army lawyer. A case known as the "Langoni Nine" was typical. Eleven young men were arrested on their way to play basketball at an elementary school in Langoni, a town in Negros Occidental. Witnesses saw the basketball players kicked and tied up by Philippine Constabulary soldiers. The next morning nine bodies (two men had escaped) were found at the PC headquarters. One of the witnesses signed a sworn affidavit about what he had seen. The government charged the witness, and the nine victims, with subversion. The witness went into hiding; the military investigation was dropped.

Lawyers who sought to represent victims of human rights abuses found themselves targets. Several were murdered, and more arrested. One lawyer was charged with "human rights lawyering." One of the victims, Romraflo R. Taojo, who had received several warnings from military officers to cease his human rights activities, was shot while watching television one evening, when a man stepped inside the front door and fired five shots from a .45-caliber pistol. Neighbors had seen armed men lingering outside the house prior to the murder. In July 1985 the president of the American Bar Association, John C. Shepherd, sent a letter to Marcos expressing concern about the treatment of human rights lawyers. It was an extraordinary action for the American lawyers' group, which is conservative and rarely injects itself into international human rights issues.

The Reagan administration, however, refused to condemn publicly the human rights abuses. "We had to do it to get [congressional] aid," a Defense Department official said, explaining why the administration remained silent and even claimed that the human rights situation was improving.

When it came to aid, the administration, rather than use the one voice that Marcos would listen to—money—gave it away. The administration's military aid request in 1985 was for $100 million in military aid, which was a 150 percent increase over what had been authorized the previous year. In the House Stephen Solarz, chairman of the Asian subcommittee, sought to cut the amount to $25 million, arguing that the larger amount would send "the wrong signal" to Marcos. Solarz proposed to compensate for the decrease in military aid by increasing economic aid from the $95 million that the administration had requested to $155 million. He also suggested that some of the proposed economic assistance be channeled through private groups instead of the Marcos government. "The issue was joined" was how a congressional aide who supported the administration's request put it. "Should we send a message to Marcos by cutting military aid?" The administration fought hard for Marcos, even bringing General Theodore Allen, the commander of U.S. forces in the Philippines, back to lobby. Allen gave the same arguments that military men and administrations have always made about military aid to repressive governments: It gives the U.S. leverage to push for reforms and improvements. Marcos, predictably, began to spout about the bases agreement: Maybe he would have to abrogate it; maybe the bases would be moved. In the end Congress, as had the administration, capitulated to Marcos, approving $70 million in military aid and sending the economic aid through the usual Philippine government channels.

What General Allen did for Marcos and the Philippine military, Secretary of State Shultz and Reagan's chief of staff, Donald T. Regan, did for Marcos and the Philippine economy, which Marcos had destroyed. Unable to meet the interest payments on the foreign debt he had accumulated, Marcos was seeking a rescheduling. One of the major banks involved, the National Commercial Bank of

Saudi Arabia, balked at the rescheduling, without which there would not be any new loans to the Philippines. The Reagan administration had been leaning hard on Marcos to dismantle the monopolies. Marcos was forever promising to do so, and in fact, he did issue some decrees and orders; but it was all a shell game: He took the sugar monopoly from Benedicto and gave it to Cojuangco. Washington wasn't fooled by Marcos's sleight of hand. But now that it had Marcos in a position to squeeze him, Shultz and Regan, rather than use the economic leverage, made several phone calls to Saudi officials, pressuring them into agreeing to the rescheduling.

With the administration so unwilling to take a firm stand with Marcos, it's understandable why he didn't take seriously all the talk about reform. It was a policy of speak softly and carry no stick. That was evident with the administration's next choice of emissaries to Marcos—CIA Director William Casey. He was the wrong man at the wrong time in the wrong place. He was much too involved with the Marcoses, their relationship dating back to the early 1970s, when he had pushed the Westinghouse nuclear reactor loan through the Ex-Im Bank. Since then he had been a frequent guest of the Marcoses. In April 1983 Casey had dined at Malacañang between Mrs. Marcos and Nguyen Cao Ky, the flamboyant former Vietnamese air marshal, prime minister, and vice president.

What transpired during Casey's visit to Manila in May 1985 has been distorted in just about every respect, principally by Marcos and Casey to suit their own ends and self-images. Soon after Casey had departed the Philippines, *Newsweek* ran a story saying that he had urged Marcos to hold an election. The story, *Newsweek*'s correspondent later told the embassy, was based on sources in Malacañang. It was another demonstration of Marcos's political shrewdness, of his using the press, particularly the American press, for his own ends. If he held an election, which, of course, he'd win, he could serve until 1991, as opposed to 1987, when his current term was to expire. But Marcos didn't know how his party and the public felt about an election. He wanted to test the political winds without being spotted. So Marcos planted the idea that Casey and the United States wanted an election. The response from his party leaders was strong and negative: The machinery wasn't in place for another election. Marcos dropped the idea, which he raised again when he needed to deflect attention from another crisis.

After Marcos did call an election, the one that led to his defeat by Corazon Aquino, Casey claimed that he discussed an early election with Marcos during that May 1985 visit. Casey's effort to enhance his role in the resolution of the Philippine crises was aided by Paul Laxalt, Republican senator from Nevada, who also engaged in a slight alteration of history to embellish his own role. The possibility of a "snap election" had been "broached" by Casey during his meetings with Marcos in May, Laxalt wrote in *Policy Review,* a conservative quarterly. Casey himself went even further, telling some reporters that during the May visit he had suggested to Marcos that he step down.

"Bullshit!" says a State Department officer who was intimately involved in Casey's visit. His explosive rebuttal to Casey's claims is supported by the other U.S. officials, at State and the CIA, who were with Casey when he met with Marcos, who talked with Casey afterward, or who saw his reports, including those of his private meetings with Marcos. All these officials state unequivocally that Casey never discussed elections with Marcos, much less that he proposed Marcos step aside. On the contrary, Casey came away from Manila persuaded that Marcos was best for the Philippines. Marcos told Casey that the Communists were not a serious threat, that he could handle them, that they had been a bigger threat in 1972 than they were at the time. It was the same presentation he made to all American officials. It wasn't just that he could lie better than the best of them. It was more that like so many dictators, Marcos had lost contact with his country. He had surrounded himself with sycophants who wouldn't tell him anything he didn't want to hear, wouldn't deliver bad news. He knew nothing about the insurgency. Though it was never mentioned in the crony-controlled press, Marcos hadn't been to Mindanao, the country's second most important island, where the insurgency was strongest, in more than a decade. Nor had his defense minister, Enrile.

American officials who knew Marcos, who knew anything about the Philippines didn't believe him. But Casey did. In Japan, where he stopped after the Philippines, the CIA director assured government officials that there was nothing to worry about in the Philippines. He made the same reassuring statements to Reagan and others when he returned to the United States. Casey's visit was another blow to those professionals in the State Department.

By the summer of 1985 the Washington bureaucracy was scrambling to find something to do in the Philippines before the place erupted into a war that the Communists were sure to win. Almost every agency hired new people. The Defense Intelligence Agency created an entire group to focus on the Philippines, staffing it with a dozen or so people. The number of CIA analysts concentrating on the Philippines was doubled. Carl W. Ford, Jr., who had spent the past five years as a member of the Democratic staff of the Senate Foreign Relations Committee, helping draft a report in September 1984 that was critical to that committee's eventual involvement in the Philippine crisis, returned to the CIA as an analyst. He instituted regular meetings devoted exclusively to the Philippines, every Monday afternoon from three to four, following the one-hour meeting on Asia. The CIA station chief in Manila upon his return to Washington was promoted to the head of the East Asia division. Over at the State Department Marjorie Niehaus, the Philippine expert from the Congressional Research Service, was brought on board, to work on Philippine affairs in the Bureau of Intelligence and Research, headed by Morton Abramowitz. Bright and hardworking (after the denouement she received a departmental award for her performance), Niehaus reinforced Abramowitz's view that Marcos the reformer was an oxymoron, that the longer Marcos was in power, the worse it would be for the United States. Maisto was of the same view. But the three of them had only limited influence—Niehaus and Maisto because they were too far down in the hierarchy; Abramowitz because as head of INR he was out of the policy-making loop.

In August everyone gathered at the National War College at Fort McNair in southwest Washington. More than sixty attended: representatives from the Defense Intelligence Agency, the Central Intelligence Agency, the State Department, the National Security Council. Ed Lansdale, now seventy-seven years old, was asked to participate, an invitation which seemed to be a manifestation of

Washington's frustration in trying to figure out how to deal with Marcos. Maybe, it was thought, Lansdale's experiences in the 1950s might have some relevance in 1986. But Lansdale, who gave the opening address, offered little more than obvious observations about how it wasn't the same situation it had been three decades before. He added that there was a deep reservoir of goodwill toward Americans among the Filipino people. Indeed, there was, although much of it had been expended during the decade of support for Marcos and martial law, and the well would almost be drained by Reagan a few months hence. A couple of "outsiders" were invited to the conference. One was Claude Buss, a professor emeritus at Stanford, with extensive knowledge and understanding of the Philippines, dating back to 1935, when he had been assigned there as a young Foreign Service officer. Another was William H. Overholt, a vice-president of Bankers Trust, who spent so much time involved with Philippine policy matters that many wondered when he ever did any bank work (he was to be very active in Mrs. Aquino's campaign). Overholt's ties to the Philippines went back to the early seventies, when fresh out of Harvard and Yale (with a Ph.D. in political science), he had worked on development programs in the islands. A conservative Democrat, whose desire to work for Brzezinski at the NSC had not been realized, Overholt was a forceful participant at the National War College conference.

For two days at the War College, the covert operators and the overt thinkers talked, divided into three sections, A, B, and C, then came together for lunch and at the end of the day to exchange ideas. "Facilitators" had been brought in, to ensure that the discussions didn't lag. They found themselves with no role; everyone had plenty to say. About the only time the participants weren't talking was when they were watching the Defense Department's slide shows, which many found simplistic. The soldiers and diplomats, the intelligence analysts and policymakers debated whether or not the United States should launch a covert operation to get rid of Marcos, an idea that was then being discussed by the Pentagon. Someone suggested that wouldn't be possible because Marcos and Ver controlled the guns. Others raised the issue of Diem and what had happened after the Kennedy administration had, actively or passively, endorsed the coup in which he was murdered. Another sug-

375

gestion actively debated was to alter the sentence in the NSDD that Reagan had signed in January 1985 which said that Marcos was part of the solution. It should first be amended to read, it was argued, that Marcos was "not" part of the solution, then be leaked to the press, thereby sending a message to Marcos that Washington was serious about reform. They discussed how in the next election, whenever it was, the United States would provide covert support for organizations such as NAMFREL, the citizens' watchdog committee. They debated how the NPA was to be defeated. Only Marcos could do that, argued a man from the CIA, a strident conservative whose views chilled some of the participants. "He was rabid," said a participant. "He saw the NPA as ten feet tall." Above all, they examined whether Marcos could be counted on to reform. No way, said Overholt. Buss agreed. So did Niehaus. In the front row, Wolfowitz, Armacost, and Armitage seemed to nod in agreement.

Those who believed that Marcos was the cause of the problem, that the longer the United States stuck with him, the deeper the quagmire would get, that, in sum, it was time for some decisive action, were about to acquire some significant support. It came from the Senate Foreign Relations Committee. The committee hadn't been paying much attention to the Philippines. On the House side the Foreign Affairs Subcommittee on Asian and Pacific Affairs had been holding hearings for several years, with a step-up in activity after the Aquino assassination. The subcommittee was chaired by Stephen Solarz, the liberal Democrat who had entered Congress with the Watergate class of 1974, at the age of thirty-four. Solarz was one of the most traveled members of Congress. His weren't junkets but learning trips, from South Africa to the Middle East to Asia, his taut energy fueled by the ambition (which he acknowledged) someday to be secretary of state or national security adviser. He wasn't widely liked by his colleagues, who thought him too brash and a bit too much of a grandstander, too anxious to dominate issues and the spotlight.

Solarz didn't have a solution for the Philippine crisis, and he rejected those that human rights organizations were urging, such as requiring the president to certify an improvement in human rights before aid could be continued. Solarz argued that the certification legislation, which he had sponsored, hadn't worked in El Salvador, where the U.S. president routinely certified an improving human right situation while thousands of Salvadorans were still being killed by the army and death squads. The effect of this certification, Solarz and many others thought, was to give a clean bill of health to a dirty government. While it is certainly true that the Reagan administration made a mockery of the certification law, it had nevertheless focused scrutiny on human rights abuses and as a result, lives were saved because of it. Moreover, the responsibility for allowing the president to sidestep the certification law was with the Congress, which should have, but didn't, enforce it. Anyway, Solarz didn't push human rights in the Philippines, even excluding from his committee hearings human rights organizations whose testimony Republican members of the committee, notably James Leach of Iowa, wanted to hear. But for whatever Solarz wasn't doing, at least he was focusing on the Philippines, forcing the administration to explain its policy in public (many say this is the only proper role for Congress because the elected representatives aren't qualified to make foreign policy).

It was more than the Senate Foreign Relations Committee was doing. Until late 1985 it had ignored the Philippines. The Subcommittee on East Asian and Pacific Affairs had been under the chairmanship of S. I. Hayakawa, the aging and conservative California Republican who actually fell asleep on the job. Hayakawa was succeeded as chairman by Frank H. Murkowski, Republican from Alaska. Murkowski, like so many others after the fall of Marcos, sought to gain credit for having played a positive and important role. But staff members on the Foreign Relations Committee had long been frustrated by Murkowski. "He had absolutely no interest" in the Philippines, says a staff member. "He had to be dragged kicking and screaming into the Philippine issue."

Two Foreign Relations Committee staff members had become interested: Frederick Z. Brown, who worked on the Republican side, and Carl Ford, who worked for the Democrats. In 1984 the two had spent three weeks in the Philippines, an unusually long period for staff members. They were disturbed by what they observed and learned, traveling extensively throughout the archipelago. But the Philippines still wasn't a pressing issue in the Senate, so they worked on the report leisurely, Ford on weekends, Brown during his vacation to Lake Michigan. A year later, in August 1985, Brown went back to the Philippines (Ford was now back at the CIA), and when he returned to Washington, he wrote an alarming memorandum.

Brown's role in the shaping of American policy in the Philippines during the last six months of Marcos was, like Maisto's at the State Department, far greater than was publicly known. A former Foreign Service officer, Brown had considerable experience in intelligence and insurgencies. As an air force lieutenant (before joining the Foreign Service) he had engaged in intelligence and photo interpretation in Libya and Morocco. For five years, from 1968 to 1973, he was in Vietnam, where he had a long stint as the deputy senior adviser for the pacification program in Vinhlong Province, the controversial program that relocated Vietnamese and put them under military control. Most of Brown's Foreign Service career had focused on Southeast Asia, as the director of State's Office of Vietnam, Laos, and Cambodia Affairs for a year and as director of the Office of Indonesia, Malaysia, Singapore, Burma, and Brunei Affairs, which included acting as regional coordinator for East Asia narcotics matters, for three years.

On his trip to the Philippines in 1985 Brown again traveled widely. During his last days he spent two hours in a private meeting with Marcos and three hours with Imelda Marcos. Back in Washington, Brown began an intense lobbying effort to convince the Senate Foreign Relations Committee chairman, Richard Lugar, to involve himself actively in the Philippines issue. Lugar was already bogged down in South Africa and Central America, but he agreed to take on the Philippines. Though he had no way of knowing it at the time, within six months he was to play a pivotal role in the successful resolution of the crisis. With Brown providing crucial support, the two of them in tandem were often way ahead of the president of the United States.

But all that was to come. In August 1985 the situation in the Philippines seemed between bleak and hopeless, "gloom and doom," Brown wrote. Within a day after returning to Washington, Brown set out his views in a confidential memorandum for Lugar. Brown's conclusions:

378

1. President Marcos's prime objective is to stay in power, not to promote change which could endanger him in the short term. . . . He does not accept his own mortality and expects to remain in power indefinitely. He hopes to manage the present crisis tactically, without yielding to terms from either the U.S. or his countrymen.
2. Marcos has not gotten our message about the urgent need for reform. U.S. demands for reform run diametrically counter to Marcos' interests. . . .
3. Marcos believes that he enjoys the support of the highest levels of the U.S. government. Congress may huff and puff, State Department Assistant Secretaries may harass him, and some of his military aid monies may be transferred to ESF [economic support funds]. But in the end, the U.S. will not dare to pull its support.
4. Marcos is convinced that Clark and Subic give him the whip handle in dealing with the U.S. He interpreted the $70 million level for military assistance as evidence of the Administration's desire to satisfy him. . . .
6. The problem in the Philippines begins at the top and expands downward. It is difficult to accept the conventional wisdom that although Marcos is part of the problem, he is also part of the solution. . . .
7. Time is short. The question is not whether the government can reverse the slide but whether it can stop the hemorrhage. . . .

It was a grim analysis, as much an indictment of the Reagan administration's timid approach as it was of Marcos. The report was considered so sensitive that it was distributed only to the members of the Senate Foreign Relations Committee. It should have been widely distributed and made public. Maybe that would have convinced the administration to act. But not necessarily. There wasn't anything in the report that Maisto, Abramowitz, Armacost, and most of the others at State wouldn't agree with and hadn't been saying.

By the fall of 1985 it had become the professionals in the bureaucracies against the ideologues in the White House. From Abramowitz to Wolfowitz, there was agreement that Marcos would not reform. Bosworth knew it, and he was adding that in much of the country there simply was no government anymore. Armacost knew it, having learned the hard way. Carl Ford and his staff at the

CIA had analyzed the situation and Marcos accurately. Over at Defense, Armitage and Admiral Crowe realized that Marcos couldn't and wouldn't change, and they were growing increasingly worried about the bases. Having Admiral Crowe, who was chairman of the Joint Chiefs of Staff, on the same policy ship as the State Department was critical, for it meant that State did not have to fight the Pentagon as it so often did over Philippine policy and in many other parts of the world.

But just as these high-level American officials couldn't influence Marcos, neither could they reach their superiors in Washington. Casey, Weinberger, Bush, McFarlane, even Shultz (though he was beginning to waver because he was listening to his professionals) clung to Marcos. They stuck with Marcos because their boss, the president of the United States, Ronald Reagan, was still loyal to Marcos. Reagan, and the conservatives around him, refused to accept the fact that Marcos was as bad as everyone said. Moreover, they argued, if we get rid of Marcos, the next person might be worse. The Philippine president was corrupt and repressive, his American supporters acknowledged. But we had better stick with him. He's pro-American; pro-bases; anti-Communist. "Nicaragua was on everybody's mind," says one high-level official. The Reagan administration and its conservative backers were still castigating the Carter administration for having abandoned Somoza. They could not very well abandon Marcos. And now it wasn't just the Communists they were talking about as possibly being worse; the administration conservatives weren't at all comfortable with many in the democratic opposition in the Philippines either. They were considered far too liberal; they talked about removing the bases; they said that to end the war with the Communists, they would negotiate, would even allow "leftists" into the government.

On this faith in Marcos, on these fears and beliefs, the policy ship was floating, then slowly sinking. Desperation reigned. The administration grabbed for the now-battered life raft: another high-level mission to talk to Marcos. The problem, the White House still believed, wasn't the message but the messenger: Marcos didn't take the reform message seriously because he was hearing only from bureaucrats. The State Department had long realized that if the policy were to be effective, the message would have to be delivered by someone with clout in the White House; only then would Marcos listen. The White House ignored State's proposal. Then, in August 1985, in an interview with Charles Krause, correspondent for the *MacNeil/Lehrer Newshour*, Marcos said:

> Your government is divided into bureaucratic factions. There is one faction there which closes its eyes to reality and has come out openly against my administration. There is another faction trying to help us. I won't mention names, but we have had some problems with some former ambassadors to the Philippines who did not see eye-to-eye with some of our people here. . . . I am told that these are the leaders in the anti-Marcos movement within that faction. The story in the diplomatic circles of course is that in Washington you need two ambassadors—one for Congress and another for the Executive Department.

Marcos didn't have to name names. Armacost was the former ambassador, and indeed, he had turned against Marcos. But more significantly, Marcos drove home what the State Department had been saying for a year or more: Marcos didn't believe he had to listen to anyone because he was convinced that he still had the support of Ronald Reagan and the White House, that other "faction trying to help us." Marcos was correct, of course, but even the Reagan White House wanted a reformed Marcos.

If, however, the U.S. president had been serious about delivering a message, he would have picked up the phone and called Marcos, as some in the State Department thought he ought to do. But Reagan wasn't about to confront his friend. Other individuals were considered for the assignment. Former President Ford was approached. He was willing to undertake the mission to Manila; but he had other commitments, and before he could rearrange his schedule, the administration decided he would not be the appropriate emissary. William ("Judge") Clark, Reagan's longtime friend from California, who had been the head of the National Security Council before moving over to the Department of the Interior, was considered, as was McFarlane, Clark's successor at the National Security Council. They were vetoed in part because the mission was to be secret, and it was thought impossible for either of those two men to slip in and out of Manila without raising suspicions. Finally, it was decided to send Senator Paul Laxalt in October.

The Nevada Republican was eager. He was just beginning to advance his presidential ambitions, and a visit such as this would give him some foreign policy experience, which he was almost completely lacking. For that reason he didn't want the visit secret. Nor did he want to alienate voters in Nevada, where he had some Columbus Day commitments. Thus, he agreed to undertake the mission, but it had to be public, the White House had to announce it (getting him off the hook with his constituents), and it had to be made clear that he was going at the president's request (which would bolster his ratings by drawing him even closer to the popular president). First, the trip was leaked to the *Washington Times;* then the White House made the official announcement.

Laxalt's mission was simple: to convince Ferdinand Marcos that it wasn't just the bureaucracy that was talking to him about reforms, that his good friend Ronald Reagan was also concerned, also wanted the economic, political, and military reforms. Laxalt carried Reagan's imprimatur. The two men were "political, personal and ideological soul mates," wrote veteran Washington political correspondents Jack Germond and Jules Witcover. Laxalt and Reagan had campaigned together for Barry Goldwater in 1964, both had been elected governors of their respective states in 1966, and Laxalt was Reagan's presidential campaign chairman in 1976, 1980, and 1984. To underscore his mission, Laxalt carried a letter from Reagan. It was handwritten, so that Marcos wouldn't think that it had been prepared by the bureaucracy and that Reagan had merely signed it. In response, Marcos wrote his own letter in longhand, a much longer one. It was filled with the same fantasies that he fed all Americans: The insurgency wasn't growing; he was in control; yes, he'd break up the monopolies; it wasn't true that there was no political freedom; martial law had been necessary in 1972; Filipinos were better off materially than they had been when Marcos became president.

The administration told the *Washington Post,* which reported the story prominently on the front page, that Laxalt had delivered "an extremely blunt message of warning," that it was "the bluntest presidential message ever delivered to a friend." But it wasn't so.

"He did not deliver a blunt message," says an embassy officer about Laxalt. It was "a love feast," says another. Laxalt assured Marcos that Ronald Reagan was still his friend. It was the darn

Congress that was causing all the trouble. So, if he'd just do a few of these things, there'd be no more problem. Laxalt told Marcos that one of his major problems was his image in the United States, which an aggressive public relations effort could correct.

The Laxalt mission was a success—for Marcos. He had expected much worse. He told American diplomats later that he thought Laxalt was going to suggest he resign. Like the Casey visit, the Laxalt mission was a disaster for the State Department. "Marcos came away the winner," a State Department official commented a few weeks after Laxalt's return. Marcos had again bought time, with Reagan, Casey, Weinberger, and the others who wanted to stick with him. Laxalt had been impressed with Marcos, and his reports on his return were positive.

Marcos was now convinced he could bypass Bosworth, the embassy, and the State Department. He had his own back channel to Reagan, through Laxalt. Marcos was continually calling the Nevada senator. He also hired a public relations firm. When she was in New York, for another opening session of the United Nations, Imelda Marcos handed over a check for $60,000 as the down payment on a one-year contract that called for a total payment of $950,000. (She told the United Nations General Assembly that the world's problems "have their roots in injustice, intolerance, greed and dominance by the strong.") The PR firm was Black, Manafort, Stone & Kelly, a young agency with impeccable conservative credentials. Roger Stone was close to Nixon, the friendship from Stone's days as a Young Republican who had played some dirty tricks during the Watergate era. Paul J. Manafort, Jr. thirty-six years old, who had worked in the Ford White House, handled the account. Manafort checked with the Reagan White House before taking on Marcos as a client. The White House said OK. There might be some in the administration who thought it was time to tilt away from Marcos—Admiral Crowe of the Joint Chiefs of Staff and Michael Armacost, the number three at State, the most senior men with those views—but the White House was still firmly behind him.*

Marcos, however, was rapidly losing control. He was under heavy

---

* Black, Manafort, which was paid $250,000 for its services in December 1985, terminated its relationship with the Marcos government on February 24, 1986, the day before Marcos fled.

medication, and all plants and carpets had been stripped from the palace because they contained chemicals that irritated his diseases. For long stretches he could work only four to five hours a day; then, in accord with the nature of his disease, he would recover and carry on long conversations with journalists and visitors. During a visit Admiral Crowe sat horrified as Marcos rambled on incoherently about World War II, his medals, his injuries. In Washington there were stories that Marcos would soon die. It seemed almost a wish, born of desperation, out of an unwillingness to act decisively with a policy. There was also talk in Washington about hastening his departure from the palace, with a coup or some other covert operation. Both Armacost and Abramowitz were members of a supersecret group known as the 208 Committee (named for the room in the Old Executive Office Building where they met). Its function was to oversee the covert wars and operations that had increased dramatically under Casey and Reagan, from the war against the Sandinistas to Angola to Afghanistan. Numerous Filipinos approached the CIA and Pentagon officials in search of support for a coup.

Though Marcos didn't know about the 208 Committee, he was convinced that Washington was out to topple him, that he was to meet the same fate as Diem. The shah had suffered from similar delusions prior to his ouster. In late October Marcos asked aides to research the fall of Diem, Allende, the shah, Somoza, and Park Chung Hee. He instructed his reseachers to study *The New York Times* stories and especially editorials prior to the ouster of these men. Reflecting an anxiety bordering on paranoia, Marcos told confidants (who told Americans) that James Nach, the embassy political officer, was a leader in the effort to destabilize his government. Marcos was sure of this because Nach had been in Vietnam—even though Nach's service in Vietnam had been many years after Diem's ouster.

In Washington the possibility of a coup or some other covert action didn't go much beyond talk and contingency planning. Marcos still had important support in the White House. Frustration reigned.

"The situation is bad. It's getting worse. Marcos is the problem. And we don't know what to do," lamented a senior State Department official in October 1985.

16: A Blunder
Leads to an Election

"**T**here's an old saying that victory has a hundred fathers and defeat is an orphan," President Kennedy remarked after the Bay of Pigs debacle. How true that proved to be in the Philippines. No one wanted to bear responsibility for the twenty years of Marcos, but many were those who sought credit for his ouster and the return to democracy, an outcome which brought hosannahs for the United States and the Reagan administration.

It was Ferdinand E. Marcos, however, who set in motion the events that led to his ignominious flight from the country. Throughout his career he had faithfully adhered to the advice his father had given him as a young man: "Don't start a fight until you know you can win it." Now he faltered. Several times. The first mistake, from which all others would follow, came on November 3, 1985. That was the day Marcos announced that he would hold a "snap election." The next regularly scheduled presidential election was not until 1987. Had Marcos not decided to advance the date, he would have (barring death or a coup, which, though being considered, was unlikely) remained as the country's president. Even if he had decided not to run in 1987, he could have probably handpicked his successor, anyone from Enrile to his son or daughter. Marcos embarked down the fatal electoral path against the advice of his wife and his closest advisers. They all were strongly opposed to an election. Marcos ignored them, making the announcement when Imelda Marcos was in the Soviet Union, where she had ventured again, after another spree in New York.

After the elections had led to Marcos's ouster and brought into office Corazon Aquino, Senator Laxalt sought some credit for having set the process in motion. Writing in *Policy Review,* the magazine of the conservative Heritage Foundation, Laxalt claimed he had "briefly discussed the idea of a snap presidential election" during his meeting with Marcos in October. "That's simply not true," says a senior embassy officer, a view supported by the embassy officers who were with Laxalt during his meetings with Marcos, those who talked with him afterward, as well as senior State Department officials in Washington who read the cables from Manila while Laxalt was there and talked with him when he returned. All emphatically insist that Laxalt and Marcos never discussed the possibility of an election during Laxalt's visit. But what the department didn't know was that after that visit Laxalt had talked with Marcos about an early election and recommended that he hold one.

The State Department was adamantly opposed to an early election. Even those officers who were most concerned about Marcos's remaining in power did not consider an election at this time to be in Washington's best interest. "I thought this was going to be a disaster for everybody," says a diplomat, reflecting back on his reaction to Marcos's announcement. "The only victor was going to be the NPA." If Marcos cheated to win, it would help the NPA. And even if he won honestly, he would continue the same economic policies and plundering, which were fueling the NPA's growth. While the State Department wanted Marcos out and wanted an election, it didn't want the election now, because it didn't believe that the opposition was strong enough or unified enough to take on Marcos. After twenty years of one-man rule it was going to take some time for the opposition to build up its organization. For that reason the official U.S. policy was to use the 1986 municipal elections as the springboard for the presidential elections a year later.

Marcos dropped his election bombshell during an appearance on *This Week with David Brinkley*. George Will, the erudite conservative columnist and commentator, served up the question. Will had been thinking about asking Marcos about the possibility of an early election; then, prior to the show, he talked to Laxalt, who was also to appear. The Nevada senator suggested that if Will inquired about an election, he "might get an interesting answer."

On the show Will asked: "President Marcos, there is a perception here that your problems derive from the fact that your mandate is gone, whatever it once was. . . . And there are some people here who wonder if it is not possible and if you would not be willing to move up the election date, the better to renew your mandate soon, say, within the next eight months or so. Is that possible, that you could have an election earlier than scheduled?"

Marcos leaned into the pitch he had been waiting for. "Well, I understand the opposition has been asking for an election. In answer to their request I announce that I am ready to call a snap election perhaps earlier than eight months, perhaps in three months or less than that . . ."

Sam Donaldson, ABC's White House correspondent, who seemed genuinely surprised, took over. "Are there any catches, Mr. President?" he asked Marcos.

"I'm ready. I'm ready. I'm ready," Marcos shot back.

Donaldson burrowed into Marcos as he often did into the American president. "Mr. President, are there any catches? Can anyone run in this election? If Corazon Aquino wants to run, if Senator Laurel wants to run? Everyone can run?"

"Oh yes," Marcos assured Donaldson and the American public. "Anyone."

After a break for the commercials Donaldson kept on. "Okay. My question is, since the allegation against you is that you have conducted massive voting fraud in the past, if you hold elections in 60 days or so, will you allow outside observers into the Philippines to oversee the elections to make certain they're fair?"

Marcos: "You are all invited to come, and we will invite members of the American Congress to please come and just see what is happening here."

State Department and embassy officers who had been watching the show and whose hearts had sunk when Marcos announced the election recovered when Marcos said he would allow observers in. "I was elated," one remembered. They were confident Marcos could not conduct a fair election and win. Inviting observers proved to be another Marcos blunder, for instead of overlooking the fraud, they screamed about it, far louder than anyone expected they would. ("No third world dictator will ever allow another observer team," a diplomat, pleased with the outcome, said with a laugh after the election.)

Marcos's election announcement on the Brinkley show seemed

spontaneous. Of course, it wasn't. On the Friday before the show Marcos had again called Laxalt and raised the idea of an election. Laxalt responded, "If you are going to do that [conduct a snap election], it would be very dramatic for you to make that announcement on the Brinkley show. That would be very effective for American consumption."

Laxalt's suggestion is a revealing insight into what lay behind Marcos's idea for the election. It was not an election for Filipinos; it was an election for Americans, specifically for the American critics of his regime. Now that he had Washington's attention (Laxalt's visit had convinced Marcos of that, if of nothing else), he would show them, put an end to all this nonsensical talk about his having lost control of the country.

While the State Department might not want an election, the conservatives around Reagan thought it was a great idea. They, too, thought an election would silence critics; of course, they thought Marcos would win. Laxalt told fellow senators that it would be a fair election. It would make no sense, he reasoned, for Marcos to announce an election if he would have to cheat to win. It was the same naïveté and faith which had marked American policy toward Marcos for twenty years. Marcos was suffering from self-delusions about his popularity; he deluded Laxalt and other Americans. This time they would be hoisted on their own ideological deceptions.

Marcos's consideration of an early election was precipitated, in part, by articles in the *San Jose Mercury News* in July 1985 about what became known as the "hidden wealth," State Department officers concluded. Three reporters working for six months documented how Marcos, his family, and his cronies, often using offshore corporations and phony names, had accumulated massive property holdings in the United States. In the Philippines, opposition leaders in the Assembly began impeachment proceedings, which, even though certain not to go very far, were unpleasant for Marcos. In the United States the articles, which later earned the Pulitzer Prize, spurred more investigations. In early August ABC's *20/20* devoted a segment to the hidden wealth. A week after that the *Village Voice* weighed in, enlarging on the scandal with details of the Marcos property holdings in New York: In September 1981, Imelda Marcos had, for $51 million, purchased the Crown Building on Fifth Avenue; five months later it was the Herald Center, on Thirty-fourth Street and Broadway, for $60 million; and more. After the *Village Voice* articles Congressman Solarz decided to hold hearings. It wasn't just that he was chairman of the Asian subcommittee; he was also from New York. Once Marcos announced the election, Solarz became determined to hold his hearings far enough in advance of voting day so that they would influence Philippine voters.

In calling for an election, Marcos had wounded himself. The blood was on the water. From every direction came help to inflict the mortal blows: American liberals; diplomats and public officials; members of Congress and their aides. In order to trap Marcos, however, U.S. officials found it necessary to maneuver Ronald Reagan into a corner from which the only exit was to abandon Marcos.

All these interlopers meant well, convinced that six more years of Marcos would be disastrous. In their involvement in Philippine affairs they were acting in the tradition of Lansdale and the CIA back in the 1950s. When the CIA had drugged President Quirino, it was because Washington had decided Ramón Magsaysay would make a better president. When the CIA had passed out money to congressional candidates (in violation of Philippine law), it justified the illegality with the rationalization that it was being done "to change their country for the better," as Joseph Smith, the CIA agent in charge of the operation, had observed. "We did not think that we were interfering in the political life of the country." That same attitude prevailed in 1986. No one seemed to be disturbed by the fact that the Philippines was a sovereign, independent nation. In the minds of many Americans, it was still an American colony. Americans had to save the Filipinos.

One of the first outsiders to involve himself in the Philippine political process was Richard Holbrooke, who as Carter's assistant secretary of state had fashioned and presided over the policy that allowed Marcos to remain in power. Now he would get behind Mrs. Aquino. Holbrooke, who hadn't been in the Philippines since the 1980 New Year's Eve blowout at Malacañang, was en route to China, in his capacity as an investment banker, and decided to stop in Manila. Since he was a former assistant secretary and had some clout within the Democratic party (the State Department was anxious for bipartisan support for its Philippine policy), the embassy welcomed him. Moreover, the embassy's political officer, Scott Hallford, had worked for Holbrooke during the Carter years and believed that Holbrooke had helped advance his career.

Hallford met Holbrooke at the airport, put him up at his home, and arranged his meetings, which included Marcos and Mrs. Aquino. The embassy hosted a breakfast for Holbrooke, so he could talk with the opposition leaders. Holbrooke had some advice: Avoid being portrayed as anti bases or soft on communism. A few weeks later Holbrooke, speaking at a conference in Los Angeles about the Pacific basin, again chastised the Philippine opposition. "I am concerned that they have not renounced completely the thought of a tactical alliance with the Communists," Holbrooke said. "This they should do, however expedient such an association might look to some of them in the short term. There are too many historical examples of democrats who were eaten alive by their erstwhile Communist allies to trust such an arrangement now." There were a few Philippine opposition leaders in the audience, and they were angered by Holbrooke's comments. His views of the Philippines and communism were the same as those of the Reagan administration. They did not take kindly to his telling them how to deal with the Communists. After all, as they saw it, the American policy of supporting Marcos had only helped the Communists grow stronger.

While in Manila, Holbrooke confused and irritated Mrs. Aquino. When the two met, she had not yet been selected as the opposition candidate. During their one-hour meeting at her house, while her daughter sat on the couch doing her homework, Holbrooke pressed her about whether she really wanted to run for president. The election would probably be fraudulent, Holbrooke said. Why should she allow herself to be used? She was perplexed but concluded that he did not want her to run. After their meeting she called several Americans and asked what Holbrooke was all about. Was he speaking officially? Was that the American position, that she not run? "It was a serious misunderstanding," says Holbrooke. "It's absolutely not true that I didn't want her to run. She misunderstood me." An embassy officer who was present agrees with Holbrooke.

Once Aquino had decided to run, the task was to unify the

opposition, because a divided opposition was just what Marcos was counting on. Though there were several men and women who wanted to run, two emerged as the most likely candidates: Corazon Aquino and Salvador ("Doy") Laurel. Laurel, whose father had written the Supreme Court decision exonerating Marcos for the Nalundasan murder, represented Philippine politics-as-usual. "Doy would be more of the same of Marcos, and worse," a leading businessman said at the time. From a wealthy family Laurel, who had a law degree from Yale, was something of a playboy. He was also conservative, and many in Washington, particularly at the White House, would have preferred him as the candidate; he was one of the few opposition leaders who were not in favor of removing the bases. Because Laurel was so much like Marcos, he could not have made an appeal that would have defeated Marcos. But Laurel had enough political power that he had to be reckoned with.

It was Cardinal Sin's job to get Aquino and Laurel on the same ticket. "He's one of the best politicians in the Philippines," says a very senior U.S. diplomat whose contacts with Sin spanned a decade. "If he hadn't been cardinal, he'd be president. If not president, the pope." As for Pope John Paul II's edict that priests should stay out of politics, it has been as inconsistently applied as was the Reagan administration's human rights policy. The pope might enforce that edict in Nicaragua but not in the Philippines. Besides, Sin had a personal relationship with John Paul, dating back to when they both had served on the same synod committee. The two men got along well, the pope enjoying his meetings with Sin. After one luncheon in Rome, as Sin was departing for Manila, the pope said with a straight face, "Say hi to Imelda."

Sin leaned hard on both Aquino and Laurel, she to accept him, he to accept the number two spot. The cardinal also made sure each of them realized that the American embassy was of the same mind, as it was. The embassy delivered that message to the two Philippine politicians through every third party the U.S. diplomats could find. "These people were bombarded," says a Foreign Service officer. "Absolutely overwhelmed." Solarz weighed in; so did John Kerry, the liberal senator from Massachusetts, who as freshman member of the Senate Foreign Relations Committee had decided to pay particular attention to the Philippines. Laurel backed off, accepting the number two spot in exchange for promises to be named prime minister and foreign minister.

Aquino's campaign had barely begun when it was dealt a severe blow. It came in the form of an interview with *The New York Times*.

"What on earth do I know about being President?" she admitted having told those who had urged her to run. "The only thing I can really offer the Filipino people is my sincerity." She told *The Times* that she did not have a specific program of government. That vagueness, that seeming lack of purpose and strength were bad enough for those American officials who had been supportive of her as an alternative to Marcos. But even more of a blow was what she said specifically. First, she said she favored removal of the bases. Then she was asked about the Communists and the NPA. Her first response was to refer to a Jesuit priest who worked in the slums and had briefed her. Then she added that the "majority" of those who supported the NPA were "not really Communists." She would, if elected, she explained, propose a cease-fire and a dialogue.

It's hard to imagine what Corazon Aquino could have said that would have sent more shudders through the White House. To the conservatives, her view of the Communists was simply naïve, at best. It is a fundamental, unalterable tenet of conservative ideology that it is not possible to negotiate with Marxists. Period. And it's not just conservative Republicans who believe that. That was precisely what Richard Holbrooke, a Democrat, had said in his speech in December.

No matter when Mrs. Aquino had expressed those views of communism and the NPA, there would have been a strong reaction in Washington. But what transformed a tremor into an earthquake was that her remarks came at about the same time an article appeared in the conservative *Commentary* magazine about the NPA. The title was "The New Khmer Rouge." Twenty pages long, written by Ross H. Munro, a *Time* magazine correspondent, it was as chilling and strident as the title suggested.* Those in the NPA, according

---

* *Time* magazine editors were not pleased with what Munro had done, and *Time's* correspondent who covered the Philippines, Sandra Burton, was even more upset. It wasn't just the polemics of the article that bothered them; it was more the fact that Munro, who had previously worked in the Philippines for *Time*, had left the impression with people he interviewed that he was writing the article about the NPA for *Time*.

to Munro, weren't just Communists. They were the next Khmer Rouge. No discussion. No debate. There was no question mark in the title, which had been selected by the author, not by the magazine. The Philippine Communists were not only brutal but everywhere, according to Munro. They had infiltrated unions, political organizations, human rights groups, and the church. He wrote shrilly of "clerics turned killers" and of "secret cells inside the Catholic Church." Lest he hadn't set off enough panic, Munro wrote that if the Communists were victorious, they would align the Philippines with the Soviet Union.

The impact of Munro's article was considerable. Stephen S. Rosenfeld, editorial writer and columnist for the *Washington Post,* devoted a column to it and acclaimed it as "arresting." The executive editor of *The New York Times,* A. M. Rosenthal, had the Munro article with him when he arrived in Manila in mid-December (he was present at the interview with Corazon Aquino). Rosenthal, a hard-line anti-Communist who believed that his correspondents had been too soft in their reporting on the Sandinistas before and after they came to power, wanted to be sure that his correspondent in Manila, Seth Mydans, didn't make the same errors when reporting about the NPA. The subsequent *Times* coverage of the NPA reflected many of Munro's conclusions.

There were, however, serious weaknesses in Munro's article, and the embassy recognized them. "It's a bit like a two-hundred-and-fifty-pound ballerina balancing on one toe," an embassy officer said at the time. "Impressive but not much support." Even Jim Nach, the author of the most authoritative study of the NPA, to whom Munro had talked at length (much of what Munro wrote is contained in Nach's cable), thought that Munro had overstated the brutality of the NPA, had stretched the facts to suggest that the Philippine Communists would be like Pol Pot. (Nach thought an NPA government would be more similar to the Marxist governments in Mozambique and Angola.)

The embassy prepared a classified analysis of the article. Bosworth noted that Munro had pursued the matter of the CPP and the NPA "as a labor of love." He had done "an excellent job describing the CPP's use of force, the party's growth, and the dangers it poses to the Philippines—and to U.S. interests." The embassy added, however, that Munro "has overstated the CPP/NPA's use of terror in the Party's successes to date." The embassy's conclusion was that "the communists are careful about using terror and specialize in 'Robin Hood'-like activities, including the liquidation of corrupt, abusive officials and, less often, especially effective ones." The embassy also faulted Munro for "unconfirmed assertions about a Soviet angle." As Nach had noted in his study, "improper links" between the Philippine Communists and the Soviet Union "cannot be demonstrated."

In Washington Munro's article was quickly overtaken by the focus on the election and most immediately by *The New York Times* interview with Mrs. Aquino. The paper had run long excerpts from the interview because Rosenthal, who had been present, was so stunned by what he heard—"it was almost embarassing," he says about the interview—that he thought only the text could convey how "vague and rambling" he thought her answers had been. Rosenthal wasn't alone in this reaction. Warren Hoge, the paper's foreign editor, who also participated in the interview, was also surprised and dismayed. Running along the edge of Manila Bay the morning after, he could talk about little else. He had interviewed a lot of politicians, domestic and foreign, during his career. He had covered Washington during the Watergate years for the *New York Post,* had been deputy metropolitan editor for *The New York Times,* and spent five years in Latin America (interviewing right-wing Bolivian generals who trafficked in cocaine and left-wing Sandinistas) before becoming *The New York Times* foreign editor in 1983. He had never, he said, found a leader who seemed so ill prepared.

That was precisely what the interview told conservatives around Reagan who wanted to continue supporting Marcos. They could point to the interview and say in effect, See, look what's going to happen if she wins. She's not strong. She's not forceful. She's a housewife. She'll force us out of the bases, and she'll make a deal with the Communists. It wasn't only the conservatives who were alarmed by what they read in *The New York Times.* The number three man in the State Department, Michael Armacost, who had played a key role in gradually moving the policy away from Marcos, was concerned about what he might have set in motion. "Armacost began asking, 'Is this lady serious?' "

While the interview had been "devastating, even more devastating was Rosenthal's observation that he thought she was naïve," says a senior State Department official who was involved in formulating the policy. In Rosenthal's own words, she was "unprepared" to be president, "not a fully developed political personality." That's what Rosenthal told Ambassador Bosworth in Manila and upon his return, what he said directly to Secretary of State Shultz as well as to guests during a White House affair he attended. "His opinion was very influential for a long, long time around the White House," Shultz said later. In the weeks that followed, Reagan himself, along with his advisers who wanted to stick with Marcos, often said in their attacks on Mrs. Aquino, "This is what the editor of *The New York Times* thinks of her."

Mrs. Aquino didn't know about what was going on in private between *The New York Times* and official Washington, but the interview alone embittered her toward *The Times,* a resentment she harbored long after the election and her victory. She said she didn't know that it was to be a formal interview; she thought it was an informal chat. But if Mrs. Aquino didn't realize it was an interview, in part it was because she was a neophyte in dealing with the press. Though the interview was in her home and on a Sunday evening, which might suggest a less than official air, Rosenthal was accompanied by his foreign editor, Hoge, and the paper's Manila correspondent, Mydans; there was a tape recorder prominently placed on the table; and Susan Meiselas moved about, taking official photographs.

No matter why Mrs. Aquino handled the questions as she did, the interview was a serious blow to her incipient campaign. Out of the destruction, however, rose the desperately needed construction. While the interview provided ammunition for Mrs. Aquino's enemies, it also convinced her friends that they had better act, quickly and decisively. And they did.

At the center of a team that stretched from Manila to London to New York and Washington was Robert Trent Jones, Jr., the golf course designer who had known Cory Aquino for twenty years and had tried to secure her husband's release from prison back in 1975. One week after *The New York Times* interview appeared, Jones, on December 23, went to the Menlo Country Club, where he knew

Shultz was playing golf. The course, on the San Francisco peninsula, was where the two men had golfed together during the years that Shultz had taught at nearby Stanford University and been the head of San Francisco-based Bechtel Corporation. That day Jones passed the time at the practice range until the secretary of state finished his round. Then they talked.

Jones explained that he was going to help Mrs. Aquino. A receptive Shultz told Jones to stay in touch with Armacost. It was a tilt toward Aquino, the first of what became a lean. When Jones discovered on the day that he was to leave for Manila that his passport had expired, he called the State Department. Within an hour he had a valid passport. Even more, Armacost, disturbed by the fallout from *The New York Times* interview, recommended to Jones that the New York-based public relations firm D. H. Sawyer & Associates be hired for Aquino's campaign. And in Manila diplomatic and military officers in the embassy would help the Aquino effort, though indirectly and very carefully. "They were straining the limits of the mandate to stay neutral," says an American who worked informally for Mrs. Aquino.

Jones moved on two fronts: in the Philippines and in the United States. His first major move was to bring Mark Malloch Brown into the Aquino campaign. One of Brown's principal missions was to avoid another *New York Times* debacle. Brown, a tall, sometimes disheveled-looking thirty-two-year-old, was "a shark in angels' clothing," as an admirer describes him. He was a journalist who in 1979 had worked for the United Nations high commissioner for refugees along the Thai-Cambodian border. For the past several years, he had been employed by the *Economist* first as a political correspondent, then as editor of the *Economist Development Report*. When Brown began working full-time for Mrs. Aquino, he left the impression that he was still working for the British magazine, no doubt to help her gain business backing.

For more than a year Brown had been discussing with D. H. Sawyer & Associates the possibility of his working for them. He was ready to join but postponed doing so. The Aquino campaign, Brown explains, "took pains to say there was no American involvement." Since Brown was British and not on Sawyer's payroll (he went on it after the Philippine election), it was possible to make this claim, but only by some considerable stretching. Jones was paying Brown's fare, and there were other Americans involved in her campaign, even if they weren't officially on her staff.

One of them was William Overholt, the Bankers Trust vice-president based in Hong Kong who had participated in the seminar at the National War College in August. He was an adviser to Mrs. Aquino's campaign policy committee, which was chaired by Jaime Ongpin, the forty-seven-year-old Harvard M.B.A. corporate executive who had always been close to the American embassy but was even more welcome there now, with many embassy officers strongly pro-Aquino. Overholt kept the embassy informed generally of what he was doing for Aquino, and he found that the embassy's diplomatic and military officers were supportive, going about as far as they could to help without exposing themselves to charges of partisan interference. One of Overholt's schemes (which didn't have any American embassy involvement) was for a rally in Hong Kong. His idea was to gather in a plaza the 30,000 Filipinos working as domestic maids there. Aquino would give a speech, and bags would be passed among the crowd; but they would already have been secretly filled with money, collected from wealthy people. Thus, there would be a double impact: raising money and leaving the impression that the average Filipino wanted Cory Aquino. Overholt was forced to drop the plan when Hong Kong officials denied him a rally permit.

Though it may not have been on Mrs. Aquino's staff, Sawyer's firm (the one Armacost had recommended) was certainly helping her, even waiving its normal fee, which would have been about $250,000. It was symptomatic of the Philippine election that both candidates had retained American public relations firms and that those firms concentrated on American, not Philippine, audiences. D. H. Sawyer was considered a Democratic firm; one or two of its associates had worked in the Carter White House, and the firm usually represented Democratic candidates in congressional races. Marcos, on the other hand, had Black, Manafort, Stone & Kelly, conservative and very Republican. Paul Manafort set out to demonstrate that Mrs. Aquino was soft on communism and would throw the United States out of the military bases. Through his own connections he was able to deliver that message to conservatives around

Reagan. To reach a wider audience, he arranged for three journalists to go to the Philippines: Robert Novak, the conservative columnist; John McLaughlin, the conservative and provocatively contentious host and spark on a political roundtable show; and Fred Barnes, the *New Republic*'s political reporter who was seen as giving the once-liberal magazine an increasingly conservative stance on foreign policy issues.

Jones, working with and through Sawyer's firm, carried out what he called the "second campaign." It was aimed at the American audience, especially the policymakers, to convince them that Corazon Aquino could be trusted. An informal advisory board, "Friends of Aquino" it called itself, was established to spread the message. The principal apostles were Solarz, Holbrooke (at first Mrs. Aquino was reluctant to have him involved because of her encounter with him in November), and Rafael Salas, who had been Marcos's executive secretary back in the 1960s but had split with Marcos and for many years had been working at the UN in New York as the executive director of the Fund for Population Activities. And, of course, Jones.

Golf being the sport of politicians, Jones had a special cachet with many members of Congress. His effectiveness was enhanced because he was considered moderate to conservative, and he had contributed to many a Democratic campaign. He focused his lobby efforts on personal friends in the Senate: Bill Bradley, who was from his native New Jersey; Sam Nunn, a longtime golfing companion from Georgia; and Alan Cranston, senator from California, where Jones now made his home.

In the Philippines Mark Brown directed Aquino's media campaign. First he had to persuade her that notwithstanding her bitter experience with *The New York Times,* she had to meet with the foreign press. He prepared her for the sessions by playing the role of the nasty reporter. Then he went to work on her image: that she was tough, trustworthy, and competent. And they framed her responses to the issues, the ones of concern in America. Those were communism and the bases. Four days after saying publicly that she would allow Communists in her cabinet if they renounced violence, she reversed herself, declaring unequivocally to a gathering of 700 businessmen, "I would like to assure everybody here that I will not appoint a Communist to my cabinet." It's doubtful that many Philippine voters were concerned about communism; that was an obsession in Washington. So was the bases issue. As the embassy had reported, based on its meetings with opposition leaders prior to the start of the campaign, "As far as the US bases are concerned . . . they would not be a major campaign issue."

Mrs. Aquino was opposed to the bases in principle. As a nationalist she didn't like the foreign influence; as a woman and Catholic she was sickened by the seediness surrounding the bases, the abuse and exploitation of women, the thousands of teenagers who had turned to prostitution. But her position on the bases didn't play well in Washington. So she modified it. She said she'd honor the agreement, which ran until 1991; then the issue would be considered anew. Brown explained to her that she could get away with that position, that Felipe González in Spain and Andreas Papandreou in Greece had campaigned against the presence of the American bases in their countries without Washington's coming down hard on them.

In general, Aquino had to demonstrate, in the Philippines and Washington, says Brown, "competence, toughness, and winnability." The last was the most difficult, there existing such fatalism and cynicism after twenty years of Marcos. Even some of those closest to Mrs. Aquino, as well as most embassy officers, didn't think she could succeed. Aquino was seen as a saint and mother figure but not a candidate who could win. After the rallies, which attracted huge and enthusiastic crowds, Brown would tell his candidate, "They're going to pray for you—and vote for Marcos." The challenge was to give a political edge to a religious campaign. "The strategy was classic dirty democratic strategy," says Brown. "We had to get her down from the high road. She had to attack Marcos personally." Mrs. Aquino was reluctant. She had said at the outset that she would not attack Marcos personally. That was not her style or her nature. Finally, she was persuaded.

The ammunition for the attacks came from the United States. First she went after corruption and hidden wealth. After the stories in the *San Jose Mercury News* and *Village Voice,* major newspapers began investigations. Solarz kept the issue alive by holding hearings, subpoenaing the Marcoses' agents in the United States to testify.

Each day there would be new revelations: another multimillion-dollar building or apartment here; another offshore corporation that was really part of Imelda Marcos's vast financial empire. Each disclosure would be trumpeted by the media. A circle was tightening around Marcos.

Then came another scandal, made for Aquino's campaign: Marcos's war record.

An American professor at the University of New South Wales in Sydney, Australia, Alfred W. McCoy, uncovered, then disseminated the smoking documents. A historian and prolific writer, McCoy lived in the Philippines for several years, researching and writing articles and books, including an account of the priests imprisoned, then later deported by Marcos. While doing research for a book about World War II in the Philippines, McCoy discovered official U.S. government records in the National Archives in Washington, D.C., which revealed that Marcos's claims about his wartime exploits were fraudulent. McCoy uncovered the lode, which he copied without the archives staff's realizing what he had, in the summer of 1985.

When Marcos announced the election, McCoy realized that now was the time to go public. He went first to the *Los Angeles Times* syndicate, hoping that he could write the article himself. The syndicate passed the material to the paper's foreign desk. No interest. So McCoy went to the *Washington Post,* to John Sharkey, the reporter who had exposed Marcos's fraudulent war medals claims back in 1983 (in an article that went virtually unnoticed at the time). Sharkey brushed off McCoy with some lame reason. Finally, McCoy called Seymour Hersh, the man to whom all journalists seem to go when they have exposés. Hersh was too busy finishing his book about the shoot-down of Korean Airlines 007 and referred McCoy to his friend at *The New York Times* Jeff Gerth. Gerth had been investigating the Marcos's financial activities for several months (and not having much success getting his stories into the paper until the Marcos empire began to crumble). He took the story to his boss, Washington bureau chief Bill Kovach. Kovach assigned not only Gerth but also Joel Brinkley and Stephen Engelberg. It was a formidable team.

Beginning on Friday night, January 17, 1986, the three of them took McCoy's material and followed up, finding other documents and locating, then interviewing men who had served with Marcos in the Philippines during World War II. MARCOS'S WARTIME ROLE DISCREDITED IN U.S. FILES was the headline at the top of page one of *The New York Times* the following Thursday. The next day the *Washington Post* had a front-page story by John Sharkey, going beyond what *The Times* had written. Sharkey had documentary evidence which suggested that Marcos's father had been a collaborator during the war and that Marcos may have been as well. It seemed astonishing that the *Post* had been able to come up with such an explosive and well-researched story so quickly. But it wasn't so quick. Sharkey had put off McCoy because Sharkey had already written his own story. It had been in the hands of editors for two months, and after McCoy had called on him, Sharkey, not wanting to be scooped, had sent memos to his editors, alerting them that someone else was on to the story. Nothing had happened.

But now it was open season on Marcos. His affair with the press was over. For twenty years so many reporters had treated him with reverence and respect. The times had changed; the hounds were loose, sniffing out corruption, tearing away the wartime fabrications. Two years earlier, in December 1983, when Sharkey had written his story about the war medals fraud, the *Post* had run it not as a news story but rather in the Sunday Outlook section, which, though a place for long and thoughtful articles, was not where the newspaper placed its most important stories. And at that time other newspapers and journalists, as well as members of Congress, had ignored it. Now *The New York Times* story was splashed across the front page; across the country the story was reprinted. It generated congressional cries for an investigation.

But though all these charges of corruption and phony medals were front-page and prime-time news in the United States, there was a serious problem for the Aquino people: how to get the news to the Filipino voters. Contrary to what Senator Laxalt believed, Marcos controlled the press and kept Aquino out. Laxalt wrote, in his *Policy Review* article, that:

> the election campaign was as free and open as any we have had in the United States. The Aquino people complained about time on television, but that was the same complaint that American

politicians usually make: you can't get time on TV unless you buy expensive time on the air. Mrs. Aquino had rallies all over the country, and she and a very vigorous opposition press were able to make the strongest statements with impunity. I don't think anyone can say that freedom of the press or freedom of assembly were [*sic*] suppressed during the campaign.

It was a description that bore no relation to reality. Aquino couldn't get time on TV, not even if she had been richer than Marcos. Marcos controlled television, and radio, and the newspapers. It was as if CBS were owned by Nancy Reagan, ABC by Maureen Reagan, and NBC by Paul Laxalt, while all the newspapers except for one in Alaska and maybe another in Alabama were owned by Reagan's friends. Even that wouldn't adequately portray what Mrs. Aquino was up against. The owners of American newspapers and television stations will sell time to anyone who has the money. The Filipino owners would not. When the major Philippine newspapers reported early in the campaign about Mrs. Aquino's rallies, Marcos personally called the editors. "He came down on them like a ton of bricks," a journalist told Seth Mydans of *The New York Times*. "Equal access, that's a laugh," another columnist said. Aquino's rallies drew tens of thousands, flashing the Laban party's *L* with the thumb and forefinger, a sea of yellow shouting "Cory, Cory, Cory." On the rare occasions that Mrs. Aquino was covered on television, the reporters had instructions not to show the size of her crowds, or to film close-ups of her, and in most cases not to include the sound of her speeches. *The Times* summed it up in its headline: IN MANILA PRESS, IT'S "CORAZON WHO?"

To overcome this press blackout, Mark Brown and the other advisers devised a scheme at once elaborate and simple. It was based on the principle in American journalism that a person about whom something negative is said is to be given an opportunity to respond. This meant that Marcos would be called upon to answer the charges about his real estate holdings and his war record. The Aquino campaigns in the United States and in Manila coordinated their efforts. Thus, McCoy alerted Brown in Manila when he knew that *The New York Times* story about the phony war medals was to run. Brown began preparing his candidate to seize the issue, while in New York Aquino advisers alerted the networks that the story was about to break. When it did, the networks called Marcos for a response. And then the linchpin of the scheme came into operation: Since anything Marcos said was news, the Philippine television stations naturally ran excerpts of Marcos's American television appearances. In order to make sense of his denials, Philippine journalists had to provide some background on the charges. Thus did the scandals reach the Philippine people.

But for all the clever efforts and overwhelming support Mrs. Aquino was gaining in the Philippines, the Reagan administration, or at least the president and his closest advisers, were still hanging in with Marcos.

Less than two weeks before the voting Reagan's chief of staff, Donald Regan, declared that even if Marcos were elected by "massive fraud," the Reagan administration, while condemning the fraud, would still "have to do business with Marcos." Regan, appearing on *This Week with David Brinkley,* added, "There are a lot of governments elected by fraud." Indeed there were, and the United States knew about the frauds, and the United States endorsed the governments. In the Panamanian election of 1984 a military strongman, General Manuel Antonio Noriega, stole the election for the military's candidate, Nicolás Ardito Barletta. The vote rigging and fraud were reported at the time to Washington by the CIA and the embassy in Panama, but Secretary of State Shultz attended the inauguration, bestowing the blessings of the Reagan administration.

Though Regan's statement that no matter what, Washington would do business with Marcos may have seemed cavalier, it was consistent with the policy of sticking with Marcos. While American liberals were working for Aquino and calling for Marcos's ouster, leading American conservatives were Marcos enthusiasts. Columnists Evans and Novak backed him by raising all the Red scares. The Philippine election was nothing less than one for "life-and-death," they intoned. An Aquino victory would mean not only change but "radical" change, they charged. They concluded that "the sound of her campaign is not liberal reform. It is revolutionary zeal for vengeance and change, promising an uncertain and dangerous future for the Philippines."

The most influential of Marcos's champions outside the government was Jeane Kirkpatrick, who in late 1985 was being championed by many on the political right as its next presidential candidate. At the 1984 Republican National Convention in Dallas, she had roused the crowd with a speech in which she sharply castigated the Democrats because of what she said was their propensity to "blame America first" for the problems in the world. Now, Kirkpatrick, in several of her syndicated columns, blamed Marcos's problems on Foreign Service officers, on Stephen Solarz, on journalists—on everybody but Marcos. "Marcos opponents in the U.S. Congress, the State Department and the press challenged his war record, his use of U.S. aid funds, his health, his ability to deal with the Communist New People's Army," she wrote. She didn't explain why there shouldn't be concern about the misuse of U.S. funds. Or even about Marcos's health. After all, hadn't Washington's lack of knowledge about the shah's cancer contributed to the devastating outcome in Iran? Nor was she troubled by the facts, for it hadn't been the State Department but a historian who had challenged Marcos's war record.* As for concern about Marcos's ability to deal with the New People's Army, no less an official than Admiral Crowe, chairman of the Joint Chiefs of Staff, was most alarmed, as well he should have been. Above all, however, Kirkpatrick blamed the press: ". . . from reading the American press, one would think that President Ferdinand Marcos is the 'focus of evil' in the world and that his government is the major threat to American interests in Asia. Day after day, American newspapers, news weeklies and network newscasts treat Marcos' real and imagined failures, inefficiencies and corruption as if they were extraordinary and unique. They are not. Of 159 member states of the United Nations, at least 100 are probably governed more poorly than the Philippines."

---

* Kirkpatrick wasn't the only one quick to blame the State Department for the wartime fraud stories. Charles Krauthammer of the *New Republic* saw them as part of "an orgy of meddling" in the Philippine election. A supporter of America's covert wars in Angola, Afghanistan, and Nicaragua, Krauthammer found "nothing covert to this operation" in the Philippines. "Administration officials," he was sure, "leak evidence, buried for 40 years, that Marcos fabricated his history as an anti-Japanese guerrilla in World War II. . . ." The next day Krauthammer was forced to run a correction when he discovered that it had not been Reagan administration officials who had leaked the documents but that the evidence had "emerged through the work of independent investigators." This correction ran before the Kirkpatrick column.

The former United Nations ambassador didn't mention any of those states that were more poorly governed. Though there certainly were some, they weren't governments that had received billions of dollars in U.S. aid over the years and had once been America's "showcase of democracy." There probably weren't more than a handful of states in that category. This was the tragic failure of the American policy: that in spite of all the U.S. aid and attention, the Philippines under Marcos was poorly governed. Kirkpatrick would have been hard pressed to come up with an example of a ruler and his wife whose corruption was more extraordinary, the Marcoses and their friends having salted away between $5 and $10 billion— in New York office buildings, European castles, Swiss bank accounts, offshore corporations. In embracing Marcos, Kirkpatrick pulled out the familiar conservative saw: Whatever Marcos was, the future might be worse. She ran through the litany: "Remember Fulgencio Batista of Cuba, Ngo Dinh Diem of Vietnam, Lon Nol of Cambodia, the shah of Iran, Anastasio Somoza of Nicaragua?" The message was clear: Better stay with Marcos. Then, for added fear, she threw in a reference to the "brutality" of the NPA, as "graphically described by *Time* magazine correspondent Ross H. Munro in the current issue of *Commentary* magazine." Kirkpatrick's comments could not be dismissed lightly. They reflected the thinking of most of those around Reagan.

Though conservative political ideology might be setting the country's political course, and Ronald Reagan was at the helm, the president and his conservative allies couldn't control everything. They couldn't control Marcos, whose cheating in the election was so massive that it couldn't be ignored. They couldn't control the media, which brought the election cheating and violence into the living rooms on the evening news and onto the breakfast tables in the morning papers. And most of all, not Ronald Reagan, not Donald Regan, not anyone else in the White House could control the one man who it seemed would be the most reliable ally. That man was Richard Green Lugar, Republican senator from Indiana. It was he who delivered a blow to Marcos, and to the White House policy, from which there was no recovery. It may not have been the final punch, but it was decisive, all the more potent because it was unexpected.

Lugar was a moderate conservative and loyal to the president.

405

But when he went to observe the election in the Philippines and saw the fraud, he refused to look the other way. Some of his aides joked that Lugar was particularly well qualified to recognize electoral fraud, being from Indiana. His press spokesman, Mark Helmke, liked to recall how as a boy, in a politically active family, his grandfather had taught him to insert a piece of metal in a voting machine to prevent the pull of the lever next to an opponent's name from registering. It was generally accepted that to win in Gary, Indiana, it was necessary to steal 20,000 votes. Lugar, a fifth-generation Hoosier, had some firsthand exposure to electoral skulduggery. In his first run for mayor of Indianapolis in 1967, Lugar, who was thirty-five, faced an opponent whose brother was the district attorney; on election day many of Lugar's poll watchers were conveniently arrested.

It was a combination of the vicissitudes of the American political system and shrewd maneuvering by Lugar's staff that set the stage for him to play the hero's role in the return of democracy to the Philippines. It had begun in 1985, when Lugar, first elected to the Senate eight years earlier, became chairman of the Senate Foreign Relations Committee. The chairmanship was available because Charles Percy, Republican of Illinois, had been defeated, in part because conservatives had campaigned against him, viewing him as too moderate. With Percy out, the conservatives wanted Jesse Helms to take over the committee chairmanship, as he could have done, being the Republican with the most seniority. How different history might have been—and in the Philippines it almost certainly would have been—had Helms, a strident conservative who routinely supported dictators as long as they were anti-Communist, become chairman. But a senator may be chairman of only one committee, and Helms, bowing to the pressures of the powerful tobacco growers in his home state of North Carolina, chose the Agriculture Committee, where he could protect tobacco subsidies.

As chairman of the Foreign Relations Committee Lugar hadn't devoted much attention to the Philippines until his aide Fred Brown returned from his two trips with the dire reports and began lobbying his senator to become involved. The Rhodes scholar learned quickly about the archipelago, and when Marcos called the "snap election," Lugar began to move. First, he sent a letter to Marcos. As committee chairman Lugar had earned a reputation for being able to fashion bipartisan support for a policy, so the letter was signed by the ranking Democrat on the Foreign Relations Committee, Claiborne Pell of Rhode Island, and the ranking Democrat on the East Asian sub-committee—and one of the most liberal members of the Senate—Alan Cranston of California. The letter, also signed by the chairman of the East Asian subcommittee, Frank Murkowski, who was now beginning to pay some attention to the Philippines, outlined what Marcos needed to do to ensure a free and fair election; in other words, congressional meddling in Philippine domestic politics was bipartisan.

One of the conditions the four senators established was "equal access to the media, including radio and television." Marcos and the Reagan White House were trapped by this condition. If Marcos allowed equal access, he would lose, and if he didn't, his critics in the United States would argue that it had been a fraudulent election because one of the very conditions set by Lugar had not been met.

In addition to the letter, Lugar and Pell asked an independent organization, the Center for Democracy, to go to Manila in early December, to examine the preparations being made for the election and determine whether the election would be fair. It was a cautious move, the delegation members being selected to ensure that there would not be any radical, or even liberal, proposals. The center was headed by Allen Weinstein, a university professor and author who described himself as a Democratic supporter of Ronald Reagan. Upon returning from a week in Manila, Weinstein and the five other members of his delegation hastily drafted their report, under pressure from Lugar, who wanted to bring it before the public before the long Christmas recess.

The center's report touched all the bases: the media, the military, ballot boxes, registration of voters, and the organizations that would monitor the election. One was the official government organization, the Commission on Elections (COMELEC). In their letter Lugar and Pell had called on Marcos to appoint "a genuinely impartial" COMELEC. It was another trap because Marcos could not win a free election. The commission was not "genuinely impartial," its members being appointed by Marcos and beholden to him. Again, therefore, if Marcos had won, his critics could argue that this con-dition had not been satisfied.

The other monitoring organization was the National Citizens

Movement for Free Elections (NAMFREL), which was, as its name implied, a citizens' organization to monitor elections. NAMFREL relied heavily on trained volunteers to observe the voting on election day. Lugar and Pell had called on Marcos to accredit NAMFREL and to ensure that it could "function freely, having full access to polling places nationwide." NAMFREL's roots went back to the early 1950s, when it was created by Ed Lansdale with CIA funds for the campaign of Ramón Magsaysay. The organization had disappeared during the martial law years but been resurrected in 1983, and it had played a vital role in Assembly elections in May 1984, elections which were considerably more fraudulent than the Reagan administration acknowledged but which were less so than they would have been without NAMFREL.

The United States was to fund NAMFREL for the 1986 election, though NAMFREL and American officials repeatedly denied that it had received any American money. NAMFREL leaders said that it had been offered but refused, while in fact NAMFREL had initiated at least one request for funding. Various stratagems were used to channel the money to the group. A principal route was through the organizations that made up NAMFREL, altogether nearly 100, from the Bishops-Businessmen's Conference for Human Development to the Girl Scouts of the Philippines to the Philippine Amateur Radio Association. The Agency for International Development (AID) gave at least $300,000 to NAMFREL through these organizations.

NAMFREL also received money from the National Endowment for Democracy (NED), which had been set up in 1983 after Reagan had called on the private sector to help spread the American way around the world. The endowment received its funds from Congress (that is, from American taxpayers) and in turn made grants to international organizations, most of them conservative and controversial. Weinstein had been NED's acting president until he was replaced by Carl Gershman, a former aide to Jeane Kirkpatrick. Congressman John Conyers, a liberal Democrat from Michigan, once blasted NED as "clearly one of the most mischievous and unjustified expenditures of public funds that we've seen in some time." The congressional law creating NED, Conyers wrote, "should really be known as the Taxpayer Funding for Foreign Elections

Act." In the 1984 presidential election in Panama $20,000 of NED money had gone to Barletta, the man who fraudulently won. In the Philippines at least $3 million was "quietly being spent to fight the communist insurgency . . . and to cultivate political leaders there," the *San Francisco Examiner* reported in July 1985. Some of that money was channeled to NAMFREL.

Altogether, according to individuals familiar with the funding and the mechanisms, slightly less than $1 million was provided NAMFREL. In addition, the organization received money, surreptitiously, from the Japanese government and Japanese businessmen. Major "contributors" were American businessmen living in the Philippines who were members of an organization called Republicans Abroad. An offshoot of the National Republican party (the Democrats have a similar organization, though not as large), Republicans Abroad chapters exist in nearly every country and are a source of donations and absentee votes. (After the Philippine election, during those tense days when the pressure was on Reagan to abandon Marcos and accept Aquino, the argument was made, somewhat impishly by those with knowledge of this funding mechanism, "But, Mr. President, the Republicans are for Cory. She's a Republican.")

NAMFREL didn't use all the money for the election. It in turn was quietly supporting the Reform the Armed Forces Movement (RAM), that group of officers who were seeking to end the corruption within the military and had the enthusiastic endorsement of U.S. officials, from Bosworth in Manila to Armacost and Armitage in Washington.

Putting aside the issue of secret American intervention in the Philippines' domestic politics, funding NAMFREL, and RAM, could be viewed as neutral, designed to foster democracy. But though ostensibly neutral, NAMFREL, again like RAM, was a haven for anti-Marcos forces, almost by definition: Anything that fostered democracy was ipso facto anti-Marcos. But the tilt toward Aquino didn't stop there. The United States also secretly funded Radio Veritas, the church-owned radio station in the Philippines, probably the most widely respected and listened-to voice of opposition to Marcos. Conservatives in the administration who were pro-Marcos allowed the funding of NAMFREL and Radio Veritas for a number of reasons. In part, it was because they were sufficiently knowledgeable about the Philippines and the organizations to realize what they were beneath their ostensibly neutral surfaces. Additionally, the conservatives were confident that Marcos could win; his victory would have a seal of approval if NAMFREL were a credible watchdog.

As election day drew near, the only major issue remaining pertained to American observers. As chairman of the Senate Foreign Relations Committee, and having sent the Weinstein team to the Philippines, Lugar was the obvious choice to lead a delegation. But he had very mixed feelings. He liked the process of politics, and his experience as an official observer to the Guatemalan elections in 1985 had had a positive impact on him. In that Central American country, Washington's intervention had been successful, a moderate Christian Democrat, Vinicio Cerezo, emerging as the first democratically elected civilian president after a succession of brutal military regimes. But the chances for a successful outcome in the Philippines weren't as great as they had been in Guatemala or in El Salvador before that. Both those elections had been virtually run by the United States, from the ballot boxes to the devices to guard against double voting to the counting of the ballots. Marcos wasn't about to allow that. So it seemed like a no-win situation to Lugar. If it were a fraudulent election and he gave a seal of approval, he would be tarnished. If Marcos cheated, and Lugar said so, the White House and conservatives would not be pleased. But Wolfowitz at State and Armitage at Defense were pressing Lugar, and Shultz himself made an appeal. Lugar agreed to go.

"This is when the White House really starts screwing around," says an aide to Lugar. Again the White House was trapped, by Lugar and the State Department, working together. The White House wasn't anxious to send observers to this election. The reports from Manila, from the embassy and the CIA, were that as in the past, Marcos was preparing to cheat to the full extent necessary and that he would have to do so in order to defeat Mrs. Aquino. It would be easier to continue supporting Marcos if Americans didn't observe the fraud. But Marcos had invited observers, and Lugar, a respected Republican leader in the Senate, had volunteered to go. It was a bit difficult for the White House to say no. Moreover, observer teams had served the administration well. They had endorsed the fraudulent Panamanian election and their endorsement of the Salvadoran elections in 1982 and 1984 (in which the CIA spent $2-$3 million to bring about the desired outcome) had been a tremendous boost for the administration's policy in that country. The White House's hope was to put together a team that would do the same for the Philippine elections, a team it could control and count on to endorse a fraud.

The members of the observer team were decided in negotiations among Lugar, who agreed to go only if he were involved in the selection process, the State Department, and the White House. Lugar wanted a bipartisan team. Solarz was the obvious Democratic leader. He declined, knowing that the election would be fraudulent and not wanting to be in the position of endorsing it. The ranking Democrat was John P. Murtha, congressman from Johnstown, Pennsylvania, who became cochair of the official delegation. Murtha's role in the ultimately successful outcome was far greater than he was publicly credited for, his failure to be acknowledged in part because of his relatively quiet demeanor, which in this case was compounded by Lugar's virtual monopoly of the media attention. Most of the other members were selected not because they knew anything about foreign policy or the Philippines (the two exceptions being Larry Niksch, the Philippine specialist at the Congressional Research Service, and Allen Weinstein, who had studied the process in December) but because of domestic politics, good old-fashioned logrolling. Thus, Senate Majority Leader Robert Dole, from Kansas, was successful in placing the Kansas secretary of state, Jack H. Brier, on the team. The White House political operatives wanted Norma Paulus, thinking the exposure would help her in her race for governor of Oregon. (It might have helped, but not enough. Paulus lost in November 1986.) One of Lugar's choices was Van P. Smith, from Indiana, a former president of the U.S. Chamber of Commerce. Lugar also wanted Otis Chandler, chairman of the *Los Angeles Times* publishing company. Chandler agreed to go, but the White House, doing all it could to subvert the observer team—"really dragging its feet" on the whole observer issue, was how a State Department officer put it—delayed so long that by the time it said yes, Chandler had other commitments.

411

As possible members of the observer team for the Philippine elections, the State Department sent eighty to ninety names to the White House. It cut most of them as too liberal, too independent, too unreliable. The White House "wanted a safe team," says a State Department officer, adding that the group that was sent was "very conservative." The White House secretly had some assistance in putting it together from Marcos's public relations firm, Black, Manafort, Stone & Kelly, which vetoed people on State's list and added names of its own. This angered Lugar, who didn't mind trading with other politicians and the White House but thought that outsiders and clear partisans should not be involved. One of those whom the White House put on the team was Fred Fielding, the president's White House lawyer. "He was our watchdog, and so be it; we all knew it," says Helmke, Lugar's press secretary, who was on the trip. Patrick Buchanan, the most ideologically conservative member of the White House staff, suggested Ben J. Wattenberg, a prominent neoconservative commentator and writer, and Mortimer B. Zuckerman, a real estate developer as well as chairman of the *Atlantic Monthly* and editor in chief of *U.S. News & World Report.** Neither of these men had been on the long State Department list. Zuckerman wasn't contacted about being an observer until five days before the group was to leave. "It came out of the blue," he says, adding that he had to cancel thirty-two appointments in order to go.

The first skirmishes within the observer team occurred on the plane, somewhere between Alaska and Tokyo. Fielding began arguing that the delegation should shorten the amount of time it would spend in the Philippines. The voting was to be on Friday, and the delegation had planned to remain until Monday. Fielding asserted that for reasons of security and safety it should not remain that long. It was a specious argument. The most significant fraud might come

---

* The members of the U.S. presidential delegation were: Lugar; Murtha; Senator Thad Cochran, Republican of Mississippi; Senator Frank Murkowski, Republican of Alaska; Senator John F. Kerry, Democrat of Massachusetts; Representative Samuel S. Stratton, Democrat of New York; Representative Robert Livingston, Republican of Louisiana; Representative Jerry Lewis, Republican of California; Representative Bernard J. Dwyer, Democrat of New Jersey; Jack Brier, secretary of state, Kansas; Fred Fielding; Admiral Robert L. J. Long; Natalie Meyer, secretary of state, Colorado; Reverend Adam J. Maida, Green Bay, Wisconsin; Larry Niksch; Norma Paulus; Van P. Smith; Ben J. Wattenberg; Allen Weinstein; Mortimer B. Zuckerman.

not on voting day but in the counting that followed. Fielding wanted the team out of the country before that happened. A bitter argument ensued. Lugar's aides were strenuously opposed to the early return, and at one point the senator snapped at them "to shut up." Upon landing in Tokyo, Fielding called the White House to bring the president abreast of what was happening; a State Department officer with the delegation, John Finney, who was Maisto's deputy, alerted Bosworth in Manila about the maneuvering to get the delegation out of the Philippines quickly. When the delegation arrived, Bosworth, who early on had urged Washington to send observers, took Lugar aside and explained why it was critical that the observers remain until Monday. They did.

Friday, February 7, was voting day. It was also the day that halfway around the world, another long-reigning corrupt dictator and his avaricious spouse were forced to flee their country: President Jean-Claude ("Baby Doc") Duvalier and his wife, Michele, of Haiti. They departed the island nation they had bled and impoverished in a U.S. military jet. In the Philippines the American observers fanned out across the country. At a high school in Makati Lugar watched as the votes were tabulated. According to the regulations governing the election, tabulated votes were to be sent immediately to the Commission on Elections (COMELEC), where they were to be posted for public observation. A few hours later, when Lugar went to the COMELEC headquarters, the Makati votes had not been posted. He was disturbed.

A key issue in the fairness of the election was the "quick count." The classic ploy of dictators around the world has long been to stop the count when results start to show that they are losing, then to resume it after the alterations have been made to provide the margin of victory. Thus, from the beginning of the involvement in the Philippine election, there had been an emphasis on a quick count. Lugar and Pell had made it one of the conditions in their letter to Marcos in November; Weinstein and the Center for Democracy had discussed its importance in their report. Lugar, once again moving Reagan into a corner, wrote in his letter to the president accepting the appointment as head of the observer delegation that the quick count would be "of special interest to the official U.S. observer delegation."

When Lugar asked the COMELEC officials why the Makati count hadn't been recorded, he was assured that it would be very soon. Lugar returned to the Manila Hotel and spoke with Bosworth, who informed him that on the basis of the reports coming in from embassy officials in the field, Aquino was doing even better than expected. After dinner Lugar returned to COMELEC. It was now about ten o'clock; the vote tabulations Lugar had seen several hours earlier in Makati still had not been recorded. Lugar was convinced he was being lied to. For him, that was the turning point.

Lugar spoke out. "I think we're in a situation where obviously the count has been slowed and obviously someone is worried," he said. He also commented on what he said was "frankly a very disturbing pattern" of fraud and violence in the election. Lugar's statement angered other members of the delegation. On the flight to Manila they had agreed that no one would make any statement until the group could gather and issue one jointly. The leader of the delegation was violating the agreement.

Down in Mindanao, where he had spent the day hopping from village to village in a helicopter, Graeme Bannerman, staff director of the Senate Foreign Relations Committee, heard his boss's remarks about the election. He was stunned. It wasn't just that Bannerman was a conservative who thought a Marcos victory in a clean election would be best for the Philippines (a view that some thought pulled Lugar one way, while Fred Brown, who was also along, pulled the senator the other). It was more that Bannerman had been sent to Mindanao to keep a leash on Senator John Kerry, the most liberal member of the observer delegation, to prevent him from spouting off, but here was his boss, the conservative Richard Lugar, speaking out.

On Sunday afternoon the observers gathered at the embassy, to hear each other's reports and to prepare a joint statement. It was a "contentious, vociferous meeting," as one described it.

"We are telling Washington," Bosworth said in reference to the embassy's reporting, "there was a systematic effort to limit the vote and manage the number. Not just computer glitches, but the insipid [sic] manipulation of a fragile process." Lugar explained that from 10 to 40 percent of the voters might have been disenfranchised, kept even from casting their vote through a purge from the registration roles of people thought to be pro Aquino. It was the "boldest stroke," Lugar said, and "something we weren't even watching for."

The conservatives in the delegation wanted to stress the positives of the process: the enthusiasm of voters; the role of NAMFREL. "We saw an extremely stirring vision of democracy," Wattenberg said. "No matter who wins, this was good for the United States." A few days later, after returning to the United States, he described the election as "a very poetic display of democracy which in many ways was more open and public than what we have in the United States." Fielding, during the meeting, urged the delegation not to issue any statement. "We shouldn't involve ourselves further."

Senator Kerry and Allen Weinstein led the effort for a statement that condemned the fraud. Kerry cautioned, however, that it not be so strong that Marcos could use it to declare the election null and void. That would have meant that Marcos could continue in office until a new election; the CIA had gathered some intelligence that Marcos was preparing to do just that. Because of his liberal politics, Kerry risked being dismissed by conservative members of the delegation, who made up a strong majority. Therefore, rather than get out front, he allied himself with Lugar, careful to avoid anti-Marcos rantings, couching his positions in moderate language. Admiral Robert L. J. Long, a former commander in chief of U.S. forces in the Pacific (CINCPAC), also stressed the importance of mentioning the fraud in the statement. "We have to make a gloved threat to Marcos."

After a discussion that lasted nearly three hours, Lugar assigned aides from his staff, Murtha's staff, and Allen Weinstein, to draft a statement. They expected to have it ready in a couple of hours. But each draft precipitated a fight, with the conservatives trying to water it down, the drafters wanting to toughen it. Back and forth the drafts went, until six o'clock in the morning. The conservatives prevailed. The statement stressed the "passionate commitment of Filipinos to democracy," the "vigorous campaign," "lively debate," and long lines of people waiting to vote, a demonstration of the Filipinos' "faith in democracy." The fraud was addressed in only one paragraph: "Sadly, however, we have witnessed and heard disturbing reports to undermine the integrity of [the electoral] process . . . serious charges have been made in regard to the tabulation system."

415

The statement would have been an even greater whitewash of the fraud and endorsement of the election had it not been for one event on Sunday evening. It was the turning point for many of the delegation, conservatives and liberals agree, and caused them later to issue individual statements stronger than the joint declaration. Francis X. Clines, of *The New York Times,* captured the event best, in one sentence of his story: "Weeping and fearful, the Government computer workers arose from their terminals and, data disks in hand, darted from the Commission on Elections to make the charge that the Marcos Government was rigging the presidential vote." The computer workers made their way to safety and refuge in the Church of Our Mother of Perpetual Help, where a crowd gathered to pray and cheer for them. Several members of the observer delegation rushed to the church. It was a dramatic moment. "The church incident revealed that many young people were willing to take risks in order to express their concerns," Zuckerman said. "What affected me was the fact that these people were willing to walk out under very dangerous circumstances." (On his return to the United States, however, Zuckerman continued to stress the positives of the election and criticized the press for dwelling too much on the fraud. "Violence, intimidation, fraud and voter disenfranchisement made headlines in the United States, but they were not nearly as newsworthy in the Philippines," Zuckerman wrote. "What is newsworthy, in my judgment, is that we have seen the creation and operation of a new structure for Philippine democracy.")

By the next morning, Monday, two of the conservative delegates, Senator Cochran and Admiral Long, had been converted, "radicalized," said one member of the delegation. Cochran, whose conservative ratings were in the eighties and who was a Reagan administration loyalist, pointedly wore his yellow golf slacks, Aquino's campaign color. When the delegation stopped in Hawaii, en route home, it became clear that Admiral Long had also turned around. Long, who after his retirement had been appointed the chairman of the commission that investigated the bombing of the Marine headquarters in Beirut in November 1983, was put on the Philippine observer team to ensure that the delegation would appreciate the strategic importance of the archipelago. In Honolulu, at his old CINCPAC headquarters, an air force brigadier general, during a briefing, routine for a delegation of this stature, defended the Philippine elections, saying that there had not been that much fraud. The retired admiral interrupted, bluntly informing the officer that he was wrong.

Before departing from the Philippines, Murtha had a conversation with Bosworth and an aide. "It's very clear to me what's happened," Murtha said. "The people want him [Marcos] out, and he doesn't want to go." The observations had an impact. Murtha is "an ex-marine who doesn't say much," an embassy officer noted. "Just the opposite of Lugar, who talks and talks. But when he [Murtha] does say something, you listen."

It was over for Marcos—at least as far as the embassy, the State Department, critical members of Congress, and many influential conservatives were concerned. After the election Marcos even lost George Will. It had been Manafort's strategy to put Marcos before the American public as often as possible, believing that he could captivate the American people as he had American officials for twenty years. Marcos was everywhere: several times on *Nightline*; NBC's *Meet the Press* and CBS's *Face the Nation;* ABC's *Good Morning America* and NBC's *Today;* CNN's *Crossfire;* PBS's *MacNeil/Lehrer* and John McLaughlin's *One on One*. The strategy backfired. Marcos exposed himself for what he was. On the Sunday after the election, he was on *This Week with David Brinkley,* again. Asked about the charges of fraud, he denied them emphatically. As for the slow count, well, he said, that was because some of the country's towns "are in the mountains," and he placed the blame on "foul weather . . . a depression and the winds are very high . . . accidents." It was becoming a verbal slapstick routine, the journalists playing straight man to Marcos. How was it possible, David Brinkley asked, that in one town Marcos had received 13,643 votes and Aquino 0? Marcos could explain that: The town was close to his hometown; the voters were "probably my relatives."

George Will brought up the war medals issue. He noted that one of Marcos's defenses to the fraudulent war record charge was that the Japanese emperor Hirohito, in his memoirs, had attested to Marcos's exploits against the Japanese during the war. How could

417

that be, Will wondered, since "the only public words by Emperor Hirohito are on marine biology and botany"? Marcos answered: "If you think—if you, the Americans, who are our allies think that I was not in this, then you should read the memoirs of his majesty, the Emperor, in his memoirs he speaks of Marcos—"

Will cut him off. "They've not been published, sir!"

Later Will called the White House. Their man Marcos, he said, was an "inveterate liar." State Department officials who learned of Will's loss of faith were delighted. Now the task was to convince the president of the United States. In the end it was the Filipino people who did so.

17 : To the End

The observer team was on the way to the Manila Airport when Ambassador Bosworth informed Senator Lugar that because of the escalating crisis, Secretary of State George Shultz would like him to come directly to Washington to brief President Reagan. In spite of all the reports the embassy had been sending about the fraud, the White House was still clinging to Marcos. Lugar had planned to go from the Philippines to Indiana, not wanting to be another Foreign Relations Committee chairman who fell victim to constituents who thought the man they elected should be paying less attention to foreigners and more to their needs. A suitcase with his winter clothes, including a cold-weather jogging suit, was waiting for him in Indianapolis. But having come this far with the Philippine election, Lugar couldn't turn back now. Nor could he say no to the president.

Lugar arrived at Andrews Air Base about midnight, and knowing that the White House was upset with his comments about the fraud, he avoided the reporters waiting in the cold rain. At ten the next morning, Tuesday, he appeared at the White House, along with Murtha. Fielding was present, as were Reagan's national security adviser, John M. Poindexter; Chief of Staff Regan; and Secretary Shultz. Knowing that Bosworth had been under bitter attack from all quarters—Fielding had sent messages from Manila accusing him of being in Aquino's camp; Imelda Marcos had unleashed her tirades about him to Nancy Reagan; Marcos himself did the same in his almost daily conversations with Laxalt—Lugar made a point of praising Bosworth and the embassy staff. (After the meeting Shultz thanked Lugar for his support of the beleaguered ambassador.) During the thirty-five-minute meeting, described by one observer as "very serious," Lugar summarized for the president the fraud and violence that had marked the election. Still concerned that Marcos was looking for a reason to declare the election null and void, the senator was careful not to go too far. Lugar realized later that maybe the strategy had been a mistake, that his caution had reinforced what the conservatives were saying: that the fraud hadn't been as bad as the embassy and press were reporting it to be. For the most part Reagan listened, asking few questions, speaking anecdotally. At one point the president made reference to having seen Aquino supporters dumping ballots in the street. Lugar didn't know what he was talking about, and his aides never were able to find when and where the purported scene had been televised.

That evening Reagan held a news conference. The first question, from Mike Putzel of the Associated Press, was, as expected, about the Philippine election: "The observers you sent to the Philippines have just returned with reports that they witnessed fraud and violence. Couldn't this undermine the credibility of the elections and strengthen the hand of the Communist insurgents in the islands?"

Reagan, behind the podium in the red-carpeted East Room, answered: "Well, Mike, I'm, I am just not going to comment on this process, just as they are not going to render an official report until the counting has finally been finished."

That was the answer the president's advisers had prepared him to give. But Putzel followed up: "Did what they tell you give you concern about the credibility there and what the impact will be for U.S. interests in the Philippines?"

Reagan answered: "Well, I think that we're concerned about the violence that was evident there and the possibility of fraud, although it could have been that all of that was occurring on both sides. . . ."

That was the clangor reported around the world. Later, after the absurdity of the remark had generated an outpouring of rage, Reagan's advisers sought to limit the damage to the president. They portrayed it as an inadvertent and innocuous misstatement, one that didn't reflect U.S. policy. The *Washington Post* wrote: "Officials said a communications failure beginning with the president caused the confusion, rather than the kind of deep-seated divisions that exist among Reagan's top advisers on many other issues." *Time* called it "a flub pure and simple."

It had not been a flub. The statement reflected the policy, at least as it existed in the White House. And there was division in the ranks. The State Department knew that Marcos had been responsible for the fraud, and it was now even more strongly convinced that the United States should not stick by him. The White House intended to stay with Marcos, fraud or not. That was precisely what Donald Regan had said the week before the election. Moreover, the president believed there had been fraud by both sides. That was what Marcos was saying. Reagan was hearing it from Nancy Reagan, who was being fed that line by Imelda Marcos. And Marcos's public relations firm, Black, Manafort, Stone & Kelly, was advancing the same line within Reagan's conservative inner circle.

To counter, Aquino's people in New York went to work immediately. John Scanlon, a New York public relations consultant who had been retained by the Aquino campaign, called Peter Jennings at ABC and introduced one of Aquino's team to the ABC anchor; for forty-five minutes they talked, the Aquino aide explaining that the fraud had been by Marcos. Scanlon made similar introductions to network anchors Tom Brokaw and Dan Rather. But all this lobbying may not have been necessary; the events now had a propulsion of their own and played out on the stage for the electronic global village.

There were a few thousand journalists, including technicians, in the Philippines for the elections. NBC's Tom Brokaw had anchored his show from there, as had Jennings. CBS had moved its entire election polling team to the Philippines, even building a transmission tower in Mindanao in order to send the results back quickly. Every night there was something on the evening news about the elections—for the four-week election period a total of some 180 minutes on the three evening network news shows, compared with an average of fewer than three Philippine stories per year between 1972 and 1981. Marcos consumed much of that television time now, and the more Americans saw him, the more they recoiled, convinced, as was George Will, that he was a liar. And everything news watchers were seeing convinced them that Marcos had stolen the election from this saintly woman in yellow. There were pictures of bodies of people who had been murdered, nearly all of them, it seemed, Aquino campaign workers. The scene of the workers' walking out of COMELEC and going to the church had been shown and re-shown. On the day of Reagan's news conference six masked gunmen chased a leader of Aquino's campaign, Evelio Javier, forty-three years old, across the square in San José de Buenavista, leveled their rifles, and shot him dead. It was reported on the front pages of American newspapers and broadcast on the evening news along with President Reagan's speech. The funeral a few days later was shown on television.

Congress was in recess the week after the Philippine election, and in districts from Maine to California senators and representatives were being told that it was time for the United States to dump Marcos. Lugar was hearing that even from his constituents. In the middle of Reagan country, they were in love with Cory Aquino. Lugar was attending Lincoln Day dinners and Chamber of Commerce lunches, and all he was hearing from Republican businessmen was adulation for Aquino. He also heard praise for his role; for once, people were telling him, America had come down on the side of the good guys instead of the dictators.

Thirty-six hours after Reagan's statement Lugar told an Associated Press reporter in South Bend that the president was "not well informed." It was a strong statement for a Republican senator about his president. It was not, however, the only one reflecting the public outrage. In Salem, Oregon, Republican Senator Mark Hatfield, who had been entertained at Malacañang on the day of Aquino's funeral, called on Marcos to resign. Republican Dole of Kansas reacted to Reagan's remark by publicly asking the Pentagon to undertake priority studies about relocating the bases. The most outspoken was Georgia Senator Sam Nunn.

Again, it was Robert Trent Jones, Jr., who had brought Nunn into the fray on behalf of Mrs. Aquino. Jones had first met Nunn during a round of golf on California's Monterey Peninsula in the late 1970s. Over the years they had played golf, and the friendship had grown. After Reagan's news conference Jones reached Nunn who was in Geneva observing the arms negotiations. En route back to the United States, Nunn prepared his response, which he read to Jones before he sent it. Declaring that Aquino was the winner, Nunn charged that Marcos was trying "to steal the election by massive fraud, intimidation and murder." He called on Reagan to notify

Marcos that all U.S. aid to the Philippines "will be terminated if the will of the Philippine voters, as expressed at the ballot box, is not followed." The protest by the Democratic senator was amplified because he was the ranking Democrat on the Armed Services Committee and, even more, because he frequently supported the president on defense, security, and foreign policy issues, including the MX and aid to the contras.

But Reagan's news conference statement struck hardest in the Philippines, sweeping away everything in the path to restoring democracy, like one of the typhoons that frequently savage the islands. For a few days Americans had been heroes, greeted more enthusiastically than they had been since their country liberated the islands during World War II. Filipinos generally considered that Marcos had been pushed to the election by Americans, and they were aware of what Lugar had been saying. Reagan's statement swiftly dissipated all the goodwill. "I have never been so ashamed to be an American," recalled Charles Krause, who had been in many parts of the world where American policy wasn't very popular, including Nicaragua and El Salvador. Krause, who had worked for the *Washington Post* and CBS before joining *MacNeil/Lehrer,* had been invited to a dinner party by some wealthy Filipinos. After Reagan's statement he wasn't much in the mood. "I wanted to crawl under the bed and hide. . . . I just did not want to see or talk to any Filipinos, I felt so ashamed." But he went, and he spent the evening unable to explain Reagan's remark to the small group of upper-class Filipinos. "They were bewildered."

Embassy officers, exhausted after weeks of numbingly long hours, were demoralized. "It was a real body blow," recalled one senior officer. "We couldn't explain to our friends; we couldn't explain to our enemies, to anyone. They just couldn't understand how the president of the United States could say that." Above all, they couldn't explain it to themselves. They had worked so hard. Practically the entire embassy staff had been pressed into service for the elections. A week before the voting two-person teams had been sent to provinces near and far, to observe the election process. Some of the teams knew their provinces well. When the reports about the insurgency began to have an impact in Washington, Morton Abramowitz had encouraged the embassy to set up a system whereby officers would become experts in provinces where the NPA was strong; it was designed to avoid another Vietnam. Now their expertise was being put to use for the election. Some of the teams were in areas so remote that they had no telephone connections to Manila. But they were equipped with the most sophisticated military communications equipment.

After voting day the teams remained out in the field, not like the international observers, who scurried back to Manila, to hot baths, clean sheets, and ample food. The embassy teams fed their reports to Manila, to the operation on the third floor set up by political counselor Scott Hallford. They were collated, analyzed, summarized, and then forwarded on to Washington. Nothing in the embassy's reporting about the election supported what the president had said about fraud occurring on both sides. Indeed, their reports and those of the CIA were unequivocal: Marcos had "stolen the shit out of this election," as one intelligence official in Washington graphically described the nature of the reports from Manila. Members of the observer team might want to deemphasize the fraud; Wattenberg might think that what he saw was "poetic democracy." To the embassy and the CIA it was theft—grand larceny. One prominent Filipino told the embassy that if he were going to write a book about the election, he would title it *How to Cheat and Lose Your People.* He told how in towns in a province controlled by the Kilusang Bagong Lipunan (KBL; Marcos's party), mayors, "some carrying sidearms, and all accompanied by armed bodyguards, had moved brazenly around on election day, brandishing guns near voting lines and 'encouraging' voters to vote for Marcos. . . . [G]oons fired guns in the air to scare off voters, and ballot boxes were stolen." Altogether the KBL had spent an estimated $1 million in the province. In general, the embassy cabled Washington, the Filipino "described a "scenario we have heard and seen all too frequently in the last few days: massive KBL vote buying, disenfranchisement in opposition strongholds, vote padding in KBL areas, widespread intimidation of voters and NAMFREL by armed thugs and to a lesser extent by the military, ballot boxes stolen in opposition areas, etc." From Cebu the embassy sent a cable with the caption "KBL caught with hand in cookie jar during provincial canvassing session." One KBL poll watcher "was caught trying to slip a fake tally sheet (at his feet under the table) into the pile of authentic ones."

By Sunday night, two days before Reagan spoke, the CIA had calculated and reported that Aquino had won about 60 percent of the vote—and that was *after* taking into account the intimidation of voters, the disenfranchisement of Aquino voters, the padding of the rolls with Marcos voters. Even the embassy was surprised. So was Marcos. "The vote that she got shocked him," said an American who talked with him a few days after the election. "He wasn't prepared for that."

The embassy's shock at Reagan's statement was mixed with anger and outrage. "Why have we been working so hard?" they cried in effect. "We might as well turn the country over to the Communists and go home!" Then they gathered their collective composure and, working with the department in Washington, set about to stop the hemorrhaging, to save the president of the United States from his own blundering. Ambassador Bosworth, who urged his staff not to let their emotions cloud their professionalism, personally went to see Mrs. Aquino. It was one of the most unpleasant missions in his diplomatic career. He was "very embarrassed, very ashamed," recalled an Aquino aide who was present. As diplomatically as possible the ambassador told Mrs. Aquino to ignore what his president had said, that sometimes the policy moved slowly, but that she should have faith, the president would be moved. Secretary of State Shultz asked Bob Jones to call on Mrs. Aquino, and Jones's message was similar.

Time was running out. Filipinos weren't waiting for Washington. On Friday, February 14, one week after the election, the Catholic Bishops' Conference of the Philippines issued a statement calling the fraud "unparalleled." The bishops condemned the "systematic disenfranchisement of voters . . . widespread and massive vote-buying . . . the deliberate tampering with the election returns . . . intimidation, harassment, terrorism and murder." Then they added pointedly, "According to moral principles, a government that assumes or retains power through fraudulent means has no moral basis."

It was a powerful statement, made more so because although there had always been some outspoken bishops, they were very few in number, and the 103-member Bishops' Conference was quite conservative. Marcos responded on the *CBS Evening News,* angrily declaring, "They [the Aquino people] used priests and nuns not only to help the opposition but to destroy the electoral process. . . . We have pictures showing how priests and nuns were intimidating and coercing people."

The bishops called for a "nonviolent struggle for justice." Meanwhile, the violence was accelerating. In the preceding few days the mutilated and decapitated bodies of ten Aquino supporters had been found in Quirino Province. Some had been hanged from trees; three young women at Quirino State College who had worked for the opposition were raped, mutilated, and killed. The opposition said altogether thirty of its workers were killed in the week following the election. Marcos on the *CBS Evening News* claimed it was his supporters who were being killed. "We can point to any number of people who have been killed, about sixty of them."

Into the storm rode the veteran diplomatic troubleshooter Philip C. Habib, the man for all crises, for all presidents. "Mr. Foreign Service" younger diplomats called him. The son of a Lebanese grocer in Brooklyn, New York, Habib began his Foreign Service career in 1949. He played a major role in the negotiations to end the Vietnam War; he was ambassador to South Korea, assistant secretary for East Asia under Ford. He was the number three man in the State Department during Vance's tenure as secretary, but only briefly, forced to retire in 1977 after a series of near-fatal heart attacks. It can hardly be said that he retired. He was sent on special assignments for Carter, and from 1981 to 1983 he was Reagan's special envoy to the Middle East, seeking the seemingly impossible: peace among the warring Syrians, Israelis, and various factions in Lebanon. Presidents liked him because he didn't talk. Gregariously gruff, the jowly Habib liked to banter with reporters, but he never revealed anything. Some of the missions he undertook in his career are still not known about publicly. Nor will they be, at least not from Habib. He didn't keep a journal or diary and has no plans to write his memoirs. That's for politicians, he says, not diplomats. The diplomat's role is to serve the president. If you disagree strongly enough about the policy, you resign. But no public statements.

Habib was on a golfing vacation in Florida when Shultz reached him the Sunday after the Philippine vote. Shultz wanted Habib to study up on four areas: South Africa, Central America, South Korea, and the Philippines. All were foreign policy hot spots, and the secretary said he'd let Habib know within a week where he'd be sent. Habib already had a ticket on a flight to return home to California; instead, he flew to Washington, not knowing where or when his next assignment would be. Within twenty-four hours he had his mission, publicly announced by Reagan during the fateful news conference.

Habib's mission further demoralized the embassy in Manila. The officers knew full well why he was being sent: The president of the United States didn't trust their reporting. Reagan was being told that the embassy had made camp with Aquino. The focus of the distrust was more than just the embassy, however. The conservative word being spread in Washington was that "it was the Carter administration running the Reagan administration's Philippine policy," as one conservative Marcos backer said scornfully. The suspect Carterites were Armacost, Bosworth, Abramowitz, Congressman Solarz, Richard Holbrooke, and Leslie Gelb of *The New York Times*. Gelb, who had served in the Carter State Department, was included because of a long article he had written about the evolution of the Reagan policy in the Philippines. The article, which began on the front page, had appeared one week before the Philippine election. Gelb wrote that during the past year "a consensus" had developed within the Reagan administration that "the departure of President Ferdinand E. Marcos" was in the best interests of the Philippines and the United States. The reaction to the article was furious. Conservatives were convinced that Gelb, "another Carter assistant secretary of state," as Evans and Novak labeled him in an attack on the Carterites, wasn't reporting policy but trying to make it. The "ringleader" behind the drive to oust Marcos, Evans and Novak declared, was Armacost. The conservative columnists conveniently overlooked the fact that Armacost had faithfully served Ronald Reagan while he was ambassador to the Philippines; it was easier to engage in "guilt" by association. With Holbrooke now solidly opposed to Marcos, Evans and Novak turned against him, forgetting that they had sided with him against Derian a few years earlier; the columnists branded Armacost for being Holbrooke's "close friend."

Shultz and Armacost were well aware that the Reagan White House and conservatives didn't trust most of the State Department types. Rather than sail into the gales, they smartly tacked with them. It was a clever maneuver to recommend Habib for the mission; Armacost had suggested it to Shultz, Shultz to Reagan. Reagan trusted Habib no matter what conservatives might holler. And Shultz and Armacost had no doubt that Habib would see, and then report, the situation exactly as the embassy had. The mission was also designed to buy time with Reagan, to keep him from making any more disastrous statements that would lock the United States into support for Marcos. The White House said it would not comment on the crisis until Habib returned with his report. Habib's job would then be "to educate the president," said a State Department officer. Though the mission was seen by some as a slap at Bosworth, the ambassador took it professionally. His ego was not so big that he could not accept assistance; it helped that he had known Habib for fifteen years. Bosworth, too, was certain that Habib would reach the same conclusions that he and his staff had. In an assignment seeming to underscore that the outcome was preordained, Habib's principal aide for the mission was John Maisto.

The day Habib and Maisto arrived in Manila, the National Assembly declared Marcos the victor, not surprisingly because Marcos's party controlled the legislature. It said Marcos had won 53.8 percent of the vote. Mrs. Aquino countered that she was the winner, with between 60 and 70 percent of the vote. "No tinsel and celebration of the president's make-believe win can hide his loss of moral and political authority," she said. "He is beaten."

Habib met first with Marcos, who tried to persuade the veteran diplomat that "it was a great election." Yes, Marcos acknowledged there had been some cheating by his followers, but there had been cheating on both sides, and more by Aquino's camp, he insisted, handing Habib a packet of alleged violations.

After Marcos, Habib called on Corazon Aquino, who told him that nothing less than Marcos's removal from office would be acceptable.

Aquino's camp had been divided after Reagan's fraud-on-both-sides statement. Some were ready to sue for peace; others wanted to stand and fight. The fighters won. They decided to take on Habib. Aquino and her aides were convinced that Habib was being sent to negotiate a peace between the Marcos and Aquino camps. That was the way Habib's mission had been widely portrayed in the American press, which noted his previous missions to the Middle East. So Aquino issued a statement that if Habib were coming to broker a deal, he might just as well stay home. Referring to Habib's inability to end the warring in Lebanon, Mrs. Aquino said, "I hope neither Mr. Reagan nor Mr. Marcos is expecting to see our beloved country go the same way." The White House, the State Department, and Habib all denied that it was Habib's mission to persuade Aquino to become the loyal opposition; his only assignment was to gather the facts and assess the situation. Though Habib had "carte blanche authority," he did not ask Mrs. Aquino to enter into any sort of arrangement with Marcos, which suggests that this had never been his intention. If it had been, it is hard to imagine that Philip Habib would have abandoned it so readily, after a mere statement by Mrs. Aquino.

The Habib-Aquino meeting went smoothly, in part because Robert Jones had delivered a message to Mrs. Aquino that she should trust Habib, that he was Shultz's man, not Reagan's. Though Habib had been in the Philippines several times during his career—coming over from Vietnam for the Manila Summit with LBJ in 1966; accompanying President Ford on his visit in 1975—he had never met Mrs. Aquino. Now that he had, he was very impressed, convinced that she was not a naïve, simple housewife, which is how she had been so widely portrayed.

During his week in the Philippines Habib was his energetic self, meeting with more than 100 individuals, usually alone or in very small groups: labor leaders; members of Marcos's party, of Aquino's party; Cardinal Sin and the bishops, who were still very divided, in spite of their joint statement about the fraud. A select group of Filipino businessmen was also gathered to give their views to Habib. They were "convinced that Marcos cannot govern, has no credibility, cannot regain any, and has got to go." One businessman described President Reagan's remark about fraud on both sides as "devastating," adding that continued United States support for Marcos would benefit only the radical left. Even the American Chamber of Commerce, which had been so enamored of Marcos for twenty years, had come to realize that the dictator did not serve its interests. The chamber's president and members of the board of directors had delivered a message to the embassy that any "whitewash of this election could gravely endager American business in the Philippines." They added that "some further visible distancing of [the United States] from Marcos regime was required."

One of Habib's earliest meetings had been with three Americans: Guy Pauker, of the Rand Corporation; Robert Shaplen, the *New Yorker* correspondent; and Claude Buss, the Philippine scholar who was also a neighbor of Habib's on the San Francisco peninsula. He also sought out the veteran Southeast Asian correspondent Stanley Karnow, who was working on a book about the Philippines. Together the four men had a combined experience of writing and reporting on, about, and from the Philippines that exceeded 100 years. Buss, who had been in the Philippines for this election, as he had been in 1935, was about to depart when he received a cable from Habib asking him to remain. When they met, Buss told Habib that he could summarize the situation in three sentences: "First, Marcos is finished. Second, Cory's for real. Third, it ain't over yet."

By the time he departed, Habib was also convinced that Mrs. Aquino would be a tough president and that Marcos was finished. The problem, he told the embassy, would be in getting that message through to the U.S. president. "I see him once a week; she sees him every night," Habib said, referring to Nancy Reagan. Habib knew that Mrs. Reagan's influence on her husband and American policy was greater than realized, that she did more than just occasionally whisper answers into her husband's ear. Another diplomat said during the final week of Marcos's rule, "Don't underestimate Nancy Reagan in all this." Mrs. Reagan and Mrs. Marcos had first met in 1969, and after Reagan became president, Mrs. Marcos pushed the friendship, bestowing gifts on Mrs. Reagan as she did on everyone. As recently as October Mrs. Marcos had sent two gowns worth $10,000 to Nancy Reagan, one a strapless red silk with a rhinestone butterfly; they were put in the National Archives. While Mrs. Marcos was in New York at that time, she and Mrs. Reagan met; after that, as the crisis intensified, Imelda Marcos frequently called Nancy Reagan for comfort and support.

The Reagan administration's Philippine policy was on icy pavement. Everyone was grabbing for the steering wheel, but no one, least of all the White House, seemed to have control.

Four days after the president's election comment, the White House scrambled to recover. From his Santa Barbara ranch, to which Reagan had adjourned for some rest, the White House issued a statement that the "widespread fraud and violence" in the Philippine election had been "perpetrated largely by the ruling party." The White House was finally forced to admit to the reality. It was a dramatic reversal, and it was widely reported as such. What wasn't reported was the maneuvering that preceded the retraction and a key reason for its having been released when the White House had said it was going to wait for Habib's report before commenting on the election.

That reason was Corazon Aquino. The small woman in yellow was slaying the giant. Thanks to television, she had become an instant international heroine. Not only did she have Marcos reeling, but she also had Reagan on the defensive, as few American politicians were ever able to do. She did not flinch from attacking the American president, often turning the language that he used in justifying aid for the contras and other rebel forces against him. Her response to his news conference assertion that the fraud had been on both sides was biting with sarcasm: "I wonder at the motives of a friend of democracy who chose to conspire with Mr. Marcos to cheat the Filipino people of their liberation." The verbal attacks continued, and by Saturday Ronald Reagan, president of the United States, was ready to cry uncle.

From the Western White House in Santa Barbara a top Reagan aide contacted Aquino's backers in New York, who in turn got in touch with her aides in Manila. The proposed statement was read to the aides. Was it OK? the White House wanted to know. Would it satisfy Mrs. Aquino? It was three in the morning in Manila when a sleepy aide had the statement read to him. He approved it, though he barely remembered it until he read it in the newspapers. It didn't quiet Mrs. Aquino immediately. In his statement Reagan continued the line that the elections "were marked by the continuing commitment of the Filipino people to the democratic process and the furtherance of a two-party system." Mrs. Aquino's barbed response to that was: "What Reagan cited as 'the heartening evidence of the continuing commitment of the Filipino people to the democratic process' was a persecuted people clinging on the ballot boxes against a government determined to trample all over their rights." Then she added, cousciously turning Reagan's support for the contras against him, "Those, who are prepared to support armed struggles for liberation elsewhere, discredit themselves if they obscure the nature of what we are doing peacefully here."

Though Reagan had now been forced to acknowledge that it was Marcos who stole the election, the administration was not calling on Marcos to resign. Indeed, Reagan in his statement had been careful not to chastise his good friend by name, blaming the election fraud and violence on the "ruling party," as if Marcos were somehow above all the skulduggery. No one in the White House was ready to push Marcos, and over at State, as the temperature rose and the room to maneuver begin to shrink, some of the policymakers grew nervous. Principal among them was Paul Wolfowitz, the boyish-looking forty-two-year-old assistant secretary of state for East Asia. For a year this self-described workaholic had been pushing for a tougher line toward Marcos than at times Shultz was willing to adopt. But now that the moment of truth had arrived, Wolfowitz wasn't so sure. On the Tuesday after Reagan had placed the blame for the fraud on the Marcos party, Wolfowitz appeared privately before the Council on Foreign Relations in New York. He focused on the mounting movement in Congress, supported increasingly by conservatives, to terminate military aid to the Philippines because of the fraud. Wolfowitz urged caution. Yes, there had been fraud; yes, it had been by Marcos. But Marcos was still the government, and the United States had to deal with him. It was the same line, the same policy that Donald Regan had expressed the week before the voting. Wolfowitz was worried about another Iran, another Nicaragua. He was worried, in those final days, that everything was happening too fast. He worried aloud, in the department, about Reagan's being railroaded into a disaster; if the Philippines tumbled into chaos, it would be a Republican disaster.

432

Wolfowitz's anxiety became public after Gelb's article about the "consensus" within the administration to put some distance between Washington and Marcos. Gelb listed the architects of the policy as Armacost; Ambassador Bosworth; Morton Abramowitz; Gaston Sigur, the senior Asian specialist on the National Security Council; Richard Armitage, assistant secretary of defense; and Paul Wolfowitz. The article was accurate. Wolfowitz was infuriated with the Gelb piece, using a long profile about him in the *Washington Post* to respond publicly, to preserve his standing with conservative Republicans, who were still very much with Marcos. Wolfowitz had studied under a hard-line conservative at the University of Chicago, earning his Ph.D. in political science, and in the 1970s he had been part of a small group of conservative intellectuals burrowing into American foreign policy. He had headed Secretary of State Haig's Policy Planning Staff. Then Shultz had asked him to take over the East Asian Bureau. He was still an "ideologue," he insisted to the *Washington Post* reporter Steve Coll, who described Wolfowitz as the "brash young hard-liner that he insists he is."

Evans and Novak came to Wolfowitz's rescue. The attempts by Armacost (the "ringleader," according to the columnists), Abramowitz, and the Carterites "to tilt the U.S. policy" away from Marcos, the conservative journalists declared, "were viewed with disdain by some middle-level officials with day-to-day responsibility for the Philippines, including Assistant Secretary Paul Wolfowitz at State, and Gaston Sigur at the National Security Council. They are moderate conservatives, free of Carterite ties and determined not to be the architects of destabilization."

The Evans and Novak column, in which the conservatives were still with Marcos, appeared on February 22, 1986. By the time the newspapers were being read by even the earliest of risers, it was too late. The policy wheel had slipped from American hands and had been seized by Filipinos; all Washington could do was try to avoid crashing.

The denouement began when Defense Minister Juan Ponce Enrile decided the time had come to break with Marcos. Once he had, others quickly followed, from military officers to church leaders to American diplomats, and, above all, to hundreds of thousands of Filipinos who had been waiting for the opportunity. Though Enrile had faithfully served Marcos for twenty years and had become im-

433

mensely wealthy in return, he was Cassius with that "lean and hungry look." He had long wanted to be president, and had been maneuvering against Marcos for a couple of years, preparing for the time to move. His vehicle was RAM. Ostensibly the RAM officers were interested only in the professionalization of the armed forces Marcos had corrupted. But it became a cover for officers who began plotting a coup d'état. By mid-1985 Enrile had become involved. The core group of officers plotting the coup worked in his office. His wealth was used to purchase weapons on the black market, which, because Enrile was minister of defense, could easily be slipped into the country without detection.

By October 1985 the plans for a coup d'état were well advanced. Then Marcos announced the "snap elections," and everything was put on hold. After the election had heightened the tensions and the animosity toward Marcos, Enrile and a handful of officers swung into high gear, preparing for an attack on Malacañang and a takeover of the country. On Thursday, February 20, Aquino's camp was approached with a proposal for a coup and subsequent junta. The members would be: Enrile, General Ramos, Cardinal Sin, Mrs. Aquino, and Alejandro Melchor, the man close to all sides at all times. Aquino flatly rejected the proposal.

Two days later, on Saturday morning, while he was having coffee, Enrile received a telephone call alerting him that Marcos had learned of the plot and was about to arrest him. Enrile was frightened. He called the loyalist officers and told them to proceed immediately to Camp Aguinaldo, the military base where the Defense Ministry was located. Then Enrile, his voice trembling, called Lieutenant General Fidel V. Ramos, the deputy chief of staff of the armed forces. Enrile's was a conversion of convenience; Ramos's, of conscience. Ramos was a member of a public service-oriented family: His father had been foreign minister in the early 1960s, and his sister, Leticia Shahani, was a diplomat highly regarded internationally. Ramos hadn't grown wealthy during the Marcos years, though he bore some responsibility for the military brutality, for he had been the head of the Philippine Constabulary. But the slight, bespectacled West Point graduate was widely respected by the army's professional officers and by the Americans.

Ramos didn't hesitate. A devout Catholic, he had been greatly affected by the bishops' statement condemning the fraud. He agreed to join Enrile. The rebellion was on, but far from over. The CIA station chief in Manila was certain it would fail, that it was the opposition's "last gasp," a view that created some tension within the embassy.

But the forces of inaction and action fused as events cascaded far more rapidly than anyone could have imagined. First was the inaction, specifically Marcos's. For at least the first twelve hours—and maybe for the first twenty-four—virtually all the nation's generals as well as many key unit commanders were loyal to their president, not to Enrile and Ramos. But Marcos failed to order them to attack, a miscalculation as fatal as had been the calling of the election. With each passing hour more and more units defected to the rebels.

More important, tens of thousands of Filipinos poured into the streets, forming a human cordon protecting the Enrile-Ramos forces from an attack by Marcos's army. The Filipino people had been called out by Jaime Cardinal Sin, as shrewd and cautious as cardinals are expected to be and now as political as the pope says they aren't supposed to be. Sin's appeal was broadcast over Radio Veritas, which the United States had secretly funded. As the tanks rolled toward the rebels, crying women stood in front of them. It became "People Power." The whole world watched and cheered as the people stood up to the dictator and the tanks.

Was the United States behind the rebellion of Enrile and Ramos? There are Filipinos and American observers who had no doubt of it (and will continue to believe it no matter what is said and written; it is part of the lore in the Philippines, as in Latin America, that nothing happens without American intervention). Both Enrile and Ramos were close to the Americans, and had been for years. Enrile in particular had established a good working relationship with all CIA station chiefs, and he began his rebellion two hours after Habib's departure. It looked and smelled like an American plot. But the evidence, though strong, is all circumstantial and tends to be rebutted by other evidence, equally circumstantial. Perhaps the strongest argument against U.S. involvement is that support of Marcos was still the official policy of the U.S. government. For the CIA to have participated in a coup would have meant that William Casey was acting not only without the approval of but, in fact, contrary to the policy of the president of the United States. That he would not have done. Finally, if the United States had been behind the coup, the Reagan administration, it seems, would have moved swiftly in calling on Marcos to resign. In fact, it was only after several intense meetings, and hard lobbying by Habib and Shultz, that Reagan, Casey, and Weinberger finally agreed that Marcos had to go.

Even though the United States may not have started the rebellion, once it had begun there was no doubt whom it wanted to win, or at least whom Bosworth, the embassy, and the State Department wanted. One of Enrile's first calls after he had talked to Cardinal Sin had been to Bosworth. The American ambassador did not promise support. Neither did he express disapproval of the rebellion. And from that moment on, "We were watching but getting more and more pregnant," says an embassy officer. There was an important American with Ramos, a lanky army colonel who had served with the Green Berets in Vietnam. He was Galen W. Radke, and until just a few months before, he had been the U.S. Army attaché in Manila. Not only was his presence a symbolic lift to the rebels, but he also provided valuable intelligence information on their activities and military needs to the embassy. Very early in the rebellion Enrile asked Bosworth for fuel (for planes and helicopters) and ammunition. Bosworth contacted Washington for authorization. Sunday night they were provided.

Washington had gone into its crisis mode, operating around the clock. On the seventh floor of the State Department, in addition to all the sophisticated government communications equipment, two ordinary commercial phone lines were opened to the embassy; everything was so chaotic that officials in the State Department in Washington had to whistle and shout in order to raise someone on the line in Manila.

The Reagan administration was desperately struggling to avert a shoot-out between the rebel forces and the Marcos forces. The Communists would have loved that; they could have just watched it all, then moved in afterward.

Late Saturday afternoon in Washington (Manila is thirteen hours ahead, so it was early Sunday morning there and the streets were mobbed with people supporting the rebellion), the White House issued its fourth statement in the two weeks since the election. It declared again that the election fraud had been "perpetrated overwhelmingly" by Marcos's party, but now it added that it was "so extreme as to undermine the credibility and legitimacy of the election and impair the capacity of the Government of the Philippines to cope with a growing insurgency and troubled economy." The statement stopped short, however, of asking Marcos to resign.

Habib, however, who was now in Washington, was delivering the message that the Marcos era "had ended." He had planned to stop on his return from Manila for some rest. But when his air force jet landed at Moffett Air Base, which he can see from his modest hillside home on the San Francisco peninsula, events were occurring so hectically that he and Maisto stepped off the plane and boarded a smaller Learjet, which had pulled up alongside with its engines running. It was the modern pony express to Washington. After a few hours' sleep Habib met with Shultz and a small group from the CIA and Defense.

On Sunday morning the group expanded, gathering at Shultz's brick colonial-style house in Bethesda, Maryland: Defense Secretary Weinberger; Chairman of the Joint Chiefs Admiral Crowe; Deputy CIA Director Robert M. Gates; National Security Adviser John Poindexter; Armacost; Wolfowitz. Once again, in his straightforward, blunt way, Habib told them that Marcos "has had it." Someone expressed concern about Mrs. Aquino's ability to govern. He assured them she was not any simple housewife. What about the bases? "I talked to her about the bases. She is going to respect the treaty."

The crisis resolution group moved over to the White House for a meeting that originally had been scheduled for Monday; events in the Philippines dictated it be held immediately. Reagan returned early from Camp David. Dressed in a plaid flannel shirt, he presided over a meeting of the National Security Planning Group that began at 3:03. During the eithty-five-minute session Chief of Staff Regan, recalling what had happened in Iran, argued that the United States could not abandon Marcos. In spite of all that had transpired, Ronald Reagan was still with Marcos. Once again Habib said, "The Marcos era has ended." Shultz forcefully agreed. The last holdouts were Weinberger (who had also denied that he had ever been a part of the consensus Gelb wrote about) and Casey. And, of course, Reagan. Finally, Shultz and Habib prevailed.

It was a win for the professional diplomats at the State Department. The ideology of the Reagan conservatives, which said to stay with Marcos, had finally yielded to the national interest, which Marcos didn't serve. Along the way the diplomats had been bolstered by Admiral Crowe and the Pentagon. The goal had been decided upon; all that remained was to reach it, peacefully. Above all, it had to be done without its appearing that the United States was acting heavy-handedly and especially, without Reagan's fingerprints on the knife.

Following the National Security Planning Group meeting, the White House, turning the ratchet another notch or two, issued a statement that the United States would cut off military aid if Marcos launched an attack on the rebels. The statement still stopped short of asking Marcos to step aside, and in response to questions, White House spokesman Larry Speakes declined to say whether Reagan thought he should. In fact, however, Reagan had already sent a message to Marcos offering him asylum in the United States, the offer delivered by Bosworth. The Reagan administration wanted to avoid Marcos's becoming another shah, left to wander from country to country, without a home, without a welcome in the United States. Every possible way of reaching Marcos, short of the most obvious, direct, and effective one, a call from Reagan, was explored. And the administration pressed into service every available person including Alejandro Melchor, a man with an uncanny ability to walk the highest wire between all camps and never fall off. He had been Marcos's executive secretary when martial law was declared and had been the point man in Washington to defend it; three years later Marcos had dismissed him because Melchor proposed cleaning up the corruption, including Imelda Marcos's gang. Yet he had remained close to, and was trusted by, Marcos while moving close enough to Mrs. Aquino so that when it was all over, she named him Philippine ambassador to Moscow.

It's not clear why Melchor was in Washington on that final weekend—not clear because he offered different reasons. At the time he told American intelligence and military officers that he had been sent by Marcos to try to hold the situation together, to tell Washington that Marcos could still control the country. Later Melchor claimed that he had come to Washington on other matters and had been contacted by the Reagan administration when it learned he was in town. Whatever the reason, Melchor still had as much cachet in Washington as he had had fourteen years before, when he had defended martial law.

On Sunday night Richard Childress and Admiral Poindexter of the NSC brought Melchor into the secure situation room in the White House. That's where Melchor remained during the final forty-eight hours. Childress told Melchor that Reagan did not want to telephone Marcos for two reasons. One was the concern that Marcos, once on the phone, would argue that he had won the election. The second, and more important, was a fear that the plan to get Marcos to step aside might not work; Reagan was not to be associated with any failure. Melchor was advising the Americans "which buttons to push" to convince Marcos to step aside. Over at the State Department another of Marcos's longtime political allies and a Marcos cabinet member, Blas Ople, was working with Armacost and Shultz, trying to reach Marcos with the message that he could have asylum in the United States.

At five o'clock Monday morning Reagan was awakened. The United States had intercepted a radio message from Malacañang giving the orders to attack the Enrile-Ramos forces. The White House issued a public statement to Marcos calling for the "peaceful transition to a new government." A retired CIA officer who had served in the Philippines was called by the White House. He still had good contacts with the Philippine military. He got in touch with General Ver, with a twofold message. First, don't use violence; secondly, you and your family can have asylum in the United States. Marcos was still hanging on, still not convinced that his friend Ronald Reagan would abandon him.

On Tuesday, at three o'clock in the morning in Manila, Marcos reached Senator Laxalt on the Hill, where Shultz, Habib, and Armacost were briefing senators on the crisis. Marcos, now a desperate man, proposed an arrangement whereby Aquino would be allowed to run the government, but he would remain as president until his term expired in 1987. He asked whether if he did resign, he could remain in the country. He didn't want exile. What Marcos really wanted to know from Laxalt was if these messages about a peaceful transition to a new government really expressed the views of Ronald Reagan. Laxalt promised to check with the president and call Marcos back. In a lightly falling snow Laxalt, Shultz, Habib, and Armacost were driven to the White House. The diplomats' minds were made up. "Hell, no!" Habib had said to the idea of a coalition government. Whether Marcos could stay in the country, well, that would be up to Mrs. Aquino, they said, knowing full well what the answer would be. Of course, they had to check with the president. Meanwhile, Imelda Marcos was calling Nancy Reagan with the same questions.

At five o'clock in the morning in Manila Laxalt called Marcos back from Admiral Poindexter's office. Again Marcos asked, Did President Reagan want him to resign? Laxalt, still protecting his president, said he couldn't answer for him.

Then came the "gut question." Marcos asked what did he, Paul Laxalt, think he should do.

"Cut and cut cleanly. The time has come."

There was a long pause, so long that Laxalt had to ask Marcos if he was still there. Then Marcos, dispirited, his voice weak, said, "I am so very, very disappointed."

Sixteen hours later, at 9:05 P.M. in Manila, four American helicopters lifted off from the grass at Malacañang. On board were Ferdinand Marcos, Imelda Marcos, their children, and close allies, such as Ver. They were fleeing, an ignominious end for an American friend.

From the embassy roof across town, Bosworth and his staff were watching. When the helicopters were in the air, the ambassador went to the phone and dialed. When the voice he wanted to hear came on the line, a relieved and happy ambassador greeted Corazon Aquino: "Madame President . . ."

Epilogue : The Price of the Policy

In Manila they stormed the palace, then danced in the streets, celebrating the dictator's departure and cheering America's help. In Washington the praise for the manner in which the United States had conducted itself at the end was bipartisan and effusive. Then the euphoria and the applause subsided, and the future had to be faced. It was the grim legacy of twenty years of the Marcoses and Washington's cozy alliance with them.

As with American support of other dictators, the policy of supporting Marcos was myopic. Along the way he may have served America's short-term interests—protecting American bases and businessmen's profits—but his rule was disastrous for America's long-term interests.

In 1972, when Marcos seized power, the Philippine foreign debt was some $2 billion; when he fled, it was a treasury-breaking $26 billion. The international bankers who were so keen on Marcos for so long faced having to bail out the sinking economy he left behind; in a time of tight budgets the American Congress, within six months after Marcos fled, was offering $200 million of American taxpayers' money to salvage the Philippine economy.

Marcos eviscerated the country's democratic institutions—the courts, the electoral process, the schools. Maybe, with enough time, they can be put back together, but even so, the loss to the country has been tremendous.

Will the Philippines become another banana republic, with coups and countercoups, juntas, colonels and generals occupying Malacañang or deciding who does? Juan Ponce Enrile and Fidel Ramos and the Philippine military were hailed for the army's role in ousting Marcos. It ought to have been a cause for concern. It remains to be seen whether it was the first step toward the post-Marcos military involvement in Philippine politics—an explosive, undemocratic, unstable mixture, as so many Latin American countries have learned. The Reform the Armed Forces Movement, which the United States had organized and funded, played a role in Marcos's ouster; nine months later the RAM officers were demanding more say in running the government, with General Ramos, the chief of staff of the armed forces, making demands on how President Aquino governed and who was in her cabinet. It was a dangerous climate, one for which Washington bore partial responsibility.

The Philippine military was created in the image of General Douglas MacArthur, its officers proudly graduating from the Philippine Military Academy, modeled after West Point. It had been one of the most professional armies, not just in Asia but in the entire third world. It saw its role as defending the country's democracy and left the governing to civilians. Like everything else he touched, Marcos polluted the Philippine military. The corruption wasn't just monetary; far more troubling, it went to the very core. It was a fully politicized army. It couldn't fight.

For Washington, the most bitter legacy of the Marcos era was the growth of the Communists. There weren't more than a few hundred New People's Army guerrillas in 1972; by 1986 there were 15,000 well-armed, motivated guerrillas and a million or so supporters. In this growth lie the seeds of what should be the most enduring lesson for American foreign policy: Outsiders don't cause Communist revolutions; internal conditions and dictators do.

That a revolution developed in the Philippines was as inexorable as mosquitoes breeding in pools of brackish water. Indeed, the revolution had been foreseen, not directly but in the reports that Americans had been filing out of the archipelago for three decades. In the early 1950s Ed Lansdale, the man Washington sent out to advance democracy in the Philippines, noted that it was "a government of the privileged few, not of the people. The troops protected only these few and made war on the people." In 1952 the American ambassador Admiral Spruance wrote: "If the shackles of the landed aristocracy are not loosened . . . there will be a revolution in the Philippines when we get off the lid—and it will not be a peaceful and bloodless one."

A decade and a half later, at the time of Marcos's first election as president, the CIA, in a Secret National Intelligence Estimate, observed that the Philippines was beset by "land hunger in the countryside; unemployment in the cities; and a grinding poverty for the overwhelming majority of the people. The situation is aggravated by widespread violence and lawlessness, and by corruption in government." If Marcos "fails to reduce economic discontent and to achieve greater honesty and efficiency in governmental affairs, public disillusionment is likely to grow and political stability could be seriously undermined." Without a program to address "basic domestic socioeconomic problems," the agency noted in another Secret report out of the Philippines, written just a few months earlier in late 1965, "nationalism and discontent are likely to lend themselves to leftist exploitation."

Six years later, in 1971, the State Department's Bureau of Intelligence and Research noted that "social inequalities in the Philippines are, if not the greatest among the countries of Southeast Asia, certainly the most visible." The result had been a number of radical movements. "Rather surprisingly," INR wrote, "in view of the grossly inequitable social structure, none of these movements has ever developed sufficient mass support to challenge seriously the oligarchy or threaten its domination of the political process."

These were the root causes of revolution in the Philippines, and elsewhere. It was the prescription that Marx had written, that Mao, Ho Chi Minh, Castro, the Sandinistas, the revolutionaries in El Salvador had exploited: screaming disparities between the rich and the poor, with a brutal army to keep the peasants and workers in line while the rich got richer.

In the Philippines the observations by Lansdale, Spruance, the CIA, and INR had been ignored. The political instability, the leftist exploitation had come about because Marcos, instead of achieving greater honesty in government, reached new levels of corruption and did nothing to alleviate the poverty. And all the while Washington watched.

Whether the followers of the Communist-led revolution can be persuaded to lay down their arms or withdraw their sympathies will depend on whether the present government addresses the root causes of problems, provides peasants with land, and redistributes some of

443

the wealth. What happened in February 1986 was not a revolution; it was the toppling of a dictator. The revolution is yet to come. It can be a peaceful, democratic one, or it will be a Communist one. If legitimate grievances aren't addressed, if the "grossly inequitable social structure" is not made more equitable, the NPA will continue to grow.

For the United States, and particularly the Reagan administration, the question is whether it will support and assist President Aquino, and the governments that follow, in implementing the needed socioeconomic structural changes, such as land reform, which the administration resisted in El Salvador. Or will Washington emphasize the military response to the insurgency, as it seemed to when the first high-level official visitor from the United States to the post-Marcos Philippines was Defense Secretary Weinberger?

If the NPA again poses a serious threat, if the Philippine military can't be resurrected to fight it, and if, as a result, Washington decides on a policy of more military aid and American advisers, the blame will lie, in part, with Washington and the policy of having supported Marcos for too long.

The Carter administration didn't challenge Marcos because it couldn't, or wouldn't, shake the *liberal* fears of being thought soft on communism. The irony was that by being soft on Marcos, it made communism possible. The Reagan administration enthusiastically embraced him because it was a captive of *conservative* dogma. Conservatives castigated the Carter administration for having abandoned the shah and Somoza, giving the world Khomeini and the Sandinistas. That was the lesson for conservatives: Don't abandon a pro-American, anti-Communist, friendly dictator because what follows will be worse. But it was the wrong lesson. The lesson of the shah and Somoza, and before them of Chiang Kai-shek, Batista, and Diem, is that by sticking with such dictators for too long, the United States sets the stage for, virtually guarantees the very outcome that it doesn't want.

It's not a moral imperative which says don't embrace dictators; it is hard, cold realpolitik. If that wasn't clear before, it should be after Marcos.

Appendix

ASSISTANT SECRETARIES OF STATE FOR EAST ASIAN AND PACIFIC AFFAIRS, 1964–1986

William P. Bundy	March 1964–April 1969
Marshall Green	May 1969–May 1973
Robert S. Ingersoll	January 1974–July 1974
Philip C. Habib	September 1974–July 1976
Arthur W. Hummel, Jr.	July 1976–January 1977
Richard C. Holbrooke	January 1977–January 1981
John H. Holdridge	May 1981–December 1982
Paul D. Wolfowitz	December 1982–March 1986
Gaston Sigur	March 1986–

U.S. AMBASSADORS TO THE PHILIPPINES, 1964–1986

William McCormick Blair, Jr.	August 1964–October 1967
James M. Wilson, Jr. (Chargé d'Affaires)	October 1967–June 1968
G. Mennen Williams	June 1968–April 1969
James M. Wilson, Jr. (Chargé)	May 1969–August 1969
Henry R. Byroade	August 1969–May 1973
William H. Sullivan	August 1973–April 1977
Lee T. Stull (Chargé d'Affaires)	May 1977–November 1977
David D. Newsom	November 1977–March 1978
Richard W. Murphy	June 1978–August 1981
Michael H. Armacost	March 1982–April 1984
Stephen W. Bosworth	April 1984–

Appendix

Author's Note

One word has propelled this book. Why? It became the question I asked over and over again, until it became monotonous to hear myself; it was the question that was etched in my mind as I wrote. Why? To expand: Why is it that the United States so often supports dictators? As I wandered about the third world in the late 1970s, principally Latin America, it was a question I was continually confronted with.

At one point Jonathan Segal, my editor at Times Books, suggested a book that would look at five dictators who have ruled with America's support: Batista, Diem, the shah, Somoza, and Marcos. I said, Why not focus on Marcos, as a case study about U.S. relations with dictators? Jon saw the value of such a book immediately, and along the way he was always there.

I began thinking about a book about the Philippines while I was working on my book about U.S. policy in El Salvador. In August 1983 Aquino was assassinated; I began clipping articles about the Philippines. Then, in late 1984, I filed my first Freedom of Information Act requests for U.S. government records pertaining to Marcos and the Philippines. By March 1985 I was beginning my interviews; the first former ambassador I talked to was G. Mennen ("Soapy") Williams, whom I interviewed in Detroit, where he was sitting as chief justice of the Michigan Supreme Court. Subsequent interviews took me to Flat Rock, North Carolina; San Diego; Kuala Lumpur; Bangkok; and beyond. More details about my research, whom I interviewed, the public records and classified documents I examined will be found in the Sources and Notes.

This is a book about Washington more than about Manila, more about American policy than about Philippine culture and society.

I have tried to do two things. One was to establish the record of what happened in America's dealings with Marcos during the twenty years of his rule. Even more, I have sought to answer the why. To the extent I have succeeded in either or both, I owe a great deal of gratitude to a number of people.

First and foremost, my thanks to Craig Nelson. I cannot thank him enough. Craig went everywhere, did everything. He spent long days at the Library of Congress reading old Philippine newspapers, located people I needed to interview, and learned about the resources at the State Department, the National Archives, and Justice Department. He examined the Hubert H. Humphrey Papers at the Minnesota Historical Society and traveled to his alma mater, Carleton, to probe the background of Michael Armacost. My file drawers brim with the material he gathered. Craig was a friend and colleague throughout. He read drafts of chapters along the way and improved them. Without Craig's dedication I would have toiled for another year.

Nor does "thank you" say enough to Les Gelb, who so willingly imparted to me his tremendous knowledge and understanding of the making of American foreign policy. He was at once a professor, a thesis adviser, a journalist, and an editor. I consulted him frequently along the way, and in the end he read the entire manuscript.

The manuscript was also read by Anthony Lake, a former Foreign Service officer who worked on Kissinger's NSC staff (resigning to protest the invasion of Cambodia), was director of the Policy Planning Staff during the Carter administration, and is currently professor of international relations at Amherst College; by Joseph Lelyveld, *The New York Times* correspondent in Asia for many years and currently the paper's foreign editor, and who opened a critical door for me when I began my research; by Johanna McGeary, diplomatic correspondent for *Time*; and by Michael Posner, director of the Lawyers Committee for Human Rights. Sandra Burton, who covered the Philippines for *Time* from 1983 to 1986, read the chapters about the Reagan period, and Diane Orentlicher, who prepared Lawyers Committee reports about the Philippines, read the chapters about human rights during the Carter administration.

Reading a manuscript is a chore; in this case, it meant lugging around and plowing through 750 double-spaced pages, which had not been finally edited. All these people read with great care. Their insights, additions, and corrections were considerable and invaluable, from small details to broad themes. I must stress, however, in fairness to each of them, that the facts, conclusions, and judgments in this book are mine.

Many are the journalists who assisted me. Early on I talked with Robert Shaplen, the veteran Southeast Asian correspondent for *The New Yorker*. In addition to his knowledge of the Philippines, he provided me with a list of his main contacts, including their phone numbers, and told me that I could use his name when I contacted them. That is a generosity rare among journalists, who zealously guard their sources. I can only "repay" Bob by doing for other journalists what he did for me. Colin Campbell deserves credit for the extensive notes in this book. As I was nearing the finish, Colin stressed the importance of notes for historical purposes. Off and on for several days, we discussed the dilemma journalists face when they write books and cannot identify their sources. Out of that discussion grew my decision to make the notes as extensive and explanatory as possible, along with the introductory comment to them. Jeff Gerth, of *The New York Times*, allowed me to look through his files about the financial activities of the Marcoses. Dale Van Atta, who works with Jack Anderson, shared many classified documents that he had acquired over the years about the Marcoses and the Philippines. John Martin of ABC found needed transcripts in the archives of his network. Along the way, Karl Meyer of *The New York Times* and Roy Rowan of *Fortune* offered critical encouragement, which their many years in the profession made more meaningful. Richard Nations, for a while the chief diplomatic correspondent in Washington for the *Far Eastern Economic Review* and an Asian hand, shared his insights.

While I was in the Philippines, several journalists were generous with their time and expertise, laying aside the feeling they must have had about an "outsider" coming in to write a book about a place they had been covering for years. Among those to whom I am most indebted are Guy Sacerdote and Lin Neumann. Seth Mydans, bureau chief for *The New York Times*, made my working in the Philippines considerably easier and more enjoyable. In the Philippines, I worked closely with Susan Meiselas, whose photojournalism in Central America has been much acclaimed. Her commitment to and breadth of understanding about the third world contributed immensely to what I was able to do and learn.

In the Philippines my special thanks to Fe Mangahas, who dug through old newspapers for many articles and photos. I shudder to think what I would have lacked without Fe's efforts. I am also grateful to Julie Amargo, Cookie Diokno, Father James Reuter, Adrian Cristobal, Leticia Shahani, Felix Bautista, F. Sionil José, Ramón Locsin, and Lupita Kashiwahara, who, though she was deep in her sister-in-law's campaign in December 1985, found time to help me arrange interviews.

As I mention in the Sources and Notes, I relied heavily on the *Far Eastern Economic Review*, which is the journal of record for the region it covers. Thanks to Roger Tam, the *Review*'s librarian, I had copies of all the Philippine articles, and Roger also provided me with his bound volumes of the *Far Eastern Economic Review Yearbook*. Thanks also to the Data Center in Oakland, California, for its clippings on the Philippines. Others who deserve acknowledgment and whose assistance surpasses their mention here: Richard Kessler, a Southeast Asian scholar at the Carnegie Endowment who was available to discuss ideas and themes and who suggested many questions for me to probe; Claude Buss, professor emeritus at Stanford University; Robin Broad, a Philippine scholar, who also introduced me to many people in the Philippines; Pamela Belluck, a young journalist, who did research, including interviews about some of the Marcos activities in the United States; Rachel Burd, who transcribed hours of interviews; Lemual Thomas, who patiently and painstakingly copied reams of documents; Eric Guyot, Walden Bello, Joel Rocamora, and Gareth Porter, who shared their years of research and knowledge; Joe Cincotti, Scott Aiges, and Victor Wright, who located, then copied *New York Times* stories; Linda Amster, who helped locate researchers; Steve Psinakis, who shared his voluminous and well-organized files on the activities of the Marcoses and their cronies in the United States; Belinda Rathbone, who deserves credit for finding the photos in this book; Elise Banducci, for her study of U.S. military assistance to the Philippines; Jim Morrell, for steering me through the myriad congressional laws on human rights; Lee Feinstein, for his knowledge about the American bases; Jay Peterzell of the Center for National Security Studies and a font of information about American intelligence activities; Ted Slate, library director at *Newsweek*; attorneys at the Center for Constitutional Rights, which represented the Aquino government in its efforts to recover money and property from the Marcoses; Narciso ("Gene") Reyes, press attaché at the Philippine Mission to the United Nations; Robert Dockery, Gary Bombardier, Martin Rendon, and Stanley Roth, congressional aides who allowed me to search their files and memories; Robert Puckett, who introduced me to his family. At the LBJ Library in Austin, Texas, where I passed several days poring through the trove there, the helpfulness of David Humphrey and Linda Hanson was surpassed only by their friendliness. It was a delight to work there; I hope my next book gives me reason to return. I also owe a special thanks to the staff of the Freedom of Information Act office at the State Department, particularly Rebecca Gonzales and Barbara Jibrin, who were most pleasant in responding to my persistent requests.

A book like this quite obviously necessitated spending considerable time in Washington. After I moved to New York in August 1985, I always had a home away from home in Washington, in the warmth and friendship of Susannah, Julie, and Walter Empson and Jonathan Fuerbringer and Johanna McGeary.

Working in Washington was easier because of the National Security Archive. Established in 1985 by Scott Armstrong, the archive is to be a repository for documents pertaining to American foreign policy. For me, it provided an office, a telephone, and, above all, a friendly staff. My thanks to Scott, Janet DiVincenzo, Louise Pierson, and everyone at the archive.

The collection of government documents I obtained was enlarged substantially because of the work of William Webber, an attorney with the Washington, D.C., office of Hughes Hubbard & Reed, which represented me pro bono in my FOIA lawsuits. As a former lawyer, one who was involved in public interest law, I want to say something more about Bill's work: He treated me as a regular client, working as hard and as diligently as if I were paying as much as any corporate client. His effort on my behalf was a model of the pro bono commitment lawyers talk about but too rarely deliver.

And on the subject of professionals, I come now to those pros who really worked on this book. My agent is Gloria Loomis. Enthusiastic about this book from its inception, Gloria is a superb agent, but much more—a great friend. Finally, but certainly not least, and maybe foremost, is my appreciation to the staff at Times Books. It is a warm publishing family. To name one without naming all would be unfair. Besides, they all know how much I care about them. Again, as with my last book, Pearl Hanig did the copy editing, and what a superb job she did. But what made this book was the attention it, and I, received from Ruth Fecych and Jonathan Segal. They worked hard—very hard. An author cannot ask for any more than they gave.

Thank you one and all.

RTB
March 1987
New York

Sources and Notes

This book is based on material from three general categories: interviews, government documents, and the public record. As for the last, I read, and have copies of, every article about the Philippines which appeared in the *Far Eastern Economic Review* and *The New York Times* since 1965. To almost the same degree I examined the *Washington Post, Wall Street Journal, Newsweek, Time, U.S. News & World Report, Washington Star* (which ceased publication in 1981), and *Washington Times*, which began publication in 1982. For selected events (such as the 1966 state visit) or critical periods of time (the weeks before martial law, for example), I read the major Philippine newspapers; in the pre-martial-law years the *Philippines Free Press, Manila Chronicle,* and *Manila Times* were the most reliable. In these notes I have not cited every fact or statement from these publications but have selected those I consider the most significant or the most likely to generate discussion or debate. When there is not a full bibliographical reference in the notes, it will be found in the Bibliography.

The muscle and bone of this book are government documents and interviews. I made some 150 Freedom of Information Act (FOIA) requests to the State Department as well as requests to the Central Intelligence Agency National Security Council, Department of Defense, and Securities and Exchange Commission. Altogether I received more than 3,200 previously classified documents, totaling some 12,000 pages. I also obtained government documents from the Lyndon Baines Johnson Library at the University of Texas at Austin; the Gerald R. Ford Library at the University of Michigan, Ann Arbor; and the Hubert H. Humphrey Papers at the Minnesota Historical Society in St. Paul. In the notes that follow each cable is cited by place of issuance (usually State Department or Manila), number, date, and classification. Unless otherwise noted, the cables and other classified government documents were released by the State Department under the FOIA. All the documents I received under the FOIA will be turned over to the National Security Archives in Washington, D.C., and will thus be available to journalists, authors, and historians.

Finally, there were the interviews. Altogether I conducted extensive interviews with some seventy American officials who were involved in the making or implementation of U.S. policy in the Philippines during the Marcos years; I talked, usually by telephone, with probably twenty more. I also interviewed a score-plus of Philippine officials. Many key officials, American and Philippine, I interviewed twice; some three or four times. The American officials interviewed include every American ambassador to the Philippines from 1964 to 1986 and, for that same period, every assistant secretary of state for East Asia, with the exception of one or two who served for only very brief periods. Additionally I interviewed most of the deputy chiefs of mission and political counselors in Manila and the Philippine desk officers in Washington.

Some of the most valuable information, not surprisingly, was provided by military and intelligence officers. At the beginning of an interview with one CIA officer, I explained, as I did in each first interview, how I was conducting my research; the individuals (by category, not by name) whom I had interviewed; the documents I had requested under the FOIA. When I finished, he said, "You can't write the history of any country without talking to the agency." Then he added, "I'm going to tell you some things you won't find in the documents." He did, as did many of his colleagues. They didn't give away the company store or any national security secrets. And I am sure they didn't tell me all that they knew, particularly about agency activities. The CIA officers were most helpful with information about the Marcoses and, as a corollary, what the United States knew.

There is always a great danger in using information provided by CIA officers. All individuals have a tendency to remember and cast information in a somewhat self-serving, or institution-serving, manner. And CIA officers are trained in disinformation. I was haunted by the fear that I was being used, that a story, or a particular interpretation of events, was being planted on me. As a result, I occasionally spent more time—or so it seemed—trying to confirm a story or piece of information than I did in extracting it.

With one exception, I have not named any of the CIA station chiefs in Manila during the Marcos years. I did not think that naming them would add anything of substance to this book. It would show little more than that I had been able to ascertain who they were.

Throughout the writing of this book I was troubled by how I was going to identify my sources. It is a real dilemma. This book would not have been possible without the interviews. But the interviews, or at least most of them, would not have been possible if those interviewed thought they were going to be named. Diplomats don't customarily speak for attribution; CIA officers almost never do. I considered a number of possibilities. One was to describe the source generically— for example, as a former station chief or even a former CIA official in Manila. Or I thought maybe I would list everyone I interviewed.

Then, in 1985, CIA Director William Casey was on a campaign to investigate leaks, aided by a special unit at the FBI. Lie detector tests were administered to government employees at the NSC, CIA, Department of Defense, and State Department. These actions had their chilling effect. Several people whom I had interviewed and who had said I could include their names in a general list changed their minds, saying they wanted no indication they had talked to me.

I have also been the subject of this U.S. government assault on journalists and their government sources. This I discovered when I made a request under the Privacy Act to the FBI for any file it might have prepared on me. The FBI acknowledged that it had such a file but refused to release it on the ground of national security. Its investigation was conducted, I assume, when I was a reporter with The New York Times and wrote about classified government documents which had been provided to me.

In this environment, general and specific, I decided that I must take extra precautions to protect my sources. Consequently I have not listed those whom I

454

interviewed. Where it has been possible to note that a particular piece of information came from an interview, rather than the public record or a document, I have done so. I regret I have not been able to be more specific.

PROLOGUE

This Prologue and Chapter 5, "Countdown to Martial Law," provide what I believe are the most complete account ever published of the developments in the days and weeks prior to martial law and particularly what the United States knew and when. The official U.S. government version—that the United States had no advance knowledge—has been the generally accepted history. One highly respected American scholar on the Philippines, for example, told me in 1985 that the embassy in Manila had been caught "completely flatfooted" by martial law. There have, of course, always been skeptics, individuals, Philippine and American, who have insisted that the United States must have known in advance that Marcos was going to declare martial law. Their principal argument is that he simply would not have acted without consulting the United States. But those who subscribe to this conspiracy theory have not offered any evidence.

One of the stories that has circulated is that Marcos discussed martial law with Senator Daniel Inouye when he was in Manila in late August 1972; also raising suspicions (among those who were aware of it) was the visit by a CIA analyst to the Philippines at the same time. I am convinced, however, on the basis of my interviews, that neither Inouye nor the CIA analyst, a woman who later wrote some reports highly critical of Imelda Marcos, were involved with, or had any advance knowledge of, martial law.

I made four FOIA requests which generated documents relevant to piecing together what happened. Two were to the State Department. One was for all cables to and from the embassy in Manila during September 1972. The other was for all documents pertaining to martial law for the period 1972 to 1981, inclusive. The latter request generated 345 documents. I also made FOIA requests pertaining to the imposition of martial law to the NSC and CIA and received important documents.

In many ways, more helpful than the documents were the recollections of persons who were directly involved in September 1972. I interviewed the top-level diplomats in the United States embassy in Manila; the principal State Department officers; members of the National Security Council; and several CIA officers who were in the Philippines, in Washington, or where they would have read the traffic. Finally, I interviewed several members of Marcos's inner circle at the time, including Defense Minister Enrile, who was a principal architect of martial law, and Filipinos who were working for the CIA.

While I am confident that this is the most complete account to date, in the future there may emerge more information (with the release of the Nixon papers, for example) which will supplement the details here.

p. 3. "Rolex 12": The twelve martial law planners were Defense Minister Juan Ponce Enrile; Fabian Ver, at the time in charge of presidential security; General Fidel Ramos, commander of the Philippine Constabulary (who, in 1986, joined in the revolt against Marcos); General Romeo Espino, armed forces chief of staff; General Rafael Zagala, head of the army; General Ignacio Paz, head of army intelligence; Air Force General José Rancudo; Navy Rear Admiral Hilario Ruiz; Tomas Díaz, commander of a key constabulary unit, whose wife once dumped a small sack of diamonds on the bed of the wife of an American army lieutenant, promising that she could get the woman as many as she wanted; Alfredo Montoya, head of the Manila Metropolitan Command; Colonel Romeo Gatan, commander of the constabulary in Tarlac, Aquino's district; and Eduardo Cojuangco, the only civilian among the twelve.

This list was provided to the author by one of the men on it and was confirmed by several U.S. intelligence officials.

pp. 3–4. Byroade as Horatio Alger: "Men Who Fascinate Women," *Look* (April 4, 1955), p. 130. Byroade's ambassadorial postings were: Egypt, South Africa. Afghanistan, Burma, Philippines, and Pakistan. The record is held by Ellis Ormsbee Briggs, who between 1944 and 1959 served in the Dominican Republic, Uruguay, Czechoslovakia, Korea, Peru, Brazil, and Greece.

p. 4. That Byroade was honored by the CIA was told to me by three persons, including a former CIA director.

p. 5. "flatly wrong" and "not informed": Transcript of State Department briefing, September 25, 1972.

p. 5. "spent the day": Lee Lescaze, "Marcos Says Martial Law Last Defense," *Washington Post*, September 24, 1972.

pp. 5–6. September 13 cable: Manila 8620, September 13, 1972, Confidential. State Department's cable for more details: State 168484, September 14, 1972, Secret.

p. 5. "evaluation of likelihood": State 171335, September 19, 1972, Secret ExDis.

1 : THE MAN AND THE WOMAN

p. 9. "If you are electing me": Spence, *Marcos of the Philippines*, p. 210. As noted in the footnote on page 10 there are several editions of the Spence "biography," which was originally titled *For Every Tear a Victory*. I used the 1982 paperback edition.

p. 9. "was in such a hurry": Ibid., p. 14.

p. 10. Marcos's mother thought he'd be a novelist: Ibid., p. 35.

p. 10. "I promise you, Mother": Ibid., p. 16.

p. 10. Marcos's father a collaborator: John Sharkey, "New Doubts on Marcos' War Role," *Washington Post*, January 24, 1986; *Far Eastern Economic Review*, February 27, 1986.

p. 10. Footnote about updating book and approach to Campbell: Related to author by Campbell in 1985.

pp. 11–14. The accounts of the Nalundasan murder are based on Philippine newspaper accounts at the time, principally the *Manila Daily Bulletin* and the *Philippines Herald*, as well as on Spence, *Marcos of the Philippines*, and Martinez, *Aquino vs. Marcos*. The government's Supreme Court brief was published in the *Philippines Herald*, October 5, 1940. Some of the details in the newspaper accounts differ from those in Spence's biography. For example, Spence (p. 50) says Marcos was arrested on December 7, 1939, the year that has been reprinted often in major American newspapers and magazines. The date December 7, 1938, is based on a story of December 8, 1938, in the *Daily Bulletin*. The cited language from the judge's decision is from the *Philippines Herald*, January 11, 1940.

p. 12. "He deeply impressed the court": Judge's opinion published in the *Philippines Herald*, January 11, 1940.

p. 13. *Lawyers' Journal*: Martinez, *Aquino vs. Marcos*, pp. 120–22; Spence, *Marcos of the Philippines*, p. 110–11.

p. 13. Marcos before Supreme Court: Spence, *Marcos of the Philippines*, pp. 115–18. The Supreme Court opinion was published in the *Philippines Herald*, October 22, 1940.

p. 13. For an examination of Laurel's role during the war, re the Japanese, see Steinberg, "José P. Laurel: A 'Collaborator' Misunderstood," *Journal of Asian Studies* (August 1965). Steinberg, a recognized Philippine scholar, concludes that Laurel "was neither a weak puppet, as was claimed by his post-war enemies, nor a martyr, as was claimed by his friends and himself." In 1985 Steinberg became president of Long Island University, where I interviewed him in October of that year.

p. 13. Marcos delivered Laurel eulogy: John Sharkey, "New Doubts on Marcos' War Role," *Washington Post*, January 24, 1986.

p. 14. "Almost invariably": Teodoro Agoncillo, *A Short History of the Philippines*, p. 13.

p. 14. "General Douglas MacArthur, pinning": Spence, *Marcos of the Philippines*, p. 126.

p. 15. Marcos exploits not mentioned: John Sharkey, "The Marcos Mystery: Did the Philippine Leader Really Win U.S. Medals for Valor?," *Washington Post*, December 18, 1983.

p. 15. Marcos saluted by Omar Bradley: Spence, *Marcos of the Philippines*, p. 207.

p. 15. Footnote about Kamm and Medal of Honor: Kamm related the incident to the author in August 1985.

p. 16. "Man in the News": *The New York Times*, November 13, 1965.

p. 16. I interviewed Manriquez and Swick by telephone in the summer of 1985, six months before *The New York Times* published a full exposé of Marcos's war medals fraud. Manriquez was living in Arlington, Virginia; Swick in Miami, Arizona.

pp. 16–17. Ang Mga Maharlika guerrilla unit: "A malicious criminal act": Memorandum from Capt E. R. Curtis to Lt Col W. M. Hanes; 24 March 48; Subject: Ferdinand E. Marcos. Marcos arrested; "enough political prestige": Memorandum from Capt E. R. Curtis to Lt Col W. M. Hanes; Subject: Radiogram Protest Non-Recognition Maharlika Guerrilla Unit. These and other documents pertaining to Maharlika unit are in the National Archives.

p. 17. Marcos as collaborator: Sharkey, "New Doubts on Marcos' War Role," *Washington Post*, January 24, 1986.

p. 18. "Don't start a fight": Spence, *Marcos of the Philippines*, p. 33. "Never make an important move": Ibid., p. 29.

p. 18. "proudly packaged": *Time* (October 21, 1966).

p. 18. "She moved heaven and earth": Author's interview with Carmen Navarro Pedrosa, March 1986, New York. Much of the information about Imelda Marcos's early years is from Pedrosa's book.

p. 19. Imelda Marcos frequently made these boasts about her father. The words I have used here are from an interview she gave Roy Rowan or *Fortune* magazine in April 1979. Rowan provided the author with a transcript.

p. 21. "Give him a jug": Agoncillo, *Short History of the Philippines*, p. 16.

p. 23. "She's lost the bloom": Interview with author.

p. 23. "flung 100-peso bills": "Special Report, Philippines," *Life* (November 26, 1965).

p. 23. Imelda Marcos's advice for Humphrey: Author's interview with William P. Bundy, Princeton, New Jersey, October 21, 1985.

p. 24. Imelda Marcos's wooing Lopez: Author's interviews with Fernando and Mariquit Lopez and Robert Puckett, San Francisco, August 1985.

p. 25. "year-long propaganda orgy": Manila 866, November 8, 1965, Confidential. Obtained from LBJ Library, Austin, Texas.

p. 25. CIA's view of Marcos as "brilliant lawyer" but "ruthless politician": Intelligence Memorandum, Directorate of Intelligence; 28 October 1965, OCI No. 2343/65, Secret. Released to the author under the FOIA.

p. 25. "few are willing to believe": R. H. Leary, "President's Progress," *Far Eastern Economic Review* (November 4, 1966). For two other excellent looks at the color and tenor of the campaign: R. H. Leary, "The Wrong Issues," *Far Eastern Economic Review* (June 24, 1965), and Bernard Ronquillo, "The Unique Campaign," *Far Eastern Economic Review* (October 21, 1965).

p. 25. CIA on Macapagal: Intelligence Memorandum; 28 October 1965, OCI No. 2343/65, Secret.

p. 25. "suffers from too much": Testimony of Ambassador William McCormick Blair before the House Subcommittee on Asian and Pacific Affairs, April 20, 1967. The testimony was delivered in executive session. A transcript of the session, classified secret, was provided to the author.

Two general accounts of the the corruption and the 1965 election: George De Carvalho, "A Dirty Campaign on the Corruption Issue," *Life* (November 26, 1965); and Alex Campbell, *New Republic* (March 12, 1966), pp. 21–24.

p. 26. Embassy cable on eve of voting: Manila 866, November 8, 1965, Confidential. LBJ Library.

p. 26. CIA views on what electorate wanted and what was needed: Intelligence Memorandum; 28 October 1965, OCI No. 2343/65, Secret.

2 : ONCE A COLONY, ALWAYS A COLONY?

pp. 28–29. A vivid account of America's war in the Philippines is *Sitting in Darkness: Americans in the Philippines*, by David Haward Bain. It is part biography (of the Philippine revolutionary Emilio Aguinaldo and the American soldier of fortune who pursued him, Frederick Funston), part adventure story (Bain retraced the final chase), and thoroughly researched history. Another excellent account is *Benevolent Assimilation: The American Conquest of the Philippines, 1899–1903*, by Stuart Creighton Miller. For general history, I also used Stephen Rosskaamm Shalom's *The United States and the Philippines: A Study of Neocolonialism*. A concise history of American policy in the Philippines is Claude A. Buss, *The United States and the Philippines: Background for Policy*. Only 152 pages, it covers the period from 1896 to 1976, with probably the most reliable and informative chapters those which cover the pre-Marcos period. Buss was first in the Philippines as a Foreign Service officer in the 1930s, was executive assistant to the American high commissioner when World War II broke out, later taught at the University of the Philippines, and retired as professor emeritus at Stanford University. Unfortunately his book has no index, and it must be read with the understanding, as he offered to this author (in a conversation in 1986), that it reflects the conservative political orientation of the publishers, jointly the American Enterprise Institute, in Washington, D.C., and the Hoover Institution on War, Revolution, and Peace, at Stanford.

p. 30. "Myth number one": Robert Pringle, *Indonesia and the Philippines: American Interests in Island Southeast Asia*, pp. 54–55. One reviewer of Pringle's book, Richard Kessler, a Southeast Asia scholar, at the time at the conservative Georgetown Center for Strategic and International Studies, expressed the hope that someday, after he had left the Foreign Service, Pringle might provide a more detailed analysis. It was clear that Kessler, who later moved to the more liberal Carnegie Endowment for International Peace, believed Pringle had held back. (Kessler's review appeared in the *Asian Wall Street Journal*, December 30, 1981.) While that may be, and while it is certainly true that Pringle does not divulge any secrets or classified information, his analysis of the American role and policies in the Philippines is far more critically objective than what one usually hears or reads from American officials, at least publicly.

p. 32. Eisenhower's view of the Philippine bases: Air Force Major William E. Berry, Jr., "American Military Bases in the Philippines, Base Negotiations, and Philippine-American Relations: Past, Present, and Future," (1981), p. 152. Major Berry's 529-page doctoral thesis is probably the most comprehensive public document on the subject of the bases. It does not suffer from excessive military jargon and benefits from a concise historical chapter.

The agreement covering the bases is officially known as: Agreement Between the United States of America and the Republic of the Philippines concerning Military Bases.

pp. 33–34. Kennan memorandum: "Review of Current Trends, U.S. Foreign Policy," PPS/23, Top Secret. Included in *Foreign Relations of the United States, 1948* (Washington, D.C.: Government Printing Office, 1976), vol. I, part 2, pp. 509–29.

pp. 34–36. Lansdale: Snippets of Lansdale's activities appear in many of the books about Vietnam. See, for example, David Halberstam, *The Best and the Brightest*, particularly pp. 124–29, which explore Lansdale's relations with the Kennedy brothers. Another valuable reference for Lansdale in Vietnam is *The U.S. Government and the Vietnam War. Executive and Legislative Roles and Relationships*, part I, 1945–1961, prepared for the Senate Foreign Relations Committee by the Congressional Research Service, 1984. Lansdale's activities in Cuba are most fully detailed in *The Man Who Kept the Secrets: Richard Helms and the CIA*, by Thomas Powers (New York: Alfred A. Knopf, 1979). The best account of Lansdale in the Philippines is in Joseph B. Smith, *Portrait of a Cold Warrior*. Valeriano's role, with Lansdale in the Philippines and later in Cuba, was related to the author by several CIA sources, who laughed about his inability to return home.

p. 35. Ky and Lansdale: Author's interview with General Landsdale, July 19, 1985, McLean, Virginia. Lansdale died in February 1987.

p. 36. Huk rebellion: A comprehensive account of the Huk rebellion is Eduardo Lachica, *HUK: Philippine Agrarian Society in Revolt*. A Philippine journalist working in Manila when he wrote his book (which was based on much of his own investigative reporting), Lachica later went to work for the *Wall Street Journal*. His book, which also traces the links between the Huks and the Communist-led New People's Army, is well researched, is carefully footnoted, and contains an index. Perhaps the best American-authored account is *The Huk Rebellion: A Study of Peasant Revolt in the Philippines*, by Benedict J. Kerkvliet.

p. 36. "with the knowledge": Agoncillo, *Short History of the Philippines*, p. 267.

p. 36. "The rebellion's main impetus": *Philippines: a Country Study*, p. 43.

pp. 37–38. Lansdale's account of the Huk war and the U.S. role in it, as well as of the first of his years in Vietnam, is contained in his book *In the Midst of Wars: An American's Mission to Southeast Asia*. It is self-censored—Lansdale doesn't even acknowledge that he was working for the CIA, and although the book was published in 1972, he writes nothing about what he did in Vietnam after 1963—and self-serving, not just to Lansdale but to the entire U.S. effort in the Philippines and then Vietnam.

pp. 37–38. Eye of God and *asuang*: Lansdale, *Midst of Wars*, pp. 72–75.

p. 37. Footnote on propaganda training and disinformation campaigns: Joseph Smith, *Portrait of a Cold Warrior*, pp. 78–80 and 85–86. Smith's book is a personal story, readable, and, above all, highly revelatory about the ways and means of the agency. To my mind one of the best books by or about the CIA, it is must reading for foreign correspondents, who should worry whether the CIA is planting stories with them.

p. 38. "Magsayay's humane approach": Agoncillo, *Short History of the Philippines*, p. 270.

p. 39. CIA not to inform State and drugged Quirino's drinks: Thomas Buell interview with General Ralph B. Lovett, July 6, 1972, Arlington, Virginia. On file in the Naval Historical Collection, Naval War College, Newport, Rhode Island. Lovett was the CIA station chief in the Philippines in the early 1950s.

p. 39. Lansdale offered $5 million: Thomas Buell interview with Lansdale, July 6, 1972, Alexandria, Virginia. On file in the Naval Historical Collection, Naval War College, Newport, Rhode Island.

p. 39. Coca-Cola contribution: Author's interview with Lansdale.

p. 39. That Sternberg worked for the CIA was told to the author by several CIA sources. That he shot an intruder: Buell interview with Lovett. Sternberg's *Foreign Affairs* article, "The Philippines: Contour and Perspective," appeared in April 1966. Sternberg was described as a "resident in the Philippines for 26 years, contributor to *The Christian Science Monitor* and on occasion adviser to A.I.D. [Agency for International Development]."

p. 40. Lansdale hit Magsaysay: Buell interview with Lansdale.

p. 40. Kaplan's role: Joseph Smith, *Portrait of a Cold Warrior*, pp. 251–52.

p. 40. Operation Brotherhood: For Lansdale's innocuous version, see *Midst of Wars*; see also Joseph Smith, *Portrait of a Cold Warrior*, pp. 171–72. In interviews American and Philippine intelligence officials added to much that has already been written about Operation Brotherhood.

p. 40. "We taught a lot": Author's interview with William Sullivan, March 7, 1986, New York.

p. 40. "neither the authority nor justification": Thomas Buell, *The Quest Warrior: A Biography of Admiral Raymond A. Spruance* (1974), p. 419.

p. 41. "orchestrated": Joseph Smith, *Portrait of a Cold Warrior*, p. 102. That the agency set up the National Press Club was told to the author by Smith. I interviewed him in Florida, October 30, 1985; we also exchanged letters, and I spoke with him many times by telephone.

p. 41. That the agency encouraged editors to send their best: Buell interview with Lovett.

p. 41. "on our side": *New York Times* editorial, June 19, 1952.

p. 41. *Time* cover on Magsaysay: November 26, 1951.

p. 41. Smugggled guns: Author's interview with Joseph Smith and with another CIA officer.

p. 42. Recto as "spearhead and brains": Agoncillo, *Short History of the Philippines*, pp. 285–90.

p. 42. Recto, CIA, and condoms: Joseph Smith, *Portrait of a Cold Warrior*, p. 248.

p. 42. Assassination plot: Buell interview with Lovett.

p. 42. "Find another": Joseph Smith, *Portrait of a Cold Warrior*, p. 248.

p. 43. "always much cagier": Author's interview with Smith.

p. 43. Grand Alliance: Joseph Smith, *Portrait of a Cold Warrior*, pp. 304–14.

p. 43. 1961 CIA backing for Macapagal: Author's interviews with CIA sources; $50,000: Smith, *Portrait of a Cold Warrior*, pp. 308–09.

p. 43. "Western oriented": Intelligence Memorandum, OCI 2343/65, 28 October 1965. Released under the FOIA.

3 : DEBUT AND CONQUEST

p. 46. The language I have cited here is taken from the text of Marcos's inaugural address that was released by Malacañang at the time.

p. 47. "tour de force": Author's interview with Jack Valenti, July 16, 1985, Washington, D.C.

p. 47. "one of the most magnetic": Memorandum from Valenti to LBJ, July 1, 1966. Obtained from the LBJ Library.

p. 47. "tough . . . guts": Memorandum from Valenti to LBJ, February 25, 1966. LBJ Library.

p. 47. "let's play golf . . . I thought, my God . . . one of the great men": Author's interview with Valenti.

p. 47. Footnote on golf statistics: Manila 2101, August 29, 1966, Limited Official Use.

p. 48. Valenti and Imelda Marcos: Author's interview with Valenti.

p. 48. "kind of his man": Ibid.

pp. 48–49. "Marcos Visit: The Plot Thickens": Memorandum from James Thomson to Walt W. Rostow, May 4, 1966. LBJ Library.

p. 49. Mounted head of a tamarau: Memorandum for Walt W. Rostow, from Benjamin H. Read; Subject: Request for Appointment with the President for Philippine Special Envoy Benjamin Romualdez, drafted August 9, 1966. LBJ Library.

p. 49. Kokoy Romualdez's Southampton estate: Based on documents provided by the Presidential Commission on Good Government, which was set up by President Corazon Aquino after Marcos's ouster in February 1986.

p. 49. "handsome, a war hero": Valenti memorandum to LBJ, July 1, 1966. LBJ Library.

p. 50. "excellent mood": Manila, September 12, 1966, Confidential. LBJ Library.

pp. 50–51. "genuine war hero": Manila 497, July 14, 1966, Secret. LBJ Library.

p. 51. *Life* cover: Asia edition, August 8, 1966.

p. 51. *Parade*: Vera Glaser, "Imelda Marcos: First Lady of Asia," October 11, 1966.

p. 51. *Time* cover: October 21, 1966.

p. 52. "political purposes": Memorandum for the President from W. W. Rostow, September 7, 1966, Secret. LBJ Library.

p. 52. McNamara's position on the engineering battalions: Memorandum for the President, September 9, 1966, Secret. LBJ Library.

p. 53. "he insisted on going head to head": Author's interview with Bundy.

p. 53. LBJ and Marcos in Australia: Ibid.

pp. 54–55. Most of the details of the White House dinner are from Jim Bishop, *A Day in the Life of President Johnson*, pp. 193–263.

p. 54. Imelda Marcos's missing Smith's party: Author's interview with Smith.

p. 55. 3,000 Chinese egg rolls: *Manila Chronicle*, September 17, 1966.

p. 55. "Imelda Stole Spotlight": *Washington Post*, September 16, 1966.

p. 55. Beale: "Marcoses a Hit, Fete Johnsons," *Washington Star*, September 16, 1966.

p. 55. Dixon: " 'Meldy' Meets Press," *Washington Star*, September 16, 1966.

p. 55. Psychiatric treatment: Author's interview with Filipino psychiatrist.

pp. 55–58. New York trip: Based on news coverage at the time in Philippine and New York newspapers and the official program released by the State Department at the time.

p. 56. "quite a scholar": Manila A-905 (Memorandum of Conversation), April 29, 1966, Secret. LBJ Library.

p. 57. "best efforts": State [no number on copy of cable obtained from LBJ Library], May 23, 1966, Secret/LimDis. In interviews with the author, Bundy and Paul Kattenburg, a Yale alumnus and the State Department officer who drafted the cable about what Bundy had told Romualdez, said that nothing had ever been done about getting Marcos an honorary degree from Yale or Harvard.

p. 57. "quite possibly": "A Night at the Opera," *Newsweek* (September 22, 1966).

p. 57. "would have no interest": State 31761, August 19, 1966, Confidential. Not even *Il Trovatore*: Manila 1788, August 19, 1966, Confidential. Other cables in this saga: State 32353, August 21, 1966, Confidential ("belief that either Marcoses have been invited Opera premiere as State guests is erroneous repeat erroneous impression on part Ben Romualdez"); Manila 1920, August 24, 1966, Confidential; State 34122, August 24, 1966, Confidential ("Department . . . informed Romualdez that President and Mrs. Marcos are invited to attend opera opening performance").

pp. 57–58. Kokoy Romualdez's efforts: Author's interview with Paul Kattenburg, June 16, 1985, Columbia, South Carolina. I had many subsequent telephone conversations with Kattenburg. His account of what happened was confirmed by Edna Barr Hubbert, in an interview with the author, July 26, 1985, Crystal City, Virginia. I also had several subsequent telephone conversations with Hubbert.

p. 58. "It came out of nowhere": Author's interview with Hubbert.

p. 58. "hungry trout": Author's interview with Bundy. This version of how the Manila Summit came about is different from reports at the time. The White House claimed (and it was reported by the press) that President Marcos had invited President Johnson to attend a conference on Vietnam to be held in Manila and that Johnson had accepted. According to the White House, it had been discussed by the two presidents during the state visit. The White House denied that the trip was politically motivated. "We could not turn down the invitation just because a political campaign is going on," said the White House spokesman. In truth, however, the Johnson administration could not turn down the invitation because the idea had come from Johnson, not Marcos, and it was principally motivated by LBJ's domestic political concerns.

pp. 58–59. Letter from Filipino farmer: Obtained from LBJ Library.

p. 61. "I have rarely seen a night": Lady Bird Johnson, *A White House Diary*, p. 434.

pp. 61–62. Barrio Fiesta: Don Moser, "Solemn Event in a Fiesta City," *Life* (November 4, 1966); Johnson, *White House Diary*, p. 435; Robert Trumbull, "Leaders Unwind at Manila Fiesta," *The New York Times*, October 26, 1966.

p. 62. Details of the 1968 private dinner: From documents obtained from LBJ Library.

p. 62. Bong Bong Marcos to Cape Kennedy: Ibid.

4 : CHASING POWER

p. 63. "but into Imelda's pockets": Author's interview with Jaime Ferrer, November 22, 1985, Manila.

p. 65. "The visit itself": Manila 9795, July 7, 1969, Secret/LimDis. Pursuant to an FOIA request, the State Department located thirty documents pertaining to Nixon's visit. Twenty-nine were released in full; one, with excisions.

p. 65. "It was incredible. . . . Rafferty was busy": Author's interview, July 1985.

pp. 65–69. Rafferty's preparations for the Nixon visit and his other activities in Manila were provided in more than a dozen interviews with ambassadors, other Foreign Service officers, CIA officials, and Filipinos who knew him. I had several telephone conversations with Rafferty, who declined to provide an in-person interview. Basic biographical data were taken from the *Biographic Register*. The department discontinued the *Biographic Register* once it realized how journalists (and presumably the Soviet Union) could use it to identify CIA officers who were operating under diplomatic cover. The last widely distributed *Biographic Register* was for 1974; I obtained a copy of one from 1977.

p. 66. "He was always an enigma": Author's interview with Evelyn Colbert, July 29, 1985, Washington, D.C.

p. 66. "He was introduced to everyone": Author's interview with Jovito Salonga, November 1985, Manila.

p. 66. "I've always assumed": Author's interview with Lewis Gleeck, Jr., December 1985, Manila.

p. 67. "after midnight": Author's interview, 1985.

p. 67. "One of the reasons": Author's telephone conversation with Rafferty, July 1985.

pp. 67–69. Dovie Beams affair: *Marcos' Lovey Dovie*, by Hermie Rotea, a Philippine journalist in exile, is an account of the affair, written in the same tone and style as the grade B affair, which is to say it might be entertaining but can hardly be considered serious journalism or scholarship. This author's account is based on interviews with diplomats and CIA officials, who also told about Marcos's affair with the wife of the American naval officer. Members of the Locsin family, including Mrs. Locsin, provided the anecdote about Imelda Marcos's call to Mrs. Locsin. Edna Barr Hubbert told about how Washington first learned about Dovie Beams.

p. 69. "I fired him": Author's interview with Sullivan.

p. 69. "We know he is only coming": Charles Mohr, "Few Issues Expected to Arise in Nixon's Brief Talks in Manila," *The New York Times*, July 26, 1969.

p. 70. Nixon's toast: From State Department archives.

p. 70. "Despite almost round the clock": Manila 7584, July 18, 1969, Confidential/ExDis.

p. 70. Semple's reaction: Interview with author, June 1986, New York.

pp. 70–73. Three lengthy articles about the Cultural Center appeared in the *Philippines Free Press*, February 22, 1969 ("Parthenon or Pantheon?"); September 13, 1969 ("A Stage for Greatness"); and September 20, 1969 ("If It's Wednesday, This Must Be the Cultural Center").

p. 71. Executive order for cultural commission: Published in the *Official Gazette*, August 1, 1966, pp. 5555–57. After Marcos had declared martial law, he dissolved the government commission, transferring all its properties, assets, and bank accounts, which were vast, to a nongovernmental body of which Imelda Marcos was chairman: Proclamation No. 1088, published in the *Official Gazette*, November 6, 1972, pp. 8659–60.

p. 71. Special Fund for Education: Philippine War Damage Legislation of 1962; P.L. 88–94, approved August 12, 1963. U.S. money for Cultural Center: Memorandum for the President, Subject: Special Fund for Philippine National Cultural Center, from W. W. Rostow, June 19, 1967 (with several attachments).

p. 71. *Parade*'s view of fund-raising: Vera Glaser, "Imelda Marcos: First Lady of Asia," October 11, 1966.

p. 72. Imelda Marcos and tax man: Author's interview with Ferrer.

p. 72. Footnote on not giving to the Kennedy Center: Related to author by a senior U.S. government official who was involved in raising money for the Kennedy Center.

p. 73. How Nixon selected Reagan: Incident related to author by a person present.

pp. 73–75. Symington hearings: *United States Security Agreements and Commitments Abroad*, hearings before the Subcommittee on United States Security Agreements and Commitments Abroad of the Committee on Foreign Relations, U.S. Senate, vol. I, parts 1–4, 1971. Through various individuals, I was able to read, make notes from, and in some instances copy, nearly all those parts of the hearings that were not publicly released.

pp. 75–76. GAO Report: B-168501, Review of Assistance to the Philippine Government in Support of the Philippine Civic Action Group, June 1, 1970. The author was permitted to read and take notes from the still-classified version.

p. 76. That Rafferty delivered checks directly to Marcos was told to the author by a diplomat who had been in the U.S. embassy at the time and who said he was relying on his own firsthand knowledge as well as on what Rafferty had told him.

p. 76. Maceda and stealing the election: Author's interview with Ernesto Maceda, October 1985, Washington, D.C. Maceda broke with Marcos a few years after martial law was declared and lived in New York for many years; he returned to the Philippines after Marcos was ousted, becoming a high-level member of Aquino's cabinet, much to the disappointment of many of her advisers who knew about his corrupt ways; in late 1986 President Aquino removed him. Pursuant to an FOIA request the State Department located twenty-four documents pertaining to the 1969 election. Twenty-one were released in full; three, with excisions.

p. 76. $50 million: Lachica, *HUK*, p. 192.

p. 76. O'Brien and Napolitan: Robert H. Phelps, "Washington Notes," *The New York Times*, December 19, 1969.

pp. 76–77. Everett Martin: "The Philippines: Making of a President," *Newsweek* (November 24, 1969).

p. 77. Footnote on whether the United States helped Marcos: Interview with Kattenburg. Author's interview with James Wilson, June 12, 1985, Bethesda, Maryland, and subsequent telephone conversations.

p. 77. "Man in the News": *The New York Times*, November 14, 1969. *Time*: (November 21, 1969).

pp. 77–78. First Quarter Storm: Based on accounts in Philippine and American newspapers at the time. For a summary and analysis, see Lachica, *HUK*, pp. 191–94.

p. 79. "social inequities": "Philippines: The Radical Movements," Bureau of Intelligence and Research, May 3, 1971, Secret/No Foreign Dissem/Controlled Dissem/No Dissem Abroad.

pp. 79–80. Plaza Miranda bombing: The *Philippines Free Press* story was on September 4, 1971. In addition to this and other newspaper accounts at the time, I relied on cables and other documents received pursuant to an FOIA request pertaining to the incident. There have been various explanations given for Aquino's arriving late and the nature of an advance warning. The one I have used comes from an embassy report to Washington: Manila 7956, August 24, 1971, Confidential.

p. 80. "remained a mystery": Seth Mydans, "Fears of a Coup Rise in Manila, But Then Ease," *The New York Times*, November 8, 1986.

p. 80. "Without question": Author's interview.

In 1986 a Philippine military officer, Victor Corpuz, who had defected to the Communist guerrillas, then returned to the military fold after six years, wrote a letter claiming that the Communists were responsible for the Plaza Miranda incident. See *The New York Times*, Mydans, "Fears of a Coup," November 8, 1986; Gregg Jones, "Aquino Asks Enrile About Plot Reports," *Washington Post*, November 8, 1986.

After this story appeared, I contacted several American officials with whom I had previously spoken about Plaza Miranda. They scoffed at Corpuz's story. "I've never heard anybody seriously allege that before," said one intelligence officer who had been in Manila at the time of the bombing.

"Do you believe it?" I asked another.

"No!"

What they couldn't explain were Corpuz's motivations, though they assumed they had something to do with the power struggle going on in late 1986 between the military and President Corazon Aquino. Since Ninoy Aquino had been linked with Communists and the bombing in 1971, if the Communists were implicated, she would be weakened. There was also a personal motivation: Corpuz was trying to rehabilitate himself with the army, and he was reinstated as a reserve officer after implicating the Communists.

p. 82. "No precedent whatsoever": Memorandum from Emil Mosbacher, Jr., to Mr. Whitehouse, October 21, 1971. Ambassador Mosbacher worked in the Office of Protocol; Charles S. Whitehouse was a deputy assistant secretary in the East Asian Bureau.

p. 82. $1,608.87: Confidential Memorandum; from Mr. Whitehouse, to Ambassador Mosbacher, October 21, 1971. That the NSC and State argued over who would pay the bill was told to the author in an interview with a diplomat working at the NSC at the time.

p. 82. "I can remember": Author's interview.

pp. 82–83. Green and Imelda Marcos: Author's interview with Marshall Green, July 17, 1985, Washington, D.C. I subsequently talked with Green by telephone and conducted another long interview, April 1, 1986.

p. 83. Usher: Author's interview, June 21, 1985, Washington, D.C.

p. 83. "share the tent": Manila 9500, October 8, 1971, Secret/LimDis.

p. 84. "It should be born [sic] in mind": Memo from Whitehouse to Mosbacher, October 21, 1971.

p. 84. "The people who control": Author's interview with Hubbert.

p. 84. "vested oligarchial [sic] interests": INR Briefing Note, October 5, 1971, Confidential.

p. 84. "through the traditional tactics": "Philippines: Marcos and the Constitutional Convention; Opportunities and Pitfalls," INR, May 7, 1971, Secret/No Foreign Dissem/Controlled Dissem/Background Use Only/No Dissem Abroad.

p. 85. CIA bribery of Vietnamese legislators: Seymour Hersh, *The Price of Power: Kissinger in the Nixon White House*, p. 435.

pp. 85–91. Byroade: Many of the details of Byroade's life and career were provided by him during several interviews, at his home in Potomac, Maryland; as well as when he and I were in Manila in December 1985. Altogether I spent probably forty hours with Byroade and had numerous telephone conversations with him. In addition, I interviewed several CIA stations chiefs who worked for him, in the Philippines and elsewhere, along with a much greater number of foreign service officers. Byroade was profiled in *Current Biography*, 1952, p. 79. For his role in the overthrow of Mossadegh, see Kermit Roosevelt, *Countercoup: The Struggle for the Control of Iran* (New York: McGraw-Hill, 1979), p. 5. Byroade's two speeches on the Middle East were printed in Department of State *Bulletins*, April 26 and May 10, 1954; the controversy was reported in *The New York Times*, May 2, 3, 4, and 6, 1954. The Byroade-Nasser relationship is described in Anthony Nutting, *Nasser* (London: Constable 1972), pp. 103–04, 116, 118–19. For Byroade and his cars, see "Body by Byroade," *American Magazine* (March 1955). "Man in the News": *The New York Times*, July 4, 1969. Byroade's reaction to *The New York Times*' publication of the *Pentagon Papers* was released as part of *United States* v. *Washington Post Co. et al.* (D.D.C.) Civil Action No. 1235-71; U.S. District Court for the District of Columbia; Attachment B to Plaintiff's Amended Second Motion for Modification of Protective Order, p. 8.

5 : COUNTDOWN TO MARTIAL LAW

See author's comments (page 455) at beginning of Prologue notes.

p. 92. Homicide rates. Harvey A. Averch, John E. Koehler, and Frank H. Denton, *The Matrix of Policy in the Philippines*, p. 120; and Robert E. Klitgaard, "Martial Law in the Philippines" (November 1972), p. 3.

pp. 92–93. "A symbol of male virility" and "This place is a hopeless mess": Letter to author from Francis T. Underhill, June 3, 1985. I interviewed Underhill in June 1985 at his home in Flat Rock, North Carolina.

p. 94. The transferred commanders were General Rafael ("Rocky") Ileto and General Manuel Yan. Ileto was made deputy chief of staff for the armed forces, and Yan was sent to Indonesia as ambassador. While those might be considered promotions—and Marcos, ever skillful in using rewards as well as punishments to keep needed supporters in line, also gave Ileto another star—it meant that they no longer had control of troops. The loyalists were Tomas Diaz and Alfredo Montoya.

p. 94. *Karagatan*: For an amusing and informative account of the incident, see Peter Kann, "An Abandoned Boat Is the Key to a Puzzle Without Any Solution," *Wall Street Journal*, September 1, 1972.

p. 94. "Everything about it": Author's interview.

p. 94. "gun-smuggling circles": A copy of a CIA analysis, dated June 28, 1975, which was classified Secret and Not for Foreign Dissemination, was made available to the author.

p. 95. The two leaders of the Communist party were interviewed by the author in the Philippines in 1985, over the space of several days, separately, and in different parts of the Philippines.

pp. 95–98. Bombings: These were reported at the time in the Philippine newspapers. A summary and recapitulation appeared in the *Philippines Free Press*, September 23, 1972.

p. 95. In early August several tentative dates set: Author's interview with a person who was present.

p. 96. "Undesirability . . . not stated in so many words": Manila 8990, September 22, 1972, Secret/ExDis.

p. 96. Byroade's meeting with Kissinger and Nixon was described by two persons who were present.

pp. 97–98. That Aquino revealed martial law plan to embassy before making it public: Manila 8738, September 15, 1972, Limited Official Use.

p. 98. Marcos told one of top aides that he had already cleared martial law with Nixon: This was related to the author by the aide during an interview in Manila in December 1985. The aide was no longer working for Marcos but was still very close to him.

p. 98. Marcos and Nixon spoke on or about the eighteenth: Raul Manglapus, "The Marcos Dictatorship and U.S. Policy," *Asian Thought & Society: An International Review* (April 1977), p. 134.

pp. 98–99. The account of the two Marcos-Nixon conversations was told to the author in an interview in Manila in December 1980 by the person to whom Romulo had related it. A few days later, in an interview with Romulo, I asked him about it. He declined to provide any details, saying that he might do so when we next talked. A few days later, Romulo, who was eighty-six years old, died.

According to a Marcos press flack, Primitivo Mijares, Imelda Marcos told him that a few days before martial law was declared, Marcos spoke with Nixon, who gave his "personal blessings" to martial law. Mijares relates this in his book *The Conjugal Dictatorship of Ferdinand and Imelda Marcos*, p. 6. There is every reason to be suspicious of Imelda Marcos on such a self-serving matter; and there is good reason to be cautious of anything Mijares said or wrote. He was somewhat of an unsavory character, "hardly an objective observer," the *Far Eastern Economic Review* noted at the time his book was published, adding: "His pen was for sale before and possibly still is" (June 4, 1976). But there is little reason for him to have fabricated this conversation. Mrs. Marcos's account of the conversation, however, is nothing short of wild. She told Mijares that Nixon wanted Marcos to try martial law "because he [Nixon] might find need for a model which he could adopt later in the United States. We are actually doing Nixon a favor by showing him here in the Philippines how martial law can be wielded to save a President from his political troubles."

The Conjugal Dictatorship is badly organized and without footnotes or index, a kiss-and-tell account written after Mijares had broken with Marcos, but it is filled with the details which as an insider Mijares was in a position to know. Mijares testified before the U.S. Congress in 1975, an appearance Marcos tried to prevent by offering Mijares $100,000. Not long thereafter Mjiraes's son was killed and Mjiares himself disappeared. His body has never been found.

For Mijares's testimony: *Human Rights in South Korea and the Philippines: Implications for U.S. Policy*, hearings before the Subcommittee on International Organizations of the Committee on International Relations, June 17, 1975. Jack Anderson wrote about the attempted bribe of Mijares: *Washington Post*, July 2, 3, 14, and 22, 1975. Anderson's articles are printed in the congressional hearings, pp. 481–84.

p. 99. "for the time being": Manila 8890, September 22, 1972, Secret/ExDis.

In his book *The Counterfeit Revolution: The Philippines from Martial Law to the Aquino Assassination*, Reuben Canoy writes that Ambassador Sullivan (Byroade's successor in Manila) saw a cable in which Byroade "thought there might be a chance that martial law would be put in [*sic*] November or early December" (p. 29). Presumably Manila 8890 was that cable. Canoy, a lawyer, politician, and writer, held positions in Marcos's martial law government, then later broke with him. His book is probably the best on the martial law and the period about which he writes. It has an index, and though there are no footnotes, Canoy is careful to indicate when he is offering opinion as opposed to fact. Thus, he says that though there is an "absence of hard evidence," he is "inclined to believe" that Byroade knew about and approved martial law in advance. See pp. 27–28.

p. 100. Attack on Enrile: In December 1985 I had two long interviews with Enrile, one at his home, the other in his office. He was emphatic that the attack on him had been not been staged, but in February 1986, after he had broken with Marcos and led the revolt that ousted the Philippine president, Enrile admitted that the attack on his car had been faked. Several American intelligence officers told me that the car attack was phony. "Flimflam," said one.

p. 100. Footnote on backdating: Author's interview with Enrile; author's interview with Roberto Reyes, December 1985, Manila.

pp. 100–101. Aquino's arrest has been widely reported. This version was taken from Lee Lescaze, "Marcos Says Martial Law Last Defense," *Washington Post*, September 24, 1972. Lescaze provided the best accounts from Manila at the time of the imposition of martial law. A short, and probably only summary of events in the Philippines preceding martial law which was written at the time is "Martial Law: How It Happened," *Far Eastern Economic Review* (September 30, 1972). On Aquino's arrest, see also Martinez, *Aquino vs. Marcos*, p. 295; Mijares, *Conjugal Dictatorship*, pp. 63–65.

p. 101. "I got bored": Nick Joaquin, *The Aquinos of Tarlac: An Essay on History as Three Generations*, p. 194. This is one of the few full-length biographies of Aquino; though it was written by a partisan and in anticipation of Aquino's expected 1973 campaign and must be read with that realization, it is generally accurate and certainly not as distorted as is Spence's biography of Marcos. It is without footnotes or even an index. About Aquino, see also "Man in the News," *The New York Times*, January 24, 1966; Robert Shaplen, "Letter from Manila," *New Yorker* (January 15, 1966).

p. 102. Aquino's jail reading: Martinez, *Aquino vs. Marcos*, p. 169. As noted, Martinez acknowledges that his book is favorably disposed to Aquino.

pp. 102–103. Aquino's views on communism, Asia, and the United States: Joaquin, *Aquinos of Tarlac*, p. 229.

p. 103. Taruc's version: Lachica, *HUK*, p. 135.

p. 103. Lansdale's account: Author's interview with Lansdale.

p. 103. Aquino at spy schools: Joaquin, *Aquinos of Tarlac*, p. 252.

p. 103. "I've worked with your CIA": *Multinational Monitor*, February 1981; see also, Rommel Corro (AP), "Marcos Foe Denies He's CIA Agent," *Washington Post*. March 11, 1978.

p. 104. The Pope bombing incident has been recounted in several of the books about the CIA. See, for example, Joseph Smith, *Portrait of a Cold Warrior*, pp. 197, 240; David Wise and Thomas Ross, *The Invisible Government* (New York: Vintage Books, 1974), pp. 136–46.

p. 104. "Absolutely not": Author's interview with Joseph Smith.

p. 104. "Kept bragging:" Joaquin, *Aquinos of Tarlac*, p. 250.

p. 106. Without due process; bar girl; shoot-outs: Martinez, *Aquino vs. Marcos*, pp. 107–89.

p. 106. "he is probably one of the smartest": Author's interview with Guy Pauker, April 31, 1986, Washington, D.C.

p. 107. *Philippines Free Press*: A copy was given to the author by the Locsin family in December 1985.

p. 108. Melchor's activities at the time of martial law were related to the author by several individuals, American and Philippine, with firsthand knowledge. All asked for anonymity on these matters, even though some of those interviewed spoke on the record regarding other events.

pp. 109–10. The press and Marcos: "The Marcos Gamble," *Newsweek* (October 9, 1972); "Marcos Details His 'Revolution from Center,' " *Washington Star*, December 14, 1972; "Man in the News," *The New York Times*, January 19, 1973; "Manila Enjoys Respite from Crisis Conditions," *Christian Science Monitor*, October 2, 1972.

pp. 110–11. Valeo's report was printed in the *Congressional Record*, February 21, 1973, S4841–44.

p. 111. U.S. reaction to martial law in Korea and the Philippines: See *Korea and the Philippines: November 1972*, staff report, Senate, Committee on Foreign Relations, February 18, 1973, pp.6–7.

6 : AMERICAN ACQUIESCENCE

p. 113. "backwater": Author's interview with Sullivan.

p. 114. "had thrown in the towel": Hersh, *The Price of Power*, p. 572, note.

p. 114. "a fait accompli": Author's interviews with Green.

p. 114. "leading expert": *The New York Times*, February 29, 1972.

p. 115. "we were ready, as usual": Robert Shaplen, "A Reporter at Large," *New Yorker* (May 5, 1986).

p. 115. Kim Dae Jung made the statement in an interview with Joseph Lelyveld of *The New York Times*, reported June 23, 1974, in the first article of a series on the United States in Southern Asia

p. 116. Proclamation 1081: Manila 9017, September 24, 1972, Unclassified. The proclamation is included as Appendix 2, David A. Rosenberg, ed., *Marcos and Martial Law in the Philippines*.

pp. 116–17. "Any idea or activity": *The Recent Presidential Elections in El Salvador: Implications for U.S. Foreign Policy*, hearings before the subcommittees on International Organizations and on Inter-American Affairs, 95th Congress, 1st Session, March 9 and 17, 1977, p. 54.

p. 117. "We in the United States": Observation of Ignacio Lozano, Jr., U.S. ambassador to El Salvador, *Religious Persecution in El Salvador*, hearings before the Subcommittee on International Organizations, 95th Congress, 1st Session, July 21 and 29, 1977.

pp. 117–18. A Philippine journalist's account of the birth, background, and orientation of the New People's Army is Eduardo Lachica's *HUK: Philippine Agrarian Society in Revolt*, ch. 9 through 12. The U.S. embassy, in a Secret cable in 1984 (Manila 15403), described Lachica's book as the "best account" of the early period of the Philippine Communist party and the NPA. I agree. One of the most complete academic papers is Francisco Nemenzo, "Rectification Process in the Philippine Communist Movement" (November 1982). More readily available is David Rosenberg, "Communism in the Philippines," *Problems of Communism* (September–October 1984), pp. 24–26.

p. 118. INR report: "Philippine Communists Under Martial Law," Dec. 11, 1973, Secret/No Forn Dissem/No Dissem Abroad/Controlled Dissem.

p. 118. Rand Corporation: Klitgaard, "Martial Law in the Philippines."

p. 119. Kann's view of the Muslim strife: Peter Kann, "The Philippines Without Democracy," *Foreign Affairs* (April 1974), p. 619. Pursuant to the FOIA, I received some 200 documents pertaining to the MNLF.

Writing in *Problems of Communism*, Tilman Durdin, who covered the region, including the Philippines, for *The New York Times* for more than two decades, beginning in the early 1950s, stated that by the summer of 1972 the Communists had "succeeded in fomenting a revolutionary situation" and that the NPA, "together with the gathering Moslem revolt in Mindanao, generally threatened his [Marcos's] regime" ("Philippine Communism [May–June 1976]," p. 42). On both counts, it is a distinctly minority view, shared by few others than Marcos and certainly not by any U.S. officials in the Foreign Service or the CIA who were in the Philippines at the time of martial law.

p. 122. "would have little choice": Manila 8378, September 15, 1972, Limited Official Use.

p. 122. Valeo's view: *Congressional Record*, February 21, 1973, S4842.

p. 122. Reports about the number of persons arrested and detained following martial law have varied widely, from 8,000 to 50,000. The 30,000 figure is from a report by Amnesty International, which took its figures from the Philippine government: *Report of an Amnesty International Mission to the Republic of the Philippines, 22 November–5 December 1975*.

p. 122. "something both cynical and presumptuous": Kann, "Philippines Without Democracy," p. 613.

p. 123. The number of newspapers, TV, and radio stations varies slightly in accounts at the time perhaps because, at least with newspapers, some were small and tended to fold after a short life. These numbers are from Klitgaard's Rand Corporation report.

p. 123. "Our analysis suggests": Averch et al., *Matrix of Policy*, p. 130.

p. 123. "essentially a police matter": The Interdepartmental Group report, dated August 28, 1972, was issued in response to National Security Study Memorandum 155, signed by Kissinger on June 28, 1972. The NSSM and the concluding report were released to the author, with substantial deletions, pursuant to an FOIA request to the NSC.

pp. 124–25. Ileto on how to defeat private armies: I had several interviews with General Ileto—February 1985, Bangkok; December 1985, Manila; and January 1986, Bangkok.

p. 126. Santos prepared and signed two lengthy affidavits, one February 13, 1984, the other March 22, 1984. They were submitted to the U.S. House Subcommittee on Asian and Pacific Affairs. The author also has copies. While there are good reasons to be suspicious of Santos's statements, in view of his own criminal conduct, an American intelligence official with knowledge of the Monkees' activities confirmed the reliability of those portions of the Santos affidavit that I have quoted here.

pp. 126–27. "knew about every": Author's interview.

p. 127. "There exists no authority": Letter from Lieutenant Colonel James U. Cross, aide to President Johnson, to Pacifico El. Macapagal, dated June 27, 1966. LBJ Library.

p. 127. "We all assumed": Author's interview, 1985.

p. 127. Psychological profile: It was mentioned publicly by John Marks, coauthor of *The CIA and the Cult of Intelligence*, in a speech in Chicago in May 1975. Marks's speech was reported by Mijares, *Conjugal Dictatorship*, p. 244. Marks, who worked in State's Bureau of Intelligence and Research from 1968 to 1970, confirmed to me in 1985 that there was such a CIA profile and that the Mijares account was generally accurate.

p. 127. "bribery and intimidation": Intelligence Note, Bureau of Intelligence and Research, "Philippines: Marcos Gambles on Martial Law," October 6, 1972, Secret/No Foreign Dissem.

p. 128. I saw the picture of Diokno and Hoover, which Hoover had inscribed, in Diokno's office in 1985. I had numerous conversations with Diokno in Manila in January and December 1985.

When Diokno died of cancer in February 1987, President Corazon Aquino declared ten days of national mourning, heralding him as "a giant of a man" who "braved the Marcos dictatorship with a dignified and eloquent courage our country will long remember."

p. 128. Kattenburg that Diokno was "mature, prudent": Paul Kattenburg, "Marcos Said They 'Chose to Stay' in Prison," *The New York Times*, July 24, 1974.

p. 129. INR on embassy reporting: "Appraisal of Political Reporting from Embassy Manila and Consulate Cebu." The first draft was prepared on July 17, 1973. It was toned down and shortened because William Hamilton, who had been the number two man in the embassy during the period being criticized, had returned to Washington and was working in INR; the modified, and shorter, report was issued on July 23, 1973. The language quoted here is from the first version.

p. 129. "By one means or another . . . no sign": "Talking Points for the Secretary's Briefing," October 31, 1972.

p. 130. Biographical material on Barber comes from author's interview, September 1985, Washington, D.C.

pp. 130–31. "The Philippines Tries One-Man Democracy": Intelligence Note, Bureau of Intelligence and Research, November 1, 1972, Secret/No Foreign Dissem. Released in response to FOIA request. The same Intelligence Note was released in response to two different FOIA requests, and in each release the deletions and excisions were different, suggesting that censorship has less to do with national security than with the whims of the censor. Thus, the italicized portion ("which he himself shares and has exploited") was deleted from one release, while it remained in another.

p. 131. Kissinger's question to Senior Review Group: Minutes of the SRG meeting, the Philippines and Morocco, November 30, 1972, Secret.

pp. 131–32. "supremely skilled, opportunistic,": "Appraisal of Political Reporting . . . ," July 17, 1973.

pp. 132–33. "Democracy is not the most important": Author's interview, September 1985, Washington, D.C.

p. 133. Kennan: Memorandum, "Review of Current Trends, U.S. Foreign Policy," PPS/23, Top Secret, February 24, 1948.

p. 133. Dulles: Cited in Buss, *United States and the Philippines*, p. 37.

p. 133. Nuclear weapons in the Philippines: The author was allowed to take notes from a Top Secret NSC document containing this information.

In a dispatch from Manila a few days after martial law was declared, Keyes Beech wrote that Marcos "promised to protect a $1 billion American economic stake in the Philippines in return for tacit U.S. approval of his declaration of martial law." "Marcos in Martial Law 'Deal,' " *San Francisco Examiner*, September 28, 1972. Beech, a Pulitzer Prize reporter for the *Chicago Sun-Times*, may have been the only American reporter to write about the U.S. role in martial law. But Beech cited no source for this assertion about the $1 billion deal, and intelligence and diplomatic officials who occupied senior positions in Manila at the time martial law was declared, and who otherwise expressed highest regard for Beech's reporting, say that this story was, as one intelligence officer put it, "absolutely, totally, without basis—totally."

pp. 133–34. For summaries of the activities of American businesses in the Philippines at the time of martial law, see *Korea and the Philippines: November 1972*, pp. 34–37; "The Republic of the Philippines: American Corporations, Martial Law, and Underdevelopment," prepared by the Corporate Information Center, National Council of Churches, New York; and Guy Whitehead, "Philippine-American Economic Relations," *Pacific Research and World Empire Telegram* (January–February 1973).

pp. 134–35. Chamber of Commerce telegram: Manila 9118, September 27, 1972, Limited Official Use.

p. 135. "ease the nationalistic restrictions": Minutes of meeting of SRG [Senior Review Group], November 30, 1972, Secret.

p. 136. The phrasing of the questions and the tabulations are taken from Filemon C. Rodriguez, *The Marcos Regime: Rape of the Nation*, pp. 108–09.

pp. 136–37. INR analysis: Intelligence Note, Bureau of Intelligence and Research. "Philippines: Marcos Abandons Constitutionality," January 15, 1973, Secret/

No Foreign Dissem. As with other INR reports, this one was released in response to two different FOIA requests; again the deletions were different in each.

7 : EMBRACING THE CONJUGAL DICTATORS

p. 138. NSDM 209 was provided to the author. This is the first time, I believe, that it has been made public. The documents which were the basis for the NSDM, including National Security Study Memorandum 155, June 28, 1972, which initiated the review of Philippine policy, were provided to the author pursuant to an FOIA request to the National Security Council.

p. 139. Policy on inaugural: State 217059; November 30, 1972, Unclassified.

pp. 139–44. The details of Imelda Marcos's visit were provided in interviews with State Department and NSC officers who were involved in her coming. I also made an FOIA request to the State Department for records pertaining to her attendance at the inauguration. Twelve documents were located; five were released in their entirety; seven, with excisions.

pp. 140–41. Lagdameo donations to Nixon: Watergate Special Prosecution Force memorandums: September 23, 1973; April 2, 1974; April 4, 1974; April 24, 1974. Transcript of proceedings, *United States* v. *Maurice H. Stans*; Criminal No. 75–163; U.S. District Court for the District of Columbia; March 12, 1975, pp. 1–17. All these documents were obtained from the National Archives. The other information about the Lagdameo contribution, including the fact that he was acting as a front for the Marcoses, as well as about the other contributions from the Marcoses to the Nixons, was provided to the author in interviews with American diplomatic and intelligence officers and with Philippine officials. Lagdameo died in 1986. The Marcoses gave more than $1 million to Nixon: Author's interview with Rafael Salas, October 13, 1986, New York. Salas died of a heart attack in March 1987.

p. 141. Usher's memorandum: Memorandum of Conversation; Subject: Mrs. Marcos' Visit to Washington; January 25, 1972; Secret.

pp. 141–42. Sharon's role in assisting Mrs. Marcos obtain inaugural tickets: State 008444, January 15, 1973, Confidential. His relationship to the Marcoses was pieced together from cables and from interviews with American officials. Mrs. Sharon, who was living in Chevy Chase, Maryland, was interviewed by telephone by Pamela Belluck, December 1985. Mr. Sharon died in 1980.

p. 142. Footnote "surrounded by 'faggots' there": Manila 13024, November 4, 1974, Confidential.

p. 142. "as soon as he had returned": Usher Memorandum of Conversation, January 25, 1972.

p. 143. Biographical information on Manglapus: I interviewed Manglapus, June 1985, Washington, D.C.

p. 144. "minimize ruffled feathers": State 100074, May 14, 1974, Confidential.

p. 144. "inappropriate": Letter from Benjamin A. Fleck, director of the Office of Philippine Affairs, to Steve E. Psinakis, dated June 30, 1976. Included in articles and documents bound by Manglapus; author has a copy.

p. 145. Lelyveld's article: "Rich Family Loses Power in Bitter Feud with Marcos," *The New York Times*, April 25, 1975.

p. 145. Imelda Marcos borrowing from Presy Lopez: Author's interview with Presy Lopez, August 1985, San Francisco.

p. 146. "took a big bite": Author's interview.

p. 146. Imelda Marcos's appearance at Lopez's funeral mass was related by an American diplomat who had been present, in an interview with the author in December 1985 in Manila.

pp. 147–48. Aquino's letter: *Far Eastern Economic Review*, October 8, 1973. The spelling of the words is as they appeared in the *Review*.

p. 148. "You may remember Bob": Letter from James W. McLane to Winston Lord, dated December 28, 1973. Copy in author's files.

p. 149. "a fresh status report": Letter from Lord to McLane, dated March 4, 1974. Copy in author's files.

pp. 149–50. "to be left to the judicial processes": Letter from McLane to Jones, dated March 12, 1974. Copy in author's files.

p. 150. Footnote on Guyana election: Author's interview with Kattenburg.

p. 151. Letter from Kattenburg to Cosell: August 20, 1975. Copy in author's files.

p. 151. "Flamboyant events": Mark Kram, "For Blood and Money," *Sports Illustrated* (September 29, 1975), pp. 22–30.

p. 151. Ali's praise for Marcos: *Philippines Yearbook*, 1975, pp. 48–49.

p. 152. "I'm personally going to set out to blast . . .": Kattenburg letter to John Helble, special assistant, Bureau of East Asian and Pacific Affairs, dated February 27, 1975. Copy in author's files.

p. 152. Kattenburg-Habib exchange: Kattenburg to Habib, February 27, 1975; Habib's first response, not dated; Kattenburg to Habib, March 31, 1975; Habib reply, April 11, 1975. All are in author's files.

p. 153. Sullivan-Jones encounter: Author's interview with Robert T. Jones, Jr., February 1986, New York. I had several subsequent telephone conversations with Jones.

p. 153. Footnote, "Marcos reneged": Author's interview with Sullivan.

p. 153. Imelda Marcos "deplores what happened to Nixon": Manila 13024, November 4, 1974, Confidential/LimDis.

p. 153. Footnote on omission, Sullivan's explanation: Author's interview.

p. 154. "confirmation of the truth": Manila 16893, December 3, 1975, Limited Official Use.

p. 154. "a success as soon as it was announced" and "pulled out all stops . . . unprecedented . . . carefully contrived": Manila 17133, December 8, 1975, Confidential. Pursuant to an FOIA request the State Department located twenty-nine documents relating to Ford's visit; eighteen were released in full; eleven, with excisions.

p. 155. Naughton: "100,000 Filipinos Welcome President,": *The New York Times*, December 7, 1975.

p. 155. Kissinger-Sullivan exchange about Imelda Marcos: Related to author by two persons who were present.

p. 156. Presidential Decree 731: This was among the papers discovered after Marcos fled.

p. 156. "Mrs. Marcos may be ready": Manila 3590, March 21, 1975, Confidential.

pp. 157–60. The account of Imelda Marcos's trip to China is based on public reports at the time and cables received pursuant to an FOIA request. Among the more enlightening cables: Peking 1644, September 1974, Limited Official Use (Zhou's greeting Imelda Marcos); Hong Kong 10486, September 21, 1974, Limited Official Use; Taipei 5935, September 24, 1974, Limited Official Use

(Zhou's declining to greet Fulbright); Manila 13024, November 4, 1974, Confidential/LimDis ("delectable foodstuffs" and "She is inclined not only to give Chinese"); Manila 11520, September 24, 1974 (Sullivan's request for "pontification"); Manila 13320, November 11, 1974, Confidential (students' reaction). Chiang Ching's view of Imelda Marcos: Roxane Witke, *Comrade Chiang Ch'ing* (Boston: Little, Brown, 1977), pp. 460–61.

pp. 159–60. Sullivan describes his encounter with Mrs. Marcos in his memoirs, *Obbligato*, pp. 257–60. He elaborated in interviews with the author.

p. 160. "Her enthusiasm for third world causes": CIA analysis, dated December 24, 1975. Provided to the author.

pp. 160–61. "diplomatic success": Tripoli 1466, November 21, 1976, Confidential. Other cables about her Libya trip: Manila 18140, November 19, 1976, Confidential; Manila 18243, November 22, 1976, Confidential ("You are a good woman" and Sullivan's comment about sand dunes in Manila Bay); Manila 17521, November 10, 1976, Confidential (". . . the college try."); Manila 17421, November 9, 1976, Secret ("incorruptibility").

p. 161. Richard Baker, "The Ten Richest Women in the World," *Cosmopolitan* (December 1975).

p. 162. CIA analysis: December 24, 1975. Provided to the author. When and where Mrs. Marcos was first publicly tagged the Steel Butterfly, or sometimes Iron Butterfly, is uncertain, at least to this author, but Edna Barr Hubbert, working in State's Bureau of Intelligence and Research was using it within the department in the late 1960s.

8 : HUMAN RIGHTS: CONFLICT AT FOGGY BOTTOM

I made an FOIA request to the State Department for all documents pertaining to human rights in the Philippines, during the Carter administration. In response I received 548 documents; 427 were released with excisions. In addition, I requested, and received (with excisions), "Presidential Review Memorandum/NSC-28 [PRM-28]: Human Rights," dated August 31, 1977. This was the bureaucracy's response to a May 20, 1977, request from the president for "a review of United States foreign policy with respect to human rights."

For summaries of the passage of the human rights legislation in Congress, see: Lars Schoultz, *Human Rights and United States Policy Toward Latin America*, pp. 189–202; and Stephen B. Cohen, "Conditioning U.S. Security Assistance on Human Rights Practices," *American Journal of International Law* (April 1982), pp. 250–54. For a broader look at the role of human rights in American policy, see Arthur M. Schlesinger, *The Cycles of American History*, ch. 5 ("Human Rights and the American Tradition").

For an overview of the transformation of Congress in the making of foreign policy, see *Our Own Worst Enemy: The Unmaking of American Foreign Policy*, ch. III. "Congress and Press: The New Irresponsibility." The book was written by I. M. Destler, who has looked at the making of foreign policy from the outside, and by two former State Department officers, Leslie Gelb and Anthony Lake.

The two basic laws prohibiting U.S. aid to countries that are gross violators of basic human rights standards are Sections 116 (economic assistance) and 502B (security assistance) of the Foreign Assistance Act of 1961.

p. 165. In his inaugural Carter also declared, "Our commitment to human rights must be absolute." It is this sentence that is usually quoted as a manifestation of the human rights policy. But Carter said it in the context of a discussion about domestic, not foreign, policy. The full paragraph from the printed text of the inaugural reads: "We have already found a high degree of personal liberty, and we are now struggling to enhance equality of opportunity. Our commitment to human rights must be absolute, our laws fair, our national beauty preserved; the powerful must not persecute the weak, and human dignity must be enhanced."

The best and perhaps the only in-depth look at the role of human rights in Carter's presidential campaign is Elizabeth Drew, "Reporter at Large," *New Yorker* (July 18, 1977), pp. 36–62. See also, Schoultz, *Human Rights*, p. 113; and Schlesinger, *Cycles*, pp. 97–99.

p. 165. Gwertzman: "Suddenly Everyone's Asia Bound," *The New York Times*, May 7, 1978.

p. 167. Footnote on Jones: State 270010, November 14, 1975, Limited Official Use.

p. 167. Embassy's response to Amnesty's report: Manila 13573, September 4, 1976, Confidential. Pursuant to an FOIA request, pertaining to the Amnesty report, the State Department located nineteen documents. Fifteen were released in full; four, subject to excisions.

p. 168. "It has become increasingly clear": State Department Briefing Paper prepared for President Ford's visit to Manila in December 1975, Confidential.

p. 168. "sanctioned Philippine authoritarianism": Pringle, *Indonesia and the Philippines*, p. 115.

p. 168. Did not persuade Marcos "to liberalize": Larry Niksch and Marjorie Niehaus, *The Internal Situation in the Philippines: Current Trends and Future Prospects*, Congressional Research Service, January 20, 1981, p. 125. Larry Niksch is an Asia scholar with a master's in foreign relations and a Ph.D. from Georgetown who was to serve on Reagan's Philippine election observer team in 1986, and Marjorie Niehaus is a Philippine specialist who was recruited by the State Department in 1984 when the crisis in the archipelago began to heat up. This is one of several reports they wrote on the Philippines, together or separately, and I found them to be among the best analyses by the CRS that I have read.

p. 169. "overweening fear": Author's interview with Leslie Gelb, November 1985, Washington, D.C. As I mention in the Author's Note, Gelb was an invaluable teacher in the workings of the foreign policy establishment.

p. 169. "Thank goodness": R. W. Apple, Jr., "For the U.S. the Toughest Philippine Policy Decisions May Yet Lie Ahead," *The New York Times*, February 26, 1986.

p. 171. "I made Philippine policy": Author's interview with Richard Holbrooke. I had two very long interviews (each about three hours) with Holbrooke, both in New York, the first on September 25, 1985, the second on July 9, 1986. In addition, he called me on several occasions, usually to clarify or add to something he had said.

p. 172. "I'm proud of it": Ibid.

p. 173. "I'm not ashamed": Ibid.

p. 173. Holbrooke and Nitze at Johns Hopkins: Related to author by a former Carter administration official who was present.

p. 173. Holbrooke's essay in *Harper's*: "The Smartest Man in the Room" (June 1965), p. 5.

pp. 173–74. "They were our role models . . . but they were very flawed": Author's interview with Holbrooke.

p. 173. Footnote on Halberstam's inscription: Tom Bethell, "The Making of Richard Holbrooke," *Washingtonian* (February 1980), p. 114. Holbrooke told me that he had provided Halberstam with many of the anecdotes in *The Best and the Brightest*.

p. 174. This biographical material—Scarsdale; Brown; Paris summit; *The New York Times*; Rusk's role—comes from interviews with Holbrooke.

p. 174. Rusk asked Sullivan to watch over Holbrooke: Author's interview with Sullivan.

p. 175. "so confident, so self-assured": Author's interview with CIA officer.

pp. 175–76. Acclaimed by *Time:* "Leadership in America. Special Section: 200 Rising Leaders," *Time* (July 15, 1974), p. 50.

p. 176. Trilateral Commission; how he joined Carter campaign: Author's interviews with Holbrooke.

p. 176. How Holbrooke became assistant secretary: Based on author's interviews with a top aide to Vance and a top aide to Brzezinski.

p. 177. "He lost his temper": Author's interview with Evelyn Colbert, July 29, 1985, Washington, D.C.

p. 178. Holbrooke's breakfast meetings and the reaction of the senator who was on the Middle East subcommittee: Author's interview with Robert Oakley, June 20, 1986, Washington, D.C. Oakley was a deputy assistant secretary to Holbrooke from 1977 to 1979.

p. 179. Holbrooke welcoming Stevens et al.: Donnie Radcliffe, "Goodbye, 'Pops'," *Washington Post*, February 7, 1980. Armacost's apology: *Human Rights in Asia: Noncommunist Countries*, hearings before the House subcommittees on Asian and Pacific Affairs and on International Organizations," p. 163. "Dear Dick" letter from Wolff: dated February 8, 1980; copy in author's files.

p. 179. "At least Dick Holbrooke won't be around": Related to author by Foreign Service officer to whom Derian made the remark.

p. 180. Early civil rights experiences: Author's interview with Derian. I interviewed Derian on two occasions, both in Washington, D.C., the first time on July 10, 1985, the second, on July 25, 1986. I had also interviewed her for my previous book, and we spoke frequently by telephone.

p. 181. "I can't tap-dance": Ibid.

p. 181. Derian in Singapore: As I indicated, the story of her encounters is frequently told. The account here is based on what I heard from a person who was present and on what Derian told me.

p. 182. Law establishing an assistant secretary of state for human rights and humanitarian affairs: Section 624, Foreign Assistance Act of 1961, as amended.

p. 182. " . . . so goddamn quick": Author's interview with Mark Schneider, July 6, 1986, Washington, D.C.

p. 183. Argentina cable: A draft of the cable was provided to the author, as was Tarnoff's "Eyes Only."

p. 184. Green's views: Testimony before the House subcommittees on Asian and Pacific Affairs and on Human Rights and International Organizations, August 10, 1982.

p. 185. Harris's experiences in Argentina were the subject of a show by Bill Moyers, "Tex Harris," which aired on CBS (as part of a short-lived series, *Crossroads*)

477

on August 8, 1984. Timmerman's quote is from the transcript of that broadcast. Other details were provided to the author in an interview with Harris, in 1985; by Derian; and by others in the Human Rights Bureau.

p. 186. Cohen and the GDR report: Based on author's interview with Stephen Cohen. I had two long interviews with Cohen at his office at the Georgetown Law School in Washington, D.C., in 1985 and talked with him on numerous occasions by telephone.

p. 186. "wasn't evenhanded": Author's interview with Holbrooke.

p. 186. Debate over the Pol Pot vote: Cyrus Vance, *Hard Choices*, p. 126.

p. 186. "single most difficult thing": Author's interview with Holbrooke.

pp. 187–88. The details of the Salzberg controversy were provided to the author by Derian and in an interview with Salzberg, June 27, 1986, Washington, D.C. I also discussed it with numerous other Foreign Service officers. About the incident Holbrooke says, "This is a guy who acted in ways absolutely hostile. I didn't see any reason I should work with a man who was at war with me."

p. 188. "I had a very complex tightrope": Author's interview with Holbrooke.

pp. 188–89. "in Asia, especially Korea and the Philippines": Caleb Rossiter, "Human Rights: The Carter Record, the Reagan Reaction," Center for International Policy, Washington, D.C., September 1984. The study was based on interviews with about forty key officials, including Holbrooke; Derian; Warren Christopher, number two man under Vance; and Anthony Lake, director of policy planning.

p. 189. Holbrooke's views on human rights: Testimony of Richard Holbrooke, before the House subcommittees on Asian and Pacific Affairs and on Human Rights and International Organizations, August 10, 1982.

Holbrooke's support of the contras: He signed a full-page ad which appeared in *The New York Times* on March 16, 1986, advocating military assistance for the contras. Asked how he squared that position with his view of himself as a liberal, he told the author (July 9, 1986), "Everyone is entitled to a little inconsistency. . . . I'm not ashamed of it [signing the ads]."

p. 190. "ideologue of the far left": Author's interview with Holbrooke.

p. 190. "supplicant for Marcos": Author's interview with Derian.

p. 190. Met "unexpectedly" and "begged off": Manila 5898, April 20, 1977, Secret/ExDis.

p. 190. "A lot of frivolity": Author's interview with Holbrooke.

pp. 190–91. Holbrooke's discussions with Marcos: Manila 5898, April 20, 1977, Secret/ExDis.

pp. 191–92. Herrera incident: As indicated, her arrest and release, after pressure by the United States, was widely reported, though Charles Salmon's name and the details have not been provided before. This account is based on interviews with three Foreign Serivce officers who were involved—two who were in the embassy in Manila at the time and one who was in Washington.

p. 192. "I wanted to be a diplomat": Author's interview with Lee Stull, June 10, 1986, Philadelphia.

p. 192. "enemies list": *Investigation into Certain Charges of the Use of the Internal Revenue Service for Political Purposes*, prepared for the Joint Committee on Internal Revenue Taxation, 1973, p. 28.

p. 193. Imelda Marcos's objection to Hummel, her desire for Hand, etc.: Based on author's interviews with a Marcos cabinet member and several diplomats who were involved, including Holbrooke, Sullivan, Stull, and a senior aide to Vance. The same aide, who spoke on background, told about the Colombian reaction to Cabranes.

p. 193. "It's not a moral issue": Author's interview with Stull.

pp. 194–95. Stull's meeting with Marcos: Manila 9145, June 14, 1977, Secret/ExDis.

p. 195. "on his own initiative": Memorandum in lieu of Efficiency Report, Lee T. Stull; prepared by Benjamin A. Fleck, Country Director, Office of Philippine Affairs; April 5, 1978. A copy was provided to the author.

p. 195. "correct but not overly cordial": Ibid.

p. 195. "In his vigorous administration": Ibid.

p. 196. "Washington was exhibiting nervousness": Lee Stull, "Moments of Truth in Philippine-American Relations," May 1, 1986.

p. 196. "the intensity of our dialogue": State 14186, June 18, 1977, Secret/ExDis.

pp. 196–97. Stull recounted the World Bank loan incident during an interview with the author.

p. 197. "Much Ado": Manila 7961, May 25, 1977, Limited Official Use.

p. 197. "Apologies on the Zilch": State 135478, June 11, 1977, Limited Official Use.

p. 199. "some of the most ugly, contentious": Holbrooke's statement was made in an on-the-record interview with Caleb Rossiter, who conducted the study of the Carter administration human rights policy for the Center for International Policy. Notes of the interview were provided to the author.

pp. 199–200. How the United States voted in the multilateral development banks: Based on unclassified State Department documents. Results of various Christopher committee meetings: Based on State Department documents provided to the author.

p. 200. "It's not the materials": Author's interview with Schneider.

pp. 200–201. Mondale's meetings with Imelda Marcos: Based on author's interviews with former Vice President Walter Mondale, June 27, 1986, Washington, D.C.

p. 201. Footnote: "I never heard": Author's interview with Derian.

p. 201. "downgraded this year": Manila 15155, September 26, 1977, Limited Official Use.

p. 201. Imelda Marcos's spending: Based on documents provided to the author.

p. 202. Holbrooke's cable for meeting with Imelda Marcos: Manila 15004, September 23, 1977, Secret/NoDis.

In his *Indonesia and the Philippines* Robert Pringle describes Imelda Marcos's meeting with Carter as "an unprecedented encounter" (p. 111). It's not clear to me what was "unprecedented" about the meeting since Mrs. Marcos had met with other presidents. I wrote Pringle in early 1986, at his post in Papua, New Guinea, asking about this, but received no response.

9 : THE BASES

I made an FOIA request to the State Department for all documents pertaining to the bases negotiations from 1976 to 1979 inclusive. The department located more than 374 documents. Of these, 103 were released without excisions; 21 were released with excisions; 226 were withheld from release; and the remainder were said either to be in the White House, and therefore not subject to the FOIA, or to have been sent for review to other agencies, such as the Defense Department.

p. 203. "if Marcos knew how much we wanted": Author's interview with Holbrooke.

p. 204. Footnote on size of bases: The data are from Lee Feinstein of the Center for Defense Information in Washington, D.C.

p. 206. "behind some of the more strident": CIA analysis, dated June 24, 1975, Top Secret. The author was allowed to look at and make notes from this analysis.

p. 206. "some form of compensation": Memorandum for Brent Scowcroft; Subject: NSSM 235. U.S. Interests and Security Objectives in the Asia-Pacific Area; Issue: Philippine Base Negotiations; April 12, 1976; Secret/Sensitive. The author was permitted to read and make notes from this document.

p. 206. "out of keeping with the spirit": Memorandum for The President [Ford]; From Henry A. Kissinger; Subject: Your Visit to the Philippines; Secret. The memorandum was not dated, but it was prepared for President Ford's December 1976 visit to the Philippines.

p. 206. General Warren testified, in secret session, before the subcommittee on October 1, 1969. Portions of his testimony were deleted from the published transcript of the hearings. The author was allowed to read and take notes from his uncensored testimony.

p. 207. "principal threat": Testimony of Admiral Kauffman before the Senate Subcommittee on U.S. Security Agreements, September 30, 1969. This statement is included in the published hearings, on p. 45, but the exchange between Symington and Kauffman which followed, when Kauffman acknowledged that the threat was "very small . . ." was deleted. I was permitted to read and take notes from portions of Admiral Kauffman's testimony.

p. 207. "the major threat": CIA analysis dated June 4, 1975. The author was permitted to take notes from a copy.

p. 207. That the U-2 flew out of the Philippines in the 1950s was told to the author by a diplomat and by a CIA officer who had been stationed there. For a summary of U.S. intelligence activities from the bases, see "U.S. Military Bases in the Philippines," *Southeast Asia Chronicle* (April 1983), pp. 12–13.

p. 209. "some cosmetic changes": Memorandum to Scowcroft, April 12, 1976.

p. 209. "out of the blue": Author's interview with Sullivan.

pp. 209–10. How the embassy learned about Kissinger offer: Related to the author by an American official who was intimately involved in the negotiations for several years.

p. 210. Footnote on Le Duc Tho: Told to the author by a CIA officer who was in Vietnam at the time.

p. 210. Confusion about the Kissinger offer, particularly how it compared to the Carter deal, has long existed. The conclusion that the two were very similar is based on interviews with several military and Foreign Service officers who were involved in the negotiations.

p. 211. "Just as there will always be a General Motors": LeRoy Hansen, "Carter's Far East Strategy: New Role for Philippine Bases," *U.S. News and World Report* (August 29, 1977), p. 30

pp. 211–12. "Immediate, complete": George Kennan, *The Cloud of Danger: Current Realities of American Foreign Policy*, pp. 98–99.

pp. 212–13. Underhill's cable on the bases: Kuala Lumpur 900, February 9, 1977, Confidential.

p. 213. "stupid," "nutty": Author's interview with Holbrooke.

p. 214. For Kattenburg's views, see his "The Philippines: It Is Time to End the Special Relationship and Leave the U.S. Bases," November 6–9, 1985.

pp. 214–15. La Rocque testified before the House Subcommittee on Foreign Operations, April 6, 1979.

p. 215. Berry testified before the House Subcommittee on Asian and Pacific Affairs, June 28, 1983.

p. 215. Underhill's views are from his cable.

p. 216. "unless the United States intends": *United States-Philippine Base Negotiations*, staff report to the Senate Subcommittee on Foreign Assistance, April 7, 1977, p. 12. Another report on the possibility of moving the bases is Edmund Gannon, *Alternative Sites for U.S. Philippine Bases*, Congressional Research Service, April 20, 1977.

p. 217. "Agreements are much easier to strike": The statement was made by Patrick M. Norton, assistant legal adviser for East Asian and Pacific affairs, during a discussion of the Philippine bases at the Foreign Service Institute, November 26, 1985. Notes from the meeting were provided to the author by a person who attended.

p. 217. Colonel Berry's observation: Testimony before House Subcommittee on Asian and Pacific Affairs, June 28, 1983.

pp. 217–18. "essentially no restrictions": This statement was made by Philip E. Barringer, director of foreign military rights affairs in the Defense Department's Office of International Security Affairs, during the meeting at the Foreign Service Institute on November 26, 1985. Notes from the meeting were provided to the author by a person who attended.

p. 218. Subic, Yokosuka, Guam labor costs: *United States-Philippine Base Negotiations*, p. 12.

p. 219. Views of Stull, Wenzel, et al.: Based on author's interviews.

p. 219. Views of Philippine scholars: At a conference of American Philippines scholars at Eastern Michigan State University in May 1980, the State Department's Stephen Cohen found that all those with whom he talked "expressed great surprise upon learning that some policymakers considered Marcos's threat credible." Cohen, "Conditioning U.S. Security Assistance on Human Rights Practices," *American Journal of International Law* (April 1982), p. 260, n. 72.

p. 219. Stockwin: "Basis for the Bases," *Far Eastern Economic Review* (May 13, 1977).

p. 220. "He was correct": Pringle, *Indonesia and the Philippines*, p. 111.

p. 221. "He was absolutely a genius": Author's interview with Oakley.

p. 221. Holbrooke's desire to send Rafferty and embassy objections: Author's interview with Holbrooke; several embassy officers confirmed this.

p. 221. "I fired him": Author's interview with Holbrooke.

p. 222. "sound analytically": Author's interview with Sullivan.

p. 222. "I learned more about the Philippines": Author's interview with Cohen.

pp. 222–23. Holbrooke's February 1986 statement: *The Philippine Election and the Implications for U.S. Policy*, hearing and markup before the House Subcommittee on Asian and Pacific Affairs, February 19 and 20, 1986, p. 45. His statement in 1979: *Foreign Assistance and Related Programs: Appropriations for 1980*, hearing before a House subcommittee of the Committee on Appropriations, February 8, 1979, p. 30.

p. 223. Footnote on Lopez-Osmeña escape: Holbrooke's statement is on p. 45 of *The Philippine Election* hearing and markup. For a detailed account of the escape, see Stu Cohen, "The Great Escape," *Boston Phoenix* (November 8, 1977); and Rodney Tasker, " 'My God, They're Not Here!'," *Far Eastern Economic Review* (October 14, 1977).

p. 223. "preoccupation of Washington": Stull, "Moments of Truth in Philippine-American Relations."

p. 223. "disincentive to a stronger": Larry Niksch, *Philippine Bases: How Important to U.S. Interests in Asia?*, Congressional Research Service, April 23, 1979 (updated, August 1, 1980), and related article in *Congressional Research Service Review*. Another overview of the bases by Niksch: Congressional Research Service, *Philippine Base Negotiations*, December 7, 1978, distribution limited; copy in author's files.

10 : VISITORS TO MANILA

pp. 224–25. Schneider's letter to Derian was provided to the author.

p. 225. "very bitter session . . . It was gutsy": Author's interview with Holbrooke.

p. 225. "I'm proud to know. . . . I'm usually pretty tough": Author's interview with Derian.

p. 226. Derian and Marcos: Author's interview with Derian and another person present.

p. 226. Enrile's response to Derian: *Philippines Daily Express*, January 12, 1978.

pp. 226–27. Malacañang luncheon for Derian: Author's interview with Derian.

p. 227. Natzke's observations about Aquino: Ibid. Derian did not give me Natzke's name; it was provided by an embassy officer. I have named Natzke because he has been previously identified as having been a station chief in Manila. He was living in San Francisco in August 1985.

p. 228. "She was a schoolgirl": Author's interview with Carlos Romulo, December 1985, Manila.

p. 229. Footnote on Evans and Novak on Derian and Argentina: " 'Undiplomatic' Incident," *Washington Post*, September 6, 1978.

p. 229. "She was rude": *Washington Post*, August 7, 1978.

p. 229. "He got wildly excited": Author's interview with Derian.

p. 229. "repair the damage": Author's interview with State Department officer.

p. 230. "I don't know what good": Author's interview with Mondale.

p. 230. "He sideswiped": Author's interview with Schneider.

pp. 230–31. Scene in the basement and White House meeting: Author's interview with Derian. Another person who was present at Mondale meeting confirmed her account of what happened at the White House.

p. 232. Holbrooke's cable: State 42011, February 17, 1978, Secret.

p. 234. "The results of the forthcoming": Manila 2940, February 22, 1978, Confidential/LimDis. In response to an FOIA request for documents pertaining to the 1978 election, the State Department located 167 documents. Of these, 101 were released without excisions, 39 with excisions, and 27 were withheld.

p. 235. "lack of even elemental subtlety": Manila 5323, April 4, 1978, Confidential.

p. 235. "Marcos will permit . . . in the counting": Cebu 0030, March 14, 1978, Confidential.

p. 235. "in an honest vote": Manila 5323, April 4, 1978, Confidential.

p. 236. "major fraud and manipulation": Manila 5500, April 6, 1978, Confidential.

p. 236. "flying voters": Manila 5323, April 4, 1978, Confidential.

p. 236. "one million fake ballots": Ibid.

p. 236. "under the table . . . We had been quite proud": Manila A-123, July 13, 1978, Limited Official Use.

p. 237. "anti-Marcos, anti-martial law protest": Manila 6011, April 15, 1978, Confidential.

p. 238. Herblock: *Washington Post*, April 12, 1978.

pp. 238–39. Complaints about Butterfield, Mathews, and Malloy: Manila 5723, April 12, 1978, Confidential. "A Real Contest": *Time* (April 10, 1978). Came: "A Chiller in Manila," *Newsweek* (April 24, 1978).

p. 239. Fraud charges "could hurt": Mathews, "Marcos' Followers Take Early Lead in Philippines' Voting," *Washington Post*, April 8, 1978. "A return to the pattern": Mathews, "Philippine Police Arrest Hundreds to Block Protest," *Washington Post*, April 10, 1978.

p. 239. "serious cracks": Manila 6953, April 29, 1978, Confidential.

p. 240. "I said about two days": Author's interview with Father James Reuter, December 1985, Manila.

p. 240. "blatantly rigged": *Human Rights in the Philippines: Recent Developments*, hearings before the House Subcommittee on International Relations, April 27, 1978, p. 4.

p. 241. "It was a lively discussion": Reported in Philippine and American press.

pp. 241–42. Aaron-Mondale: The exchange was first told to the author in an interview with a Mondale aide. Mondale, in an interview with the author, confirmed and added some details.

Pursuant to an FOIA request for all records pertaining to Mondale's visit, the department located twenty-eight documents. Twenty-two were released in full; three were released with excisions; three were withheld.

p. 242. Diamond for Abell: Author's telephone interview with Elizabeth Abell, March 1986.

p. 242. "toed the line": "The Wrath of Cardinal Sin," *Far Eastern Economic Review* (June 2, 1978)

p. 242. Footnote on "sharply critical": Terence Smith, "Mondale, in Manila, Sees Marcos Critics," *The New York Times*, May 4, 1978.

p. 243. Footnote on "Damage limiting": Author's interview with Derian. *The New York Times* report on compromise: Terence Smith, "Mondale After Debate Will Include Manila on Trip," April 29, 1978.

p. 243. Hotels: Bernard Wideman, "Overbuilt, Underbooked," *Far Eastern Economic Review* (January 21, 1977); Fox Butterfield, "14 New Hotels, Only Half Full, Trouble Manila," *The New York Times*, November 20, 1977; George McArthur, "Philippine Ills Blamed on Marcos and Wife," *Los Angeles Times*, November 26, 1976.

p. 244. "nothing to be ashamed of": Author's interview with Jovito Salonga, November 20, 1985, Manila.

p. 244. "He sure tricked me": Author's interview with President Macapagal, November 22, 1985, Manila.

p. 244. "military aid . . . to kill Filipinos": Author's interview with Reuter.

p. 245. "I feel greatly disappointed": Alan Riding, "El Salvador's Dissidents Disappointed at U.S. Silence," *The New York Times*, May 8, 1978.

p. 245. definite "squeamishness": Author's interview with Foreign Service Officer.

p. 245. "human rights diplomacy was less active": Niksch and Niehaus, *Internal Situation in the Philippines*, pp. 124–25.

p. 246. *Bulletin Today* editorial: May 6, 1978.

p. 246. none . . . "more egregiously": Bernard Gwertzman, "Suddenly Everyone's Asia Bound," *The New York Times*, May 7, 1978.

p. 247. "the noble dimensions": *Bulletin Today*, July 8, 1978.

pp. 247–48. Imelda Marcos's purchases: Based on documents provided to the author.

pp. 248–49. Imelda Marcos's session with members of Congress: An unofficial transcript was made from the taping of the session.

p. 249. "Barbarians": Stephen Barber, "First Lady in Distress," *Far Eastern Economic Review* (August 11, 1978), p. 22.

p. 250. "sharing a laugh": Author's interview with Holbrooke.

p. 251. Inouye, Marcos, Murphy, etc.: Ibid.

p. 251. Opposition letter: Copy in author's files.

p. 252. "euphoric": Author's interview with Holbrooke.

11 : MARCOS GROWS STRONGER

pp. 254–55. Pauker study: Author's interview with Pauker.

p. 255. Stock title for journalists: See, for example, Richard Kessler, "The Philippines: The Next Iran?" *Asian Affairs* (January/February, 1980); Larry Niksch, "The Philippines: The Next Iran?," *Congressional Research Service Review*, (April 1981).

p. 255. "After the shah falls": Author's interview with Holbrooke.

pp. 256–57. "Enough to break"; "can't avoid stealing": Natzke made these comments to Foreign Service officers in the embassy. The words here are from notes taken at the time.

pp. 256–57. For coverage of the twenty-fifth wedding anniversary, see Roy Rowan, "Silver Anniversary for the Iron Butterfly," *Life* (July 1979).

p. 257. "functioning increasingly": Cable from the Defense Intelligence Agency to various posts around the world, September 14, 1979, Secret/NoForn. A copy of this cable was provided to the author.

p. 258. Doctor ratios are from the *Far Eastern Economic Review Yearbook, 1980*, p. 10.

p. 259. Olympic Towers: Based on documents from the Presidential Commission on Good Government, which was appointed by President Aquino after Marcos's ouster.

p. 259. Philippine National Bank: Carl M. Cannon, "Sources Link Bank to First Lady's Trips," *San Jose Mercury News*, March 21, 1986.

pp. 259–60. Gambling and jai alai: See Bernard Wideman, "Winning Ways of the Marcos Cabal," *Insight* (September 1978). Amounts generated are also based on documents discovered after Marcos fled; see, for example, Joel Brinkley, "Marcos Papers Show a Fortune Around World," *The New York Times*, March 20, 1986.

p. 260. Pagcor: Manila 07385, March 13, 1985, Confidential.

p. 260. "one of the most notorious": Ibid.

p. 261. Benedicto's real estate purchases: Based on documents provided by the Presidential Commission on Good Government.

p. 261. California-Overseas Bank: Wideman, "Winning Ways of the Marcos Cabal"; Pete Carey, Katherine Ellison, and Lewis M. Simons, "Hidden Billions: The Draining of the Philippines," *San Jose Mercury News*, June 23, 24, and 25, 1985.

p. 261. Floirendo and SuCrest deal: See Edward Pound and Eduardo Lachica, "Philippine Tales: Did Fugitive Tycoon Operate as Front Man in Marcos Investments?," *Wall Street Journal*, January 30, 1985.

The best overview of the cronies and their activities is a study, "Some Are Smarter Than Others," which was clandestinely prepared in the Philippines by a group of businessmen and professional managers in 1979. See also Carey, Ellison, and Simons, "Hidden Billions: The Draining of the Philippines." For sketches of Disini, Cojuangco, and another Marcos crony, Rodolfo Cuenca, see Paul Gigot, "Favored Friends: In Philippines, to Be President's Pal Can Be Boon for a Businessman," *Wall Street Journal*, November 4, 1983.

For a summary of sugar monopoly, see Manila 01905, January 21, 1984, Confidential.

p. 262. Takeover of Aquino bank: Fox Butterfield, "Once-Powerful Families in the Philippines Lose Heavily Under Government Pressure," *The New York Times*, June 18, 1978.

p. 262. Coconuts: Manila A-47, "Concentration of Power in the Philippine Coconut Industry: Implications for Investment and Trade," May 9, 1980, Confidential. Manila 05607, "The Philippine Coconut Monopoly," March 2, 1985, Confidential.

p. 263. Rowan: "The High-Flying First Lady of the Philippines," *Fortune* (July 2, 1979).

p. 263. Footnote about Imelda Marcos's phone call to Rowan: Related to author by Rowan in 1986.

p. 263. "intense drive to power": Manila A-47, May 9, 1980, Confidential.

pp. 264–67. The Disini-Westinghouse deal has been widely written about. Pursuant to an FOIA request for all records pertaining to Westinghouse and the nuclear power plant, the State Department located 359 documents. Of these, 266 were released in full, 28 with excisions, and 65 were withheld. Two of the best stories are by Fox Butterfield in *The New York Times*, "Marcos, Facing Criticism, May End $1 Billion Westinghouse Contract," January 14, 1978, and "Filipinos Say Marcos Was Given Millions for '76 Nuclear Contract," March 7, 1986. Also: Peter Pringle and James Spigelman, *The Nuclear Barons* (New York: Avon Books, 1981), pp. 393–96; Walden Bello, Peters Hayes, and Lyuba Zarsky, " '500-Mile Island': The Philippine Nuclear Reactor Deal," *Pacific Research* (First Quarter 1979). On the Ex-Im loan and its approval: Ann Crittenden, "Behind the Philippine Loan," *The New York Times*, February 12, 1978.

pp. 267–68. Articles about Marcos corruption: Fox Butterfield, "5 Years of Philippine Martial Law Builds Personal Power of Marcos," *The New York Times*, January 9, 1978; "Marcos, Facing Criticism, May End $1 Billion Westinghouse Contract," *The New York Times*, January 14, 1978; "Marcos Inner Circle Gains Under Marcos," *The New York Times*, January 15, 1978; "Huge Profits Linked to a Marcos Agency," *The New York Times*, January 17, 1978. Barry Kramer, "Ties to the Top: In the Philippines, It's Whom You Know That Can Really Count," *Wall Street Journal*, January 28, 1978. Jay Mathews and Bernard Wideman, "Marcos Seized Airline After Wife Got Bill," *Washington*

Post, April 23, 1978. Brennon Jones, "Marcos's Influential Enemies," *Nation* (October 4, 1980).

p. 268. Embassy knowledge of Westinghouse payments to Disini: Interviews with embassy officers.

p. 268. "executive branch had done:" State 265668, October 10, 1979.

p. 269. GTE transaction: The SEC's civil suit was filed with the U.S. District Court for the District of Columbia, January 12, 1977. See also Jeff Gerth, "The Marcos Empire: Gold, Oil, Land and Cash," *The New York Times*, March 16, 1986.

p. 269. Footnote on Japanese payments: Joel Brinkley, "Marcos Papers Show a Fortune Around World," *The New York Times*, March 20, 1986.

p. 269. "I never could": Author's interview with David Newsom, July 29, 1985, Washington, D.C.

pp. 269–70. "Almost eight decades": "War on Hunger," Agency for International Development, December 1977.

p. 271. A most comprehensive analysis of the effects of martial law on the poor is Robert B. Stauffer, "Philippine Authoritarianism: Framework for Peripheral 'Development'," *Pacific Affairs*, (Fall 1977), pp. 365–86. Also, Keith Dalton, "The Undernourished Philippines," *Far Eastern Economic Review* (September 1, 1978).

p. 271. Infant mortality rates are from the *Far Eastern Economic Review Yearbook*, 1978, p. 53.

p. 271. World Bank study: Draft, "The World Bank Philippine Poverty Report, 1979," Confidential, p. 25.

pp. 271–72. Joseph Lelyveld: "Workers in Richest Sugar Region Are Still Untouched by Boom," *The New York Times*, November 8, 1974. Barry Kramer: "Ill-Paid Sugar Workers in the Philippines Stir After Years of Passivity," *Wall Street Journal*, September 12, 1980.

p. 272. "POWDER KEG": *Time* (September 24, 1979).

p. 273. Tull, Wenzel, and Maisto made their comments to Stephen Cohen in July 1979. Cohen took copious notes, as he did during all his meetings, from which he read during an interview with the author in 1985.

pp. 273–74. How Cohen was hired: Author's interview with Stephen Cohen.

p. 274. The Pentagon's trust of Cohen was told to Caleb Rossiter in an interview for his study about the Carter administration and human rights, "Human Rights: The Carter Record, the Reagan Reaction," which was published by the Center for International Policy.

pp. 274–75. A copy of Cohen's letter to Murphy, July 3, 1979, was provided to the author. The copy provided was double-spaced and appeared to be a draft, but Cohen confirmed that it was the letter that had, in fact, been sent. Oakley's response was a memorandum dated July 23, 1979.

pp. 275–76. How Murphy became ambassador to Philippines: Author's interviews, including with Holbrooke and Oakley, and as well as Richard Murphy, whom I interviewed, July 24, 1986, Washington, D.C.

p. 277. "I thought he was an agent": Concepción made his comments to Cohen during his visit to the Philippines in 1979. Cohen recorded them verbatim at the time and read them to the author during our interviews.

pp. 277–78. Chamber of Commerce and Imelda Marcos; "being in the pocket": Manila 16108, October 11, 1977, Limited Official Use.

p. 278. Marcos was "very sensitive": "Problems in the Philippines Chill an Economic Boom," *Business Week* (August 27, 1979), p. 50.

p. 278. Suter "a known apologist": Manila 7324, May 13, 1977, Confidential.

p. 278. Minimum wages and "effective cost of labor": Robin Broad, "Behind Philippine Policy Making: The Role of the World Ban and International Monetary Fund," June 1983, pp. 292, 284.

p. 278. "soft dictator": Author's interview with Holbrooke.

pp. 278–79. *The Politics of Torture*: ABC, December 27, 1978. Cables in the exchange: State 326476, December 29, 1978, Confidential; State 028087, February 2, 1979, Limited Official Use; Manila 02686, February 7, 1979, Limited Official Use.

p. 280. Morrell's testimony: *Human Rights in Asia: Noncommunist Countries*, p. 200. Holbrooke's testimony: *Foreign Assistance Legislation for Fiscal Year 1981 (Part 4)*, hearings and markup before the Subcommittee on Asian and Pacific Affairs, February 11, 21; March 4 and 6, 1980, p. 55. Jeffords's testimony: Ibid., p. 29.

p. 280. "becoming worse every day.": Henry Kamm, "Philippine Cardinal Calls for End to Martial-Law Rule by Marcos," *The New York Times*, September 15, 1979. "We expected": Henry Kamm, "Ex-President of Philippines Attacks Carter over U.S. Support of Marcos," *The New York Times*, September 18, 1979.

pp. 281–83. Hall's effort: Based on newspaper accounts at the time and on author's interview with Tony Hall, June 19, 1986, Washington, D.C.

pp. 283–84. Senate-House conference committee: An official transcript of the joint conference committee session, November 19, 1980, was provided to the author. The list of church organizations and Murphy's cable are from that transcript.

p. 284. Imelda Marcos's purchases: From documents provided to the author.

p. 284. Glenn's position: Transcript of conference committee.

p. 285. Loan amounts are from unclassified government documents. PISO: The department was advised in a letter from Congressman Hall, dated December 9, 1980; the department responded December 19, 1980. More details were provided by the Center for International Policy in a letter to Hall, May 12, 1981. All these letters are in the author's files.

p. 286. "bolster domestic support": Manila 07643, April 19, 1980, Confidential.

    I made an FOIA request for all records pertaining to Marcos's appearance at the ANPA meeting. The State Department located sixty documents. Of these, thirty-nine were released without excisions; nine were released with excisions; twelve were withheld.

p. 286. "Mrs. Graham, publisher": *Bulletin Today*, April 12, 1980, as cited in Manila 7137, April 14, 1980, Unclassified.

p. 286. "You know how sentimental . . . I suspect": Manila 04484, March 6, 1980, Secret.

p. 286. Holbrooke memo to Vance: Action Memorandum; Appropriate Reception for President Marcos When He Visits Honolulu; March 27, 1980, Confidential.

p. 287. "we concocted": Author's interview with Holbrooke.

p. 287. The letter from Carter to Marcos as drafted by the State Department was provided to the author pursuant to an FOIA request.

p. 287. Armacost and "quiet diplomacy": *Human Rights in Asia: Noncommunist Countries*, p. 182.

p. 288. "Nixon and Ford never talked about human rights": Maria Karagianis, "Marcos Foe Endures; He Says 'Carter Gave Us New Hope," *Boston Globe*, December 28, 1980.

pp. 288–89. Holbrooke's assurances to Marcos about Aquino: Author's interview with Holbrooke.

pp. 289–90. The memoranda in the Open Forum controversy were provided to the author. Holbrooke's position was provided to the author in an interview.

p. 290. Lake's views on affair: Author's telephone interview with Anthony Lake, December 1986.

p. 291. Holbrooke's last fling in Manila: Author's interview with Holbrooke.

p. 291. "We knew his was a repressive government": Author's interview with Mondale.

12 : A NEW DAY FOR DICTATORS

pp. 293–94. "Dictatorships and Double Standards": *Commentary* (November 1979).

p. 294. The Metzenbaum-Kirkpatrick exchange came during a seminar sponsored by the Members of Congress for Peace Through Law, February 1981. Transcript in author's files.

p. 295. Kirkpatrick made the statements about the deaths of the nuns to a reporter for the *Tampa Tribune*, in which they appeared on December 25, 1980. After the article was published, Kirkpatrick denied having made the statements. The reporter said he had a tape recording of the interview. Kirkpatrick claimed she had been quoted out of context. She had not been; the article was in a question-and-answer format, and her response was to very specific questions. See this author's account in *Weakness and Deceit*, pp. 80–81.

p. 295. Haig's view on killing of the nuns: *Weakness and Deceit*, pp. 75–76.

p. 295. Schlesinger: Arthur M. Schlesinger, *Cycles*, p. 58.

p. 295. "must be abandoned": Tamar Jacoby, "The Reagan Turnaround on Human Rights," *Foreign Affairs* (Summer 1986), p. 1069. This is a very good overview of the Reagan administration's initial approach to human rights.

p. 296. Reagan's column on Patt Derian: *Miami News*, October 20, 1978.

p. 297. "Pakistan's biggest success": *Far Eastern Economic Review Asia Yearbook*, 1982, p. 216.

p. 298. "foreign policy objectives and the U.S. role": Memorandum from Pedro A. Sanjuan, State Department Transition Team, Office of the President-Elect, to Ambassador Robert Neumann; subject: Interim Report on the Bureau of Inter-American Affairs and Related Bureaus and Policy Areas, Department of State. The transition team paper was provided to the author.

p. 298. Hit list: Caleb Rossiter, "The Financial Hit List." Part one in a series on Human Rights and the International Financial Institutions, published by the Center for International Policy, February 1984.

p. 298. "music to Marcos's ears": Author's interview, 1986.

p. 298. Reagan administration relationship to Aquino: Based on interviews with several Foreign Service officers.

p. 299. Ungo's statement: See author's *Weakness and Deceit*, p. 236.

p. 300. "almost euphoric": *Time* (February 2, 1981). The Reagan-Imelda Marcos meeting was described to me by two individuals involved, one American and one Filipino.

p. 300. Imelda Marcos and Percy: Letter from Senator Charles Percy to Secretary of State Edmund Muskie. Released pursuant to an FOIA request for all documents pertaining to Mrs. Marcos's visits to the United States.

p. 300. "converging on Manila": Manila 01317, January 16, 1981, Limited Official Use.

p. 301. Footnote on what Imelda Marcos told Psinakis: Psinakis describes his meeting with her in his book, *Two "Terrorists" Meet*.

p. 301. "Focus of world attention": Manila 25667, December 26, 1980, Confidential.

p. 301. "Marcos has lifted": Keyes Beech, "Martial Law in Philippines Ends Today," *Los Angeles Times*, January 17, 1981.

p. 301. "have been adequately institutionalized": Manila 25667, December 26, 1980, Confidential.

p. 301. "With this legislation": Manila 18102, September 16, 1980, Confidential.

p. 302. "no return to normalcy": International Commission of Jurists, *The Philippines: Human Rights After Martial Law*, p. 15.

p. 303. Henry Kamm on the scene at Malacañang: "Creating a Dynasty in the Philippines," *The New York Times Magazine*, May 24, 1981.

p. 304. "Public reaction": Manila 04259, February 24, 1981, Confidential. I made an FOIA request for all documents pertaining to the pope's visit to the Philippines. Eighteen documents were located. Of these, fourteen were released without excisions; one with excisions; three were withheld altogether.

pp. 306–307. House resolution: H. Res. 133, April 29, 1981. Reaction in the Philippines: Manila 10012, May 5, 1981, Limited Official Use; State 132599, May 21, 1981, Limited Official Use; Manila 11640, May 26, 1981, Confidential.

p. 307. Mrs. Bush: State 166719, June 24, 1981, Confidential. Pursuant to an FOIA request for documents pertaining to the Bush visit, the State Department located fifty-two documents. Of these, thirty-nine were released in full; three, subject to excisions; and ten withheld.

p. 307. *The New York Times* editorial: September 15, 1982.

p. 308. "I'll repeat it": Lindy Washburn, Associated Press, July 2, 1981.

p. 308. "I'm sure the president": Associated Press, July 6, 1981.

pp. 309–311. Imelda Marcos's spending and the town house: Based on public reports, documents provided to the author, and author's tour of the town house.

p. 311. "Who Kidnapped Tommy Manotoc?": Manila 00057, January 4, 1982, Limited Official Use. Other cables in the saga: Manila 04082, February 16, 1982, Confidential; Manila 01393 ("Government Cites New Twist in Manotoc Case—Emotional Terrorism"), January 18, 1982, Confidential; State 030539 ("We have heard reports here that 'the Australians' . . ."), February 4, 1982, Limited Official Use.

pp. 311–12. Imelda Marcos and the scientists: Related to the author by a person who was present.

p. 312. "It's just an example of totalitarian power": Author's interview with embassy officer who was present during the Manotoc affair.

13 : THE BEST OF TIMES . . .

p. 313. Within six months: Bush discussed the state visit with the Marcoses during his trip to Manila in July 1981, according to documents pertaining to the trip received pursuant to an FOIA request.

p. 313. "because of the great value": Manila 17095, July 14, 1982, Unclassified.

p. 314. Imelda Marcos's meetings with Bush and Casey: State 199316, July 19, 1982, Confidential; Manila 17831, July 22, 1982, Confidential.

p. 314. Imee Manatoc's purchases: Based on documents provided to the author.

p. 314. "in a buoyant mood": Manila 17831, July 22, 1981, Confidential. Pursuant to an FOIA request for all records pertaining to the state visit, the State Department located eighty documents. Of these, twenty-four were released without excisions, twelve with excisions, and forty-four were withheld.

pp. 314–15. Amnesty report: No date, but it was released in September 1982.

p. 316. University of Pennsylvania: "University Plans No Award," *The New York Times*, September 17, 1982.

p. 316. "Whatever the trips costs": William Branigin, "Marcos' Visit Here Aims at Bases Pact, Improved Image," *Washington Post*, September 13, 1982.

pp. 316–17. Manila in Georgetown restaurant: Based on documents on file with the Alcoholic Beverage Control Board, District of Columbia. The documents were provided to the author by *New York Times* reporter Jeff Gerth, who wrote about the restaurant, "The Marcos Connections in the Capital," *The New York Times*, November 12, 1985.

p. 317. "I see Kokoy": Related to author by person to whom Imelda Marcos spoke the words.

p. 317. Rosellini story: "The Panoply of Preparation for the Marcos Visit," *The New York Times*, September 15, 1982. See also: Richard Nations, "Marcos' Circus Comes to Town," *Far Eastern Economic Review* (September 24, 1982); and Caryle Murphy, "Philippine Embassy Works Hard, Turns Out Crowd for Marcos," *Washington Post*, September 16, 1982.

pp. 318–19. Reception and White House dinner: Donnie Radcliffe and Elisabeth Bumiller, "Dinner, Dancing & Demonstration," *Washington Post*, September 17 and 18, 1982.

pp. 319–20. *Philippine News*: Week of September 15–21, 1982.

p. 320. Marcos's meeting with *Washington Post* editors and reporters was described to the author by several persons who were present. In addition, another *Post* reporter provided the author with a long memorandum written after that meeting on September 24, 1982.

p. 320. "greatly exceeded": Letter from Ambassador Armacost to Secretary of State Shultz, October 29, 1982.

p. 321. Sin's remarks were published by the church in Manila.

pp. 321–22. "Who's this Sheenboom?": The story was widely circulated among diplomats, and I heard it from several, always with slightly different words. The account here is based on an interview with someone who was present. The Sheinbaum report: Manila A-03, April 13, 1982, Confidential. State Department's response: Caryle Murphy, "Governmental Abuses Toughen Philippines Guerrilla Movement," *Washington Post*, August 12, 1982, p. A20.

p. 323. "It is also likely": Manila 30017, December 8, 1982, Confidential.

pp. 323–24. Floirendo role in evicting Kroes: Manila A-30, April 13, 1982, Confidential.

pp. 324–25. "Creeping State Capitalism": Manila A-008, April 6, 1983, Limited Official Use.

pp. 324–25. Letters of instruction and decrees, and government role in the economy in general: Emmanuel S. De Dios, ed., *An Analysis of the Philippine Economic Crises*.

p. 325. Gigot: "Favored Friends: In Philippines, to Be. . . ."

p. 326. "This timely action contributed": Shultz's letter, dated October 4, 1982, was released pursuant to an FOIA request for all documents pertaining to Westinghouse and the nuclear plant project in the Philippines.

p. 326. Sugar losses; De Dios, *Analysis of Philippine Economic Crisis*, pp. 42–49.

p. 327. "pulled no punches": Manila A-47, May 9, 1980, Confidential. The subject of this airgram is "Concentration of Power in the Philippine Coconut Industry: Implications for Investment and Trade." It is eighteen pages, including an appendix of the officers of the United Coconut Planters Bank and UNICOM, and is a comprehensive examination of the coconut monopoly. It was released to the author pursuant to a FOIA request. The released document contains many excisions. It is quite apparent that what was excised was a particular person's name, and it is obvious that the name deleted was Enrile. Cojuangco's name was not deleted. In one place, apparently overlooked by the State Department officer who reviewed the document prior to its release, Enrile's name was not deleted. A State Department officer who read the document told me that it was indeed Enrile's name that was deleted throughout.

p. 327. Details of UNICOM's activities were provided by Rafael Fernando in an interview in Los Angeles, August 1985. He also provided me with eleven pages, single-spaced, that he had written earlier, at the time of the federal investigation. See also the file of affidavits and motions, In Re Coconut Oil Antitrust Litigation, U.S. District Court for the Northern District of California, MDL No. 474, 1986.

p. 329. "we understood their concerns clearly": State 034796, February 10, 1981, Confidential.

p. 329. "That's ridiculous": Author's telephone interview with Shelley Taylor Convissar Olander, September 1986. She was living and practicing law in San Diego.

p. 329. "Dept considers Justice's": State 038077, February 13, 1981, Confidential. Pursuant to an FOIA request for all records pertaining to UNICOM, the State Department released twenty-two without excisions, eight with excisions, and withheld eighteen. Some of the released documents had been generated by the Justice Department. Included in the released documents were handwritten notes taken during the meetings.

About the only media attention paid to the UNICOM scandal and settlement was by National Public Radio on March 4, 1981, and Eduardo Lachica "Coconut-Oil Price Scheme Is Said to Have Burned Manila," *Asian Wall Street Journal*, August 6, 1981.

p. 330. Pauker study: Holdridge's and Armacost's reactions were told to the author by two persons.

p. 331. "Why is it, sir": Author's interviews with embassy officers who were present.

pp. 331–33. Why Armacost chose Carleton: Author's interview with Michael Armacost, May 16, 1986, Washington, D.C. Much of the biographical material about Armacost comes from the files at Carleton, which provided them to Craig Nelson. Nelson also located and interviewed several of Armacost's former classmates and professors.

p. 333. Fulbright letter to White: June 16, 1981. Copy in author's files. For more on the purge in the Latin American bureau and embassies, see author's *Weakness and Deceit*, ch. 12.

pp. 335–36. The most complete account of the right-wing attack on Abramowitz:

491

Don Oberdorfer, "Diplomat's Enemies Play Role In Blocking His Appointment," *Washington Post*, May 21, 1982. Also Anthony Lewis, "Poisoning the Well," *The New York Times*, May 24, 1982.

p. 336. Shawcross on Abramowitz: *The Quality of Mercy*, May 24, 1982, especially pp. 178–80.

p. 337. Inserting eighth paragraph: Related to author by a diplomat who was involved in the negotiations.

p. 338. Shultz's reaction to floor show and reception by Marcos: Shultz made these remarks to aides who were with him on the trip.

p. 338. "I wonder what": Author's interview.

14 : . . . AND THE WORST

p. 339. "beyond a doubt": Shaplen, "A Reporter at Large: From Marcos to Aquino—I," *New Yorker* (August 25, 1986).

p. 340. That Marcos had secreted a kidney dialysis machine in his baggage during the 1982 state visit was told to author by a Foreign Service officer who learned about it afterward. The CIA's difficulty in identifying the doctors was told the author by a CIA officer.

p. 341. Much has been written about Aquino's return. One of the best accounts is by his brother-in-law, Ken Kashiwahara, who was on the plane with him. Kashiwahara, "Aquino's Final Journey," *The New York Times Magazine*, October 16, 1983.

p. 343. Maisto's role in drafting the statement was first told to me by embassy officers in Manila. It was confirmed by State Department officers. I interviewed Maisto on July 16, 1985, and March 31, 1986, both times in Washington, D.C.

p. 344. "For such a relatively low-level": Author's interview with Stanley Roth, May 2, 1986, Washington, D.C. Roth was staff director of the House Subcommittee on Asian and Pacific Affairs, which was chaired by Stephen Solarz. I spoke with Roth many times.

p. 344. "The Philippines seems to be one country": Letter to author from Donald R. Toussaint, October 11, 1985. I talked with Toussaint several times by telephone; he died of a heart attack in January 1986.

p. 345. "The Administration is prepared": Bernard Gwertzman, "U.S. Would Cool Ties with Marcos If Guilt Is Found," *The New York Times*, August 25, 1983.

p. 345. "As a group": Manila 29310, November 8, 1983, Confidential. I made an FOIA request to the State Department for all records pertaining to the Aquino assassination. The department released 142 documents.

p. 346. "enough so that [he] could live well": Author's interview with the Philippine diplomat.

p. 346. Effort to intercept: Phil Bronstein, "Philippine Jets Tried to Divert Aquino," *San Francisco Examiner*, July 14, 1985. Bronstein and the *Examiner* were frequently ahead of the journalistic pack on the Philippine story from the Aquino assassination until the final days.

p. 347. "Ver was deeply involved": Author's interview. "There is no question": Ibid. "He wouldn't have acted": Ibid. "The last person": Ibid.

p. 348. Ver's real estate: Based on documents from the Presidential Commission on Good Government. "long-time mistress": Phil Mintz, "Marcos Aide Has LI Link," *Newsday*, February 26, 1985.

p. 348. Research on assassinations: Told to author by a person who was involved in the research.

p. 348. Abadilla's mission: Based on author's interviews with three embassy officers.

pp. 348–49. "It was Marcos": Author's interview, 1986.

p. 349. Solarz's and Armacost's meeting with Marcos: Described by two persons who were present.

p. 350. "She owned him": Author's interview.

p. 351. "Our analysis here": "A Welcome-Home Murder," *Newsweek* (September 5, 1985).

p. 351. Deaver's advance work described by several embassy officers in interviews with author.

pp. 351–52. Cancellation of Reagan's visit: Pursuant to an FOIA request for all records pertaining to the cancellation, the State Department released fifty-six documents in full, twenty-five with excisions, and it withheld twenty. Among the documents was Reagan's letter to Marcos.

p. 352. Bush's statement: "Criticism of Marcos Is Unfair, Bush Says," *Chicago Tribune*, October 7, 1983.

p. 352. "I was deeply impressed": Author's interview.

p. 353. "I can't believe it": Author's interview with embassy officer to whom remark was made.

p. 353. Hatfield's report "fortified" Reagan: Reagan's letter to Marcos.

p. 353. Imelda Marcos and Armacost before Santo Niño: Related to author by a person present.

p. 354. Sin's relationship with Armacost was described to the author by a senior aide to Sin.

15 : IN SEARCH OF A POLICY

p. 355. "The question is not": Author's interview.

pp. 355–56. Nach's cable: Manila 15403, June 9, 1984, Secret. The cable was released, with deletions, pursuant to the FOIA. I interviewed Nach on two occasions, in December 1985 in Manila and in August 1986 in Washington, D.C.

p. 357. "What they're trying to do": A copy of this letter was provided to the author by the person to whom it was sent, on the condition that the author not use the sender's name.

pp. 358–59. "Sometimes for us moderates": Author's interview, January 1985, Manila.

p. 358. "textbook case": "Communist Interference in El Salvador," Department of State, February 23, 1981; published in *The New York Times*, February 28, 1981.

p. 359. "The Filipino people": Bosworth expressed this view frequently. The words here are from the notes of a person who met with the ambassador.

pp. 359–60. "justice cannot be obtained": Bureau of Intelligence and Research, "Politics and the Philippine Military," Report No. 1353, March 27, 1980, Secret.

p. 361. Footnote on Mondale and debate: Author's interview with Mondale.

p. 362. Reaction of embassy in Manila and Maisto's role: Interviews with Foreign Service officers who were in Manila and the State Department at the time.

p. 362. "I don't think that the President": Steve Lohr, "Reagan Remark on Philippines Assailed," *The New York Times*, October 23, 1984

pp. 362–63. The NSSD was leaked to the press, but the *Washington Post* and *Far*

Eastern Economic Review were about the only publications that paid much attention to it.

pp. 364–65. Bosworth's schedule in Washington: Provided by the State Department pursuant to an FOIA request for all documents pertaining to Bosworth's visit.

p. 365. I interviewed Bosworth in December 1985 in Manila and in July 1986 in New York.

p. 366. Scene at Leyte: Described to author by an embassy officer who had been present.

p. 366. Bosworth's relations to Sin: Author's interview with senior Sin aide.

p. 366. Ongpin and Bosworth: Author's interview with Jaime Ongpin, November 1985, Manila.

p. 367. "Cannot afford a business as usual approach": House Subcommittee on Asian and Pacific Affairs, March 12, 1985.

p. 367. "military abuse against civilians": Paul Wolfowitz, "Challenges in the Pacific," Honolulu symposium, National Defense University, February 22, 1985.

p. 368. Wolfowitz column in *Wall Street Journal*: "U.S. Encourages Constructive Change in the Philippines," April 15, 1985.

p. 368. Reagan interview with *The New York Times*: February 12, 1985.

p. 368. Secret support for RAM: Author's interviews.

p. 368. "broad press freedom": Wolfowitz testimony before the Subcommittee on Asian and Pacific Affairs, February 20, 1985.

pp. 369–70. Human rights abuses: Author's interviews in January 1985. I went to the Philippines on behalf of the Lawyers Committee for Human Rights. The report of that human rights mission, though not all the incidents described here, is " 'Salvaging' Democracy: Human Rights in the Philippines," issued by the Lawyers Committee for Human Rights, December 1985.

p. 370. "cover-up": Author's interview.

pp. 370–71. ABA's letter: Behind the ABA's action were the efforts of Diane Orentlicher, deputy director of the Lawyers Committee for Human Rights. Orentlicher drafted the letter, then lobbied many members of the ABA whose approval was needed before its president would send it.

p. 371. "We had to do it": The Defense Department official made this statement in a meeting, the notes of which were provided to the author.

p. 371. Allen's role: Author's interviews with staff aides to the Senate and House foreign affairs committees.

pp. 371–72. Saudi bank and pressure from Shultz: Related to author by Philippine businessman in August 1985. Also, Jeff Gerth, "Banks Pressed to Aid Manila," *The New York Times*, November 2, 1985.

p. 372. *Newsweek* story about Casey and Marcos: "Casey: A Message for Marcos" (May 27, 1985).

p. 373. Laxalt on Casey: Paul Laxalt, "My Conversations with Ferdinand Marcos: A Lesson in Personal Diplomacy," *Policy Review* (Summer 1986).

pp. 373–74. Reaction to Casey mission: Author's interviews.

pp. 374–76. National War College gathering: Author's interviews with about a dozen people who attended.

pp. 376–77. Solarz's views on certification: I discussed this with Solarz during an evening with him in January 1986 in Sydney, Australia. On Solarz, see Christopher Madison, "Solarz's Brash Style Tempers His Quest for Influence in the Foreign Policy Arena," *National Journal* (October 26, 1985), pp. 2413–17;

and Rachel Flick, "The Solarz System: A Brooklyn Congressman's Global Ambitions," *New York* (August 4, 1986), p. 44.

pp. 378–79. Brown's memorandum to Lugar: Subject: Situation in the Philippines: Initial Impressions. Dated August 19, 1985. A copy was provided to the author. With modifications it was published in April 1986: *Visit to the Philippines, August 2–15, 1985*, staff report prepared for the Committee on Foreign Relations.

p. 381. Krause interview with Marcos: A transcript was provided to the author.

p. 382. "political, personal": Jack W. Germond and Jules Witcover, "The Wild Card," *Washingtonian* (August 1986), p. 81.

p. 382. "an extremely blunt message": Lou Cannon and Bob Woodward, "Reagan Warning Marcos on Peril of Overthrow," *Washington Post*, October 15, 1985, p. 1.

p. 382. "He did not deliver a blunt" and "love feast": Author's interviews.

p. 383. Black, Manafort: Documents in the Justice Department, filed pursuant to the Foreign Agents Registration Act, and author's interviews.

p. 384. The 208 Committee: Patrick E. Tyler and David B. Ottaway, "Casey Enforces 'Reagan Doctrine' with Reinvigorated Covert Action," *Washington Post*, March 9, 1986.

p. 384. Marcos researchers: Author's interview with one of Marcos's researchers.

16 : A BLUNDER LEADS TO AN ELECTION

pp. 385–86. Laxalt: "My Conversations with Ferdinand Marcos."

p. 386. "I thought this was going to be": Author's interview, March 1986.

pp. 386–87. Transcript, *This Week with David Brinkley*, November 3, 1985.

p. 388. "If you are going to do that": Laxalt, "My Conversations with Ferdinand Marcos."

p. 388. Laxalt told fellow senators that it would be a fair election: Author's interviews.

p. 388. "hidden wealth": Carey, Ellison, and Simons, "Hidden Billions: The Draining of the Philippines." Series reprinted by the *San Jose Mercury News*.

pp. 388–89. *Village Voice* exposé: William Bastone and Joe Conason, "Marcos Takes Manhattan," *Village Voice* (October 15, 1985).

p. 389. "to change their country for the better": Joseph Smith, *Portrait of a Cold Warrior*, p. 283.

p. 390. Holbrooke in Manila: Author's interviews with Holbrooke and with embassy officers. The breakfast meeting is described in a cable from the embassy, which was provided to the author. The cable was dated November 6, 1985; subject: Snap Elections.

p. 390. Holbrooke at Pacific basin conference: His speech on December 7, 1985, was entitled "Transitions in the Pacific Rim." A text was released. The anger of the Philippine opposition was described in interviews with the author by persons who were present.

p. 390. "It was a serious misunderstanding": Author's interview with Holbrooke. In addition to Holbrooke, several persons, including an embassy officer and a person whom Mrs. Aquino called afterward, told me about the Aquino-Holbrooke meeting.

p. 391. "Doy would be more of the same": Author's interview, November 1985, Manila.

p. 391. "He's one of the best politicians": Author's interview.

p. 391. "Say hi to Imelda": Author's interview with aide to Sin.

p. 392. Aquino's *New York Times* interview: December 16, 1985.

pp. 392–393. Munro: "The New Khmer Rouge," *Commentary* (December 1985).

p. 393. Rosenfeld's column: "Another Vietnam—or Another Cambodia?," *Washington Post*, December 6, 1985.

p. 393. "It's a bit like": Author's interview with embassy officer, December 1985.

pp. 393–94. Embassy's analysis: Manila 00207, January 4, 1986, Confidential.

p. 394. "it was almost embarrassing": Author's telephone interview with A. M. Rosenthal, December 3, 1986. "vague and rambling": A. M. Rosenthal, "Journey with Tyrants," *The New York Times Magazine*, March 23, 1986. I was in Manila when Rosenthal and Hoge were there. I ran with Hoge along Manila Bay the morning after the interview.

p. 394. "Armacost began asking": Author's interview with embassy officer.

p. 395. "devastating, even more": Author's interview with senior diplomat, October 1986.

p. 395. Rosenthal's views: Author's interview with Rosenthal.

pp. 395–98. The roles of Jones, D. H. Sawyer's, Mark Brown, et al. in the campaign were described by several people, including diplomats. I interviewed Jones on February 27, 1986, in New York and spoke with him by telephone thereafter. I interviewed Mark Brown on August 11, 1986, in New York.

p. 397. Hong Kong rally: Related to author by a person involved.

p. 399. Bases not a campaign issue: Confidential cable from the embassy, November 6, 1985; subject: Snap Elections. Provided to author.

pp. 400–401. War medals fraud and *The New York Times*: Author's conversations with Hersh, Gerth, and Kovach. The *Times* story appeared on January 23, 1986; Sharkey's *Washington Post* story, "New Doubts on Marcos' War Role," January 24, 1986.

p. 401. Sharkey and McCoy: Author's telephone interview with Sharkey.

pp. 401–402. "the election campaign": Laxalt, "My Conversations with Ferdinand Marcos."

p. 402. "He came down on them": Seth Mydans, "In Manila Press, It's 'Corazon Who'?, " *The New York Times*, January 20, 1986.

p. 403. Donald Regan on *Brinkley* show: January 26, 1986.

p. 403. Panama election fraud: Seymour Hersh, "Panama General Said to Have Told Army to Rig Vote," *The New York Times*, June 21, 1986.

p. 403. "life-and-death": Evans and Novak, "Cory Aquino's Zeal," *Washington Post*, January 22, 1986.

p. 404. "Marcos opponents in the U.S. Congress": Kirkpatrick column, "Aquino Campaign Is Lesson in Freedom," *San Francisco Chronicle*, February 10, 1986.

p. 404. Footnote on Krauthammer: "Intervening for Democracy," *Washington Post*, February 4, 1986. Correction, February 5, 1986.

pp. 405–406. "from reading the American press": Kirkpatrick column, "Strong Philippines a Major U.S. Goal," *San Francisco Chronicle*, December 16, 1985.

p. 406. Helmke's political family and Lugar's election as mayor: Author's interview with Mark Helmke, August 9, 1986, Washington, D.C.

pp. 407–408. Lugar et al. letter to Marcos: November 22, 1985. Copy in author's files.

p. 407. The center's report: *The Presidential Election Process in the Philippines*, a report to the Committee on Foreign Relations by the Center for Democracy, January 1986.

pp. 408–409. NAMFREL and NED and Conyers' statement: Phil Bronstein and David Johnston, "U.S. Funding Anti-Left Fight in Philippines," *San Francisco Examiner*, July 21, 1985.

Details about the funding of NAMFREL were provided to the author by diplomatic and congressional sources and documents released pursuant to an FOIA request. NAMFREL's request for funding: See, for example, Manila 35263, November 13, 1985, Confidential; Manila 37955, December 5, 1985, Confidential ("Namfrel requests status of its proposal for National Endowment for Democracy Funding . . . ").

p. 409. The U.S. funding of Veritas was first reported by Alan Berlow of National Public Radio, April 30, 1986. Berlow was relying on Walden Bello, a Filipino active in the anti-Marcos movement in the United States. Bello, who has a Ph.D. from Princeton and is the author of numerous books and articles about the Philippines, had been invited to attend a session at the Foreign Service Institute; the speaker was Undersecretary Armacost. Armacost's comments were to have been off the record, but because Bello was not part of the press, he did not feel bound by the restriction. Among other things, Armacost said, "Radio Veritas enjoyed our financial support and that of the Asia Foundation, among others." When NPR asked the State Department about Armacost's remarks, the department's spokesman, Charles Redman, said the United States "did not and does not provide direct financial support to Radio Veritas. . . ." And the spokesman for the Bureau of East Asian Affairs said that no money had been "designated" for Veritas.

According to this author's sources, which include priests affiliated with Veritas, the United States did indeed provide funding for the radio station. But as with NAMFREL, it was channeled to the station through other organizations—that is, it was "indirect." See also "A Proposal for Funding Assistance on Project Information," from UNDA/Philippines to Carl Gershman, president, National Endowment for Democracy. The eight-page proposal was released pursuant to an FOIA request for all documents pertaining to the calling of the "snap election." Altogether in response to this FOIA request, the department released 135 documents without excisions and 41 with excisions and withheld 57.

p. 410. "This is when the White House": Author's interview. In addition to Mark Helmke, Lugar's press secretary, I interviewed three other Lugar aides who were involved in the observer team. On the matter of the observer team, I also interviewed several State Department officers and a person who represented the White House position.

p. 411. That Lugar wanted Chandler: Author's interview with Helmke.

p. 412. "wanted a safe team . . . very conservative": Author's interview.

p. 412. "He was our watchdog": Author's interview with Helmke.

p. 412. "It came out of the blue": Author's interview with Mortimer B. Zuckerman, November 6, 1986, New York City.

p. 413. Lugar's letter to Reagan: January 31, 1986. Copy in author's files.

p. 414. Bannerman and Kerry: Related to auther by Graeme Bannerman, August 9, 1986, Washington, D.C.

pp. 414–15. Sunday meeting: Described by several persons who were present; one person's notes of the meeting were provided to the author.

pp. 414–15. "We are telling"; "boldest stroke": Based on notes of the meeting provided to the author.

p. 415. "We saw an extremely stirring": Based on notes of the meeting.

p. 415. "a very poetic display": Robert Pear, "U.S. Observers Disagree on Extent of Philippine Fraud," *The New York Times*, February 17, 1986.

p. 415. Views of Fielding, Kerry, and Long: Based on notes of meeting.

p. 416. Clines: "30 Computer Aides Say Vote Is Rigged," *The New York Times*, February 10, 1986.

p. 416. "What affected me": Author's interview with Zuckerman. For Zuckerman's view on the election, see his editorial, "End of an Era," *U.S. News & World Report*, February 24, 1986. Many journalists questioned whether Zuckerman should have accepted a position on the observer delegation, arguing that in doing so, he crossed the inviolable line between writing about government and being a part of it. Zuckerman, in an interview with the author, said that it was a "fair question" but added that he did not feel he sacrificed his journalistic independence.

p. 417. Embassy officer's comments about Murtha: Author's interview with the officer.

pp. 417–18. Marcos on *Brinkley*: February 9, 1986.

17 : TO THE END

I made an FOIA request for all records pertaining to the political situation in the Philippines prepared between February 10 and 20, 1986, inclusive. The State Department located 303 documents. Of these, 155 were released in full, 42 with excisions, and 106 were withheld.

p. 420. Text of press conference: *The New York Times*, February 12, 1986.

p. 420. "Officials said": Lou Cannon, "President's Remarks Undercut U.S. Efforts in Philippines," *Washington Post*, February 15, 1986.

p. 420. "a flub pure": *Time* (February 24, 1986).

p. 421. Scanlon's efforts: Author's interview with John Scanlon, October 3, 1986, New York.

p. 421. 180 minutes versus three per year: David Haward Bain, "Tipping the Balance Against a Tyrant," *Columbia Journalism Review* (May/June 1986).

pp. 422–23. Nunn's letter: Copy in author's files.

p. 423. "I have never been so ashamed": Author's interview with Charles Krause, November 1986, New York.

p. 423. "It was a real body blow": Author's interview.

p. 424. "stolen the shit": Author's interview.

p. 424. "How to Cheat and Lose Your People": Manila 4898, February 13, 1986, Confidential.

p. 424. "KBL caught with hand": Cebu 81, February 11, 1986, Confidential.

p. 425. "The vote that she got shocked him": Author's interview with the American.

p. 425. Bosworth and Aquino: Based on interviews with several people, including two who were present.

p. 426. Jones and Aquino: Author's interview.

pp. 425–26. Text of bishops' statement: *The New York Times*, February 15, 1986.

p. 426. Ten deaths in Quirino: Francis X. Clines, "10 More Killed in Philippines, Opposition Says," *The New York Times*, February 15, 1986.

pp. 426–29. Habib's mission: There was extensive reporting about it at the time. But much of what I have written here comes from interviews with three persons who were intimately involved at the highest levels, as well as documents released pursuant to my FOIA requests.

p. 427. "It was the Carter administration": Author's interview.

p. 427. Gelb's article: "Marcos Reported To Lose Support In Administration," *The New York Times*, January 26, 1986.

p. 427. "ringleader": Evans and Novak, "The Philippines Struggle," *Washington Post*, February 22, 1986.

p. 428. Habib's meeting with Marcos: Described to the author by a person who was present.

p. 429. "carte blanche authority": Author's interview with State Department official involved in Habib mission.

pp. 429–30. Habib meeting with businessmen: State 54515, February 22, 1986, Confidential/ExDis.

p. 430. American Chamber of Commerce views: Manila 4421, February 10, 1986, Confidential.

p. 430. Buss told Habib: Author's telephone interview with Buss, October 1986.

p. 430. Habib on Nancy Reagan: Author's interview with embassy officers.

p. 430. "Don't underestimate": Author's interview.

p. 430. Imelda Marcos's gifts to Nancy Reagan: Sarah Booth Conroy, "The President's Presents," *Washington Post*, March 7, 1986.

p. 431. That the White House checked with Aquino's staff before issuing statement was told to author by two persons involved.

p. 432. Wolfowitz at the Council on Foreign Relations: Author's interview with Ambassador William Sullivan, who was present, and with others present. Wolfowitz's nervousness within the department was related in several interviews.

p. 433. Coll's description of Wolfowitz: "Along the Philippine Watershed," *Washington Post*, February 7, 1986.

pp. 433–35. Probably the most detailed account of Enrile's relationship to RAM and their coup plotting is a very long article which appeared in the *National Times on Sunday*, an Australian newspaper, on October 5, 1986. The article was the first of two parts about the downfall of Marcos; the second was published on October 12. They were researched and written by Alfred McCoy, the professor-author who had uncovered Marcos's war medals fraud; by Gwen Robinson, who covered the Philippine election for the *National Times*; and by Marian Wilkinson, its correspondent in Washington.

One of the best recapitulations of events during the final days: Mark Fineman, "The 3-Day Revolution: How Marcos Was Toppled," *Los Angeles Times*, February 27, 1986. Also, Jim Mulvaney and Jeff Sommer, "The Final Days, Marcos' Fall: The U.S. Role," *Newsday*, March 2, 1986. For a more impressionistic look, a sense of the mood in Manila: James Fenton, "The Snap Revolution," *Granta 18* (Spring 1986).

I made an FOIA request for all records pertaining to the political situation in the Philippines prepared during the period February 21–26 inclusive. The

State Department located 242 documents. Of these, 95 were released in full, 53 with excisions, and 94 were withheld.

p. 434. Proposed junta: Author's interview with American intelligence and diplomatic officers.

p. 435. "last gasp": Author's interview.

p. 436. "We were watching": Author's interview.

p. 436. Radke: Based on author's interviews; also, Jim Mann and Rone Tempest, "American Saw Rebellion Unfold," *Los Angeles Times*, March 4, 1986.

p. 437. Sunday morning meeting: Bernard Gwertzman, "Reagan Sent Marcos Secret Message 12 Hours Before White House's Plea," *The New York Times*, February 28, 1986.

pp. 437–38. White House meeting: Don Oberdorfer and David Hoffman, "Marcos' U.S. Support Ended Sunday Night," *Washington Post*, February 27, 1986.

pp. 438–39. Melchor: Several persons who talked with Melchor while he was in Washington told me that he (Melchor) had come at Marcos's request. In a memorandum to Armacost, Wolfowitz wrote that Marcos "is sending four senior GOP officials to Washington in an attempt to make a case for his Administration." The four were Labor Minister Blas Ople; Kokoy Romualdez; the deputy director of the National Economic and Development Authority, Ramón Cardenas; and Melchor, described by Wolfowitz as a "Presidential Advisor." Copy of this Confidential memorandum was released pursuant to an FOIA request. Melchor told President Corazon Aquino that he had gone to Washington on personal matters which were unrelated to Marcos.

Melchor's presence in the situation room and what he did there were described to the author by several persons who were present.

pp. 439–40. Marcos's call to Laxalt: This was described at the time in much of the reporting, but Habib's response is based on author's interviews.

p. 440. "Madame President": Told to author by a diplomat who was present.

EPILOGUE : THE PRICE OF THE POLICY

p. 442. Lansdale: *Midst of Wars*, p. 28.

p. 442. Spruance: Buell, *Quiet Warrior*, p. 406.

p. 443. "land hunger in the countryside": National Intelligence Estimate. "Prospects for the Philippines," NIE 56–66 ADVCON, 17 February 1966. Secret/ Controlled Dissem. Obtained from LBJ Library.

p. 443. "basic domestic socioeconomic": Intelligence Memorandum, "Philippine Elections." OCI No. 2343/65. 28 October 1965. Secret. Obtained from LBJ Library.

p. 443. INR report: "Philippines: The Radical Movements," May 3, 1971, Secret/ No Foreign Dissem/Controlled Dissem/No Dissem Abroad.

Bibliography

BOOKS

Agoncillo, Teodoro A. *A Short History of the Philippines*. New York and London: Mentor, 1975.

Amnesty International. *Report of an Amnesty International Mission to the Republic of the Philippines, 22 November–5 December 1975*, 2d ed. London: AI Publications, 1977.

Aquino, Benigno S., Jr. *Testament from a Prison Cell*. Manila: Benigno S. Aquino, Jr. Foundation, Inc., 1984.

Area Handbook for the Philippines, 2d ed. Foreign Area Studies, American University. Washington, D.C.: Government Printing Office, 1976.

———. *Philippines: a Country Study*. Foreign Area Studies, American University. Washington, D.C.: U.S. Government Printing Office, 1983.

Averch, Harvey A., John E. Koehler, and Frank H. Denton. *The Matrix of Policy in the Philippines*. Princeton, N.J.: Princeton University Press, 1971.

Bain, David Haward. *Sitting in Darkness: Americans in the Philippines*. Boston: Houghton Mifflin Company, 1984.

Bello, Walden, David Kinley, and Elaine Elinson. *Development Debacle: The World Bank in the Philippines*. San Francisco: Institute for Food and Development Policy, 1982.

Bishop, Jim. *A Day in the Life of President Johnson*. New York: Random House, 1967.

Bohlen, Charles E. *Witness to History, 1929–1969*. New York: W. W. Norton & Company, 1973.

Bonner, Raymond T. *Weakness and Deceit: U.S. Policy and El Salvador*. New York: Times Books, 1984.

Brzezinski, Zbigniew. *Power and Principle: Memoirs of the National Security Adviser, 1977–1981*. New York: Farrar, Straus & Giroux, 1983.

Buell, Thomas B. *The Quiet Warrior: A Biography of Admiral Raymond A. Spruance*. Boston: Little, Brown and Company, 1974.

Buss, Claude A. *The United States and the Philippines*. Washington, D.C.: American Enterprise Institute; Stanford, Calif.: Hoover Institution on War, Revolution, and Peace, 1977.

Canoy, Reuben B. *The Counterfeit Revolution: The Philippines from Martial Law to the Aquino Assassination*. Manila: Philippine Editions, 1981.

Carter, Jimmy. *Keeping Faith. Memoirs of a President.* New York: Bantam Books, 1982.
Cottrell, Alvin J., and Robert J. Hanks. *The Military Utility of the U.S. Facilities in the Philippines.* Washington, D.C.: Center for Strategic and International Studies, Georgetown University, 1980.

Day, Beth. *The Philippines: Shattered Showcase of Democracy in Asia.* New York: M. Evans and Company, Inc., 1974.
De Dios, Emmanuel S., ed. *An Analysis of the Philippine Economic Crises.* Manila: University of the Philippines Press, 1984.
Destler, I. M., Leslie H. Gelb, and Anthony Lake. *Our Own Worst Enemy: The Unmaking of American Foreign Policy.* New York: Simon & Schuster, 1984.

Far Eastern Economic Review. Yearbooks, 1965–1974.
———. Asia Yearbooks, 1975–1986.
Fookien Times Yearbook. Manila: Fookien Times Company, 1971–1984–1985.

Gregor, A. James, ed. *The U.S. and the Philippines: A Challenge to a Special Relationship.* Washington, D.C.: Heritage Foundation, 1983.
———. *Crisis in the Philippines: A Threat to U.S. Interests.* Washington, D.C.: Ethics and Public Policy Center, 1984.

Haig, Alexander M., Jr. *Caveat: Realism, Reagan, and Foreign Policy.* New York: Macmillan Publishing Company, 1984.
Halberstam, David. *The Best and the Brightest.* New York: Random House, 1972.
Hardy, Richard P., ed. *The Philippine Bishops Speak (1968–1983).* Manila: Maryhill School of Theology, 1984.
Hayes, Peter, Lyuba Zarsky, and Walden Bello. *American Lake: Nuclear Peril in the Pacific.* Ringwood, Australia: Penguin Books, 1987.
Hersh, Seymour. *The Price of Power: Kissinger in the Nixon White House.* New York: Summit Books, 1983.
Herz, Martin F., ed. *Contacts with the Opposition: A Symposium.* Lanham, Md.: University Press of America, 1986.

IBON Databank. *What Crisis?: Highlights of the Philippine Economy, 1983.* Manila: IBON Databank Phils., Inc., 1984.
International Commission of Jurists. *The Decline of Democracy in the Philippines.* Geneva, Switzerland: August 1977.
———. *The Philippines: Human Rights After Martial Law.* Geneva: 1984.

Joaquin, Nick. *The Aquinos of Tarlac: An Essay on History as Three Generations.* Manila: Cacho Hermanos, Inc., 1983.
Johnson, Lady Bird. *A White House Diary.* New York: Holt, Rinehart & Winston, 1970.

Kennan, George F. *The Cloud of Danger: Current Realities of American Foreign Policy.* Boston: Little, Brown and Company, 1977.
———. *Memoirs, 1925–1950.* Boston: Little, Brown and Company, 1967.

Kerkvliet, Benedict J. *The Huk Rebellion: A Study of Peasant Revolt in the Philippines.* Berkeley and Los Angeles: University of California Press, 1977.

Khan, Azizur Rahman. "Growth and Inequality in the Rural Philippines." In *Poverty and Landlessness in Rural Asia.* Geneva: International Labor Organization, 1977.

Kirkpatrick, Jeane J. *Dictatorships and Double Standards.* New York: American Enterprise Institute and Simon & Schuster, 1982.

Kissinger, Henry. *White House Years.* Boston: Little, Brown and Company, 1979.

———. *Years of Upheaval.* Boston: Little, Brown and Company, 1982.

Kwitny, Jonathan. *Endless Enemies: The Making of an Unfriendly World.* New York: Congdon & Weed, 1984.

Lachica, Eduardo. *HUK: Philippine Agrarian Society in Revolt.* Manila: Solidaridad Publishing House, 1971.

Lansdale, Edward Geary. *In the Midst of Wars: An American's Mission to Southeast Asia.* New York: Harper & Row, 1972.

McCoy, Alfred W. *Priests on Trial.* Ringwood, Australia: Penguin Books, 1984.

Macapagal, Diosdado. *A Stone for the Edifice: Memoirs of a President.* Quezon City: Mac Publishing House, 1968.

———. *The Philippines Turns East*, 2d ed. Quezon City: Mac Publishing House, 1970.

Manglapus, Raul S. *Philippines: The Silenced Democracy.* Maryknoll, N.Y.: Orbis Books, 1976.

Marcos, Ferdinand E. *Notes on the New Society of the Philippines.* Published by Ferdinand E. Marcos, 1973.

———. *The Democratic Revolution in the Philippines*, 2d ed. Englewood Cliffs, N.J.: Prentice-Hall International, 1979.

Martinez, Manuel F. *Aquino vs. Marcos: The Grand Collision.* Hongkong: A P & G Resources (HK) Co., Ltd., 1984.

Mijares, Primitivo. *The Conjugal Dictatorship of Ferdinand and Imelda Marcos I.* San Francisco: Union Square Publications, 1976.

Miller, Stuart Creighton. *"Benevolent Assimilation": The American Conquest of the Philippines, 1899–1903.* New Haven: Yale University Press, 1982.

Newsom, David D., ed. *The Diplomacy of Human Rights.* Lanham, Maryland, and London: University Press of America; Washington, D.C.: Institute for the Study of Diplomacy, Georgetown University, 1986

Paez, Patricia Ann. *The Bases Factor. Realpolitik of RP-US Relations.* Manila: Center for Strategic and International Studies of the Philippines, 1985.

Payer, Cheryl. *The Debt Trap: The International Monetary Fund and the Third World.* New York: Monthly Review Press, 1974.

Pedrosa, Carmen Navarro. *The Untold Story of Imelda Marcos.* Rizal: Tandem Publishing Company, Ltd., 1969.

Plischke, Elmer. *Presidential Diplomacy: A Chronology of Summit Visits, Trips and Meetings.* Dobbs Ferry, N.Y.: Oceana Publications, 1986.

Poole, Fred, and Max Vanzi. *Revolution in the Philippines: The United States in a Hall of Cracked Mirrors.* New York: McGraw-Hill Book Company, 1984.

503

Pringle, Robert. *Indonesia and the Philippines: American Interests in Island Southeast Asia.* New York: Columbia University Press, 1980.

Psinakis, Steve. *Two "Terrorists" Meet.* San Francisco: Alchemy Books, 1981.

Pye, Lucian W., with Mary W. Pye. *Asian Power and Politics: The Cultural Dimensions of Authority.* Cambridge: Belknap Press of Harvard University Press, 1985.

Reynolds, Quentin, and Geoffrey Bocca. *Macapagal the Incorruptible.* New York: David McKay Company, Inc., 1965.

Rodriguez, Filemon C. *The Marcos Regime: Rape of the Nation.* New York: Vantage Press, 1985.

Rosenberg, David A., ed. *Marcos and Martial Law in the Philippines.* Ithaca: Cornell University Press, 1979.

Rotea, Hermie. *Marcos' Lovey Dovie.* Los Angeles: Liberty Publishing, 1983.

Rubin, Barry. *Secrets of State: The State Department and the Struggle over U.S. Foreign Policy.* New York: Oxford University Press, 1985.

Salas, Rafael M. *More Than the Grains: Participatory Management in the Philippine Rice Sufficiency Program 1967–1969.* Tokyo: Simul Press, Inc., 1985.

Salonga, Jovito R. *Land of the Morning: A Collection of Speeches and Lectures.* Manila: Regina Publishing Company, 1967.

Schlesinger, Arthur. *The Cycles of American History.* Boston: Houghton Mifflin Company, 1986.

Schoultz, Lars. *Human Rights and United States Policy Toward Latin America.* Princeton, N.J.: Princeton University Press, 1981.

Shalom, Stephen Rosskaamm. *The United States and the Philippines: A Study of Neocolonialism.* Quezon City: New Day Publishers. 1986.

Shawcross, William. *The Quality of Mercy: Cambodia, Holocaust and Modern Conscience.* New York: Simon & Schuster, 1984.

Simbulan, Roland G. *The Bases of Our Insecurity: A Study of the US Military Bases in the Philippines.* Manila: Balai Fellowship, Inc., 1983.

Smith, Gaddis. *Morality, Reason, and Power: American Diplomacy in the Carter Years.* New York: Hill and Wang, 1986.

Smith, Joseph B. *Portrait of a Cold Warrior.* New York: Ballantine Books, 1976.

Spence, Hartzell. *Marcos of the Philippines.* Published by Ferdinand E. Marcos, 1982.

Stannard, Bruce. *Poor Man's Priest: The Fr. Brian Gore Story.* Sydney: Collins/Fontana, 1984.

Steinberg, David Joel. *The Philippines: A Singular and a Plural Place.* Boulder, Colo.: Westview Press, 1982.

Sullivan, William H. *Obbligato, 1939–1979: Notes on a Foreign Service Career.* New York: W. W. Norton & Company, 1984.

Vance, Cyrus. *Hard Choices: Critical Years in America's Foreign Policy.* New York: Simon & Schuster, 1983.

CONGRESSIONAL MATERIALS

Senate

Committee on Foreign Relations. *United States Security Agreements and Commitments Abroad.* Hearings before the Subcommittee on United States Security Agreements and Commitments Abroad. Vol I, 91st Congress, September 30, October 1, 2, and 3, 1969. Printed in 1971.

———. *Security Agreements And Commitments Abroad.* Report to the Committee on Foreign Relations by the Subcommittee on Security Agreements and Commitments Abroad, 91st Congress, 2d Session, December 21, 1970.

———. *Korea and the Philippines: November 1972.* A staff report for the Committee on Foreign Relations, 93d Congress, 1st Session, February 18, 1973.

———. *Economic and Political Developments in the Far East.* Report by Senator Charles H. Percy to the Committee on Foreign Relations on a study mission to the Far East, November 26–December 23, 1972, 93d Congress, 1st Session, March 30, 1973.

———. *Foreign Assistance Authorization: Examination of U.S. Foreign Aid Programs and Policies.* Hearings before the Subcommittee on Foreign Assistance, 94th Congress, 1st Session, June 3 and 13, July 17, 21, 23 and 29, and September 17 and 23, 1975.

———. *Winds of Change: Evolving Relations and Interests in Southeast Asia.* A report by Senator Mike Mansfield, majority leader, U.S. Senate, 94th Congress, 1st Session, October 1975.

———. *Foreign Assistance Authorization: Arms Sales Issues.* Hearings before the Subcommittee on Foreign Assistance, 94th Congress, 1st Session, June 17 and 18, November 19 and 21, and December 4 and 5, 1975.

———. *Charting a New Course: Southeast Asia in a Time of Change.* A report by Senator Mike Mansfield, majority leader, U.S. Senate, 94th Congress, 2d Session, December 1976.

———. *United States Development Assistance Programs in Pakistan, the Philippines, and Indonesia.* Staff reports to the Subcommittee on Foreign Assistance, 95th Congress, 1st Session, February 1977.

———. *United States-Philippine Base Negotiations.* Staff Report to the Subcommittee on Foreign Assistance, 95th Congress, 1st Session, April 7, 1977.

———. *United States Foreign Policy Objectives and Overseas Military Installations.* Prepared for the Committee on Foreign Relations by the Foreign Affairs and National Defense Division, Congressional Research Service, Library of Congress, 96th Congress, 1st Session, April 1979.

———. *Human Rights and U.S. Foreign Assistance. Experiences and Issues in Policy Implementation (1977–1978).* Prepared for the Committee on Foreign Relations by the Foreign Affairs and National Defense Division, Congressional Research Service, Library of Congress, 96th Congress, 1st Session, November 1979.

———. *Situation in the Philippines and Implications for U.S. Policy.* Hearing before the Subcommittee on East Asian and Pacific Affairs, 98th Congress, 2d Session, September 18, 1984.

———. *The Situation in the Philippines.* A staff report for the Committee on Foreign Relations, 98th Congress, 2d Session, October 1984.

———. *Administration Review of U.S. Policy Toward the Philippines.* Hearing

before the Committee on Foreign Relations, 99th Congress, 1st Session, October 30, 1985.
———. *Insurgency and Counterinsurgency in the Philippines.* Prepared for the Committee on Foreign Relations by the Foreign Affairs and National Defense Division, Congressional Research Service, Library of Congress, 99th Congress, 1st Session, November 1985.
———. *The Presidential Election Process in the Philippines.* A report to the Committee on Foreign Relations by the Center for Democracy, 99th Congress, 2d Session, January 1986.
———. *Visit to the Philippines, August 2–15, 1985.* A staff report for the Committee on Foreign Relations, 99th Congress, 2d Session, April 1986.

House of Representatives

Committee on Foreign Affairs. *Our Asian Neighbors.* Hearing before the Subcommittee on Asian and Pacific Affairs, 93d Congress, 1st Session, March 28, 1973.
———. *Human Rights in the World Community: A Call for U.S. Leadership.* Report of the Subcommittee on International Organizations and Movements, 93d Congress, 2d Session, March 27, 1974.

Committee on International Relations. *Human Rights in South Korea and the Philippines: Implications for U.S. Policy.* Hearings before the Subcommittee on International Organizations, 94th Congress, 1st Session, May 20, 22; June 3, 5, 10, 12, 17, and 24, 1975.
———. *Shifting Balance of Power in Asia: Implications for Future U.S. Policy.* Hearings before the Subcommittee on Future Foreign Policy Research and Development, 94th Congress, November 18, December 10, 1975; January 28, March 8, April 7, and May 18, 1976.
———. *Foreign Assistance Legislation for Fiscal Year 1978 (Part 6).* Hearings before the Subcommittee on Asian and Pacific Affairs, 95th Congress, 1st Session, March 10, 17, and 22, 1977.
———. *Security Assistance to Asia for Fiscal Year 1978.* Report of a special study mission to Asia, April 8–21, 1977, by members of the Subcommittee on Asian and Pacific Affairs, 95th Congress, 1st Session, June 19, 1977.
———. *Foreign Assistance Legislation for Fiscal Year 1979 (Part 6).* Hearings before the Subcommittee on Asian and Pacific Affairs, 95th Congress, 2d Session, March 7, 9, 14, 16, 21, and 22, 1978.

Committee on Appropriations. *Foreign Assistance and Related Programs: Appropriations for 1980.* Hearings before the Subcommittee on Foreign Operations and Related Programs, 96th Congress, 1st Session, 1979.

Committee on Foreign Affairs. *Foreign Assistance Legislation for Fiscal Years 1980–81 (Part 4).* Hearings and markup before the Subcommittee on Asian and Pacific Affairs, 96th Congress, 1st Session, February 27; March 1, 6, 7, and 12, 1979.
———. *Human Rights in Asia: Noncommunist Countries.* Hearings before the subcommittees on Asian and Pacific Affairs and on International Organizations, 96th Congress, 2d Session, February 4, 6, and 7, 1980.
———. *Foreign Assistance Legislation for Fiscal Year 1981 (Part 4).* Hearings and

markup before the Subcommittee on Asian and Pacific Affairs, 96th Congress, 2d Session, February 11, 21; March 4 and 6, 1980.

―――. *Asian Security Environment: 1980.* Report of a special study mission to Asia, January 5–23, 1980, 96th Congress, 2d Session, May 1980.

Committee on Banking, Finance, and Urban Affairs. *Human Rights and U.S. Policy in the Multilateral Development Banks.* Hearings before the Subcommittee on International Development Institutions and Finance, 97th Congress, 1st Session, July 21 and 23, 1981.

―――― and Committee on Foreign Affairs. *U.S. Policy Toward the Philippines.* Hearing before the subcommittees on Asian and Pacific Affairs and on Human Rights and International Organizations, 97th Congress, 1st Session, November 18, 1981.

―――. *Reconciling Human Rights and U.S. Security Interests in Asia.* Hearings before the subcommittees on Asian and Pacific Affairs and on Human Rights and International Organizations, 97th Congress, 2d Session, August 10; September 21, 22, 28, 29; December 3, 9, 15, 1982.

―――. *United States-Philippines Relations and the New Base and Aid Agreement.* Hearings before the Subcommittee on Asian and Pacific Affairs, 98th Congress, 1st Session, June 17, 23, and 28, 1983.

―――. *The Consequences of the Aquino Assassination.* Hearing and markup before the Subcommittee on Asian and Pacific Affairs, 98th Congress, 1st Session, September 13; October 6, 18, 1983.

―――. *The Situation and Outlook in the Philippines.* Hearings before the Subcommittee on Asian and Pacific Affairs, 98th Congress, 2d Session, September 20 and October 4, 1984.

―――. *Recent Events in the Philippines, Fall 1985.* Hearings and markup before the Subcommittee on Asian and Pacific Affairs, 99th Congress, 1st Session, November 12 and 13, 1985.

―――. *The Philippine Election and the Implications for U.S. Policy.* Hearing and markup before the Subcommittee on Asian and Pacific Affairs, 99th Congress, 2d Session, February 19 and 20, 1986.

Human Rights Reports

Human Rights and U.S. Policy: Argentina, Haiti, Indonesia, Iran, Peru, and the Philippines. Reports submitted to the House Committee on International Relations by the Department of State, 94th Congress, 2d Session, December 31, 1976.

The Status of Human Rights in Selected Countries and the U.S. Response. Prepared for the Subcommittee on International Organizations of the House Committee on International Relations by the Foreign Affairs and National Defense Division, Congressional Research Service, Library of Congress, 95th Congress, 1st Session, July 25, 1977.

Country Reports on Human Rights Practices. Report submitted to the House Committee on International Relations and Senate Committee on Foreign Relations by the Department of State, 95th Congress, 2d Session, February 3, 1978.

Human Rights Conditions in Selected Countries and the U.S. Response. Prepared for the Subcommittee on International Organizations of the House Committee on International Relations, by the Foreign Affairs and National Defense Division, Congressional Research Service, Library of Congress, 95th Congress, 2d Session, July 25, 1978.

Report on Human Rights Practices in Countries Receiving U.S. Aid. Submitted to the Senate Committee on Foreign Relations and the House Committee on Foreign Affairs by the Department of State, 96th Congress, 1st Session, February 8, 1979.

Country Reports on Human Rights Practices for 1980. Submitted to the Senate Committee on Foreign Affairs and the House Committee on Foreign Relations by the Department of State, February 2, 1981.

——— *for 1981.* Submitted to the House Committee on Foreign Affairs and the Senate Committee on Foreign Relations by the Department of State, February 1982.

——— *for 1982.* Submitted to the Senate Committee on Foreign Relations and the House Committee on Foreign Affairs by the Department of State, February 1983.

——— *for 1983.* Submitted to the House Committee on Foreign Affairs and the Senate Committee on Foreign Relations by the Department of State, February 1984.

——— *for 1984.* Submitted to the Senate Committee on Foreign Affairs and the House Committee on Foreign Relations by the Department of State, February 1985.

——— *for 1985.* Submitted to the House Committee on Foreign Affairs and the Senate Committee on Foreign Relations by the Department of State, February 1986.

Congressional Research Service, Library of Congress

Bowen, Alva M. *Philippine Bases: U.S. Redeployment Options.* No. 86–44 F, February 20, 1986.

Erickson, R. Lynn. *U.S. Assistance to the Philippines: Foreign Aid Facts.* Updated April 8, 1985.

Gannon, Edmund J. *Alternative Sites for U.S. Philippine Bases.* April 20, 1977.

Human Rights & U.S. Foreign Assistance: Experience & Issues in Policy Implementation. February 27, 1979.

Niehaus, Marjorie. *Aquino Assassination: Consequences for U.S.-Philippine Relations.* October 21, 1983.

Niksch, Larry A. *The Internal Situation in the Philippines: Factors Affecting Future Trends.* February 10, 1980.

———. *U.S. Assistance to the Philippines: Foreign Aid Facts.* Updated October 28, 1985.

Niksch, Larry A., and Marjorie Niehaus. *The Internal Situation in the Philippines: Current Trends and Future Prospects.* No. 81–21 F, January 20, 1981.

Comptroller General/General Accounting Office

Review of Military Assistance Provided to the Republic of the Philippines. B-133359, March 26, 1965.

Review of Economic Assistance Provided to the Republic of the Philippines for Development Purposes. B-146984, April 21, 1965.

Military Assistance and Commitments in the Philippines. April 12, 1973.
Better Use Could Be Made of U.S. Assistance and Other Support to the Philippines. B-133359, March 2, 1973.
Economic Support Fund Assistance to the Philippines. GAO/NSIAD-84-44, January 27, 1984.
Use of Special Presidential Authorities for Foreign Assistance. GAO/NSIAD-85-79, May 20, 1985.

Articles, Pamphlets, Reports,
Dissertations, Other

Amnesty International. "Human Rights Violations in the Philippines: An Account of Torture, 'Disappearances,' Extrajudicial Executions and Illegal Detention." Amnesty International USA, N.d. Released in 1982.
Aquino, Belinda A., ed. "Cronies and Enemies: The Current Scene." Philippine Studies Occasional Paper No. 5. Philippine Studies Program, Center for Asian and Pacific Studies, University of Hawaii, August 1982.
Aquino, Benigno S., Jr. "What's Wrong with the Philippines?" *Foreign Affairs*, Vol. 46 (July 1968), pp. 770–79.

Bain, David Haward. "Letter from Manila." *Columbia Journalism Review* (May/June 1986), pp. 27–36.
Baker, Richard. "The Ten Richest Women in the World." *Cosmopolitan* (December 1975), p. 160.
Barnes, Fred. "The Shaking of a President." *New Republic* (February 10, 1986), pp. 16–20.
Bello, Walden. "The Pentagon and the Philippine Crisis." *Southeast Asia Chronicle* (November 1984), pp. 20–24.
Belluck, Pamela J. "Off-Base? The Impact of U.S. Security Policy on Political Development in the Philippines." B.A. thesis, Princeton University, 1985.
Berry, William E., Jr. "American Military Bases in the Philippines, Base Negotiations, and Philippine-American Relations: Past, Present, and Future." Ph.D. thesis, Cornell University, 1981.
Bethell, Tom. "The Making of Richard Holbrooke." *Washingtonian* (February 1980), p. 114.
Bird, Kai. "Right Turn in the Foreign Service." *Nation* (June 16, 1968), p. 737.
———. "Inside the Manila Embassy." *Foreign Service Journal* (September 1984), p. 24.
———. "The Decline of Dissent." *Foreign Service Journal* (February 1985), p. 26.
Boyer, Neil A. "The Dissent Channel: Who's Using It?" *Department of State Newsletter* (October 1976), p. 28.
Branigin, William. "The Philippines: A Society Adrift." *Washington Post*, August 12–17, 1984.
Broad, Robin. "Behind Philippine Policy Making: The Role of the World Bank and International Monetary Fund." Ph.D. dissertation, Princeton University, Woodrow Wilson School of Public and International Affairs, 1983.
Brown, Mark Malloch. "Aquino, Marcos and the White House." *Granta 18* (Spring 1986), pp. 160–69.
Buckley, William F., Jr. "Marcos and the Philippines." *National Review* (December 23, 1977), p. 1512.

Bundy, William P. "Dictatorships and American Foreign Policy." *Foreign Affairs*, Vol. 53 (October 1975), pp. 51–60.

Campbell, Alex. "The Philippines. 'Sugar, Rice and a Great Deal of Vice.' " *The New Republic* (March 12, 1966), p. 21.
Campbell, Colin. "Looking Beyond Marcos." *The New York Times Magazine*, January 8, 1984, p. 52.
Chappell, David. "U.S. Security and the Philippines: An Exchange." *Bulletin of Atomic Scientists* (May 1985), pp. 38–40.
Cheevers, Jack, and Spencer A. Sherman. "The Palace Plot." *Mother Jones* (June 1983), p. 31.
Clines, Francis X. "Putting It Together." *The New York Times Magazine*, April 27, 1986, p. 30.
Cohen, Stephen B. "Conditioning U.S. Security Assistance on Human Rights Practices." *American Journal of International Law*, Vol. 76 (April 1982), pp. 246–79.

Davies, John Paton. "America and East Asia." *Foreign Affairs*, Vol. 55 (January 1977), pp. 368–94.
Diokno, José. "On the Struggle for Democracy." *World Policy Journal*, Vol. I (Winter 1984), pp. 434–45.
Drew, Elizabeth. "A Reporter at Large: Human Rights." *New Yorker* (July 18, 1977), pp. 36–62.
Durdin, Tillman. "The Philippines: Martial Law, Marcos Style." *Asian Affairs*, Vol. 3 (November/December 1975), pp. 67–82.
———. "Philippine Communism." *Problems of Communism*, Vol. 25 (May–June 1976), pp. 40–48.

Falk, Richard. "Views from Manila and Washington." *World Policy Journal*, Vol. I (Winter 1984), pp. 421–32.
Fenton, James. "The Snap Revolution." *Granta 18* (Spring 1986), pp. 33–155.
Flick, Rachel. "The Solarz System. A Brooklyn Congressman's Global Ambitions." *New York* (August 4, 1986), p. 44.

Gelb, Leslie H. "The Mind of the President." *The New York Times Magazine*, October 8, 1985, p. 21.
———. "Reagan and the Philippines: A Winning Style." *The New York Times Magazine*, March 30, 1986, p. 30.
Greenberg, Jonathan, and John Taylor. "Secret Agents." *Manhattan, Inc.* (May 1986), pp. 77–85.

Heritage Foundation. "The Key Role of U.S. Bases in the Philippines." January 10, 1984.

Jacoby, Tamar. "The Reagan Turnaround on Human Rights." *Foreign Affairs*, Vol. 64 (Summer 1986), pp. 1066–86.
Jones, Brennon. "Marcos's Influential Enemies." *Nation* (October 4, 1980), p. 311.

Kamm, Henry. "Creating a Dynasty in the Philippines." *The New York Times Magazine*, May 24, 1981, p. 15.

Kann, Peter R. "The Philippines Without Democracy." *Foreign Affairs*, Vol. 52 (April 1974), pp. 612–32.

Kattenburg, Paul M. "The Philippines: It Is Time to End the Special Relationship and Leave the U.S. Bases." Paper prepared for the 1985 annual meeting of the Southern Political Science Association, November 6–9, 1985, at Nashville, Tennessee.

Kennan, George F. "Morality and Foreign Policy." *Foreign Affairs*, Vol. 64 (Winter 1985/86), pp. 205–18.

Kerkvliet, Benedict J. "Land Reform in the Philippines Since the Marcos Coup." *Pacific Affairs*, Vol. 47 (Fall 1974), pp. 286–304.

Kessler, Richard J. "Marcos and the Americans." *Foreign Policy*, No. 63 (Summer 1986), p. 40.

———. "The Philippines: The Next Iran?" *Asian Affairs*, Vol. 7 (January/February 1980), pp. 148–60.

———. "The Philippines: A U.S. Policy Dilemma." *Bulletin of Atomic Scientists* (January 1985), pp. 41–44.

Klitgaard, Robert E. "Martial Law in the Philippines." Santa Monica, Calif.: Rand Corporation, November 1972. Written for the 301st Civil Affairs Group, U.S. Army Reserve, November 1972.

Kwitny, Jonathan. "Plundering the Philippines." *Inquiry* (December 1982), p. 24.

Lande, Carl H. "Philippine Prospects After Martial Law." *Foreign Affairs*, Vol. 59 (Summer 1981), pp. 1147–68.

Lansdale, Major-General Edward G. "Viet Nam: Do We Understand Revolution?" *Foreign Affairs*, Vol. 43 (October 1964), pp. 75–86.

Lawyers Committee for International Human Rights. "The Philippines: A Country in Crisis." New York: December 1983.

———. " 'Salvaging' Democracy: Human Rights in the Philippines." New York: December 1985.

Laxalt, Paul. "My Conversations with Ferdinand Marcos: A Lesson in Personal Diplomacy." *Policy Review* (Summer 1986), p. 2.

Lind, John E. *Philippine Debt to Foreign Banks*. Northern California Interfaith Committee on Corporate Responsibility, San Francisco, November 1984.

Lohr, Steve. "Inside the Philippine Insurgency." *The New York Times Magazine*, November 3, 1985, p. 40.

McPherson, Harry, and Richard Holbrooke. "A Foreign Policy for the Democrats." *The New York Times Magazine*, April 10, 1983, p. 30.

Madison, Christopher. "Solarz's Brash Style Tempers His Quest for Influence in the Foreign Policy Arena." *National Journal* (October 25, 1985), pp. 2413–17.

Manglapus, Raul S. "The State of Philippine Democracy." *Foreign Affairs*, Vol. 38 (July 1960), pp. 613–24.

———. "The Marcos Dictatorship and U.S. Policy." *Asian Thought & Society: An International Review*, Vol. II, No. 1 (April 1977).

Manning, Robert A. "The Philippines in Crisis." *Foreign Affairs*, Vol. 63 (Winter 1984), pp. 392–410.

511

Mecklin, John M. "The Philippines: An Ailing and Resentful Ally." *Fortune* (July 1969), p. 119.

Morrell, Jim. *Aid to the Philippines: Who Benefits?* Washington, D.C.: Center for International Policy, October 1979.

Munro, Ross H. "The New Khmer Rouge." *Commentary*, Vol. 80 (December 1985), pp. 19–38.

Mydans, Seth. "A Dilemma of a Priest in the Philippines." *The New York Times Magazine*, September 14, 1986, p. 68.

———. "The Philippine Middle Class: Turning Against Marcos." *The New York Times Magazine*, February 2, 1986, p. 19.

Nemenzo, Francisco. "Rectification Process in the Philippine Communist Movement." Paper presented to the Institute of Southeast Asian Studies, Singapore, November 17–19, 1982.

Neumann, A. Lin. " 'Hospitality Girls' in the Philippines." Joint issue: *Southeast Asia Chronicle* (January–February 1979) and *Pacific Research* (July–October 1978), pp. 18–23.

Niksch, Larry A. "The Philippines: The Next Iran?" *Congressional Research Service Review* (April 1981), pp. 6–8.

———. "Bases of Understanding." *Foreign Service Journal* (November 1983), p. 17.

O'Hare, Joseph A. "The Other Side of Smiling." *America* (November 19, 1977), p. 353.

Overholt, William H. "Land Reform in the Philippines." *Asian Survey*, Vol. 16 (May 1976), pp. 427–51.

Paglaban, Enric. "Philippines: Workers in the Export Industry." *Pacific Research*, Vol. IX (March–June 1978).

Philippine Resource Center. *Sourcebook on the Philippine Economic Crisis: Analysis and Clippings.* Berkeley: Philippine Resource Center, n.d.

"Republic of the Philippines: American Corporations, Martial Law, and Underdevelopment." Published by the Corporate Information Center, National Council of Churches, 1973.

Rosenberg, David A. "Communism in the Philippines." *Problems of Communism*, Vol. 33 (September–October 1984), pp. 24–46.

Rosenthal, A. M. "Journey with Tyrants." *The New York Times Magazine*, March 23, 1986.

Rossiter, Caleb. "The Financial Hit List." Part One in a Series on Human Rights and the International Financial Institutions. Washington, D.C.: Center for International Policy, February 1984.

———. "Human Rights: The Carter Record, the Reagan Reaction." Part Two in a Series on Human Rights and the International Financial Institutions. Washington, D.C.: Center for International Policy, September 1984.

Rowan, Roy. "The High-Flying First Lady of the Philippines." *Fortune* (July 2, 1979), p. 93.

Schirmer, Daniel B. "Marcos—Sophisticated Dictator." *Commonweal*, Vol. 102 (April 11, 1975), p. 44.
———. "The Philippine Bases: Bulwark of Dictatorship." *Progressive* (April 1978), p. 41.
Shaplen, Robert. "Letter from Manila." *New Yorker* (January 15, 1966), p. 84.
———. "Letter from Manila." *New Yorker* (December 20, 1969), p. 87.
———. "Letter from Manila." *New Yorker* (April 14, 1973), p. 97.
———. "Letter from Manila." *New Yorker* (March 26, 1979), p. 56.
———. "Letter from the Philippines." *New Yorker* (February 4, 1985), p. 60.
———. "A Reporter at Large: The Captivity of Cambodia." *New Yorker* (May 5, 1986), p. 66.
———. "A Reporter at Large: From Marcos to Aquino—I." *New Yorker* (August 25, 1986), p. 33.
———. "A Reporter at Large: From Marcos to Acquino—II." *New Yorker* (September 1, 1986), p. 36.
"Some Are Smarter Than Others." Clandestinely published by Philippine businessmen, 1979.
Stauffer, Robert B. "Philippine Authoritarianism: Framework for Peripheral 'Development.' " *Pacific Affairs*, Vol. 50 (Fall 1977), pp. 365–86.
Steinberg, David. "José P. Laurel: A 'Collaborator' Misunderstood." *Journal of Asian Studies*, Vol. XXIV (August 1965), pp. 661–65.
Sternberg, David T. "The Philippines: Contour and Perspective." *Foreign Affairs*, Vol. 44 (April 1966), pp. 501–11.
Stull, Lee. "Moments of Truth in Philippine-American Relations." A paper presented to the Conference on the Philippines and U.S. Policy, sponsored by the Washington Institute for Values in Public Policy, Washington, D.C., May 1, 1986.
Sullivan, William H. "Living Without Marcos." *Foreign Policy*, No. 53 (Winter 1983–1984), p. 150.
Szulc, Tad. "The Moveable War." *New Republic* (May 12, 1973), p. 21.

Tilman, Robert O. "The Philippines Under Martial Law." *Current History*, Vol. 71 (December 1976), p. 201.
"Tribal People and the Marcos Regime: Cultural Genocide in the Philippines." *Southeast Asia Chronicle* (October 1979).

"U.S. Bases in the Philippines: Assets or Liabilities?" *Defense Monitor*, Vol. XV, No. 4 (1986).
"U.S. Military Bases in the Philippines." *Southeast Asia Chronicle*, No. 89 (April 1983).

Vance, Cyrus R. "The Human Rights Imperative." *Foreign Policy*, No. 63 (Summer 1986), p. 3.

Walsh, Tom. "Martial Law in the Philippines: A Research Guide and Working Bibliography." Southeast Asia Working Paper No. 4. University of Hawaii, 1973.

Bibliography

Whitehead, Guy. "Philippine-American Economic Relations." *Pacific Research &
World Empire Telegram*, Vol. IV (January–February 1973), pp. 1–8.
Wideman, Bernard. "Winning Ways of the Marcos Cabal." *Insight* (September
1978).

Youngblood, Robert L. "Philippine-American Relations Under the 'New Society.'" *Pacific Affairs*, Vol. 50 (Spring 1977), pp. 45–63.

Index

ABOUT THE AUTHOR

This is Raymond Bonner's second book about the making of U.S. foreign policy. His first, *Weakness and Deceit: U.S. Policy and El Salvador*, received the Robert F. Kennedy Book Award for 1985.

Time magazine, in 1982, described Bonner as the "most energetic and controversial reporter on the scene" in Central America. He was a Poynter Fellow lecturer at Yale University in 1983 and the following year won the Latin American Studies Association Award for outstanding media coverage of Latin American affairs.

Mr. Bonner graduated from MacMurray College in 1964 and Stanford Law School in 1967. After three years as an officer in the U.S. Marine Corps, including a tour of duty in Vietnam, he became a practicing attorney, working for Ralph Nader in Washington, D.C. He moved back to San Francisco, where he established the West Coast office of Consumers Union, followed by two years at the San Francisco district attorney's office. He also taught at law school.

In 1979 Bonner set out to travel in Latin America, beginning in Bolivia, where he launched what was to become a journalism career, filing dispatches for *Newsweek*, the *Washington Post*, CBS Radio, and National Public Radio. He was forced to flee from Bolivia in July 1980, when the military government sought to arrest him because of what he was writing about the army's drug trafficking and brutality. In December 1980 Bonner went to El Salvador on what was to have been a one-week assignment for *The New York Times*. When "almost all of us went home for Christmas," Christopher Dickey, the *Washington Post*'s Central America correspondent, wrote later, "Raymond Bonner stayed." In February 1981 he was hired by *The New York Times* as a full-time reporter. During much of 1981 and 1982 he was in Central America. In July 1984 Raymond Bonner left *The New York Times*. In addition to writing, Bonner, who lives in New York, lectures regularly across the country.